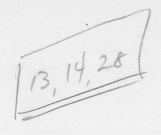

Financial History of the United States

FINANCIAL HISTORY
OF THE UNITED STATES

Fiscal, Monetary, Banking, and Tariff,
including Financial Administration
and State and Local Finance

PAUL STUDENSKI
Professor of Economics
New York University

and

HERMAN E. KROOSS
Associate Professor of Economics
New York University

FIRST EDITION

New York Toronto London
McGRAW-HILL BOOK COMPANY, INC.
1952

FINANCIAL HISTORY OF THE UNITED STATES

Library of Congress Catalog Card Number: 51–12649

THE MAPLE PRESS COMPANY, YORK, PA.

To My Wife Nastia
who contributes immeasurably
to all my work
and
To the pursuit of better financial policies
P. S.

To Helen
and all other
timorous students
H. E. K.

All sciences have the faculty of prediction, and this is especially true of the science of finance. It will, therefore, pay politicians who by the vagaries of elections are placed at the helm of public affairs as well as businessmen and citizens generally to familiarize themselves with this science. There are sciences so lofty as to forgive those who treat them with contempt. But the science of finance is not one of them. It has a terrible fashion of avenging itself upon governments and peoples who ignore or defy it.

Leroy-Beaulieu
Traité de la Science des Finances, 1876
Preface to the 5th edition

PREFACE

The vast expansion of public finance and of governmental monetary, credit, and foreign trade controls currently taking place has made the public keenly interested in the political and economic issues involved in these fields of governmental activity. This keen interest seems to create an ideal setting for a new financial history of the United States, a history which would help toward a better understanding of the genesis, interrelationships, and effects of governmental fiscal, monetary, banking, and tariff policies and institutional arrangements.

The present book attempts to meet this need. It is designed not only for the professional economist, political scientist, and student, but also for the layman seeking enlightenment on the current financial problems of the nation and its subdivisions.

The book is written out of an extensive teaching experience, embracing the training of hundreds of graduate and undergraduate students. Its writing was prompted by the keen interest of the students in the subject matter and by the absence of acceptable texts, the earlier ones all being out of print. A preliminary draft in mimeographed form was prepared first and was used in the authors' classes for three succeeding years. As the experiment seemed to turn out favorably, the work was put into permanent form so that it could have wider use.

Dr. Johnson, according to Boswell, once said that "a man will turn over half a library to make one book." Something of this nature could be said about the labors involved in the preparation of this book. Many works and documents were consulted—in fact, many more than could be listed in the appended bibliography. Among the earlier works, the greatest debt is owed to Davis Rich Dewey's *Financial History of the United States*, which will continue to be a classic in the field.

Special acknowledgment is due to Dr. Robert T. Patterson, Professor John Bryson, and Professor Ernest Kurnow for having gone over the manuscript and checked much of the factual data presented in it; and to Mulford Martin, associate director of libraries of New York University, and to C. B. Allen, one of his assistants, for extending to the authors many courtesies in the procurement and use of library materials.

PAUL STUDENSKI
HERMAN E. KROOSS

NEW YORK, N.Y.
November, 1951

vii

CONTENTS

CHAPTER 1: THE MEANING AND BASIC TRENDS OF FINANCIAL HISTORY

Financial history, in addition to embracing the history of fiscal policies—Federal, state, and local—covers the development of governmental monetary, banking, and foreign-trade-control policies, their mutual interrelationships, and their institutional setting. It is concerned not only with changes in financial legislation, but also with changes in financial administrative policy, practice, and organization. As conceived by the authors, it goes beyond financial practice and tries to trace the development of the theories which underly it and to test their correctness in the light of the produced results.

If one feature distinguishes this book in financial history from others which preceded it, it is the authors' belief that we not only can but do learn from past experience. Consistent with this belief, the authors have attempted throughout the work to indicate the forces which shaped events and, above all, to point out the advances as well as the mistakes made by each generation in handling its basic financial problems—state and local as well as national. In making such appraisals, the authors have endeavored to be as objective as possible, but they do not regard historical objectivity as an injunction against interpretation. History is an illumination of events. It begins with the discovery of a theme, but lest it deteriorate to mere antiquarianism, it must generalize. It must go beyond the historical events themselves to discover their broader meaning and causal relationships.

Financial history is permeated with the materials of both political and economic history. It lies on the border line between the two and is neither completely independent nor a branch of the one or of the other. The dynamics of financial history are interwoven with economic development and changing social institutions; the ebb and flow of financial development cannot be separated from the great political controversies which shook the country from time to time. Moreover, the action is reciprocal, for while economic and political developments influence financial policy, financial policy also influences political and economic developments. The substance of financial history is rich, for in finance are mirrored and through it are effected most of the political and economic actions of men.

The Changing Goals of Public Finance. The goals of American public finance—local, state, and especially national—have changed as the economy has advanced and new economic groups have attained political power and impressed their economic philosophies upon the government.

1

State and local activity and finance were limited during the colonial period and the succeeding half century. In the early nineteenth century with the rapid westward expansion of population, the beginnings of urban development, and the shift of political power in the direction of small property owners and city workers, state and local activity expanded to include a variety of social-welfare functions as well as internal-improvement projects. The expansion continued on an accelerated scale among the cities, the counties, and the smaller municipalities. But state governments during the second half of the century ceased to be an active developmental factor, limiting their activities to supervising municipal operations and regulating private enterprise. With the revolutionary changes in industry and transportation which occurred in the beginning of the twentieth century and the appearance at the same time of new social needs and centralizing forces, the states came to life again as active service agencies, taking over from the local governments many of their financial and administrative responsibilities. In the 1930's with the appearance of the "New Federalism," state and local government activities were totally overshadowed by expanding Federal operations.

The historical development of national finance was completely different. In the seventeenth century under the influence of mercantilistic thought the national government was regarded as a tool for regulating the economy and stimulating the expansion of national commerce. During the early nineteenth century as the small farmer achieved political control, agrarian *laissez faire* became the prevalent economic philosophy, and the scope of Federal activity and finance became increasingly restricted to a minimum of services. After the Civil War, as industrial capitalism became dominant and an atmosphere of ambivalent *laissez faire* became prevalent in national affairs, the aim of Federal activity was enlarged to include active aid to private enterprise. While expected not to interfere with business in any way, the Federal government was required to furnish a variety of aids to business. In short, it was to be a subsidiary agent which should respond to business commands and give business every required support.

With the opening of the twentieth century, simultaneously with the consolidation of business and the growth of trade-unionism, the goals of Federal finance and activity were still further broadened, and the Federal government assumed the role of a limited arbiter between business and labor. At first the Federal government moved gingerly, but as a result of two world wars and an intervening disastrous business depression, Federal finance was charged with a new responsibility. This responsibility embraced the permanent stabilization of the economy at a high level of employment and production. During the 1930's public finance abandoned, one by one, the traditions of orthodox economic theory and adopted a new rationale. In this new rationale the economic importance of government was freely accepted, but whether it was to be a controlling factor in the economy remained a matter of controversy.

According to one school of thought, government spending was to be maintained at a continuously high and expanding level to compensate for the supposedly insufficient distribution of purchasing power by private enterprise. High spending was to be assisted by continuous borrowing. Debt reduction, because of its deflationary effects, was declared to be unnecessary and even harmful. Taxation was to be concentrated on incomes with high propensities to save, that is, high and middle incomes, rather than on incomes with high propensities to consume, that is, low incomes. According to another school, fiscal policy was to be flexible, "compensatory," and countercyclical. Government spending was to be increased, debt incurred, and taxation lowered in times of business depression, while reduction in government spending, retirement of debt, and increased taxation were to be followed during boom times.

It still is not clear to what extent this new fiscal thinking represents merely a fad of limited practical value or a lasting development translatable into practical politics. There can be no doubt, however, that in the future the economic effects of fiscal policies will be examined more closely than they have ever been before and that in this examination practical politicians and the lay public will participate along with professional economists.

Trends of Government Spending and Taxation.[1] From the furnishing of mere rudimentary protection, which individuals had to supplement with protective measures of their own, the scope of government activity broadened to include complete and elaborate internal and external protective measures as well as a multitude of developmental, social-welfare, and economic functions. The remote protective state became the all-pervasive

[1] Throughout the text, a series of tables is presented showing receipts, expenditures, surplus, and debt of the Federal government for each year from 1789 to 1950. The figures given are taken from the annual reports of the Secretary of the Treasury. In some cases they differ vastly from the figures published in the historical series of the Treasury reports which are most generally quoted. The divergence is due to differences in accounting. The figures given for each year in the report for that year are based on a variety of methods (warrants issued, warrants paid, checks issued or collected, and daily Treasury statements). The historical series, on the other hand, is based for the years 1789 to 1915 on warrants issued and from 1916 on, on the basis of daily Treasury statements. For the years beginning 1933 the figures currently reported for the year and those published in the historical series are identical. In the text we have used the figures given in the individual reports of the Secretary of the Treasury rather than those in the historical series for two reasons: (1) because they are more detailed and (2) because they were used by the authorities in determining financial policy at the time. However, for the convenience of the reader accustomed to use the historical series and as a cross check to the other figures we are reproducing the historical series in the Appendix.

protective state, then the "welfare" or "social" state, and according to some prophets, it is fast becoming an "economic-control" state.

Government expenditures—national, state, and local combined—rose from 2 or 3 per cent of the national income at the beginning of the nineteenth century to between 8 and 10 per cent at the beginning of the twentieth century and to more than 25 per cent by the middle thereof. Government became a colossal employer of labor, a purchaser of goods and services from business, a disburser of cash benefits, and an influential determinant of the levels of employment, consumption, and production.

The whole structure of state, local, and Federal expenditures changed. In state and local government, expenditures for education, recreation, health, sanitation, social welfare, and road construction and maintenance became primary, while those for protection and general government became secondary. In the Federal government, the expenditures for past and future wars continued to be dominant, but expenditures for social welfare, farm subsidies, and grants-in-aid to states—which were insignificant or nonexistent in the earlier period—also became important.

Taxation has grown from humble beginnings, when it imposed imperceptible burdens and was mainly indirect and regressive, into an elaborate system of direct and indirect levies whose combined impact is heavy and progressive. In 1950 it took 15 per cent of the low incomes and as much as 90 per cent of the high incomes and showed no promise of abatement. At first, the Federal government, the states, and the localities each had different tax sources and simple tax systems. But as time went on, each class of government added new taxes, and the additions were in large part of the same nature. Thus, Federal, state, and local tax systems became multiform and overlapping; and duplicate and triplicate levies of the same kind, though at different rates, became quite general. With this multiplication and pyramiding of taxes, tax administration and tax compliance became difficult processes.

During most of its early history the Federal government relied on customs duties as its only tax source, but after the Civil War its permanent tax system included liquor and tobacco taxes. With the further growth of its fiscal requirements, as well as with the development of more democratic tax ideas, the Federal government in 1913 was given the constitutional power to levy personal and corporate income taxes. In addition to developing these sources to the utmost, it adopted an inheritance tax and a multiplicity of other direct and indirect taxes during the succeeding three decades.

The states, after losing the customs duties to the Federal government following the adoption of the Constitution, became dependent upon the property tax and a few nondescript revenue sources, such as auction duties, lotteries, income from investments, and bank taxes. But in the second half of the nineteenth century state taxation became multiform in nature, embracing, in addition, inheritance taxes and a variety of corporation levies. In the twentieth century it was further broadened through the addition of the personal income tax, the general sales tax, and consumer excises. On the other hand, many states in the meanwhile had abandoned the property tax to the localities.

Local governments relied first on land taxes and taxes on special types of personal property, but these were quickly consolidated into a general property tax designed to treat all property alike and to distribute the burdens of government support among the citizens in proportion to their wealth. Eventually, in the second half of the nineteenth century, the taxation of personal property broke down, and the property tax became in substance a real estate tax. In the meanwhile, as local property taxes were proving insufficient to support the expanding local services, the states began to apportion a part of their revenue among the localities. Thus, state and local tax revenues became closely interlocked. Finally, in recent years some states granted the localities power to levy supplemental nonproperty taxes, such as personal income and retail sales taxes. Local tax systems accordingly also became multiform in character.

With government expenditures being made increasingly for the benefit of middle- and low-income groups and taxation, especially on the Federal level, being concentrated increasingly upon the rich, public finance became a huge funnel for the redistribution and equalization of advantages and income in society. Increasingly, the ultimate distribution of income was determined not by economic forces operating in the market, but by political forces—the struggle of pressure groups—operating in the legislative and administrative arenas. This being so, the continued progress of the economy came to depend upon the ability of the contending pressure groups to effect successful compromises under a democratic political system.

Trends in Public Borrowing and Debt Management. Public debt during colonial times took the form of paper-money issues which transferred goods and services from private individuals to the government through price inflation. Modern forms of public debt first appeared with the issuance of interest-bearing stock for sale to the public during the Revolutionary War. Thereafter, as the public debt grew, it became increasingly complex. New forms were elaborated until governments were issuing securities designed to fit the needs of every type of investor.

During the nineteenth century the generally accepted theory of public finance on all levels of government was that revenues and expenditures should be kept in balance. But in practice this could not always be done. State and local governments financed most of their capital construction by borrowing, and Federal revenue fluctuated sharply with changes in business activity, resulting in heavy surpluses during prosperity and large deficits during depressions. Moreover, all governments lacked effective systems of budgetary control, and revenue and expenditure programs were opportunistic rather than well planned. The theory of keeping revenues and expenditures in balance began to be applied effectively only in the twentieth century, when the executive budget system was generally adopted. But very soon thereafter during the depression of the 1930's the beneficence of a balanced budget as applied to the Federal government came to be seriously questioned. The Federal debt, which was substantial as a result of World War I, was permitted to increase further, but the greatest increase resulted from World War II.

Throughout our financial history, whenever large debts were incurred, they posed a multitude of difficult financial problems. They often produced violent price inflation, always saddled the Treasury with huge interest charges, and created the inevitable problems of debt management, that is, of funding, refunding, and retirement. In the nineteenth century debt management was guided by the conditions of the money market; funding and refunding of the public debt were adjusted to market interest rates and the other requirements of the private economy. But after World War II, when for the first time in the nation's history the national debt exceeded the annual national income as well as the aggregate private debt, the requirements of the private money market were subordinated completely to the requirements of the government-bond market, and the Treasury came to dictate monetary as well as fiscal policy.

Not only did the concept of the relation of debt management to monetary policy change, but the traditional belief in the necessity of rapid debt retirement lost its vigor. Consistently in the past, Federal debt was reduced rapidly through the application of surpluses, and state and local debts were reduced through regular amortization and redemption from current revenue. But with the gigantic increase in the Federal debt and in the size of Federal expenditures and taxation, it became doubtful whether the economy could again achieve rapid debt retirement.

Changed Relation of Federal to State-Local Finance. During the colonial period national finance, which was then imperial finance, was of no concern to the colonial population. National finance in the true sense of the term began only with the setting up of a central government during the Revolution and its permanent confirmation and reformation with the adoption of the Constitution.

For the first few years of national government, Federal expenditures, tax revenues, and borrowings exceeded aggregate state and local expenditures, tax revenue, and borrowing as may be readily seen from Table 1. It should be noted that this table exaggerates the relative importance of nineteenth century local expenditures, for it gives the per capita expenditures of only the larger cities, which were much higher than those of the rural sections.

TABLE 1. POPULATION AND PER CAPITA NATIONAL INCOME, GOVERNMENT
EXPENDITURES, AND DEBT, 1799–1950

Year (actual, or nearest)	Population, continental United States (millions)	National income	Government expenditures				Government debt			
			Federal	State*	Local†	Total	Federal	State	Local	Total
1799	5.2	$ 131	$ 1.88	$ 0.39┐	$ 1.37┐	....	$ 15.96	‡	‡	
1809	7.0	130	1.43	0.42	2.06	....	7.60	‡	‡	
1819	9.4	93	2.29	0.47	2.18	....	9.68	‡	‡	
1829	12.6	78	1.21	0.20	3.21	....	3.86	$ 2.00	‡	
1839	16.7	98	1.60	0.37	2.85	....	0.30	10.20	$ 1.46	$ 11.96
1849	22.6	107	2.00	0.25	3.91	....	2.80	8.19	‡	
1859	30.7	140	2.26	0.43	7.27	....	1.91	8.18	‡	
1869	39.1	175	8.55	1.30	14.69	....	65.17	9.14	13.37	87.68
1879	49.2	147	5.46	1.04┘	19.54┘	....	46.72	4.52	16.37	67.61
1889	61.8	173	4.84	1.14	7.74	$ 13.72	20.23	3.37	14.79	38.39
1902	79.2	220	5.96	2.30	11.22	19.48	14.88	3.41	24.32	42.61
1913	97.2	324	7.01	3.89	15.02	25.92	12.27	4.35	41.91	58.53
1919	105.1	599	144.77	6.70	28.93	180.40	242.54	6.61	50.62	299.77
1932	124.8	334	36.16§	15.78§	52.07	104.01	156.10	23.29	133.61	313.00
1939	130.9	554	63.73§	27.01§	46.89	137.63	308.98	26.72	126.70	462.40
1950	151.7	1,576	250.05§	58.64§	77.33	386.02	1,696.00	35.00	121.00	1,852.00

SOURCES: Federal expenditures from *Treasury Bulletin*, March, 1951; *Annual Report of the Secretary of the Treasury*, 1866, 1893, 1920, 1949, and Debt, *ibid.*, 1872, 1949. State and local finance from U.S. Bureau of the Census, *Historical Review of State and Local Government Finances*; National Industrial Conference Board, *Economic Almanac*; Studenski, *Public Borrowing*; Sowers, *Financial History of New York*; Stokes, *The Finances and Financial Administration of Providence*. National income to 1919, from Robert F. Martin, *National Income in the United States, 1799–1938*; after 1929, from U.S. Department of Commerce.

* 1799–1879 average expenditures derived from New York.
† 1799–1879 average expenditures of Providence. Providence was selected because among the cities for which figures are available, its per capita expenditures were the lowest and therefore closer to the average per capita for the local governments of the period. But even the Providence figures were undoubtedly higher than average local expenditures. Hence, the series 1799–1879 is not comparable with that of 1889–1950 which is based on the census collations and covers all local government expenditures.
‡ Not available.
§ For own operations; not including aid paid to other governments.

The rapid westward movement of the population, the growth of cities, the extension of the suffrage, and the ascent of laissez-faire philosophy terminated for a time the predominance of Federal activity and finance. Beginning with the 1820's, government activity, expenditures, revenues, and borrowings, except during wartime, grew more rapidly at the periphery than at the center.

The contrast was not quite so sharp in the growth of revenues as it was in the growth of expenditures and productive (nonwar) debts. From the outset, the ability of the Federal government to raise revenue exceeded its need for revenue, whereas the abilities of the states and localities to raise revenue lagged behind their expenditure needs. For this reason the Federal government frequently had large surpluses, but in the state and local governments the reverse was generally true. To correct this unbalance, the Federal government made land grants to the states for the support of internal improvements and higher education, and the scheme of distributing casual Federal surpluses to the states was conceived and on one occasion actually carried out. Later, annual financial grants were made to the states for agricultural experimentation and extension, road construction, vocational education, rehabilitation, child welfare, public-health control, and the like.

In the early 1930's the largely decentralized system of government finance was changed completely by the demands of the depression, and the change was further accentuated by the requirements of World War II and the postwar international unsettlement. Federal expenditures, taxation, and borrowing swelled, while state and local finance contracted. Moreover, through its grants-in-aid, which supplied close to 15 per cent of state and local revenue, the Federal government came to exercise substantial controls over state and local government activities and spending. With the proportion of Federal expenditures increasing from 35 to 70 per cent of total government spending and with Federal controls being exercised over a substantial portion of state and local expenditures, Federalism lost some of its original meaning. Students of government asked themselves whether this centralization of government activity and finance was permanent, or would subside to permit the restoration of a more balanced form of Federalism.

Trends in Financial Administration. Government financial administration developed in fits and starts. Throughout the nineteenth century government finances were loosely managed. Tax burdens were light, and the public was not particularly concerned over government spending. Congress, the state legislatures, and the municipal councils, which controlled the financial machinery, appropriated funds to various departments without bothering to estimate the total or to assure enough revenue to cover it. Neither expenditure nor revenue was planned but rose and fell in accordance with the changes in the business cycle. If a deficit resulted, debt was incurred; if a surplus occurred, spending was increased sharply; and if a surplus still remained, it was disposed of in the most opportunistic fashion. Some improvements were introduced in accounting and auditing. Also the increase in the debt had given some concern, and controls over the exercise of public credit and its management were instituted. But none of these improvements in financial management was startling.

With the increase in Federal, local, and state tax burdens at the beginning of the twentieth century, the situation changed. The people began to demand more careful planning and management of expenditures and revenues. Financial administrative organization increased in size and became more coordinated and functionalized, and its procedures grew ever more complicated and technical. Responsibility for financial planning and management became increasingly vested in the chief executive. Executive budget systems were installed, and staffs of technically trained budgeteers were set up. While the chief executive was made responsible for the preparation and execution of annual budgets, the legislature became the scrutinizer of executive proposals. The systems of accounting and auditing were further improved, and the powers of the comptroller were strengthened. Emphasis was placed on "independent audits," which would give Congress, the state legislature, or the municipal council a means for checking executive performance. Central purchasing of goods was inaugurated in order to correct incompetent and wasteful buying. Assessment and collection of revenue were centralized and streamlined. The system of reporting accounts and financial performance to the public was improved. While all these developments began on the state level, they were also adopted gradually by the Federal government, and by the middle of the century, the improvement in financial administration on all levels of government could be clearly recognized.

Trends in Tariff Policy. The development of tariff policy over the greater part of national history was attended with continued controversy and changes from one extreme to another. The battles were waged first along national lines between the manufacturing East and the cotton-growing South, with the West holding the balance of power. As manufacturing spread throughout the country, the division ceased to be along sectional lines and followed more strictly economic lines. Omitting short-run changes, the development can be divided into four main periods. From 1789 to 1833 tariffs were becoming more protectionist, but the movement outreached itself. From 1833 to 1860 tariffs were only moderately protectionist. After the Civil War, however, they were highly and militantly protective. In 1933 the trend was reversed sharply. Through trade agreements, tariffs were greatly moderated, and in time the whole tariff issue became much less controversial. The change in our international financial position from that of an import and debtor country to that of an export and creditor country had much to do with bringing about this reorientation, and the impoverishment of our foreign competitors by World War II caused this reorientation to become even more accentuated after the war was over.

Trends in Monetary and Banking Policies. The development of monetary and banking policies was turbulent and tortuous. It was influenced throughout by conditions incident to the settlement of a new country, the uneven economic development of its various sections, and the political struggle of the agricultural debtor classes of the South and West and the commercial and industrial creditor classes of the East. The Southern planters and the Western settlers, lacking capital, favored cheap and abundant money. They distrusted banks and were particularly opposed to central banking and to a nationally controlled banking system. In so far as government had to exercise control over private credit, they favored easy-money policies. The Eastern industrial and commercial classes on the other hand favored "sound currency," which they identified with the gold standard. They also advocated central banking or at least a nationally controlled banking system and currency.

In the course of the struggle between the opposing forces of "sound" and "easy money," there was scarcely a type of currency or banking policy which was not tried. For about a century bimetallism was followed, although in accordance with Gresham's law, only one metal, usually gold, circulated. In time bimetallism was replaced by a limping standard, and then after one of the sharpest political contests between East and West, the gold standard was officially adopted at the opening of the twentieth century. Yet thirty-three years later, in keeping with the new faith in the ability of the government to influence economic activity, the gold standard was abandoned in favor of managed money—an irredeemable domestic paper currency and a controlled international gold-bullion standard.

We began, under our dual Federal-state political system, with a hybrid banking system consisting of a Federally chartered and partly Federally owned central bank and of state-chartered and either state-owned or privately owned local banks. Under the influence of agrarian *laissez faire*, we abandoned central banking and all direct Federal controls over private credit, divorced Federal financial operations from the banking system, and, in a manner reminiscent of the ancient monarchies and republics, placed them for a time on a coin basis, with the Treasury acting as the custodian of its own funds. In the 1860's, with industrial capitalism efflorescing, relations between the Treasury and the banks were reestablished under the Federally controlled national banking system. In 1914, with the expansion of Federal powers, the Federal Reserve System was established. Starting with a somewhat diluted form of central banking, there was a constant trend toward more complete centralization until in the middle 1930's the

Federal Reserve Board and the Treasury exercised substantial control over the nation's banking structure. Whereas monetary policy had been rigid, it now became flexible. Infrequent changes made by Congressional legislation after prolonged battle gave way to frequent changes made relatively quietly by administrative decisions of the Federal Reserve Board and the Treasury.

In the meanwhile, beginning in the 1920's and continuing through the 1930's, a whole network of new Federally owned banking institutions was established. Finally, after World War II, the Federal government became the principal partner in the International Bank for Reconstruction and Development. All this development of government banking, as well as the increase of corporate savings and the separation ordered in the 1930's of the investment functions of commercial banks from their loan functions, divested the commercial banks of much of their original dynamic role in the economy as the suppliers of the lifeblood of business expansion.

Federal monetary and banking policy was always somewhat interlocked with Federal fiscal policy. Thus, Federal debt was used to facilitate the founding of the first and second central banks, and Federal bonds were made the basis of the national-bank-note currency and later of Federal Reserve notes. However, throughout the nineteenth and early twentieth centuries monetary and banking policy generally had the upper hand, while fiscal policy was being adjusted thereto and operated as its handmaiden. Beginning with the 1930's this historic relationship was overturned, and as already indicated, fiscal policy was made dominant, with monetary and banking policy being reduced to a subsidiary role.

In the light of this historical development, will monetary and banking policy resume its original important role in the management of the economy, or will it continue to diminish? History can furnish partial answers to this and the other questions of fiscal, monetary, and banking policy raised in the course of this broad survey. But these answers are valid only for the foreseeable future. What will happen in the more remote future depends on a myriad of unforeseeable events, many of them hidden in the political and social currents which are sweeping the globe.

PART I

FROM THE COLONIAL PERIOD
TO THE CIVIL WAR

Chapter 2: COLONIAL FINANCE

The American economy in 1620 was just emerging from the frontier stage. Yet the aggressive individualists who comprised the colonial population desired to expand their trade and raise their standard of living. In this they were greatly handicapped for the next century and a half by a constant insufficiency of domestic money supply and foreign exchange. They sought to overcome these handicaps by various experiments ranging from commodity money to private or governmental issues of paper money.

At the same time the type of colonial government had profound effects on finance. Each of the 13 colonies existed separately, the only common tie being allegiance to the Crown and Parliament. For its part, the British government was guided by doctrines of mercantilism. Although these offered many advantages to the colonies, the colonists chose to disregard them, emphasizing instead their obvious disadvantages. As time passed, they stressed the righteousness of self-government and engaged in interminable conflicts with the English government and its colonial representatives over the right to tax and the right to spend public moneys.

These continual monetary experiments and fiscal conflicts left a profound imprint on future American history and served to color and influence the theories, prejudices, and institutions of future American finance.

The Scarcity of Specie. In order to raise their standard of living, the colonists had to import the capital goods necessary to increase home production. This necessitated the use of some form of money, such as specie or bills of exchange, that could be utilized in foreign trade.

However, the colonists had not brought with them any significant amount of specie, and the colonies possessed no mines from which gold or silver could be obtained. Furthermore, whatever specie was obtained tended to be exported in exchange for goods for which there was more urgent need, namely, tools and capital goods which could be used in a productive process. Therefore, imports from England continually exceeded exports. This unfavorable balance of trade, only partly offset by service items, drained the colonies of acceptable specie and made them even more dependent on investments from England. In 1766 Franklin estimated that Pennsylvania alone imported £500,000 of goods annually from England while exporting only £40,000. In short, the colonies suffered from a "pound sterling shortage."

On the other hand, the balance of payments with the West Indies was favorable, and Spanish dollars (pieces of eight) tended to be imported. The best of these were collected and sent to England to help pay for imports. The sweated and clipped specimens circulated in the colonies. Thus, while the colonists carried their accounts in English money, they usually made payments in Spanish dollars, necessitating constant conversion of values.

Although the colonial supply of specie increased, the rate of growth was not sufficient to cope with the rapid increase in domestic and foreign trade and the consequent growing demand for money.[1]

Commodity Money. A barter system of exchange came into use automatically. But as the economy of the colonies progressed, it became necessary to provide an objective medium of exchange. Naturally, the next step was to use the leading commodities in each section as money. "Country pay," as this system was sometimes called, included fur skins, powder, and shot in the hunting sections; corn or livestock in the farming sections; wampum (sea shells) in New England and the Middle Atlantic states; and tobacco and rice in the South.[2]

Wampum was made a legal tender in Massachusetts in 1643. Used for years by the Indians as jewelry and money, it appeared to be a satisfactory means of exchange. Unfortunately, however, its supply could be easily expanded, and in a short time, it depreciated in value. By 1649 Massachusetts prohibited its use in the payment of taxes, and its career as legal tender ended in the early sixties.

Tobacco, the staple crop of the upper South, soon became an accepted medium of exchange in that part of the country. In Virginia, in 1619, the value of tobacco was fixed for exchange purposes at "three shillings the beste" and "the second sorte at eighteen pence the pound." Since anyone with a modicum of ambition could grow money in his own back yard, the cultivation of tobacco increased so rapidly that its price in terms of silver fell 80 per cent within a few years. The legislature tried all sorts of tricks to stop the runaway depreciation. The right to grow tobacco was restricted, and certain persons were specifically prohibited from growing the crop. But depreciation continued, and in 1639 a revaluation of existing debts was ordered so that exchange transactions would have some reality.

---

[1] Charles J. Bullock (*Essays on the Monetary History of the United States*, p. 14) disputes the scarcity of specie, but most historians of the period confirm it.

[2] Students of Harvard College for many years paid their bills in produce or articles raked up from the family closets. One student, later president of the college, settled his bill in 1649 with "an old cow," and the accounts for the construction of Harvard's first building included a melancholy entry: "Received a goat 30s plantations of Watertown rate which died." (Davis R. Dewey, *Financial History of the United States*, 12th ed., p. 19.)

In 1642 contracts payable in coin were prohibited, but this availed little, and tobacco never did succeed as money.

In addition to being subject to depreciation because its supply could be easily increased, commodity money was not uniform in quality, it was subject to spoilage, and it was difficult to transport. Worst of all, it could not be used as a medium of international exchange. By the end of the seventeenth century, therefore, its use was confined almost wholly to the frontier.

Devaluation of British Coin. In the early period some of the colonies resorted to another well-known device for increasing the supply of money. They devalued English money in terms of the Spanish dollar, hoping to attract the dollar from neighboring colonies as well as from the Spanish territories.

Like all devaluations, the colonial experiments gave only temporary relief. In time prices of commodities, in Spanish dollars, increased, and the advantage of spending the overvalued "pieces of eight" ceased. Moreover, what one colony could do, others could do, and competitive devaluation set in with its usual chaotic effects. In New York a "real," whose metallic content was slightly less than 7 pence, was given a value of 10 pence, while in Pennsylvania it was valued at 11 pence, and in Massachusetts at 9. Finally, in 1704, in an effort to restore order, England introduced "proclamation money," declaring the maximum value of the "piece of eight" to be 6 shillings and making a "real" worth 9 pence at the utmost.

Meanwhile, Massachusetts established a mint. Between 1652 and 1684, when it was closed by order of the Crown, the mint produced silver coins in denominations of shillings, half shillings, and quarter shillings. These "pine tree shillings," as they were called, were debased deliberately in order to prevent export. They contained 72 grains of silver as compared with 93 in the English shilling. However, the need for hard money was so great that the debasement did not prevent their export.

Bills of Credit. Since metallic money was scarce and commodity money was unsatisfactory, the colonists began to issue paper money. There were three types: bills of credit issued by the legislatures, bank notes issued by publicly owned banks, and bank notes issued by private banks.

Bills of credit were a cross between short-term notes issued in anticipation of tax collection and outright fiat money. Since they were used to pay government expenses, they were a form of borrowing setting a precedent for the issuance of non-interest-bearing "continentals" during the Revolution and of "treasury notes" during the War of 1812 and the Civil War. The first bills of credit (the first paper money in the British Empire) appeared in 1690 when Massachusetts issued £7,000 of one-year notes to pay the soldiers returning from the unfortunate campaign against Quebec.

They were to be redeemed from taxes, but since the colonists loathed paying taxes, and paper money seemed an easy method of paying government expenses, the levying of taxes was postponed and more and more new bills were issued to retire the old bills, as well as to pay new expenses. By 1710 about £160,000 had been issued, and maturities were successively lengthened to two, four, six, and finally thirteen years. At first, the bills maintained their value, but when the likelihood of their eventual redemption in coin became dim, they began to depreciate even though they were accepted in payment of taxes at a 5 per cent premium. By 1727 the bills were worth in silver less than one-third their nominal value, and as emissions continued on an ever-growing scale, their value dropped to one-tenth.

Meanwhile, the other colonies, learning of the marvels of paper money, also began to emit bills of credit. Price inflation became general throughout the colonies, although it varied in degree. In Rhode Island, where the issues were particularly numerous, paper declined to 26 to 1 in terms of specie. In the middle colonies it held up reasonably well, while in South Carolina it was worth about one-eighth of specie. In the colonies where depreciation was greatest, partial repudiation occurred. Old notes were replaced by new at a fraction of their nominal value, so that there eventually existed old tenor, new tenor, middle tenor, new tenor firsts, new tenor seconds, etc., causing much hardship to consumers and creditors and offering an attractive opportunity to speculators. To alleviate these hardships, the colonies resorted to novel arrangements. Massachusetts operated under a crude tabular standard in the 1740's, fixing by law the degree of depreciation for each issue so that the claims of creditors could be adjusted and their rights protected.

Parliament also became concerned over the inflation created by the bills of credit. In 1751 it passed a law prohibiting any further issues of legal-tender bills in the New England colonies, and in 1764 it extended this restriction to all colonies. This put an end to the main abuse but did not prevent the colonies from accumulating further floating debts. Following Parliament's action, some colonies attempted to redeem their outstanding bills in coin at a fraction of their value. Massachusetts, for example, redeemed her currency at 7½ to 1.

The First Banks and Bank Notes. The colonies had very little need for banks as we know them today. The functions of deposit and discount were performed by merchant houses for their customers as an incident of their trading business, and banks were organized primarily to issue and lend paper currency ("bank notes").

Most of the colonial banks were privately organized by associations of landowners who subscribed for mortgages on their land and in return received bank notes which passed as currency. The few publicly owned banks, on the other hand, were really public loan offices.

Banks existed in almost every colony, but those of Massachusetts and Pennsylvania were most typical. Attempts to organize a bank in Massachusetts began as early as 1671, but the first operating bank about which anything of importance can be ascertained was formed in 1733. This was similar to a pawnshop and was formed by a group of Boston merchants who wanted to keep the badly depreciated Rhode Island paper from circulating in Massachusetts. They issued £110,000 of notes redeemable in silver. As silver increased in value, these notes went to a premium, but they did not accomplish the intended purpose, for they were hoarded and thus ceased to fulfill the functions of money.

In 1740 the Massachusetts Land Bank was formed. Its capital was £150,-000. Subscribers obtained bank notes by mortgaging land at 3 per cent interest with the principal amortized at 5 per cent annually in notes, manufactured goods, or agricultural produce. The supporters of the "silver bank" objected vehemently to the land bank and were supported by the governor and the council. But the lower house favored the land bank. Thus, the controversy was an incident in the age-old struggle between the cheap- and hard-money forces.

The Massachusetts bank was only short-lived, for in 1741 the English government made stockholders personally liable for the debts of their companies, effectively ending the careers of all land banks. In any case, the land-bank scheme gave little hope of providing a stable currency, for there was no arrangement for regular retirement of notes. Each new loan increased the outstanding issues and the probability of depreciation.

In sharp contrast to the Massachusetts experiment, the Pennsylvania Land Bank, a public bank, provided a stable and adequate currency. It was organized in a period of economic hardship when a cabal of four or five men monopolized goods and retailed them on credit at high interest rates. To break this monopoly, Francis Rawle, one of the prominent radicals in the assembly, suggested a paper-money issue, arguing that depreciation could be prevented if the amount of paper money was not excessive, if it was full legal tender, and if it bore interest at the same rate as other currency. The bank was formed in 1723 and began to lend notes on 5 per cent mortgages, granted up to 50 per cent of land value. The issue was limited to £15,000 (later increased to £45,000), and the limit on loans was £100 to any one person. The loans were repayable within eight years and in bank notes only. Thus, provision was made for continuous retirement of the issues.

Appraisal of Paper-money Issues. The depreciation of colonial paper money has usually been exaggerated. Where the bills were used in moderation and not as substitutes for taxes to pay current expenses, and where the bank notes were issued cautiously and subject to rigid redemption, they did not have a bad history. Indeed, in seven colonies the experience was favorable while in the six others it was unfavorable.[3]

Where depreciation occurred, it was not because of lack of security, for currency which was known to be counterfeit often circulated as money. Nor was it because taxes for redemption were postponed or because interest was not paid on the notes. It was because notes were issued beyond the needs of trade and confidence in their worth was completely lost.

The British government made no effort to assist the colonies in overcoming their money shortage. It made only one shipment of specie £180,-000 in 1749. At all other times it prevented the expansion of the money supply. Closing the colonial mints and banks, fixing the exchange value of the dollar, and prohibiting legal-tender notes were examples of the English anti-inflation policy. This policy was followed because inflation would violate the mercantilist philosophy by benefiting American trade at the expense of agriculture, because British merchants complained bitterly as inflation depreciated their claims as creditors, and because coinage was a prerogative to be exercised only by the Crown.

But the overwhelming majority of the colonists favored paper money and inflationary policies in general, regarding them as economically beneficial. Indeed, if paper money, or money inflation, had not been resorted to, the colonies would not have been able to import so great a volume of finished goods and economic progress would have been much slower. Franklin was correct in listing the British anti-inflation policy among the five factors which lessened the colonial respect for Parliament and led to the Revolution.[4]

The Colonial System of Government. Legally, the government of the colonies was completely unitary, all authority being derived from the Crown and from Parliament. But in actuality, the government soon broke into two semi-independent parts: the central government in London and the local government in the colonies. The central government was represented in the colonies by the governors, commanders of the troops, and the naval officers. The local governments consisted of general assemblies and other agencies created in accordance with the particular conditions

[3] Richard A. Lester, *Monetary Experiments*, Chap. 1; Curtis P. Nettels, *The Money Supply of the American Colonies before 1720*, Chap. 10. For an opposite opinion, see A. B. Hepburn, *History of the Currency*; Charles J. Bullock, *Essays on the Monetary History of the United States*.

[4] Carl Van Doren, *Benjamin Franklin*, p. 102. Franklin defended paper money in a pamphlet published in 1729 (*A Modest Enquiry into the Nature and Necessity of a Paper Currency.*)

of each colony and its various subdivisions. These colonial governments were not much concerned in international politics and economics or even in intercolonial affairs, leaving them to be attended to by the imperial government. On the other hand, the central government allowed each colony to manage its own affairs, provided it complied with certain broad imperial political and commercial policies.

Whereas the officials of the Crown were paid from the British Treasury, the locally appointed or elected officials were paid from locally raised revenues. The governors and colonial agents, although appointed by the Crown or the proprietors and sent from England, received their pay from local revenue and were thus tossed between allegiance to the London office and dependence on the colonists. The practical responsibility of serving two jurisdictions, which were often at odds, made the exercise of their duties most difficult.

This dual system of government was inconsistent with the legal theory of a unitary, imperial state as well as with the theories of representative government which England herself had established through two violent revolutions. Furthermore, it was too complicated to run smoothly, and it produced constant friction between the Crown and the colonies. But it was a form of "check-and-balance" government which appealed to the sceptical mind of the "Age of Reason."

Contest over the Control of the Public Purse. While the colonists conceded that the British government had the power to regulate external commerce and levy customs duties, they took the position that internal taxes could be imposed on them only with the approval of their own representatives.

The same contest between the colonists and the representatives of the Crown took place over the control of appropriations, that is, over who should decide how the money was to be spent. The colonists believed that these decisions belonged to the taxpayers acting through their chosen representatives rather than to the governor, who too often pursued his own, rather than the people's, interests. In this struggle, the upper house of the legislature usually supported the governor, while the lower house, representing the people, fought tenaciously to confine his authority. In Virginia the assembly very early passed an act declaring, "The governor shall not lay any taxes or impositions upon the colony," except by authority of the general assembly.[5] In all the colonies, the governor was not granted funds, except in accordance with specifications of his needs. The colonists insisted that these needs be approved by their representatives through appropriations.

In time of war, the controversy sharpened. The governors, at the re-

[5] William Z. Ripley, *Financial History of Virginia*, p. 20.

quest of their home government, insisted on larger appropriations or attempted to raise revenue on their own authority. The assemblies were reluctant to grant these demands, insisting instead that the Crown send more troops. There were also acrid controversies among the colonies themselves, each colony maintaining that it was contributing more than its fair share. Theoretically, the British authorities were responsible for apportioning the cost of military operations. But actually, each colony determined for itself how much it would contribute. In financing a common war effort, this system was most inefficient.

The controversy over who had the right to levy taxes and control expenditures was never finally settled. It was to influence fiscal administration after independence was achieved, and the same distrust of the executive, of centralized power, and of lump-sum appropriations was to be demonstrated after the formation of the Federal government.

Colonial Expenditures. The expenditures of the local colonial governments were very small. During the latter part of the colonial period, total civil expenditures for all the colonies were estimated at £60,000, or $300,000, annually. The largest ordinary expense was for the maintenance of the governor. The other typical expenditures were for defense, administration of justice, protection of life and property, and collection of taxes. Social expenditures were unknown, except in New England, where the pay of ministers and slight amounts for education entered the budget. The New York colony appropriated a total of £4,645 in 1767. The governor received £2,000; the chief justice, £300; three judges, £200 each; an agent in England, £500; and the treasurer, £300. The remaining appropriations covered minor officers and supplies.[6]

Many officials, including sheriffs, constables, and registers of deed, received no salaries for their services but collected fees from the citizens who had to transact business with them. The rates of these fees were fixed by law, but their proceeds were treated by the officials as private income and were never accounted for. How much was spent by the public for governmental services in this way was therefore unknown. Time and again, the governors, in an effort to secure for themselves an independent revenue, tried to charge fees for their services. However, since these services were of a general and intangible nature, fees could not be imposed. Moreover, the colonial assemblies, not wishing the governor to become independent of their control, generally refused to sanction such charges.

Colonial Taxation. The amounts collected in taxes by the colonial governments were so small that they were inadequate to meet even the piddling expenses of government. The colonists were manifestly opposed to taxes, taking the view that they received little in return. Moreover, since

[6] *N.Y. State Documents Relating to Colonial History*, Vol. 7, p. 908.

the supply of money was small, the payment of any tax became a hardship even though taxes were often payable in kind. Therefore, wholesale evasion of tax payments was the rule rather than the exception. Then, too, the administration of tax collections was inefficient. Confronted with all these problems, the collection of taxes was a hit-or-miss affair, and in the words of Professor Sumner, "Taxes in the colonies were nothing but subscriptions to a club."

Such taxes as were levied differed from section to section because of different political heritages and economic conditions. Thus New England, with her relatively equal distribution of wealth, favored direct taxation, whereas the Southern colonies, because of the nature of their land tenure, drifted away from direct taxation. In the Middle Atlantic colonies, with their mixed economies, direct and indirect taxation was fairly balanced.

Taxation was expected to pay not only for the expenses of the colonies but also for some of the colonial expenses of the Crown. Up to 1750, the British government poured more money into the colonies than it took out, and its deficit would have been even larger if the Crown had not excluded the colonies from sharing in certain sources of revenue, such as quitrents.

The first internal tax in the English colonies was imposed in 1619 when Virginia levied a per capita, or poll, tax of 1 pound of tobacco to meet the salaries of civil officials. Since the receipts from the poll tax did not increase when the colony needed additional revenue, such as in time of war, property taxes were imposed intermittently. However, the economy of Virginia, with its great dependence on tobacco, lent itself to the imposition of export and import duties. The stage was thus set for the first great contest over the respective merits of direct and indirect taxation. The small landholders of the Piedmont, not owning many slaves, favored property and poll taxes. On the other hand, the plantation owners of the Tidewater favored import and export duties, and since they had political control, the general trend in Virginia was toward indirect taxation. The same tendency was found in most of the other Southern colonies.

In New England, on the other hand, property and poll taxes were the first to be imposed, and all through the colonial period, direct taxes were important, since there were no large landholders and no large slave owners to oppose them. In time, the general property tax was extended to include personal property as well as realty. Subsequently, a crude form of income tax, called "faculty tax," was introduced in order to equalize the tax burdens between individuals who had real property and those, particularly in the towns, who did not own real estate but who had an income. In 1634 Massachusetts Bay assessed each man "according to his estate and with consideration of all his other abilities whatsoever." "Every laborer, artificer, and handicraftsman that takes over 18 d. per day," said the law of 1646, "shall pay 3s. 4d." over and above the regular poll tax. Eventually, as cities and towns grew in size and the number of nonproperty owners increased, it became impossible to administer the faculty tax and it was abandoned.[7]

However well direct taxation worked in theory, it did not work well in practice. Difficulties of assessment and inefficient administration by the officials united with a burning zeal for tax evasion and a knack for concealment of property by citizens, with the result that tax collections were not adequate to cover expenditures. To increase receipts, New England turned in desperation to excises and tariffs. At the same time the Puritan conscience compromised with reality, and a lottery was instituted. In no case, however, were the revenues sufficient to meet the extraordinary expenses of ambitious military campaigns. When these took place, the printing press went into action.

Colonial Tariffs. To expand their revenues, the colonies turned more and more to the txation of foreign and intercolonial trade. Export duties, widely used in the early period, began to fade away in the eighteenth century. On the other hand, tariffs on imports grew more important. However, since British regulation limited rather closely the range of dutiable articles, the first tariffs were imposed on raw materials, farm commodities, and certain luxuries rather than on manufactures. Had the colonies been given a free hand, they would have undoubtedly adopted a more protective system, for whenever the opportunity arose, there was no hesitation in granting protection. Indeed, Massachusetts imposed an embargo on certain foodstuffs; Virginia, on tobacco; and others, on horses, cattle, and liquor.

The colonial system of tariff administration was of major influence in the later development of American finance, for it was taken over lock, stock, and barrel by the Federal government after the adoption of the Constitution. As long as duties were payable in kind and specific rates prevailed, it was not necessary to place a value on imports. However, as soon as money appeared in sufficient quantities, the almost insoluble problem of evaluating goods presented itself, for since most duties were ad valorem, or "according to the value," the money payments under the tariff were determined by the method of evaluation. Lawmakers could arbitrarily set a value, or they could use as a basis specific purchase price, foreign-market value, export value, domestic value, cost of production, or landed cost.

After deciding upon the basis of evaluation, the administrators had to apply it to a specific shipment of goods. Evidence of value might be obtained through examination of an invoice, by appraisal, or by sworn statement of the importer. The final problem, probably the most imperative,

[7] Charles H. J. Douglas, *The Financial History of Massachusetts*, p. 31.

was to prevent smuggling, an outdoor sport which the colonists played with ineffable skill, since the seacoast was extensive enough to prevent satisfactory patrol.

Very early in colonial history, most of these problems were solved, if not scientifically and efficiently, at least satisfactorily. And by the time of the Revolution, the four cornerstones of tariff administration—the basis of foreign evaluation, the use of invoices as evidence of value, appraisal by an expert in doubtful cases, and a system of moieties or fees to informers—were in use. All of these were to persist in the American administrative system for the better part of a century.

Local Finance. Local government activities were carried on largely with the aid of services in kind by the citizens themselves. In the farming districts, roads were laid and repaired by a turnout of the able-bodied men, each contributing a required number of days of labor or paying a fee which would enable the hiring of a substitute.

Even in the larger cities expenditures were small. In New York City, for example, total expenditures in 1710 were only £277, for a number of public tasks which later were performed with hired labor, such as lighting and cleaning the streets, were required to be done by the citizens individually.[8] Even by the time of the Revolution, after the services of paving and grading the streets, etc., had been taken over, the city spent about £10,000, or less than 7 shillings per capita.

Because many services were voluntary or were paid for by fees, taxes were not greatly needed. However, some levies became unavoidable. At first these took the form of taxes on land, buildings, and selected items of personal property. Later a general property tax was introduced. From the very beginning, in addition to unscientific assessment of realty, there was much evasion of the tax with respect to the ownership of personalty. Nevertheless, the general property tax was a great step forward, for it was far in advance of any other form of taxation available for local use and it immediately placed local government activity upon a solid financial foundation.[9]

British Colonial Expenditures. The functions of a national or central government performed by the British for the colonies were both extensive and expensive. Embracing the defense of the colonies on land and on the high seas, the protection and fostering of colonial navigation and foreign

[8] The mayor and city council not only received no salaries but were subject to fine for failure to serve, and for a long time, poor relief was taken care of through the established church, the requisite levies not passing through the city treasury.

[9] The general property tax was collected in the late summer or early fall when the farmers had money from the sale of their crops. Since the fiscal year generally coincided with the calendar year, this meant that the locality was getting its revenue toward the end of the fiscal period and meanwhile had to live on borrowed funds. This difficulty has plagued many American local governments ever since.

trade, and civil and judicial administration through the Board of Trade, the Office of Foreign Affairs, and other agencies, they were paid out of the pockets of the citizens of the British Isles.

Up to the middle of the eighteenth century the British abstained from levying customs duties or internal taxes in America for revenue purposes. Customs duties and other port charges were levied to enforce the Navigation Laws and were not rigorously enforced. At best the customs were supposed to cover the pay of the inspection officers. However, they ran at the rate of about £2,000 per year, while costing almost £8,000 to collect. Of course, these and other restrictions on American trade increased prices of English goods to the colonists, thereby putting into the pockets of British merchants money which could be taxed by the royal authority. The extent of the "secondary taxation" of the colonists, as Franklin called it, was unknown, and the legal right of the English to impose it was never questioned by the colonists.

In time as the colonies became more populous and more involved in the wars with France, the British began to believe that it was time for the colonies to contribute their share of the expense of the central functions performed for their benefit. On the other hand, the colonists, not realizing how great were the services of the British central government, were inclined to understate the costs of the defense and administration of the colonies, while overstating the economic and financial gains which England obtained.

The drift of events was brought to an issue when Great Britain drastically changed its colonial fiscal policy in 1764. The government was reorganized, and a ministry was appointed which undertook to enforce Britain's trade regulations and to impose taxes on the American colonies for their share of the costs of defense and civil administration.

The new ministry estimated the cost of maintaining the British garrisons in America at £360,000 a year, and it proposed to provide one-third of this sum from moneys raised in the colonies. However, it was idle to expect the colonists to provide such an amount voluntarily, since by that time they were antagonistic toward the central government. Accordingly, in April, 1764, Parliament repealed the Molasses Act, which had been regulatory in theory, and replaced it with a set of duties which it intended to enforce. It was estimated that these new taxes would yield £45,000 a year. In the following year, Parliament passed a law requiring the colonies to provide quarters and supplies for British troops. In addition, various documentary stamp taxes and duties on tea and other imported articles were imposed.[10]

[10] The stamp duties were imposed on every legal paper and were high: on legal papers, from 1 shilling to £6; on a college diploma, £2; a liquor license, £4; a pack of cards, 1 shilling; a pair of dice, 10 shillings; a newspaper, penny per sheet; a pamphlet, 1 shilling; an advertisement, 2 shillings; an almanac, 2 pence; etc.

The colonists refused to admit the right of the British government to impose taxes without the consent of their legislatures. To do so would be to relinquish whatever rights of self-government they had acquired in practice, if not in legal theory. Some English statesmen, admitting that there was some justification for the American outcry against "taxation without representation," proposed to grant the colonies representation in the British Parliament. But most of the men in authority thought that such a plan would weaken British prestige and would result in the contamination of the British populace with the more radical or equalitarian American ideas. Moreover, the proposal was unpopular in the colonies, for it was thought that distance would not permit the people to follow the deliberations in Parliament or to instruct their representatives on how to act upon the matters at issue, with the result that approval might be given by the representatives to policies which would be inimical to colonial interests.

Benjamin Franklin and a few other American statesmen advocated the establishment, under the authority of the Empire, of a Union of Colonies, to which could be delegated certain functions then performed by the Crown and in which the colonies could vest limited powers of taxation. But the British feared that this proposal would result in a loss of control over the colonies. The colonists, on the other hand, were concerned in the affairs of their own particular colony and did not wish to be tied too closely with the other colonies or to be subordinated to a continental supergovernment.

Thus, the problem of more effective organization of continental defense and taxation remained unsolved, and an issue was joined which contributed importantly to the eventual armed break with England.

Prelude to Revolution. In September, 1774, delegates from the thirteen colonies met in a "Continental Congress" at Philadelphia to consider measures for the defense of their liberties. After organizing, through committees in each colony, measures of resistance to the offensive British measures, they issued a Declaration of Rights and Grievances and a petition to the King. Following the armed conflicts at Lexington and Concord, the Second Continental Congress assembled in Philadelphia in May, 1775, and issued the Declaration of the Causes and Necessity of Taking up Arms. Early in 1776, several colonies declared themselves independent states, and in May, Virginia adopted a formal constitution. In June, Congress advised all colonies to establish independent governments, and on July 4, it issued the Declaration of Independence, proclaiming all colonies to be states and to be bound in a union for the defense of their independence. During the succeeding four years all the other states either framed and adopted constitutions or at least declared their existing colonial charters to be constitutions of independent states.

Chapter 3: FINANCING THE REVOLUTION

When the Revolutionary War began, the colonies had a central government in name only. The Continental Congress was little more than a debating society or an assembly of ministers of states. It had the power to borrow money and spend it, but it could not levy taxes. It could pass resolutions, but it could not enforce them without implementation by the states. It could appeal to the states for money but could not force them to supply it, for each one of the thirteen colonies had retained its full sovereignty at the time it entered into a union for the common defense.

Congress tried to persuade the states to contribute to its treasury. When they failed to respond, it was forced to resort to the crudest method of raising funds—printing paper money. In time these paper-money issues depreciated and either were converted into a new tenor at a fraction of their value or completely disappeared from circulation as worthless money. Meanwhile, specie was circulated in the colonies by the English and the French, and a line of credit was opened to Congress in Europe, making it possible to change radically the methods of war finance. As the war progressed and assumed a more crucial character, Congress developed bolder action. After the adoption of the Articles of Confederation, it actually began to be spoken of as the "national" or "Federal" government, even though it continued to lack the most important single attribute of a government—the power of taxation. At the same time the states responded better to Federal requisitions.

The Revolutionary War, therefore, divides itself into two periods: 1775 to 1780, when paper money provided most of the funds, and 1780 to 1783, when foreign loans and requisitions on the states were the mainstay of the finances.

Organization of Fiscal Machinery. Immediately after fighting began, Congress proceeded to organize its fiscal machinery. Beginning in June, 1775, it appointed several committees, each to attend to different phases of finances, and two joint treasurers to receive and disburse money.[1] In 1776, it replaced most of these committees by a single standing committee "for superintending the treasury" and dispensed with one of the two treasurers. It also established an Office of Accounts headed by an auditor general. This was the beginning of the present Treasury. But henceforth,

[1] One committee was to recommend financial measures; another, to supervise printing the bills of credit; a third, to number and sign them; a fourth, to prepare estimates; and a fifth, to pass on public claims.

25

the organization began to be complicated. In 1777, three commissioners were appointed to aid the committee in examining public claims, and commissioners of loan offices were established. In 1778–1779 the Treasury was reorganized completely. A Board of Treasury comprised of five commissioners, not members of Congress, was established to direct all operations of the department.[2] The Congressional Committee on the Treasury, otherwise referred to as the Committee on Finance, was continued as a policy-making agency. Robert Morris, the leading merchant of the time, was appointed as its chairman. Thus, Congressional and administrative financial functions were clearly separated for the first time. At the same time the internal organization of the Treasury was expanded by the creation of an office of comptroller, in addition to those of auditor, deputy auditor, and treasurer; and of two chambers of accounts, one on claims and one on debts, each composed of three commissioners; and in 1779, a secretary was added. The organization was cumbersome, and the duties of the various officials overlapped, producing constant disagreement and confusion. The Treasury was reorganized once more in 1779. Two members of Congress were placed on the Board of Treasury, and the appointed commissioners were reduced to three. But this had little positive effect. In November, 1780, the Congressional Committee after thorough inquiry reported to Congress that "the Demon of Discord pervaded the whole Department" and there was but one solution: " . . . the Treasury should be under the direction of a single officer accountable to Congress for the conduct of his Department."[3]

Accordingly, in February, 1781, Congress established the office of Superintendent of Finance, with complete authority over the Department, and abolished the Board of Treasury.[4] It appointed to that office Robert Morris, who, as chairman of the Standing Committee on Finance in 1778,

[2] The Resolution of Apr. 15, 1778, gave the Board complete powers "to superintend the affairs of the Treasury"; prepare estimates of expenditures; appoint subordinate officials; and to report to the Congressional committee on the state of the treasury. For full text of the various resolutions, organizing and reorganizing the department, and committee reports of this period, see Fred W. Powell, *Control of Federal Expenditures*, pp. 1–19.

[3] *Ibid.*, p. 33.

[4] The Superintendent of Finance was "to examine into the state of the public debt, the public expenditures, and . . . revenue, to digest and report plans for improving and regulating the finances, and for establishing order and economy in the expenditure of the public money; to direct the execution of all plans which shall be adopted by Congress respecting revenue and expenditure; to superintend the settlement of all public accounts; to direct and control all persons employed in procuring supplies for the public service; . . . to obtain accounts of all the issues of specific supplies furnished by the several states; to compel the payment of all moneys due to the United States." The chamber of accounts and the various commissioners were abolished and replaced by an assistant superintendent of finance, a secretary, a comptroller, a treasurer, a register, auditors, and clerks. (*Ibid.*, pp. 33–36.)

had reported a plan of expenditures and financing which, though crude, was the first national budget in American history.

Paper-money Issues. The exact cost of the Revolution to the Continental Congress is impossible to ascertain, because the expenditures were made in money which constantly changed in value, and because the accounts were complicated and none too well kept. But a conservative estimate would be $100 million in specie. By far the largest share was covered by printing paper money, lesser amounts being raised by domestic and foreign loans, requisitions on the states, lotteries, and miscellaneous sources. The individual colonies levied taxes, but collections were poor, and they also relied on paper money and loans in paying requisitions to the Federal Treasury or financing their separate war expenditures.

Congress could not resort to taxes to finance the war, since it had no power to levy them. Nor could it even ask for this power, since the war had been undertaken as a protest against centralized taxation. Furthermore, the primitive nature of the economy and the occupation of much of the territory by British troops would have prevented effective tax collection.

Congress also found it impossible to borrow to cover its expenditures until very late in the war. (1) In the first place, the outcome of the Revolution was by no means certain. (2) The colonists lacked capital funds which could be tapped through loans. (3) With no power to tax, Congress was not a safe borrower. (4) There was no precedent in colonial history for any governmental borrowing through the issuance of salable securities.

Since both taxes and loans were not immediately possible, Congress began to print paper money, a course of action fully in line with American colonial tradition and popular among both the people and the delegates to Congress.[5] On June 22, 1775, Congress resolved to issue bills of credit up to 2 million Spanish milled dollars. It was assumed that all the bills would be retired by the states through taxes and that the war would be short. Neither of these assumptions was correct, and paper-money issues increased steadily and remained unredeemed. Before the end of 1775, $6 million had been issued, but like the Massachusetts issues of the colonial period, continental currency did not depreciate immediately. It began to lose its value in 1776 after $19 million more had been issued, and by the end of the year it was worth only 70 per cent of its face value.

Congress realized full well what was taking place and in 1777 adopted

[5] As one congressman expressed the prevalent sentiment, "Do you think, gentlemen, that I will consent to load my constituents with taxes, when we can send to our printer, and get a wagon-load of money, one quire of which will pay for the whole?" (Albert S. Bolles, *The Financial History of the United States from 1774 to 1789,* p. 38.)

a resolution, declaring, "When a quantity of money of any denomination exceeds what is useful as a medium of commerce, its comparative value must be proportionately reduced." Yet it went right on issuing more paper money—$13 million in 1777, $63 million in 1778, and $140 million in 1779. Altogether, $241.6 million with a specie value of $41.0 million was issued.[6] If Congress recognized the nature of the problem, why did it continue to issue paper money? (1) Because there was no other alternative, (2) because it still hoped that the states would levy taxes to redeem the issues, (3) because it hoped that government price fixing and legal-tender laws would be effective, and (4) because it began to regard depreciation as a crude form of taxation. But the states were neither willing nor able to raise enough in taxes to sink the enormous issues. In fact, at first they swelled the total by issuing their own bills. But in late 1777 at the request of Congress, they stopped further issues, and many passed price- and wage-fixing laws and made continental bills legal tender. These laws were largely ineffective. However, a new rationale for paper money and its depreciation was being developed. It became recognized that, since each noteholder lost part of his equity in favor of the government, which presumably had first received full value, depreciation operated as a tax. There was little justice or equity in such a scheme of taxation, since it fell most heavily, not upon those who were best able to pay, but on those who held the notes the longest. Far from regarding its crudity as a disadvantage, many urged that depreciation made unnecessary the levying of other taxes. Wrote a contemporary:

There is at present no absolute necessity for high government taxes. The natural unavoidable tax of depreciation is the most certain, expeditious, and equal tax that could be devised. Every possessor of money has paid a tax in proportion to the time he held it. Like a hackney coach, it must be paid for by the hour.[7]

By 1780, $80 in paper money was worth only $1 in specie. Following Gresham's law, all specie disappeared, even though the existing stock of specie was far larger than at the beginning of the war. Many citizens sought to circumvent depreciation by accepting payments only in commodities or by eluding their debtors who sought to pay them off in paper.

A plan of retirement and contraction of currency was now adopted which was the first of its kind in monetary history and was as well conceived as any system of currency stabilization adopted anywhere since that time. The states were requested to levy a tax of $15 million a month for thirteen months in continental bills (now called "old tenor") or in specie

---

[6] For the amounts and dates of issue, see *American State Papers, Finance*, Vol. 5, pp. 763–774.

[7] Quoted by Bolles, *op. cit.*, p. 201.

on a basis of 1 silver dollar for 40 paper dollars and were to turn the proceeds over to Congress. Congress would replace the old bills with "new tenor," redeemable in five years and bearing interest at 5 per cent, on a basis of 1 new dollar for each 20 of the old. Sixty per cent of the new issues were to be returned to the states, while 40 per cent were to be retained by the national government.

The monetary reform was a ringing success for the conservatives, for $119 million of the old bills were turned in and destroyed, further paper-money issues were ended, specie came out of hoarding, and the currency was put on a "sounder" basis, even though the "new tenor" immediately depreciated to one-sixth of silver value. The old bills which had not been surrendered depreciated in time to 1,000 to 1. Later, under the terms of the Funding Act of 1790, any old bills which were offered for redemption were converted into bonds at a ratio of 1 to 100. However, at that time only $7 million of the old currency was turned in, the rest having been lost or destroyed.

Domestic and Foreign Loans. The Continental Congress first attempted to borrow money domestically in October, 1776. A loan office was opened, and 3-year certificates were offered at 4 per cent, but the rate was too low, and only a few certificates were sold. The rate was raised to 6 per cent, and after September, 1777, sales began to increase. Three factors induced people to buy Congressional stock: Congress began to receive contributions from the states, it had received a cash loan from France, and currency had depreciated to a point where its conversion into stock became attractive. When sales were suspended, $63.3 million of certificates with an estimated specie value of $7.7 million had been sold.

At first interest was paid in cash, but in March, 1782, Congress was forced to suspend cash payments. Interest was then paid in indents (evidences of interest due). Immediately the value of the loan certificates fell sharply, and many holders, deprived of income, were forced to sell their certificates at a loss to those who had funds and were willing to speculate on the future credit of the United States.

Early in the war, gifts came clandestinely from the French government, which naturally felt a certain satisfaction at England's difficulties. But foreign loans were extended only later in the war, when the military fortunes of America improved. Nevertheless, it was because of these loans that American finances were finally placed on a sound basis.

Altogether $7.8 million in specie value was obtained from foreign loans: $6.4 million from France (after the consummation of the alliance in February, 1778), $1.3 million from Holland, and $174,017 from Spain. Interest was at 4 to 5 per cent and was generally paid from new loans. Five million of the total went for purchases abroad or for discounting drafts issued to foreign or domestic supply houses, but some of the loan proceeds were delivered in this country in specie. Thus, in 1781 a shipment of $462,862 came from France, helping to establish the Bank of North America.

Requisitions on States; Financing by States. The first requisition on the states was made informally as part of the first paper-money issue and met with little success. It was followed in 1778 by a formal requisition of $5 million apportioned according to population. From then on, requisitions continued until the ratification of the Constitution. Even though the requisitions were regarded as loans to be repaid with interest, apportionment was difficult, collections were slow, and a large part was never collected. Some requisitions were to be paid in paper money, some in specie, and others in commodities. But the total paid up to the close of fighting was estimated at only $2.4 million in specie.

The aggregate costs of the campaigns independently conducted by the individual states cannot be estimated. Most of the states, with much less excuse than the national government, relied on paper money, issuing an estimated $209 million in bills of credit. Some of these were interest-bearing evidences of debt, but since they circulated, they could scarcely be distinguished from other types of paper money. Presumably, these issues were supported by some form of security—in Delaware by real estate, in New Hampshire by the taxing power, and in Georgia by confiscation of loyalist property. But this did not prevent them from depreciating, and in time they were redeemed at rates ranging from 40 to 1, to 1,000 to 1.

Late in the war, substantial resources, estimated at $15 million, were obtained from the sale of property confiscated from the loyalists. The unsold confiscated property also contributed to war finance, for it became a reserve against future state borrowings.

Because of the apparent painlessness of paper money, taxes were much lighter than they should have been and were not imposed until relatively late in the war. As in earlier colonial times, they were evaded and inefficiently collected. Everywhere, people complained about taxes, but only the patriotic and the conscientious paid them.

Administration of the Finances by Robert Morris. When Robert Morris accepted the job of Superintendent of Finance on May 7, 1781, the financial situation was already improving. Foreign loans and the large circulation of specie made domestic financing easier. Military operations largely ended in October, 1781, with the battle of Yorktown, thus reducing the need for funds; and the establishment of the Bank of North America increased the efficiency of existing capital funds. But most of Morris's contributions were in financial administration.

Morris knew that most of his measures did not deal with the root of the matter, which was the lack of Federal taxing power. Upon taking office, he had three objectives: to reduce expenditures, to obtain the maximum revenue domestically, and to borrow the remainder abroad. He succeeded in the first and third objectives, but not in the second, which was the most important. Incessantly he called upon Congress and the states to provide him with revenues, but his recommendations were ignored, and he had to rely on superficial measures.

To begin with, Morris insisted on a grant of wide powers and proceeded to apply them. He cut spending drastically, introduced order into the accounting and spending methods, persuaded the states to repeal all their legal-tender legislation, and began to contract the outstanding paper money by accepting it in payment of taxes and refusing to reissue it. But his attempts to obtain contributions from the states fell far short of his expectations.

The payments from the states having proved inadequate, Morris recommended, in 1781, that the several states give Congress the power to levy a 5 per cent ad valorem duty on imports, except arms, clothing, wool cards, and cotton cards. All the states except Rhode Island assented, but since unanimous consent was necessary, the recommendation was not adopted. In 1783 a similar measure met the same fate.

Morris also sought to stop the practice of obtaining specific supplies from the states in lieu of taxes. Under the existing arrangement, quartermasters issued certificates to the states in exchange for supplies. The states then presented them to the Treasury to be credited against their quotas under the requisition system. It was impossible to ascertain the amount of the certificates issued, but Hamilton eventually estimated them at $16.7 million. Morris considered this system wasteful and conducive to corruption. He wanted to supply the Army by private contracts, and he succeeded in effecting this reform in July, 1781.

The Bank of North America. Since taxes were not adequate to cover expenditures, Morris sought to improve borrowing methods. England had a central bank which was of inestimable value to her war financing, and it was clear that the states needed a similar instrumentality.

Accordingly, in May, 1781, Morris presented to Congress a plan for the establishment of a bank of deposit, discount, and issue. In December, 1781, Congress granted a perpetual charter to the Bank of North America, which opened in Philadelphia in January, 1782. This was the first American bank in the modern sense and also the first central bank in the history of the nation. Its initial capital was fixed at $400,000, which could be increased to $10 million. Actually, the bank started with a paid-in capital of only $253,000 subscribed by the Continental Congress from the proceeds of the specie loan from France and $85,000 subscribed privately.

The bank was operated conservatively under its first president, Thomas Willing, who for many years had been Morris's partner. Its notes were redeemable in specie on demand and circulated at close to par with specie, except in the beginning, when, in spite of the redemption privilege, they circulated at 10 to 15 per cent discount.

The bank loaned money to the government, held its deposits, and otherwise acted as its fiscal agent. Most of the government loans were for short terms, and the highest amount outstanding at any one time was $400,000. In December, 1782, when the bank requested some repayment, Morris sold $200,000 of the government's stock holdings, and in July, 1783, he sold the remainder to Dutch bankers. In 1787 the bank received a charter from the state of Pennsylvania. Gradually, its connections with the government became attenuated, and in recommending a national bank in 1790, Hamilton specifically excluded the possibility of using the Bank of North America in that capacity, declaring that its state charter "so narrows the foundation of the institution as to render it an incompetent basis for the extensive purposes of a national bank."

CHAPTER 4: FROM COLONIAL ORGANIZATION TO STATEHOOD AND FEDERALISM

The Revolution estàblished on a broader and firmer foundation the political and fiscal organizations developed by the colonists out of their own experience. It also gave birth to new political and fiscal arrangements borrowed from British practice or suggested by the political philosophers of the age—Locke, Montesquieu, Rousseau, Harrington, and others. These existing as well as new patterns first became embodied in the constitutions of the individual states. They were then carried over into the Articles of Confederation and finally, in a much more vigorous form, into the Constitution of the United States.

The post-Revolutionary period marked the beginning of the interchange of institutional experiments between the states and the Federal government, which has been one of the most significant features of American political development. The equally dynamic interchange of experiments between the local and the state governments which had its roots in the colonial development continued even more vigorously than before. Leading statesmen of the time moved freely between the government of the town in which they resided and the government of the state and the nation. In moving from one level of government to another, they brought with them a wealth of experience plus an ability to transplant the innovations successfully achieved at each level. It was thus that the ideas of popular sovereignty, elective office, separation of powers, bicameralism, and checks and balances, which were first developed in the state constitutions, were carried over into the Federal Constitution. Vice versa, the idea of a centralized executive who possessed the power of appointment and veto, was first fully developed on the Federal level and later seeped through into the revisions of state constitutions.

The Character of State Constitutions. Eight states framed and adopted constitutions for their own government in 1776. Three adopted constitutions in 1777, and one in 1780. Two states—Connecticut and Rhode Island —found their existing colonial charters so satisfactory that they simply declared them to be constitutions of independent states and did not replace them with new constitutions until twenty or more years later.

Because of the disturbances of war and the need for haste, all except two[1] of the constitutions were framed by legislative bodies and, contrary

[1] Massachusetts in 1780 and New Hampshire's second constitution in 1784.

to the theory of government by the consent of the people, were not submitted for popular ratification. Subsequently, the framing of constitutions by elected conventions and their ratifications by referendum became standard practice everywhere.

The writers of the state constitutions were college-educated men, familiar with the evolution of British parliamentary and administrative institutions and the writings of European political philosophers. They affirmed and gave more vigorous expression to those colonial institutions which had been born of the democratic aspirations of the people, while uprooting those which stemmed from British aristocratic traditions or had served as instruments of British imperialism. They also introduced bold experiments in popular government suggested by the writings of the political philosophers. Several constitutions contained preambles expounding the principles of equality of men, popular sovereignty, separation of powers, maintenance of checks and balances, freedom of election, rotation in public office, and the right of a majority to alter its government. To fit the spirit of popular government more completely, they reshaped the four basic institutions of colonial government: the popularly elected assembly, the governor appointed by the Crown and directly or indirectly exercising a veto power over the acts of the assembly, the governor's council, and the judges appointed by the Crown. They provided for a bicameral legislature, a governor elected by the people or by the legislature and more or less subordinate to the legislature, and a judiciary elected by the legislature. While declaring for the principle of separation of powers, so eloquently developed by Montesquieu, they seldom followed it consistently. Instead, they deferred to the popular distrust of executive power and sharply restricted the governor's authority. The Virginia constitution, despite its theoretical expression in favor of separation of powers, permitted the legislature to elect the governor, the council, and the judiciary. The authors of the Pennsylvania constitution went even further, providing for a unicameral legislature and doing away with the governor altogether, substituting an executive council elected by the legislature. They also prohibited any member of the legislature from serving more than four years and any member of the council more than three years in every seven, so that "the danger of establishing an inconvenient aristocracy" might be avoided. New York, adhering more closely to the theory of separation of powers, provided for popular election of the governor. But it subordinated him to the legislature by vesting all powers of appointment in a Council of Appointments and by giving him no veto power. The legislature was to appoint a treasurer and an auditor general (renamed "controller" in 1797) and thus kept fiscal administration completely in its own hands. The Massachusetts constitution gave the most complete expression to the doctrine of separation of powers, and it was the only one to give the governor a veto power.[2]

Although declaring all men to be equal, the state constitutions retained the colonial property restrictions on suffrage, and some, such as that of Massachusetts, even raised them. Similarly, while proclaiming freedom of conscience, several required religious qualifications for the holding of public office.[3]

Most of the constitutions made no reference to the taxing and appropriating powers, but these were implied to be contained in the legislative powers. Few established any limitations on the exercise of these powers or introduced any new principles. The Maryland constitution of 1776, however, gave expression to the popular wrath against the poll tax and prohibited its use in the future. It laid down the rule that "every person should contribute his proportion of public taxes for the support of government according to his real or personal property within this state," thus expressing the democratic idea of taxation according to ability to pay as it was then understood. It also recognized, however, that "fines, duties or taxes may properly and justly be imposed or laid with a political view for the good government of the State."[4]

In providing for a bicameral legislature, some of the constitutions, such as Maryland's, following the colonial and also the British parliamentary practice, made the point that only the lower house, which was expected to represent the common man, was to originate money bills. The Maryland

[2] John Adams expressed the underlying theory of separation of powers in his *Defense of the Constitution of the Government of the United States* (Vol. I, p. xiii): "If there is one certain truth to be collected from the history of all ages, it is this: that the people's rights and liberties can never be preserved without a strong executive, or, in other words, without separating the executive from the legislature. If the executive power, or any considerable part of it, is left in the hands of either an aristocratic or democratic assembly, it will corrupt the legislature as rust corrupts iron, or as arsenic poisons the human body; and when the legislature is corrupted, the people are undone." According to Adams, the Senate was to represent the rich and protect them against being robbed by the poor; the House was to represent the poor and protect them against being robbed by the rich; " . . . but neither the rich nor the poor can be defended by their respective guardians in the constitution without any executive power, vested with a negative, equal to either, to hold the balance even between them, and decide when they cannot agree." (*Ibid.*, Vol. III, p. 294.)

[3] The Massachusetts constitutional convention declared that those who did not possess property were just beginning life or were living off their parents or were guilty of "idleness of life and profligacy of manners." The two Carolinas and the New Jersey constitutions required legislators to be Protestants; Delaware that they be Trinitarians; and Pennsylvania that they believe in the inspiration of the Bible, while Massachusetts and Maryland excluded non-Christians from all public office. (H. C. Hockett, *Political and Social Growth of the United States*, p. 245.)

[4] H. S. Hanna, *Financial History of Maryland, 1789–1848*, p. 27.

constitution also provided that no money bill shall be attached as a "rider" to a bill of another character, thus safeguarding the integrity of the appropriating process.

None of the constitutions introduced any changes in the existing power of local government. For the moment this framework did not clash with the precepts of popular government, having been the child thereof from the beginning.

Having adopted constitutions and having set up new legislative, executive, and judicial establishments, the states proceeded to liberalize the statutes inherited from the colonial regime. Under the leadership of Thomas Jefferson, Virginia disestablished the church, abolished the taxes levied for its support, freed the ownership of property of feudal entailments, and otherwise brought the whole field of civil and property relations into closer conformance with republican institutions. Other states did the same, although not so rapidly and sweepingly.

The finances of the states continued in confusion for some years after the war. Business and agriculture were depressed. Currency, although nominally on a specie basis, was still replete with paper issues of diverse values. Soldiers besieged legislatures with demands for payment for their past services, and debtors asked for laws that would release them of their private debts. Holders of state obligations demanded payment of principal and accumulated interest in specie. The people at large insisted that they were unable to pay taxes, only a portion of existing levies were collected, and the state treasuries were empty. Public lands were offered for sale, but the buyers were few and bought only on credit. The legislatures deemed it futile to enforce new levies and reverted to the issuance of paper money to meet payments to soldiers, interest on debt, and extraordinary expenditures.[5] In addition, all states were anticipating with great disquietude the time when they would have to assume their respective shares of the continental debt.

Articles of Confederation. While the states were framing their constitutions, they also gave formal status to the loose union formed in 1775 to carry on the rebellion against England. The colonists designedly labeled it a "Confederation," meaning that it was a mere temporary banding together of independent states for the achievement of certain common ends. The national government was given no such vast power as it had assumed on occasions during the Revolution, and the states did not surrender any of their sovereignty.

In 1776 the Second Continental Congress appointed a committee to prepare Articles of Confederation. Its report was debated for more than a

---

[5] As during the colonial period, depreciation of paper money was heavy in some states, while in others it was small.

year and was finally passed by Congress in November, 1777, but it took four more years for the Articles to be ratified, and then they merely gave legal substance to a system already long in effect.

The delay in ratification occurred because those states which had no claims to Western lands insisted that the others surrender their claims in favor of the union so that the lands would be used for the benefit of all. The establishment of a national jurisdiction over the Western lands made possible a unified policy for their sale and disposition. Moreover, it provided a source of revenue for the central government and later, through distribution to the states, a source of support for internal improvements and education.

Under the Articles, each state specifically retained its sovereignty, freedom, and independence and every power which was not expressly delegated to the United States Congress. The relationship of the states to one another was that of a "firm league of friendship for common defense, security of liberties and their mutual and general welfare."

The administrative structure of the national government was too clumsy to permit efficient operation. There was a Congress, to which each state sent from two to seven delegates. Delegates could not serve for more than three in any six years, and they were appointed, paid, and subject to recall by their individual states. Every state, regardless of size, population, or number of congressmen, had only one vote. Congress appointed one of its own members as presiding officer, but he could not serve for more than one year in any three-year term and was in no sense an executive.

Congress's powers were rigidly circumscribed. It could spend money for the common defense and the general welfare but could not levy taxes on individual citizens. It could make assessments on the states for its required revenue in proportion to the value of their real property, but it could not compel the payment of the assessments. Congress could also coin money and regulate the value thereof, emit bills of credit, borrow money on the credit of the United States, and appropriate money. But each action required the consent of at least nine states. Amendments to the Articles required unanimous consent. Congress was thus made entirely dependent upon the good will of the states. It lacked the main attribute of a government—the power of coercion—and was, therefore, scarcely a government at all.

Fiscal Affairs after the War. During the first years following the conclusion of peace in 1783, the finances of the government deteriorated badly. The advent of peace weakened the will to cooperate, and each state became immersed in its own internal affairs. Collections from the states fell to 25 per cent of the sums levied and between 1783 and 1789 provided only $2 million in specie (plus $2 million in indents, which reduced the debt but could not be used as money). Sales of public lands brought $960,000, and sales of other properties $300,000. Total receipts, $7.5 million, fell far short of the requirements of government. Consequently, Congress had to borrow $2.3 million from Dutch bankers. The domestic and some of the foreign debt continued in default, the arrears of interest on the first mounting to $8 million and on the second to $1.5 million. The United States was bankrupt, and no state seemed to care.

Robert Morris struggled to persuade the states to establish the national credit by granting the central government an independent revenue which would enable it to resume payments on the debt. Finding himself completely blocked, he resigned in 1784, prophesying disaster for the nation unless a firmer union was formed and the national government was more adequately supported.[6] The office of Superintendent of Finance was abolished, and a Board of Treasury, composed of three commissioners appointed by Congress, was reestablished.

Economic Background of the Constitution. Wartime economic prosperity ended in 1785, and the hardships of the time caused the usual dissatisfaction. Debtors insisted upon new issues of paper money, while wealthier classes demanded a stronger central government. States were engaging in economic warfare by imposing tariffs on one another's commerce. The credit of the national government was low, and the securities issued in financing the Revolution were depreciating continuously. Congress could not negotiate any treaties to encourage international trade, it had no army or navy to give protection to property, and it could not levy tariffs on foreign commerce. Moreover, radical movements, culminating in Shays' Rebellion, caused widespread fear.

Finding political and commercial conditions intolerable, conservative leaders called a convention to amend the Articles. Meeting in Philadelphia in 1787, the convention wrote the Constitution of the United States. Far from being simply amendments to the Articles, the Constitution was a completely new document. Nevertheless, after a spirited campaign it was ratified in 1788 by nine states and became effective in 1789.

The Constitution revolutionized the governmental structure by establishing a more closely knit and permanent type of union. It created a dual government, consisting of a national authority, with sovereign powers in certain spheres, and of state authorities, with supreme powers in other fields. Thus a type of organization, known in political science as the "federal state," came into being in America. Under the new arrangement,

---

[6] "The inhabitants of a little hamlet may feel pride in a sense of separate independence," said Morris. "But if there be not one government which can draw forth and direct the combined efforts of our united America, our independence is but a name, our freedom a shadow, and our dignity a dream." (Ellis P. Oberholtzer, *Robert Morris*, p. 212.)

the states surrendered part of their sovereignty to an indissoluble union. But just how much, not even the best informed men could tell, for it took many years for the full implications of the Constitution to develop and for the substance of the "federal state" to crystallize in the public consciousness and governmental practice.

The Power to Tax. The Constitution gave Congress the power to levy and collect taxes, duties, imposts, and excises "to pay the debts and provide for the common defence and general welfare of the United States" (Art. I, sec. 8). However, all taxes had to be uniform throughout the United States, a direct tax could be levied only by apportionment among the states in accordance with population, and no export duty could be levied (Art. I, sec. 9).

The grant of taxing power was broad, for the "general welfare" clause came in time to be interpreted as almost all-embracing. Hamilton thought that general welfare included anything which was not purely local. The definition was within Congress's discretion and undoubtedly included "whatever concerns the general interests of learning, of agriculture, of manufactures, and of commerce."[7] On the other hand, the Jeffersonians believed that the phrase added nothing to the enumerated powers. Hamilton's concept prevailed in the beginning and, despite powerful opposition from state rights advocates, also in time.

The requirement of uniformity in Federal levies related to geographic uniformity, being inserted to prevent discrimination in favor of one section against another. The requirement for apportioning direct taxes according to population (slaves being counted only as three-fifths of free persons) was included at the request of the land-rich, slave-owning states, which had found from experience that such a tax bore most heavily upon them.

The exact meaning of the term "direct tax" proved perplexing. Recurrently, over more than a century, questions arose as to whether real property and poll taxes were the only direct taxes or whether income taxes and taxes on personal property were also direct. The Supreme Court first inclined toward a limited interpretation of the term but at the end of the nineteenth century switched over to a more inclusive interpretation. The whole problem had to be settled eventually by a constitutional amendment permitting Federal levies on personal and corporate incomes without apportionment.

The taxing powers of the Federal government and the states were concurrent in nature. But to prevent the possibility of one class of government taxing the activities of the other out of existence, the Supreme Court, at an early date, held that the instrumentalities of each were con-

[7] *Report on Manufactures,* 1791.

stitutionally immune from taxation by the other. At the same time, the states were specifically prohibited from levying either import or export duties except with the consent of Congress and only for the enforcement of their inspection laws (Art. I, sec. 10). By abolishing at one stroke the power of the states to impose conflicting tariffs on foreign and interstate commerce, the Constitution fused the entire country into an economic entity with a single international commercial policy and with free internal trade over its entire expanse. Thus, it opened the way for the most efficient use of the resources of each section of the country. It also established a basis for a possible separation of Federal and state revenues.

The Constitution provided that all revenue bills had to originate in the House of Representatives (Art. I, sec. 7). However, the Senate was given the power to amend revenue bills, and this was interpreted to mean that it could substitute entirely new bills. Moreover, it has been held that a bill introduced in the House and not acted upon in the same session might be introduced in the Senate during a succeeding session without being first reintroduced in the House.

The Power to Borrow. The Constitution gave Congress unlimited power to borrow money on the credit of the United States (Art. I, sec. 8). The original draft also gave Congress the power to emit bills of credit, *i.e.*, to issue paper money, but after lengthy debate, this clause was eliminated. Some delegates believed that Congress had to have this power, but they agreed to strike out the clause because it might encourage unnecessary emissions and because the power was inherent in the power to borrow money and did not need to be mentioned specifically. Others voted for the omission because they were opposed to paper money under any circumstances. Actually, Congress eventually issued bills of credit, and the courts ruled that it was within the borrowing power.

Although the power to borrow money was unlimited, there were implicit provisos which did impose a check. The phrase "on the credit of the United States" was later held to mean that "Congress is authorized to pledge that credit as an assurance of payment." Since the Constitution contains no vain promises, it was held that Congress could not ignore or withdraw that pledge. In short, while Congress could borrow or print money, it could not repudiate contract obligations. However, Congress, by exercising its sovereign powers, could refuse to allow the Federal government to be sued, and in such event debts could be repudiated.[8]

The Power to Spend. The spending power was limited by four qualifications: (1) to ensure proper budgetary practice and the complete responsibility of the Executive to Congress, it was provided that "no money

---

[8] *Perry v. United States*, 294 U.S. (1935).

shall be drawn from the Treasury but in consequence of appropriations made by law"; (2) "a regular statement and account of the receipts and expenditures" had to be published from time to time (Art. I, sec. 9); (3) in order to prevent the establishment of a strong military clique, the Constitution restricted appropriations for the army to a two-year period (Art. I, sec. 8); (4) although not specifically stated, it was deduced from the taxing power that all spending had to be for the general welfare.

The spending power was held to be as broad as the taxing power, and in practice it proved to be even broader, for its exercise could not be challenged in court. The courts took the view that no single taxpayer could sue to estop the Federal government from making an expenditure, for he could not show that he had been injured. As a result, the Federal government could, and eventually did, spend funds for distribution to the states, thus influencing state action.

The Power to Coin Money and Regulate the Value Thereof. The Constitution not only gave Congress power "to coin money and regulate the value thereof," but it specifically prohibited the states from emitting bills of credit or making anything but gold or silver a legal tender (Art. I, sec. 10). Eventually, an issue arose as to whether this debarred a state bank from issuing notes, but it was decided that it did not. The phrases "coin money" and "regulate the value thereof" have also been hotly debated. Was the term "to coin" applicable only to hard money or also to currency? Did "money" mean gold or silver or both? Could Congress refuse to coin silver, or did the Constitution guarantee free coinage of both metals? Could Congress declare anything but gold and silver a legal tender? Did the phrase "value thereof" mean value in terms of metallic content, or did it also mean value in terms of purchasing power? Over a period of time, all these questions, except the last, have been answered, if not by judicial opinion, at least by estoppel, and the power of Congress over money seems unlimited.

Enumerated and Implied Powers. The powers of the Federal government were specifically enumerated. In addition to the fiscal powers, they included maintaining an army and a navy; declaring war; calling out state militia to execute the laws of the union; regulating foreign and interstate commerce; regulating naturalization, bankruptcy, patents, and copyrights; and establishing post offices and post roads (Art. I, sec. 8). In addition, Congress was authorized "to make all laws which shall be necessary and proper for carrying into execution the foregoing powers, and all other powers vested by this Constitution in the government of the United States or in any department or office thereof" (Art. I, sec. 8). No part of the Constitution was more bitterly debated in the early years of the Republic. Liberal constructionists, led by Hamilton, maintained that the words "necessary and proper" gave Congress "implied powers" to take any measures which might expedite the accomplishment of the enumerated powers. Strict constructionists, led by Jefferson and Madison, held that Congress was limited to expressly stated powers and interpreted the phrase as giving Congress the right to take only such measures as were indispensable in putting into effect the enumerated powers. By and large, the liberal interpretation prevailed, making possible a consistent broadening of the operation of the national government and adapting the Constitution to changing conditions.[9]

The President and the Judiciary. By creating the office of the President, the Constitution provided a strong and completely centralized executive authority, thus correcting one of the most glaring defects of the Articles of Confederation. The President was to be commander in chief of the Army and Navy and of state militias when called into service and the head of the executive department. He was to appoint, with the advice and consent of the Senate, ambassadors, judges, and other officials and to make treaties with the Senate's concurrence (Art. II, secs. 1 and 2).

The Constitution also gave the President influence over legislation by giving him the power to veto and by directing him from time to time to inform Congress on the state of the Union (Art. I, sec. 7, and Art. II, sec. 3). Under this authority the practice of an annual message with recommendations of needed legislation developed from the very outset, and the practice of submission of an annual budget was established 130 years later. The right to veto was an ever-present threat in all legislation, and the appointing power, by giving him control over patronage, offered him a subtle means to compel recalcitrant members of Congress to support his legislative program.

Thus, from the very beginning, there tended to be a conflict of authority between Congress and the Executive. To resolve this conflict and complete the system of checks and balances, the Constitution established the Judiciary as the third branch of government. Without this balance wheel, the whole constitutional structure, with its division of powers between the national and the state government as well as within the national government itself, would have fallen apart.

Limitations on the Fiscal Powers of the States. The only direct limitation which the Constitution placed on the taxing powers of the states was to prohibit them from levying import, export, and tonnage duties (Art. I, sec. 10). Later, other prohibitions were implied. Thus, the clause vesting the regulation of interstate commerce in the Federal government (Art. I, sec. 8) was interpreted as inhibiting the states from taxing interstate

[9] See particularly sections on the Bank of the United States, internal improvements, national banking, and paper money (pp. 60, 85, 101, 155, 168, 186).

transactions, greatly limiting their ability to levy sales and consumption taxes. The provision for a dual government, as already stated, was held to bar the states from taxing Federal instrumentalities, and the war powers of the Federal government were held to give its fiscal measures priority over state levies in times of war.

Other Provisions and the Impact of the Constitution. The only other fiscal provision in the Constitution declared all debts of the Confederation valid under the new government (Art. VI, sec. 1). In addition, a few political provisions had fiscal implications. The authority giving Congress control over the territory and properties of the United States (Art. IV, sec. 3) imposed certain expenditure responsibilities, while providing a source of revenue.

Several political restrictions on the states indirectly limited their taxing powers. Prohibited from passing laws impairing the obligations of contracts (Art. I, sec. 10), the states could not withdraw tax exemptions once granted or alter the debt obligations of local communities. The provision guaranteeing the citizens of each state all privileges and immunities of citizens in the several states (Art. IV, sec. 2) protected citizens of other states against discriminatory taxation. The declaration that treaties made by the United States were the supreme law (Art. VI, sec. 2) established the supremacy of international agreements over state tax laws.

Some of the few amendments adopted during the succeeding 160 years had fiscal implications. In 1791 the Fifth Amendment to the Bill of Rights declared that no person shall be deprived of life, liberty, or property without due process of law. The Ninth and Tenth Amendments reserved to the states and to the people all powers not delegated to the United States or prohibited to the states. This was a most important conceptual limitation on all Federal powers, fiscal as well as administrative.

In 1868 the Fourteenth Amendment applied the "due process" clause to state governments, and it became the basis for many court decisions, enjoining state and local taxation beyond territorial jurisdiction or in violation of other individual rights.

In 1913 the Sixteenth Amendment permitted Congress to levy personal and corporate income taxes without apportionment among the states, thus opening a most prolific source of revenue. The Eighteenth Amendment, in 1919, established prohibition, eliminating liquor taxes as a source of Federal and state revenue, but the Twenty-first Amendment repealed prohibition in 1933.

The Constitution vested the Federal government with almost unlimited fiscal powers. From the very beginning the Federal government was given a fiscal advantage over the states, for every form of taxation, whether or not used by a state, was made available to the Federal government, and the taxation of imports was reserved exclusively to the Federal government. The exclusive and unlimited jurisdiction over the public lands gave the central government another important fiscal advantage. The Federal spending power was limited only by Congress's definition of "general welfare," and the Federal borrowing power was unlimited.

In a word, while establishing a system of Federalism or dualism in the discharge of public administrative and fiscal powers, the Constitution was weighted heavily in favor of the central government. In this respect, it expressed completely the wishes of the more nationalistically inclined trading and propertied groups in the country.

Chapter 5: ESTABLISHMENT OF THE NATIONAL FINANCIAL SYSTEM

The financial policies of the Federalist administration were dominated by its first Secretary of the Treasury, Alexander Hamilton. He was the architect of the new national financial system, and some of his policies were permanently adhered to while others were reverted to from time to time during the succeeding 160 years.

Long before coming to office, Hamilton had developed the philosophy which was to determine his activities as Secretary. His outlook was aristocratic rather than democratic, capitalistic rather than agrarian, mercantalistic rather than laissez-faire. His whole program was dedicated to the achievement of a strong government which would be closely allied with the merchant and financial groups. The individual parts of the program, being intermeshed, formed a consistent fiscal, monetary, economic, and political system.

To establish the national credit and to rally all public creditors to the support of the national government, Hamilton proposed to fund the national debt, *i.e.*, to convert it into long-term bonds and provide sufficient revenue to pay its interest charges and ultimately to retire it. He also proposed that the Federal government assume the obligations of the state debts under a similar funding system. The funding was also intended to create a supply of readily marketable bonds, which investors could use to subscribe for capital in large-scale business ventures, such as the Bank of the United States. Created by government authority but controlled privately, the Bank was to be an instrument through which government and business could function in unison in fostering the development of national commerce by extending commercial credit in addition to facilitating government fiscal operations.

Hamilton projected a revenue system based on import duties supplemented by internal taxes. He proposed a protective tariff to accelerate the country's industrial development and to make it self-sufficient in time of war as well as to tie business interests more closely to the national government. Finally, he proposed to sell public lands in large parcels and on credit in order to attract large "investors," to increase revenue, and to keep administrative selling expenses low.

The Organization of the Treasury. When the First Congress convened on the first Wednesday of March, 1789, the immediate financial tasks were to organize the Treasury, to establish a revenue system, to straighten out

45

the government's debts, and to provide a national monetary system. After taking the initial steps to create a revenue, Congress turned to the organization of the Treasury. In the meanwhile, the old Board of Treasury was temporarily continued. The Congressional debate on the subject demonstrated the ever-present fear of the American people that power might become too concentrated.[1] Two basic issues were involved: was the Treasury to be headed by a single individual or a board; and if by a single individual, how much power was he to be given?

Those who wanted a single head denounced the board arrangement as utterly unsystematic and irresponsible. They pointed out that the old boards had never closed their books and were engaged in endless wrangles, while management under the Superintendent of Finance had been far more responsible and efficient. The opposition argued that one man would not have enough ability to fill the exacting demands of the position. On the other hand, a board would offer the checks and balances lacking in a one-man system. The idea of a single head prevailed. He was to be appointed by the President and completely responsible to him.

The bill establishing the Treasury was drafted by Hamilton, who was slated to be its first head. He thought of that office as the fountainhead and executor of all the financial plans of the government. He was to have direct access to Congress by presenting his plans in person. Serving both the President and Congress, he was to occupy a semi-independent position and could use his own initiative and discretion in the performance of his duties. He was to be the second most important officer in the government, yielding precedence only to the President.

In drafting the bill, Hamilton followed the text of the resolution establishing the office of Superintendent of Finance. He called the Treasury a "department" rather than an "executive department." He also spelled out in detail the duties which the Secretary was to perform for Congress, while avoiding any reference to duties to be performed for the President. Thus, the Secretary was

. . . to digest and report plans for the improvement and management of the revenue and for the support of public credit; to prepare and report estimates of the public revenue and the public expenditures; to superintend the collection of the revenue; to decide on the forms of keeping and stating accounts and making returns; and to grant . . . warrants for money to be issued from the Treasury, in pursuance of appropriations by law; to execute such services relative to the sale of the lands belonging to the United States as may be by law required of him; to report and give information to either branch of the Legislature, in person or in writing (as he may be required) . . . , and generally, to perform all such services, relative to the finances, as he shall be directed to perform.

[1] For the debates, see Fred W. Powell, *Control of Federal Expenditures*, pp. 43–64.

Nowhere did Hamilton incorporate the sentence which appeared in the bills establishing the other departments—" . . . such principal officer of the department . . . shall perform and execute such duties as shall from time to time be enjoyned on or entrusted to him by the President of the United States, agreeable to the Constitution." Yet the Secretary could be removed at any time by the President, and thus he was the President's creature.

Congress's response to Hamilton's proposal was somewhat mixed. On the one hand, some members liked to have the Secretary attached to Congress. On the other hand, Gerry and others feared that this attachment might result in the Secretary's dominating Congress. They objected particularly to the word "report," claiming that permitting the Secretary the right of personal appearance before Congress would give him an opportunity to influence its judgments and proceedings. A compromise was adopted, substituting the word "prepare" for "report," leaving the choice of presentation to Congress.

The importance of this amendment extended far beyond the issue of the relation of the Secretary to Congress, for it allowed Congress to exclude executive officials from open appearance, thus condemning the relations between the Executive and the Legislature to backdoor conferences.

In addition to the Secretary, the Act created several subordinate officers—a Comptroller, an Auditor, a Treasurer, and a Register to be appointed by the President and an Assistant Secretary to be appointed by the Secretary.

The Auditor was to examine all public accounts and transmit them to the Comptroller, who was to examine and certify them for payment, superintend their adjustment, countersign warrants drawn by the Secretary, and prosecute delinquencies in revenue collections and bring public debtors to account.[2] The Treasurer was to receive and keep the public moneys, disburse them on warrants signed by the Secretary and countersigned by the Comptroller, and give Congress a statement of accounts on the third day of each session. The Register was to keep all accounts of receipts, expenditures, and debts; preserve and record vouchers and certificates; and transmit to the Secretary copies of certified balances of settled accounts.

Obviously, it was intended to create an elaborate system of checks and balances in order to prevent tampering with Federal funds. However, the arrangement was clumsy and resulted in confusion. The Secretary was not required to give an annual report until 1800, and in a number of cases money was paid out without legal authority. Thus, no one—auditors,

[2] Three years later, in 1792, the customs service was placed under the direction of the Comptroller and internal-revenue collection, under a commissioner.

Comptrollers, Treasurers, Secretaries, or congressmen—had any understanding of what was taking place.

Financial Organization of Congress. The basic features of the Act establishing the Treasury Department have survived to the present day.[3] But
except for the short period when Hamilton was in office, the position of
the Secretary has never attained the preeminence which he planned for it.
Before long Congress began to take financial matters into its own hands
and succeeded in confining the Secretary to administrative work. However, in the beginning, Congress followed the procedures of the British
House of Commons, allowing the Secretary (like the Chancellor of the
Exchequer) to initiate revenue and appropriation bills, always, however,
in writing.[4] As soon as his reports were received, the House would resolve
itself into a Committee of the Whole on Ways and Means. A debate would
be held, and a committee appointed to put the proposal into bill form. This
committee would confer with the Secretary and leave it to him to draft
the bill, since he was best equipped to do the job.

This procedure gave Hamilton a great advantage even in the absence
of direct appearance before Congress, and he took full advantage of it. In
quick succession he presented to Congress one measure after another, each
dealing with an urgent problem and worked out in such complete detail
as to leave Congress little choice but to adopt it in its entirety. In presenting his estimates of appropriations, Hamilton did not itemize them but
submitted them in lump sum.[5] Whether this was necessitated by the newness of the operations or was intentional is uncertain, but it restricted Congressional appropriation action to that of a rubber stamp. Congress specified the revenue from which appropriations were to be paid and set up
some permanent appropriations. One of the difficulties in the way of a
sound system was that the fiscal year coincided with the calendar year.
With Congress convening in December, there was not time enough to
legislate appropriations before the beginning of the new year. In the
interim, the departments had to depend on permanent appropriations, informal advances from the bank, and departmental funds not transferred
to the Treasury. In paying off the advances, the departments became short
of funds toward the end of the year.[6]

Eventually Congress revolted against domination by the Secretary. In

[3] The Act was signed Sept. 2, 1789, and Hamilton became Secretary on Sept. 11.
[4] The Secretary's right of personal appearance before Congress was rejected in
1790, when Hamilton wrote the House that he would like to present in person a
plan for funding the debt. In the ensuing debate, Gerry and Madison contended that
better consideration could be given to the plan if it were presented in writing, and
they won their point. (Henry J. Ford, *Alexander Hamilton*, pp. 226ff.)
[5] For example, the first appropriation act of 1789 contained only 13 lines.
[6] The pernicious mechanism of making appropriations to cover deficiencies, that is,
money already spent, was not inaugurated until 1804.

1796 it established a standing committee on Ways and Means in the House with duties of inquiring continuously into the financial requirements of the government and initiating and preparing revenue and appropriation measures. The Secretary was requested to report his estimates to the committee and was thus reduced to a secondary place in the government. The whole plan of American financial management became fundamentally different from the British system, giving more power over fiscal arrangements to the Legislature than to the Executive. Whether or not this was a beneficial reform was open to serious question.

The Establishment and Expansion of Customs Revenue. Even before organizing the Treasury, Congress took up the problem of raising money to support the government. It was apparent to all members that taxation of imports was the most natural source of revenue. It was relatively easy to collect and was bound to be productive because of the importance of foreign trade. Yet it took Congress three months to frame and pass a tariff law, for the issue of protection for domestic manufactures immediately arose. Even though there were few manufacturers in the country, they were quite vocal in their clamor for protection, and the tariff law of July, 1789, was mildly protective.[7] It set up basic collection processes and administration and imposed tonnage duties of 6 cents a ton on American-owned ships and 50 cents on those built and owned by foreigners.

Ad valorem duties accounted for about one-third of the total revenue collected in customs. Goods were evaluated by the importer on the basis of the actual cost as evidenced by an invoice. To this was added 20 per cent if the goods came from the Cape of Good Hope or beyond or 10 per cent if the goods had been shipped from any other place. The colonial system of "moieties" was reestablished, providing rewards for information in regard to false appraisal or smuggling. There was also a provision for appraisal if the invoice on the goods was challenged. All duties were to be paid in cash or by bond. However, 10 per cent discounts were allowed for prompt payment or on goods imported in American ships. In 1795 evaluation was changed to "actual cost at place of export." In 1799 evaluation reverted to the 1789 method.

The tariff of 1789 did not produce enough revenue, nor was it high enough to satisfy Hamilton's desire to encourage domestic manufactures. In his famous *Report on Manufactures* in December, 1791, he suggested 21 increases in current rates, five reductions in rates on raw materials, and four government subsidies to industry. Above all, he developed the philosophy of protection, arguing that everything possible should be done to

[7] Seventeen commodities were placed on a free list. Specific duties were imposed on 36 commodities, including cocoa, coffee, spirits, nails, steel, and twine. Rates of 7½, 10, and 15 per cent were levied on a selected list, including iron, glassware, stone, and carriages. A flat duty of 5 per cent was placed on all other commodities.

stimulate domestic industry and protect it against foreign competition. In March, 1792, Congress passed a new tariff bill, increasing the average rate to 13½ per cent and adopting 18 of Hamilton's recommended increases and three of his suggested reductions. Even at that early date sectional interest in the tariff was strong. The bill was passed by the House, 37 to 20, with all but two of New England's votes and all of Pennsylvania's being favorable.

In the early years the administration of the tariff was characterized by expediency and improvisation. Then, in March, 1799, the previous tariff administration acts were consolidated in one act which became the basis of future development.

An Internal-revenue System. Hamilton soon became convinced that the revenue from customs duties alone would not be sufficient to sustain the government's military and civil establishments in addition to covering its debt obligations.[8] Accordingly, he persuaded Congress to impose internal taxes in 1791 and 1794 and, after he had left office, in 1797. Probably the most famous of these excises was the whisky tax. Imposed in March, 1791, at rates of 9 to 30 cents a gallon, it evoked widespread protest among the farmers who were operating stills universally. In western Pennsylvania the so-called "Whisky Rebellion" broke out in 1794. It was suppressed by the militia, giving the Federalists an opportunity to demonstrate the power of the national authority. But the tax produced little revenue, only $347,354 in 1794, or half the estimated yield, while it cost $70,000 to collect.

Other levies included excises on the ownership of carriages, the manufacture of snuff, the refining of sugar, and sales at auctions; license taxes on sales of wine; and, after 1797, stamp taxes on legacies and other documents. The revenue from these taxes was small, being only $170,941 in twelve typical months in the middle nineties.[9] The carriage tax resulted in the first interpretation of what the Constitution meant by a direct tax. In the case of *United States v. Hylton*, the Supreme Court held that the carriage tax was not a direct tax, but an excise tax. Therefore, it did not have to be apportioned among the states according to population. The inference was that only per capita taxes and those on land and buildings were direct. Thus, it was an important precedent in later litigation over the income tax.

In July, 1798, on Secretary Wolcott's recommendation, Congress levied a $2 million direct tax. Each state was assigned a quota in proportion to its population. Slaves were taxed at 50 cents, and houses were taxed ac-

[8] In January, 1790, he estimated the ordinary expenditures, exclusive of debt service, at $600,000 and the revenue from customs duties and miscellaneous sources at $1.1 million.

[9] *American State Papers, Finance,* Vol. I, p. 403.

cording to their value on a graduated basis. The state's land acreage was then taxed according to its value at rates sufficient to supply the balance. The administration of the tax was complicated, the valuations of land and houses were imperfect, and the states were lax in imposing the tax. As a result, only half the levy had been collected as late as 1801.

Revenue from the Sale of Public Lands. The Treasury and Congress, including the Jeffersonian Republicans, viewed the public domain, then mainly in the Northwest Territory, as a source of revenue. Hamilton estimated the public domain at 21 million acres. Anticipating only bulk sales, he said, "This quantity, at twenty cents an acre, would yield a sum of $4.2 million. But . . . if it ultimately yields $3 million, it will probably equal every reasonable expectation."[10] In the long run, these estimates fell far short of the mark, but for the immediate future the proceeds were practically nil.[11]

From the beginning, the "investor," or, less euphemistically, the speculator, was favored by the land policy. By the Act of 1785, 640 acres was the minimum which could be purchased. The price was $1 per acre, but larger tracts could be bought at wholesale rates. In 1796 Congress adopted a permanent land ordinance, providing for the sale of 640 acres at $2 per acre, one-half payable in cash and the remainder in one year.

Funding the National Debt. Aside from raising revenue and organizing a fiscal machinery, the most pressing problem was to improve the credit of the government. In his *First Report on the Public Credit,* Hamilton estimated the national debt at $54.1 million[12] and the state war debts at $25 million.

The various certificates issued during the war were selling at 20 to 25 cents on the dollar in January, 1789, but by November when it became evident that measures to reestablish public credit would be recommended, speculators began to purchase the war certificates, and they rose 33⅓ per cent. By January when Hamilton made his report, they had increased another 50 per cent.

Hamilton proposed that the Federal government fund the old certificates at par with accrued interest through exchange for new long-term

[10] *Second Report on the Public Credit.*

[11] Between 1787 and 1796, 1.3 million acres was sold. John C. Symmes bought 272,540 acres, paying for them with certificates of the public debt. The Ohio Company bought 892,900 acres, paying certificates of debt and army land warrants. The total purchase money for the 1.3 million acres was $1.1 million, but the Treasury did not receive any cash until 1796, and by 1798 it had collected little more than $100,000. (*Annual Report of the Secretary of the Treasury,* 1835.)

[12] $10.1 million represented principal due to foreign governments and $27.4 million was owed domestically. Unpaid interest on the foreign debt was $1.6 million, and unpaid interest on the domestic debt, $13.0 million. There was also an estimated $2 million of continental bills of credit.

bonds. He argued that, by honoring the debt in full, the Federal government would establish its credit so firmly as to make it easier to raise money in the event of another great national emergency. He also thought that the new bonds could be used as money. This monetization of the public debt would alleviate the existing shortage of stable money, lower interest rates, stimulate trade and manufacturing, and enhance the value of land.

Hamilton's opponents, led by Madison, objected to his plan because it would give a windfall profit to speculators who had acquired the certificates from the original holders at low prices. They agreed that the debt be funded at par. But they insisted that the current holder of a bond be paid only the current market price and that the difference between par and the market price be paid to the original holder. Hamilton rejected this counterproposal, because it would constitute a breach of contract and would be completely impracticable. Although the Republican proposal was more ethical, Hamilton's plan provided the only workable solution. But his greatest difficulty was in persuading Congress to assume the state debts. His main contentions were that the state debts were contracted in a common cause and should, therefore, be commonly provided for and that assumption would cement the union more firmly and would establish the superior fiscal powers of the central government. He also thought that the securities involved would constitute a better investment for individuals if provided for by the same authority under the same interest and retirement provisions. Finally, he believed that the debts would be taken care of more quickly and efficiently.

However, the opposition insisted that the debts be regarded as contributions by the states to the winning of independence and that under Hamilton's plan, some states, which had originally paid a large part of their war expenditures out of taxes, would indirectly be bearing the burden of other states which had not been so efficient. Finally, the assumption of state debts would necessitate Federal internal levies and would be in contravention of state rights and of the superior efficiency of the states in internal taxation.

By dint of political maneuvering, Hamilton succeeded in having his entire funding program adopted in August, 1790. The principal of the national debt was funded into 6 per cent bonds, but one-third were not to bear interest until 1800. The arrears of interest were funded into bonds paying 3 per cent. Subscriptions to the new bonds could be in government obligations at their specie value, except in the case of continental currency, $100 of which was acceptable as $1 of specie.

To fund the state debts, the Treasury was authorized to issue $21.5 million of bonds, which was the estimated amount of the state debts incurred in financing the war. Four-ninths bore interest at 6 per cent payable immediately, two-ninths were at 6 per cent with interest to begin in

1800, and the remaining three-ninths were at 3 per cent, interest payable immediately. All the 3 per cent debt was redeemable "whenever provision shall be made by law for that purpose," but annual payments for principal and interest on other stock were limited to 8 per cent. Hence, the 6 per cent stock was really an annuity which would be retired by 1818 and 1824 if maximum payments were made every year.

In assuming the state debts, the Federal government assigned to each state a quota of Federal bonds to be distributed to holders of state certificates. Actually, the distribution was greater than necessary, for individuals turned in only $18.3 million of state certificates. The Federal government endeavored to recapture the excess payments and also to collect the balances owed to it by the states under the requisitions made before 1789, but the effort failed, as no state was willing to pay. Gallatin later insisted that assumption was done too hastily, costing the Federal government $10 million more than necessary.

The Funding Act also laid down some rules for the management of the debt. The proceeds from the sale of Western lands were earmarked for retiring the principal, and payment of interest was given priority over all other government expenses except for $600,000 allowed for general administration. The highest priority was given to interest on the foreign debt, and the lowest to interest on the assumed state debts.

Establishment of a Sinking Fund. Although the term "sinking fund" was not used in the law, the Funding Act contemplated the retirement of the debt gradually by a sinking-fund arrangement. Hamilton himself was very partial to the sinking-fund device, regarding it, like all other phases of fiscal policy, as an instrument for influencing the economy.

Urged on by Hamilton, Congress gradually extended the sinking fund. First, it set aside the surplus from customs and tonnage for the retirement of the public debt at par or less. It authorized the President to borrow $2 million at rates not exceeding 5 per cent, the proceeds to be used to purchase debt obligations. It also set up a board to supervise purchases of public stock and gave its members—the president of the Senate, the Chief Justice, the Secretaries of the Treasury and State, and the Attorney General—wide discretionary power. Since Hamilton naturally assumed a dominant position on the board, Congress's action gave him considerable authority to regulate the money market. He could contract the market by borrowing from the banks and building up the Treasury's cash fund. He could expand the market by having the fund purchase government securities. Indeed, he possessed half the power over credit given to the Federal Reserve Open Market Committee a century and a quarter later. Moreover, he could also support the market price of government bonds, a power which was not to be given to another Secretary until World War I.

In March, 1795, Hamilton presented in his *Second Report on Public Credit* a plan for speedier debt retirement which Congress adopted. The device was officially named a sinking fund. Its income consisted of a sum from current receipts equal to the interest on the debt already purchased, dividends on bank stock, proceeds from the sale of public lands, and any surplus remaining at the end of the year. The Sinking Fund Commissioners were given complete authority over the retirement of the debt and were empowered to borrow any sums needed to pay installments on the principal of the debt.

Increase in Expenditures. Interest payments absorbed 50 to 60 per cent of the entire Federal budget—an unprecedented situation in the annals of

TABLE 2.   FEDERAL RECEIPTS, EXPENDITURES, AND DEBT, 1789–1800*
(In millions of dollars)

	1789–1791	1792	1793	1794	1795	1796	1797	1798	1799	1800
Receipts:										
Customs......	$ 4.4	$ 3.4	$ 4.3	$ 4.8	$ 5.6	$ 6.6	$ 7.5	$ 7.1	$ 6.6	$ 9.1
Internal excises	.....	0.2	0.3	0.3	0.3	0.5	0.6	0.6	0.8	0.8
Bank stock....	.....	.....	.....		0.3	0.2	1.2	0.4	0.1	0.1
Miscellaneous.	.....	.....	0.1	.....	0.1	0.1†	0.2†	0.1	0.1	0.8‡
Totals......	$ 4.4	$ 3.7	$ 4.7	$ 5.4	$ 6.1	$ 8.4	$ 8.7	$ 7.9	$ 7.5	$10.8
Expenditures:										
Civil.........	$ 0.8	$ 0.4	$ 0.4	$ 0.4	$ 0.4	$ 0.4	$ 0.5	$ 0.5	$ 0.6	$ 0.7
Foreign......	.....	0.1	0.1	0.1	0.9	0.2	0.7	0.5	0.3	0.4
Navy........	.....	.....	.....	0.1	0.4	0.3	0.4	1.4	2.9	3.4
War.........	0.6	1.1	1.1	2.6	2.5	1.3	1.0	2.0	2.5	2.6
Pensions......	0.2	0.1	0.1	0.1	0.1	0.1	0.1	0.1	0.1	0.1
Interest.......	2.3	3.2	2.8	3.5	3.2	3.2	3.3	3.1	3.2	3.4
Miscellaneous.	0.3	0.2	0.1	0.1	0.1	0.3§	0.2	0.1	0.2	0.2
Totals......	$ 4.3	$ 5.1	$ 4.5	$ 7.0	$ 7.5	$ 5.7	$ 6.1	$ 7.7	$ 9.7	$10.8
Annual surplus ..	$ 0.1	$−1.4	$ 0.2	$−1.6	$−1.4	$ 2.7	$ 2.6	$ 0.2	$−2.1	$ 0.1
Debt at end of year	$77.2	$ 80.4	$78.4	$ 80.7	$ 83.8	$82.1	$79.2	$78.4	$ 83.0	$83.0

SOURCE: *Annual Report of the Secretary of the Treasury*, 1866, pp. 304–309.

* Fiscal year was same as calendar year until 1843 when it became July 1 to June 30. Figures for 1789–1791 are for approximately 2½ years.

† Including $4,000 in 1796 and $80,000 in 1797 from sale of public lands.

‡ Including $734,000 from direct tax.

§ Including $114,000 for Indian affairs.

any government. But the task of financial management, made almost insuperable by Hamilton's liberal provisions for the payment of the Federal and state debts, was made even more formidable by the unexpected increases in military expenditures due to the outbreak of wars with Indians, international conflicts with France and Spain, and payments of damages to Algiers under international awards. All the expenditures combined increased from a few hundred thousand dollars in 1789 to $7 million in 1794, with the prospect of a further increase in 1795.[13] As a result, despite all his efforts to increase the revenue, Hamilton did not succeed in taking the Treasury out of the red.

Rising Indebtedness. Many opinions to the contrary notwithstanding, Hamilton did not believe that a public debt was necessarily a public blessing.[14] He advocated that Congress ordinarily provide adequate revenue to meet appropriations, thus avoiding unnecessary debt. In his *Report on Manufactures*, he said,

As the vicissitudes of nations beget a perpetual tendency to the accumulation of debt, there ought to be a perpetual, anxious, and unceasing effort to reduce that which at any time exists, as fast as shall be practicable, consistently with integrity and good faith.

On the other hand, Hamilton did not agree with the "respectable individuals who, from a just aversion to an accumulation of public debt, are unwilling to concede to it any kind of utility." His desire to reduce the debt was offset by his desire to maintain a strong Federal government and the concomitant necessity for a high level of Federal expenditures.

During the Federalist administration, 1789 to 1801, net ordinary receipts were $67.8 million while total ordinary expenditures were $68.7 million. With a deficit of $900,000, the sinking-fund arrangement could not reduce the debt but could only change its composition. Thus, the total gross debt increased from $77.2 million in 1791 to $80.7 million in 1795 and $83.0 million in 1801. However, this increase was in part offset by a substantial cash balance in the Treasury and stock in the Bank of the United States.

In covering the increase in the gross debt, the Treasury borrowed extensively from European and American bankers. Between 1791 and 1794 Hope and Co. in Amsterdam sold six bond issues totaling $7.2 million, partly to fund the original foreign debt and partly to fund short-term loans. Bearing interest at 4 to 5 per cent, they were sold at 94½ to 96. In addition, temporary loans were arranged with the Bank of North America and the Bank of New York. In 1791, in order to pay for its subscription to the stock of the Bank of the United States, the establishment of which is described below, the Treasury borrowed $2 million from the Bank at 6 per cent, repayable over a ten-year period. Additional borrowing raised the government's indebtedness to the Bank to almost $5 million in January, 1795, when Hamilton resigned, and to $6 million in the following December.

[13] Expenditures were approximately $1.50 per capita. At the same time New York City's expenditures were $2 per capita and those of New York State less than $1.
[14] *Second Report on the Public Credit.*

The large loan to the government restricted the Bank's power to make private loans. Therefore, it asked the government to reduce its debt. The Treasury tried to raise money by offering $5 million of 6 per cent bonds, but the issue could not be sold at par and proved a failure. Thereupon, Congress authorized the Treasury to sell bonds below par and to sell the government's holdings of Bank stock. Even at a discount, only $80,000 of the loan was sold. The Treasury, therefore, was forced to sell part of its stock. In August and September, 1796, Wolcott sold 2,160 shares for $1.1 million and, in July, 620 more shares for $304,260, reducing the government's holdings to 2,220 shares with a nominal value of $888,000 but a considerably higher market value.

In 1796 the Treasury endeavored to relieve the pressure of the debt by resorting to a policy which was to hamper its operations for the next century. It began to issue noncallable, long-term securities. The 6 per cent stock of 1796, already cited as a complete fiasco, was a 24-year noncallable issue. Then, under the Act of July, 1798, $5 million of 8 per cent 15-year noncallable stock was sold, followed in 1800 by a similar issue of $1.5 million.

State Revenue. The sweeping financial measures of the Federalist administration had tremendous direct and indirect effects on the finances of the states. Almost overnight most of them became completely debt free, and others, such as Massachusetts, which had continued to borrow after the war, were freed of at least their largest and most troublesome debts. Several states, such as New York and Maryland, in the course of the settlement of their debts with the Federal Treasury, had even come into the possession of substantial net assets, for they had bought continental certificates at bargain prices in anticipation of eventually being required to pay their shares of the continental debt. Under the Hamiltonian funding program, they received new interest-paying certificates in exchange for these fortuitously acquired debt holdings.[15]

By the middle of the 1790's state revenue had been built up to the point where, instead of deficits, large annual surpluses began to appear. Most states were able to realize substantial revenue from the sale of some of their vast land holdings. Many of these lands were sold to speculators or to individuals who financed their purchases by borrowing from the newly organized branches of the Bank of the United States and the newly chartered state banks.[16]

[15] In 1786 Massachusetts had a debt of approximately $5 million and was charged with an equal amount of continental debt. But in 1794, after completing its accounting with the Federal Treasury, it had a net investment of $1.2 million in Federal stock. New York emerged from its settlement with the Federal government with $2.1 million in Federal stock, earning an immediate interest of $75,000 a year.

[16] In the early 1790's New York sold 5½ million acres for $1 million in cash, or an average of 18 cents per acre. Alexander McComb purchased more than 3 million

Tax collections also picked up. New levies were introduced, either to replace import duties which had been ceded permanently to the Federal government or to replace poll taxes which no longer harmonized with the spirit of the times. Several states introduced or reintroduced a state property tax—a levy which had always appealed to the common people, since it purported to apportion tax burdens proportionately to wealth. But a state property tax was not so easily administered as a local property tax, for local assessors in the different districts varied in their methods of assessment and great interdistrict inequalities resulted. The states had no more success in solving this problem than the provincial assemblies had had many years before. New York and Maryland abandoned the property tax after a few years. Massachusetts, on the other hand, retained the tax, trying to perfect state equalization tables in the face of constant objections from the towns. Many states introduced or increased the rates of auction duties, which produced large revenues.[17] Some states revised their excises on liquor and other commodities, extending their list to include sugar, tea, coffee, iron, glass, carriages, etc., or they increased or introduced license taxes on innkeeping and other occupations. In some states, such as Massachusetts, these excises were repealed after a few years, for they were exceedingly unpopular. Although many banks were chartered during this decade, they were not generally taxed, inasmuch as they were new and had not yet demonstrated their financial strength.

A prolific new source of revenue—state lotteries—was discovered during this time. Legislatures were besieged with demands to authorize the holding of a lottery for this or that public purpose—the founding of a college, the building of roads, etc. As the gains to the treasury were large, legislatures readily yielded.

In addition to land sales, taxes, and lotteries, many states, as already mentioned, derived substantial revenue from their holdings of Federal securities, and many ventured into business, investing in banks or establishing loan funds for farmers.[18]

---

acres, and most of the rest was sold in parcels of more than 100,000 acres. In 1795 more than half of the state's revenue ($325,000 of $559,000) came from land sales. (Don C. Sowers, *The Financial History of New York State from 1789 to 1912*, p. 39.)

[17] In New York, auction duties were imposed originally in 1784 at a rate of 2½ per cent of sales. This rate was raised in 1801 on auctions held in New York City to 3½ per cent. The revenue from auction duties increased from $6,219, or 5 per cent of the total state revenue, in 1790 to $55,493, or 18 per cent of the total revenue, in 1800. (*Ibid.*, p. 324.)

[18] New York, in 1795, purchased salt springs from the Onondaga Indians for $1,000 plus a royalty of 100 to 150 bushels of salt a year. It leased the saltworks to individuals in 10-acre lots, charging a duty of 4 cents a bushel (salt sold at $2 a bushel). The state invested over $1 million in the Bank of New York in 1797. Its revenues from investments increased from $24,000 in 1790 to $125,000 in 1800. (*Ibid.*, pp. 138, 258, 325.)

State Expenditures. Relieved of their troublesome debt charges by the Federal government, the states were able to meet their other expenditures without difficulty.[19] Judged by today's standards, their expenditures were low—only 42 cents per capita in Massachusetts in 1794 and only 40 cents in 1790 and 65 cents in 1800 in New York. They were also low compared with Federal and municipal expenditures, each of which varied between $1.50 and $2 per capita.

The maintenance of the legislature was one of the largest items of state expenditure, but the administrative and judicial departments required relatively small amounts. Legislators were paid a small per diem compensation (in New York $3 a day while in attendance and $1.50 while in travel). Governors usually received $3,000, and other high officials, $1,000 to $1,250 a year. Some states spent substantial sums for the reequipment of the militia, and under the pressure of public demand, several states began to take over correctional administration from the counties.[20]

Few states, if any, established and maintained charitable institutions, but limited grants were made to existing private institutions, and Massachusetts as early as 1789 assumed responsibility for certain categories of paupers. Several states initiated public-health measures, since local governments were slow to take action. New York in 1792 inaugurated annual appropriations to the New York Hospital and also for quarantine service in the port of New York. It followed these grants in 1794 with annual appropriations for the suppression of contagious diseases.

A number of states began to supplement the educational activities formerly conducted by the churches. New York as early as 1784 established a "Board of Regents of the University of the State of New York," first with a view to founding a secular state university in place of the church-dominated King's College and later, when this project failed in 1787, with the authority to charter private colleges and academies. In 1790, New York established from the proceeds of the sales of land a Literature Fund the income of which was to be used by the Regents to aid the institutions which they chartered. The first appropriation under the Literature Fund was $19,750 to Columbia College in 1792.

At the same time some states began to promote the common schools

[19] Illustrating the startling change in the size and structure of state expenditures resulting from Federal assumption, Massachusetts' expenditures in 1786 aggregated $352,400, of which $278,700 was for interest and $73,700 for other purposes. In 1794 expenditures dropped to $215,200, but interest was only $114,900, while other expenditures had risen to $100,300.

[20] New York, in 1796, built a model state prison in New York City at a cost of $253,000. Its total expenditures in 1799 were $252,000—$55,000 for the legislature, $29,000 for administration, $9,500 for judiciary, $17,000 for prison operation, $17,000 for charity, $12,000 for public health, $9,500 for Indian affairs, $7,000 for internal improvements, and $13,000 for interest. (*Ibid.*, p. 304.)

with financial subsidies. As early as 1786 the New York legislature set aside in each township one lot of public lands for "gospels and schools" and one lot for the "promotion of literature," and in 1795 it made its first appropriation, $50,000, in aid of common schools.

Few states made any expenditures for highways.[21] But since investments in internal improvements were greater than the counties and towns were willing to make, many states granted charters and subsidies to private companies enabling them to build and maintain turnpikes, bridges, and canals and to charge tolls. Thus, a beginning was made in the internal-improvements movement which eventually resulted in substantial state and Federal investment. Maryland, as early as 1784, chartered a company to build a canal around the unnavigable portions of the Susquehanna River, and in 1800 it loaned the company $30,000 which was never repaid. In 1791, the Pennsylvania legislature chartered a company to build a canal connecting the Susquehanna and Schuylkill rivers. Whenever dividends amounted to 15 per cent net, 1 per cent was to be reserved for education.

Conservatism in Local Finance. The political and economic stabilization of the country did not affect local finance so much as it did state finance, for the obvious reason that local government had not been so much disturbed by the Revolution and postwar dislocations.

By 1800 there had been little expansion in the services offered by local governments. Even in the larger cities only the main thoroughfares were paved and had drains or sewers. Street lighting and a night watch were maintained, but there were no day police, and fire protection was supplied by volunteers. No city or town had an organized water supply, but pumps and wells were generally erected in the city squares. Public-health control was almost nonexistent, and few localities maintained schools. Accordingly, total municipal expenditures of New York City in 1798 amounted to only $1.80 per capita (1.4 per cent of average per capita national income), and those of most other cities were about that size.[22]

Although the city fathers tried to confine local financing as much as possible to indirect taxes, the property tax was the main source of revenue, and auction duties, lotteries, liquor licenses, fees, and fines were supple-

[21] Pennsylvania, in 1785, appropriated £2,000 from "import monies" for a road from western Cumberland County to Pittsburgh.

[22] New York City, with a population of 60,000 in 1798, had a tax levy budget of $108,000, apportioned as follows: schools, $2,000; poorhouse and bridewell, $40,000; contingencies, $30,000; night watch, $23,000; and lamps, $13,000. (Edward D. Durand, *The Finances of New York City,* p. 30.) Providence, population 7,600 in 1800, spent $15,400 as follows: general government and finance, $800; night watch, $800; streets, sewers, etc., $2,700; schools, $500; poor relief, $2,800; interest, $1,500; miscellaneous, $1,400; debt repayment, $5,000. (H. K. Stokes, *Finances and Financial Administration of Providence,* pp. 134ff.) National income figures for the early years are admittedly crude.

mentary. With increased reliance on the property tax, it became necessary to improve its administration, either through state legislative or local action. In most states, following the precedent established by the provincial assemblies, the legislature retained some control over local property taxes by specifying the types of property to be taxed and the procedures to be followed in evaluation and collection, by establishing a limit on the rate of the tax, or by requiring that all property be assessed locally at full value. Notwithstanding this last requirement, local assessors continued to underassess property, and tax rates at the end of the century had risen to between 50 and 75 cents in each $100 of assessed value.

Establishment of a National Bank. The debate over Hamilton's proposal to establish a Bank of the United States anticipated many of the issues that were to fill the pages of American banking history over the next century and a half.

In his *Report on a National Bank* in December, 1790, Hamilton argued that such a bank would make a threefold contribution to the economy: it would increase the country's active or productive capital, because under the principle of a fractional reserve, a bank could issue two or three dollars in paper money for every dollar it had in specie; it would help the government in borrowing; and it would facilitate the payment and collection of taxes. "It is evident," he wrote, "that whatever enhances the quantity of circulating money, adds to the ease with which every industrious member of the community may acquire that portion of it of which he stands in need," and by having more money, every "industrious member" would find it easier to pay taxes.

The Jeffersonian party opposed the Bank as unconstitutional, for the power to create a bank was not among the enumerated powers. It also thought the Bank would dangerously extend Federal powers. In answering the constitutional objections, Hamilton advanced the theory of "implied powers," holding that the Constitution gave Congress the power to establish any instrument that would aid the national government in performing its constitutionally designated functions. The Bank was such an instrument, for it would help the government to regulate coinage, collect taxes, borrow money, and disburse funds.

The opponents of the Bank did not confine themselves to political arguments but insisted that banks increased usury, diverted funds from agriculture, increased speculation, and drove specie out of the country. While conceding that these charges were true in certain cases, Hamilton argued that it would be to the Bank's interest to "succor the wary and industrious; to discredit the rash and unthrifty; to discountenance both usurious lenders and usurious borrowers." In addition, he insisted that a national bank would promote lower interest rates by increasing the supply of money. Nor would it diminish the supply of funds for agricultural loans, since there would always be lenders who, "from a spirit of caution, will incline to vest their funds in mortgages on real estate, [rather] than in the stock of a bank, which they are apt to consider as a more precarious security." Anticipating by over one hundred years the future debate over the effect of security loans on the availability of commercial loans, Hamilton declared, "Stock may indeed change hands, but the money which the buyer takes out of the common mass to purchase the stock, the seller receives and restores to it." In answering the Smithian criticism that paper money would drive specie out of circulation, Hamilton pointed out that the abundance of a country's precious metals was not so important as the "quantity of the productions of its labor and industry" and that "in the early periods of new settlements, the settlers not only furnish no surplus for exploitation, but they consume a part of that which is produced by the labors of others." Therefore, "precious metals will not abound in any country which has not mines, or variety of manufactures." To the charge that banks encourage speculation—a charge that was to be made for many years in the future and was eventually to become an important component of business-cycle theory—Hamilton merely questioned whether it would be wise to root out the advantages of credit because it now and then ran to excess.

In spite of the objections of the Jeffersonians, the bill to charter the Bank was passed along the lines suggested by Hamilton and was signed by Washington in February, 1791. In the House vote (39 to 20) only three Southerners voted for and only one Northerner against. The more important provisions of the Bank Charter were:

1. Charter to be in effect for twenty years.
2. Capital to be $10 million (25,000 shares of $400 par value) of which the Federal government was to subscribe one-fifth.
3. Private subscriptions to be made, one-fourth in specie and three-fourths in 6 per cent government stock; no subscription except government's to be for more than 1,000 shares.
4. There were to be 25 directors. Foreign stockholders could not vote by proxy, and voting was to be regressive; i.e., as stockholdings increased, number of votes did not increase proportionately.
5. All debts of the Bank, including notes but not including deposits, were not to exceed the capital.
6. Bank was not permitted to buy or sell goods or real estate except where acquired as forfeited collateral. It was also prohibited from purchasing stock of the Federal government.
7. Interest on loans and discounts was not to exceed 6 per cent.

The subscription books for Bank stock were opened in July, 1791, and closed in one hour with a 20 per cent oversubscription. Since only a small down payment was required, a portion of the Bank's capital consisted of the "IOU's" of the subscribers, and in actual practice, only a little more than $675,000 in hard money was paid into the Bank's capital.

Establishment of a Coinage System. During the entire colonial period, there had never been a satisfactory system of coinage. After the country broke away from England, it continued to use the English monetary terminology even though Spanish dollars and "reals" were far more common than pounds, shillings, and pence. In 1782 Robert Morris recommended a system in which the dollar was divided into 1,440 units so as to make the existing vast variety of coins easily convertible into it. Morris's plan was not adopted, but Jefferson later simplified it, proposing a decimal system which became the base upon which American coinage was finally built. In 1785 Congress adopted the dollar as the unit of currency, but no coins were minted under this resolution.

In April, 1791, at the request of the House, Hamilton submitted a *Report on the Establishment of a Mint.* Although he preferred a monometallic gold standard, he proposed a system of bimetallism, since "to annul the use of either of the metals, as money, is to abridge the quantity of the circulating medium; and is liable to all the objections which arise from a comparison of the benefits of a full, with the evils of a scanty circulation." Although completely cognizant of Gresham's law, he hoped to circumvent it by making the market and the mint ratio coincide and thus prevent the disappearance of either metal. In this, he was completely mistaken, for the market price of the two metals varied from day to day and could not continue to be equal to the arbitrary value fixed at the mint.

In April, 1792, Congress adopted Hamilton's coinage recommendations. A mint was established to coin a gold eagle ($10) containing 247.50 grains of pure gold (270 grains, 11/12 fine), a silver dollar containing 371.25 grains of silver (416 grains, 0.89242 fine), and fractional money from ½ to 50 cents.[23] An ounce of gold was thus worth at the mint 15 ounces of silver. The mint began to coin silver in October, 1794, and gold in July, 1795, but a mistake by the first director resulted in coins 9/10 fine.

Soon after coinage began, the international market price of silver began to fall, and by 1799, 1 ounce of gold was worth 15.75 ounces of silver in the open market. This meant that a person with gold bullion could sell it in the market for 3/4 of a grain more silver than he could receive at the mint. Gold naturally began to be hoarded or exported to Europe, since it commanded a better price as a commodity than as money. Silver dollars also tended to disappear from domestic circulation. They were accepted at their face value in the Spanish possessions, even though they were

[23] A seigniorage charge of ½ of 1 per cent was made when a person bringing bullion to the mint demanded coins immediately.

minted slightly lighter than the Spanish coins. Therefore it became profitable to export American silver dollars. This practice came to an end in 1806 when Jefferson stopped the coinage of silver dollars. In brief, the mint stopped operations almost completely because of the operation of Gresham's law.

Since the United States still did not have an effective monetary system, a barter system continued to prevail over most of the country. However, in the towns, some paper money was used in the form of notes issued by state banks or by the United States Bank and its eight branches. These United States Bank notes added substantially to the money supply, although their circulation never exceeded $6 million and no note was ever issued for less than $5. Hamilton accepted them in payment of government dues, although the Revenue Act of July, 1789, specified that all payments due to the government were to be made in gold, silver, or foreign coins of specific fineness.

Where small coins were needed, prices were quoted in fractional Spanish currency, such as two bits, inasmuch as no American coin higher than 5 cents circulated. Recognizing this situation, Congress gave legal-tender quality to foreign coins of a specified fineness.

Hamilton's Resignation and a Summary of Federalist Finance. Hamilton succeeded in effecting almost all of his program, but in so doing, he gave ammunition to those who opposed Executive leadership. In line with the tradition developed in the colonial assemblies, the Constitution vested Congress with vast fiscal powers. It proposed to exert them in full, and it resented Hamilton's domination. Meanwhile, political differences with the New England Federalists caused Hamilton to lose prestige in his own party. Moreover, his private life was unconventional, and this was unforgivable in a public figure. Then, too, many of his associates had profited enormously by speculating in government stock. Politically, his position became untenable, and he was forced to resign in January, 1795. He continued to influence Treasury policy indirectly until the end of the Federalist administration through his successor, Oliver Wolcott. But after Hamilton's resignation, Congress began to develop machinery to prevent any future Secretary from usurping its powers.

On the whole, the record of the Federalist administration in the development and management of the national finances was one of solid achievement. A comprehensive national financial system was established, national credit was placed on a firm foundation, every debt obligation was met, and great encouragement was given to the development of commerce. However, the record also had its weak spots: Federal fiscal operations were overextended; the country was not yet ready for a national internal revenue and resented its establishment. Moreover, Hamilton was not much interested in administrative routine. He did not bother about breaking down the expenditure requests of the departments into smaller items. Nor did he keep the accounts or report on the state of the Treasury in a detailed and understandable fashion. It was impossible to ascertain from his accounts the exact amount of government receipts, expenditures, or national debt. Indeed, no clear statement of the debt was ever presented by Hamilton or by Wolcott. In 1800 the latter told the Ways and Means Committee that the debt had increased $1.5 million since 1789. A special debt committee, on the other hand, concluded that the debt had declined by $1.1 million. Gallatin presented still another estimate showing a $6.7 million increase. In short, Hamilton's administration demonstrated brilliance and executive genius, but it lacked the ability to supervise efficiently the unspectacular administrative details entailed in operating a Treasury Department.

Chapter 6: JEFFERSONIAN FINANCE

Being more a state of mind than an organized political party, Federalism gradually faded away, leaving the field to agrarian Republicanism for the next twenty-four years.

In general, the National Republican party, under the leadership of Jefferson, was opposed to the increase of industrialism. It favored a society composed of small landholders and repudiated the Hamiltonian ideal of an alliance between the government and the capitalist group. Representing the small farmer who had little to gain from a strong government, its economic philosophy was *laissez faire*. It wanted a "happy and not a powerful nation," believing "that government best which governs least." The Jeffersonians, therefore, opposed the cornerstones of the Hamiltonian system: a protective tariff, internal taxation, a national bank, and a strong Federal government. They won popular support on a platform which pledged frugality, tax reduction, rapid debt retirement, and the decimation of government bureaucracy. Despite these pledges, the necessities of the times forced the Jefferson and Madison administrations, much against their will, to do more to strengthen the Federal government and advance industrialism than even Hamilton had thought possible.

Reorganization of Expenditures. Jefferson appointed Albert Gallatin, for many years the principal Republican Congressional critic of Hamiltonian finance, Secretary of the Treasury. Gallatin's primary aim was to reduce the public debt, chiefly by reducing expenditures. Unlike Jefferson, he had little hope of cutting civil expenditures significantly, but from the beginning, he believed that great economies could be achieved in the military establishment. Even after it appeared probable that the United States would become involved in the war between England and France, Gallatin urged Congress to reduce, rather than increase, military expenditures. For a time he was successful, but his program of extreme economy was eventually blocked because it antagonized a large group of government officials and congressmen, including the Smith brothers, Robert, the Secretary of the Navy, and Samuel, the leader of the Senate.

Although Gallatin thought that public expenditures were generally unproductive, he twice was willing to unloosen the strings of the public purse. In 1803 he strongly supported the purchase of Louisiana from France for $15 million. The cost was covered by $2 million from current revenue and the sale of $11¼ million of 15-year 6 per cent stock and $1¾ million of temporary obligations. Under the terms of the treaty, $11¼ million was paid directly to France, and the United States assumed an estimated $3¾ million of debts owed to American citizens by the French government.

In borrowing most of the purchase money, Gallatin departed from his antidebt philosophy and unwittingly demonstrated that Federal expenditures could be productive, for the half billion acres of Louisiana doubled the area of the United States at a cost of less than three cents an acre and increased Federal revenue and private wealth by many times the cost of the debt.

TABLE 3. FEDERAL EXPENDITURES, 1801–1811
(In millions of dollars)

Year	Civil	Foreign*	Navy	War	Pensions	Indians	Interest	Misc.	Total
1801	$0.5	$0.3	$2.1	$1.7	$0.1	....	$4.4	$0.3	$ 9.4
1802	0.6	0.6	0.9	1.2	0.1	$0.1	4.1	0.3	7.9
1803	0.5	1.1	1.2	0.8	0.1	0.1	3.8	0.2	7.9
1804	0.6	1.2	1.2	0.9	0.1	0.1	4.3	0.4	8.7
1805	0.6	2.8	1.6	0.7	0.1	0.2	4.1	0.4	10.5
1806	0.7	1.8	1.6	1.2	0.1	0.2	3.7	0.4	9.8
1807	0.7	0.6	1.7	1.3	0.1	0.2	3.4	0.5	8.4
1808	0.7	0.3	1.9	2.9	0.1	0.2	3.4	0.4	9.9
1809	0.7	0.2	2.4	3.3	0.1	0.3	2.9	0.3	10.3
1810	0.7	0.1	1.7	2.3	0.1	0.2	2.8	0.3	8.2
1811	0.6	0.3	2.0	2.0	0.1	0.2	2.5	0.5	8.1

SOURCE: *Annual Report of the Secretary of the Treasury*, 1866, pp. 308–309.

* Not including $11,250,000 paid directly to France for Louisiana in 1803, but including $3,750,000 of assumed French claims, 1803–1806.

Gallatin again departed from his doctrine that government expenditures were unproductive when he joined Jefferson in advocating Federally financed internal improvements. As early as 1796 the Federal government had made some small grants for state internal improvements, and in 1802 5 per cent of the sale of public lands in the newly admitted state of Ohio were set aside for building public roads. In his second inaugural address, Jefferson recommended that surplus revenue should "be applied to rivers, canals, roads, arts, manufactures, education, and other great objects within each state." Following his suggestion, Congress, in March, 1806, authorized the construction of a National Turnpike. Three-fifths of the Ohio land fund were to be spent within the state, and two-fifths in building a connecting link with the East. However, construction did not begin until 1811 and was interrupted by the War of 1812.

Gallatin, in his anxiety to reduce the debt, was slow in endorsing the program. But the enormous revenue surplus of 1807 changed his mind, and in 1808 he offered the essentially Federalist suggestion of using surplus revenue at a rate of $2 million a year for 10 years to construct a system of internal improvements.[1] This was the first Federal long-range capital investment program in history and was not to be matched until the 1920's. But the agrarians, unwilling to overcome their constitutional scruples, refused to accept it.

Reorganization of Revenue. During the campaign of 1800 and in his first message, Jefferson promised to repeal all internal taxes and to rely on the tariff and public land sales alone to support the government and to discharge the debt. However, Gallatin, though opposed in principle to internal taxes, feared that their immediate repeal would interfere with the speedy repayment of the debt.

Congressional Republican leaders, with John Randolph, chairman of the Ways and Means Committee, as their spokesman, swept aside the Secretary's objections, and after assuring him that any loss in annual revenue would be balanced by an equal reduction in military expenditures, they introduced bills to repeal the whole excise system.

Against Randolph's proposal, the Federalists argued that internal revenues were more stable than customs, which would melt away in times of difficulty. They insisted particularly that it was unwise to destroy the rather elaborate machinery for the collection of excises which had been developed with great care over a period of years, since it would be difficult to reconstruct it in an emergency. As an alternative they proposed that customs duties on necessities be reduced or eliminated.

The Federalist protests proved unavailing, and the entire internal-revenue system (producing $600,000 annually and capable of producing much more) was repealed in 1802. The extremists among the Republicans went even further and in 1807, against Gallatin's protests, repealed the tariff on salt, which had for years produced over $500,000.

[1] The plan provided:

	In Millions of Dollars
Inland canals from Massachusetts to North Carolina	$ 3.0
Turnpike from Maine to Georgia	4.8
Improvements of four great rivers emptying into the Atlantic Ocean	1.5
Four turnpikes connecting these rivers with the Western rivers	2.8
Canals around the falls of the Ohio	0.3
Improvement of roads to Detroit, St. Louis, and New Orleans	0.2
Canal between Lake Champlain and the Hudson River	0.8
Canal between the Hudson River and Lake Ontario	2.2
Canal around Niagara Falls	1.0
Local improvements	3.4
Total cost for 10 years	$20.0

Source: *American State Papers, Miscellaneous,* Vol. I, p. 740.

In spite of the elimination of these sources, revenues during the years 1801 to 1808 were very high. The Napoleonic Wars created a great demand for American products, and foreign trade was brisk. The Louisiana Purchase brought into the Union the port of New Orleans, thus augmenting the tariff revenue. Moreover, to finance the war with the Barbary powers, Congress in 1804, at Gallatin's recommendation, increased the average tariff rate to 16 per cent by imposing an additional 10 per cent duty on goods imported in foreign vessels and adding 2½ per cent to all ad valorem rates.[2] Although this so-called "Mediterranean Fund" was to expire automatically three months after the conclusion of peace, Congress renewed it at intervals until the War of 1812.

TABLE 4.   FEDERAL REVENUES, 1801–1811
(In millions of dollars)

Year	Customs	Internal excises	Direct tax	Public lands	Bank stock	Misc.	Total revenue	Annual surplus	Gross debt at end of year
1801	$10.8	$1.0	$0.5	$0.2	$0.1	$0.3	$12.9	$3.5	$80.7
1802	12.4	0.6	0.2	0.2	1.3	0.2	15.0	7.1	77.1
1803	10.5	0.2	0.1	0.2	....	0.1	11.1	3.2	86.4
1804	11.1	0.1	0.1	0.5	....	0.1	11.8	3.1	82.3
1805	12.9	*	*	0.5	....	*	13.6	3.1	75.7
1806	14.7	*	0.1	0.8	....	*	15.6	5.8	69.2
1807	15.8	*	*	0.5	....	*	16.4	8.0	65.2
1808	16.4	*	*	0.6	....	*	17.1	7.1	57.0
1809	7.3	*	*	0.4	....	*	7.8	−2.5	53.2
1810	8.6	*	*	0.7	....	0.1	9.4	1.2	48.0
1811	13.3	*	*	1.0	....	0.1	14.4	6.4	45.2

SOURCE: *Annual Report of the Secretary of the Treasury,* 1866, pp. 304–307.

* Less than $50,000.

The prosperous foreign trade with the European belligerents came to an end after 1807 when the Jefferson administration attempted to isolate the United States economically from the rest of the world in order to keep her out of war. As a result, customs revenues declined. At the same time, Army and Navy expenditures increased. Gallatin therefore recommended that existing customs rates be doubled, but Congress did not act, and total receipts fell below $8 million in 1809. Since expenditures were over $10 million, the Treasury experienced a deficit, the only one during the Jefferson administration.

[2] Although Gallatin favored free trade, he considered the tariff the best source of revenue and, while administering the Treasury, was willing to compromise with protective duties.

In 1810 the administration began to relax its restrictions on trade with the belligerents, and customs receipts again increased. Gallatin, being ever-mindful of the probability of another stoppage in trade and decline in revenue, "respectfully suggested a considerable and immediate increase of the present duties." But Congress ignored the suggestion, and shortly thereafter the Treasury's problem changed, as war became a reality instead of a possibility contemplated from afar.

Meanwhile, the revenue from the sale of public lands—heretofore quite unimportant—increased sharply, and agitation for a more liberal land policy became faintly discernible. Both Jefferson and Gallatin were sympathetic to this movement, but Gallatin's enthusiasm was restrained by his concern for public revenue. Since his views on financial matters always prevailed in the administration, the public domain continued to be regarded as a revenue producer. The land law was somewhat liberalized in 1800 when the minimum purchase was reduced to 320 acres. The minimum price—$2 an acre—remained the same, but the credit system was extended so that purchases could be made with a down payment of $320 instead of $640 as formerly.

By 1804 unpaid balances on land sales were very large, and Gallatin suggested abandoning the credit system, but instead, Congress liberalized the law by lowering the minimum purchase to 160 acres. Thereafter, the unpaid balances decreased both absolutely and relatively.[3]

Gallatin's Debt Philosophy. Unlike Hamilton, Gallatin could not see much advantage in a public debt. Moreover, he was possessed with the idea that its reduction "was certainly the principal object" in bringing him into office.[4] Although he did not think that a growing national debt would lead to national bankruptcy, he did consider it inflationary and discouraging to private investment.

He denied Hamilton's theory that a public debt could create capital, for "a public debt does not increase the existing amount of cultivated lands, of houses, of consumable commodities; it makes not the smallest addition either to the wealth or the annual labor of the nation."[5] He had a complicated notion that taxes came out of unproductive income whereas government borrowing absorbed capital funds which would ordinarily be used productively. Finally, he thought that, if the government borrowed and monetized its debt, a time would come when the supply of the circulating medium would exceed the demand and prices would increase. Thus,

[3] By Oct. 1, 1807, 2.7 million acres had been sold for $5.5 million, of which $2.4 million, or 44 per cent, remained unpaid. By Oct. 1, 1811, 3.4 million acres had been sold for $7.1 million, of which only $1.7 million, or 24 per cent, remained unpaid. (*Annual Reports of the Secretary of the Treasury*, 1807, 1811.)

[4] Henry Adams, *The Life of Albert Gallatin*, p. 270.

[5] Henry Adams, *Writings of Albert Gallatin*, Vol. III, p. 145.

Gallatin was the first American champion of a consistently balanced budget, and his views supplanted the Hamiltonian concepts which were not to return to prominence until a century later.

Reorganization of the Sinking Fund. With the help of large operating surpluses in eleven of the twelve years 1801 to 1812, and despite the Louisiana Purchase, Gallatin successfully reduced the debt by $37.8 million.[6]

In order to establish systematic debt repayment, Gallatin urged Congress to simplify Hamilton's sinking fund, which he held to be unrealistic. He said:

I know but one way that a nation has of paying her debt, and that is "Spend less than you receive." If you spend more than you receive, you may have recourse to sinking funds, you may modify them as you please, you may give a scientific appearance to additions and subtractions; you must still necessarily increase your debt.[7]

He recommended that, before any other appropriations were made, a definite sum be set aside from each year's revenue for debt repayment. In April, 1802, Congress adopted his recommendations, created a new sinking fund, and undertook to appropriate annually to it $7.3 million (the amount of the surplus in 1801). This was increased to $8.0 million annually after the purchase of Louisiana. The appropriations were used to retire maturing bonds as well as to purchase bonds in the market. The Gallatin sinking fund was a great improvement over the English system adopted by Hamilton, for it provided a definite goal of debt repayment and a definite revenue policy. However, the most important change was that interest payments ceased on the purchased bonds, which were destroyed instead of being retained as a sinking-fund investment.[8]

Not only was a large part of the debt paid off, but its structure was entirely reorganized through the elimination of the bank debt and the conversion of the Revolutionary debt into new bonds.

In 1802 the Treasury had difficulty in procuring exchange to meet debt installments payable in Holland. The Bank of the Manhattan Company offered Dutch guilders at 43 cents, but Alexander Baring, the British private banker, offered them at 41 cents provided the United States government would sell him its remaining equity in the Bank of the United States. Gallatin was reluctant to accept this offer, but the majority of the

[6] *Annual Report of the Secretary of the Treasury*, 1815.

[7] Chien Tseng Mai, *The Fiscal Policies of Albert Gallatin*, p. 49; *American State Papers, Finance*, Vol. II, p. 413.

[8] With the exception of the one after the War of 1812, future sinking funds did not conform to either the Gallatin or Hamilton plan. They provided for the appropriation of an amount equal to a specific percentage of the debt together with interest on the retired portion. But the retired bonds were destroyed, not retained in the fund.

Jeffersonians, being opposed to the Bank, were more than willing. Therefore, the last 2,220 shares of the Bank stock were sold, but at a premium of 45 per cent. The proceeds were used to pay off the debt owed to the Bank. All told, the Bank investment paid the Federal government a profit of $671,860.[9] In addition, the Treasury received dividends which not only paid the interest on the money borrowed from the Bank but also helped to meet other interest obligations.

Gallatin was farsighted enough to realize that the current rate of debt retirement would soon exhaust all the redeemable bonds. Difficulties would then be encountered in purchasing bonds in the market. At his recommendation Congress in 1807 authorized the conversion, at the holder's choice, of the 6 and 3 per cent stock into new 6 per cents, redeemable at the pleasure of the government, with the 3 per cent stock converted at 65 per cent of its par value.[10] The conversion was not a complete success, for of about $50 million of outstanding stock, only $8.1 million was exchanged.

Gallatin's Fiscal Administration. In fiscal management, Gallatin emphasized order and method and was a more able financial technician than Hamilton, but he lacked the latter's driving force and was never his equal in formulating broad programs.

As a member of Congress, Gallatin had consistently opposed three Hamiltonian policies: lump-sum appropriations, the broad discretionary powers given to the President and the Secretary of the Treasury in fiscal matters, and the lack of formal, regular reports on the state of the finances.

Early in his career as Secretary, Gallatin urged Jefferson to advise Congress to make specific appropriations whenever practicable, to limit discretionary power in the application of funds, and to prohibit the transfer of money to any object other than that for which it had originally been appropriated.[11]

Gallatin did not revolutionize fiscal management so much as he had hoped, but he gave it the essential characteristics which persisted well into the twentieth century. It was at his suggestion that Congress extended its controls. Specific appropriations replaced lump-sum appropriations, which were not to return to the Federal financial scene until the 1920's.

[9] In August and September, 1796, 2,160 shares were sold for $1.1 million, yielding a $216,000 profit. In July, 1797, 620 shares were sold for $300,000, the profit being $56,260. In July, 1802, the last 2,220 shares were sold for $1.3 million. (*American State Papers, Finance*, Vol. I, pp. 467, 498; Vol. II, p. 6.)

[10] See *ibid.*, Vol. II, p. 213, for Gallatin's argument.

[11] Hamilton immediately stated his disagreement. "Nothing," he wrote, "is more just or proper than that the Legislature ought to appropriate specific sums for specific purposes; but nothing is more wild than to appropriate a specific sum for each specific purpose, susceptible of definition." (Powell, *Control of Public Expenditures*, p. 178.)

At the same time, Congress curtailed the power of the Executive by forbidding him to transfer funds appropriated for one object to another object even if the transfer were within the same department. In order to provide regular information on the "state of the finances" and to make the Secretary more accountable, Congress, in 1800, required the Secretary of the Treasury to submit an annual report to Congress. Under Gallatin's encouragement, the House Ways and Means Committee achieved permanent status in 1802, and until the Civil War it controlled appropriation bills as well as revenue measures. By thus assuming the planning of expenditures in addition to revenue, Congress created a legislative budget system which was not to be replaced until 1921.

It was also at Gallatin's suggestion that Congress retained a firm hold over the power to borrow money by specifying the amount and terms of every loan authorization. After 1800 it gave the Treasury little discretionary power in borrowing operations, and it began to relax its controls only in 1919.

The Refusal to Recharter the United States Bank. In the course of his day-to-day contact with the Bank of the United States, Gallatin, unlike the other members of his party, became convinced of its usefulness. The Bank issued a sound and uniform currency and made loans, accepted deposits, and transferred funds for the Treasury. Therefore, in 1809, when the Bank applied for a renewal of its charter, Gallatin supported the application. But somewhat apprehensive over the Bank's private and centralized control, he proposed to give the states a share in its management, particularly over the operation of its branches.

He proposed that the Bank's capital be increased from $10 million to $30 million, with $5 million to be subscribed by private citizens and $15 million by such states as desired to do so. The states would have the right to appoint a portion of the directors of each branch, and the Federal government would appoint a portion of the directors of the parent institution. The Bank would be obliged to lend the government a sum not exceeding $18 million at a rate not in excess of 6 per cent.

In May, 1810, the House voted, 75 to 35, for renewal, but before the Senate voted, Congress adjourned. During the recess, Gallatin's many enemies carried on an extensive and effective propaganda campaign, charging that the Bank was controlled by foreigners and was an unconstitutionally created monopoly, far less efficient than the state banks. In February, 1811, the charter was defeated when Vice-President George Clinton voted in the negative after a 17-to-17 vote in the Senate.

The failure to continue the Bank had profound repercussions on the economy. The Bank had cooperated closely with the Treasury in attempting to stabilize the money market and protect the banking system.

Of the eleven banks which acted as government depositories, it was the most important, and through it Treasury funds could be transferred easily to state banks which required help. In 1801, $50,000 was deposited in the Bank of Columbia to stop a run. In 1802 the Bank of Pennsylvania was assisted when the Treasury deposited $300,000 and the Bank of the United States delayed its collections.

In addition, the failure to recharter the Bank eliminated the only agency which could possibly provide a uniform currency. With its demise, banking had no regulating agency and became completely chaotic. Finally, the specie stock was seriously reduced by the export of $7 million to pay off foreign stockholders.

Condition of State Banks. The data on state banks (those chartered by state rather than Federal government) are scant, but it is certain that most were in continuous difficulties.[12] The principal reasons for these difficulties were unequal distribution of available specie, establishment of banks in areas where they could not possibly succeed, lack of understanding of the nature of commercial banking, insufficiency of paid-in capital, and general lack of able bank management.

The stock of specie for all banks seems to have been adequate, for it is estimated to have exceeded total bank-note circulation all through the period. However, it was unequally distributed, tending to concentrate in city banks in accordance with the movement of exchange and leaving banks in the newer and smaller centers with insufficient reserves to secure their note issues. Yet the newer and poorer communities wanted banks, because it was generally believed that, by creating money, they could create capital in excess of actual savings. Thus, commercial banks were often started where business was too limited to make them profitable. Moreover, the shortage of capital funds caused subscribers to buy bank stock on credit. Consequently, most banks were started on less than a shoestring.

There was no understanding of the nature of demand deposits or of commercial banking. Outside the cities, the people demanded long-term loans, for short-term loans were of no help in financing purchases of land and livestock. When a bank made loans, it gave the borrower paper money instead of crediting his account as is done today. When these bank notes were presented for redemption in specie, while the loans on which they were based were still outstanding, specie reserves rapidly evaporated and the bank became insolvent. The only way of avoiding this gloomy fate was to prevent the redemption of notes, either by putting them in circulation far from the point of redemption ("out where the wildcats howled")

---

[12] State banks were not numerous before 1811. In 1805 there were only 75, all in the East. (*Annual Report of the Comptroller of the Currency*, 1876.)

or by persuading citizens not to redeem them. Neither alternative could avert disaster for more than a short period of time.

All the weaknesses of state banking might have been overcome if bank management had been conservative and strong-willed. But this was not the case. Bank charters were obtained by special acts of the legislature, usually by bribery or political influence. Hence, banking was filled with financial adventurers, long on daring and short on wisdom. Their interests were often best served by loose banking practices. For example, most of the stock in the Union Bank of Florida was owned by a small group of men who raised their subscriptions by mortgaging land to the bank. The more inefficient the bank and the greater the depreciation of its notes, the easier it became for them to pay off their loans.

Since the difficulties of state banking were more prominent in newer communities, they were to repeat themselves as the frontier advanced westward. Bank regulation began to appear in each section only after its economy had progressed from a less primitive to a more advanced stage of capital accumulation. Naturally, it first appeared in Massachusetts, for even before 1800 her cities had amassed enough capital to desire protection against the depredations of banks in the country areas where capital was scarce. In 1799, in order to increase specie in circulation, a law was passed prohibiting note issues in denominations below $5, but it was largely disregarded. Four years later, semiannual statements to the governor and council were required, and in 1810 a penalty of 2 per cent a month payable to the billholder was imposed for failure to redeem notes on demand. In 1811, bankers were required to swear that paid-in capital would not be removed after a charter had been granted, and the issue of notes in excess of 150 per cent of capital was prohibited.

In other states no serious attempts were made to improve bank operation. Therefore, when the charter of the Bank of the United States was not renewed, state banks could proceed as they pleased.

Chapter 7: FINANCING THE WAR OF 1812

By the time the United States entered the European war, the Jeffersonians had completed their reorganization of the national fiscal and monetary system. However, this reorganization left the nation unprepared for war. The abolition of internal taxes made the Treasury dependent on the tariff for most of its funds, and these shrank as trade with Europe declined. The failure to recharter the bank depleted specie reserves and made it impossible to support an expanding currency with safety. The reduction in Navy and Army expenditures left the country unprepared militarily. Moreover, the war was altogether unpopular in New England, the only section where pocketbooks were thick. Hence, the War of 1812, which was ill-managed militarily, was even more bungled financially.

Gallatin's Principles of War Finance. From the beginning, both Jefferson and Madison tried to keep the United States out of war and ignored the possibility of involuntary involvement. In his first annual message Jefferson said, " . . . sound principles will not justify our taxing the industry of our fellow-citizens to accumulate treasure for wars to happen we know not when." At first, he had the full agreement of Gallatin, who thought that there was no reason for imposing taxes too early, since the people would be more than willing to pay them if war actually came. But in time, Gallatin became more concerned over financial preparedness, and in his annual report of 1807 he presented his principles of war finance.

He proposed to provide revenue "at least equal to the annual expenses on a peace establishment, the interest of the existing debt, and the interest on the loans which may be raised." But believing that the "losses and privations caused by the war should not be aggravated by taxes beyond what is strictly necessary," and despite his aversion to public debts, he favored borrowing from banks to cover the expenditures of the war itself, believing that "the return of peace . . . will afford ample resources for reimbursing whatever may have been borrowed during the war."

Estimating peacetime expenditures and interest on the existing debt at less than $7 million and not expecting the current revenue of $14.5 million to fall more than 50 per cent in case of war, he thought new revenue would be required only for interest on the war loans. He therefore recommended the revival of the duty on salt, the revival of the Mediterranean Fund, and, if war did occur, an increase, perhaps a doubling, of existing tariff duties. However, he did not press these recommendations, for he

75

estimated that he would have a cash balance of $11 million in 1808, or enough to finance a whole year of war even without added taxes.

Considering the size of the national income in 1807 and the difficulties of collecting taxes in a completely rural economy, Gallatin's theories were well in advance of their time. But he did not present them vigorously enough. Moreover, he had made many enemies who had sufficient power to defeat almost anything that he proposed.

Rejection of Gallatin's Recommendations. In each of his next four reports Gallatin reiterated his belief that no internal taxes were necessary, but he politely suggested that the Mediterranean Fund be renewed and that all existing duties be doubled. Each time, Congress chose to ignore his recommendations. Finally, he became impatient, and in January, 1812, he told the House Ways and Means Committee that, because of Congress's refusal to increase revenue and to recharter the Bank, it had become necessary to impose internal taxes in addition to increasing the tariff, for not only had the revenue declined sharply but the Treasury cash balance had been dissipated. In order to increase the total revenue to $10 million, Gallatin recommended the imposition of a $3 million direct tax and $2 million of indirect taxes, similar to those levied under the Federalists, including taxes on liquor, refined sugar, licenses, auction sales, carriages, and documents.

A bill incorporating Gallatin's recommendations passed the House but failed in the Senate, for the Federalists attacked it as a glaring example of inconsistency, and many Republicans found it "truly odious," while the young "War Hawks" of the South and the West, although demanding war against Great Britain, were not enthusiastic about raising the money to pay for it. Consequently, when war broke out in June, 1812, Gallatin's plan of war finance had been completely rejected and the revenue from taxes was not sufficient to cover even peacetime expenditures.

Early Reliance on Loans. Although the military campaign was unpretentious and in some sections of the country the general citizenry seemed unaware that war was taking place, nevertheless expenditures were $2\frac{1}{2}$ to 4 times higher than in peacetime.

In July, 1812, Congress finally took the step recommended by Gallatin five years before. It doubled the existing duties, reimposed the Mediterranean Fund, added a 10 per cent duty on goods imported in foreign vessels, and imposed a special tax of $1.50 per ton on foreign-owned vessels. As Table 5 demonstrates, this increase was totally inadequate to meet the war costs, and the Treasury was forced to resort continuously to loans.

In March, 1812, Congress authorized a loan of $11 million. But by June Gallatin was becoming desperate for funds, and at his suggestion, Congress authorized $5 million of Treasury notes, which were only a step removed

TABLE 5. EXPENDITURES AND RECEIPTS, 1812–1815
(In millions of dollars)

	1812	1813	1814	1815	Total
Receipts:					
Customs...................	$ 9.0	$13.2	$ 6.0	$ 7.3	$ 35.5
Internal excises............	.....	.....	1.7	4.7	6.4
Direct tax.................	.....	.....	2.2	2.2	4.4
Public lands...............	0.7	0.8	1.1	1.3	3.9
Miscellaneous.............	0.1	0.3	0.2	0.3	0.9
Totals.................	$ 9.8	$14.3	$11.2	$ 15.7	$ 51.0
Expenditures:*					
War.....................	$11.8	$19.7	$20.4	$ 14.8	$ 66.7
Navy....................	4.0	6.4	7.3	8.7	26.4
Civil....................	0.8	0.8	0.9	0.9	3.4
Interest..................	2.5	3.6	4.6	5.8	16.5
Miscellaneous.............	1.2	1.2	1.5	2.6	6.5
Totals.................	$20.4	$31.7	$34.7	$ 32.7	$119.5
Deficit at end of year........	$10.5	$17.3	$23.5	$ 17.0	
Gross debt at end of year.....	56.0	81.5	99.8	127.3	

SOURCE: *Annual Report of the Secretary of the Treasury*, 1866, pp. 304–309.

* Treasury estimated peacetime expenditures at $7.5–$9 million.

from the paper currency issued during the Revolutionary War. Eventually, $37 million was issued, but the maximum outstanding at any one time was about $17 million. The notes were issued in denominations as low as $3, and most of them paid 5⅖ per cent interest, although some were non-interest-bearing. They were receivable in payment for public dues but were not legal tender for private transactions. Nevertheless, some of them circulated as money, thus increasing the total currency supply and contributing to inflation. Since they usually matured in one year, they had to be continuously replaced with other notes or with long-term bonds, adding to the difficulties of Treasury financing.

Before the end of 1812 the Treasury had sold about $13.1 million of bonds and notes, $3.9 million to individuals and $9.2 million to banks. Since most of the latter subscriptions were paid for with new issues of bank notes and since many of the Treasury notes entered circulation, each loan increased the nation's money supply. In addition, purchasers of bonds often paid for them in installments and then borrowed from the banks on their equity. This procedure, which was a forerunner of the "borrow-and-buy" policy of World War I, added further to the inflationary pressures on prices. Traceable to Congress's failure to tax, it reflected disastrously on the nation's credit.

In February, 1813, Congress authorized a new $16 million loan. But because New England refused to cooperate, only a small part of the issue was sold at par even though a thirteen-year annuity was offered in addition to the regular 6 per cent interest. Most of the loan was finally purchased at 88 plus ¼ per cent commission by David Parish, Stephen Girard, and John Jacob Astor, acting as the first American banking syndicate in history.[1]

Ineffective Taxes and Cumulative Overborrowing. In July, 1813, Congress finally enacted the internal-revenue system requested by Gallatin a year and a half before. The goal was $5 million of additional revenue a year, but since it took some time to establish a reasonably efficient system of tax collection, no revenue was collected from the new taxes during the balance of the year 1813 and only $3.9 million was collected in 1814. Unfortunately, in 1814, the addition of internal revenue was more than offset by a sharp drop in customs revenue. Instead of being higher, total revenue was therefore $3.1 million lower than in 1813. Since current revenue covered only 45 per cent of the expenditures in 1813 and only 32 per cent in 1814, loans had to be used on an increasing scale.

By this time Gallatin was out of the picture. It being recognized that his opponents were making his work ineffective, he was appointed to an important diplomatic mission, and later, in February, 1814, he officially resigned. His immediate substitutes and successors, William Jones and George W. Campbell, were unable to cope with the complexities of the situation. Not until Alexander J. Dallas took over in October, 1814, did the administration of the Treasury return to its previously high level.[2]

Altogether five loans were authorized and sold during the war years; they had a face value of $55 million (see Table 6). But after deduction of discounts, the proceeds were only $48 million, which represented only $28 million in specie, since most of the bonds were sold for bank notes worth in specie only 65 per cent or less of their face value. In addition to their colossal cost and inflationary nature, the loans were badly distributed. For example, of the $10 million lot offered in March, 1814, one-half was sold at 88 to Jacob Barker, Quaker merchant. When a second lot of $6 million went at 80, Barker demanded and received enough additional stock to bring his purchase price down to 80.

As of September 30, 1815, the total debt was $119.6 million compared with $45.2 million on January 1, 1812. It consisted of unpaid prewar debt,

[1] Parish and Girard bought $7.1 million, and Astor, $2.1 million. Subsequently, the same terms were offered to the original subscribers. (*American State Papers, Finance*, Vol. II, p. 647.)

[2] In the meantime, the business of negotiating loans was turned over to the chief clerk of the Treasury, who was opposed to the war. By refusing to issue stock to subscribers until the full purchase price had been paid, he succeeded for a while in obstructing the progress of the war by discouraging individuals from buying government securities. (Albert S. Bolles, *Financial History of the United States from 1789 to 1860*, pp. 230ff.)

TABLE 6. WAR LOANS, 1812–1815
(Dollar figures in millions)

Date	Interest rate (per cent)	Redeemable	Face amount	Cash received
Long-term issues:				
Mar. 14, 1812.......................	6	1825	$10.3	$10.3
Feb. 8, 1813........................	6	1826	18.1	16.0
Aug. 2, 1813........................	6	1826	8.5	7.5
Mar. 24, 1814.......................	6	1827	16.0	12.9
Nov. 15, 1814.......................	6 and 7	1827	1.5*	1.5
Feb. 24, 1815 (funding loan).........	7	1825	9.1	9.1
Totals.............................	....	....	$63.5	$57.3
Short-term issues (Treasury notes):				
June 30, 1812.......................	5⅖	....	$ 5.0	$ 5.0
Feb. 25, 1813.......................	5⅖	....	5.0	5.0
Mar. 4, 1814........................	5⅖	....	10.0	10.0
Dec. 26, 1814.......................	5⅖	....	8.3	8.3
Feb. 24, 1815.......................	Non-interest	....	3.4	3.4
Feb. 24, 1815.......................	5⅖	....	5.0	5.0
Totals.............................	....	....	$36.7	$36.7
Special issues:				
July 6, 1812 (refunding loan)..........	6	....	$ 3.0	$ 3.0
Mar. 31, 1814 (Mississippi stock†).....	....	....	4.3	$ 4.3
Jan. 9, 1815 (direct tax loan‡)........	....	....	0.2	0.2
Feb. 24, 1815 (refunding Treasury notes)............................	....	....	$ 1.5	$ 1.5
Totals.............................	....	....	$ 9.0	$ 9.0

SOURCE: Bayley, *History of the National Loans;* DeKnight, *History of the Currency and of the Loans of the United States.*

* Treasury notes could be used to purchase this loan.
† To indemnify claimants to public lands in the Mississippi Territory.
‡ Redeemed during 1815.

$39.1 million; the funded debt contracted during the war, $63.1 million; and the short-term, or floating, debt, $17.4 million.

Suspension of Specie Payments. With the Bank of the United States no longer present to exercise a restraining influence, the war years saw a great growth of state banks with a resultant rash of state-bank notes. Between 1811 and 1815 the number of state banks increased from 88 to 208, their capital increased from $42.6 million to $82.3 million, while their circulation increased from $22.7 million to $99.0 million.[3]

Since government spending was very heavy and taxes were not imposed to mop up the excessive volume of currency, price inflation resulted. In a

[3] Figures are estimated and fragmentary. (*Annual Report of the Comptroller of the Currency*, 1876.)

short time, the public lost its confidence in bank notes and began to present them for redemption. In addition, bankers themselves lost their faith in bank paper and refused to accept notes drawn in other states. As a consequence, what little specie was left went into hoards, and in the summer of 1814 the banks had to suspend specie payments. Thereafter, there was no circulating medium which could be used universally, and the entire banking and currency system broke down.

The effect on Treasury finances was completely demoralizing. Since most of the specie was in the East and especially in New England, the Treasury could not insist upon payment of taxes or loans in specie, for this would have made tax collections and bond sales impossible. Operating with a large deficit, the Secretary could do nothing but accept whatever money was offered, biding his time until the finances improved sufficiently to allow him to demand specie.

What made matters worse, the Treasury had no fiscal agent to act as a central depository. It could not even confine its deposits to a few state banks but had to use more and more of them as time went on, because they would not freely accept one another's notes. By 1814 the government had deposits in 94 banks. Moreover, depository banks insisted that each type of money be segregated and maintained in an easily identifiable account. Therefore, the Treasury had to keep four different accounts in each bank: one for local currency, one for out-of-state bank notes, another for interest-bearing Treasury notes, and a fourth for non-interest-bearing Treasury notes.

For practical purposes, much of the Treasury's revenue was useless, for it was collected in state-bank notes, which were not acceptable to citizens in other states. Therefore, the Treasury could operate only if its revenue collections in each state equaled what it owed in that state. This being obviously impossible, the Treasury by 1814 could not meet its obligations in some sections of the country.

Belated Taxation and Dallas's Attempt to Reestablish the Bank. Faced with a continuing deficit and a disheartening breakdown in credit facilities, President Madison called a special session of Congress in September, 1814, to deal with the crisis. Secretary Dallas proposed sweeping tax increases in order to provide an added $7 million, and Congress enacted them at once. The direct tax was raised to $6 million annually, although collections during the war never exceeded half that amount. The excises, imposed in the previous year, were raised. The postage rate was increased 50 per cent, and new taxes were imposed on certain domestic manufactures and on the use of gold and silver watches and household furniture in excess of $200. As a result of this legislation and a slight increase in customs revenue, collections in 1815 were $4.5 million higher than in 1814.

The ratio of expenditures covered by revenue rose to 48 per cent, but the gain was not so large as expected. Accordingly, in 1815 Dallas proposed an income tax on salaried officers, lawyers, and solicitors. This was rejected by the Committee on Ways and Means on the ground that "such a tax . . . would be an admission . . . that, in fixing the salaries of public officers, more than a just compensation [had been] allowed."[4]

Although there was a great deal of sentiment in favor of government paper-money issues, Dallas refused to consider them. Instead, he recommended that Congress improve the government's borrowing power by establishing a new United States Bank to be capitalized at $50 million, of which $30 million would be immediately loaned to the government. Congress passed a bank bill in January, 1815, but it was vetoed by President Madison, not because he thought it unconstitutional, but because it departed from Dallas's recommendations.

[4] *American State Papers, Finance*, Vol. II, p. 873.

Chapter 8: THE SEARCH FOR NEW GUIDEPOSTS, 1816 TO 1828

The United States emerged from the War of 1812 into a maelstrom of new developments and changing trends in social, political, and economic life. These years marked the beginning of the westward movement and commercial farming, of nascent manufacturing and slowly awakening trade-unionism, of stimulated cotton cultivation and solidification of the slavocracy. Against this background stood in sharp relief the money, banking, and fiscal problems of the postwar years—price inflation and deflation, broken-down banking and a disordered currency, a magnified national debt, swollen government expenditures, and high taxes.

Faced with these new trends and problems, the American people and their political spokesmen sought new viewpoints and philosophies. These were not easily developed, and it was not until the middle twenties that each section and each economic group were finally successful in arriving at an ideology which would best advance their own economic welfare.

The Congressional debates of this period, in fact for the next forty years, were dominated by Daniel Webster, the leading spokesman for New England; John C. Calhoun, who represented the Southern point of view; and Henry Clay of the new West of Kentucky and Tennessee. Each of these shifted his position from time to time, reflecting changes in the condition of his own section and of the country as a whole. Webster spoke first for the shippers, later for the industrialists. In the early postwar period, he was a leading exponent of free trade, but as New England manufacturing developed, he switched to a policy of protection, emphasizing a large spread between duties on raw materials and those on finished goods. John C. Calhoun, at first an advocate of nationalism and protection, transferred his allegiance to state rights and free trade. Henry Clay, originally an anti-Bank agrarian, became the political sponsor of a new Federalism, emphasizing high tariffs, internal improvements, and the beneficence of a central bank.

The two Presidents of this period, Monroe and John Quincy Adams, allowed their Secretaries of the Treasury to dominate the national financial scene. For a year after the war, the Treasury remained under the control of Secretary Dallas, a champion of national banking, rapid debt repayment, and protective tariffs. His successor, William H. Crawford, held office until 1825 and also supported the national bank, conservative fiscal policy, and high tariffs. Richard Rush (1825–1829) was an intense protectionist, and since the fiscal affairs of government met with few complications in the four prosperous years of his administration, he devoted himself almost exclusively to long and involved arguments for high protective tariffs.

Chartering the Second Bank of the United States. There was general agreement among national leaders that the most pressing problem was to restore order in the banking and currency system by returning to specie payments. But the state banks would not resume specie payments. Indeed, the current chaos enabled them to earn extraordinary profits, for they were able to issue notes and lend money on a much greater scale than would have been possible under a sound banking system. Debtor classes also opposed the return to specie. They wished depreciation of state-bank notes to continue, as it lightened their debt burdens.

It was clear that specie payments could be restored only if Congress applied some compulsion. But since it was generally believed that Congress did not have the constitutional power to regulate state banks, the only compulsion which it could apply was to establish its own competing note-issuing and specie-paying national bank. Reluctantly, the agrarian party, which controlled the government and had always opposed the idea of national banking, recommended the creation of a second bank with greater powers than the first. However, not all the members of Congress were ready to go along with such a program, and the Bank Act (a substantial improvement on the wartime bill) did not become law until April, 1816. Its main provisions were as follows:

1. The charter was limited to twenty years.
2. Capital to be $35 million, of which the government was to subscribe one-fifth and private individuals four-fifths, but no one subscriber could obtain more than 3,000 shares.
3. The government's subscription could be made in government stock. Private subscriptions were to be made in at least 25 per cent specie and the balance in government stock.
4. The Bank was to pay the government a bonus of $1.5 million in three equal installments.
5. There were to be 25 directors, of whom 5 were to be appointed by the President and the others to be elected by regressive voting. Foreign stockholders could not vote by proxy.
6. Notes were to be issued only in denominations of $5 or more, and the total circulation was not to exceed the capital.
7. Failure to redeem its notes in specie on demand was to make the Bank liable to the noteholder for 1 per cent per month on the value of the unredeemed note.
8. Notes of the Bank were to be acceptable in payment of all public dues.

9. Government funds were to be deposited with the Bank, or if the Secretary chose not to make such deposits, he was required to explain his reasons to Congress.

10. Transfers of government funds were to be made by the Bank without charge.

11. Government stock owned by the Bank was not to be sold without being first offered to the Treasury.

12. Bank was to deal only in bills of exchange, gold or silver bullion, or the sale of goods truly pledged as security for money loans.

13. No loans were to be made to the government in excess of $500,000.

The subscription books for the Bank shares were opened in July, 1816. When $3 million of the stock remained unsubscribed, it was taken by Stephen Girard, who with John Jacob Astor and David Parish had been instrumental in promoting the charter.

As a corollary to the Bank Act, Congress provided that after February 20, 1817, all payments to the government were to be made in coin, Treasury notes, notes of the Bank of the United States, or bank notes payable on demand in specie. The effect of this resolution was to give the state banks ten months to reorganize their note issues if they wished to have them accepted by the Treasury.

Every bank had to exert itself to the utmost to accumulate specie and to contract its loans and note issues before the deadline. In the meanwhile, the Bank opened in January, 1817, and accelerated the movement toward restoration of specie payments by discounting large volumes of importers' bonds which would have gone to the state banks. Under the pressure of the government and the Bank, the state banks throughout the country resumed specie payment on February 20, the day originally scheduled.

The Bank's Early Difficulties. When the Bank opened, the country was in the midst of a postwar speculative inflation, and unfortunately the atmosphere affected the Bank's management. Its first president, William Jones, ex-Acting Secretary of the Treasury, was not an astute banker. Moreover, he did not operate in strict conformity to the charter. The Bank became the plaything of speculators and almost collapsed. Subscribers, using the names of dummies, bought stock in excess of the legal limit. Shares were purchased in part with personal notes, and as the price of the stock rose in the bull market, these margin holdings increased.[1]

The Bank's method of making loans and handling exchange was far worse than the speculation in its stock. The branches of the Bank in the South and the West overexpanded their circulation by freely extending

[1] When Jones resigned in 1819, loans were approximately $40 million, of which $3 million represented purchases of Bank stock on margin by Bank officers. After going to a 56 per cent premium, the stock collapsed, leaving a group of bankrupt speculators.

illiquid long-term loans. Since the pioneer communities were always in debt to the older settlements, the notes of these branches tended to come East and were presented at the parent bank for redemption, creating a constant pressure on its specie reserves. The pressure might have been alleviated if the parent bank had pursued an aggressive policy in redeeming state-bank notes. It had an ample supply, for in 1817 and 1818 it received government deposits of $10.8 million, mostly in state-bank notes. It not only refused to press for redemption but insisted that its branches pay out their own notes instead of those of the state banks.[2] The situation was further aggravated by the use of "race horse bills," drafts drawn against one branch to pay maturing discounts at another branch, thus permitting Southern and Western branches to renew their discounts indefinitely. As the parent bank's holdings of branch- and state-bank notes increased, it obtained the specie to redeem its own note issues by importing some $7 million from Europe at a loss.

In paying out its liquid assets and replacing them with illiquid ones, the Bank imperiled its position. By 1818 credit could not be expanded any further but actually had to be contracted, as specie was being exported to the East Indies and less was being imported from Spanish America. Under the circumstances, the speculative inflation exploded. The Baltimore branch, in which stock speculation was unusually prominent, collapsed, and the Bank's prestige suffered a terrific blow.

Constitutionality of the Bank Sustained. Meanwhile, the opposition to the Bank was carried into the state legislatures. In 1817 Maryland imposed a stamp tax on the notes of all banks in the state not chartered by the legislature. Other states in the South and West followed suit with other types of taxes on the Bank's branches. The Maryland branch refused to pay the tax, and in 1819 the Supreme Court of the United States, in the famous case of *McCulloch v. Maryland,* ruled that the Bank had been constitutionally established, since it was a necessary and proper instrument for carrying on Federal fiscal operations. Moreover, as a Federal instrumentality it was immune from state taxation. The decision not only saved the Bank from destruction but also strengthened Federal powers generally.

Reorganization of the Bank. Realizing his own limitations, Jones resigned in 1819. After a short interval he was succeeded by an efficient, conservative, but ruthless administrator, Langdon Cheves. Cheves was not a banker, but he saved the Bank by pursuing an uncompromising policy of credit deflation and by acquiring precious time in which to liquidate the Bank's assets.

[2] See the report on the investigation of the Bank in *American State Papers, Finance* (Vol. III, pp. 306*ff*).

TABLE 7. SELECTED ASSETS AND LIABILITIES OF THE BANK OF THE UNITED STATES,
1817–1822
(In millions of dollars)

	1817	1818	1819	1820	1821	1822
Resources:						
Loans and discounts.............	$ 3.5	$41.2	$35.8	$31.4	$30.9	$28.1
Stocks.......................	4.8	9.5	7.4	7.2	9.2	13.3
Real estate...................	.....	.....	.....	.....	.....	0.6
Banking houses................	.....	0.2	0.4	1.3	1.9	1.9
Due from state banks...........	8.8	1.2	2.6	2.7	1.2	1.7
Notes of state banks...........	0.6	1.8	1.9	1.4	0.7	0.9
Due from foreign banks.........	.....	1.0	0.6	0.3	0.1	1.1
Specie.......................	1.7	2.5	2.7	3.4	7.6	4.8
Liabilities:						
Circulation...................	1.9	8.3	6.6	3.6	4.6	5.6
Deposits.....................	11.2	12.3	5.8	6.6	7.9	8.1
Due to foreign banks...........	.....	1.4	1.4	2.1	2.1	2.0

SOURCE: *Annual Report of the Comptroller of the Currency*, 1876, p. 193.

As shown in Table 7, Cheves cut discounts drastically. He caused
Southern and Western branches to curtail their note issues, arranged to
defer payments due the government, floated a three-year loan in Europe
for $2 million in specie, took steps for immediate collection of balances due
from state banks, and foreclosed securities on unpaid loans so aggressively
that the Bank soon became the principal owner of real estate in many
Western cities. The net loss which the Bank incurred as the result of the
inflationary-deflationary cycle of 1819 to 1822 was estimated at $4 million,
but it would have been far greater if the lands taken over in foreclosure
sales had not later increased substantially in value. It was in this period
that the popular resentment against the Bank solidified, for Cheves's deflationary policies were held to have caused the panic of 1819, even though
they were precipitating, rather than fundamental, factors. Feeling was
particularly intense in the pioneering communities of the South and West,
where currency and credit contraction induced by the Bank caused particularly severe hardship. Debtor classes were not interested in conservative banking methods. Anxious to extricate themselves from their economic difficulties, they demanded financial relief from the government.
The Federal government did little, but some state governments moderated
their laws on imprisonment for debt and encouraged the creation of new
banks to issue additional paper money. In Kentucky and Tennessee virtual
moratoriums on debts were declared. Some of these debt-relief laws were
eventually declared unconstitutional by the state courts, thus aggravating
the animosities between debtors and creditors and setting the stage for the
great bank and hard-money war of the later Jacksonian period.

Expansion of the Bank under Biddle. Cheves, who was distinguished for his negative management, was succeeded in 1823 by Nicholas Biddle, who intended to be an aggressive and positive banker. Whereas Cheves emphasized contraction and economy, Biddle wanted to expand the Bank's note issue and make the institution a central bank with effective power over the nation's money market. The Bank had all the tools by which this goal could be accomplished. It was the government's fiscal agent, it issued money and dealt in foreign exchange, it had intimate relations with foreign commercial and investment bankers, and it did a large discount business.

With the help of business prosperity, Biddle accomplished his goal of expanding the currency. By the terms of the Bank's charter, notes could be issued only by the parent bank and had to be signed by the president and the cashier. Hence the branches, eventually 29 in number, could not issue any notes of their own, and since the maximum number of notes which the president and the cashier could sign in one day was about 1,500, it would have taken four years to increase the circulation as much as Biddle desired. Attempts to persuade Congress to permit the branches to issue their own notes failed. Therefore, in 1827 Biddle invented the "branch draft." This was really a check drawn against the parent bank by an officer of a branch and payable to another officer, who endorsed it, thus making it a negotiable instrument which circulated like a bank note.

Control over its own circulation gave the Bank one method of regulating the money market. Indirect control over state banks provided another method. In dealing in foreign exchange and making extensive transfers of funds through its branches, it was brought into daily contact with the state banks. As the government's fiscal agent, it would not accept, in payment of government dues, any notes which were not redeemable in specie on demand. Furthermore, it could regularly send state-bank notes back for redemption and thus prevent their overexpansion, for in order to redeem $1 million of notes in specie, it was necessary for a state bank to contract its loans by an estimated $4 million to $5 million.

Biddle's policy expanded the Bank's circulation, deposits, loans, and ownership of real estate and stocks. But Biddle also increased the specie reserve and kept the amounts due from state banks at a low figure. At the same time, state banks exercised a check over the national Bank's paper-money issues, for they, too, could call for redemption.

Although the Bank's enemies insisted that the use of the branch draft violated the charter and would eventually weaken the currency, the Bank's notes were among the safest in the world. At all times, the $5 notes and drafts were receivable everywhere at par, and while notes of higher denomination circulated at slight discounts, it was actually cheaper to settle exchanges with them than by shipping specie.

The circulation of the United States Bank varied from section to section.

being greatest in the West and South, of lesser importance in the Middle Atlantic states, and unimportant in New England, where capital funds were more plentiful.

TABLE 8.   OPERATIONS OF THE BANK, 1823–1828
(In millions of dollars)

	1823	1824	1825	1826	1827	1828
Loans.........................	$30.7	$33.4	$31.8	$33.4	$30.9	$33.7
Stocks.........................	11.0	10.9	18.4	18.3	17.8	17.6
Real estate.....................	0.6	1.3	1.5	1.8	2.0	2.3
Due from state banks.............	1.4	1.3	2.1	0.7	1.7	
Notes of state banks.............	0.8	0.7	1.1	1.1	1.1	1.4
Specie.........................	4.4	5.8	6.7	4.0	6.5	6.2
Circulation.....................	4.4	4.6	6.1	9.5	8.5	9.9
Deposits.......................	7.6	13.7	12.0	11.2	14.3	14.5

SOURCE: *Annual Report of the Comptroller of the Currency*, 1876, p. 193.

The power for good or evil of the United States Bank was to a great extent in the hands of "Tsar Nicholas," as his enemies called him, for he made all the important decisions. And his policies were not opposed by either the private or the five government directors. In fact, Biddle himself was a government appointee. Well aware of his position, he foolishly boasted that he had the power of life and death over state banks and that he had more power than any President of the United States. These fatuous claims were not without influence in the eventual failure of the Bank to obtain a renewal of its charter.

State Banking Reform—the Suffolk System. It is impossible to state accurately what happened in state-bank operations from 1816 to 1828. However, in a long report on the currency in 1820, Secretary Crawford wrote, "There is no recorded example in the history of nations of a reduction of the currency so rapid . . . as that which has been exhibited in the United States."[3]

Undoubtedly, the depression of 1819 and the pressure of the United States Bank prevented the continued growth of state banks. But while the volume of their notes declined, the notes still circulated at a discount. To correct this situation in the older states, legislatures or the banks themselves introduced important reforms.

Even before the war, Massachusetts had imposed a penalty for failure to redeem notes, but this did not stop depreciation as long as the issuing agency succeeded in distributing its notes sufficiently far from home to make redemption expensive and time-consuming. Therefore, country-

[3] *Ibid.*, Vol. III, p. 496.

bank notes circulated in Boston at 1 to 5 per cent discount, and following Gresham's law, they drove the sounder notes of the Boston banks out of circulation. As a result, the Boston banks, with more than 50 per cent of the banking capital, had only 4 per cent of the circulation. Even before the war, the New England Bank had tried to improve the situation by sending country-bank notes back for redemption. But the first step toward really effective regulation came in 1825 when a group of Boston banks formed the Suffolk system.[4] Through the agency of the Suffolk Bank, the members of the system sent the notes of all out-of-city banks back for redemption in specie as fast as they were received. However, any country bank could have its notes redeemed at par in Boston by maintaining with the Suffolk Bank a permanent deposit of $2,000 or more, depending on its size, plus an additional deposit to cover its current redemptions.

The solid front presented by the Boston banks soon persuaded the country banks to join and did much to stabilize the value of New England bank notes.

The New York Safety Fund. In New York revelations of wholesale corruption and a series of crises in the money market aroused so much popular resentment that a statute of banking regulation was adopted in 1827, limiting bank loans to three times the paid-up capital, imposing double liability on stockholders, and requiring annual reports to the state comptroller. However, the regulations were too severe and discouraged applications for new charters.

In 1829 as a result of Governor Van Buren's recommendations, a new banking law was passed, establishing the safety fund system. Supposedly patterned after an arrangement originated by the Hong merchants of China under which the stronger merchants supported the weak, the Act provided that any bank applying for a new charter or a renewal of an existing charter had to contribute annually for six years ½ of 1 per cent of its capital, or a total of 3 per cent, to a fund which was to be used to assist insolvent banks. The Act also limited note issues to twice the bank's capital and loans to 2½ times the capital and established a commission of three men to inspect the state's banks.

The safety fund system was never popular with the stronger banks in New York City, for they had four times as much capital and five times as much specie as the country banks, but less than two times the loans and discounts. Therefore, they made larger contributions while receiving fewer benefits than the country banks. Yet the system worked fairly well until the panic of 1837. Its basic weakness lay in the fact that it sought to do the impossible by giving protection to depositors as well as to noteholders. Eventually, in 1842 noteholders were given prior protection.

[4] The Suffolk Bank itself began to redeem notes in 1819.

The Tariff of 1816. The war-imposed tariff, which was to expire automatically in February, 1816, was extended to June while Congress considered the problem of protecting war-born American manufacturers from the competition of revitalized Britishers.

Although the enthusiasm for protection was not general, the War of 1812 had produced an intense nationalism mixed with desire for self-sufficiency and a great need for revenue to pay off the war debt. Under the circumstances, Congress regarded a tariff increase as a necessity and passed it forthwith.

Under the new tariff the average rate of duty was approximately 20 per cent—less than the average rate during the war. But added protection was given to many strategic commodities. On textiles, the duty was fixed at 25 per cent for the next three years and 20 per cent thereafter. Moreover, the Act introduced for the first time the so-called "minimum principle," under which goods were valued, not at their exact worth, but in round figures. Thus, cottons costing less than 25 cents a square yard were valued at 25 cents. In future tariff legislation, one of the most bitter controversies was to center around attempts by protectionists to extend this principle.

The Economic and Financial Setting of the Tariff. Although the Tariff of 1816 was intended to emphasize protection more than revenue, it was also intended to be only temporary. But as sectional interests began to solidify and protection became more and more involved with fiscal policy, internal improvements, and the public land policy, the trend toward protectionism became more vigorous.

The divergent economic interests of the manufacturer and the would-be commercial farmer were brought together by a common desire for assistance against the economic pressures of the depression of 1819. Both wanted a market for their products, and a rationale was quickly found in the so-called "home markets" argument. It was argued that protective tariffs would help American manufacturers by stimulating the growth of American industry. Concurrently, this would help the farmer by contributing to the growth of cities, and raising the demand of their populations for food and raw materials. But a market for farm products could not be exploited in the absence of means of transportation. Therefore, demands for Federal internal improvements financed from tariff revenue became dominant among commercial agriculturalists. Henry Clay was the leader in amalgamating protectionism with internal improvements. He euphoniously labeled his platform "The American System," and for years he used it as his chief talking point in seeking the Presidency.

The depression of 1819 also emphasized the close connection between the tariff and fiscal affairs. During depression when government income was low, the proponents of protectionism sought to increase it by raising tariffs, the most important source of revenue. On the other hand, during prosperity when revenues exceeded expenditures and operating surpluses presented an embarrassing problem, free traders tried to reduce tariffs. Hence, protectionists thrived in periods of depression; free traders in periods of prosperity. Consequently, protectionists favored high expenditures and reduction of noncustoms revenue and supported internal improvements, veterans' pensions, and a liberal land policy or the distribution of the proceeds of land sales among the states, while free traders favored economy and nontariff sources of revenue. They tended to oppose Federal internal improvements, liberal pensions, free land, and distribution of money to the states. As time went on, the issue of the protective tariff interfered more and more with the development of consistent expenditure policies. At the same time, the fluctuations of government revenue interfered with the pursuit of either a consistent protective or free-trade economic policy.

Against this economic background, the tariff became a sectional issue. The home market argument had its greatest appeal among the manufacturers and growers of marketable grain crops in the Middle Atlantic states. But it was also favored in the new West, where internal improvements and the desire for cheap land were fundamental issues. New England was still largely commercial. What manufacturing did exist was concentrated in the textile industry, where entrepreneurs were not so much interested in the principle of protection as in widening the gap between the prices of raw materials and finished goods.

By 1820 the rapid development of the rich cotton lands in the Gulf basin made it abundantly clear that the South would continue to be a plantation economy, dependent upon the exportation of cotton and the importation of finished manufactures. Its economic future thus determined, the South naturally opposed high tariffs which would increase the cost of European imports as well as cut European power to buy Southern staples. It also opposed the accompanying demands of the Eastern and particularly the Western states for internal improvements and a liberal land policy.

Tariff of 1824. As early as 1818 manufacturers won for themselves some favorable minor tariff changes. The temporary textile rates, which were about to expire, were extended until 1826; the duty on manufactured iron was increased; and appraisers were employed to determine the value of imported goods in the event of dispute.

In 1820, during a period of temporary Treasury deficits, free traders of the South and New England defeated by one vote Secretary Crawford's attempt to increase revenue by increasing tariffs. But the West and the Middle Atlantic states were growing, while New England and the

South remained practically stationary. As a result, the votes for protection outran those for free trade, and in 1824 a general increase in tariffs was adopted, increasing the average rate from 20 to 33⅓ per cent. The rates on textiles, iron, lead, glass, and hemp were raised, but because equal or greater increases on raw materials were included, the manufacturers were disappointed.

Restoration of Finances to a Peacetime Basis. The great increase of imports immediately after the war, the belated collections of internal revenue under the last wartime revenue act, and the increased sale of public lands as the westward movement began in earnest raised the aggregate revenue far above any previous level. In 1816 the revenue aggregated $48 million as compared with $16 million in 1815. Under the circumstances, there seemed little reason for the internal taxes established during the war, and they were repealed in December, 1817.

TABLE 9. FEDERAL REVENUES, 1816–1828
(In millions of dollars)

Year	Customs	Internal excises	Direct tax	Public lands	Bank dividends	Misc.	Total
1816	$36.3	$5.1	$4.3	$1.7	....	$0.3	$47.7
1817	26.3	2.7	1.8	2.0	$0.2	0.1	33.1
1818	17.2	1.0	0.3	2.6	0.5	0.1	21.6
1819	20.2	0.2	0.1	3.3	0.7	0.1	24.6
1820	15.0	0.1	....	1.6	1.0	0.1	17.8
1821	13.0	0.1	....	1.2	0.1	0.2	14.6
1822	17.6	0.1	....	1.8	0.3	0.5	20.2
1823	19.1	....	....	0.9	0.4	0.1	20.5
1824	17.9	....	....	1.0	0.4	0.1	19.4
1825	20.1	....	....	1.2	0.4	0.1	21.8
1826	23.3	....	....	1.4	0.4	0.1	25.3
1827	19.7	....	....	1.5	0.4	1.3	23.0
1828	23.2	....	....	1.0	0.5	0.1	24.8

SOURCE: *Annual Report of the Secretary of the Treasury*, 1866, pp. 306–307.

Meanwhile, expenditures were reduced substantially from their wartime level, but in 1818 they were still 2½ times the prewar level, for the interest charges on the postwar debt were almost equal to the entire prewar expenditures and Army and Navy expenditures were greatly increased.

High revenue and reduced expenditures produced large annual surpluses, making possible rapid debt reduction. In 1817 the Treasury funded the outstanding $17 million of short-term notes and at the same time

TABLE 10. FEDERAL EXPENDITURES, 1816–1828
(In millions of dollars)

Year	Civil	For- eign	Navy	War	Pen- sions	Inter- est	Misc.	Total	Surplus (+) or deficit (−)	Debt
1816	$1.2	$0.4	$3.9	$16.0	$0.2	$7.2	$1.7	$30.6	$+17.1	123.5
1817	1.0	0.3	3.3	8.0	0.3	6.4	2.6	21.8	+11.3	103.5
1818	1.1	0.4	3.0	5.6	0.9	6.0	2.8	19.8	+ 1.8	95.5
1819	1.1	0.3	3.8	6.5	2.4	5.2	2.1	21.5	+ 3.1	91.0
1820	1.2	0.3	4.4	2.6	3.2	5.1	1.4	18.3	− 0.5	90.0
1821	1.1	0.2	3.3	4.5	0.2	5.1	1.4	15.8	− 1.2	93.5
1822	1.2	0.2	2.2	3.1	1.9	5.2	1.2	15.0	+ 5.2	90.9
1823	1.1	0.3	2.5	3.1	1.8	4.9	1.1	14.7	+ 5.8	90.3
1824	1.3	5.1*	2.9	3.3	1.5	5.0	1.1	20.3	− 0.9	83.8
1825	1.3	0.4	3.0	3.7	1.3	4.4	1.8	15.9	+ 6.0	81.1
1826	1.3	0.2	4.2	3.9	1.6	4.0	1.9	17.0	+ 8.2	74.0
1827	1.2	0.7	4.3	3.9	1.0	3.5	1.6	16.1	+ 6.8	67.5
1828	1.5	1.0	3.9	4.1	0.9	3.1	1.9	16.4	+ 8.4	58.4

SOURCE: *Annual Report of the Secretary of the Treasury*, 1866, pp. 304–309.

* Florida purchase.

proceeded toward discharging the funded indebtedness. At the suggestion of the Secretary, Congress approved a regular $10 million annual appropriation to the sinking fund, as well as an additional $9 million for 1817. It also provided that any future annual surplus over $2 million was to be used similarly for debt retirement. To give more discretion in debt management, the sinking-fund commissioners were authorized to purchase bonds in the open market but not above certain prices specified by Congress. Since these prices were below market prices, the power was of little use.

Increased Expenditures, 1816 to 1819. The surplus acted as a spur to new expenditure projects, among which the most popular were pensions of $8 to $20 a month to poverty-stricken veterans of the Revolutionary War. Previously, pensions were paid only to veterans who had been disabled in the war. A minority in Congress opposed the suggested legislation as introducing a dangerous principle which would in time cost the Treasury immense sums. But the bill became law in March, 1818. Instead of costing $300,000 a year, as contended by its sponsors, the new pension system cost more than $2 million during the first full year of its operation.

The surplus also caused the revival of Gallatin's program of internal improvements. In February, 1816, Calhoun proposed that the government use the $1.5 million bonus and the dividends paid by the United States

Bank to finance internal improvements. Immediately a controversy developed over Congress's constitutional power to construct public works. In the long run, sectional jealousy and complaints by congressmen that their districts contributed more revenue to the Federal government than they received were to determine which governments—Federal, state, or local—constructed internal improvements. But the immediate issue was decided in favor of strict construction, President Madison vetoing Calhoun's bill and Monroe threatening to veto similar bills.

However, money for some internal improvements was provided from special appropriations. The Cumberland Road was finished from Cumberland, Maryland, to Wheeling on the Ohio River in 1818, at a total expense of $1.6 million. Miscellaneous military roads were constructed in the territories, and by 1820 total Federal expenditures for internal improvements since 1791 aggregated a little more than $15 million, of which about half was spent after 1815.[5]

Treasury Deficits during the Depression, 1819 to 1821. The 1819 business reversal instantly affected Federal fiscal affairs. Customs revenue fell, and sales of public lands declined as speculative values collapsed. Expenditures also declined but not so quickly, because disbursements for interest, the general government, and the Navy were inelastic. Veterans' pensions were cut substantially by the passage, in May, 1820, of a law requiring pensioners to submit sworn statements of their assets and income.

As a result of the sharp drop in revenue, operating deficits appeared in each of the two depression years. Thus, the pattern of declining revenues, inelastic expenditures, deficits, and government borrowing, which featured all subsequent business depressions, was inaugurated.

Public Land Sales Placed on a Cash Basis. When the depression of 1819 began, settlers who had bought land on credit owed the Treasury about $22 million, and there was little prospect of payment. To prevent the recurrence of a similar situation, Congress in 1820 required all future land payments to be made in cash. At the same time it reduced minimum purchases to 80 acres and the minimum price to $1.25 an acre. Then in 1821 Congress eliminated most of the land indebtedness by giving debtors full title to an amount of land proportionate to the cash they had actually paid and reclaiming the balance. These two acts signified that the goal of public land policy was beginning to shift from revenue to rapid settlement.

Reappearance of Revenue Surpluses, 1822 to 1828. With the improvement in business conditions after 1822, Treasury surpluses reappeared. Customs receipts tended to increase, although the sharp increase in tariff rates in 1824 caused imports to fall off temporarily. Public land sales did

[5] The largest items in the $15 million total were forts and arsenals, $8.6 million; light stations, $2.4 million; and roads and canals, $1.9 million. (U.S. Treasury. *Statement of Appropriations and Expenditures for Public Works.*)

not recover so rapidly, for they always lagged behind changes in the business cycle, rising rapidly in periods of superspeculation or following a major liberalization of government land policy.[6] Since miscellaneous revenue was very small, customs produced over 90 per cent of the revenue, which averaged $20 million annually.

While receipts increased, Federal expenditures changed considerably in type, although the total was below the predepression level. Civil and military expenditures resumed their upward climb, reflecting the growth of the country, the public pressure for more adequate national defense, and larger appropriations for internal improvements. Prosperity made Congress more lenient about pension administration, and in March, 1823, it restored to the pension rolls a great many who had been dropped in 1820. These increases were balanced to some extent by reduced interest payments as the debt was paid off.

The Surplus Problem. The reappearance of surpluses of $5 million to $8 million a year permitted the Treasury to resume the debt reduction so successfully begun during the postwar boom. However, an unexpected difficulty appeared, for debt maturities were not evenly distributed. Unlike 1816 to 1819, when a large portion of the debt was constantly maturing, the debt now consisted of the 12-year bonds issued during the war and the 3 per cent Revolutionary debt. None of these was as yet maturing. As a result, the Treasury had surplus cash in 1822 to 1825 which it could not use advantageously. On the other hand, in 1826 and 1827 the redeemable debt would be about $18 million in excess of the Treasury's available cash, while in 1829 to 1831 the surplus would again be far in excess of the redeemable debt.

Faced with this problem, Crawford, in 1823, attempted to persuade Congress to permit him to purchase the debt at the market price, but this was refused. He then proposed to spread maturities by exchanging the 6 per cent stock redeemable in 1825 and 1826 for 5 per cent stock redeemable at later dates. This was authorized by Congress, but only a few bonds were exchanged, since the transaction entailed a 1 per cent annual loss in interest. Crawford now suggested floating a new loan at a low rate of interest, using the proceeds to refund the redeemable debt. Congress compromised. It authorized 4½ per cent exchange stock, and if exchanges were not offered, a new 4½ per cent loan was to be issued. Unfortunately, less than $2 million of the existing bonds were exchanged, and no offers were made for the new loan.

When Rush became Secretary in 1825, he also prodded Congress to authorize new loans at reasonable rates, but he met with no greater success. Consequently, when the 6 per cent bonds became callable, he retired as many as possible from the surplus and exchanged an additional portion.

[6] As in 1819, 1835–1836, 1854–1856, 1867–1869, 1883–1890, 1902–1904 (pp. 92, 100, 264).

On the remainder he continued to pay higher interest than was demanded by market conditions.

TABLE 11.   DEBT STRUCTURE, JAN. 1, 1816–1828
(In millions of dollars)

	1816	1819	1822	1825	1828
Old 6% stock	$ 17.3	$ 3.3	$ 1.5		
3% stock	16.2	13.5	13.3	$13.3	$13.3
Deferred stock	9.4				
Louisiana stock	10.9	5.0			
Exchanged 6% of 1812	3.0	2.7	2.7	0.1	
6%, redeemable 1825–1828	62.0	51.1	51.0	46.6	25.4
Funded Treasury notes	3.9	10.1	10.1	1.5	
5% bank subscriptions	......	7.0	7.0	7.0	7.0
6% of 1820	......	......	2.0		
5% of 1831–1835	......	......	5.7	5.8	5.8
4½% Florida loan of 1832	......	......	.....	5.0	5.0
Exchanged 4½% of 1833–1834	......	......	.....	4.5	11.0
Totals	$123.9*	$92.8†	$93.4	$83.8	$67.5

SOURCE: *Annual Reports of the Secretary of the Treasury*, 1816–1828, *American State Papers, Finance*, Vol. 5.

* Includes $1.1 million of temporary bank loans and $0.1 million of 6% stock of 1796.
† Includes $0.1 million of 6% of 1796.

Since it seemed probable that surpluses would continue for some years, the question arose as to what could be done with them when the last of the debt had been retired. The most popular proposal was to distribute the surplus among the states in aid of internal improvements and education. In his first annual message, President John Quincy Adams went further, urging the establishment of a national university and a national observatory, as well as various internal improvements. As a Hamiltonian, he believed that the Federal government could act more efficiently than the states in taking care of the interests of the entire population. However, his ideas were ridiculed and did not receive much consideration. Instead, expenditures for the usual type of public works were stepped up, $9.7 million being expended between 1821 and 1828 ($6.8 million during Adams's administration). In addition, the Federal government invested in private enterprises. In the period 1826 to 1831, for example, it acquired stock in the following companies: the Chesapeake and Delaware Canal Company, $257,500; the Dismal Swamp Canal Company, $200,000; the Louisville and Portland Canal Company, $233,500; and the Chesapeake and Ohio Canal Company, $550,000.[7] But this was not sufficient, and the surplus problem was to reappear, intermittently for the next fifty years, in a much sharper form.

[7] See the *Annual Reports of the Secretary of the Treasury*, 1826–1831.

Chapter 9: FINANCES OF AN EMERGING DEMOCRACY, 1828 TO 1836

Economically, the nine years covered in this chapter were featured by a great speculative boom. Politically, the most important development was a continued extension of the suffrage to Western farmers and Eastern working classes. These new voters wrested power from the declining aristocracy in state and local governments, and they formed the backbone of a new national political party, which, under Andrew Jackson's leadership, claimed to be the champion of the "common man." By its victory in 1828, it gained the opportunity to provide its own answers to the problems of tariff protection, internal improvements, debt management, currency, and banking which were carried over from the impasses and gropings of the early 1820's.

In making its decisions on these issues, Jacksonian Democracy was not distinguished for consistency, for it was a coalition of widely divergent interests thrown together by a common antagonism toward the Hamiltonian tradition as represented by the Adams-Clay National Republicans. The Jacksonian party was democratic, antimonopolistic, and laissez-faire, but within its ranks it harbored at one time or another the remnants of the Jeffersonian hard-money, anti-Bank school; agrarians from the new West, who believed in easy money; state rightists, who supported low tariffs; nationalists, who looked toward the West and not toward Europe; city laborers, who opposed paper money; and budding entrepreneurs, who sought a political and economic milieu conducive to the development of industrialism.

The Tariff of Abominations of 1828. Jacksonian Democracy rose quickly and sensationally, but its more impatient adherents saw in the tariff issue a means of obtaining even broader victories. Therefore, while in its long-run aspects the Tariff of 1828 was the culmination of the protective movement begun in 1816, in its immediate origin it was concerned, as John Randolph aptly put it, with "manufacturers of no sort or kind but the manufacture of a President of the United States." In the original bill, Jackson's supporters included high rates on raw wool. Since these were distasteful to New England's woolen manufacturers, it was expected that President Adams would oppose the measure, causing him to lose the support of the raw-materials producers of the West. However, the plan went awry, for when the bill was amended to increase the duty on finished woolens, it was accepted by New England and received enough votes to become law.

The Tariff of 1828 was immediately dubbed the "Tariff of Abominations." It imposed especially heavy rates on iron, wool, hemp, and finished woolens, and its average rate on dutiable articles, 41 per cent, was the highest of any tariff before the Civil War. Moreover, the protectionist nature of the bill was accentuated by extending the minimum evaluation principle to woolen goods.

Protectionism Retreats. In helping to enact this tariff, the protectionists overshot their mark. Government revenues were pushed up to new heights, laying the foundation for a perplexing surplus problem. Furthermore, many manufacturers were dissatisfied with the Act, since its extremely high duties on raw materials tended to offset the high duties on finished goods. Most importantly, the "Black Tariff" aroused white-hot indignation in the South, even though the Carolinians John C. Calhoun and George McDuffie had participated in the conspiracy out of which the tariff came.

After the election of 1828, the South was confident that Jackson would press for a tariff reduction, for he was a slaveholder and a plantation owner. However, it was Henry Clay who made the first overtures for reduction. In 1830 he moved to reduce or eliminate the duties on imports which did not compete with domestic products. Naturally, this was unsatisfactory to the South, and McDuffie countered with a proposal that rates be reduced to a maximum of 12½ per cent. Although the Clay and McDuffie plans were both rejected, there was a disposition to make some concessions to the South. After considerable debate, Congress passed the Tariff of 1832, reducing duties to 33 per cent, the average level in effect in 1824; repealing the principle of minimum evaluation; and shortening the allowable time for payment of duties from two years to six months.

The Compromise Tariff of 1833. The reduction of 1832 was not sufficiently drastic to satisfy the South, for it still embodied the hated principle of protection. Following Calhoun's interpretation of the Constitution, South Carolina issued an Ordinance of Nullification, declaring the Acts of 1828 and 1832 null and void and threatening seccession if the Federal government attempted to impose the tariff by force.

With a display of strength and executive ability, Jackson maintained that the laws of Congress were the supreme law of the land, that the Union was indissoluble, and that if necessary he would use the Army and Navy to enforce the tariff. However, at heart he was opposed to extreme protection, and he was well satisfied when Clay and Calhoun reached an agreement. Under the Compromise Tariff of 1833, all rates were to be gradually reduced to a maximum of 20 per cent by 1842.[1] In addition, the principle of "home evaluation" (evaluation at average American prices) was adopted for all goods imported after 1842.

Skyrocketing Revenues and Surpluses. Federal revenue collections during the Jackson administration exceeded all previous records, doubling from $25 million to $50 million between 1829 and 1836. Tariff increases and decreases had little effect on customs revenue, for imports steadily mounted. At the same time, the prosperity of the thirties, characterized as it was by land speculation, resulted in a phenomenal increase in the revenue from the sale of public lands.

By the Act of 1820 public lands had to be paid for in cash, which included notes issued by specie-paying banks. Since loans were easy to obtain from state banks, the government's change in policy did not interfere with the purchase of land on credit; it merely changed the identity of the creditor, land buyers becoming indebted to state banks instead of to the government.

After October 1, 1833, when the United States Bank ceased to receive public deposits and to act as a brake on the money market, the terms of borrowing became even easier. Land buyers paid the government in borrowed bank notes which were deposited in "pet banks." Since government deposits were considered to be the same as specie, they became reserves on which credit could be further expanded. Consequently, a vicious circle developed. Land speculation and currency and credit expansion increased the government surplus, which in turn increased bank reserves, causing further credit inflation and a fantastic increase in public land sales. Whereas 1.2 million acres were sold in 1829 for $1.5 million, 20 million acres were sold in 1836 for $25 million, surpassing customs as a revenue producer.

The continual rising price of land tended paradoxically to increase the demand, for buyers expected to resell immediately at higher prices. The spiral whirled ever higher. Chicago offered the most spectacular example of inflated land prices, but the boom was not confined to the West. Between 1831 and 1837 the valuation of the city of Mobile increased from $1.3 million to $27.5 million, and New York City real estate increased in assessed value from $300 million to $600 million.

Although revenue increased, expenditures remained approximately the same until the last year of the Jackson administration. Therefore, the annual surplus grew progressively larger. In 1835 at $17.9 million it was more than the total expenditures for that year, and in 1836 it reached a high of $20.4 million. At first, it was used for debt retirement, but when

[1] Rates above 20 per cent were to be reduced 10 per cent after Dec. 31, 1833; 1835; 1837; and 1839; 50 per cent after 1841; and to 20 per cent on July 1, 1842.

the last of the interest-bearing debt was paid off in January, 1835 (for the first and only time in history), a problem arose as to what to do with it. It did not seem safe to keep on accumulating deposits in the banks, for the banks would use them to expand credit. There seemed to be no way of eliminating surpluses by reducing taxes and other public revenue, for the Compromise of 1833 prevented the reduction of customs duties and public lands could not be turned over to the states.

TABLE 12. FEDERAL RECEIPTS, EXPENDITURES, AND DEBT, 1829–1836
(In millions of dollars)

	1829	1830	1831	1832	1833	1834	1835	1836
Receipts:								
Customs.......	$22.7	$21.9	$24.2	$28.5	$29.0	$16.2	$19.4	$23.4
Public lands.....	1.5	2.3	3.2	2.6	4.0	4.9	14.8	24.9
Bank dividends..	0.5	0.5	0.5	0.7	0.6	0.6	0.6	0.3
Miscellaneous...	0.1	0.1	0.6	0.1	0.3	0.1	0.7	2.2
Totals.......	$24.8	$24.8	$28.5	$31.9	$33.9	$21.8	$35.4	$50.8
Expenditures:								
Civil..........	$ 1.3	$ 1.6	$ 1.4	$ 1.8	$ 1.6	$ 2.1	$ 1.9	$ 2.1
Foreign........	0.2	0.3	0.3	0.3	1.0	0.2	0.8	0.5
Navy..........	3.3	3.2	3.9	4.0	3.9	4.0	3.9	5.8
War..........	6.3	6.8	4.8	5.4	6.7	5.7	5.8	11.8
Pensions.......	0.9	1.4	1.2	1.2	4.6	3.4	2.0	2.9
Indians........	0.6	0.6	0.9	1.4	1.8	1.0	1.6	5.0
Interest.......	2.5	1.9	1.4	0.8	0.3	0.2	0.1	0.1
Miscellaneous...	1.6	1.4	1.4	2.5	3.2	2.1	1.5	2.7
Totals.......	$16.7	$17.1	$15.2	$17.3	$23.0	$18.6	$17.6	$30.9
Surplus..........	$ 8.1	$ 7.7	$13.3	$14.6	$10.9	$ 3.2	$17.9	$19.9
Gross debt at end of year........	48.6	39.1	24.3	7.0	4.8	0.4	0.3	1.9

SOURCE: *Annual Report of the Secretary of the Treasury*, 1866, pp. 304–309.

Expansion of Expenditures for Internal Improvements. The first impulse was to expand Federal activities. Congress, following recommendations by Secretary of the Treasury McLane in his annual report of 1831, increased appropriations for the improvement of national defense, extinction of Indian claims, prosecution of various Indian wars, and construction of public buildings. Although money was spent extravagantly and often scandalously, the surplus ran at a larger rate than ever.

Accordingly, there were renewed demands for expenditures for internal improvements, and the debate over the issue continued throughout the Jackson administration. The issue was not whether government rather than private enterprise should carry on internal improvements but whether the Federal or the state governments should do it. Those who followed the Hamiltonian tradition believed that the Federal government could make a great contribution to national welfare through internal improvements and that it had the constitutional power to make them under the "general welfare" clause as well as under its implied powers. The followers of the Jeffersonian philosophy, on the other hand, feared that through internal improvements the Federal government would become all-powerful and state autonomy would be destroyed. They held that the Federal government could constitutionally finance internal improvements only in the organized territories which were indisputably governed by it. Jackson belonged to the Jeffersonian school. He was opposed to centralization and "big government" and regarded Federal financing of enterprise as a potential threat to the freedom of the individual citizen.

In 1830 Congress authorized a financial contribution to assist in the construction of a road from Maysville to Lexington, Kentucky. Jackson vetoed the bill on the ground that the project was of purely local nature and therefore outside Federal jurisdiction. Several subsequent bills to accomplish similar purposes in other localities were passed by Congress and vetoed by Jackson.

However, the practical aspects of the issue—the continued growth of the West and the unprecedented prosperity of the Federal Treasury—overshadowed ideological and constitutional scruples and forced the Jackson administration to spend more money on internal improvements than all previous administrations combined.[2] The growth of the West not only increased the agitation for national help in improving transportation facilities but also broadened the geographical area in which projects could be undertaken, while the continued collection of surplus revenue, the disposition of which was daily becoming more difficult, fostered favorable consideration of the demand.

Distribution of the Surplus among the States. Yet the Federal internal-improvement program hardly satisfied the citizens of the growing West or disposed of the surplus. Secretary Woodbury, anticipating in a crude way the cyclical-budget concept of many years later, proposed the accumulation and careful investment of the surplus for a short period "as a provident fund to be ready to meet any contingencies attending the great reduction contemplated in our revenue hereafter."[3] Congress ignored this suggestion and showed more interest in a proposal to distribute the money among the states. Most of the states were deeply in debt, and be-

[2] Between 1829 and 1836 Federal public works cost $25.1 million ($6.8 million for roads and canals, $6.3 million for forts and arsenals, $5.0 million for rivers and harbors, $3.4 million for the Cumberland Road, $2.4 million for lighthouses, and $1.2 million for public buildings). (U.S. Treasury, *Appropriations and Expenditures for Public Works.*)

[3] *Annual Report of the Secretary of the Treasury*, 1835.

cause of the Maysville veto, their citizens were pressing them to under-take internal-improvement programs.

Henry Clay, fearing that the surplus would endanger the protective tariff, supported the distribution of land revenue among the states. At first, Jackson also supported distribution if and when the debt was paid off. However, he later turned against it in favor of a more liberal land policy, and when Congress passed Clay's distribution bill, Jackson vetoed it.

The controversy was finally solved in June, 1836, by providing for the distribution of the surplus in excess of $5 million in four equal quarterly installments as a loan among the states in proportion to their representation in the House and Senate. The loan feature was a subterfuge, since the loan was to bear no interest. However, Jackson, for one, continued to insist that the deposit was a loan, not a gift. Actually, it was a precursor of the Federal grants-in-aid to the states which became a regular and exceedingly important feature of Federal-state-local finance at a much later period.

On January 1, 1837, the accumulated surplus was approximately $42.5 million, leaving $37.5 million to be distributed. But only about $28 million was actually loaned to the states, for a panic broke out in October, government revenue declined, and the distribution of the last installment had to be postponed indefinitely.

The distribution had an alarming effect. Many of the states used their shares to inflate the economy further by either investing them in capital projects or distributing them among their citizens, thus increasing purchasing power. The movement of funds from the original place of deposit to the state treasuries also had a disrupting effect on the money market, and when the Treasury began to withdraw its deposits in specie, the banks found themselves in a most embarrassing position.

Internal Improvements and Borrowing by the States. While the Federal government followed a policy of economy and debt reduction, the states did just the opposite. Between 1820 and 1838 the states borrowed $60 million for canal construction, $53 million to capitalize state banks, $43 million for railroads, $7 million for turnpikes, and smaller amounts for state universities, hospitals, statehouses, schools, and jails. Total state debts increased from $26 million in 1830 to about $175 million in 1838, Pennsylvania, Louisiana, and New York having the largest increases—$27 million, $24 million, and $19 million, respectively. And Indiana, Illinois, Maryland, and Alabama each increased its debt by over $10 million.[4]

Most of this debt was placed with Europeans, who invested in America

[4] Hunt's *Merchants Magazine*, August, 1839, p. 178.

largely because of the phenomenal success of the Erie Canal, the rapid repayment of the Federal debt, the extraordinary outward prosperity of the country, and the high interest rates offered. British investments alone increased from an estimated $20 million in 1805 to almost $70 million in 1835 and $175 million by 1838.[5]

The influx of European capital was mostly used to purchase imports, but it also produced a large net inflow of specie.[6] In 1836 the United States had an import balance of $52.2 million on the merchandise account and $9.1 million on the specie account. As this foreign capital flowed in, investment spending increased sharply, adding to the strong inflationary pressures of the period.

The improvements which were constructed were economically successful in the long run, but on a short-term investment basis, they were failures. Since taxes were low, disaster could be averted only as long as the European capital flow continued.

Prologue to the Bank Controversy. While Federal fiscal policies and state borrowings for internal improvements encouraged speculative investment, the United States Bank remained a controlling factor against extreme credit expansion. But the Bank's charter was to expire in 1836, and the election of 1828 had brought into office a group of men and a set of economic interests philosophically opposed to the Bank and all it symbolized. Jackson himself was a hard-money agrarian who distrusted all banks and all paper money, believing that they inflated the currency and created speculative booms. He was ably supported by Senator Benton, whose predilection for hard money earned him the title "Old Bullion" Benton. These hard-money views were shared by urban laborers who suffered from the depreciation which often characterized paper money.

Other supporters of the Jackson party opposed the Bank because it tended to exert a control over the money market and imposed a check on credit expansion. Among them were agrarians who needed capital funds and favored credit expansion, state bankers who regarded the central bank as an obstacle to their expansionist ambitions, and would-be entrepreneurs who favored *laissez faire* and objected to any institution with even a faint tinge of monopolistic privilege.[7] The charge of monopoly was potent, for in making it, the leaders of the "New Democracy" convinced the rank and file that the Bank was a threat to the preservation of American democracy. As such, its powers should be clipped at once.

[5] Leland H. Jenks, *The Migration of British Capital*, p. 85.
[6] The devaluation of the gold dollar (see p. 109) also encouraged specie imports.
[7] Curiously, one of these budding entrepreneurs was James A. Hamilton, Alexander Hamilton's son.

In one sense, the opposition to the Bank represented small business against big business, *laissez faire* against monopoly, and the masses against the few. Yet in another sense, it represented state rights opposed to Federalism and free local banking against the restraints of central banking.[8]

The First Round of the Bank Battle. The struggle over rechartering the Bank came to a focus in 1829 shortly after the inauguration when Jackson told Biddle that he had been afraid of all banks ever since reading the history of the South Sea Bubble. He might have added that his distrust of the Bank was increased by charges that the officers of some of its branches had actively opposed him in the previous election. In his first message to Congress in December, 1829, Jackson openly demonstrated his hostility by questioning the constitutionality of the Bank and charging that it had failed to establish a uniform and sound currency. Though willing to have the Bank rechartered if its functions were greatly curtailed, he preferred an institution "founded on the credit of the government and its revenues."

The majority report of the House Ways and Means Committee, written by Chairman McDuffie, dismissed Jackson's vague suggestion, saying, "There is no species of trade in which the government should embark, especially banking." It maintained that the Bank provided a sound and uniform currency and regarded the issue, not as hard money vs. paper money, but as central-bank notes vs. state-bank notes.

In May, 1830, the House twice expressed its confidence in the Bank, leading many to believe that the matter was settled, but in his message of 1830 Jackson proposed a bank as a branch of the Treasury with the function of deposit but not of making loans. Little notice was taken of this proposal, but on the floor of the Senate in early 1831, Benton gave new life to the forces opposing the Bank. His speech was the most complete statement of the anti-Bank position, not only expressing his own hard-money views, but appealing to agrarians, laborers, and state rightists and giving the controversy an emotional tinge that was to be the most effective weapon in the whole contest. He asserted that the Bank was controlled by "private individuals, many of them foreigners." It had too much power and was too much disposed to exercise that power to the prejudice of the freedom and equality which should prevail in a republic. It tended "to make the rich richer and the poor poorer." It was "unfavorable to small capitalists . . . and injurious to the laboring classes." Instead of a national-bank currency, Benton advocated gold and silver as the money which best suited "the men of middle property and the

---

[8] There is a mass of material on the bank controversy. Ralph C. H. Catterall's *The Second Bank of the United States* is the most definitive. Arthur M. Schlesinger, Jr. (*The Age of Jackson*) presents the anti-Bank point of view. The articles by Bray Hammond in the *Journal of Economic History* (Vols. VI and VII, May, 1946, and May, 1947) give a forceful presentation of the pro-Bank view.

working people." But rather than proposing the complete abolition of paper money, Benton would leave "every species of paper . . . money to the states."[9]

Despite its tremendous appeal, Benton's speech was hardly realistic. The Bank was not a monopoly, for it had only 25 per cent of the total note circulation. It was not controlled by foreigners. On the other hand, its note issues were as good as any in the world, and the cause of hard money could be dealt no severer blow than to give state banks complete control over paper-money issues.

Jackson Vetoes the Bank's Recharter. While Jackson and his closest advisers opposed the Bank, most of his cabinet, including Secretary McLane, favored it. It appeared for a while as though they were softening the President's attitude, for in his message of December, 1831, Jackson said that he would leave the question to the decision of an enlightened people, but he was careful to state that he had not changed his own opinion.

However, in the same month the anti-Jackson forces met at Baltimore and nominated Henry Clay for President. The majority of the convention decided to make the Bank the chief issue of the campaign, and Clay accepted the decision. In turn, he successfully convinced Biddle to appeal at once for a new charter. A bill, with some limiting provisions designed to appease Jackson, was introduced on January 9, 1832. After long debate, it was passed on July 3. Strongly characterized by sectionalism, the vote in the Senate was 28 to 20 and in the House, 107 to 85. The issue was now squarely up to Jackson. The Whigs were convinced that, if he vetoed the bill, he would lose the vote of Pennsylvania; if he signed it, he would lose the vote of the South. Nevertheless, on July 10, 1832, Jackson vetoed the recharter, emphasizing the same charges made by Benton but making no mention of the economics of the case and omitting all his hard-money views.[10]

Although it could not muster enough votes to override the veto, the anti-Jackson coalition was delighted. Incorrectly convinced that the public supported the Bank, it circulated 30,000 copies of the veto message, but in the election of 1832, Clay was badly defeated.

The Removal of Deposits. For over a year the pro-Bank group continued to attempt to pass another bill for recharter, and during this period the antagonism between Biddle and the administration became most in-

[9] Theodore Roosevelt, *Thomas Hart Benton*, pp. 106ff.

[10] Biddle called the message "a manifesto of anarchy, such as Marat or Robespierre might have issued." The conservative Boston *Daily Advertiser* observed that "for the first time, perhaps, in the history of civilized communities, the chief Magistrate of a great nation . . . is found appealing to the worst passions of the uninformed part of the people, and endeavoring to stir up the poor against the rich."

tense. Two incidents added fuel to the fire. One involved the retirement of the last of the 3 per cent Revolutionary debt, which was held largely abroad. Biddle deemed the repayment inadvisable on the ground that the existence of a cholera epidemic required the Bank to maintain ample cash resources to prevent a financial calamity. Without consulting the Treasury, he arranged with the Barings for the extension of the debt, the Bank pledging itself to meet future interest payments. McLane regarded Biddle's action as a violation of the Bank's charter inasmuch as it was tantamount to the acquisition by the Bank of government stock, and Jackson became more determined than ever to teach the Bank that it was not bigger than the government.

The second incident occurred in February, 1833. The government, through the Bank, drew a draft on the French government for nearly $1 million in satisfaction of claims for damages growing out of the Napoleonic Wars. When the French government refused to accept it, Biddle submitted a bill to the Treasury for the costs of the unsuccessful attempt at collection plus 15 per cent damages to which he claimed the Bank was entitled under a statute of the District of Columbia. McLane refused to pay, and Biddle withheld part of the dividends due on the government's Bank stock. The case was taken to the courts, and eventually in 1847, it was held that the Bank was not entitled to damages. But in the meanwhile, Jackson recommended an investigation of the Bank's solvency. Once again, the majority of the Ways and Means Committee favored the Bank, and the House concurred 109 to 46. But Jackson was not satisfied, and in July he sent Amos Kendall on a mission to see whether state banks would take government deposits on satisfactory terms so that relations with "Biddle's Bank" could be terminated.

In August, 1833, Biddle, still hoping to procure a recharter, began to contract credit severely. Within a year, he reduced discounts and exchange by over 20 per cent and outstanding state bank balances from $2.2 million to $500,000. Simultaneously, the Bank's specie holdings increased to a record level.

Biddle's deflationary program lost him many of his remaining friends, since it caused much financial stringency throughout the country. But it did not cause Jackson to change his attitude. On September 18, 1833, he announced that he would take full responsibility for withdrawing government deposits from the Bank. McLane, who refused to go along with the plan, was appointed Secretary of State. His successor Duane, who also refused to cooperate, was dismissed. Finally, Attorney General Taney, who was extremely hostile to the Bank, was appointed Secretary of the Treasury, and on October 1, 1833, he began to deposit newly collected government funds in various state banks, or "pet banks" as they came to be called. By January 1, 1835, 29 depositories had been selected. Technically, Taney did not withdraw the deposits in the United States Bank but drew upon them to pay expenditures and made no new deposits in the Bank.[11]

Biddle's expectations that enough Whig congressmen would be elected in 1834 to override a second Presidential veto did not come true. Under the circumstances, he had no choice except to begin liquidation. In March, 1837, he delivered four bonds totaling approximately $7.9 million in payment for the government's stock. After obtaining a charter from the Pennsylvania legislature, he reorganized the Bank as a state institution. It suffered severely in the panic of 1837 and failed in the subsequent depression.

The Expansion of State Banking. Although the administration was opposed to all banks of issue and supported hard money, its refusal to recharter the United States Bank and the withdrawal of government deposits caused state banking to enter its second era of great growth. In 1829 there were 329 state banks with a capital of $110 million, in 1834 there were 506 capitalized at $200 million, and by 1837, 788 with $300 million capital. Between 1830 and 1837, state-bank-note circulation more than doubled, and loans and discounts increased from less than $200 million to over $500 million.

State governments encouraged the formation of banks, since they helped to foster commerce and facilitated the raising of capital funds for use in public works. At the same time, the upsurge of *laissez faire*, which accompanied the development of industrialism, encouraged the expansion of banking by preaching the right of anyone to engage in the business. The Federal government also encouraged the inflationary expansion of state banks by accepting their notes in payment for public lands and by building up their reserves through the deposit of public moneys. Finally, the public itself lent encouragement to state banking. Particularly in frontier sections, where capital was scarce, the public demanded long-term loans on poor security, regarded with equanimity the existence of wildcat banking, favored expansion of paper money, and resented attempts to redeem it.

The shortage of capital funds would appear, in retrospect, to have been the basic cause of the inefficient banking system of the time. The most inefficient banks existed where capital was scarcest, whereas the most efficient ones were confined to areas in which conditions were the reverse. Inefficient banking produced overexpansion of note issues, drove specie out of circulation, and caused bank notes to circulate at heavy discounts. It brought in its wake a top-heavy credit structure, overextension of state

[11] The *Annual Report of the Secretary of the Treasury* (1832 and 1833) contains the documents on the relations between the Bank and the Treasury.

and local borrowing, a general shortage of liquid assets, and eventual panic.

Yet inefficient banking had some advantages. It was one of the roots of prosperity as well as panic, and it is questionable if a conservative banking policy would have made possible the rapid economic development of the West which took place under loose banking. Moreover, even if sound banking had been desired, it probably could not have been instituted. There was no single pattern of sound banking, for that which succeeded in one area might have readily failed in another. The essence of sound banking was not a thing of law or rule or structure but of conservative management—a thing which was neither popular nor in supply.

Measures to Protect Federal Funds. As credit expanded, the administration became concerned over the safety of its state-bank deposits. As the first important step to safeguard them, it instructed all collectors in April, 1835, not to accept any bank notes of less than $5 denomination. A year later, it announced that it would not pay out any bank note which was not redeemable in specie at its place of issue and was not circulating at par with specie at the place where offered.

Finally, in June, 1836, Congress, on the recommendation of the Treasury, enacted a comprehensive law regulating the deposits of public money. In addition to distributing the surplus, the Act prohibited government depositories from issuing notes in denominations of less than $5 or from refusing to redeem notes in specie. At the same time they were instructed to consider all government deposits to be specie deposits. It was also provided that, whenever the Federal deposits exceeded 25 per cent of a bank's capital for more than three months, 2 per cent interest was to be paid by the bank on the excess and the Secretary was authorized to require security against public deposits.

All these measures taken together showed the unmistakable intention of the government to impel greater caution on the part of banks in their note issues and other operations. But the chief tool of regulation was based on a widely held opinion, for which there was little factual support, that any restriction of bank-note circulation to denominations of $5 or more would encourage the use of specie.

Devaluation of the Gold Dollar. In addition to its attempts to increase the use of specie in banking, the hard-money administration also tried to stimulate its use in the money system. For many years gold coins had not circulated in the United States because the mint ratio of gold to silver (1 to 15) was below the market ratio. Silver dollars had not been minted since 1806 because it was more profitable to export them to South America. The nation's currency, therefore, consisted of United States

Bank notes, state-bank notes, and foreign coins, together with some subsidiary coins.

The discovery of gold in the Appalachian Range of the upper South gave the Jackson-Benton hard-money coalition another opportunity to strike a blow for specie. Accordingly, in 1834 the gold weight of the dollar was reduced to 23.2 grains (23.22 by amendment in 1837), while the silver dollar was maintained at 371.25 grains, thus changing the coinage ratio to approximately 1 to 16. Since the market ratio in Europe was about 1 to 15.75, the new mint ratio prompted the possessors of gold to bring it to the American mint, while discouraging the owners of silver from doing so. In six months in 1834, $4 million of gold coin was minted, compared with an annual average of only $400,000 in the previous years. On the other hand, it became impossible for the administration to substitute specie for notes of small denomination, for silver coins would not circulate, since they were worth more in the bullion market than at the mint.

The Specie Circular. In addition to its uneasiness concerning the safety of its deposits, the administration was for a number of years disturbed by the speculative fever in public lands. It was apparent that purchases of land with bank credit were helping the speculator rather than the settler, besides creating a fictitious picture of banking strength. The deposits to the credit of the government were in terms of specie, but they had been actually made in paper money, producing a totally impossible condition. As Table 13 demonstrates, the government's "specie deposits" exceeded the total specie holdings of the deposit banks.

TABLE 13.   CONDITION OF 36 DEPOSIT BANKS, JUNE 1, 1836
(In millions of dollars)

Assets		Liabilities	
Loans and discounts	$108.5	Public deposits (nominally in specie)	$ 41.0
Real estate	1.9	Other deposits	16.0
Due from banks	17.9	Circulation	28.0
Bank notes	11.0	Due to banks	17.1
Specie	10.5	Capital	46.4
Other investments	12.6	Other liabilities	13.8
Total	$162.3	Total	$162.3

SOURCE: *Annual Report of the Secretary of the Treasury*, 1836.

After much preliminary thought, Jackson finally took action. In July, 1836, by an executive order known as the "specie circular," he directed that, effective August 15, 1836, all sales of public lands, except to bona fide settlers or actual residents of the state in which the land was sold, were to be for specie or Virginia land scrip and after December 15, 1836, all land sales were to be for specie or Virgina land scrip.

The specie circular immediately stopped further credit expansion and brought the land boom to an end, precipitating a panic. However, Jackson's action was not fundamental. The great overinvestment in state-financed capital projects and the overspeculation in land during the period of prosperity were much more responsible for the eventual collapse. Over-expansion was fed by capital imports from abroad, by vast expansion of bank credit, and by the government's fiscal and banking policies. The rapid repayment of the national debt provided funds which the states borrowed. The Maysville veto surrendered the function of internal-improvement construction to the states. The land policy encouraged speculation. The failure to recharter the Bank removed the only control over the credit structure. While deposited in the state banks, the surplus acted as a source for credit inflation, and when distributed among the states, it added to the investment boom.

When capital funds from Britain stopped flowing into the states upon the outbreak of a crisis abroad, the floor on which the American investment boom was built collapsed. And when the specie circular was issued, the banking system was confronted with a demand for specie, which it did not have and which it could not raise. Therefore, banks began to suspend specie payments, and by May, 1837, suspension was country-wide. At the same time investment fell off, and liquidation and deflation began to take place on a large scale.

Chapter 10: FINANCING THROUGH THE DEPRESSION, 1837 TO 1843

During the depression which followed the panic of 1837, Democrats and Whigs clashed sharply over questions of fiscal and monetary policy. The Democrats favored a reduction of government spending, a restricted Federal government, the separation of the Treasury from the banks, and the payment of public dues in hard money. The Whigs, on the other hand, advocated increased government spending for internal improvements, easy-money policies, reestablishment of the United States Bank, and general increases in tariff rates for the replenishment of the Treasury as well as for the greater protection of manufacturers.

Van Buren's View on the Depression. When the panic broke out, Jackson was no longer President. But his successor and long-time political associate, Martin Van Buren, followed the Jacksonian theories of limited Federal powers and *laissez faire*. Despite pleas from business and threats from opponents, he refused to ease money conditions or to rescind the specie circular.

The suspension of specie payments by the banks in May, 1837, threw government fiscal operations out of gear. By law, the government could not make deposits in banks which did not redeem their notes in specie, and it could not accept notes which were not so redeemable. Temporarily, collectors kept government funds in the mint or in improvised strong boxes, safes, and vaults, and all payments of public dues were required to be made in coin. Difficulties were encountered in enforcing the latter rule, and collectors were often compelled to accept paper money. Nevertheless, the bulk of Treasury operations were made in hard cash.[1]

Thus by force of circumstances, Treasury operations became separated from the banks, but this could not continue indefinitely without Congressional authorization and provision for more adequate physical facilities for keeping funds. In addition, revenue declined sharply, and the prospect of a deficit arose. Accordingly, in September, 1837, Van Buren called a session of Congress to deal with the emergency problem.

In his message to the special session, Van Buren identified the panic as part of a world crisis, but he ascribed its domestic aspects more particularly to overaction in business, excessive issues of paper money, foreign loans contracted by states, overextension of short-term credits to mer-

[1] In 1838, as business recovered slightly, some banks resumed specie payments, but in 1839, as the depression began in earnest, they again suspended.

chants, diversion of labor from agriculture, and the disturbances caused by the movement of public funds under the Surplus Distribution Act. He refused to regard the Federal government as in any way responsible for causing or alleviating the "revulsion," saying:

Those who look to the action of this government for specific aid to the citizen . . . lose sight of the ends for which it was created and the powers with which it is clothed. . . . The less government interferes with private pursuits, the better for the general prosperity.

Most of the message was devoted to the twin problems of where to deposit government funds and what to accept in payment of government dues. Van Buren dismissed the possibility of reviving a central bank, since it had been repudiated by the public, did not prevent "economic revulsions," and represented a concentrated money power dangerous to republican institutions. The use of state banks as depositories was equally unthinkable. In Van Buren's judgment all banks were prone to overissue bank notes, but the temptation was especially strong among state banks. Therefore, the deposit of Federal funds in state banks would increase loans and circulation and give a new stimulus to speculation. Van Buren also opposed the use of paper money in payment of government dues, for he considered that to accept it was unconstitutional and that its depreciation would result in a loss for the government. Under the circumstances, the only sound course for the government to follow was to have nothing to do with banks and bank-note issues of any sort. It should conduct all its affairs in specie and take care of the custody and disbursement of its own funds.

Independent Treasury Act of 1840. Congress was not greatly impressed with the President's address. Indeed, in May, 1838, by joint resolution, it repealed the specie circular. In addition, it refused for a long while to enact the President's recommendations for a separation of government from the banks. But finally, in June, 1840, the Independent Treasury bill passed the House by a vote of 124 to 107 and was approved by the President in July.

The bill provided that government funds were to be held in its own subtreasuries. From June, 1840, to June, 1841, at least one-quarter of any payment due to the government had to be made in specie. This was to be gradually increased, and after June 30, 1843, all government dues were to be payable in specie only.

Attempts to Establish a Third Bank. The provision for 100 per cent specie payments never became effective, for Van Buren was defeated for reelection in 1840 and one of the first acts of the Harrison administration was to repeal the Independent Treasury Act.

The victory of the Whigs brought to office a group of men distinguished more for their opposition to Jacksonian laissez-faire democracy than for any consistent political philosophy of their own. Henry Clay was recognized as the leading member of the party, but when William Henry Harrison died and John Tyler, an anti-Jackson, state rights Democrat, became President, Clay's expansionist program was completely blocked. As a result the Tyler administration was spent in continuous wrangling between the President and the Whig majority in Congress.

After the Independent Treasury Act was repealed, Clay introduced a bill to create a Fiscal Bank, which would have been similar to the Second United States Bank. Tyler vetoed it and suggested that Secretary of the Treasury Ewing draft a substitute. Ewing brought in a plan for a Fiscal Corporation, which would be limited to dealing in exchange, but Tyler also vetoed that. The President then recommended the formation of an Exchequer Bank which would issue notes upon deposit of specie, deal in domestic bills and drafts, and hold government deposits. But Congress refused to consider it. In the meanwhile, the old system of using state banks as government depositories was readopted without any formal legislation.

State Banking in the Depression. The return to the use of state banks as depositories did not work out well, for state-bank failures were widespread during the depression of 1837 to 1843, and the Treasury was hard pressed to find safe banks in which to deposit its funds. In 1843 it had only 19 general deposit banks—12 on the East coast, 2 in the South, 4 in Ohio, and 1 in Michigan—and 9 special deposit banks, all in the East and South.

TABLE 14. OPERATIONS OF STATE BANKS, 1837–1843
(In millions of dollars)

	1837	1838	1839	1840	1841	1842	1843
No. of banks	788	829	840	901	784	692	691
Principal resources:							
Loans and discounts	$525	$486	$492	$463	$386	$324	$255
Stocks	12	34	36	42	65	25	28
Notes of other banks	37	25	27	21	26	19	13
Specie	38	35	45	33	35	28	34
Principal liabilities:							
Capital	291	318	327	358	314	260	229
Circulation	149	116	135	107	107	84	59
Deposits	127	85	90	76	65	62	56

SOURCE: *Annual Report of the Comptroller of the Currency*, 1876, pp. 204–205.

Free Banking. Widespread bank failures caused a revulsion of public feeling against banking and bankers. The public objected strongly to the monopolistic organization of banks under special charters and demanded that banking be operated as free enterprise, subject to special government regulation.

This movement toward "free banking" was best illustrated by the experiences of New York and Michigan. In New York the safety fund system broke down in the panic of 1837. Eleven banks became insolvent, and although two recovered, the other nine drew $2.6 million from the fund, making heavy drains on its resources. Consequently, in 1838 under the pressure of labor and hard-money Locofocoism,[2] New York ended the system of granting bank charters by special legislative acts and adopted a free banking system under which any group of people could incorporate a bank by depositing with the state comptroller United States bonds, state bonds, or real estate bonds or mortgages. In exchange, the bank would receive an equivalent amount of bank notes for circulation. Every bank was required to submit periodic reports to the comptroller and to redeem in specie on demand any note with a value below $1,000. Failure to redeem entailed a 14 per cent penalty payable to the holder of the unredeemed note, and if it continued, the comptroller was to sell the security and redeem as much of the bank's circulation as possible. The New York law was copied widely in later years, and it became the basis of the national banking system adopted by the Federal government in 1863.

However, free banking did not assure soundness and efficiency. It produced an inelastic currency, and it was only as safe as the securities deposited against the notes. In the beginning, New York banks posted bonds issued by Southern and Western states. These were poor, and when banks failed, the comptroller could not realize sufficient funds to settle the claims of noteholders. Up to 1843, 29 banks failed with a circulation of $1.2 million, but the sale of their securities produced only $1.0 million. Indeed, free banking at first provided less security than the safety fund. However, in time, the law was changed limiting the security to New York and Federal bonds, and the system became increasingly successful.

On the other hand, Michigan's Free Banking Act of 1837 (the first in American history) was a complete fiasco. Every bank was required to deposit securities up to the full amount of its debts, but the securities might be the personal bonds of stockholders or bonds and mortgages on real estate. In addition, at least 30 per cent of a bank's capital had to be paid in specie, and provision was made for regular examination of each bank. Unfortunately, these rigid requirements were vitiated by lax enforcement. Real estate security was grossly overvalued, and the personal bonds of stockholders were mere promises to pay. Many so-called bankers disap-

[2] A term originating with "loco-foco" (self-propelled) friction matches and applied in the 1830's to the more radical segments of the Democratic party.

peared, leaving their state-bank notes without a redeemer. Specie was shipped from bank to bank, always a step or two ahead of the bank examiner, and kegs of nails or broken glass were given a thin icing of gold coins to deceive the public and the bank examiners as to the size of the bank's gold reserves. In many cases, bank examiners winked at fraud and joined in the collusion. Under such a system, failures were common. In the first year more than 40 banks were formed even though the state had only a little more than 200,000 population. Two years later, more than 40 banks had failed. In the last analysis, the unsoundness of Michigan's banking was caused by the area's lack of capital and was characteristic of frontier conditions. If the law of 1837 had been effectively enforced, Michigan would have had no banks at all.

State-owned Banks. In the last years of prosperity the withdrawal of the Federal government from banking caused many states to venture upon bank ownership. These experiments, like free banking, met with mixed success. The State Bank of Indiana, founded in 1834, was successful, for its management was efficient and conservative. The state owned outright half of the parent bank's capital and made loans to subscribers to the bank's stock. Commercial loans were made only after most careful consideration and were in small amounts and highly diversified. In spite of its success, the bank, with its 17 branches, was not popular. As a monopoly, it was vulnerable to attack and was forced to wind up its affairs in 1855.

The experience in Mississippi with a state-owned bank was altogether different. In 1838 after the branch of the United States Bank in Mississippi was closed, the state chartered the Union Bank with a capital of $15 million, $5 million of which was subscribed by the state through the sale of bonds. About two-thirds of the bank's loans were made on overinflated real estate and could not be liquidated quickly during the succeeding money stringency. The bank failed, and the state of Mississippi repudiated the bonds which had been floated to start the bank.

Louisiana Banking System. In Louisiana private enterprise continued to control banking, but under strict government regulation. After the failure of a land bank in 1842, the state adopted a free banking system, requiring a 100 per cent reserve against all public liabilities (33⅓ per cent in specie and 66⅔ per cent in 90-day commercial paper). A bank could not be started with less than 50 stockholders. No bank could pay out any notes except its own, and a system of weekly clearing was instituted. State regulation was so complete and so well enforced that only one important bank was started, with the result that the Louisiana banking system became a branch system with the parent bank in New Orleans. In many respects, it was the best bank of the period, being a model for other states and countries. But its chief importance lay in the fact that it contained many features of the later Federal Reserve System, such as reserves in commercial paper, prohibition of payment of any notes but the bank's own, and a weekly settlement.

Government Fiscal Policy. While attempting to reorganize the banking system, the Van Buren administration also proposed to attack the depression by pursuing a frugal fiscal policy. Woodbury, who continued as Secretary of the Treasury, estimated the deficit for 1837, even after using all the Treasury balances, at $6 million. He recommended that Congress suspend the fourth installment of the distribution to the states, extend the period of time allowed for the payment of customs duties, and authorize the issue of treasury notes in anticipation of revenue. Van Buren supported Woodbury's recommendations and also suggested that Congress might "promote the prosperity of the country by using forbearance in making appropriations."

TABLE 15.   FEDERAL RECEIPTS, EXPENDITURES, AND DEBT, 1837–1844
(In millions of dollars)

	1837	1838	1839	1840	1841	1842	1843*	1844
Revenues:								
Customs.............	$ 11.2	$ 16.2	$ 23.1	$ 13.5	$ 14.5	$ 18.2	$ 7.0	$ 26.2
Public lands...........	6.8	3.1	7.1	3.3	1.4	1.3	0.9	2.1
Bank stock...........	1.4	4.5	......	1.7	0.7			
Miscellaneous.........	5.6	2.5	1.3	0.9	0.3	0.4	0.3	1.1
Totals.............	$ 25.0	$ 26.3	$ 31.5	$ 19.5	$ 16.9	$ 20.0	$ 8.2	$ 29.3
Expenditures:								
Civil................	$ 2.4	$ 2.7	$ 2.1	$ 2.7	$ 2.6	$ 2.9	$ 1.2	$ 2.5
Foreign..............	4.6	1.2	1.0	0.7	0.4	0.6	0.4	0.6
Navy...............	6.6	6.1	6.2	6.1	6.0	8.4	3.7	6.5
War....	13.7	13.1	9.2	7.2	9.0	6.7	3.1	5.2
Pensions.............	2.7	2.2	3.1	2.6	2.4	1.4	0.8	2.0
Indians..............	4.3	5.3	2.2	2.3	2.3	1.2	0.4	1.3
Interest on debt........	......	......	0.4	0.2	0.3	0.8	0.5	1.9
Miscellaneous.........	2.9	3.3	2.6	2.6	3.5	3.3	1.6	2.6
Totals.............	$ 37.2	$ 33.9	$ 26.9	$ 24.3	$ 26.5	$ 25.1	$ 11.8	$ 22.5
Surplus (+) or deficit (−)	$ −12.2	$ −7.6	$ +4.9	$ −4.8	−9.6	$ −5.2	$ −3.5	$ +6.8
Gross debt at end of fiscal year.................	4.9	12.0	5.1	6.7	15.0	......	27.2	24.7

SOURCE: *Annual Report of the Secretary of the Treasury,* 1866, pp. 304 309.

* Half year only. Fiscal year was changed from Jan. 1–Dec. 31 to July 1–June 30.

But the economy policy could not be instituted immediately, as projects started in the last years of prosperity had to be finished and government salaries were fixed by law. However, in time the government's capital investments in roads, canals, and other public works were cut. During the eight years of the Van Buren and Tyler administrations, public-works expenditures declined to $19.6 million, or an average of $2.4 million a year, and near the end of the depression amounted to less than $2 million annually. When the Whig administration first assumed office, Beverly Tucker, professor of law at William and Mary, anticipating many professors of a century later, recommended meeting the depression by a "judicious increase in the national debt."[3] But this suggestion was not accepted.

Although expenditures did not decline at once, revenue fell off one-half and, after a substantial recovery in 1839, declined even further during the remainder of the depression. Consequently, the government operated with a deficit in every year of the depression but one.

The Treasury, which had been debt-free in 1836, found itself with a gross debt in excess of $25 million at the end of the depression. In each year of the depression, the Treasury sold short-term notes at interest rates of $\frac{1}{10}$ of 1 per cent to 6 per cent. Including reissues, $47 million were issued. There were also three long-term loans beginning in 1841, aggregating $21 million. They bore interest at 5 and 6 per cent and were redeemable at the pleasure of the government.

Public Lands and the Tariff of 1842. The decline in government revenues and depressed business conditions caused a new outbreak of agitation for increased tariff duties. At the same time the West demanded a liberalization of Federal land policy. But conservatives, led by Clay, feared that a liberal land policy would be detrimental to industrialism and to the older, more settled regions of the country. On the other hand, revenue from land sales had to be cut lest it endanger protectionism. Conservatives, therefore, proposed to distribute the proceeds of land sales among the states. Finally, in the Preemption Act of 1841 a compromise was reached. To satisfy the frontier, squatters were given the right to buy up to 160 acres of land at $1.25 an acre. To please conservatives, Clay's distribution plan was adopted, but in order to appease the South, it was to take place only if the average rate of the tariff remained at the 20 per cent level fixed under the Compromise of 1833.

Subsequently, Clay twice introduced bills to raise the tariff and at the same time retain the distribution clause, but Tyler vetoed both bills. Clay finally abandoned the distribution clause and introduced a bill to increase the tariff to the general average in effect in 1824. Calhoun insisted that the proposed bill dishonored the pledge made in the Compromise of 1833. Nevertheless, it was passed. It increased the rates to an average of 33⅓ per cent. While it emphasized specific duties, it also provided for minimum

---

[3] Quoted by Hugh R. Fraser, *Democracy in the Making*, p. 166; Joseph Dorfman, *The Economic Mind in American Civilization*, Vol. II, p. 915.

evaluation. The home-evaluation clause of the Compromise of 1833, which was to be effective in 1842, was dropped, and all duties were payable in cash.

State Defaults. The depression was felt far more by the state governments than by the Federal government, for they were more deeply involved in internal improvements and had incurred large debts. Their railroad and canal works were not earning enough revenues to cover interest charges, their bank ventures were mostly failures, and their taxes were unproductive. In Pennsylvania, for example, $24 million had been invested in canals, railroads, and turnpikes, carrying an annual interest charge of $1.2 million but returning a revenue of only $210,000. The state had a low level of taxation, and in 1842, at the bottom of the depression, it was forced to default on interest payments. Mississippi, Arkansas, Florida, Illinois, Indiana, Maryland, and Michigan had already defaulted. Eventually, Pennsylvania resumed interest payments and met her indebtedness in full, but Mississippi, Arkansas, and Florida, with carefully rationalized arguments, repudiated.

Foreign investors were alienated by the failure of the states to meet their debts, and when attempts to persuade the Federal government to assume the state obligations failed, European capital ceased to be available to American borrowers. However, the bitter experience was finally forgotten in the 1850's and European money markets were again opened to American securities.

Chapter 11: FINANCES OF THE LAST AGRARIAN ADMINISTRATIONS

During the years 1844 to 1860, Federal financial and monetary problems became less dramatic as the spotlight played on the much more crucial economic, social, and political conflicts between the North and the South. At the same time, the political administrations (Polk, Taylor, Fillmore, Pierce, and Buchanan) were increasingly dominated by agrarianism, and the trend was therefore toward a more and more limited exercise of Federal powers.

The monetary and fiscal problems which did exist were solved along previously determined lines. The Federal government returned to the Independent Treasury system, and state banking continued to develop according to the pattern set in the previous decade. Little need was felt for any great expansion of Federal improvements, and the greatest Federal ventures of the time—the Mexican War and the acquisition of California and other Mexican territory—were easily financed. Fiscal and monetary developments were affected over the first thirteen years of the period by a continually mounting prosperity and during the last three, by sharp economic recession.

Revival of the Independent Treasury System. The election of a Democratic administration in 1844 made it certain that new attempts would be made to separate the government from the banking system. In August, 1846, Congress reestablished the Independent Treasury system, and with various modifications, it remained in existence until 1921. Under its operation before the Civil War, government finance was theoretically separated from the banking system. Government dues were payable only in specie or Treasury notes. Government funds were held in government subtreasuries scattered around the country, and all collectors of government revenue were instructed, first by a ruling and after 1857 by a law, not to deposit any government funds in private banks. Under the limitations imposed by the agrarian thinking which prevailed during the era, the Independent Treasury was the only logical system. It was an attempt to save the government from the allegedly baneful influences of an overly powerful central bank, as well as from dependence on an irresponsible state-banking structure. In another sense, it was a hard-money compromise between conservative, centrally controlled paper circulation and aggressive, but overly loose, state-bank circulation.

Its most astute champions claimed that the system increased the amount of specie in circulation, prevented the suspension of specie payments, weakened the forces which made possible spasmodic bank expansion and contraction, prevented the loss of public funds, and prevented the derangement of business which might result from the floating of government loans based on bank credit.[1] Undoubtedly, the Independent Treasury system placed a checkrein on credit expansion and increased the use of specie, privately as well as publicly. But it also had enormous disadvantages, and the fundamental principle upon which it was based—the separation of the government from the banks—could never be achieved completely. The Treasury's operations continued to influence the money market, since payments by and to the government caused a huge daily stream of hard cash to circulate between individuals and the Treasury. Unless Treasury disbursements were equal to collections, the system tended to drain specie out of commercial channels into government vaults.

In periods of prosperity, revenue surpluses accumulated in the Treasury, correspondingly reducing hard-money circulation, tightening credit, and restraining the legitimate as well as the speculative expansion of trade and production. During panics and depressions, when many banks suspended specie payments and hard money was hoarded, insistence on the payment of government dues in specie or treasury notes aggravated economic difficulties and tended to retard recovery by preventing the expansion of credit. Nor could the system work effectively in a time of crisis such as a great war. Although it functioned well enough during the comparatively minor Mexican War, its limitations were clearly revealed by the problems encountered in financing the Civil War.

Creating a Subsidiary Coinage. To put as much of the economy as possible on a specie basis, it was necessary to provide a subsidiary coinage, because the devaluation of the gold dollar in 1834 to 1837 had made the half dollar worth 52 cents in the bullion market and had caused it and other silver coins to disappear from circulation. In 1853, therefore, Congress reduced the weight of the half dollar from 206.25 to 192 grains, 9/10 fine. Thereafter, it was no longer profitable to sell silver coins in the bullion market, and the circulation of half dollars, quarters, and dimes immediately increased. With an assured monetary circulation from the lowest coin to the highest, it was no longer necessary to rely on foreign coins to fill the void in the currency, and in 1857 the government finally removed the legal-tender status of foreign coins. As a result, they soon disappeared from circulation.

Further Reforms in State Banking. While the Federal government was endeavoring to separate its fiscal affairs from the banks, state banking was

[1] For views in opposition to the Independent Treasury, see *The Writings and Speeches of Daniel Webster* (Vol. 9, pp. 244ff.). For the supporting view, see the contemporary writings of William Gouge.

continually improving along the lines established in the thirties. Free banking systems were adopted by state after state. Many more states limited circulation to a specific percentage of a bank's capital. Double liability for bank stockholders was imposed. More efficient systems of bank examination were adopted. Banks were prevented from paying out any notes but their own, and notes below a minimum denomination were prohibited.

Most of these extensions in the regulation of banking were adopted in the more mature states of the East and the older West. In the frontier states of the Middle West, however, limited capital, excessive note issue, inefficient management, and public satisfaction with bad banking led to numerous failures and contributed to antibank sentiment. By 1852 resentment against banks had grown so great that there were no incorporated banks in the seven states of Arkansas, California, Florida, Illinois, Iowa, Michigan, and Wisconsin; in the Oregon and Minnesota territories; and in the District of Columbia. In Indiana and Missouri, banking was a state monopoly.

TABLE 16.   SELECTED ITEMS OF STATE-BANK OPERATIONS, 1844–1860
(In millions of dollars)

Year	No. of banks	Capital	Loans	Deposits	Circulation	Specie
1844	696	$210.9	$264.9	$ 84.6	$ 75.2	$49.9
1846	707	196.9	312.1	96.9	105.6	42.0
1848	751	204.8	344.5	103.2	128.5	46.4
1850	824	217.3	364.2	109.6	131.4	45.4
1854	1,208	301.4	557.4	188.2	204.7	59.4
1856	1,398	343.9	634.2	212.7	195.7	59.3
1858	1,422	394.6	583.2	185.9	155.2	74.4
1860	1,562	421.9	691.9	253.8	207.1	83.6

SOURCE: Estimates of the Comptroller of the Currency, *Annual Report*, 1876, pp. 204–205.

In the late fifties the situation in the West began to change for the better, but although improvement in banking undoubtedly took place, state banking was still far from perfect. There were too many kinds of paper money in circulation, and depreciated and fraudulent currency was common. Merchants of any consequence referred constantly to the "bank-note reporter," for dishonesty in issuing bank notes was both varied and ingenious. Notes were freely counterfeited, and denominations were altered. Signatures were forged, and the notes of insolvent banks or of banks long out of existence continued to circulate. In 1859, one of the well-known bank services contained descriptions of 5,400 different types of spurious notes. Fifty years of banking experiment under diverse state laws had thus produced a money system chaotic beyond description.

Development of Clearinghouses. Continuous expansion of banking in the larger cities made old methods obsolete. This was especially true of clearing arrangements. Before 1853 banks in all cities settled their accounts with one another in full in specie or specie certificates. In New York City Friday was settlement day, and every bank dispatched runners to every other bank to settle accounts. Ordinary banking operations practically closed down, loans were called, credit tightened, and large amounts of specie left bank vaults for a tour of the financial district. The arrangement was wasteful and inefficient, for it required more time and more specie than if settlements had been made on balance. It could no longer be tolerated when, in the middle fifties, the use of checks and demand deposits became more important than bank notes.

Finally, in 1853 New York established a clearinghouse for daily settlement of interbank balances. In 1855 Boston established a similar clearinghouse, and in the subsequent year the idea was adopted in other large cities. From its inception, the clearinghouse system was a great success. It economized the use of specie, saved time, and made for smoother operation of the money market.

The Walker Tariff of 1846. Soon after its inauguration, the Polk administration showed a definite sentiment for free trade. Secretary of the Treasury Walker, who favored tariffs primarily for revenue, sought maximum yields to facilitate rapid debt retirement. He wrote a concise tariff bill which, for the first time in national history, attempted to give a fairly consistent expression to free-trade ideas—an attempt not repeated until 1913. Dutiable articles were classified into a number of schedules, each subject to a different rate. Luxuries, such as brandy, were placed in schedule A carrying a 100 per cent duty, while semiluxuries—spices, cigars, and the like—were placed in schedule B carrying a 40 per cent duty. Duties of 10 to 30 per cent were levied on other manufactured goods, a 5 per cent duty was imposed on raw materials and unfinished products, and some commodities were placed on a free list.

Goods were to be valued at the market price at the place of export, plus packing and other costs to the exporter up to the time and point of shipment. The Walker tariff also established a warehouse system under which importers could deposit goods in a government warehouse for one year without paying any duty.

Congress agreed with most of Walker's proposals, but because of the large surplus revenue, it placed coffee and tea on the free list. The vote on the bill was along sectional and party lines, demonstrating the close relationship that was beginning to exist between economic interest and political alignment.[2]

[2] Only 18 Democrats voted against the bill, and only 2 Whigs in favor of it.

The Walker tariff was not a free-trade measure, for its average rate—25 to 30 per cent—was not low and it retained many protective duties on manufactured goods. However, it was a step in the direction of freer trade and more scientific tariff legislation.

Financing the Mexican War. With the support of the agrarians and against opposition from industrial centers, the Polk administration went to war with Mexico over the annexation of Texas and the acquisition of California.

Since the enemy was inferior in power and victory was assured, the Mexican War did not pose any great financial problem. It lasted from May, 1846, to February, 1848, and its costs were small. Approximately $63.5 million was spent for military operations, and later, the United States paid Mexico $15 million as purchase money for an area greater than France and Germany combined. It also assumed $3.5 million of claims for damages held by American citizens against Mexico.

The war was over so quickly that there was neither time nor need to impose new taxes. Furthermore, the private economy was not in the least restricted, and trade actually increased. Therefore, revenues from existing taxes continued at a high level, covering not only ordinary expenditures but also part of the military outlays.

The remaining expenses of the war were covered by loans. Including reissues, $33.8 million of 1-year Treasury notes, with interest of $\frac{1}{10}$ of 1 per cent to 6 per cent, was issued in July, 1846, and January, 1847. In addition, $49.2 million of 6 per cent 10- and 20-year bonds was issued in July, 1846; January, 1847; and March, 1848. Some of the proceeds from these issues were used to refund the short-term notes. All the bonds were noncallable and were to present a serious problem in the postwar period when the Treasury began to operate with a sizable surplus.

To provide funds for the postwar acquisition of territory, to make land grants to the veterans of the war, and to reimburse Texas for disputed lands which were ceded to the Federal government, an additional $5.5 million of 5 and 6 per cent obligations was issued.[3]

The Treasury acted as its own broker in floating its loans, and for the first time in history it sold its obligations for specie. More important, it sold them above par, even though the distribution was not any wider than in 1812. In the 1848 loan of $16 million, for example, Corcoran and Riggs, Washington bankers, paid a 3.02 per cent premium in specie for $14 million of the bonds, disposing of more than $5 million in Great Britain.

The Secretary of the Treasury regarded the Independent Treasury system as the key to the success of the war financing, but prosperous

---

[3] William F. DeKnight, *History of the Currency and of the Loans of the United States;* Rafael Bayley, *The National Loans of the United States.*

economic conditions as well as the popularity of this almost costless war were undoubtedly more important.

Receipts, Expenditures, and Debt. The increased expenditures of the Federal government during the Mexican War contributed to the enormous agricultural and business boom which took place in the fifties. But they were a less significant factor than the sharp increase in immigration,[4] and the vast spending by private enterprise in extending railroad mileage from 9,000 to 25,000 between 1850 and 1857, and the heavy capital outlays made by state and local governments. A large part of the capital for these expanded activities came from European investments, making possible a great increase in merchandise imports. By 1853 it was estimated that Europeans owned approximately $225 million of American securities compared with $170 million in the previous boom. Gold discoveries in California in 1848 also helped to increase imports and were a most important factor in creating the bank credit which helped finance business activity. Half of the $128.4 million produced between 1848 and 1853 was exported, and half was used to swell bank reserves. Merchandise imports, therefore, increased from $173 million to $348 million between 1850 and 1857, while exports increased from $135 million to $279 million. During the same period, bank loans increased from $364 million to $685 million. Under the stimulus of heavy investment spending, the estimated national income increased from $2 billion to $4 billion during the decade, or from $107 to $140 per capita.

Receipts from customs doubled in this period under the impact of expanding foreign trade. Land revenues were also unusually high, partly due to the Graduation Act of 1854, providing for the sale of previously unsold land at sharply reduced prices.

Expenditures showed the usual increases accompanying prosperity and the growth of population, but there were also some unusual increases: interest payments on the war debt, payments in 1849 to 1852 of $18.5 million on Mexican claims, and an additional payment to Mexico in 1853 and 1854 of $10 million for lands in southern Arizona and New Mexico. These increases, though large, were not so great as the growth of revenue, and between the end of the war and 1857, there were large annual surpluses, the highest being $19.6 million in 1854.

The Problem of the Surplus. Secretary Guthrie was well aware that, under the Independent Treasury system, the Federal surplus was so much dead weight on the economy. Therefore, he exerted all his efforts to pour the surplus back into circulation. In March, 1849, he persuaded Congress

---

[4] Whereas in the twenties only 140,000 immigrants entered the United States and in the thirties, 600,000, the number increased to 1.7 million in the forties, especially after 1845, and to 2.6 million in the fifties.

TABLE 17. FEDERAL RECEIPTS, EXPENDITURES, AND DEBT, 1845–1860

(In millions of dollesr)

	1845	1846	1847	1848	1849	1850	1851	1852	1853	1854	1855	1856	1857	1858	1859	1860
Receipts:																
Customs	$ 27.5	$ 26.7	$ 23.7	$ 31.8	$ 28.3	$ 39.7	$ 49.0	$ 47.3	$ 58.9	$ 64.2	$ 53.0	$ 64.0	$ 63.9	$ 41.8	$ 49.6	$ 53.2
Public lands	2.1	2.7	2.5	3.3	1.7	1.9	2.4	2.0	1.7	8.5	11.5	8.9	3.8	3.5	1.8	1.8
Miscellaneous	0.3	0.3	0.3	0.6	0.3	0.7	1.2	0.4	1.2	1.1	0.8	1.1	1.3	1.4	2.2	1.1
Totals	$ 29.9	$ 29.7	$ 26.5	$ 35.7	$ 30.4	$ 42.2	$ 52.6	$ 49.8	$ 61.8	$ 73.8	$ 65.4	$ 74.1	$ 69.0	$ 46.7	$ 53.5	$ 56.1
Expenditures:																
Civil	$ 2.4	$ 2.5	$ 2.6	$ 2.6	$ 2.9	$ 3.0	$ 3.5	$ 3.4	$ 4.3	$ 4.6	$ 6.4	$ 6.5	$ 7.6	$ 7.1	$ 5.9	$ 6.1
Foreign	0.7	0.4	0.4	0.4	6.9	6.0	6.3	4.2	1.0	*7.8	1.0	3.6	1.0	1.4	1.0	1.1
Navy	6.3	6.5	7.9	9.4	9.8	7.9	8.9	8.9	11.1	10.8	13.3	14.1	12.7	14.1	14.7	11.5
War	5.8	10.4	35.8	27.8	16.6	9.7	12.2	8.5	9.9	11.7	14.6	17.0	19.2	25.7	23.2	16.5
Pensions	2.4	1.8	1.7	1.2	0.2	1.9	2.3	2.4	3.9	1.4	1.5	1.3	1.4	1.2	0.2	1.1
Indians	1.5	1.1	1.5	1.1	0.5	1.7	2.8	3.0	3.9	1.4	2.7	2.6	4.2	5.0	4.6	3.0
Interest	1.1	0.8	1.1	2.4	3.6	3.9	3.7	4.0	3.7	3.1	2.3	2.0	1.6	1.7	2.6	3.1
Miscellaneous	2.8	3.8	3.9	2.6	3.1	7.0	8.1	9.9	12.2	13.5	16.7	15.3	18.9	17.8	16.9	20.7
Totals	$ 23.0	$ 27.3	$ 54.9	$ 47.6	$ 43.5	$ 41.1	$ 47.8	$ 44.4	$ 47.7	$ 54.2	$ 58.6	$ 62.5	$ 56.6	$ 73.9	$ 69.0	$ 63.2
Surplus (+) or deficit (−)	$ +7.0	$ +2.4	$ −28.4	$ −11.9	$ −13.1	$ +1.2	$ +4.8	$ +5.5	$ +14.0	$ +19.6	$ +6.7	$ +11.8	$ +2.3	$ −27.3	$ −15.5	$ −7.1
Gross debt at end of fiscal year	17.1	16.8	39.0	48.5	63.1	63.5	68.3	66.2	59.8	42.2	35.6	32.0	28.7	44.9	58.5	64.8

SOURCE: *Annual Report of the Secretary of the Treasury*, 1886. Gross debt beginning 1849, *Annual Report*, 1876, p. 8.

* Includes $7 million for Mexican idemnity.

to give him the power to buy bonds in the open market above par, and during the fifties he bought bonds at premiums as high as 21 per cent, paying total premiums of $40.3 million. In addition, he bought silver for the reestablishment of the subsidiary coinage. However, the effectiveness of these measures was limited. The subsidiary coinage could not be increased without limit, and bond purchases in the open market were an expensive business, for, when the Treasury began to buy, it caused the price of the bonds to rise, making the Secretary reluctant to pursue the policy.

Meanwhile, the surplus aroused agitation for increased expenditures and reduction of the tariff. As early as 1845 Congress provided subsidies to steamship companies for carrying the mails. In 1847 these subsidies were liberalized, and in 1848 the famous Collins line obtained a ten-year subsidy of about $3 a mile, which was increased to $5 a mile in 1852.

There were also demands for Federal expenditures for social welfare. Such expenditures had been made at least twice before: in 1812, $50,000 had been contributed to victims of an earthquake in Venezuela, and in 1827, $20,000 was given to the victims of a fire in Alexandria, Virginia. But these were small and constituted no departure from the agrarian doctrine of limited Federal activity. Consequently, when Congress, in 1854, made a land grant to the states to help pay for the care of the insane, President Pierce vetoed it. A few years later, his successor Buchanan vetoed a bill to give Federal land to the states for the support of education. According to Buchanan, "When the state governments look to the Federal Treasury for the means of supporting themselves and maintaining their systems of education . . . the character of both governments will be greatly deteriorated."[5]

Despite administration objections, Federal expenditures did expand, and just as in the Jackson years, the increased spending occurred primarily in internal improvements. Whereas in four years of the Polk administration, $7.1 million was spent on public works (public buildings, rivers and harbors, forts, lighthouses, and roads and canals), in the extreme agrarian administrations of Pierce and Buchanan, these expenditures reached $18.7 million and $25.0 million, respectively.[6]

The administration did not look with favor on the increased expenditures. It preferred to reduce the surplus through reductions in tariffs. On the other hand, manufacturers clamored for a larger gap between the duties on raw materials and those on finished products, either by reducing the former or by raising the latter.

[5] James D. Richardson, *Messages and Papers of the Presidents*, Vol. 5, p. 545.

[6] For the opposing views on capital expenditures in this period, see Mentor L. Williams, "The Chicago River and Harbor Convention, 1847," *The Mississippi Historical Review*, Vol. XXXV, No. 4, March, 1949.

Early in 1857 industrialists helped to pass a bill which reduced tariff rates and seemed to be a victory for the administration and the South. However, the reductions were much more substantial on raw materials than on finished goods and thereby represented a victory for the manufacturers at the expense of Western producers of raw materials.

Panic of 1857. In the spring of 1857 the boom reached its peak. The large Treasury surplus continued to drain off the marginal specie reserve, the Treasury cash balance reaching the very high level of $15.7 million. Capital imports from Europe were declining and the flow of gold from California decreased. Consequently, money became tight. On August 24, the Ohio Life Insurance and Trust Company failed, New York banks began to contract their loans, and the panic began.[7]

The panic had an immediate effect on government fiscal affairs. Receipts fell off, and since it was not possible to reduce expenditures as rapidly, deficits resulted. To meet them the government issued $52.8 million of Treasury notes and floated a $20 million, 15-year loan at 5 per cent.

In accordance with its extreme agrarian views and its philosophy of a limited Federal government, the administration did not believe that it could do anything to help the businessman or the unemployed worker. President Buchanan thought that bank currency was chiefly responsible for the panic, but he did not believe that the national government could regulate state banks. He recommended that the states prohibit the issue of paper money in denominations below $20 and that they require a 33⅓ per cent specie reserve. But as far as the Federal government was concerned, both Buchanan and Secretary Cobb thought it could do nothing except pursue a policy of economy in an effort to make revenues and expenditures equal. "No statesman," said Buchanan, "would advise that we should go on increasing the national debt."[8] Under the prodding of the administration, expenditures were reduced beginning in 1858. Among other economies, the subsidy to steamship companies was dropped.

Left to their own devices, the banks muddled through. In the absence of cash, they issued clearinghouse certificates—scrip issued against frozen assets—to settle interbank balances. Almost without exception they suspended specie payments. But this was one of the few periods of major economic crisis in which the Federal government did not suspend specie payments. The Secretary attributed this to the Independent Treasury system. By 1860 economic conditions were slowly improving when the threat of war made all such matters of secondary importance.

[7] It was apparent that the initial liquidation came from the banks. Loans were liquidated faster than deposits, while specie reserves in the banks actually increased. (J. S. Gibbons, *The Banks of New York and the Panic of 1857*.)

[8] James D. Richardson, *Messages and Papers of the Presidents*, Vol. 5, p. 521.

Chapter 12: STATE AND LOCAL FINANCE, 1800 TO 1860

During the first three decades of the nineteenth century, state and municipal activities were getting slowly under way. But beginning with the thirties state and local governments began to bear the brunt of the demand of the rapidly increasing urban and rural populations for new social services and public improvements. Their increased expenditures, particularly in the forties and fifties, more than made up for the Federal passivity of the period, described in the previous chapter.

Expansion of State Functions and Expenditures. The states became active service agencies, reasserting their original primary position in the scheme of government. They took over from the Federal government the responsibility for internal improvements and from the local communities a considerable share of responsibility in the field of correction and charities. They also opened up new areas for government responsibility. They built penitentiaries, reformatories, and institutions for the aged, the mentally unfit, and the disabled. They inaugurated aid to common schools, usually by segregating the proceeds from the sale of public lands in special funds. Later, they supplemented these funds from their shares of Federal surplus and provided additional aid from general revenue or from special taxes.[1] They furnished aid to private colleges, and several states in the South and the new West established state-supported universities, while others, with New York leading, established free normal schools for the training of teachers.

State subsidies were furnished to county and state agricultural societies for the dissemination of information and the improvement of agriculture. Regulation of business vested with special public interest—banks, insurance companies, and railroads—was also inaugurated.[2]

[1] New York established a Common School Fund in 1805. In 1851 it imposed a special property tax for school purposes, raising the annual apportionment to $800,000. However, free common schools did not become generally established in New York until the 1840's, although Pennsylvania had established them in 1834, and public high schools began only a decade or so later.

[2] New York State established regulation of banks by a board of bank commissioners in 1829 and a state banking department in 1851, supervision of insurance companies in 1850 and an insurance department in 1859, supervision of railroads in 1850, and a general incorporation law for manufacturing enterprise as early as 1811. It established a board of agriculture to administer grants to county agricultural societies in 1819 and a subsidy to the state agricultural society in 1841.

As correctional, charitable, and educational expenditures assumed a dominant position in state budgets, those for general government and protection dropped to a secondary place. Although the statistical evidence is not too reliable, state operating expenditures (exclusive of those made from special funds) averaged 50 cents per capita for the period as a whole, compared with $1.50 for Federal expenditures (excluding wartime) and about $3 for the larger cities. State expenditures were deeply affected by fluctuations in business activity, increasing sharply during business booms and declining during depressions.[3]

The most important developments in state finance during these years were the expansion of state expenditures for internal improvements and the consequent vast increase in state indebtedness. The westward movement and the expansion of business after the War of 1812 resulted in a popular demand for improved means of transportation. Only the states could raise the large amounts of capital necessary to defray the costs of such projects, for there was not enough assurance of profits to attract sufficient private capital and the Federal administration, with its laissez-faire philosophy, refused to enter the field on a large scale.

The vast investments by the states in internal improvements began when New York State launched the construction of the Erie Canal in 1817. The project was completed in 1825 at a total cost of $11 million, of which $3.1 million came from the proceeds of auction duties and other current sources and $7.9 million from long-term loans. The canal proved an instant financial success, paying for itself within ten years. The success of the Erie Canal fired popular imagination in other states. In 1825 to 1833 Ohio, at a cost of more than $3 million, built the Ohio Canal, which complemented the Erie Canal in opening up the West. Maryland in 1826 ventured upon an extensive internal-improvement program, making grants or loans of $15 million during the next ten years toward the construction of the Baltimore and Ohio Railroad, the Baltimore and Susquehanna Railroad, the Chesapeake and Ohio Canal, and other smaller projects. Pennsylvania, finding herself outstripped commercially by New York, built almost a thousand miles of canals during the 1830's, thereby increasing her debt by

---

[3] In Massachusetts, expenditures other than those for internal improvements increased during the boom of 1825 to 1837 from $199,000 (35 cents per capita) to $510,000 and dropped after the panic under the pressure of rigid economy to $370,000 by 1843. Then with business improvement they rose to $1,360,000, or $1.27 per capita, by 1857. Per capita operating expenses in New York fluctuated with changes in business activity and other factors between 20 and 47 cents. Because of the practice of making disbursements from a number of different funds, the published collations of expenditures are not very reliable. The figures for New York include capital outlays other than for canals and other enterprises, but they do not include payments out of the Common School Fund or all correctional expenditures. The Massachusetts figures exclude all capital expenditures financed from loans.

$16.6 million. New York, in the late 1820's, started on a second round of internal improvements. In 1835 it began to enlarge the Erie Canal, a $30 million project which was not completed until 1862. The state also subscribed $3 million in 1836 to the company organized to build the Erie Railroad.

Regularizing State Taxation. Increased state expenditures made necessary regular and continuous, rather than intermittent, taxation. Investment and windfall revenues, such as dividends on bank stocks, sales of lands, and lotteries, were no longer sufficient to maintain activities from year to year, and new types of levies had to be introduced. A lucrative source appeared after the War of 1812 when bank taxes were imposed, usually on capital stock. But the most important addition was the state general property tax. It had been levied intermittently before, but after 1842 it was imposed regularly and rapidly became the chief source of revenue.[4]

State government activity and finance were thus expanding, while Federal were contracting. So impressed was De Tocqueville by this development that, disregarding entirely the effects of the greater fiscal resources of the central government, he wrote in 1830 that "the Federal government is visibly losing strength." Predicting that within a century the nation would have a population of 100 million scattered over 40 states, he wrote that "the continuance of the Federal government can only be a fortunate accident."[5]

However, De Tocqueville was wrong, for while governmental activity and expenditures, owing to the social and economic conditions of the time as well as public preference, continued to be decentralized, the Federal government had great advantages in raising revenue which were bound in time to influence the distribution of power. It had a huge overflowing revenue from customs duties and land sales, while the states were continually struggling against the insufficiency of their revenue resources. Time and again during this period efforts were made to correct this discrepancy by distributing to the states a substantial portion of the Federal lands or setting aside and apportioning among them the proceeds from the sale of these lands as a capital fund for the support of specific state functions. But each time that these measures were passed by Congress, they were vetoed by the Presidents on the ground that they would under-

---

[4] In 1820 New York State revenue totaled $1.2 million. The property tax accounted for 25 per cent; land sales, lotteries, and the saltworks, for 12 per cent; business taxes, for 14 per cent; and investments, for 48 per cent. In 1860, the property tax accounted for over 80 per cent of revenues, aggregating $3.0 million; business taxes, for 7 per cent; and land sales, saltworks, and income from state institutions, for 13 per cent. In Maryland in 1830 the property tax provided only $1,279 of $210,372 of total revenue, but in 1848 it provided $435,647 of a total revenue of $989,000.

[5] Quoted from Maxwell, *The Fiscal Impact of Federalism*, p. 20.

mine the political and administrative independence of the states and destroy the constitutional system.

Reckless State Borrowing. Because of insufficient revenue, the states financed many of their expenditures, especially internal-improvement investments, by the use of state credit. Easy-money conditions (induced by huge imports of capital, the rapid repayment of the Federal debt, and the inflationary rise in bank credit) encouraged the use of state credit. By the late 1830's, when the Federal government was debt-free, state debts, which had practically been liquidated in 1800, rose to $175 million ($10 per capita). Where capital ventures were private, the states substituted for the weak credit of the companies their own stronger credit, by issuing bonds to the public, turning over the proceeds to the companies, and taking the latter's bonds or stocks as security. The states seldom levied additional taxes to meet interest and principal payments on their debts, preferring to depend on the future earnings of the enterprises. This was a foolhardy procedure, as the enterprises did not pay their way until many years later, if at all.

As the money market tightened in the late thirties, the states found themselves unable to obtain the funds necessary to complete the projects in which they were engaged. At the same time the canal and railroad companies, in which the states had invested their funds, became unable to meet their obligations and were compelled to suspend. The states were caught with huge debts, some of which were about to mature and all of which called for large interest payments. Defaults of interest and repudiation of principal became widespread. Some states, such as Pennsylvania, sold their investments and properties for a fraction of their original costs. Some, such as New York, pulled out of the difficulty by imposing a substantial emergency property tax.

Foreign bondholders had no recourse against state default or repudiation, for under the Constitution the states were sovereign and could not be sued or even interfered with by the Federal government. A Congressional committee was appointed to investigate the claims of foreign bondholders, and it recommended Federal assumption. But nothing came of this recommendation.[6]

---

[6] Sidney Smith, in a letter printed in the *Morning Chronicle*, expressed the feelings of the British creditors in biting words. He confessed that he had never met a citizen of Pennsylvania at a London dinner "without feeling a disposition to seize and divide him—to allot his beaver to one sufferer and his coat to another—to appropriate his pocket-handkerchief to the orphan, and to comfort the widow with his silver watch, Broadway rings, and the *London Guide* which he always carries in his pockets. How such a man can set himself down at an English table without feeling that he owes two or three pounds to every man in company, I am at a loss to conceive. He has no more right to eat with honest men than a leper has to eat with clean men." (Hesketh Pearson, *The Smith of Smiths*, pp. 295–296.)

Public demand for state financial participation in the improvement of internal communications again became active with the recovery of business after 1844. States which had not participated heavily in the borrowing spree of the 1830's borrowed heavily in the fifties. These were the states of Virginia, Missouri, Tennessee, the two Carolinas, and Georgia. Most of the loans floated by them were for railroad construction, as the public interest definitely switched from canal to railroad transportation. In a few cases the loans were used to supply a capital subsidy to construction companies at so much per constructed mile. In one or two cases, North Carolina for example, loans were employed for the construction of wholly state-owned railroad lines.

By and large the state borrowings of this period were characterized by less boldness. Altogether, state debts increased from $190 million in 1841 to $257 million in 1860—an amount more than four times the size of the Federal debt. The actual borrowings were greater than indicated by these totals, however, inasmuch as some of the borrowers of the previous period, such as Alabama, Illinois, and Louisiana, had reduced their debts substantially by liquidating their banking or canal ventures and using the proceeds to settle with the bondholders.

In the meanwhile, in a number of states conservative opinion organized against a repetition of the same financial disasters. The remedy appeared simple: either the state should henceforth be prohibited by constitutional provision from borrowing money for internal improvements, or else it should be permitted by the constitution to borrow only after a favorable referendum. When several states revised their constitutions in the forties and the fifties, restrictions of this sort were incorporated. Henceforth, in those states the task of raising capital for the construction of improved communications was left entirely to private enterprise and to local governments, and one of the most dynamic economic functions was taken away from the states for many years to come.[7]

Changes in State Financial Administration. During the sixty-year period profound changes took place in most states in the organization of their government and financial administration. The extension of the suffrage in the 1820's and 1830's under the influence of Jacksonian Democracy brought in its wake demands for the popular election of administrative officials instead of the existing system of appointment by the state legislature. The people discovered that the legislature was not necessarily a

[7] In New York, civic leadership in the Constitutional Convention of 1846 insisted on the incorporation in the constitution of what was called at the time the "People's Resolution," prohibiting the lending of state credit to any individual or corporation under any circumstances, permitting unlimited state borrowing only for the suppression of an insurrection, and allowing borrowing for public improvements only by a public referendum. Ohio in its 1851 revision of the constitution provided succinctly that "the state should never contract any debt for purposes of internal improvement."

better guardian of public interest than the chief executive, and conservatives were particularly concerned over the frequent abuse by the legislatures of their vast spending, taxing, and borrowing powers.

Accordingly, the revised constitutions incorporated many features designed to strengthen popular control and to eliminate specific abuses. They provided for popular election of various fiscal and administrative officers—the comptroller, treasurer, superintendent of instruction, superintendent of public works, etc.—for fixed terms, gave the governor a suspensive veto over the acts of the legislature, prohibited the disbursement of any funds from the treasury except pursuant to appropriations, required that the appropriations be specific rather than in lump sums and limited their duration, required regular accounting of all expenditures, imposed curbs on the borrowing powers of the legislature as already noted, required that property taxes be imposed in accordance with uniform rules, and, in some states, required that every law imposing a new tax specify the purpose for which the tax was to be used.

Not all these changes in the state constitutions were soundly conceived. The gains in popular control through popular election of administrative officials were illusory. Although the administrative officials were freed of control by the legislators, they were not made more responsible to the electorate, which had no way of checking on their performance. They were made responsible to no one except possibly the party boss, whose invisible control over state government was greatly strengthened. State administrations became more decentralized, and orderly budgeting more difficult. The earmarking of taxes for specific purposes led to the establishment of a multiplicity of special funds, making orderly and flexible financing as well as intelligible accounting impossible, while the imposition of extreme curbs on the use of state credit, as already mentioned, reduced to impotence state finance in one of its most import applications—internal improvements.

Expansion of Municipal Functions and Improvements. During the period 1800 to 1860 municipal activity expanded tremendously and assumed some of its modern characteristics. Not only were the cities growing in population as a result of increasing immigration and industrial development,[8] but their governments were becoming more democratic and, hence, more subject to public pressure for additional services. In a great many cities popular election of top executive officials was substituted for the older system of appointment by the city councils, and the councils themselves became more representative of the working classes. Political machines

[8] New York City's population grew from about 200,000 in 1830 to 500,000 in 1850 and 800,000 in 1860. In 1800 there were only six cities with more than 10,000 population. Together they comprised only 3½ per cent of the country's total population. By 1860 there were 93 such cities, and their combined population was 11½ per cent of the national total.

were formed everywhere, and they sought votes by catering to public demands.

To protect their increasing populations against the dangers of disease, crime, and fire, as well as to provide them with other desired conveniences, the city governments constructed water works and sewer systems; paved miles of streets and sidewalks; provided for street lighting; organized full-time police, fire, and health departments; established city hospitals; and introduced systems of free public education. Some cities became organized as independent school districts with separate taxing powers and governing boards. Others organized schools under their general municipal governments.

One of the largest municipal undertakings of the time was the construction of the Croton reservoir and aqueduct by New York City in the late 1830's and early 1840's. Before it was approved in a local referendum, the project was hotly debated. At the time the city budget was below $1 million and the funded debt was only $0.5 million, or less than ½ of 1 per cent of the assessed valuation. The construction of the water works would increase the debt to $9 million, and many citizens thought that such a debt would result in financial disaster. Actually, the water works proved self-supporting soon after their installation. The success of this venture in municipal ownership encouraged other cities to engage in similar ventures. For example, Boston in 1846 undertook the construction of municipal works at a cost of $5 million, a large investment for a city whose annual budget was in the neighborhood of a million dollars.

In the 1830's, cities also began to vie with one another for railroad connections. With the permission of their states they offered loans and subsidies to companies undertaking to build lines through them or to them. Thus, Baltimore lent more than $4 million to the Baltimore and Ohio Railroad, the Baltimore and Susquehanna Railroad, and the Susquehanna Canal, increasing its debt thereby from less than $1 million to $5 million in the course of a few years.

Among operating expenses, those for police and fire protection, streets, education, and debt service grew fastest. In New York City, police expenditures increased from $23,000 in 1800 to $99,000 in 1830 and $1.4 million in 1860; expenditures for education increased from $2,000 (3 cents per capita) in 1800 to $1.3 million ($1.62 per capita) by 1860; debt service increased from nothing in 1800 to $909,000 ($1.14 per capita) in 1860. Total municipal per capita expenditures rose from $2 to $12 over the period.

Growth of City Taxes and Debts. The increased municipal operating expenditures were met by increased city taxation. The rate of the property tax was raised from less than ½ of 1 per cent of assessed value in 1800 to more than 1 per cent in 1860, while the per capita assessed value more than doubled.[9]

. Despite the increase in taxes, most of the extensive capital outlays had to be financed by loans. Municipal indebtedness, which had scarcely existed in 1800, increased to $27 million in 1843 and to $200 million by 1860—almost as much as the combined state debt and three times as much as the Federal debt.[10] To borrow money, the cities required additional powers from their state legislatures, but they generally obtained these powers without undue difficulty. The propensity to borrow was strongest during business booms, and then taxpayers and legislators were inclined to be lenient. But during business depressions indebtedness became a headache to the cities, and during the depression of the 1850's many of them defaulted. Taxpayers, who had previously found little fault with the use of municipal credit for financing local improvements, began to press for constitutional and statutory restrictions on municipal borrowing. But the restrictions which they were able to impose never attained the severity of those on state borrowing.

Reforms in Municipal Financial Administration. The charters granted to cities during this period gave clearer expression to the principle of separation of powers, broadened the powers of the mayor (although still retaining the supreme authority in the municipal council), provided for an elective comptroller with greatly strengthened powers of audit and control over administrative expenditures, and established some elements of a budgetary system.

New York City's charter of 1830 was one of the most advanced of the time. It established a bicameral council, made the mayor and comptroller popularly elected officials, and gave the mayor the veto power. It required the council to organize the executive branch into departments and to appoint their heads, provide appropriations for the departments, and supervise their accounts. Departments were required to submit their requests for appropriations annually in detail, and the comptroller was charged with the duty of transmitting these requests in consolidated form together with his estimates of revenue to the council so that the latter could pass appropriation and tax levy ordinances. The declaration of the convention expressed the conviction that this system "will bring the whole disbursement of the city annually before the corporation and their constituents,

[9] New York City's tax rate per $100 of assessed value increased from ½ of 1 per cent to 1.69 per cent, while the per capita assessed valuation rose from $345 to $721. In Baltimore the rate was ¾ of 1 per cent in 1800 and 1 per cent in 1860.

[10] New York City's per capita debt increased from nothing in 1800 to $23 in 1860; that of Boston, from nothing to $43; Baltimore's, from $6 to $71; and Providence's, from $3 to $10.

and by showing the several heads of expense distinctly, will indicate the proper place and mode of reform and retrenchment."[11]

The reforms in municipal administration introduced by the charters of the time did not go far enough. Members of the council continued to meddle in administration with the result that no responsibility could ever be placed upon any officials for any particular acts and much of the government was invisible. Since the cities, particularly after 1830, engaged in large expenditures, involving substantial contracts, and since they issued a multitude of licenses, permits, and franchises, invisible government opened the doors to graft and corruption. For the first time in the history of local government abuses became widespread. In New York City the council earned for itself the nickname "The Forty Thieves," and in other cities the municipal councils deteriorated to the point where no honorable citizen wished to serve on them.

In state after state civic leaders induced their legislatures to take control over municipal affairs away from the municipal councils and other locally elected or appointed officials and to vest it in state-appointed boards endowed with full tax-levying and spending powers. But this was a false remedy, for state interference and control did not stamp out graft and corruption. It merely introduced a new type of corrupt politics into local affairs. The state commissioners were responsible to nobody and did as they pleased. The city budget was split between half a dozen or more independent tax-levying and spending authorities—some locally elected, some state appointed—and became completely disorganized.

Suburban areas developed some of the same needs for additional services and the same difficulties in financing them as did the cities. Some suburbs were annexed to the cities and obtained services through a consolidated local government. Others preferred to continue to operate under their own local governments and provided services and financing as best they could. In rural areas local government and finance developed more slowly. Counties and towns built roads and maintained judicial and protective services, financing them from the property tax without increasing the debt substantially. The most important governmental and fiscal development in the suburban and rural areas was the rapid and, by 1860, almost universal organization of school districts. Through these completely self-governing tax-levying authorities, the suburban and rural areas established free elementary schools.

[11] E. D. Durand, The Finances of New York City, p. 44.

Part II
FROM THE CIVIL WAR TO WORLD WAR I

Chapter 13: CIVIL WAR FINANCING: THE FIRST MISTAKES

In order to finance the Civil War, it was necessary for the Federal government to reorganize its entire fiscal and monetary structure. Naturally, many mistakes were made. The government had never been called upon, not even in any of its previous wars, for an all-out effort of the type required by this war. Without the benefit of past experience to guide them, few among those in authority recognized the magnitude of the task involved. Fortunate as this was from a psychological point of view, it was equally unfortunate from the viewpoint of efficient financial management.

Everyone agreed that the war could not last more than a few months. As far as economic resources were concerned, the North's confidence in a short conflict seemed well founded. It had two-thirds of the population, the national wealth, and the national income. It was economically diversified, while the South had few heavy industries and was almost completely dependent on cotton. But the South was equally confident, placing its faith in the superior morale of its population and the economic power of "King Cotton."

Even if there had been a realistic appraisal of the future, no tools were available which could be used efficiently in financing the war. The American economy was overwhelmingly agricultural. The national income was low (estimated at $4.3 billion, or $140 per capita), and savings were not available in large enough quantities to make it easy for the government to obtain large funds. Moreover, the revenue system, being based on customs, sales of public land, and miscellaneous sources, lacked the elasticity required for overnight expansion. Excise taxes had not been levied for a generation, and the income tax was unknown. The methods of borrowing were not much more efficient. The minutest details of each loan—the amount, interest rates, and terms of sale—required Congressional authorization, thus tying the hands of the Secretary and making it impossible for him to adjust the forms and terms of borrowing to the continually changing conditions of the money market.

Neither side possessed a strong banking or currency system. The Federal government had no central bank which could act as its fiscal agent, and not having had any contact with banks for nearly twenty years, it did not know how to deal with them in placing loans. The banking business was conducted by 1,600 state banks, each going its own merry way; 7,000 different kinds of bank notes circulated, with more than half being spurious. Total currency was about $450 million—$250 million in specie and $200 million in private paper issues of dubious character—with about 25 per cent of the paper money circulating in the South. Since the government, under the Independent Treasury, used only hard money, the dual-currency system was completely unsuited to the conditions of a war economy and had to be replaced in part by a new system.

Until these difficulties were ironed out, the Treasury and Congress had to resort in hit-or-miss fashion to every conceivable method of raising money. The Federal government issued long-term bonds of varying maturities, short-term Treasury notes, non-interest-bearing demand notes, evidences of temporary deposit, and certificates of indebtedness. It printed and circulated paper money. Belatedly, but on an increasingly comprehensive scale, it resorted to a wide variety of taxes. Tariffs were increased, a direct tax was levied on the states, an income tax was adopted, and a variety of manufacturers' sales, license, and excise taxes were imposed. In addition, revenue was obtained from public land sales, from confiscation of Confederate property, and from buying and selling specie.

Federal Finances under Gathering Clouds of War. As the Civil War approached, the Treasury, which had been greatly weakened by three years of deficits, began to experience incredible difficulty in borrowing money. In June, 1860, Congress authorized a $21 million bond issue to fund the accumulated short-term debt. In September Secretary Cobb offered $10 million of bonds at 5 per cent, and they were taken at or above par. But before payment became due, the increasing talk of secession, especially after Lincoln's election, caused a loss of confidence. Many investors withdrew their subscriptions, thereby forfeiting their 1 per cent deposits. As a result, only $7 million was sold immediately. Congress thereupon authorized $10 million of notes. Meanwhile Cobb had resigned. His successor, Philip Thomas of Maryland, was able to sell $5 million of the new authorization at 12 per cent.[1] Yet, even at that exorbitant rate, the issue was barely sold partly because investors feared that Thomas favored secession. In January, 1861, John A. Dix, who became Secretary after Thomas resigned to drum up Confederate sympathy, sold the remaining $5 million, but only at similarly high rates. In February Congress authorized $25 million of 6 per cent bonds of which Dix sold $8 million at 90 or above.

The Appointment of Chase. South Carolina seceded in December, 1860, and the Confederate States of America came into being on February 4, 1861. Buchanan took no action, taking the position that, while the states

---

[1] At the same time New York State 7's were selling at a premium, evidencing the weakness of Federal credit.

had no constitutional power to secede, the Federal government had no power to prevent secession. Events therefore drifted along until Lincoln's inauguration in March.

Because of political expediency, Lincoln appointed Salmon P. Chase of Ohio as Secretary of the Treasury. Chase was a leader of the antislavery wing of the Republican party, but in his other views he was a Jacksonian Democrat. He was sympathetic toward hard money and was commonly considered a supporter of state, rather than national, banking. He had had no experience in finance, and except for some acquaintance with Western banking, he showed only a mediocre knowledge of monetary and financial history, theory, and practice. His personality was also peculiarly unsuited to the needs of his office. Prone to overestimate his prospects and without a sense of humor, he was also suspicious, dogmatic, and pompous. As a result, he did not understand that, in order to finance the war successfully, it was often necessary to compromise.

However, it must be said in Chase's defense that he accepted the Secretaryship reluctantly. Moreover, the war broke out so suddenly—only slightly more than a month after inauguration—that there was little time to prepare any plans.

The Morrill Tariff and Interim Financing. Two days before the new administration took office, the outgoing Congress enacted the Morrill Tariff Act, restoring duties to the rates in effect before 1857. Although it was originally framed to correct the insufficiency of revenue caused by the depression and was never intended as a war measure, many statesmen, including Chase, hoped that it would produce substantial Federal revenue. Actually, these hopes proved to be false. The outbreak of war brought about a sharp curtailment in foreign trade and resulted in much lower revenue collections than expected.

Almost immediately, Chase was confronted with extraordinary expenditures for military preparations. The national debt stood at $75 million, of which $18 million had been incurred since the secession movement started. Fortunately, there was available for use some $41 million of loan authorizations left over from the previous administration,[2] but of this sum, $14 million could not be borrowed at less than par.

In March, even before the war began, Chase offered to sell $8 million of bonds. Subscriptions for $28 million were received, showing an improvement in the government's credit, but some bids were as low as 85. Chase rejected all bids below 94 and placed $3.1 million of bonds at an average price of 97.69. In addition he sold $4.9 million of Treasury notes. By refusing to accept lower bids, Chase alienated the bankers. At the same time

[2] $14 million under the authority of June, 1860; $17 million under authority of February, 1861; and $10 million granted by Congress on Mar. 2, 1861.

he officially adopted the policy of depending on short-term issues, thereby creating a difficulty that was to plague the Treasury throughout the war. Not only was the Treasury forced to raise new funds to finance the war, but at the same time, it had to refund short-term obligations continually.

In May Chase sold $4.3 million of notes at par and $7.3 million of bonds at 85.34, exhausting the loans which could be sold below par. Still in desperate need of funds, Chase offered an issue at par, but since governments were selling in the market considerably below par, only $12,000 of bids were received, and even these were quickly withdrawn.

Meanwhile, revenues covered only a small part of the Treasury's requirements. In the first three months of the war, expenditures totaled $23.5 million and ordinary receipts only $5.8 million, but Chase managed to get along by borrowing from hand to mouth and by postponing the payment of bills.

Loan and Tax Acts of July and August, 1861. In July, 1861, Congress met in special session to find ways and means to finance the war. In his report to Congress Chase expressed his theory of war finance. He proposed to produce enough revenue through taxes to pay all peacetime expenses as well as interest on the public debt, thus following Gallatin's ideas of fifty years before. He did not realize that the higher national income and greater industrialization of the country called for a more vigorous policy. He placed too much reliance on borrowing and too little on taxation, entertaining the erroneous belief that the war would be over shortly and that an all-out tax effort was not necessary even if it could be organized in so little time.

Basing his calculations on President Lincoln's call for 140,000 volunteers for the Army and 18,000 for the Navy, Chase estimated the expenditures for the fiscal year beginning July 1, 1861, at exactly $318,519,581.87 (after allowing for certain recommended cuts in salaries and postal expenditures). He suggested that $80 million, one-fourth, be raised by taxes and $240 million by loans. He proposed that duties be imposed on tea and coffee, then admitted free, and that duties be increased on sugar and certain other articles. He estimated that this would yield an additional $27 million, raising the tariff revenue to $57 million. But he left it to Congress to determine how to raise the remaining $23 million, observing merely that this might be done either by levying a direct tax or by imposing excises. Chase's program was singularly weak, and his failure to recommend immediate and vigorous taxation soon reflected on the government's credit.

On July 16, 1861, Congress authorized a $250 million loan in any of the following forms: 7 per cent, 20-year bonds; 7.3 per cent, 3-year Treasury notes; 3.65 per cent, convertible, 1-year notes; and up to $50 million of non-interest-bearing Treasury notes redeemable on demand in specie. The last, the so-called "demand notes," were acceptable in payment of public dues and could be used to pay salaries of government employees.

On August 5, 1861, Congress passed an omnibus revenue bill, levying a $20 million direct tax on real property in both the Northern and Southern states, a 3 per cent income tax effective January, 1862, on all incomes over $800 earned in the calendar year 1861, and new or higher customs duties on sugar, coffee, tea, etc. The law also made the first modification in the Independent Treasury Act by allowing the Secretary of the Treasury to deposit government funds in such solvent, specie-paying banks as he might select.

Chase did not favor the income and direct taxes, and since Congress failed to provide means for enforcing them, he took no steps to put them into effect. Nor was he willing to modify his hard-money views and compromise with the original principles of the Independent Treasury. In spite of Congressional intent, he insisted that the subtreasuries continue to collect and pay specie only.

The $150 Million Bank Loan. Although they were not full legal tender and were accepted reluctantly, Chase used the non-interest-bearing demand notes to pay government salaries.[3] However, these were soon exhausted, and it became imperative to negotiate a substantial loan. In August, Chase persuaded the major banks to make an immediate loan to the government of $50 million by purchasing 3-year, 7.3 per cent notes with the privilege of taking an additional $50 million in October and the same amount in November, or altogether $150 million.

The banks had only $63 million in specie, obviously not enough for the contemplated loan. Furthermore, they were apprehensive lest the transfer of a large portion of specie to the Treasury shake public confidence in their ability to redeem their bank notes. However, they hoped to replenish their available funds continuously by reselling the notes to the public. In addition, they expected that Chase would keep government funds on deposit in the banks and would make payments by check and that only a few of those receiving the checks would cash them for specie. In modern terminology, the bankers were hoping that Chase would "monetize the debt" and facilitate the handling of the loan without serious diminution of specie reserves.

But Chase insisted on adhering to the traditional practice of the Inde-

---

[3] These notes were made full legal tender in March, 1862, and in time came to be worth considerably more than their face value, because they could be used in place of coin in paying customs duties.

pendent Treasury, demanding the advancement of the loan to the Treasury in specie.[4] He erroneously believed that the credit of the Treasury, as well as of the banks themselves, would be strengthened thereby. The bankers pleaded with him to make at least one concession and not issue any more demand notes through which additional specie would be withdrawn from their vaults, but they were unsuccessful, since he was determined to adhere to his hard-money theories from beginning to end. Under the circumstances, the banks had no choice but to go along with a banking policy which they believed would end disastrously. They agreed to deliver $5 million in coin immediately and the remaining $45 million in coin as needed for disbursement by the Treasury.

√   Having agreed to Chase's proposal, the banks could only hope that the specie would come back within a week or so either by redeposits in the banks or by the resale of treasury notes to the public for specie. However, the expected circular operation did not work so well in practice as in theory. As political and military affairs worsened, sales of the notes by the banks fell off and specie went into hoarding instead of being redeposited. The banks sold $45 million of the first $50 million issue, being forced to retain $5 million for their own account. The entire $50 million bought in October was retained, and in November the banks refused to buy notes, taking instead $50 million of 6 per cent bonds (known as 5–20's because they were redeemable in 5 years and matured in 20) for $45.8 million, a price equivalent to par for 7 per cent bonds.

In the meanwhile, expenditures were running considerably in excess of estimates, and the revenues from customs duties had unexpectedly fallen off sharply. Chase was forced to issue some $33 million of demand notes, which were quickly presented to the banks for conversion into specie, causing a further drain on their already diminished specie reserves.

Chase's Report of December, 1861. While Chase was trying to raise money, the prospects of the North lost much of their brilliance both domestically and internationally. Military affairs were not progressing successfully, and in mid-December the Union became embroiled with Britain over the Trent affair. In the same month Chase's annual report threw a pall of gloom over the financial affairs of the Union. The Secretary acknowledged that his previous report had underestimated the costs for the fiscal year 1862. Instead of $318 million, he now estimated expenditures at $532 million. On the other hand, revenue would be only $55 million, instead of the estimated $80 million. Even worse, his report contained few recommendations for meeting the large sums required. He recommended "retrenchment and reform" in expenditures and $50 million in

[4] Chase told the bankers that, unless they took the loan on his terms, he would issue paper money "until it takes $1,000 to buy a breakfast." (Albert Bushnell Hart, *Salmon Portland Chase*, p. 223.)

new taxes—a direct tax of $20 million (this time only on the Northern states), excise taxes to provide $20 million, an income tax which might possibly produce $10 million, and small increases in customs on coffee, tea, and sugar. Altogether, total revenue would be around $100 million. The only innovation in his report was a strong recommendation for the establishment of a national banking system which would create a uniform currency, provide a market for government bonds, and prevent over-expansion and depreciation of the currency. But this proposal caused consternation in financial circles, since the banks did not relish being brought under Federal control, which would undoubtedly be more rigid than state control.

Suspension of Specie. Congress passed a slight tariff increase on December 24, 1861, but before it could act on Chase's other recommendation, the private banks of the country suspended specie payments on December 30, the government suspending a day later. Although specie payments might have been continued for a short period, since the banks had reserves of about 20 per cent, suspension was inevitable. In New York City alone the banks were losing $7 million of specie a week, and the drain was constantly increasing.

Banking leaders believed that suspension was due primarily to Chase's stubborn insistence upon the delivery of specie and to his obstinate refusal to stop the issue of demand notes. However, this was a superficial explanation. Much more fundamental causes were the colossal increase in government expenditures, the government's hesitancy in levying new taxes, and the adverse nature of the news from the front. These shook public confidence in the government's ability to handle the situation and caused an increase in hoarding. Even if wiser financial policies had been followed by the Secretary, suspension of specie payments would probably have occurred. At best, its occurrence might have been postponed for a short time.

After the suspension of specie, gold was still needed by private individuals to pay international obligations and customs duties and by the Federal government to pay interest on its bonds. Therefore, a market opened in New York on January 13, 1862, where gold could be bought and sold for paper money by private individuals and government agents.

First Issue of Greenbacks. For a time after the suspension of specie payments, Chase and the fiscal leaders of Congress functioned in a state of bewilderment. Much of the program in Chase's annual report became inapplicable. The proposed national banking currency had to be forgotten for the moment, as it would take too long to bring it into being. Moreover, opposition by state bankers was so powerful that a bill to establish a national bank was adversely reported on by the Ways and Means Committee in January, 1862. The money market was completely disorganized, and until it was stabilized, it could not absorb any new Federal loans. The Ways and Means Committee, addressing itself to the problem, appointed two subcommittees, one under Morrill to consider revenue measures and the other under Spaulding to consider means of obtaining loans.

Spaulding was convinced that under existing arrangements the Treasury's funds would be exhausted in 30 days. He considered new taxes impractical, since they could not be collected quickly enough. He was even more sceptical in regard to new loan flotations, since with government bonds selling far below par it would be impossible to sell new 7 per cent bonds for more than 75 or even 50. Therefore, on grounds of necessity, rather than choice, he proposed that the government issue on its own faith $50 million of non-interest-bearing Treasury notes which would be legal tender even though not redeemable in specie.[5]

A delegation of bankers led by James Gallatin opposed the fiat-money scheme and suggested an alternative plan, calling for $125 million in taxes over and above customs, the abandonment of further issues of demand notes, the use of banks as government depositories, the issue of $100 million of interest-bearing Treasury notes, and the sale of government bonds at any price which the market might bring. The bankers' plan, although basically sound, was unpopular even among businessmen and had no appreciable effect. Nevertheless, the debate on the Spaulding bill was long and spirited. It was not until February 25, 1862, that it was finally passed, and then, one of the decisive factors was a statement by Chase, supporting the measure as the only possible way to provide funds.

The Legal Tender Act provided for the issue of $150 million of United States notes in denominations of $5 or higher, authorized $500 million of 6 per cent bonds to be sold at the market price, and allowed the Secretary to accept up to $25 million[6] of deposits in United States notes from private holders in exchange for 5 per cent certificates of deposit. The notes, which in time came to be called greenbacks, were the first real paper money ever issued by the United States government, although some of the Treasury notes of 1812 and the demand notes of 1861 were pseudo paper money and could be considered as precursors. The greenbacks were made legal tender for all private and public debts, except payment of customs duties and payment of interest on United States bonds and notes. Duties still had to be paid in specie so that the Treasury could pay interest on its debt in specie.

The greenbacks were made convertible at par into 5–20 bonds, for it

[5] Wesley Mitchell (*History of the Greenbacks*, p. 73) implies that greenbacks were not necessary, since taxes could have been raised in the same time that it took to issue greenbacks and bonds could have been sold at the same price.

[6] Later increased to $50 million, $100 million, and finally $150 million.

was thought that since they bore no interest, people would eagerly exchange them for the interest-bearing bonds. Then by reissuing the notes,
the Treasury would be in the center of a continuous circle of conversion
and would be able to sell at least $500 million of bonds for the original
$150 million of constantly reissued greenbacks. Unfortunately, the public
did not respond to the convertibility feature, as a 6 per cent bond at par
was not sufficiently attractive. But convertibility did put an effective ceiling price on government bonds, for no one would pay a premium for a
bond which could be purchased at par in greenbacks.

As a gesture toward the ultimate retirement of the debt, Congress
stipulated that after July 1, 1862, 1 per cent of the debt was to be repurchased for a sinking fund. But this provision was not enforced during the
war years, since the Treasury did not have operating surpluses.

Additional Authorizations of Greenbacks. Neither the greenbacks nor
the 5–20's alleviated the Treasury's embarrassment as quickly as anticipated. Greenbacks did not begin to circulate until late in April. Even
though Chase was authorized by the new law to sell 5–20's at the "market
price," he arbitrarily interpreted the phrase to mean the price he was
seeking to maintain. Since the public would not buy the bonds at his price,
a stalemate resulted. For a while Chase used demand notes and certificates
of deposit to raise funds. Once the greenbacks were available, he used a
substantial part of them to redeem demand notes, leaving only about $100
million for fresh expenditures. Since the government was spending more
than $1 million a day, the Treasury's financial position was, by June, 1862,
as bad as in February if not worse.

Chase therefore asked for another issue of legal tenders and an expansion of the certificates of deposit. Although Congress had insisted that the
first batch of paper money would also be the last, it authorized another
$150 million on July 11, 1862, and a third issue of $150 million in January
and March, 1863.

Although only tacitly supporting the first issue of greenbacks, Chase
initiated the second and third issues, which were in part in denominations
of less than $5. At the same time, Chase committed one of his worst
mistakes. Under the illusion that bonds could be sold at less than 6 per
cent interest if greenbacks were not convertible into bonds at par, he
persuaded Congress to withdraw the convertibility feature. Under the Act
of March, 1863, therefore, holders of greenbacks were given until July 1
to exercise the option of conversion. The withdrawal of conversion, far
from helping government finance, made it difficult to retire greenbacks
after the war was over.

Thus, by the middle of 1863 Chase had made at least five major mistakes,
each of which had dire consequences: he failed to recommend vigorous

taxation; he refused at a crucial time to use banks as government depositories and checks as means of payment; he was unwilling to sell bonds
below par, thus bringing bond sales to a standstill; he endorsed the overissue of paper currency with legal-tender quality, thereby providing fuel
for inflation; and he obtained the repeal of the convertibility feature for
the greenbacks. Yet somehow he did secure all the funds that were necessary to conduct the war, and this, after all, was most important.[7]

[7] An editorial in a British paper praised Chase's financial administration by saying,
"The hundredth part of Mr. Chase's embarrassments would tax Mr. Gladstone's in-
genuity to the utmost, and set the [British] public mind in a ferment of excitement."
(Jacob W. Schuckers, *The Life of Salmon P. Chase,* p. 226.)

After the spring of 1863, Union finances improved. News from the military front was more reassuring; loan operations became more successful; and revenue collections under the vigorous tax measures passed by Congress increased, bolstering the credit of the government. Though mistakes were made, they were fewer and less serious than those of the earlier period.

Depreciation of the Greenbacks. Greenbacks began to depreciate in terms of specie almost immediately after they were first issued in the spring of 1862. Speculators and those who needed specie in their business transactions bought it at a premium with greenbacks in the New York gold market, while its possessors tended to hoard it. Consequently, its price in paper money increased until in time $1 in gold was worth $2.85 in paper or, conversely, $1 in paper was worth only 35 cents in gold. At the same time greenbacks (and other paper currency) depreciated in terms of goods; that is, prices of commodities, which were all being purchased in paper money (inasmuch as gold was being hoarded), rose steadily. Price inflation hit the laboring classes most severely, for they were paid in paper money and their wages lagged far behind prices. The government also suffered from rising prices, for it was the largest purchaser of goods and collected only a portion of its total receipts in specie.

The basic causes of the depreciation of paper money were the great increase in demand induced by the government's war spending and the consequent expansion of currency, credit, and income. But in addition, the price of gold was affected by the news from the military front, the ebb and flow of imports payable in gold, and the government's gold payments of interest on its bonds. Bad news caused gold to be hoarded and its price in terms of paper to rise, while good news caused gold to be thrown on the market and its price to drop.[1]

Some writers have ascribed the price inflation almost entirely to the issuance of greenbacks, but this is a mistaken view.[2] Even if greenbacks

[1] When Lee invaded Pennsylvania in early 1863, greenbacks declined from 72 to 67 cents in gold. When Grant captured Vicksburg and the Confederates were stopped at Gettysburg in July, 1863, greenbacks rose from 69 to 75 cents. When Grant was repulsed in the bloody battle of Cold Spring Harbor, greenbacks went into a tail spin.

[2] See Wesley C. Mitchell, *Gold, Prices, and Wages Under the Greenback Standard*, p. 249; and Davis R. Dewey, *Financial History of the United States*, 12 ed., p. 293.

had not been issued and bonds had been sold at whatever price they would bring in the market, inflation would have taken place. It would have merely taken another form—that of monetization of the debt through the issue of bank currency or the creation of bank credit. The basic mistake was the failure to impose taxes vigorously. Once the government was forced to rely on credit, the exact form of credit expansion was not so important as assumed by some historians.

TABLE 18.   GOLD PRICES, COST OF LIVING, AND WAGES IN PAPER MONEY, 1862–1865
(1860 = 100)

Year	Prices of gold in greenbacks			Cost of living	Wages
	Low	Average	High		
1862	100½	113.3	134	112	101
1863	122⅛	145.2	172½	129	112
1864	151½	203.3	285	156	130
1865	128⅝	157.3	233¾	168	150

SOURCE: Wesley C. Mitchell, *Gold, Prices, and Wages under the Greenback Standard*, pp. 4, 279.

The Treasury, blandly ignoring its own contribution to price inflation, insisted that the phenomenon was caused by the expansion of state-bank currency and the activities of speculators in gold. Chase was especially obsessed with the theory that speculators were responsible, and in this he was supported by public opinion. In June, 1864, he persuaded Congress to pass an act prohibiting short sales of gold. Together with current Union military reversals, this action caused a further loss of confidence in paper money. In thirteen days, greenbacks declined from 51 to 35 cents, and nineteen days after its passage, the Act was repealed, much to the embarrassment of Chase, its foremost progenitor.

Disappearance of Subsidiary Currency. The depreciation of the greenbacks also caused the disappearance of subsidiary coins. Under the Coinage Act of 1853, a dollar in subsidiary coins was worth 97 cents in gold. When greenbacks depreciated to less than 97 cents in gold, holders of half dollars, quarters, or dimes began to hoard them. By early 1862 it was profitable to ship $100 of silver to Canada to be exchanged for $97 in gold, which, in turn, could be used to purchase more than $100 in greenbacks. By July, 1862, $100 in silver could be converted into $108 of paper money, and no coin higher than 1 cent remained in circulation.

To make up for the disappearance of small coins, Chase proposed that postage stamps be used, and on July 17, Congress made stamps acceptable in payment of government dues up to $5. But no provision was made for printing any special stamps. Daily sales of stamps at the New York post office jumped from $3,000 to $24,000, and clerks were kept busy redeeming old stamps. Since ordinary postal business was impeded, Postmaster General Blair refused the further issue of stamps for currency, and the government in September began to issue bits of unglued paper which could be used as small currency. Finally, in March, 1863, Congress authorized the Treasury to issue up to $50 million of fractional notes in denominations up to $5, acceptable for all government dues except customs duties. Although they have long since ceased to circulate, there are still $15 million outstanding of which the Treasury carries approximately $2 million as part of the non-interest-bearing debt.

Congress Adopts a Vigorous Tax Policy. Chase's tax proposals of December, 1861, which contemplated increasing annual revenue to about $100 million, were highly unimaginative, for they included only the imposition of the direct tax and a few of the historic excises imposed in the Hamiltonian era and during the War of 1812. Fortunately, Congress was more cognizant of the needs of the hour and had greater faith in the people's willingness to be taxed. The Ways and Means Committee proposed, in early 1862, to increase the revenue to $150 million. The bill was thoroughly debated over a period of three months and passed on July 1.

The Act was more comprehensive than any tax measure ever enacted before. It incorporated all the internal duties used by the Federal government during the War of 1812—excises on spirits, tobacco, carriages, auction sales, sugar, and other products; license taxes on retailers of liquor; and stamp duties on legal instruments. In addition, it imposed, at stiffer rates, a number of internal taxes theretofore levied only on the state level, such as taxes on yachts, billiard tables, plate, insurance dividends, and bank capital and deposits. It levied taxes—some at specific rates, others ad valorem (at 3 per cent or more)—on every manufactured article, as well as 1½ and 3 per cent taxes on gross receipts of railroads, ferryboats, steamships, toll bridges, and advertisements. It applied stamp taxes to a much broader list of legal documents and transactions than in 1814, including the sale of stocks and bonds, checks, drafts, bills of exchange, bills of lading, express parcels, insurance policies, and telegrams and, as in England, to a variety of commodities, such as patent medicines, cosmetics, and playing cards. To retain the existing margin of protection for domestic manufacturers, it provided for additional compensatory duties on imports. Finally, the Act materially extended the income tax and imposed an inheritance tax.

In brief, instead of concentrating on a few objects at high rates, the Act of 1862 attempted to diffuse the burden on as many objects as possible at low rates. Therein lay its main strength as a revenue producer, but also its main difficulty in administration. The office of Tax Commissioner established in 1861 was abolished and replaced by a Commissioner of Internal

Revenue in the Treasury Department. The country was divided into collection districts, more deputies and agents were added, and the Commissioner was authorized to issue regulations.

The tax on liquor manufacture was levied at 20 cents a gallon—almost 100 per cent of the cost of the product. Distillers were required to take out Federal licenses and to make periodic reports on grain purchases and daily output. Every cask had to be inspected and labeled by a government official before it could be sold. Since whisky required aging, distillers were permitted to place it in bonded warehouses and pay the tax at the time of withdrawal. Beer was taxed at $1 a barrel, or approximately 20 per cent of its cost. The excise on snuff was imposed at a uniform rate, while that on cigars and chewing tobacco was roughly graduated.

The income tax was made slightly progressive, with a 3 per cent rate on incomes of $600 to $10,000 and 5 per cent on those over $10,000. All recipients of income in excess of $600 were required to file returns, but these returns were to be kept confidential. The tax on inheritances was imposed on personalty in excess of $1,000 at rates of ¾ of 1 per cent to 5 per cent, according to the relationship of the heirs, but transfers to husband or wife were exempt.

The direct tax, ordained by the Act of 1861, had in the meanwhile been reluctantly put into effect by Chase. But its application was limited by subsequent amendments to the Union states (with others to pay it when conquered). Credit was allowed for any expenses incurred by the states in raising and equipping troops. Actually, therefore, very little cash was collected, less than $2 million in the fiscal year 1861–1862, less than $1.5 million in the succeeding year, and even smaller sums thereafter.[3]

The immediate collections under the 1862 Act were extremely disappointing, for it took time to organize a staff of collectors and, even though the law was detailed and covered 57 pages, its administration had to be clarified. In the meanwhile, there were much confusion and evasion. Instead of $100 million, as expected, internal-revenue collections in the fiscal year 1863 amounted to only $39 million.

To increase the revenue, Congress passed new tax laws in 1863, 1864, and 1865, those of 1864 being the most important. The tax on liquor was raised to 60 cents in March, 1864, $1.50 in June, 1864, and $2 in February, 1865, or to ten times the original cost of the product. The tax on cigars was trebled and quadrupled, until it was equivalent to between 60 and 100 per cent of their cost. The license taxes were applied to a number of additional trades and occupations and were made roughly proportional to

[3] Receipts from the direct tax, mostly in the form of credits for services rendered by the states, kept on coming in during the next 25 years. By 1888, they amounted to $15.4 million. In 1891, Congress voted to return to the states this contribution in cash (see p. 205, below).

output or size of the establishment, instead of uniform as before. The gross-receipts business taxes were extended to telegraph and express companies, canalboats, stagecoaches, theaters, circuses, and museums and, in the case of railroads and steamships, to receipts from freight. Stamp duties were affixed to matches, and the rates of other duties were increased. The general ad valorem tax on manufactures was increased from 3 to 5 and finally to 6 per cent, and specific rates were variously increased. The income tax was made more progressive at rates of 5 per cent on incomes of $600 to $5,000, 7½ per cent on $5,000 to $10,000, and 10 per cent on over $10,000. In July, 1864, an additional income tax of 5 per cent on all incomes in excess of $600 was voted, but this was repealed in March, 1865, when the rate on all income over $5,000 was set at 10 per cent. In 1863 and 1864, in addition to the deduction of Federal, state, and local taxes allowed under the 1862 Act, deductions were allowed for house rents (including rental value of owner-occupied homes), mortgage interest, repairs, and losses from the sale of land. The rates of the inheritance tax were raised to 1 to 6 per cent.

Increase in Revenue Despite Widespread Tax Evasion. The cheapest and easiest taxes to collect were stamp duties; the most difficult were those on liquor, tobacco, income, and inheritance. When the whisky tax was only 20 cents on a gallon, evasions were relatively few. But when the rate was tripled, and especially when it was increased to $2, evasion became widespread. With the connivance of government inspectors, huge quantities of liquor were diverted into bootleg channels. In addition, illicit stills were set up all over the country. Bootleg liquor, selling at a fraction of taxed liquor, displaced the latter in the market. As a result, liquor-tax revenue, after increasing from $3.3 million in the fiscal year 1863 to $28 million in the fiscal year 1864, dropped to $16 million in the fiscal year 1865.

The income tax was also extensively evaded. People objected to the complicated returns and resented the government's scrutiny of their private affairs. The various allowable deductions and the difficulties of verifying returns offered a fruitful field for dishonest persons. Fortunately, in collecting the tax, the government made considerable use of withholding at the source. This was done in collecting the tax on salaries of Federal employees and incomes of stockholders and bondholders of certain types of corporations. Thus, in 1865, out of $32 million, nearly 40 per cent was collected at the source.[4] Despite the evasions, 460,000 individuals made returns in 1866. This was 1 out of 76 inhabitants or 1 out of 15 gainfully employed persons and evidenced the relatively high rate of taxation prevailing at the time.

Manufacturers' sales taxes were fairly well enforced. Every manufac-

[4] For further details of Civil War taxation, see Frederick C. Howe, *Taxation and Taxes in the United States, 1791-1895.*

TABLE 19. FEDERAL RECEIPTS, EXPENDITURES, AND DEBT, 1861–1865
(In millions of dollars)

	1861	1862	1863	1864	1865
Receipts:					
Customs................	$ 39.6	$ 49.1	$ 69.1	$ 102.3	$ 84.9
Income tax....?.........	....	....	2.7	20.3	61.0
Direct tax..............	....	1.8	1.5	0.5	1.2
Excises*...............	....	....	34.9	89.4	148.5
Spirits and liquor.......	....	....	6.8	32.6	22.5
Tobacco..............	....	....	3.1	8.6	11.4
Manufactures..........	....	....	16.5	36.2	73.3
Stamps...............	....	....	4.1	5.9	11.2
License..............	....	....	4.8	5.2	9.8
Gross receipts.........	....	....	1.7	3.4	9.9
Other................	....	....	1.3	4.9	12.0
Sale of public lands.......	0.9	0.2	0.2	0.6	1.0
Miscellaneous...........	1.0	0.9	3.7	30.3	25.4
Premiums on gold sales...	....	0.1	0.6	21.2	11.7
Totals................	$ 41.5	$ 52.0	$ 112.7	$ 264.6	$ 333.7
Expenditures:					
Civil.................	$ 6.1	$ 5.9	$ 6.3	$ 8.0	$ 10.6
Foreign...............	1.1	1.3	1.2	1.2	1.3
Navy.................	12.4	42.6	63.3	85.7	122.6
War.................	23.0	389.2	603.3	690.4	1,030.7
Pensions..............	1.0	0.9	1.1	5.0	16.3
Indians...............	2.9	2.3	3.2	2.6	5.1
Interest...............	4.0	13.2	24.7	53.7	77.4
Premium on purchase of gold..................	....	....	....	....	1.7
Miscellaneous..........	16.1	14.2	15.7	18.4	31.1
Totals................	$ 66.6	$ 469.6	$ 718.7	$ 865.0	$ 1,296.8
Surplus (+) or deficit (−)..	$ −25.1	$ −417.6	$ −606.0	$ −600.4	$ −963.1
Gross debt†..............	90.6	524.2	1,119.8	1,815.8	2,680.6
Interest-bearing debt........	90.4	365.4	707.8	1,360.0	2,217.7

SOURCE: *Annual Report of the Secretary of the Treasury,* 1893; *Annual Report of the Commissioner of Internal Revenue,* 1876.

* Receipts from specific excise taxes were reported by the Commissioner of Internal Revenue on basis of collections and therefore will not add up to totals.

† Including various government paper currency.

turer was required to furnish on prescribed forms his monthly production and sales, and the taxes were made a lien upon his real and personal property. The largest revenue was obtained from raw and fabricated cottons and wool, iron and steel products, leather goods and shoes, oil, sugar and confectionery, paper, soap, and coal. The taxes were pyramided in the price of the final product, and it was estimated that in 1865 they amounted to 8 to 20 per cent of the cost of nearly all manufactured products, in the case of sugar equaling the entire labor cost of production. Prices were increased generally by more than the amount of the tax. Manufacturers often anticipated projected tax increases by raising prices liberally, and dealers added their markups to the price inclusive of the tax. In the meanwhile, the $20 million direct levy was repealed in 1864. The Northern states paid their apportionments, but in the Southern states collections were enforced only as occupation was extended.

All in all, despite their various defects, the tax-legislation and enforcement measures of 1862 to 1865 rolled up an internal revenue of $117 million in 1864 and $211 million in 1865. Taxes which had paid only 10 per cent of total expenditures in 1862 paid 25 per cent of total expenditures in 1864 and 1865.

Although the internal taxes, which were preeminently indirect, contributed to price inflation, they also checked consumer purchases and were less inflationary than loans. It was estimated that the consumption of coffee, sugar, textiles, and shoes fell off 50 per cent between 1860 and 1865. This was quite natural, as the war could not have been financed except by curtailing consumption.

Jay Cooke's Bond Campaign. In the meanwhile, the depreciation of the greenbacks made it profitable for individuals to convert them into government bonds. Therefore, by the fall of 1862 the prospects for marketing a large issue became bright. In October, 1862, Chase signed a contract, making Jay Cooke, a highly imaginative and enterprising banker who had sold more than 20 per cent of the notes marketed in 1861, general agent in the sale of the 6 per cent, 5–20 bonds authorized under the Loan Act of February, 1862. Cooke was to receive a commission of ½ of 1 per cent on the first $10 million sold and ⅜ of 1 per cent on the remainder and was to pay out of this commission all the expenses of the loan campaign.

Cooke hired some 2,500 subagents to comb the country, selling bonds in every whistle stop to anyone who could raise $50. He advertised in all the foreign-language newspapers, distributed throwaways, and rang doorbells. He carried on an educational campaign which explained in simple terms the fundamentals of bond investment. The technique was extraordinarily successful. By July, 1863, Cooke had sold $157 million and by January, 1864, $362 million. What was more remarkable, the bond drive cost the Treasury less than if it had been handled directly. Cooke paid his subagents ⅛ of 1 per cent, and he claimed that, after expenses, his net commission was only $220,000. Nevertheless, it was popularly supposed that Cooke had reaped an immense profit, and under the pressure of public criticism, Chase ended the Cooke agency in January, 1864.

The success of the loan was due not only to the depreciation of greenbacks and Cooke's techniques but also to the improved military situation, increased tax collections, and the passage in February, 1863, of the National Bank Act with the consequent prospect of an eventual sound and uniform bank-note currency.

The Third and Fourth Loan Acts, 1863 and 1864. In March, 1863, Congress authorized loans up to $900 million, either in 10–40 bonds or up to $400 million in Treasury notes. But the 10–40's proved unpopular, only $75 million of them being sold. The Treasury then resorted again to the short-term notes. Like the greenbacks, they were made legal tender and were used by banks as reserves. In effect, therefore, they inflated the money supply by more than the actual amount issued.

In March, 1864, the Fourth Loan Act permitted the Treasury, in lieu of the bonds authorized in 1863, to issue $200 million of bonds redeemable any time after five years but not later than after forty years and bearing interest not over 6 per cent. Proud of the fact that he had been able to reduce interest rates from 7.3 per cent in 1861 to 6 per cent in 1863, Chase decided to reduce the rate on his new flotations to 5 per cent. His plan ended in a complete fiasco. Of his proferred $200 million bonds only a little over $73 million was sold by June 30, 1864, and further sales had to be suspended. The Treasury was compelled to return to the issue of 1-, 2-, and 3-year notes, all of which were highly inflationary in nature.

Establishment of the National Banking System. Though suffering grievous disappointments in many of his endeavors, Chase at least had the satisfaction in February, 1863, of having Congress pass the National Bank Act. However, the enactment of this program by no means assured its successful establishment. Bankers preferred to operate under their state charters, inasmuch as state regulation was less stringent than national regulation. By October, 1863, only 66 banks, mostly in the Middle West, had taken national charters and the total note circulation was less than $4 million.

To speed the conversion of the banks, Congress liberalized the law in June, 1864, and also imposed a 2 per cent tax on state-bank notes. But by October, 1864, the number of national banks had grown to only 508 and their combined note circulation was only $45.3 million. Nor had Chase's hopes of securing a substantial market for government bonds been realized, total national-bank holdings of government securities amounting to only $108.1 million. The provisions of the National Bank Act as amended in 1864 were as follows:

1. Five or more persons could obtain a twenty-year national-bank charter from the Comptroller of the Currency—a new office established in the Treasury.

2. Minimum capital ranged from $200,000 for a bank in a city of 50,000 or more to $50,000 in a city with 6,000 population. Stockholders were subject to double liability.

3. Each national bank was required to deposit with the Comptroller of the Currency United States bonds equal to one-third of its capital, but not less than $30,000. In exchange, the bank received national-bank notes equal to 90 per cent of the par or market value of the deposited bonds.

4. Total issue of national-bank notes was limited to $300 million, one-half distributed among the states on the basis of population and the remainder on the basis of existing banking facilities.

5. National-bank notes were receivable for all public dues except customs and payable for all government obligations except interest on the public debt or redemption of national currency.

6. National banks in so-called reserve cities were required to maintain in their own vaults a 25 per cent reserve in lawful money against deposits. Those in other cities, while also required to maintain a 25 per cent reserve, could keep one-half of it on deposit in New York City. Country banks had to maintain a 15 per cent reserve, three-fifths of which could be deposited in a city bank.

7. All banks had to maintain a 25 per cent reserve against their note circulation and were taxed semiannually ½ per cent on the average amount in circulation, ¼ per cent on their total capital other than that invested in government bonds, and ¼ per cent on their deposits.

8. National banks could own real estate only if it were necessary for the transaction of business or had been acquired as a result of foreclosure.

9. National banks could be used as depositories for government funds other than customs duties. The Secretary of the Treasury was directed to require security "by the deposit of United States bonds and otherwise."

In March, 1865, Congress increased the tax on state-bank circulation, beginning July 1, 1866, from 2 to 10 per cent, making it unprofitable for state banks to issue notes.[5] More than any other feature of the law, this tax exerted pressure on the remaining state banks to convert to national charters. By October, 1865, there were 1,513 national banks with $171.3 million circulation, and by October, 1866, there were 1,644 with $280.3 million circulation. Thus, the great banking and currency reform first conceived in 1861 did not become fully a reality until after the war. Even then, although it was a great improvement on the old system, it did not proceed altogether smoothly.

Chase's Resignation and Fessenden's Administration. At the end of the fiscal year 1864, Chase, aggrieved by the reverses with which his policies had met and piqued by a rejection of a patronage request, submitted his resignation.[6] Much to his surprise, Lincoln accepted it and appointed as his successor William P. Fessenden, chairman of the Senate Finance Com-

[5] The Supreme Court held [*Veazie Bank v. Fenno*, 8 Wall. 533 (1869)] that the tax was within Congress's power to regulate money.

[6] Chase's resignation was surrounded by complicated political and personal clashes. (Albert Bushnell Hart, *Salmon Portland Chase*.)

mittee. The prospects which greeted Fessenden were not too encouraging. Chase had just withdrawn the 5 per cent issue, and the attempt to halt speculation in gold was proving a boomerang. The Treasury's cash balance was $18.8 million, against which there were unpaid requisitions of $71.8 million. Yet the picture was not completely dismal, for tax revenue was increasing daily and the chances of victory were brighter.

TABLE 20.   CIVIL WAR BORROWINGS
(In millions of dollars)

	Date of original authorization	Amount issued (including reissues)
Long-term issues:		
Twenty years, 6%.	July 17, 1861	$189.3
Five-twenties, 6%.	Feb. 25, 1862	514.8
Ten-forties, 6%.	Mar. 3, 1863	75.0
Ten-forties, 5%.	Mar. 3, 1864	196.1
Five-twenties, 6%.	June 30, 1864	125.6
Five-twenties, 6%.	Mar. 3, 1865	203.3
Short-term issues:		
Demand notes.	July 17, 1861	60.0
Seven-thirties of 1861, 7.3%.	July 17, 1861	140.1
Legal-tender notes.	Feb. 25, 1862	915.4
Certificates of deposit, 4, 5, and 6%.	Feb. 25, 1862	120.0
Certificates of indebtedness, 6%.	Mar. 1, 1862	561.8
One-year notes of 1863, 5%.	Mar. 3, 1863	44.5
Two-year notes of 1863, 5%.	Mar. 3, 1863	166.5
Coin certificates*.	Mar. 3, 1863	562.8
Compound-interest notes, 6%.	Mar. 3, 1863	266.6
Seven-thirties of 1864 and 1865, 7.3%.	June 30, 1864, Mar. 3, 1865	830.0

SOURCE: *Annual Report of the Secretary of the Treasury*, 1876, pp. 47–51.

* These were issued to individuals entitled to gold payments and could be converted by them into coin at any time. They were also issued in exchange for deposits of gold. They were in denominations of $20 and more and the total issued could not be more than 20 per cent in excess of total coin and bullion in the Treasury. The gold certificates henceforth became a permanent part of the country's currency system and were issued in varying amounts. In 1933 they were taken out of circulation and allowed to be used only by Federal Reserve banks.

On the last day of the fiscal year 1864, Congress passed the Fifth Loan Act, authorizing an additional $400 million issue of which half could be in 7.3 per cent notes.

During the last few months of the war Fessenden had little trouble in selling government securities. On January 28, 1865, he reappointed Jay Cooke as Treasury Agent. In six months Cooke sold $700 million of 7.3 per cent notes at a commission of ¾ of 1 per cent on the first $50 million and ⅝ per cent on the remainder. In March, Congress passed its sixth loan authorization for $600 million in bonds or notes.

Confederate Finance. If the North had difficulty in financing the war, the Southern experience was far worse, for the South was handicapped by its predominantly agricultural economy. This made taxation more difficult and caused an even heavier resort to the apparently painless method of printing paper money.[7]

The total cost of the war to the South in paper money was approximately $2 billion. Total receipts were $2.3 billion, of which $2 billion was raised by paper money and loans.

TABLE 21.   CONFEDERATE RECEIPTS AND EXPENDITURES
(In millions of dollars)

Receipts	
Current revenues:	
Taxes	$ 122.5
Sequestration	6.4
Customs	3.4
Tax on notes	14.4
Repayments	91.4
Miscellaneous	10.3
Total	$ 248.4
Borrowings:	
Bonds	$ 546.2
Notes	1,360.0
Bank loans	12.4
Call certificates	144.3
Total	$2,062.9
Total receipts	$2,311.3
Expenditures:	
War	$1,356.8
Navy	93.0
Civil	46.4
Debt service	603.6
Total	$2,099.8

SOURCE: Emory Q. Hawk, *Economic History of the South*, p. 414.

The first actions taken by the Confederate government were the imposition of a small tax on cotton exports and the authorization of an 8 per cent loan for $15 million. Later, a tariff for revenue averaging 12½ per cent was imposed. However, these import and export duties provided little revenue, for the Northern blockade imposed early in the war was highly efficient. Confiscation of specie belonging to the Federal Treasury provided approximately $1 million. Some contributions of indeterminate

[7] For the details of Confederate finances, see John C. Schwab, *The Confederate States of America;* and E. Merton Coulter, *The Confederate States of America,* Chap. 8.

value came from those who supplied their own equipment when they joined the army. But all these sources were relatively trivial. Consequently in March, 1861, the Confederate Congress authorized $1 million of 3.65 per cent, 1-year notes, and in May it authorized $50 million of 8 per cent, 20-year bonds, $20 million of which could be in non-interest-bearing notes convertible into bonds. In August, 1861, a direct tax of ½ of 1 per cent was imposed on all property except Confederate bonds and money in hand, but it was to be collected through the states, and a discount was provided for rapid payment. In order to obtain the discount, states borrowed the money, nullifying the effect of the tax and competing with the Richmond government in the loan market.

In January, 1863, Confederate agents in Europe appeared to have accomplished a ten-strike. The French bankers Erlanger and Co. underwrote a £3 million 7 per cent loan, to be sold at 77 and amortized annually at 5 per cent payable in cotton and, after peace, in specie. At first, it went well, and the British allotment was oversubscribed at 90, but the price began to sag, and in a vain effort to support the market, the Confederacy expended so much that it realized only $6.5 million from the loan. In April, 1863, the Confederacy passed its first meaningful tax legislation, imposing an 8 per cent tax on certain kinds of personal property, a 1 per cent normal and 2 per cent surtax on earned income, a 5 to 15 per cent tax on unearned income, a 10 per cent tax in kind on agricultural income, a 10 per cent war-industries profit tax, a 5 per cent corporation capital-stock tax, a heavy distillers' tax, and a miscellany of occupational license taxes.

Meanwhile, the Confederate government increased the issue of non-interest-bearing Treasury notes, and state governments and state banks continued to issue notes. By 1863 money in circulation was over $1 billion, and Confederate notes, which, unlike the Northern greenbacks, were not legal tender, began to depreciate rapidly. Military affairs were not going well, the Southern economy was not able to produce, the Northern blockade was improving in efficiency, and confidence evaporated. But while the clamor for taxes was enormous, the government took the viewpoint that acts of Congress would stop the rise in prices and the depreciation of the currency. In early 1864 the non-interest-bearing notes were partially repudiated. Notes of $5 or less were fundable until July, 1864, after which they would be reduced in value 33⅓ per cent. Notes of $100 or more were fundable until April, 1864, after which they were to be devalued 33⅓ per cent plus an additional 10 per cent per month until valueless.[8] A great storm of protest arose throughout the South, and Secretary of the Treasury Memminger resigned. In February, 1864, the second tax law was passed imposing the following taxes in addition to those of the April, 1863, Act: a 10 per cent tax on holdings of gold and silver plate, a 5 per cent tax

[8] Compare with the 1780 Act of the Continental Congress.

on all property not otherwise taxed, a 10 per cent general business-profits tax, and a 25 per cent excess-profits tax. This was followed by a third act the following June, increasing all tax rates by one-fifth and imposing an additional 30 per cent sales tax, and in March, 1865, by a fourth tax law, raising all existing rates and imposing a capital levy of 25 per cent on coin, bullion, and foreign exchange. But by this time, inflation was running wild and the whole system of Confederate finance was in a state of chaos.

Near the close of the war, the value of Confederate currency was less than state-bank currency. Army paymasters paid 15 Confederate dollars for 1 Northern greenback, and the value of the Confederate dollar averaged over the four years of war only about 12 cents.

Summary of Civil War Financing. The war cost the nation in paper money from April 1, 1861, to July 1, 1865, $5.2 billion ($3.2 billion for the Union and $2.0 billion for the Confederacy). In addition, there were vast unestimated economic losses in human life and disability, destruction of property, interest payments on the Union debt, pension payments to veterans and their survivors, and costs of Southern reconstruction.

In the first full year of the war, Federal expenditures were more than seven times greater than the annual prewar expenditures, and in the final year, they were almost twenty times the prewar figure. H. C. Adams estimated that Federal expenditures in 1865 were "in excess of 26 per cent of the gross product" of the nation as compared with 2 per cent in 1861.[9] W. E. Smith estimated expenditures by both sides at approximately 17 per cent of the country's total wealth in 1860.[10]

When heavy taxes were finally imposed in the North, few possibilities were overlooked, but excises were most prominent, and being passed on to consumers in higher prices, they were sharply regressive. Confederate taxation was even more belated and less effective.

The war was financed mainly by loans and paper-money issues. In the North, only 22 per cent of total receipts came from tax revenue, and in the South, only 5 per cent. The net debt of The Federal government at its peak was $2.8 billion—thirty-three times greater than the prewar debt and equal to more than one-half the national income. Annual interest payments ($133.1 million in 1865–1866) were approximately 2.4 per cent of the national income.

The Southern debt, which was in excess of $2 billion, was repudiated automatically with the defeat of the Confederacy and more directly by

[9] H. C. Adams, *The Science of Finance*, p. 535. Using Martin's estimates for the National Industrial Conference Board, the Committee on Public Debt Policy (*Our National Debt*, p. 12) calculated the national income at $5.4 billion. Under this estimate, the ratio of Federal expenditures to national income would not be very different (24 per cent).

[10] Carl R. Fish, *The Civil War*, p. 443.

the adoption of the Fourteenth Amendment to the Constitution of the United States.

The increase in government expenditures and debt caused a simultaneous increase in currency and bank deposits, for the various legal-tender issues were not only currency, but reserves for bank credit.[11] Per capita coin and paper currency in circulation was $13.82 in 1860 and $30.35 in 1865.

One of the effects of the stupendous war financing was to make the Federal government far more important in the postwar economy than it had ever been before. The separation of government from the economy which the agrarians had desired was no longer a possibility. In its fiscal policy alone, the national government was henceforth forced to influence the money market and the price level. Its revenues, expenditures, and debt management affected the incomes and assets of practically every family and business firm in the country. Its $400 million paper-money issue gave it a most important influence over the monetary system, while the National Bank Act brought it back into close contact with the banking system.

Each one of the far-reaching measures which extended Federal power over fiscal, monetary, and banking affairs was passed as a war measure and was not resisted by people ordinarily opposed to centralization. No one of these measures was adopted deliberately to broaden Federal power or to give the Treasury more influence over the money market. The debt and the tax structure were increased and greenbacks were issued as necessary parts of a fight for survival, and the National Bank Act could have been accepted only in an extreme emergency such as the Civil War. The continued existence of the Union was central in the minds of the people, and the heavy war outlays and the extensions of Federal power were deemed to be necessary incidents thereto.

[11] While expanding reserves by issuing greenbacks, the Federal government at the same time reduced reserves by accepting greenbacks in exchange for certificates of deposit.

Chapter 15: FISCAL READJUSTMENTS AFTER THE CIVIL WAR

During the twenty years after the Civil War, the nation's fiscal affairs became the subject of a sharp debate between higher and lower income groups. The fortunes of war decreed that victory in the controversy would go to the chief beneficiaries of industrial capitalism, for they presented a united front while the agrarian and labor lower income groups were badly split.

The higher income groups supported a regressive tax structure, emphasizing tariffs, and an orthodox debt policy, which would eliminate the greenbacks and help to restore specie payments. In general, lower income groups favored retention of progressive taxation and the payment of more liberal veterans' pensions. However, they disagreed over debt management. Farmers, favoring high prices and easy credit, demanded the retention of greenbacks, but urban workers, favoring lower prices, supported the industrialists in their demands for contracting greenbacks.

By themselves, the farmers could accomplish little, for the West was quantitatively weak and the South was relegated to political impotence. Hence, the Jeffersonian dream of a simple society was once and for all doomed, while the Hamiltonian vision of an industrial society began to come into its full flower.

Although the war greatly expanded Federal powers, the Federal government, with popular approval, refrained from competing with private enterprise. It remained a dispenser of rights and privileges and tried to create favorable conditions for the effective operation of private enterprise. Among all the Presidents during these twenty years—Johnson, Grant, Hayes, Garfield, and Arthur—only Johnson supported the agrarian view. He saw quite clearly that "an aristocracy based on nearly two and one half billion of national securities has risen in the northern states to assume that political control which was formerly given to the slave oligarchy."[1] However, Johnson was the least effective President in a period when Congress was dominant and the Presidency was superlatively ineffectual.

Most of the Secretaries of the Treasury of this period were conservative in their approach to the issues of the day. Hugh McCulloch, the first postwar Secretary, thought that the restoration of specie payments was

[1] Howard K. Beale (*The Critical Year*) gives an analysis of agrarian-industrial rivalry in the first year after the war.

TABLE 22. FEDERAL RECEIPTS, EX
(In millions

	1866	1867	1868	1869	1870	1871	1872	1873
Receipts:								
Customs...............	$ 179.0	$ 176.4	$ 164.5	$ 180.0	$ 194.5	$ 206.3	$ 216.4	$ 188.1
Income tax...........	73.0	66.0	41.5	34.8	37.8	19.2	14.4	5.1
Spirits excise..........	33.3	33.5	18.7	45.1	55.6	46.3	49.5	52.1
Fermented liquors......	5.2	6.1	6.0	6.1	6.3	7.4	8.3	9.3
Tobacco..............	16.5	19.8	18.7	23.4	31.4	33.6	33.7	34.4
Banks and bankers.....	3.5	2.0	1.9	2.2	3.0	3.6	4.6	3.8
Stamp taxes..........	14.3	15.2	14.0	15.5	15.6	14.5	15.3	7.1
Manufacturers........	127.2	91.5	61.6	3.3	3.0	3.6	4.6	3.8
Occupations tax.......	14.1	13.6	11.9	9.9	11.0	5.0		
Sales and gross receipts..	15.3	11.4	10.9	14.5	15.7	6.4		
Inheritance...........	1.2	1.9	2.8	2.4	3.1	2.5		
Miscellaneous excise....	6.5	4.0	2.5	1.8	1.7	1.0	0.4	0.5
Premiums*.............	38.1	27.8	29.2	13.8	15.3	8.9	9.4	11.6
Miscellaneous†..........	31.7	20.4	20.9	18.7	16.5	25.1	17.7	20.3
Totals...............	$ 558.0	$ 490.6	$ 405.6	$ 370.9	$ 411.3	$ 383.3	$ 374.1	$ 333.7
Expenditures:								
Civil.................	$ 12.0	$ 15.1	$ 13.1	$ 26.2	$ 15.9	$ 18.8	$ 16.1	$ 19.3
Navy.................	43.3	31.0	25.8	20.0	21.8	19.4	21.2	23.5
War..................	284.4	94.0	119.7	75.0	54.2	31.4	30.4	40.0
Pensions..............	15.6	20.9	23.8	28.5	28.3	34.4	28.5	29.4
Indians...............	3.3	4.6	4.1	7.0	3.4	7.4	7.1	8.0
River and harbor.......	0.3	1.2	3.5	3.5	3.5	4.4	5.0	6.3
Interest..............	133.1	143.8	140.4	130.7	129.2	125.6	117.4	104.8
Miscellaneous‡........	29.0	36.0	39.9	30.3	37.3	41.7	44.9	54.0
Premiums§............	0.1	10.8	7.0	1.7	16.0	9.0	7.0	5.1
Totals...............	$ 520.8	$ 357.5	$ 377.3	$ 322.9	$ 309.7	$ 292.2	$ 277.5	$ 290.3
Surplus...............	$ 37.2	$ 133.1	$ 28.3	$ 48.1	$ 101.6	$ 91.1	$ 96.6	$ 43.4
Gross debt.............	2,773.2	2,678.1	2,611.7	2,588.5	2,480.7	2,353.3	2,253.3	2,234.5
Interest-bearing debt.....	2,332.3	2,248.1	2,202.1	2,162.1	2,046.5	1,934.7	1,814.8	1,710.5

SOURCE: *Annual Reports of the Secretary of the Treasury,* 1866–1886, 1921. Figures will not necessarily add to totals because of rounding and differences in accounting methods.

* On sale of gold and on bond sales in 1877–1879; not usually included in ordinary receipts.

† Includes sale of public lands, direct tax, sale of surplus property, tax on national banks, etc. In 1874, $15.5 million Geneva award for Alabama claims.

‡ Expenses for national loans, tax collection, tax refunds, various public works, etc. In $1874, 15.5 million in settlement of Alabama claims.

§ On purchase of gold and in 1880–1881 purchase of bonds in the open market.

the most important problem. He favored drastic cuts in expenditures and a tax level high enough to yield a large annual surplus for the speedy contraction of the greenbacks. His successors, except possibly John Sherman, shared the same view. Representing the Middle West, which was neither completely agrarian nor completely industrial, Sherman became the great compromiser in many of the financial controversies of the period.

Gradual Reduction of Federal Expenditures. At the end of the war the demands on the Treasury were too heavy and the dollar too depreciated to permit a return to the $60 million annual prewar level of spending. A

PENDITURES, AND DEBT, 1866–1884
of dollars)

1874	1875	1876	1877	1878	1879	1880	1881	1882	1883	1884
$ 163.1	$ 157.2	$ 148.1	$ 131.0	$ 130.2	$ 137.3	$ 186.5	$ 198.2	$ 220.4	$ 214.7	$ 195.1
0.1	....	0.1								
49.4	52.1	56.4	57.5	50.4	52.6	61.2	67.2	69.9	74.4	76.9
9.3	9.1	9.6	9.5	9.9	10.7	12.8	13.7	16.2	16.9	18.1
33.2	37.3	39.8	41.1	40.1	40.1	38.9	42.9	47.4	42.1	26.1
3.4	4.1	4.0	3.8	3.5	3.2	3.4	3.8	5.3	3.7	
5.7	6.1	6.0	6.0	5.9	6.2	7.1	7.4	7.6	7.1	0.2
3.4	0.9	0.5	0.2	0.4	0.3	0.2	0.1	0.1	0.1	
0.4	0.5	0.4	0.4	0.3	0.3	0.4	0.2	0.2	0.3	0.3
5.0	4.0	4.0	0.4	0.3	1.5					
34.4	16.8	25.3	31.4	16.7	21.5	23.0	27.4	36.6	38.9	31.9
$ 305.0	$ 288.0	$ 294.1	$ 281.4	$ 257.8	$ 273.8	$ 333.5	$ 360.8	$ 403.5	$ 398.3	$ 348.5
$ 17.6	$ 17.3	$ 17.2	$ 16.6	$ 16.6	$ 16.4	$ 15.7	$ 17.9	$ 18.0	$ 22.3	$ 22.3
30.9	21.5	19.0	15.0	17.4	15.1	13.5	15.7	15.0	15.3	17.3
36.6	34.7	32.4	32.4	28.4	32.1	30.0	31.4	32.0	35.3	31.2
29.0	29.5	28.3	28.0	27.1	35.1	56.8	50.1	61.3	66.0	55.4
6.7	8.4	6.0	5.3	4.6	5.2	5.9	6.5	9.7	7.4	6.5
5.7	6.4	5.7	4.7	3.8	8.3	8.1	9.1	11.6	13.6	8.2
107.1	103.1	100.2	97.1	102.5	105.3	95.8	82.5	71.1	59.2	54.6
67.5	53.8	56.4	42.3	36.6	49.4	39.0	46.5	39.3	46.4	48.6
1.4	....	....	....	....	....	2.8	1.1			
$ 302.6	$ 274.6	$ 265.1	$ 241.3	$ 237.0	$ 266.9	$ 267.6	$ 260.7	$ 258.0	$ 265.4	$ 244.1
$ 2.3	$ 13.4	$ 29.0	$ 40.1	$ 20.8	$ 6.9	$ 65.9	$ 100.1	$ 145.5	$ 132.9	$ 104.4
2,251.7	2,232.3	2,180.4	2,205.3	2,256.2	2,349.6	2,120.4	2,069.0	1,918.3	1,884.2	1,830.5
1,738.9	1,722.7	1,710.7	1,711.9	1,794.7	1,797.6	1,724.0	1,639.6	1,463.8	1,338.2	1,226.6

year after the war, expenditures were approximately $520 million. There-after, they declined gradually, but it was not until the late seventies that they found a new level at about $250 million a year. Expressed in another way, Federal per capita expenditures were $2 in 1860, $37 in 1865, $14 in 1866, and $4.40 in 1884. From approximately 1.5 per cent of the national income in 1860, expenditures rose to between 20 and 25 per cent during the war and then dropped to 4 per cent in the late seventies.[2]

The reduction in dollar sums resulted from decreases in interest pay-ments and military expenditures and was partially offset by increases in civil expenditures, pension payments, and outlays for public works.

Interest on the public debt accounted for about 40 per cent of all ex-penditures, about twice as much as aggregate prewar spending. In later years, through debt repayment and refunding, interest payments were cut to about one-third, accounting for less than 20 per cent of all Federal spending. Within six months, the Army was reduced from 1 million to

[2] *Historical Statistics of the United States*, pp. 14, 26.

200,000 and within a year, to 50,000. But the savings from this rapid demobilization were offset to some extent by the high costs of Southern occupation and sporadic skirmishes with the Western Indian tribes. Gradually, by 1871 the Army outlays dropped to $30 million, at which they continued for the next fifteen years despite a substantial growth in the country's population. As the private mercantile marine was disintegrating,[3] interest in developing the Navy dropped to a vanishing point. Naval expenditures decreased almost constantly, and by the eighties they were back to the prewar level.

Increase in Veterans' Pension Payments. Unlike Army and Navy expenditures, payments for pensions increased steadily, accounting for more than 20 per cent of all Federal expenditures in 1884 compared with 3 per cent in 1866. For many years, pensions to veterans were paid only in cases of disability arising directly from military service. In 1871 and 1878 the requirement of a service-connected disability was waived for veterans of the War of 1812 and their unremarried widows, but it was retained for all others.

It was often difficult to decide whether or not a disability was due to military service, and many disabled veterans did not bother to file pension claims. This led to the development of a new profession—the pension agent, who, for a specific fee, would file a pension claim for a veteran or his widow and try to prove that a service-connected disability or death was involved in the case. If the application was successful, the pension was paid from the date of filing the claim.

The restrictive features of the pension laws irritated the Grand Army of the Republic, the veterans' organization of the time, which wanted pensions to be paid for service without any disability requirement. Or if this were not possible, it wanted pensions to be paid from the date of discharge. The moment was never more propitious for this demand, as many members of Congress thought that increased pension payments were an ideal method for reducing the Treasury surplus. In 1879 the so-called "Pension Arrears" Act provided that all pensions should be counted from the time of discharge from the service and that their accrued amounts should be paid in lump sums. These "arrears" were estimated to average $1,000 per case—enough to buy a small farm or house. It was claimed that the aggregate costs would not exceed $20 million, but $179 million was paid in the first six years alone. Within one year, the number of pensioners

---

[3] In the fifteen years after the Civil War, the government paid shipping subsidies of $1.5 million to the Brazil Mail Steamship Co., $4.5 million to the Pacific Mail Steamship Co., $425,000 for service to the Sandwich Islands, and $75,000 a year for service to Hawaii by the California, Oregon, and Mexico Line. Yet the value of the entire merchant marine was less than $10 million in 1880 when the subsidy system stopped temporarily.

increased from 26,000 to 138,000, and in two years the annual outlays more than doubled.

The Pension Arrears Act weakened the original principle of compensation for service-connected disability or death. It paved the way for the enactment in 1890 of the vicious principle of universal "service" pensions for all aged veterans and their survivors. However, service pensions were partially justifiable. They were the earliest and crudest form of social security payments. Besides care of Indians, they were the only Federal expenditure of the "social-welfare" type for the benefit of the low-income group. Moreover, unlike the social security system of fifty years later, the pensions, under the regressive tax system of the time, were paid for largely by the low-income group itself.

Civil Expenditures and Public Works. The expansion of the United States, the growth of population, and the increasing importance of the Federal government caused a slow but constant increase in Civil expenditures. The costs of Southern reconstruction were heavy, loans of $16,000 to $48,000 a mile were made to the transcontinental railroad, and loans were made to Mexico. In 1866, while increasing the civil pay, Congress voted itself, despite popular protest, a 66 per cent salary increase. Yet on the whole, the civil list was small and the civil emoluments low. In 1880 there were 21,000 Federal employees other than those in the Post Office. One-half earned less than $1,000 a year, and less than one-tenth earned more than $2,000. Excluding Justices and congressmen, scarcely 150 received $5,000 or more.

TABLE 23. FEDERAL PUBLIC-WORKS EXPENDITURES, 1866–1882
(In millions of dollars)

	1866	1870	1875	1880	1882
Roads and canals..................	$0.1	....	$ 0.1	$ 0.1	$ 0.1
Forts, armories, etc...............	2.2	$1.3	1.4	0.4	0.4
Light stations, etc................	1.4	2.6	2.9	2.4	2.4
Public buildings..................	0.3	2.2	8.6	2.8	2.8
Rivers and harbors...............	0.3	3.5	6.4	8.1	11.6
Totals........................	$4.3	$9.6	$19.4	$13.8	$17.3

SOURCE: Treasury of the United States, *Statement of Appropriations and Expenditures for Public Works*, 1882.

Although expenditures for public works increased sharply, they amounted to only 7 per cent of total expenditures and were an insignificant factor in the national income.

River and harbor expenditures were commonly denounced by conservatives as "pork barrel" legislation, and in 1882 President Arthur was applauded when he vetoed an $18.7 million river and harbor appropriation bill on the ground that some of its projects were not for the "common defense and general welfare, but for the benefit of small localized areas." Since he could not veto specific sections, he rejected the entire bill. But Congress overrode the veto. In retrospect, it appears that the criticisms of river and harbor expenditures were exaggerated, for most of the projects were in the national interest and it was hardly possible to construct projects which would not benefit local areas.

Reduction of Excises. While expenditures were cut drastically, the public, especially in the farm regions, thought that spending could be reduced to the prewar level. However, spending aroused resentment only because it necessitated high taxes. Once taxes were reduced, the new level of government spending was accepted. In 1866 the Federal tax burden was $13 per capita, or between 8 and 10 per cent of the national income, and much lower relatively than the $300 per capita, or more than 20 per cent of the national income, at the end of World War II.

Most taxes had been imposed with the understanding that they would be reduced immediately after the war. However, opinion differed as to which taxes should be reduced first. In general, farmers favored reductions in tariffs, while the industrialists, who were much more influential and articulate, insisted on the repeal of the income tax and certain "nuisance" taxes.[4]

In March, 1865, Congress appointed three experts—David A. Wells, Stephen Colwell, and S. S. Hayes—to recommend revisions in the tax system. Although regularly employed in Britain, this was the first time that a "select commission" of nonpolitical experts was used in the United States. The commission was dominated by Wells, who supported rapid tax reduction rather than rapid debt reduction. He thus differed from the earlier principles laid down by Albert Gallatin but anticipated the later views of Andrew Mellon. In January, 1866, the commission recommended abolishing or reducing "all taxes which tend to check development" and retaining "those which, like the income tax, fall chiefly on realized wealth." Specifically, it urged complete repeal of a multitude of excise and nuisance taxes and the progressive rates in the income tax.

Under pressure of public opinion, Congress, in July, 1866, repealed the taxes on coal, pig iron, books, and magazines and reduced most manufacturers' taxes by 20 to 33⅓ per cent. Having tasted the delights of tax reduction, Congress proceeded to gorge itself. In 1867 and 1868 it repealed all manufacturers' excises and the gross-receipts tax on advertisements

---

[4] Albert S. Bolles (*Financial History of the United States from 1861 to 1885*, p. 405) contended that the income tax was the most unpopular tax. Yet only 1 out of 15 income earners paid an income tax, while every income earner paid excises.

and toll roads and reduced the tax on liquor from $2 to 50 cents a gallon. The losses in revenue from these tax reductions were much smaller than anticipated, as they were partially offset by the greater yields of the lower rates and increased consumption at lower prices.[5]

The excise reductions had mixed effects on the economy. Prices, to the consumer's dismay, often failed to respond correspondingly. Indeed, in many cases they actually advanced, and manufacturers reaped profits at the expense of the Treasury. Where prices were reduced, business failures were common among marginal firms and those having heavy inventories purchased at high prices.

McCulloch, who favored a substantial surplus, was apprehensive over the effects of excise cuts on revenue and recommended the reinstatement of manufacturers' excises or the imposition of a general sales tax. But Congress was dominated by protectionists, who were anxious to eliminate all nontariff revenue. In 1870 "Pig Iron" Kelly of Pennsylvania, the champion of extreme protectionism, introduced a bill to abolish the entire internal-revenue system. Although his plan was not adopted, Congress did repeal the taxes on inheritances and sales. In 1872 many of the stamp taxes were repealed, and in 1883 the last two stamp taxes on matches and patent medicine and the taxes on bank capital and deposits were repealed, leaving only taxes on liquor and tobacco, the 10 per cent tax on state-bank-note circulation, and the ½ of 1 per cent semiannual tax on national-bank notes.

Elimination of the Income Tax. The fate of the income tax was not as easily settled. Eastern conservatives, led by Morrill and Conkling, proposed that the graduated rates of the income tax be eliminated immediately and that the tax itself be repealed in a short time. They were signally successful despite Senator Sherman's plea that the tax be retained. In March, 1867, the exemption was raised from $600 to $1,000 and the rate was reduced to a flat 5 per cent, with an understanding that in 1870 the tax was to end altogether. In the latter year Western congressmen successfully prevented its repeal. They argued that it was the only levy in the whole Federal tax system based on ability to pay and that its abolition would unjustly shift more of the burden of taxation upon the poorer people and dangerously reduce governmental revenue. A compromise was worked out, continuing the income tax for another two years, but with the exemption raised to $2,000 and the rate lowered to 2½ per cent.

Meanwhile, the opponents of the income tax effectively charged that it

[5] The classic demonstration of the greater productivity of a lower rate was the liquor tax, which at the 50 cent a gallon rate produced 3½ times as much revenue in 1869 as it did in 1868 under the $2 rate. The rate reduction practically stopped bootlegging and brought back legitimate production. In 1875, the rate was raised to 90 cents, but this time without permanent ill effect on tax collections.

was unconstitutional, and it was not until 1880, years after the tax was repealed, that the Supreme Court in *Springer v. United States* unanimously decided that the income tax was not a direct tax and therefore not unconstitutional. "Our conclusions," declared the Court, "are that direct taxes, within the meaning of the Constitution, are only capitation taxes and taxes on real estate, and that the tax of which the plaintiff complains is within the category of an excise or duty."[6]

In 1871 the debate broke out again. Sherman pleaded with the members of his own class—property owners and industrialists—to retain the income tax permanently, pointing out that British industrialists and landowners had made peace with it. He contended that the tax not only was necessary as a matter of justice to counteract the regressive consumption levies, but it was also exceedingly productive and, next to the bank tax, cheapest to collect. But conservative opinion viewed the tax as socialistic and favored its repeal in order to reduce government revenue and thereby relieve the pressure for tariff reduction. Therefore, the income tax was repealed completely in 1872. For the next forty years, the Federal tax system was to be heavily regressive resting solely on consumption.

Improvements in Tax Administration. Much of the inefficiency in the administration of the internal excises during the war and the years immediately thereafter was due to the multiplicity of the taxes employed, their newness, and the inexperience of the personnel. The repeal of most of these taxes opened the way for a vast improvement in the administration of the excise system. The system of affixing tax stamps to the taxed package, having shown its worth in the collection of taxes on matches, patent medicines, playing cards, etc., was extended in 1868 with most satisfactory results to the collection of liquor, beer, wine, and tobacco taxes and license duties. At the same time, the local staffs of tax collectors, appointed through local patronage, were abolished, and the work of assessment was centralized in Washington. In addition, the adoption of civil service in 1883 promised further improvements in administration.

In short, out of the colossal financial effort of the war came a reasonably efficient, but scarcely just, permanent Federal internal-revenue system which was destined to exceed the tariff as a revenue producer.

Tariff Revision. In theory, the tariff was closely related to internal taxes, since it was raised during the war to offset the adverse effects of internal excises on the competitive position of American manufacturers. Therefore, it was expected that, as excises were reduced, tariffs would be reduced correspondingly. However, at this juncture the rationale for wartime tariff increases was conveniently forgotten, emphasis being

[6] *Springer v. United States,* 102 U.S. 586 (1880).

shifted to the need of a high tariff revenue in order to retire the public debt. Under the guise of fiscal requirements protectionism was consolidated, and attempts to reduce tariffs met with little success. In 1866, under David Wells's influence, an attempt was made to modify the tariff. Not only was it defeated, but in 1867 and 1869 the protectionists took advantage of the backwash in sentiment to increase the duties on woolens and copper. In 1870, as revenue continued to exceed expenditures, duties on tea, coffee, sugar, wine, molasses, and spices were reduced without disturbing the principle of protection. A slight concession was made to free trade by lowering the rate on pig iron, but the duty on steel rails was raised.

In 1872 the opponents of protection won their first unqualified victory, but it was extremely crude and short-lived. Congress reduced all duties 10 per cent, placed tea and coffee on the free list, and reduced the duties on salt and coal 50 and 40 per cent, respectively. However, the 10 per cent reduction was repealed in 1875, following a decline in revenue induced by the depression of 1873. Thus, protectionism was more solidly entrenched than at the close of the war.

Tariff Revision of 1883. The recovery of business in 1878 and the consequent rise in revenue surpluses encouraged importers and Western farmers to renew their demands for tariff reduction. The existing tariff was attacked as an excrescence of the Civil War, a barrier to trade with other nations, and an unfair and unnecessary tax on the necessities of life, maintained more for the benefit of manufacturers and of a few trusts than for the good of the overflowing Treasury.

Although President Arthur was a staunch protectionist, he did not insist on retaining existing rates in the face of a mounting surplus, for he realized that, if tariff reductions were not effected by the friends of protection, they would be effected by its enemies. In 1882 when an unprecedented surplus of $146 million appeared, Congress, at Arthur's recommendation, created a commission to inquire into the possibility of tariff and excise reductions. Arthur appointed four representatives of industry and five government officials as commissioners, with John L. Hayes, secretary of the Wool Manufacturers Association, as chairman. Hayes frankly stated that he hoped to save the principle of protection by an unwilling "concession to public sentiment."[7] The Commission traveled all over the country, heard 604 witnesses, and brought in recommendations for tariff reductions estimated at 25 per cent. But these were largely disregarded. In the "elegant eighties," industrialists of high-tariff inclinations were increasing their political influence. The representatives of iron, sugar, and wool made their presence felt wherever congressmen discussed tariff rates. Under the

[7] F. W. Taussig, *Tariff History of the United States*, p. 249.

circumstances the Tariff Act of 1883 made little dent in the armor of protection. By and large, duties were reshuffled rather than reduced.[8] In fact, the general level was raised, the average duty collected being 45.9 per cent in 1885 compared with 42.5 per cent in 1883.

After the Democrats gained control of the House, they attempted in 1884 to pass a horizontal reduction of 20 per cent. Unscientific as this measure was, it offered a means for reducing the tariff. But it was opposed by a substantial segment among the Democratic congressmen themselves and was defeated, 159 to 155.

Amid the attempts to reform tariff rates, changes occurred in customs administration. During the Civil War—in 1862 and 1863—two important acts were passed, setting up machinery for consular invoices and creating the office of foreign agent. Imports continued to be valued at the foreign-market price, but in no case below the invoice value. The system of moieties, under which all fines, forfeitures, and compromises were divided 50 per cent to the Treasury and 25 per cent each to the informer and the collecter, was continued. In time the moieties arrangement demonstrated abuses. Collectors encouraged tax evasion, and it was impossible for an import business to live up to the technicalities of the law. As a result, the moieties system was repealed in June, 1874.

Fiscal Results of Tax Revision. The steady reduction in internal taxes caused a decline in revenue, but not to the extent estimated. It was expected that the 1866 to 1868 excise tax reductions alone would reduce revenue by $200 million, but the expansion of consumption and improvement in tax administration limited the loss to only $112.6 million.

Since tariffs were not markedly reduced, customs receipts increased, under the influence of industrial prosperity, from $179 million in 1866 to $200 million in the eighties.

Receipts from the sale of public lands, though relatively unimportant, continued to follow the business cycle. They increased from $665,000 in 1866 to $4 million in 1869, declined during the depression of 1873, and then swelled to $9.8 million in 1884. This surprising increase took place despite the Homestead Act of 1862, which made it possible for a settler to obtain 160 acres free by improving a claim for a period of five years. However, claims could also be preempted in six months by paying $1.25 an acre. This benefited the speculator, since he could file claims through dummies and preempt the land at the minimum price.

It was clear that the flow of Federal revenue was much more closely synchronized with changes in business activity and national income than

---

[8] Thus, the duties on steel rails, pig iron, copper, raw wool, and cheaper textiles were lowered slightly, without, however, impairing their protective nature. The duties on finer cotton and woolen goods were raised.

was the flow of expenditures. The long-run tendency of revenue was toward expansion, while Federal expenditure tended to stabilize at a low level. As a result, surpluses were realized in every year from 1866 to 1893.

Funding Short-term Obligations and Greenbacks. The aggregate Treasury surplus of about $1.3 billion in the years 1866 to 1885 made possible a great reduction in the Federal debt. But to accomplish this, it was also necessary to reorganize the debt.

The debt reached a peak on September 1, 1865, at $2.8 billion (see Table 24). Over 46 per cent was in short terms and, since cash was unavailable to pay it off, had to be refunded with long-term bonds. This was a delicate operation and required careful planning.

In addition to the short-term obligations, more than 15 per cent of the net debt was in the form of non-interest-bearing greenbacks. When first issued, they were clearly a monetization of the debt and thus were both debt and money. It was originally agreed that they would be retired as rapidly as possible after peace, but like all other types of paper money, they were not redeemable in specie.

Conservatives, in general, supported a fiscal policy which would contract greenbacks rapidly. A few, including ex-Secretary Chase, favored immediate redemption in specie without formal contraction. But the majority, including Secretary McCulloch and David Wells, recommended retirement and cancellation either by the use of the large Treasury surplus or by funding into long-term bonds.

In his annual report for 1866, McCulloch contended that depression was inevitable unless specie payments were quickly resumed. He thought resumption could be accomplished only by deflating the American price level, thereby stimulating exports and increasing the domestic gold supply. Although rejecting the quantity theory of money, McCulloch inconsistently believed that prices could be lowered by taking the greenbacks out of circulation. This deflationary program was opposed by those who believed that contraction would reduce prices, hurt debtors, lower the national income, and reduce government revenue. The most influential member of this group was Senator Sherman, who favored a debt-management policy under which greenbacks would be left strictly alone while the interest-bearing debt was paid off or refunded.

From the standpoint of the money cost to the Treasury, Sherman's proposal was much more economical. But McCulloch's plan offered a quicker resumption of specie payments. Furthermore, it would reduce the money stock and would not increase the amounts available for private investment or speculation, whereas Sherman's plan would take cash obtained from regressive taxes and transfer it, through bond purchases, to investors and speculators. In the long run, Sherman's plan of debt management was adopted, but at first McCulloch's program prevailed, although not so completely as he wished.

The Funding Act of April 12, 1866, gave McCulloch much of what he wanted. It authorized him to convert the short-term notes and certificates into 6 per cent 5–20 bonds and to retire $10 million of greenbacks within six months and $4 million per month thereafter. McCulloch wasted no time. By February, 1868, he had reduced the greenbacks to $356 million, eliminated the certificates of indebtedness and the 5 per cent notes, almost eliminated the compound-interest notes, and reduced the 7.3 per cent notes by more than half.

Instead of contracting the currency with Treasury surpluses, McCulloch should have recommended that the holders of greenbacks be given the privilege of converting them into United States bonds at par. Had this privilege, which had been a part of the first legal-tender act, been re-adopted in 1866, the legal tenders would have been refunded gradually without provoking political controversy. As it was, poor crops and a panic in Great Britain caused a business recession and a sharp drop in prices. The contraction program was immediately blamed, and in February, 1868, the Funding Act was repealed, and retirement of the greenbacks was suspended. Then, in his report of 1868, McCulloch belatedly recommended that Congress reestablish the conversion privilege, but Congress ignored the recommendation and deferred the solution of the problem to the future.

Controversy over Payment of Debt in Coin. There was also an ethical aspect to the greenback controversy. During the war the government sold bonds at par for greenbacks, enabling those who possessed gold to reap a windfall profit by buying greenbacks at depreciated values and converting them into bonds at par. The government also paid interest in gold, even though some bond issues did not specifically require it.

The debtor classes contended that debt payments in specie gave bondholders enormous profits. Calling for the same money "for the bondholder and the plowholder," they demanded that interest on the debt be paid in currency, that is, in greenbacks.

Conservatives were horror stricken. To them the "Ohio plan," as the scheme to pay interest in greenbacks came to be known, was not only heresy but outright dishonesty. They recalled that in selling the war obligations, Cooke, acting as the government's agent, had promised coin (gold or silver) payment, and they asserted that, if the government should break this binding promise, its credit and honor among nations would be lost.

The Ohio plan was popularly ascribed to Senator Pendleton, one of the leading contenders for the Democratic nomination for President.

President Johnson also defended the greenback position. He went even further and suggested that henceforth payments of interest be credited against the principal of the debt. However, Johnson had little influence, since the gap between his ideas and those of the radical Republicans was steadily widening.

The agrarians could do nothing but win a few futile and temporary victories. The Democratic platform of 1868 endorsed the Ohio plan, but the Democratic nominee, the New York banker Horatio Seymour, immediately repudiated it. Another hollow victory was gained when President Johnson, on March 3, 1869, vetoed a bill pledging payment of both bonds and United States notes in coin. The Republicans, with Grant as nominee, had declared for gold payments, and when Grant was inaugurated, the gold-payment bill was immediately repassed and became law on March 18, 1869. Thus, the conservatives gradually approached their goal of resumption of specie payments, but the method of accomplishing it still remained to be worked out, and complete victory was not to be gained by the hard-money forces until 1900, if then.

Refunding the Long-term Debt. By 1868, practically all of the short-term debt had been funded, and the fundamental problem of debt management changed. As the supply of capital funds increased because of rising national income, rapid debt repayment, and large capital imports, market interest rates declined considerably below the 6 per cent paid by the Treasury on its long-term obligations. Fortunately, most of the outstanding bonds were callable after five years and could be refunded into lower interest-bearing securities. George C. Boutwell, the new Secretary of the Treasury, was determined to take advantage of the decline in interest rates. At his recommendation Congress passed the refunding acts of July, 1870, and January, 1871, authorizing the issue at par for gold of $500 million of 10-year 5 per cents, $300 million of 15-year 4½'s, and $1 billion of 30-year 4's, but not more than $1½ billion in the aggregate. The bonds were not callable, they were payable in coin and were nontaxable, and the Treasury was allowed ½ of 1 per cent on their face value for the defrayment of selling expenses.

The fixing of a thirty-year term for the 4's without privilege of call was a mistake. But Congress erroneously believed that 4 per cent bonds could be sold only if a long term was provided. The possibility that interest rates would continue to fall and that the government might have the funds necessary to repay the bulk of the existing debt before maturity was not considered. Yet this is exactly what eventually happened.

Disturbances in Europe caused by the Franco-Prussian War and the low commissions which the Treasury was able to allow from its expense allowance delayed refunding operations. The first issue was offered in

1871, but refunding was not completed until 1879. At the same time the Treasury continued to retire large blocks of the debt, and as a result of refunding and retirement, the whole debt structure was revolutionized.

TABLE 24. CHANGES IN FEDERAL DEBT, 1865–1889
(In millions of dollars)

	August 31, 1865	July 1, 1870	July 1, 1875	July 1, 1880
Funded debt:				
3 per cent bonds........	$ 14.0	$ 14.0	$ 14.0	$ 14.0
4 per cent bonds........	0.6	....	0.7	739.3
4½ per cent bonds......	....	....	....	250.0
5 per cent bonds........	235.2	221.7	607.1	484.9
6 per cent bonds........	859.8	1,765.3	1,100.9	235.8
Totals.............	$1,109.6	$2,001.0	$1,722.7	$1,724.0
7.3% notes.............	$ 830.0			
Other short-term debt*....	443.2	$ 45.5		
Matured debt............	1.5	3.7	$ 11.4	$ 7.6
Non-interest-bearing debt:				
United States notes.....	433.2	356.1	375.8	346.7
Fractional currency.....	26.3	39.9	42.1	7.2
Other.................	2.1	34.5	80.3	34.9
Totals.............	$ 461.6	$ 430.5	$ 498.2	$ 388.8
Gross debt.............	$2,845.9	$2,480.7	$2,232.3	$2,120.4
Cash balance............	88.2	149.5	142.2	201.1
Net debt...............	$2,757.7	$2,331.2	$2,090.0	$1,919.3

SOURCE: *Annual Reports of the Secretary of the Treasury*, 1867, 1870, 1875, 1880.

* Includes 6% certificates of indebtedness, $85.1 million; temporary loans (4, 5, and 6%), $107.1 million; 5% notes, $34.0 million; and 6% compound interest notes, $217.0 million.

Secretaries Boutwell, Richardson, Bristow, and Morrill sold bonds through syndicates headed at first by Jay Cooke and later by Drexel, Morgan and Co.[9] The syndicates received a commission of ¼ to ½ of 1 per cent, the latter rate being allowed when a syndicate assumed all expenses of preparation and shipment of the bonds and the cost of transmitting the proceeds. For a time Sherman continued the contract negotiated by Secretary Morrill for the sale of the 4½ per cent bonds. He then terminated it, and a new contract was drawn for the sale of the first $75 million of the 4 per cent issue. Thereafter, he made use of the syndi-

[9] The arrangement was well illustrated by the contract of August, 1876, between Secretary Morrill and a syndicate composed of Belmont, Drexel, Morgan, Seligman, Morton, and Bliss. The bankers agreed to sell $40 million of 4½ per cents with the right to subscribe for an additional $260 million. They were to receive ½ of 1 per cent commission and assume all the expenses of printing and issuing the refunding bonds.

cate arrangement for the sale of some 4's and 4½'s in Europe, but for the greater part of the 4 per cent issue the Treasury served as its own agent. After some experimentation with this method of sale, the Secretary settled upon a flat discount of ⅛ of 1 per cent on subscriptions of $1,000 or more. It is estimated that this direct sale of bonds saved the Treasury over $1 million.

The refunding operations cut interest costs substantially. Because of constant retirement, the debt was cut in half, from $78.25 per capita in 1865 to $37.74 in 1880. However, the per capita annual interest charge was reduced by more than 60 per cent from $4.25 in 1865 to $1.56 in 1880. Nevertheless, the refunding operations might have been more successful if the bonds had been made callable. In a short time the market interest rate sank below 3 per cent, with the result that the government was saddled with excessive interest charges on its frozen 4, 4½, and 5 per cent noncallables, which immediately went to a premium. Although the Treasury had large revenue surpluses, it could not retire the debt except by purchase in the open market at heavy extra cost. As in the 1830's and 1850's, surpluses once again became a financial headache.

The Economic Effects of Federal Fiscal Policy. The revenue system which emerged from the postwar tax revisions was completely regressive, since it placed a relatively heavier burden on the lower income group. On the other hand, government expenditures for the benefit of lower income groups were only moderate. Debt management, with its emphasis on rapid debt retirement, tended to transfer money assets from nonsavers in the lower income brackets to those in the upper brackets who saved most of their incomes. Fortunately, there were ample investment outlets for savings, and in the long run, debt retirement benefited society by increasing capital accumulation, investment, and productivity. Nevertheless, at times the channels of investment were temporarily clogged by excess savings.[10]

On the whole, therefore, Federal fiscal policy was deflationary. But its influence in causing the secular price decline of the last half of the nineteenth century was exaggerated. The Federal tax burden averaged about 3 per cent of national income, while the combined state and municipal tax burden was twice as great. The Federal gross debt in 1892 was $14.74 per capita, while private debt was $515 per capita. The Federal government's economic role was, therefore, far less important than that of state and local government and insignificant compared with that of private enterprise.

[10] In pre-Keynesian 1874, one of the leading metropolitan newspapers criticized the rapid debt-repayment policy, charging that it depressed business because investments could not be found for the capital that was being thrown into the market and because it depressed interest rates and discouraged capital funds from seeking investment. (Quoted from H. C. Adams, *Public Debts*, p. 42).

Chapter 16: POST-CIVIL WAR MONETARY AND BANKING READJUSTMENTS

In the decades after the Civil War, the clash over fiscal policy was mild in comparison with the bitter disputes between debtor and creditor classes over greenbacks, free silver, and national banking. These issues were intermeshed with fiscal problems, but above all, they were related to secular and cyclical changes in prices, especially farm prices.

As a result of heavy war expenditures financed by currency and credit expansion, the price level in September, 1864, was more than double the prewar average. After the war, as industrial and agricultural production increased phenomenally, prices began to decline. Debtor classes complained that they had to pay their debts in scarcer and dearer dollars. Believing in a crude quantity theory of money, farmers and impecunious seekers of capital blamed their difficulties on an insufficient supply of money and demanded that the government increase the circulation, either by printing more greenbacks or, at a later date, by remonetizing silver.

The advocates of "sound money"—the creditors and financiers—contended, more correctly, that the secular price decline was caused by increased production. The majority denied that increasing the money supply would raise prices. But some frankly favored a contraction of the money supply and a deliberate deflation of prices in order to make possible a quick return to a specie standard.

In the monetary controversy which raged for the next thirty years, the advocates of sound money prevailed just as they did in fiscal policy. The supporters of easy money pressed their claims only when prices fell. When prices rose and relative prosperity came to the farm, agitation for monetary panaceas declined. The creditor classes then breathed more easily and mistakenly thought that the so-called "monetary heresies" had passed away.

Changes in the Banking Structure, 1865 to 1890. While currency and the price level were being bitterly debated, important changes took place in American banking. Only one of these, the steadily declining importance of national-bank currency, was clearly recognized. Yet even more important, though much less discussed, were the constant growth of checkbook money, the resurgence of state banking, the secular growth in the percentage of total assets represented by loans, and the close correlation between business activity and changes in total bank loans.

Up to 1874 changes in the National Bank Act and the declining importance of state banks caused a relative as well as an absolute increase in national-bank-note circulation. In the decade after 1874 the quantity of national-bank notes remained about the same, while other forms of money increased. After 1884 the volume of national-bank notes declined, since they could not be profitably issued with government bonds selling at a premium and yielding only 1.4 to 2.7 per cent, or less than enough to cover taxes on circulation and other costs.

TABLE 25. BANK OPERATIONS, 1863–1888
(Dollar figures in millions)

Year	National banks								State banks			
	No.	Loans	Hold-ings of gov-ern-ment obli-ga-tions	Other in-vest-ments	De-pos-its*	Ratio of reserve to deposits (New York City) (per cent)	Cir-cula-tion	Ratio of national bank notes to total circula-tion (per cent)	No. re-port-ing†	Loans and dis-counts	De-posits	Cir-cula-tion
	(1)	(2)	(3)	(4)	(5)	(6)	(7)	(8)	(9)	(10)	(11)	(12)
1863	66	$ 5	$ 6	...	$ 8	....	......	..	1,466	$649	$394	$238.7
1864	473	71	93	...	119	....	$ 31.2	4	‡	‡	‡	179.2
1865	1,294	362	394	...	456	....	146.1	19	‡	‡	‡	142.9
1866	1,634	550	450	$18	572	....	276.0	37	‡	‡	‡	20.0
1870	1,612	719	429	24	557	....	288.6	42	‡	‡	‡	2.2
1874	1,983	926	424	27	635	33.4	340.3	44	‡	154.4	137.6	1.2
1876	2,091	934	395	32	659	30.7	316.1	42	633	179.0	165.9	1.0
1878	2,056	835	424	36	653	26.8	311.7	41	475	169.4	142.8	0.8
1880	2,076	995	407	44	846	26.4	337.4	29	650	281.5	298.8	
1882	2,239	1,209	404	67	1,086	25.4	352.5	25	704	404.6	426.7	
1884	2,625	1,270	376	73	995	35.6	330.7	23	852	489.1	514.1	
1886	2,809	1,399	324	83	1,164	27.2	307.7	20	891	488.0	557.0	
1888	3,120	1,628	260	96	1,358	28.2	245.3	15	1,523	682.7	667.9	

SOURCE: Columns (1) to (5), Federal Reserve Board, *Banking and Monetary Statistics*, p. 20; column (6), *Annual Report of the Secretary of the Treasury*, 1893; columns (7) and (12), *Annual Report of the Secretary of the Treasury*, 1949; column (8), *National Monetary Commission*, Vol. 21; columns (9) to (11) *Annual Reports of the Comptroller of the Currency*, 1876–1888.

* Not including interbank.
† Data on state banks estimated.
‡ Not available.

Inflationists used the decline of national-bank currency as ammunition in fighting for expansion of currency. But while they threw brickbats at Wall Street, their argument was vitiated by the continuous increase in the use of checks.[1] Sound-money men were quick to point out that this

[1] Checks had first become more important than bank notes during the late thirties in the city areas and in the middle fifties for the country as a whole. By the late eighties the Comptroller of the Currency estimated that less than 10 per cent of the total volume of business transactions were in currency.

growth in checkbook money more than offset the decline in the circulation of currency and coin. However, in the West and in the South, where the quantity theory had its largest following, farmers were unimpressed, for unlike city dwellers, they still transacted their business in currency.

Checkbook money also helped to stop the expansion of national banking at the expense of state banking. In the early postwar years, when bank notes were still of great importance, the 10 per cent Federal tax made it unprofitable for state banks to issue notes. More and more of them took out national charters,[2] and during the next decade, the number of state banks declined almost 60 per cent and their loans, about 70 per cent. However, with the increased use of checkbook money, state banks began to regain their importance. Another factor in their favor was the fact that state regulation of banking was on the whole less rigid than national regulation. Most state laws required less capital and lower reserves, and they permitted branch banking and loans on real estate, while the National Bank Act prohibited the latter and permitted the former only in exceptional cases.

In one sense the increased use of checkbook money illustrated the pervasiveness of industrial capitalism in post-Civil War America. Equally illustrative was the fact that commercial banks were able to put more of their assets into commercial loans in contrast to the earlier period of heavy real estate loans and the later period of large investments, especially in government bonds. This was therefore the golden age of banking as it was viewed by the orthodox, for it was the heyday of the "real bills" doctrine and bank assets were distinguished for liquidity. Consequently, the banking system was flexible, with banks expanding their loans up to the limit of their reserves in prosperity, liquidating quickly in panics, and emerging into the depression with very heavy reserves.

Defects of the National Banking System. The national banking system was immeasurably superior to the old state banking system. It replaced a heterogeneous mass of paper issues with a uniform currency and tended to strengthen the banking system against failures and overissue. But it was not completely satisfactory. The volume of its bank notes was inelastic. Reserves were pyramided and immobile; the geographic distribution of circulation was arbitrary; and central-bank functions could not be performed efficiently.

In the long run, national-bank currency was inelastic and could not conform to the needs of business, for it was secured by United States bonds and depended not on the requirements of business, but on the current market rate of interest, the state of the government-bond market, and the fiscal policy of the United States Treasury. During the thirty-five years

[2] As Comptroller of the Currency Clarke said with unintentional irony in his annual report for 1865: "Nearly all of the state banks have voluntarily changed."

after the Civil War, market interest rates were declining. Since the interest on government bonds was fixed, they naturally went to a premium, prompting the banks, as already described, to sell them and to contract their circulation.

But even over short periods, national-bank currency did not expand and contract with the needs of business. In periods of prosperity, when the business community wanted more money, national-bank circulation invariably declined, because the banks had more attractive outlets for their funds than government bonds. In periods of recession, the situation was reversed, and currency expanded even though the demand for it was lacking. At the same time the system hampered government fiscal operations, because the Treasury was reluctant to pay off the debt upon which the national-bank notes depended.

Nor was national-bank currency well adapted to the needs of commercial agriculture. Rigidly restricted as it was by government securities and the possibilities of profit on bond sales, it could not satisfy the farmer's need for extra funds in the spring for planting and in the fall for moving crops.

Perhaps the greatest weakness of the system lay in the fact that it encouraged the tendency for bank reserves to concentrate in New York City. For many years out-of-town bankers had deposited their excess funds in New York City because it had a thriving call-loan market in which funds could be invested without sacrificing liquidity, because many New York banks offered interest on out-of-town deposits, and because New York banks were well known, for the city was the chief center for export and import trade.

The National Bank Act encouraged this flow of funds by allowing out-of-town banks to deposit part of their reserves in New York banks. Thus, reserves were pyramided, since both the depositing bank and the depository bank counted the same funds as reserves. In addition, the practice made reserves immobile and continued to subject the commercial banking system to the peculiar demands of the farming communities. In order to take care of the increased demand for farm loans during spring planting and fall harvesting, country banks drew extensively on their deposits in New York. Consequently, twice a year, credit in the New York money market tightened and interest rates rose, creating a mild crisis. But as soon as the seasonal burst of activity in agriculture spent itself, the financial community returned to normal. Unfortunately, there were times, such as 1873, 1893, and 1907, when the demand for funds was larger than anticipated or loans could not be easily liquidated. Then credit would be unobtainable at any price, cash would go into hoarding, and panic conditions would prevail.

Under the national banking system, there was no central organization or institution which could act as a stabilizing influence in the money market during periods of rapid inflation or deflation. The Treasury, operating through the subtreasuries, and a few national banks, such as the First National of New York, did exert some central banking influence, but it was weak and ineffective. Local clearinghouses also assumed some leadership, but most of their activities were undertaken after a crisis had begun, not before. The other advantages of central banking were also completely lacking. There was no agency to act as a link between the banks and the Treasury, the government lacked a centralized fiscal agent, there was no central control over the nation's gold supply or discount rate, and there was no bankers' bank which could rediscount paper for individual banks.

The most annoying weakness of the national banking system was that clearing of checks between different geographic areas was carried on through correspondent banks in an antiquated and costly manner. The classic example was the clearance of a check drawn on Sag Harbor, Long Island, and deposited in Hoboken, New Jersey. Before it made the return trip of 93 miles to Sag Harbor, the check traveled for ten days, covered 1,223 miles, and passed through ten banks. The mobility of capital funds, under the circumstances, was not at its optimum efficiency.

Other Criticisms of National Banking. From its very outset, the national banking system failed to gain favor with the public at large. The ever-popular charge of monopoly was levied against it, even though it was based on the New York free banking system which had been expressly passed as an antimonopoly measure. The government's practice of favoring some national banks with deposits was also criticized as inimical to the American tradition of equal opportunity. Finally, it was commonly believed that the national banks made a double profit—one from interest on the securities deposited with the Comptroller of the Currency, another from interest on the bank notes issued against the bonds. Despite its wide acceptance and superficial logic, the charge was not true, for the constant decline in national-bank-note circulation offered conclusive evidence that the expenses and restrictions involved in issuing notes were so great that it actually did not pay banks to take advantage of the privilege. The national banks had to pay the cost of redeeming national-bank notes. In addition, they had to pay a ½ of 1 per cent semiannual tax on circulation. Note issues also restricted a bank's lending power, for neither national-bank notes nor government bonds could be counted as reserves and until 1874 a 25 per cent reserve had to be maintained against note issues. Furthermore, notes could be issued only up to 90 per cent of the par value of bonds. Since bonds always sold at a premium, banks had to tie up large amounts of their funds against which nothing could be issued.

The public was on more solid ground in contending that the limit imposed on total note circulation and the method of its distribution among the states were neither fair nor economically wise. Originally, the limit was $300 million. By the amendment of March 3, 1865, half was distributed according to population and half by the Secretary of the Treasury according to the existing banking capital, resources, and business of the states and territories. Thus, the older states, having the largest populations and banking capital, received the lion's share of the national-bank-note circulation. The state of Connecticut had more circulation than Michigan, Iowa, Minnesota, Kansas, Missouri, Kentucky, and Tennessee combined, and the per capita circulation of Rhode Island was $77.16, while that of Arkansas was 13 cents.

The Banking System and the Panics of 1873 and 1884. The severe depression of 1873 and its preceding circumstances clearly illustrated how an inefficient banking system could accentuate economic difficulties. During the first eight months of 1872, bank loans increased slowly but continually. In the latter part of August large amounts of cash were withdrawn from the New York banks and the money market tightened. The Treasury gave some assistance by buying some $5 million of bonds to increase bank reserves, but the pressure on the banking system was not relieved until the movement of farm crops had been completed. In the spring of 1873, another similar seasonal difficulty developed, but this time liquidation of loans and securities was difficult because of weaknesses in railroad securities. In May three brokerage houses suspended, but by June the situation was so much improved that businessmen decided that a new spurt of prosperity was about to begin. Unfortunately, this optimistic view was ill-founded. Railroads could not continue to meet their fixed charges, capital imports declined from their high level, and the stock market began to fall. Banks began to contract credit, country banks clamored for funds, and hoarding by individuals increased. In September seven New York banks, holding 72 per cent of total interbank deposits, could not liquidate their loans fast enough to meet the increasing demand for funds, and in a short time they were operating with a reserve deficiency. Businessmen and banks had nowhere to turn, and with progressively accelerated speed, the New York money market headed to inevitable disaster. Then on September 18 came the shock of the decade, when the great banking house of Jay Cooke failed.[3]

On the day after Cooke's failure, Secretary Richardson announced

---

[3] In addition to acting as government agent in refunding operations, Cooke was financing the construction of the Northern Pacific Railroad. Besides pouring his own funds into this project, he tapped the resources of Europe, but he had no close connections with any important European banking house to ensure a continuous flow of funds. The Northern Pacific, therefore, dragged Cooke into bankruptcy when capital imports stopped.

that the government would act to relieve the financial crisis. On September 20 it began to buy 5–20 bonds at par in gold and to pay interest in advance on the debt. At the same time the New York Stock Exchange was closed, and the Clearing House authorized $10 million of clearinghouse certificates to be used in settling interbank balances.[4] By September 25 the Treasury had poured $24 million into the money market and was to pour in $2 million more.[5] But these sums had no perceptible effect, for the amount was too small. By this time, too, cash was at a premium and the Treasury's offer to purchase bonds at par in gold was quickly accepted by potential hoarders. Had the Treasury offered to buy bonds at par in greenbacks, instead of gold, hoarders would probably not have been attracted, and those who needed cash desperately might have obtained more of it.

The events of 1873 were repeated on a smaller scale in the spring of 1884. The usual seasonal demand for funds combined with difficulties in railroad financing sent the banking system into convulsions. Loans and discounts were called, wiping out secondary deposits. Primary deposits were withdrawn into hoards, and rapid deflation took place. The New York Clearing House again resorted to certificates in a crude attempt to act as a central bank. Altogether $24.9 million of certificates were issued, and at one time $21.9 million were in use. Fortunately, the repercussion of 1884 was comparatively short. By the latter part of 1885 business activity was recovering, and the demand for funds again caused an expansion of bank deposits.

Ineffectual Attempts to Strengthen National Banking. During the two decades after the Civil War, many ineffectual attempts were made by Congress to correct the decline in circulation, the maldistribution of circulation, and the poor competitive position of national banks in relation to state banks.

In 1870 the limit on national-bank notes was increased to $354 million, and under the Resumption Act of 1875 it was abandoned altogether. But because it was already becoming unprofitable to issue bank notes, little advantage was taken of the privilege, and the scarcity and maldistribution of national-bank circulation continued. In 1876 the banks of New Bedford, Massachusetts, had a larger circulation than that of any state in the South. Many authorities recognized that only a fundamental change could increase the circulation. For many years Comptrollers of the Currency regularly recommended that Congress reduce the tax on circulation and allow banks to issue notes up to 100 per cent of the par value of deposited

[4] They were similar to those of 1857 (p. 127) and were again issued against 75 per cent of the value of frozen assets.

[5] The panic reached its high point on Oct. 4 when bank reserves in New York City were down to 12.79 per cent.

bonds. However, the argument over inflating the coinage was too absorbing, and these recommendations were not acted upon until 1900.

Only one effort was made to improve the competitive position of the national banks. In 1882 banks with a capital of less than $150,000 were required to deposit only one-fourth of their capital in bonds with the Comptroller of the Currency instead of one-third (or $30,000), as previously.

Resurgence of Greenbackism. The contraction in the currency supply[6] was accompanied by a continued demand for an increase in the volume of greenbacks, and Secretary Richardson did reissue some notes in 1870 and 1871, but these were quickly withdrawn.

The panic and depression following 1873 stimulated the farmer's interest in greenbackism and caused many businessmen to give temporary support to the movement.[7] Monetary conservatives explained once more that the decline in the price level was caused by increased production and was necessary in order to readjust American prices to world prices and to help the United States restore the specie standard. For the moment, the Treasury was more impressed by the viewpoint of the expansionists, and between March, 1873, and January, 1874, Richardson increased the circulation from $356 million (to which McCulloch's contraction policy had reduced it) to $382 million, and in April, 1874, Congress (29 to 24 in the Senate and 140 to 102 in the House) increased the greenback circulation and raised the limit on national-bank currency to $400 million each. After some hesitation, President Grant vetoed the bill with a stinging anti-inflation message.

Passage of the Resumption Act. The defeat of the inflation bill gave added courage to the sound-money advocates. In June, 1874, they succeeded in limiting the circulation of greenbacks by law to $382 million. Progress toward eventual resumption of specie payments was further accelerated by a paradoxical political development. Having lost the Congressional election in 1874, the Republicans, while still in control of the outgoing Congress, passed the Resumption Act in January, 1875, expecting to saddle the Democrats with the responsibility of enforcing it.[8]

Under the Act, the Treasury was directed beginning January 1, 1879, to redeem in coin any greenbacks presented for redemption. Technically, "coin" meant gold and silver, but since silver had not circulated in forty

[6] See Table 26.

[7] Commodore Vanderbilt, for example, called upon the Treasury to deposit $20 million to $40 million of greenbacks in various banks to relieve the extraordinary tightness in money and credit. (Wheaton J. Lane, *Commodore Vanderbilt*, p. 277.)

[8] The Act was passed, 32 to 14 in the Senate and 136 to 98 in the House. (John Sherman, *Selected Speeches and Reports, 1859–1878*, and *John Sherman's Recollections of Forty Years.*)

years, the word was interpreted to mean gold. To accomplish redemption, the Secretary was authorized to use any unappropriated surpluses in the Treasury or, if necessary, to sell at par for coin bonds of the type authorized under the Funding Act of 1870. The limit on the issue of national-bank notes was removed entirely. For every $100 of national-bank currency issued after 1875, $80 of greenbacks were to be retired until the total greenbacks were reduced to $300 million. The seigniorage on gold coinage was abolished, and subsidiary silver coins were to be substituted for fractional paper currency.

The Act was regarded as an empty gesture, and there was little expectation that it would succeed in its ultimate objective. In fact, on the day the bill became law, the price of greenbacks fell in the New York gold market.

The law was obscure as to the exact meaning of redemption. Sound-money supporters insisted that greenbacks were to be retired as new national-bank notes were issued, even though total national-bank circulation might be declining. On the other hand, the inflationists contended that greenbacks could be retired only if there was a net addition to national-bank circulation.

Secretaries Bristow and Lot Morrill, being conservatives, retired the greenbacks as new national-bank notes were issued. Accordingly, by November, 1876, they had retired $14.5 million of greenbacks despite a net decline of $29.1 million in national-bank circulation. At the same time $22 million of subsidiary silver had been added, and $13 million of fractional currency was taken out of circulation, resulting in a net contraction of $34.6 million in sixteen months.

The proponents of paper money, incensed by the contraction of the currency, formed the Greenback party and nominated a candidate for President in 1876. Their platform demanded the complete repeal of the Resumption Act, the issue of legal-tender notes convertible at par into 3.65 per cent bonds, the suppression of all bank notes, and the abolition of sales of gold bonds in foreign markets. Although the party had great success in various local elections, it was of small importance nationally.

Accomplishment of Resumption. After the inauguration of President Hayes in 1877, responsibility for resuming specie payments devolved upon John Sherman, the new Secretary of the Treasury. Sherman believed that resumption could not succeed unless the Treasury had a gold fund equal to at least 40 per cent of the outstanding greenbacks. When he took office, the Treasury's gold stock was approximately $25 million, and outside the Treasury there was an additional $100 million, of which the national banks had $23 million. The possibilities of obtaining gold from abroad appeared slim, for both France and Germany were in great need of gold to reorganize their monetary systems.

These obstacles made Sherman's task difficult, but he was equal to the situation. He made American bonds attractive to foreign investors by offering a higher rate of interest than offered by European governments. Each month he sold bonds for gold, using part of the proceeds for refunding and placing the remainder in the Treasury's general fund. Thus, he increased the gross, but not the net, debt. At the same time he prevented a critical drain on the money market by making deposits in the national banks. He also obtained memberships for the Federal subtreasuries in the various clearinghouses, thus making more economical use of the Treasury's gold stock by confining it to the payment of balances.

In the meanwhile, the greenbackers failed in their attempts to repeal the Resumption Act but did succeed in May, 1878, in passing a law stopping further cancellation of greenbacks and freezing them at the amount then outstanding ($346,681,016).

Sherman's ingeniousness and financial ability, although considerable, were not sufficient in themselves to assure the continued success of specie redemption. But fortunately, he was helped by a favorable turn in economic conditions in the latter seventies. At that time there were widespread crop failures in Europe while the United States produced bumper crops, enabling American farmers to sell enormous quantities of foodstuffs. As a result, favorable export balances, which began in 1876, became very large in the four years from 1878 to 1882 and brought in gold which Sherman tapped into the Treasury by means of bond sales. Europe's misfortune and the phenomenal export of American food products also changed the domestic economic scene from depression to recovery.

By November, 1878, the Treasury had built its gold reserve up to $141.9 million. The premium on gold, which measured the depreciation of the greenbacks, fell rapidly, and on December 17, 1878, greenbacks reached par in gold. The free-gold market, after nearly seventeen years of exciting activity, went out of business. On January 2, 1879, according to schedule, the Treasury began to pay out gold for all greenbacks which were presented for conversion. On the first day of resumption, only $135,000 of notes was redeemed for gold, whereas $400,000 of gold was exchanged for paper money.[9] Thus, the nation returned to a metallic standard after seventeen years with an irredeemable paper currency. Monetary conservatives appeared to have won a solid victory against the forces of money and price inflation. Yet in reality, deflation, rather than inflation, had distinguished the period when the nation was on an irredeemable paper standard, and at the very moment of resumption, a new monetary "heresy," "free silver," was appearing.

Resumption was accomplished more easily than had been hoped by even the most optimistic, but specie payment was still on uncertain

[9] For a fuller account of resumption, see *Specie Resumption and Refunding*, House Ex. Doc. 9, 46th Cong., 2d sess.

ground. In restoring the specie standard, too high a gold value had been placed on the dollar, for although American prices had declined sharply since the Civil War, European prices had declined even more sharply. Moreover, greenbacks were not eliminated from circulation, and although their total amount was not excessive, like all paper-money issues they could become an extreme irritant. If business activity declined or the trade balance turned unfavorable or individuals and institutions lost confidence in the currency, paper money would be constantly converted into gold, the gold would be exported or hoarded, and an endless chain would be set in motion which would eventually exhaust the Treasury's gold reserve and make suspension of gold payments merely a matter of time.

Constitutionality of the Greenbacks. All through the great argument over expansion and contraction of the greenbacks, their constitutional status remained uncertain. During the Civil War, the New York State Supreme Court decided that Congress had the constitutional power to issue greenbacks. However, it was not until 1869 that the United States Supreme Court ruled on the matter. In *Hepburn v. Griswold* by a 4-to-3 decision (one justice having resigned before the decision was announced), with Chief Justice Chase writing the majority opinion, the Court decided that greenbacks were not legal tender in payment of debts incurred before 1862 and inferred that they were unconstitutional at all times.

Attorney General Hoar immediately brought a new case before the Court. In the meanwhile, President Grant appointed two new justices, one to replace a recent resignation and the other to increase the panel to nine. By these fortuitous appointments, the minority became the majority, and in *Knox v. Lee* (1872), the Court decided that Congress had the power to issue bills of credit and make them legal tenders during wartime. Eventually, in the case of *Juilliard v. Greenman* (1884) the Court, by liberally interpreting Congress's powers to borrow and to coin money, held, with only one judge dissenting, that Congress had power to issue legal tenders in peacetime as well as in war. Thus the government's right to issue fiat money, or to "emit bills of credit," was finally established after having been debated from the time of the signing of the Constitution.[10]

Outbreak of the Free-silver Movement. In the meanwhile, greenbackism had aroused the traditional American distrust of fiat money, and silver—a commodity of value—had become the hope of those who believed that more money would increase prices.

Before 1873 the United States was legally on a bimetallic standard, the mint being obliged to coin silver or gold whenever either of the

[10] For a fuller discussion of these cases, see John Jay Knox, *United States Notes*, Chap. 11 and Appendix.

metals was presented. But bimetallism existed only in law, not in practice, for from 1792 to 1873 only 8 million silver dollars had been coined. The devaluation of the gold dollar in 1834 had made it more profitable for anyone who owned silver to sell it in the market rather than at the mint.

In 1870 Deputy Comptroller of the Currency Knox drafted a bill to revise, combine, and make more concise all the laws relating to the mints, assay offices, and coinage. In the report accompanying the bill, Knox pointed out that silver dollars did not circulate because their bullion content was worth $1.0312 in gold. He therefore eliminated provision for their coinage.

Knox's report was substantially adopted in the Coinage Act of February 12, 1873. It discontinued the standard silver dollar, increased the silver content of subsidiary coins, and created a new coin of 420 grains of silver, 9/10 fine. This trade dollar was made legal tender up to $5 and was deliberately given an excess bullion content to enable it to compete with the Mexican dollar and other silver coins in the Far Eastern trade. It could not circulate domestically because its bullion value was more than $1.04.

Those who favored an increase in the money supply were not disturbed by the Coinage Act, for owners of silver rarely sold it to the mint and there did not seem to be any possibility that they ever would. However, in a short time the market value of silver began to decline, thereby giving a new and totally unintended meaning to the new law. In July, 1873, Germany adopted a monometallic gold standard and thereafter not only stopped buying silver, but even began to sell it, and soon France and other members of the Latin Union did the same. Of even greater importance were the discoveries of Western silver mines, which made the fabulous Eldorados of the past seem picayune indeed. From a mere $2 million a year in 1861, silver production jumped to $29 million in 1872 and $40 million in 1876. One new mine alone, the Consolidated Virginia, produced $645,000 of silver in 1873 and $16 million in 1875. As production climbed upward, the price of silver spiraled downward.

In the bullion market of 1861, 15.29 ounces of silver was worth 1 ounce of gold. Silver was therefore worth $1.35 an ounce. In 1873 the ratio was 15.92 to 1, making silver worth $1.298 in the market as compared with $1.292 at the mint. But in 1874 silver fell to 16.7 to 1, or $1.238 an ounce. If bimetallism had still been in effect, the silver producer would have been able to sell his silver at the mint for $1.292 an ounce. Accordingly, he denounced the Coinage Act as the "Crime of 1873" and accused it of defrauding him of 5.4 cents on every ounce of silver, the difference between the market price and the old mint price.

Although they supported the restoration of bimetallism most enthusiastically, there were not enough silver-mine owners to cause a change in national policy. The political strength of the movement came from Western and, to a lesser extent, Southern farmers, who were attracted to silver because they thought it would increase prices by increasing the money supply. However, agrarian enthusiasm for silver varied in intensity. It became articulate only when prices fell, and this usually took place when Europe had bumper crops and its demand for American food products declined.

The silver cause also had a moral appeal. Some supported it because they believed that the demonetization of 1873 had been plotted by bloated Eastern capitalists to deprive the farmer of his just share in the social product. Others thought that silver, like gold, had been created to serve as money, and they regarded its demonetization as a sacrilege and a great waste of one of America's most plentiful natural resources.[11]

The Bland-Allison Act. By the middle of the depression of 1873 to 1879, "free silver" was a robust economic force. The passage of the Resumption Act had weakened greenbackism, while tumbling prices brought about a coalition of silver and farm interests. By 1876 the price of silver had fallen so far that it even became profitable to take silver to the mint for coinage into trade dollars, but Congress repealed the legal-tender quality of the trade dollar in 1876 (and abolished it altogether in 1887), thus completely eliminating one of the remaining monetary outlets for silver. The Resumption Act offered some hope to the silverites by providing for the replacement of fractional paper currency with subsidiary silver coins. But these hopes were frustrated in late 1877, when the declining price of silver brought back into circulation many of the subsidiary coins which had disappeared during the Civil War. Moreover, there was little prospect of a new demand for silver to replace worn-out coins, since they were not redeemable at the mint.

The silverites would not accept the apparently inexorable world-wide subordination of silver money. They attempted instead to reestablish bimetallism at the old ratio of 16 to 1 whenever prices became relatively depressed and whenever the farmer was unable to sell his surplus crops in the export market. The first attempt to restore free coinage was made in 1876 by Representative Kelly of Pennsylvania. Since it was introduced shortly before Congress was to adjourn, the bill required suspension of the House rules by a two-thirds vote. The silverites could not obtain this majority, although the vote was 119 to 68 in favor of the bill, demonstrating its widespread popularity.

In 1877 Richard Bland of Missouri introduced another free-coinage bill, which passed the House 164 to 34. Although overwhelmingly outnumbered, the sound-money forces in the Senate, led by Allison, succeeded in modifying the bill considerably. Nevertheless, President Hayes

---

[11] See *Annual Report of the Secretary of the Treasury*, 1889, and Richardson, *Messages and Papers*, Vol. IX, p. 40.

TABLE 26. CHANGES IN CURRENCY AND PRICES, 1866–1884
(July 1)

	1866	1868	1870	1872	1874	1876	1878	1880	1882	1884
	In millions of dollars									
United States notes:										
In Treasury	$73.0	$27.4	$31.0	$11.3	$10.6	$38.3	$25.8	$18.8	$21.4	$28.0
In circulation	327.8	328.6	325.0	346.2	371.4	331.4	320.9	327.9	325.3	318.7
National-bank notes:										
In Treasury	5.5	5.4	11.1	8.6	11.7	16.9	12.8	7.1	6.3	8.8
In circulation	276.0	294.4	288.6	329.0	340.3	316.1	311.7	337.4	352.5	330.7
Subsidiary silver:										
In Treasury	……	……	……	……	……	6.4	6.9	24.4	28.0	29.6
In circulation	……	……	……	……	……	21.1	53.9	48.5	46.4	45.7
Silver dollars:										
In Treasury	……	……	……	……	……	……	15.1	49.5	90.4	139.6
In circulation	……	……	……	……	……	……	1.2	20.1	32.4	40.7
Silver certificates:										
In Treasury	……	……	……	……	……	……	1.5	6.6	11.6	23.4
In circulation	……	……	……	……	……	……	……	5.8	54.5	96.4
Gold coin:										
In Treasury	……	……	……	……	……	……	……	126.1	148.5	204.9
In circulation	……	……	……	……	……	……	……	225.7	358.3	340.6
Gold certificates:										
In Treasury	……	……	……	……	……	……	……	……	……	27.2
In circulation	……	……	……	……	……	……	……	8.0	5.0	71.1
Other currency in circulation*	69.7	57.2	61.6	63.1	64.4	59.0	41.4	……	……	……
	In dollars									
Per capita money in circulation	$18.99	$18.39	$17.50	$18.19	$18.13	$16.12	$15.32	$19.41	$22.37	$22.65
	Index numbers									
Gold price of bushel of spring wheat at Chicago (annual average)	$1.32	$1.70	$0.96	$1.24	$1.08	$1.03	$0.96	$1.05	$1.16	$0.82
Wholesale prices in United States (1860 = 100)	190.7	160.2	142.2	138.6	132.8	118.1	101.2	106.8	108.4	99.2
British wholesale prices (1860 = 100)	102.9	99.9	96.9	110.3	102.9	96.2	88.1	88.8	85.1	77.0

SOURCE: *Annual Report of the Secretary of the Treasury, 1893;* U.S. Census Bureau, *Historical Statistics of the United States; Annual Report of the Director of the Mint, 1898;* Clough and Cole, *European Economic History.*

* Specie on Pacific Coast, state-bank notes, fractional currency.

vetoed it. In February, 1878, Congress overrode the veto, 46 to 19 in the Senate and 196 to 73 in the House. The overwhelming support for the bill came from Western and Southern farmers.[12]

The Bland-Allison Act established a "limping standard," for it was neither fully monometallic nor fully bimetallic. It provided for the purchase of between $2 million and $4 million of silver bullion per month at the market price, to be coined into silver dollars of 412½ grains, 9/10 fine, *i.e.*, at the old ratio of 16 to 1. Part of these dollars were used to pay for the silver purchases. The remainder, which constituted a seigniorage or profit to the government, was covered into the Treasury's general fund. Thus, as the price of silver declined, the number of ounces of silver purchased, the number of dollars coined, and the seigniorage increased correspondingly. Holders of silver dollars could exchange them for silver certificates, but only in denominations of $10 or higher. The silver dollars were full legal tender, but the silver certificates were not legal tender for private transactions, although they were acceptable in payment of public dues, including customs duties.

Although it seemed to be a concession to the inflationists, the Bland-Allison Act was unsatisfactory to both the silverites and the sound-money men. The former continued to agitate for the restoration of free and unlimited coinage of silver. The sound-money men, on the other hand, were hopeful that something would happen to halt the silver movement. Conservative hopes were temporarily satisfied. Per capita money in circulation reached its lowest point in 1879 at $16.64. Thereafter, it began to increase. With the appearance of an export balance, the nation entered a period of prosperity which put an end for the moment to the demand for free coinage of silver.[13]

Difficulties of Putting Silver into Circulation. During the early operation of the Bland-Allison Act, the Treasury found it impossible to get silver into full circulation. It was the first type of money which tellers in the New York banks used in making change or in cashing checks, for it could not be used in settling international balances. Moreover, the New York Clearing House, at the time it admitted the subtreasury to membership, prohibited its use in settling balances of more than $10. Individuals in the East also fought shy of silver and used it to pay taxes and customs duties. The government was meanwhile paying its obligations in gold. By July, 1879, the Treasury had coined $41.3 million in silver and printed $2.5 million in certificates, but it had in its own vaults $33.2 million of the former and $2.1 million of the latter.

[12] The South and West voted 174 to 9 for the bill; New England and the Middle Atlantic states voted 64 to 22 against it.

[13] The last free-silver bill to be introduced for many years passed the House, 114 to 97, in 1878 but failed in the Senate, 23 to 22.

The difficulty disappeared when the economy became prosperous. Increased economic activity required more currency, but the greenback circulation was frozen and national-bank circulation kept on declining. Under the circumstances, silver was the only currency other than checkbook money which could fulfill the requirements of expanding domestic trade. In addition, the Treasury stimulated the use of silver. In 1880 Secretary Sherman agreed to ship silver to the interior free of freight charges, making it possible for Middle Western farmers, who were shipping their crops to Europe, to collect their New York balances without paying transportation costs. In the succeeding year, the Treasury put into circulation $23.6 million of silver from the subtreasuries in New Orleans, St. Louis, Cincinnati, and Chicago, and in the last five months of 1880, Treasury holdings of silver fell from $46.3 million to $18.2 million, and gold holdings rose from $115 million to $150 million.

As long as high-level economic activity continued, the silver coinage prevented the currency famine which would have resulted because of the inelasticity of the monetary system. But if business declined and the balance of payments became unfavorable, silver would become redundant and the Treasury stocks of gold would evaporate, for silver would be used to pay government dues and gold would be exported. The danger would be somewhat mitigated if a government revenue surplus continued, because silver could then accumulate in the Treasury as a hoard, leaving enough other money with which to make government payments.

Difficulties with silver began to appear in 1881 when exports declined and imports increased, resulting in an outflow of gold to cover American obligations on capital account. By June, 1882, gold shipments totaled $32.5 million. Simultaneously, a slight decline in business activity caused silver to accumulate in the Treasury vaults. In order to relieve its monetary indigestion, the Treasury tried to force the banking system to make greater use of silver. In 1882 Congress refused to renew the charter of any national bank which belonged to a clearinghouse refusing to accept silver in the settlement of interbank balances. This government "ukase" had little effect, for although the clearinghouses repealed their restrictions, the banks voluntarily refused to present silver in payment of balances.

The situation became worse in May, 1884, when a decline in business activity made a large fraction of the silver coinage redundant and it began to pile up in the Treasury. It became apparent that, in the absence of a high level of business activity, any attempt to force an increase in silver circulation by government edict would result in hoarding by the banks, private citizens, or the government. In the relatively mild business depression of the eighties the hoarding was done, quite unwillingly, by the government. Yet the farmers, harassed once again by declining prices, returned to their demands for free silver.

Chapter 17: STATE AND LOCAL FINANCE, 1860 TO 1900

The scope of the combined state and local government services, though fluctuating considerably over the period 1860 to 1900, kept pace with the expansion of private-enterprise activity and was far more extensive than the scope of corresponding government activity in most of the other advanced countries of the time. In fact, the scope of state and local activity in this country was altogether unique and can be understood only in the light of the peculiar development of the American pioneer economy. Its characterization by such ideological clichés, borrowed from past European political and economic thinking, as *"laissez-faire"* or, contrariwise, as "government interference" was scarcely proper.

Although the states were forced by conservative public opinion not to engage in internal improvements or lend their credit to private enterprise which engaged therein, they gave ample powers to their subdivisions to carry on such improvements on a local scale and to aid private enterprise in their organization. The states also gave their local communities vast powers to organize essential educational and other social services. At the same time, the states continued to maintain and improve the educational and social-welfare services which they had organized during the preceding half a century. They also extended their regulation of business in order to ensure fair competition and protect consumers and labor against possible abuse and exploitation.

State Expenditures. The development of state finance from 1860 to 1900 can be divided into three periods—the sixties, the seventies, and the last two decades. During the sixties state expenditures were intimately affected by the Civil War and its aftermath and rose sharply. The states made large outlays for bounties to volunteers and afterward for aid to veterans and their survivors and borrowed heavily to that end, with the result that they had large interest charges and debt payments to meet in subsequent years. Their costs of operation were also sharply increased by the rise in wage and price levels. During the seventies state expenditures decreased or at best only kept pace with the growth of population, for the states were paying off their debts and consequently had to pay less for debt interest. At the same time the sharp drop in wage and price levels enabled them to economize. During the period 1880 to 1900, however, state expenditures began again to rise. The states began to extend moderately their regulative services, their care of the poor and mentally ill, their correctional services, and their supports to education, and they also established the first extensive measures for the conservation of natural resources.[1] These three periods in the development of state expenditures are well illustrated by the following per capita expenditures in two states:

Year	Massachusetts	New York State
1860	$0.97	$0.80
1870	3.74	2.32
1880	2.19	1.85
1900	2.51	3.27

SOURCE: Bullock, *Historical Sketch of the Finances of Massachusetts*, pp. 96, 130; Sowers, *The Financial History of New York State from 1789 to 1912*, pp. 314ff.

State Revenues. To finance their increasing expenditures, the states needed new sources of revenue. The state general property tax was proving an ever less satisfactory means for reaching the expanding fiscal capacity of an industrial community, while impinging on the property taxes levied by local communities. The problem of equalizing the burdens of the tax among the communities whose assessments of property were unequal was becoming ever more difficult, and the equalization tables prepared by the state were being constantly challenged by the localities. The required new sources were found in taxes on insurance companies; franchise taxes on railroads, transmission and public-utility companies, and corporations generally; liquor-license taxes; and inheritance taxes. At the same time a number of states reduced the rate of their property tax. By 1902 aggregate state tax revenue reached $1.97 per capita. It was still only 1 per cent of the national income and less than one-third the per capita Federal tax burden of $6.64.[2]

[1] In 1860 New York State spent only $50,000 for regulative services other than public health, by 1880 it spent $300,000, and by 1900, $900,000. It established a railroad commission for the regulation of rates in 1882, a Bureau of Labor Statistics in the same year, and a Board of Mediation and Arbitration and a Board of Factory Inspection four years later; mine inspection in 1890; and sweatshop and bakery inspection in 1892 to 1895. A state board of health was established in 1880 with powers to collect vital statistics, enforce pure food laws, and investigate disease. State expenditures for the mentally ill and for social welfare increased from $263,000 in 1860 to $1,230,000 in 1880 and to $6,500,000 in 1900. A state agricultural experiment station was established in 1880 and a Department of Agriculture, inaugurating cattle inspection and eradication of bovine tuberculosis and plant and nursery diseases, in 1893. Conservation of state resources started in 1868 with the creation of Commissioners of Fisheries, and a Forest Reserve Commission was established in 1885. The Federal land grants under the Morrill Act of 1862 prompted all states to establish agricultural colleges.

[2] The changes which occurred in state tax systems during this period are exempli-

State Debts. During the beginning of the period state debts increased almost everywhere. Loans were floated by the states to pay bounties to veterans and, in some states, to finance internal improvements or to extend loans to railroad companies and other private enterprises. The loans of the latter kind were not very large in the Eastern and the newer Western states, but in the Southern states under the "carpetbag" governments, they reached more than $100 million in seven years on top of previous debts of $146 million. Substantial portions of the funds were misappropriated, while the projects themselves generally ended in failure. When the carpet-baggers were driven out after 1876, the new governments completely repudiated $62 million of the debt and wrote off $88 million of the re-mainder by scaling down the principal and interest on the ground that illegal procedures were followed in issuing the bonds. The combined debts of all the states, after increasing from $257 million in 1860 to more than $450 million ($9.98 per capita) in the middle 1870's, dropped to $211 million ($3.37 per capita) by 1890 and amounted to $270 million ($3.41 per capita) in 1902.

State Administrative Improvements. In the meanwhile, as state expendi-tures increased and covered many more purposes, the administrative or-ganization and procedures devised years before proved increasingly in-adequate. In 1863, the comptroller of the state of New York in his annual report referred to the appropriation bill as an "annual abomination" and "a general avenue to the treasury for claimants and beggars of every description, . . . turning the capitol into an almshouse instead of a seat of government." In many states reform was sought by giving more power

fied by the following figures covering the tax revenues of Massachusetts and New York.

(In thousands of dollars)

Tax	Massachusetts			New York		
	1860	1880	1900	1860	1880	1900
Property......................	$249	$1,495	$1,500	$2,511	$4,941	$ 8,625
Bank..........................	646	1,824	1,873	26	20	89
Insurance company..............	4	222	537	7	83	283
General corporation franchise, includ-ing railroads, etc..............	1	526	1,245	5	165	3,054
Liquor license.................	....	156	805	.....	.....	4,236
Inheritance....................	....	.....	400	.....	.....	4,335
Auction.......................	....	.....	.....	126	33	
Miscellaneous..................	14	16	19	.....	.....	96
Totals.....................	$914	$4,239	$6,379	$2,675	$5,242	$20,718

SOURCE: Bullock, *Historical Sketch of the Finances of Massachusetts*, pp. 121, 134; Sowers, *The Financial History of New York State from 1789 to 1912*, pp. 328–331.

to the governor. In New York State in 1872, the constitution was amended, giving the governor the power to veto individual items or parts of appropriation and other bills. Theretofore, he could veto a bill only as a whole and was frequently restrained from exercising this power by the fact that the greater part of the bill was unobjectionable. By another amendment, the power of the legislature to override the executive veto was further restricted by requiring a two-thirds vote of all the elected members of each house instead of merely the members present. With the multiplication of taxes, a number of states centralized the assessment and collection of all taxes in a single tax commission. Indiana led the movement by establishing the first such commission in 1891, and New York established one in 1896.

Overexpansion and Retrenchment in Municipal Finance. The trend toward urbanization, which had been one of the chief characteristics of the two decades preceding the Civil War, was even more conspicuous in the last half of the century. As a result of the great influx of immigrants and the constant drift of population from the farm to the city, urban population increased in the years 1860 to 1900 from 20 to 40 per cent of total population.

Under the circumstances, municipal services and spending continued to expand. But this expansion did not proceed evenly. It tended to concentrate in periods of business boom and to halt or even to reverse itself in periods of business depression.

Thus, during the years 1866 to 1873 cities everywhere opened and paved miles of new streets; enlarged their water works and sewer systems; built scores of new police and fire stations; reequipped their police and fire forces; constructed new public schools; added high schools (and in New York City free municipal colleges) to their former purely elementary school systems; erected giant bridges, imposing city halls, and courthouses; and founded or laid out municipal museums, zoological and botanical gardens, and public parks. In the larger metropolitan cities private companies built elevated steam railroads which made it possible for the city populations to spread out and build up the outlying city and suburban areas. At the same time the larger cities annexed tremendous suburban areas and having become supercities proceeded, at large additional capital investment and operating costs, to unify and enlarge the municipal facilities throughout the entire area on a metropolitan basis. In addition to borrowing extensively for their own vast construction works, the cities, with the enthusiastic approval of their citizens, continued to lend their credit freely to railroads in hope of obtaining better transportation and attracting more industry and population. Municipal expenditures, tax levies, and debts doubled and trebled. This tremendous expansion in municipal financial operations (in an atmosphere of ruthless industrial buccaneering) afforded an unexcelled opportunity for dishonest municipal officials to divert to themselves a substantial share of public funds. Nearly everywhere corruption blossomed as it never had before.[3]

With the collapse of the business boom in 1873, municipal finance and credit also collapsed. Municipal services were curtailed sharply, and all public improvements were suspended. Many cities defaulted on their obligations and ruined their credit for many years to come. A strong reaction similar to that which had occurred thirty years before in state finance developed against municipal spending and borrowing. By constitutional amendment or statute, municipalities were prohibited from lending their credit to private individuals or corporations, were required to hold referendums before issuing bonds, and were not allowed to borrow in excess of a certain percentage of the assessed valuation or to levy the property tax above a certain rate. For example, in New York State a constitutional amendment, adopted in 1884, limited the debt, other than for water, of cities with more than 100,000 population to 10 per cent of the assessed valuation of real estate and limited tax rates for any purposes other than debt service to 2 per cent of the assessed valuations. After the depression of the 1870's was over, these legal restrictions, taken together with the impaired financial condition of the municipalities, forced many of them to operate at low gear.

As the public need for additional services continued to be very great owing to the continued concentration of population, the expansion of municipal activity was soon resumed, but on a much more restrained scale. With the drop in general wage and price levels and more careful management, the municipal governments were able to furnish more and better services without commensurate increases in expenditures. Having learned their lesson in the 1870's the citizens were much more careful in the 1880's and 1890's. They selected their officials more discriminately and watched their performance more closely.

The whole structure of municipal expenditures changed considerably during these forty years. Public-works expenditures, embracing the construction and care of streets and bridges, water supplies, and sewer systems, took a much larger proportion of the budgets in 1900 than in 1860, while police and fire protection took a smaller proportion. The expenditures for public schools either maintained their position or advanced to a more important position in the total capital and operating spending, and debt service was everywhere a heavier drain than before.

[3] In New York City, the infamous Tweed Ring obtained control over both the state legislature and the city in 1868 and succeeded during the next four years in stealing from the city treasury more than $50 million. All bills for contracts and purchases were rigged, and of every audited bill, 25 per cent went to Tweed, 20 per cent to the comptroller, and 20 per cent to three other top officials.

TABLE 27.   DEVELOPMENT OF FINANCES OF SELECTED CITIES, 1860–1900

Year	New York City	Boston	Providence	Baltimore
Per capita operating expenditures				
1860	$10.10	$19.68	$ 8.04	$13.60
1870	30.90	46.15	23.77	19.80
1880	29.70	34.11	16.25	18.40
1885	34.10	35.94	20.15	16.00
1890	35.10	38.14	21.85	14.30
1900	49.50*	47.42	22.79	†
Tax rates (per cent of assessed valuation)				
1860	1.69	0.93	0.51	1.00
1870	2.25	1.53	1.10	1.50
1880	2.53	1.52	1.23	1.37
1885	2.40	1.28	1.33	1.60
1890	1.97	1.33	1.32	1.85
1900	2.25	1.47	1.42	2.25‡
Per capita debt				
1860	$22.90	$42.55	$ 9.64	$37.00
1870	78.00	50.30	17.33	30.00
1880	88.30	76.73	84.38	24.70
1885	42.30	63.00	69.44	20.90
1890	65.30	69.29	62.21	18.40
1900	26.40	104.00	80.06	15.70

SOURCE: Durand, *The Finances of New York City;* Hollander, *Financial History of Baltimore;* Huse, *The Financial History of Boston;* Stokes, *The Finances and Financial Administration of Providence.*

* 1897.

† Not available.

‡ 1898.

The local property tax became an 80 per cent real estate tax even though realty represented a much lower proportion of total community wealth. The rate of the tax increased from an average of 1 per cent of assessed valuation to more than 2 per cent, while the assessed valuation also rose considerably.

Municipal Financial Reforms. After the disclosures of the early seventies, considerable improvements in municipal management and financial administration were introduced in many places under the influence of reform groups who, temporarily at least, drove the despoilers out of power. State intervention having been a failure, municipal governments not only were restored to local control but received vaster powers of home rule than ever before. New charters were adopted providing for a better framework of municipal government. These charters centralized executive responsibility in the mayor, enlarged his veto powers, and reduced the councils to a subordinate role by depriving them of their powers to let contracts and prohibiting them from granting franchises except through open proceedings and competitive bidding. More orderly processes were provided for the preparation and adoption of the budget and for the authorization of bond issues and management and retirement of debt.

Typical among the reform charters were those of New York City of 1873 and 1898, Boston of 1885, and Baltimore of 1898. In New York City, particularly under the consolidation charter, all appointive powers were centralized in the mayor and all the financial powers in a small board of estimate, dominated by the mayor, comptroller, and president of the council. The charter wiped out the innumerable hidden departmental funds and placed all miscellaneous revenue in a general fund which was subject to the same appropriating process as the general tax levy. It centralized the preparation of the budget in the board of estimate, limiting the municipal council's authority to mere reduction of proposed appropriations. The board of estimate was also authorized to issue bonds, and no approval of the issue by the state legislature was required, but a sinking fund for each loan was made mandatory.

The Boston charter of 1885 separated executive and legislative authorities more clearly, gave the mayor full powers of appointment and removal, enlarged his veto power, and reduced the participation of the council to mere confirmation of appointments. The Baltimore charter followed the lines of the greater New York charter as well as the principles of municipal reform which were being formulated at the time. It made the mayor a real chief executive, reorganized municipal departments, provided checks on wasteful spending and on the incurrence of floating debts, removed the school system from political control, and strengthened the powers of the board of education. The preparation of the budget was taken away from the city council and vested in the small board of estimate, and the municipal council was permitted to reduce debt but not to increase proposed appropriations.

Revelations of Federal Corruption. The reform movement which characterized municipal government in the eighties and nineties had its counterpart in Federal government. However, instead of expanding the power of the executive, reform in the Federal government meant the separation of the civil service from politics.

Throughout the latter nineteenth century, "business is business" was the prevalent philosophy in the Federal government. Congress was dominated by a group who maintained their positions as party leaders through the use of government patronage. The strength of the political organizations of such senators as Logan of Illinois, Chandler of Michigan, Cameron of Pennsylvania, and Conkling of New York was based on the army of followers whom they appointed to positions in the postal service, the customhouses, and other Federal departments and bureaus. Politicians who were so securely placed could sell government favors to the highest bidder, the industrialists and capitalists who, believing implicitly in Social Darwinism, honestly thought that whatever was good for their financial interests was good in itself, regardless of the means by which it was attained. Therefore, in the twenty years after the war, scandal after scandal revealed a sordid picture of privateering businessmen and corruptible politicians. President Grant's brother-in-law was involved in the Gould-Fisk scheme for cornering the gold market which ended in the "Black Friday" panic of September, 1869. In 1872 came the unsavory Credit Mobilier affair, revealing gifts of stock by a railway construction company to leading members of Congress and to the Vice-President of the United States. In the same year one of the most revered figures in the Republican party, James G. Blaine, was charged with having received gifts in return for his support of railroad legislation. This was followed by the "Whisky Ring" affair, in which President Grant's private secretary was accused of collusion in tax frauds. In 1876 Secretary of War Belknap was impeached for selling Indian contracts, and in 1880 the reputations of some of the leading political figures of the day, including President Garfield's campaign manager, were badly besmirched by disclosures of frauds in awarding mail contracts.

Federal Civil Service Reform. The sordid revelations shook public confidence in the honesty of their government and embittered many against big business. Yet big business itself was not satisfied with the state of affairs. Although not concerned about the lack of ethics in government, it did not relish the idea of being dependent on politicians. It preferred control to bribery and, as Horatio Seymour expressed it, wanted "men in office who will not steal but who will not interfere with those who do."[4]

The agrarians of the West wanted increased regulation of big business by state governments. Others proposed a widespread adoption of the "merit system" or "civil service reform" in governmental appointments. President Hayes appointed some of the leaders of this group to his cabinet, and Garfield's election in 1880 accelerated the movement toward reform. Men like Garfield and Blaine, who previously had not hesitated to levy assessments on Federal officeholders, began to realize that the Republican party could no longer count on easy victories. They therefore established a reform wing, contemptuously called "Half Breeds" by the "Stalwarts," who frankly believed in the spoils system.

[4] De Alva S. Alexander, *Political History of the State of New York*, Vol. III, p. 311.

In time it became clear to almost all political leaders that the "Half Breeds" were right in believing that it was no longer advisable to depend upon Federal patronage for political victory or to sell political favors to the highest bidder. The advisable policy was to support reform and act as an ally of finance and industrial capitalists, rather than as a seller of favors.

After fifteen years of agitation, Congress in 1883 passed the Pendleton Act, providing for competitive examinations in certain classified jobs, including those in customhouses or post offices employing more than 50 persons, and giving the President discretionary power to extend the classified list. No Federal employee could lose his position for failure to contribute to a political fund, and no person in the Federal service had the right to use his position to influence the political action of any person or body.

The Pendleton Act marked the beginning of a development which eventually placed the whole day-to-day work of administration in the hands of civil service employees. Great political "revolutions" could occur, but the men who did the ordinary work of the day, those who took care of the many little details in the operation of a modern complicated government, remained at their jobs. If bureaucracy means routine procedure in the conduct of administration, the Pendleton Act marked the real beginning of bureaucracy in the Federal government. This was an inevitable development, because an expanding government not operated by a permanent civil service would lead to chaos.

Civil service reform was next taken up by state and local governments, with New York State, Massachusetts, and Wisconsin leading.

Although civil service reform did tend to eliminate much corruption, those who idealistically thought it a panacea were in every way mistaken. It is true that civil service took away from political machines their most important source of funds—contributions from officeholders. But since no political machine or party could operate without funds, politicians became the hired hands of pressure organizations whose money bags provided the new financial ammunition of politics.[5] Moreover, the establishment of a permanent civil service introduced a certain rigidity into the operations of government which in time posed serious problems in the enforcement of popular controls and preservation of the democratic process.

[5] The new relationship was explained by Senator Boies Penrose to a group of businessmen. He said: "I believe in a division of labor. You send us to Congress; we pass laws under the operation . . . of which you make money; . . . and out of your profits you further contribute to our campaign fund to send us back again to pass more laws to enable you to make more money. It is your duty to help keep us here and our duty to legislate. .. .." (James E. Watson, *As I Knew Them*, p. 294.)

Chapter 18: FAILURES OF A REFORM ADMINISTRATION

By the time of the presidential election of 1884, the people needed no Marcellus to impress upon them that there was something rotten in the state of their national financial affairs. The nation was in the midst of a business depression, the balance of payments was heavily unfavorable, the silver currency could not be forced into circulation, the national banking system was not fulfilling its purposes, a surplus revenue was piling up in the national Treasury, and the tariff was unsatisfactory both to protectionists and to free traders. Yet the platforms of both parties were practically identical on monetary and financial issues, which were scarcely discussed during the campaign. If any issue was present, it was the issue of honesty and businesslike management in government.

Once elected, the Cleveland administration accomplished a great deal in reforming government administration, but it made little progress toward solving the basic financial problems. Economically, Cleveland believed firmly in *laissez faire*. His accomplishments and his failures, therefore, offered a good yardstick for measuring the success of the laissez-faire philosophy in the last decades of the nineteenth century.

Resurgence of the Silver Controversy. About a month before Cleveland's inauguration, monetary affairs reached a critical stage. As a result of the unfavorable trade balance, the flight of foreign capital, and the business recession, gold was flowing out of the Treasury at an increasing rate. At the same time a smaller proportion of customs duties were being collected in gold.[1] Consequently, the Treasury's gold reserve was declining at the rate of $4 million to $5 million a month and was dangerously close to $100 million, the minimum deemed necessary to maintain specie payments.

Far from being alarmed over the dwindling gold reserve, the inflationists of the West and the South, representing two-thirds of the Democratic party, tried to persuade Cleveland to support increased government silver purchases. On the other hand, the more conservative members of the party sought to impress upon him that, if the silver program were continued, the Treasury and the banks would most certainly have to suspend gold payments. As Abram Hewitt, chairman of the Ways and Means Committee, expressed it,

The stock of gold in the Treasury is being exhausted, and cannot be replenished, except through purchase, which will soon put gold to a premium—

[1] 35 per cent in late 1884 compared with 100 per cent in 1877.

already the banks and trust companies are hoarding gold, or investing in sterling exchange. The Secretary of the Treasury is striving to maintain gold payments until the 4th of March, so that the inevitable suspension shall take place under a Democratic Administration.[2]

Cleveland was favorably impressed by the conservative argument, and in his first message to Congress in December, 1885, he asked for the repeal of the Bland-Allison Act. He pointed out that, since its passage, the government had coined 215.8 million silver dollars, but only 50 million of them and $100 million of silver certificates were in circulation. The rest had returned to the Treasury in exchange for gold. "If continued long enough," Cleveland declared, "this operation will result in the substitution of silver for all the gold the government owns." When and if that occurred, the gold standard would have to be abandoned and the country would *ipso facto* be on a silver standard. According to Cleveland this would impair confidence and result in an economic depression of cataclysmic proportions.

Neither the silverite nor the sound-money group was strong enough to achieve its aims. In April, 1886, stimulated by the business depression, the declining price level, the crop failure of 1885, and economic hardship among the farmers, the silverites introduced another silver bill, which was defeated, 163 to 126. But at the same time an attempt by the administration to repeal the Bland-Allison Act was defeated, 201 to 84.

Meanwhile the Treasury under Secretary Manning took whatever steps it could to conserve its cash surplus and gold reserve and to increase the circulation of silver currency and certificates. It temporarily stopped further debt retirement, persuaded the banks to buy $6 million of subsidiary silver coins, induced Congress to amend the Bland-Allison Act to permit the issue of silver certificates in denominations of $1, $2, and $5 instead of $10 or higher, and discontinued the issue of greenbacks below $5.

Manning's tactics merely postponed the inevitable day when the gold reserve would fall below $100 million. The conservation of the surplus was clearly a delaying maneuver. The advantage gained by exchanging subsidiary silver for gold was lost within six months, because the banks immediately began to exchange the subsidiary silver for legal tenders, which in turn were exchanged for gold. The use of small-denomination silver certificates was effective only until all the small-denomination greenbacks had been replaced.

The silverites scoffed at the administration's tactics and insisted that the readoption of bimetallism was the only solution for the supposed difficulties. In reply, Manning asserted that all the evidence of financial history proved that bimetallism could work only if adopted internationally. If the United States acted alone, Gresham's law would operate and all gold would disappear, leaving a silver standard. But this did not in the least disturb the inflationists, for they favored bimetallism, not as a matter of principle, but as a means of increasing circulation. They were perfectly agreeable to having a silver standard in the guise of bimetallism.

The Surplus-revenue Problem. While free silver temporarily reached an impasse, the more urgent problem of the surplus revenue required a solution.

TABLE 28. FEDERAL RECEIPTS, EXPENDITURES, AND DEBT, 1885–1889
(In millions of dollars)

	1885	1886	1887	1888	1889
Receipts:					
Customs..................	$ 181.5	$ 192.9	$ 217.3	$ 219.1	$ 223.8
Internal revenue............	112.5	116.8	118.8	124.3	130.9
Other receipts..............	29.7	26.7	35.3	35.9	32.3
Totals..................	$ 323.7	$ 336.4	$ 371.4	$ 379.3	$ 387.1
Expenditures:					
Civil.....................	$ 23.8	$ 22.0	$ 22.1	$ 22.9	$ 25.6
Foreign...................	5.4*	1.3	7.1*	1.6	2.0
War......................	32.2	30.2	30.8	31.5	33.2
Navy.....................	16.0	13.9	15.1	16.9	21.4
River and harbor............	10.5	4.1	7.8	7.0	11.2
Pensions..................	56.1	63.4	75.0	80.3	87.6
Indians...................	6.6	6.1	6.2	6.2	6.9
Interest..................	51.4	50.6	47.7	44.7	41.0
Other....................	58.2†	50.9	56.1	56.8	70.4‡
Totals..................	$ 260.2	$ 242.5	$ 267.9	$ 267.9	$ 299.3
Surplus...................	$ 63.5	$ 94.0	$ 103.5	$ 111.3	$ 87.8
Gross debt (end of year)........	1,864.0	1,775.1	1,657.6	1,692.9	1,619.1
Interest-bearing debt...........	1,196.2	1,146.0	1,021.7	950.5	829.9

SOURCE: *Annual Reports of the Secretary of the Treasury*, 1885–1889.

* Expenses involved in settling the Alabama claims.

† Includes $10.4 million expenses of revenue collection; $8.6 million customs drawbacks; $4.5 million postal deficit.

‡ Includes $7.7 million for lighthouses, customhouses, etc.; $10.8 million for expenses of revenue collection; $7.4 million for tax refunds; $3.3 million for judgment payments; $3.9 million for postal deficit; $5.2 million for District of Columbia.

Throughout the late 1880's, Federal receipts continued to increase, but the Cleveland administration succeeded in preventing any considerable rise in spending. Hence, from 1886 on, annual revenue surpluses ran at about $100 million. There were no longer any convenient outlets for the application of these surpluses, but they could not be hoarded in the

Treasury under the Independent Treasury Act, for that would withdraw money from circulation, contract bank reserves, and prevent credit expansion.

Aside from clearly impossible proposals emanating from the lunatic fringe, such as the construction of a town hall in every city of more than 10,000 inhabitants, the surplus could be used for further reduction or reorganization of the debt; deposited in the national banks; distributed among the states; spent for internal improvements, subsidies, and pensions, or eliminated through further tax reductions and tariff changes.

The Surplus and Debt Retirement. There were many disadvantages in using the surplus for debt retirement. For one, it meant a continuous reduction of national-bank circulation. Then, too, there were no large blocks of bonds immediately maturing, and since the last of the callable debt was paid off in 1887, bonds could be purchased only in the open market at high premiums. Every Secretary objected to this practice, for it was a waste of public money for which he was held directly responsible. Nevertheless, there was no satisfactory alternative, and furthermore, the sinking-fund law required the Treasury to retire a part of the debt each year. During the Cleveland administration, therefore, bonds were purchased at premiums. In the fiscal year 1888 the Treasury bought $51.5 million. It paid as high as 129, but the average price was 116 and total premiums were $8.3 million. In the fiscal year 1889 premiums were $17.3 million on $120.7 million of bonds, the average price being 114.6. Altogether, the interest-bearing debt was reduced from $1.2 billion on July 1, 1885, to $830 million on July 1, 1889. The reduction included $194 million of the callable 3's and $172 million of the noncallable 4's and 4½'s.[3]

Since it was not possible to continue debt retirement, Comptroller of the Currency John Jay Knox proposed to convert the entire existing debt into a 2½ per cent issue and to pay the difference in interest costs to the bondholders from the surplus in cash. The proposal rested too much on long-run effects to be generally acceptable, although something similar was adopted in 1900.

Secretary of the Treasury Manning suggested that the surplus be used to retire the $346.7 million of greenbacks, thereby eliminating the continuous redemption of greenbacks for gold. To avoid contracting the currency, Manning proposed to issue new gold or silver dollars for each dollar of retired greenbacks. But this solution was totally unacceptable to the inflationists of the farming regions.

---

[3] Prior to 1888 premiums were paid only on sinking-fund purchases—$2.8 million in 1880, $1.1 million in 1881, and $2.9 million in 1887. For details of the open-market purchases, see *Annual Report of the Secretary of the Treasury*, 1887, p. xxvii; 1888, p. lxxxiii; and *Annual Report of the Treasurer*, 1888, p. 6; 1889, p. 9.

Depositing the Surplus in the National Banks. Under the terms of the National Bank Act, the Treasury could deposit its funds in any national bank, provided such funds were secured by "the deposit of United States bonds and otherwise" as designated by the Secretary of the Treasury. The security ordinarily required was $100 of government bonds for every $90 of deposits. Being primary, government deposits always increased bank reserves, enabling credit to be expanded. But when the deposits were secured by bonds previously used to secure circulation, the expansion of credit money was offset by a smaller reduction of outstanding national-bank notes. In addition, government deposits tended to make the money market more sensitive, for their withdrawal from the banking system was an ever-present possibility. Prior to 1887 only a small amount of Treasury cash was deposited in the banks. But after the last of the callable debt was retired, Secretary of the Treasury Fairchild increased the deposits substantially, even though both the Cleveland administration and the opposition recognized that using the banks opened doors to favoritism and was opposed to the spirit of the Independent Treasury system. From $12.9 million in December, 1885, deposits were increased to $61.2 million in March, 1888, when 290 national banks acted as depositories.

Proposals to Distribute Surplus among States. In 1882 when the surplus first became a problem, Secretary Folger recommended that it be distributed among the states. Nothing came of this suggestion. Later in March, 1886, the Blair bill to distribute $77 million to the states for the support of education on the basis of illiteracy passed the Senate but then bogged down. However, state pressure for distribution continued, and in 1889 Congress enacted legislation to return to the states the $15.4 million credited to them under the Civil War direct tax. Cleveland vetoed the bill, but it was repassed in 1891. Ironically enough, the Treasurer of the United States still carried the $28 million "loan" of 1837 on his books as "unavailable funds."

Proposals to Spend the Surplus on Internal Improvements. Many investment projects were proposed for the disposal of the surplus. John Sherman recommended more comprehensive coastal defenses, subsidies for the merchant marine, the construction of an Isthmian canal, and "assistance and encouragement to all American republics founded upon our example." Professor Richard J. Ely urged the adoption of a broad program of river and harbor improvements to control floods and to prevent erosion of the soil. He warned the country that "if we are as niggardly in the future as in the past" in appropriations for the improvement of rivers, "the recent appalling catastrophe . . . of the Yellow River in China will be repeated in our Mississippi Valley."[4] But proposals for increased internal-improve-

[4] Albert Shaw (ed.), *The National Revenues*, p. 64.

ment expenditures met with opposition from the Eastern conservatives. Finding it easy to ridicule river and harbor bills which appropriated money for deepening the Wing Wang River in Oregon and improving Cheesequakes, Wisconsin, the press, especially in New York, led the public to regard an essentially beneficial program as ludicrous. Internal-improvement programs also aroused Cleveland's opposition, for he considered them as an unnecessary government entry into the economic system. Furthermore, internal-improvement expenditures would interfere with tariff reduction, which had become Cleveland's pet project. Accordingly, he vetoed a large river and harbor bill in 1887.

As a result of Cleveland's economy bent, Federal investment expenditures fell off sharply, averaging $14 million annually between 1885 and 1889, even though many projects, carried over from the previous administration, had to be completed.[5]

Veterans' Pensions and the Surplus. Veterans' organizations, mainly the Grand Army of the Republic, maintained that the best way to dispose of the surplus was to liberalize pensions. They demanded that pensions be paid to all indigent veterans, not simply to those with service-connected disability. Actually, despite whatever vigilance the Pension Bureau was able to exercise, the pension list was rapidly becoming a national scandal. It was estimated that about one-fourth of it was fraudulent, being comprised of individuals who had no disability or at least no service-connected disability and of widows who had long since remarried. Congress had also developed the practice of annually enacting hundreds of private bills granting pensions to specific individuals whose claims had been previously rejected by the Pension Bureau. Cleveland justifiably vetoed 233 of these bills, thereby inviting the denunciation of the Grand Army of the Republic, the pension claim agents, and the Republican opposition.[6] But despite his vetoes, more special pension bills were enacted than rejected.

In the meanwhile, the lobbying efforts of the veterans' organizations began to bear fruit. In 1886 Congress increased widows' pensions to $12 a month, and in 1887 it granted pensions to all Mexican War veterans who were either disabled or sixty-two years of age. In January, 1887, Congress also passed the Blair bill, granting generalized pensions of $12 a month

[5] Public building construction expenditures dropped from the $2.9 million annually of Arthur's administration to $2.6 million, and those for rivers and harbors, from $13.5 to $10.5 million. (U.S. Treasury, *Combined Annual Statement of Receipts, Expenditures and Balances*, 1880–1888; and *A History of Public Buildings under the Control of the Treasury Department*.)

[6] Among other bills Cleveland vetoed those which would have given pensions to a veteran who had fallen into a cellar while on a furlough, a veteran of "long and faithful service" who had spent most of it in jail as a deserter, and a widow whose husband had been accidentally killed by a neighbor who was hunting an owl. (James D. Richardson, *Messages and Papers of the Presidents*, Vol. VIII, pp. 415ff.)

to all Civil War veterans who had served 90 days or more and who were "unable to earn support." Senator Blair estimated that the bill would cost $35 million to $50 million a year and would do much toward solving the surplus problem. Cleveland immediately vetoed the Blair bill. He contended that the pension rolls should be regarded as an honor roll, not as a means of distributing charity; that pensions should take care liberally of service-connected disability or death, but not of general dependency; that, in general, the soldiers of the Civil War had been well treated; that the costs of the bill would be so high as to entirely disappoint "the expectation of the people in their desire and hope for relief from war taxation in time of peace"; and that the phrase "unable to earn support" was incapable of definition.

The convictions expressed in the veto message guided Cleveland's thinking not only in pension claims but in other pleas for government assistance. In February, 1887, in vetoing a $10,000 appropriation for seed grain to be distributed among drought-ridden counties of Texas, he wrote that it was wrong "to indulge a benevolent and charitable sentiment through the appropriation of public funds." He could "find no warrant for such an appropriation in the Constitution" and did not "believe that the power and duty of the General Government ought to be expended to the relief of individual suffering which is in no manner properly related to the public service or benefit." In the same message, he gave the laissez-faire philosophy probably its most oft-quoted phrase: " . . . though the people support the Government the Government should not support the people."

The statement was in the best tradition of the old agrarian view that the power of the central government should be limited. It was the philosophy to which Jefferson and Jackson had given theoretical allegiance and to which Pierce and Buchanan had given complete support. It was also the philosophy which continued to prevail for the succeeding forty-five years. But it prevailed in peculiar and inconsistent fashion. In most cases it did not include tariffs and subsidies for the merchant marine or the railroads, but it did apply against payments for unemployment relief and public works. President Hoover quoted from Cleveland's message when he tried to prevent Federal assistance to the unemployed in 1930 to 1932. But by then *laissez faire* was impossible, and the philosophy was shelved completely in 1933 to 1940 with the establishment of Federal unemployment relief, farm aid, and a comprehensive system of social security.

Tax Reorganization and the Surplus. There were three proposals for eliminating the surplus by reorganizing taxes—repeal of the remaining internal revenues, increases in tariff rates, and reduction in tariff rates. None of these was adopted in the eighties, although eventually the surplus was to be eliminated by tariff reorganization.

For many years "Pig Iron" Kelly, speaking for the protectionists, proposed that the liquor and tobacco taxes and the tax on oleomargarine (adopted in 1886) be eliminated. But this could not be done, because they had come to be considered as moral, social, and punitive devices, and it was thought that they added an element of stability to the Federal revenue system. Having failed to wipe out the remaining excises, protectionists proposed to reduce revenue by raising tariff rates to levels high enough to keep out most imports. The opponents of protection, on the other hand, demanded tariff reductions in order to reduce revenue.

Cleveland was sympathetic to the pleas of the tariff reformers. But he feared that extreme tariff reductions would create difficulties for American manufacturers and was by no means a free trader. He also lacked confidence in his own knowledge of the subject, and for the first year and a half of his administration he avoided taking a position on the issue. However, in the summer of 1886 the low-tariff group introduced the Morrison bill, providing for a general reduction in tariff rates, and Cleveland was persuaded to support it. Nevertheless, the House, 157 to 140, refused to consider it.

Accepting the vote as a challenge, Cleveland determined to press the battle for tariff revision more aggressively. In his annual message of December, 1886, he denounced the tariff party as "an army of mercenaries and monopolists with a treasury filled by millions of dollars wrung remorselessly year by year, from an overburdened, overtaxed people." Unable to persuade Congress to take action, Cleveland decided to take the issue to the people in the next presidential election. Some of his intimates advised Cleveland not to confine his forthcoming message (1887) entirely to the tariff or at least to temper the controversy by also recommending reductions in excises and in the tariffs on luxuries. But as was his custom, Cleveland refused to compromise. He considered that taxes on luxuries represented only a small burden on the upper-income groups and that all the benefits of tax reduction should go to the overburdened lower-income groups.

The Tariff Battle of 1888. The vigor of Cleveland's message of December, 1887, with its characterization of the existing tariff as a "vicious, inequitable, and illogical source of unnecessary taxation," exceeded all the expectations of the tariff reformers and the worst forebodings of the protectionists. After describing the fiscal emergency and the threat to business stability produced by the surplus revenue, Cleveland asserted that tariff reduction was the only satisfactory solution, and he called upon Congress to reduce the especially high duties on articles of general consumption, such as sugar and clothing, which placed the burden of taxation on the poor. After ridiculing the claim of the so-called "infant industries," he charged that the tariff enabled trusts and other combinations to neutralize the effects of competition and maintain high prices.

The violence of Cleveland's message bewildered the public, which was scarcely aware of the "heavy tax burdens" about which he spoke. If he had started a more determined and more subtle campaign for tariff revision earlier in his administration, he might have aroused more opposition to high protectionism among the people. By violently attacking the whole doctrine of protection, Cleveland was true to his own character, but he unwittingly played into the hands of the most extreme protectionists and caused a consolidation of their forces. For the next twenty years protectionists ceased to speak of protectionism as a temporary expedient but declared boldly that its permanence was necessary for American prosperity. Far from conceding the propriety of moderating existing tariff rates, they began to demand higher rates. They denied that customs duties increased the cost of living, insisting that they were really paid by foreign producers, who had to lower their prices and accept lower profits or lower wages in order to sell their products in the American market. In a famous debate on the tariff with the English statesman William Gladstone, Justin Morrill, the elder statesman of protectionism, called the British tax system onerous, since it was based on income, excise, and stamp taxes, as compared with the American tax system under which revenue was raised "by duties on imports scarcely felt by tax payers."[7]

Following Cleveland's message, Chairman Mills of the Ways and Means Committee introduced a bill to reduce the average rate of duty by 7 per cent, but even this moderate reduction was unacceptable to the protectionists. It passed the House 162 to 49 with only four Democrats opposing it, whereas 35 had voted against the last Morrison bill. But it was buried in the Senate and was thus an empty victory for tariff-for-revenue principles. The Senate Republicans prepared a rival measure, which was destined to become the McKinley tariff law of 1890.

Administrative Reorganization. The Cleveland administration did not succeed in solving either of the two great problems of the day: the silver coinage and the surplus revenue. Its one great accomplishment was the infusion of more businesslike methods in the operation of government.

Civil service reform was strengthened despite the pressure of office-hungry Democrats, who tried to repeal what they called the "Goody Two-Shoes" reform. The Navy and Interior Departments were completely reorganized, and conservation of natural resources was begun in a small way. By reasserting the independence of the Executive from Congressional interference in appointing and removing officers, Cleveland enormously increased the prestige of the Presidency, reversing a trend

[7] "Justin Morrill," *Harper's Encyclopedia of American History.*

which had been continuous since the Lincoln administration and making possible the adoption of more businesslike methods in all the executive departments.

No changes of fundamental nature were introduced in the organization of the Treasury. A Select Senate Committee, under the leadership of Senator Cockrell, was created in 1887 to inquire into the business methods of the executive departments. The committee published several voluminous reports and also caused the Treasury and War Departments to create special intradepartmental commissions to investigate their internal operations. As a result, a number of changes in operations, requiring no legislative action, were made.

No attempt was made to enlarge the fiscal functions of the Secretary of the Treasury or to make him a real budgeteer of the government. Department heads continued to submit greatly exaggerated expenditure estimates to the Treasury, and except in extraordinary cases, such as during the financial stringency following the crisis of 1873, it was not the practice of the President to go over these estimates. The Treasury, in turn, submitted them to Congress without any analysis or suggestion. Therefore, government expenditures continued to be managed in a hit-or-miss fashion without any central administrative planning and control.

Splitting up the Congressional Fiscal Organization. The original Congressional fiscal organization, headed by the Ways and Means Committee in the House and the Finance Committee in the Senate, remained substantially intact up to the time of the Civil War. Though far from perfect, it was fairly efficient, but unfortunately, it was changed in the wrong direction during the war. To relieve the committees of some of their work load, Congress left only revenue measures in their hands and created a new Committee on Appropriations in each house, thereby separating the function of raising money from the function of spending it.

Even this procedure was not allowed to operate for very long. Department heads began to submit their appropriation requests to the committees which governed their departments, realizing that in this way their estimates would be given more friendly treatment. In 1877 the Committee on Rivers and Harbors was given charge of this class of appropriation, and in 1880 the agricultural appropriation bill was taken from the Appropriation Committee. In 1885 the trend was formally solidified by taking five more general appropriation bills away from the Appropriation Committee and giving them to the corresponding legislative committees. In addition, various other committees authorized appropriations as the spirit moved them.[8]

Although department estimates were given liberal treatment, actual

[8] For details, see Selko, *The Federal Financial System*, pp. 84–92.

expenditures often exceeded appropriations, and requests were regularly submitted for additional appropriations to cover deficiencies. It was almost impossible for Congress to refuse these deficiency requests, since the expenditures had already been contracted for or actually spent.[9]

The Congressional fiscal system was therefore superlatively inefficient and unbusinesslike. There was no coordination between receipts and expenditures or among the various expenditures themselves. There was no central authority to evaluate the suggested expenditures, and requests for funds were usually exaggerated. It was impossible to hold anyone responsible for excessive spending or bad budgeting or for duplication of activities, because everyone had a finger in the pie. The chaos was obvious, but instead of fixing central responsibility, Congress kept on setting up separate committees on expenditures for each department.

[9] In 1879, for example, the Postmaster General requested an appropriation of $2 million over and above the $5.9 million which he had already received for rural mail service. Of this $2 million, $300,000 was for expansion of facilities and $1.7 million was for commitments already made. As the Postmaster General's office frankly stated, Congress had no choice but to grant the amount. (Lucius Wilmerding, *The Spending Power*, p. 144.)

Chapter 19: FINANCES OF THE GILDED AGE: DISAPPEARANCE OF THE SURPLUS

The four preceding chapters described how many of the basic financial problems of the post-Civil War period grew in intensity. It is the purpose of this chapter and the next to show how these problems were temporarily solved during the "gilded age" of the nineties to the more complete satisfaction of the group whose influence on society was greatest, namely, the industrial and financial capitalists.

In the monetary sphere, the defense of the *de facto* gold standard against the silver currency was carried on heroically, even though the fiscal resources of the government were badly strained. Then in the campaign of 1896, the whole issue of bimetallism vs. gold monometallism was thoroughly and dramatically aired and decided by the people in favor of gold.

In the fiscal sphere, the problem of the revenue surplus was solved, if not satisfactorily, at least thoroughly. Veterans' pensions were increased, and government revenue was reduced, partly as a result of lowering the non-protective-tariff schedules and partly as a result of a business depression.

With the appearance of deficits, a need arose for additional taxation, and the agrarians in the West and the South and the labor groups in the urban centers succeeded in reestablishing the income tax only to have it invalidated by the Supreme Court. In the meanwhile, the industrial group not only successfully resisted a downward revision of protective tariff rates but even obtained a material increase. Moreover, through the incorporation of a so-called "reciprocity clause," the tariff was employed to obtain concessions from foreign countries, thus becoming an instrument of the newly emerging American economic imperialism.

While dramatic developments took place in the monetary, fiscal, and tariff fields, only minor corrections were made in the national banking system. The inelastic, bond-secured national-bank currency was continued in spite of criticism by monetary and banking authorities, and the principal weakness in the banking structure—the lack of a central bank—could not be corrected in the existing social and political atmosphere. In fact, commercial banking became increasingly decentralized as state banks grew more rapidly than national banks and finally surpassed them in importance in 1892.

The McKinley Tariff of 1890 and the Revenue Surplus. The Harrison administration came to office in March, 1889, pledged to increase protective-tariff rates and to reduce government revenue. Although the two aims seemed to conflict, Representative William McKinley, chairman of the Ways and Means Committee, prepared a bill to accomplish both. Passed over the vehement protests of tariff-for-revenue spokesmen in October, 1890,[1] the McKinley Tariff was entitled "An Act to Reduce the Revenue . . . ," and it succeeded remarkably well in accomplishing its purposes. It repealed the duty on raw sugar which produced $50 million annually and paid in its stead a subsidy of 2 cents a pound to domestic sugar producers, thereby reducing the surplus by more than $60 million a year. The sugar bounty cost the Treasury $7.3 million in the first year of its operation, but within two years, the amount rose to $12.1 million, for the subsidy caused sugar growers to double production.

Aside from its repeal of the sugar duty, the McKinley Tariff was unapologetically protectionist, its average rate being estimated at 48 per cent. The minimum-evaluation principle, abandoned in 1846, was reintroduced on a number of commodities, and for the first time in American history a complete schedule of protective duties was levied on agricultural commodities. In addition, a 70 per cent duty was imposed on tin plate, all of which had been imported prior to 1890. However, the duty was to lapse unless, in any one year before 1897, domestic production equaled $33\frac{1}{3}$ per cent of the total imports of any year between 1890 and 1896. Since the infant tin-plate industry developed rapidly under tariff protection, the duty remained in existence.

At the instigation of Secretary of State James G. Blaine, the so-called "reciprocity clause" was inserted in the McKinley Tariff. The President was authorized to impose duties on five commodities imported in large volume from South America—sugar, molasses, coffee, tea, and hides—if, in his opinion, the nations exporting them imposed unequal and unreasonable duties on imports from the United States.

Reciprocity was not a new device. It had existed by treaty with Canada from March, 1855, to March, 1866, and also by the 1876 treaty with Hawaii. But there was a real exchange of concessions under the earlier treaties, while there was no real reciprocity in the 1890 tariff, since it included no grant of special concessions on the part of the United States. However, it did represent the beginning of an ever-widening movement which culminated in 1934 with the passage of the Reciprocal Trade Agreement Act.

Agreements granting concessions to the United States were concluded chiefly with Latin-American countries. On the other hand, penalizing

---

[1] The House vote was 164 to 142, with Southern and city labor districts solidly opposed and Western districts solidly supporting.

duties were imposed on Venezuela, Colombia, and Haiti, which refused to grant the demanded concessions. To the surprise and irritation of the countries involved, all the treaties were terminated by the unilateral action of the United States in 1894, when a new tariff was enacted by Congress.

In addition to changes in rates, the McKinley Act introduced an important improvement in tariff administration. The procedure of having private merchants act as referees in valuation controversies was finally abandoned, and a Board of General Appraisers composed of nine full-time men was established.

Pension Act of 1890 and the Disappearance of the Surplus. The Harrison administration also attacked the surplus revenue by increasing pension expenditures. Having pledged that he would not weigh "the claims of old soldiers with apothecary's scales," Harrison appointed as Commissioner of Pensions Corporal James Tanner, one of the leading lobbyists for the Grand Army of the Republic. In granting pensions with a profligate hand, Tanner was faithful to the remark which he is alleged to have made upon taking office: "God help the surplus."

The Harrison administration also passed the pension bill previously vetoed by Cleveland. It provided pensions for veterans of ninety days or more of military service who were prevented by disability, no matter what its cause, from earning their own support. It also provided survivor pensions to widows married to veterans before 1890 and not subsequently remarried. In 1892 and 1893, liberalizing amendments were passed in favor of veterans and veterans' widows of the Indian Wars of 1832 to 1842 and of the Mexican War.

These laws opened the pension rolls to thousands of new applicants. Between 1885 and 1893 the number of pensioners increased from 345,125 to 966,012, while pension payments almost tripled. In 1947 Civil War pensions were still being paid to 18,806, and it was estimated that they would be paid for still another fifty years, or for more than 130 years after the war.

Altogether the Harrison administration increased spending by $100 million a year, or one-third above that of the Cleveland administration.[2] Federal public-works expenditures averaged $25.9 million annually from 1890 to 1896 compared with $14.0 million annually in the four previous years. River and harbor expenditures alone averaged $15.7 million annually, and construction of customhouses, courthouses, and post offices aggregated $18.3 million, or $2.6 million annually.[3]

In the general hunt for projects upon which money could be expended,

[2] Conservatives querulously referred to the "Billion-dollar Congress," to which Speaker Reed replied, "Isn't this a billion-dollar country?"

[3] Including a post-office courthouse for over $1 million each in Detroit, Buffalo, and Milwaukee and an appraisers' warehouse for $1.8 million in New York City.

the Harrison administration did not forget the Navy and the merchant marine. In 1891 Congress granted a subsidy of 66 cents to $4 a mile to steamship companies ostensibly for carrying the mails, but in reality to develop an efficient merchant marine convertible into naval cruisers in time of war. The ships had to be built, owned, and partially operated by American citizens, and construction of the vessels was to be supervised by the Navy. Payments under the subsidy began modestly at $82,000 in 1892 but increased to over $1 million in 1897, at which level they approximately remained.

TABLE 29. FEDERAL RECEIPTS, EXPENDITURES, AND DEBT, 1889–1896
(In millions of dollars)

	1890	1891	1892	1893	1894	1895	1896
Receipts:							
Customs.....................	$ 229.7	$ 219.5	$ 177.5	$ 203.4	$ 131.8	$ 152.2	$ 160.0
Internal revenue.............	142.6	145.7	154.0	161.0	147.1	143.2	146.8
Premium (on bond sales)......	....	....	....	....	8.6	11.3	11.2
Sale of public lands...........	6.4	4.0	3.3	3.2	1.7	1.1	1.0
Other revenue................	24.4	23.4	20.2	18.2	17.1	16.7	19.2
Totals....................	$ 403.1	$ 392.6	$ 354.9	$ 385.8	$ 306.4	$ 324.7	$ 338.1
Expenditures:							
Civil......................	23.6	$ 27.1	$ 25.2	$ 28.2	$ 26.9	$ 29.2	$ 28.4
Foreign....................	1.6	2.0	1.7	2.0	1.7	1.7	1.6
War.......................	32.9	36.4	33.9	34.8	34.7	31.9	32.7
Navy......................	22.0	26.1	29.2	30.1	31.7	28.8	27.1
River and harbor............	11.7	12.3	13.0	14.8	19.9	19.9	18.1
Pensions...................	106.9	124.4	134.6	159.4	141.2	141.4	139.4
Indians....................	6.7	8.5	11.2	13.3	10.3	9.9	12.2
Interest...................	36.1	37.5	23.4	27.3	27.8	31.0	35.4
Other.....................	76.6	91.4	72.9	73.5	73.3	62.4	57.2
Totals....................	$ 318.0	$ 365.8	$ 345.0	$ 383.5	$ 367.5	$ 356.2	$ 352.2
Surplus (+) or deficit (−)......	$ +85.0	$ +26.8	$ +9.9	$ +2.3	$ −61.2	$ −31.5	$ −14.0
Gross debt (at end of year)......	1,552.1	1,546.0	1,588.5	1,546.0	1,632.3	1,676.1	1,769.8
Interest-bearing debt...........	725.3	610.5	585.0	585.0	635.0	716.2	847.4

SOURCE: *Annual Reports of the Secretary of the Treasury,* 1890–1896.

While expenditures increased, annual revenues fell off sharply. As a result, deficits began to appear in 1894, and the Treasury, after an interval of almost thirty years, had to incur new debt. Although never clearly anticipated, this reversal of the Treasury's position was to have a most embarrassing effect on the gold reserve and the solvency of the nation's currency.

Sherman Silver Purchase Act of 1890. The issues in the campaign of 1888 were the tariff and the surplus revenue, not the currency. But the silver question was by no means dead; it merely lay dormant because of the relatively prosperous condition of the economy. When the balance of trade turned against the United States in 1888, the farm regions were hard hit, and there was a new outbreak of agitation for more currency.

In his report for 1889, Secretary of the Treasury Windom reviewed all the possible solutions to the silver question: international bimetallism, continuation of the Bland-Allison Act, free coinage of silver, and coinage of silver dollars containing a dollar of bullion. All these he dismissed for one reason or another and, instead, suggested a plan under which the government would purchase at its market value all the silver produced in the United States and issue against it silver certificates redeemable in silver at its market price. Windom believed that his plan would overcome the two great difficulties inherent in a currency consisting partly of silver: the operation of Gresham's law, and the accumulation of silver in the Treasury.

Meanwhile, the protectionists were having difficulty in obtaining the enactment of the McKinley Tariff. They therefore offered to support more liberal silver legislation if the silver interests would vote for the McKinley bill. Out of this deal grew the Sherman Silver Purchase Act of July, 1890.[4] The object of the act was stated to be the maintenance of parity between silver and gold. It repealed the Bland-Allison Act; directed the Treasury to purchase 4½ million ounces of silver per month at the market price, payment to be made in Treasury notes, which were full legal tender and redeemable in gold or silver at the discretion of the Secretary of the Treasury; and prohibited the coinage of silver dollars after 1891, except for the redemption of Treasury notes.[5]

The Sherman Act differed considerably from the Bland-Allison. (1) Under the Bland-Allison Act the money expended for silver was fixed; under the Sherman Act the lower the price of silver, the less the Treasury expended for silver purchases. (2) Under the Bland-Allison Act the number of silver dollars increased as the price of silver declined; under the Sherman Act as the price of silver declined, less new money was added to the circulation. (3) The Sherman Act authorized the Secretary of the Treasury to redeem treasury notes in silver or gold as he so desired; under the Bland-Allison Act silver certificates were specifically redeemable in silver. (4) The paper money issued under the Sherman Act was full legal tender, whereas the Bland-Allison silver certificates were not legal tender for private transactions. (5) The members of the New York Clearing House freely accepted the Treasury notes of 1890, whereas they had never used Bland-Allison silver certificates in settling interbank balances.

Although the Sherman Act was by no means satisfactory to the inflationists, it seemed to be more acceptable to all groups than the Bland-

---

[4] Sherman reluctantly allowed his name to be attached to the bill, which passed the Senate, 39 to 26, and the House, 123 to 90.

[5] The Sherman Act increased the number of currencies in circulation to nine: gold coin, gold certificates, silver dollars, silver certificates, subsidiary coins, United States notes, national-bank notes, Treasury notes of 1890, and certificates of deposit.

Allison Act. During the twelve years in which the latter was in force, the government purchased 291.3 million ounces of silver at a total cost of $308.3 million and coined $378.2 million. Yet, the Bland-Allison Act had failed to fulfill its purposes, for the price of silver fell from $1.20 to 93 cents per ounce, the general price level was not raised, and agricultural conditions were not improved. Indeed, the only accomplishment of the Bland-Allison Act was to provide an artificial market for one of the commodities of the West. But the Sherman Act did not succeed any better than the Bland-Allison Act. At first, it is true, there was a flurry in silver which brought the price to $1.22 an ounce, but this was purely ephemeral and due solely to speculative activity. In the long run, the Sherman Act raised neither the market price of silver nor the price of farm commodities, for it was not possible to put the additional money into circulation. As in the eighties, money could be kept in circulation in periods of high business activity, but it tended to be redundant in periods of inactivity. The situation was made worse because the factors which had lessened the difficulties of a redundant currency in the eighties were no longer present. After 1893 the surplus revenue disappeared, and the Treasury was no longer able to hoard silver. Hence, the safety valve which made it possible to maintain a gold standard and at the same time to issue an excess amount of silver no longer existed. Moreover, relative price levels in the United States and Europe continued to diverge and tended to give the United States a persistently unfavorable balance of trade. On top of this, a business depression developed of much more severity than the one in 1884.

The Run on the Gold Reserve. When the currency became redundant, its holders, preferring gold, presented paper money at the Treasury for redemption, causing heavy pressure on the Treasury gold reserve. It had long been assumed that the minimum amount required to meet the demand for the redemption of paper money was $100 million. In early 1890 the Treasury had a comfortable net gold balance of almost $200 million, but by May the balance began to fall. Then, in November, Baring Brothers suspended. In the ensuing liquidation of American securities, the foreign demand for gold increased substantially, and means for replenishing the gold reserve were not available. Therefore, by June, 1891, the Treasury's gold was down to $117.6 million.

Temporarily, the drain was alleviated by resorting once again to the policy of shipping silver to the interior free of freight charges. More importantly, the balance of trade again became favorable in the latter part of 1891, and the demand for gold for international payments declined. But this was only a breathing spell, and in 1892 the run on Treasury gold was resumed.

At the same time silverites and farmers, still true to the quantity theory of money, were again demanding an increase in the total money stock in order to raise commodity prices. The main plank in the Populist platform in the campaign of 1892 demanded an increase in circulation from the existing $25 per capita to $50, and in 1892, a free coinage bill passed the Senate, 29 to 25, but died in the House upon the adjournment of Congress.

The new outbreak of silver agitation unquestionably diminished European confidence in American securities, and immediately after the second inauguration of Cleveland in 1893 the pressure on Treasury gold became more intense. European investors were selling their American securities, and through their American bankers, they were obtaining gold by redeeming legal tenders at the Treasury. In the fiscal year 1893, $72.3 million of gold was exported, the largest amount on record up to that time. In addition, domestic holders of paper currency were constantly presenting it for redemption. The Treasury was not permitted to retire the redeemed greenbacks but was compelled to reissue them while constantly adding new notes under the Sherman Act. Thus, the Treasury was in the center of an endless chain. It was paying out paper money at the front door, redeeming it in gold at the backdoor, and paying it out again at the front door. To make matters worse, the percentage of customs duties paid in gold declined from 90 per cent or more before 1890 to below 4 per cent in 1892 (payments being accepted in paper currency and silver). This eliminated the most important source for replenishing the gold reserve.

The silverites continued to urge the Treasury to pay out silver instead of gold. Technically, the Treasury had the power to do so. By law, greenbacks were redeemable in coin, which meant gold or silver, and Treasury notes of 1890 were redeemable in gold or silver as the Secretary might decide. If the silverites' plan had been adopted, the endless chain would have been slowed down, for Treasury notes of 1890 could not be reissued once they had been redeemed for silver. But Cleveland's Secretary of the Treasury Carlisle refused to redeem in silver, for that would have been tantamount to abandoning the gold standard and adopting a silver standard.

The endless chain continued, and on April 22, 1893, the gold reserve, which Cleveland rightly characterized as being regarded "with a sort of sentimental solicitude," fell below $100 million for the first time since the resumption of specie payments in 1879. In the following months the situation materially worsened. In May, a financial panic broke out. In June, India, one of the world's largest users of silver, announced that her mints would accept no more silver. Consequently, it became even more difficult to dispose of silver stocks, which were already excessive, and by June the average price of silver had fallen to 65 cents an ounce (a 50 per cent depreciation from the 16 to 1 ratio).

The Panic of 1893. In its details there were numerous new features in the panic of 1893, but in general it revealed the same characteristic breakdown of the banking system as all other panics under the National Bank Act. Between May and October loans in national banks contracted by $317.8 million and individual deposits by $298.8 million. The rate on call money rose to 70 per cent, and the best commercial paper could be discounted only at rates of 15 per cent and higher. The same preference for liquidity was demonstrated by individuals. Gold exports were the heaviest in history, and hoarding became so prevalent that currency commanded a premium over checks. Banks again relied on clearinghouse certificates to settle interbank balances, New York banks issuing $38.3 million and banks in other large cities, $24.8 million. The use of clearinghouse certificates again illustrated two basic weaknesses in American banking: the lack of a central bank which could create reserves in times of stress and the impracticability of the "real bills" doctrine.

Interestingly enough, the premium on cash temporarily stopped the domestic run on Treasury gold, since all money, paper as well as gold, appeared desirable for purposes of hoarding. But unfortunately, the panic also reduced the government's revenue and increased the deficit. As a result, the Treasury had to use gold to pay current expenses, thus lowering its reserve further.

Conservatives were quick to blame the panic on silver, but more fundamental factors than a loss of confidence in the currency were at the root of the collapse. Failures were more common in the West, where the silver program did not cause any loss of confidence. On the contrary, Westerners believed that the panic was deliberately planned and created by Eastern "gold bugs" who wished to discredit silver. Pointing out that national-bank circulation had consistently declined and convinced that gold production was inadequate for the money needs of an expanding economy, Westerners insisted that the panic could be ended by increasing the currency through the free coinage of silver. They did not realize that money in circulation varied with business activity, and they ignored the fact that checks and demand deposits, which were constantly growing, were far more important monetarily than cash.

Repeal of the Sherman Silver Purchase Act. President Cleveland shared the conservative view that silver coinage, by undermining confidence, was responsible for the nation's economic troubles. He therefore called Congress into special session, and when it met in August, 1893, he urged it in the strongest terms to repeal the Sherman Silver Act. "Financial distrust and fear," he said, "have sprung up on every side." He pointed out that the government had purchased $147 million of silver under the Sherman Act. The treasury notes issued in exchange were being regularly converted into gold. He was certain that, if the Sherman Act were allowed to continue, silver would very shortly replace gold as the *de facto* monetary standard,[6] the credit of the United States would be destroyed, and the nation would no longer be able to claim "a place among nations of the first class."

When Representative Wilson introduced the administration bill for repeal of the Sherman Act, the opposing forces quickly lined up. It was not a struggle between political parties, or of state rights vs. central government, or of haves against have nots. It was a struggle in which the agrarian forces of the West and the South were pitted against the industrial forces of the big cities, especially in the East. Although Representative William Jennings Bryan presented the case for silver as a crusade of the underprivileged against bloated plutocracy, the debate quickly centered on inflation and the quantity theory of money.

The House immediately repealed the Sherman Act, 239 to 108. But in the Senate, where the agrarians were not handicapped by their relatively small populations, the contest dragged on throughout the summer and part of the fall. At times it appeared that repeal could not be achieved, and many administration supporters reluctantly recommended compromise, but Cleveland refused to compromise. He used his patronage powers to good advantage and freely cracked the party whip. Finally in late October, when the price of silver was down to less than 75 cents an ounce, the Senate passed the repeal bill 43 to 32. But repeal did not have the anticipated curative effect, for it only stopped the issue of new notes without providing for retiring the old. The drain on the Treasury continued, and the worst was still to come.

The Depression of 1893 and the Appeal to the Government. During the course of the depression of 1893, profits declined, spending for capital goods diminished, and few new enterprises were started. As a result the depression hit the urban population most severely. There was nothing "gay" about the nineties for the thousands of workers who lost their jobs. And to those who considered themselves "the disinherited," it seemed natural to go to the government for help. In various parts of the country, groups of unemployed gathered together into "armies" to march to Washington to demand that Congress take action to provide employment. The most famous of these "armies" was led by "General" Jacob Coxey, a Populist of Massillon, Ohio. Starting in the Middle West and carrying banners proclaiming the arrival of the "Commonweal of Christ," and announcing

---

[6] Much of the currency issued under the Bland-Allison Act remained, and although it was not a factor in the "endless chain" because it was specifically redeemable in silver and not gold, it was a factor of annoyance, since it released a considerable amount of treasury notes and greenbacks for redemption in gold.

"Death to interest on bonds," it reached Washington on April 26 and was joined by two other ragged "armies."

The legislation for which the "armies" pleaded had already been introduced by Senator Peffer of Kansas. One of his bills authorized the Federal government to issue $500 million of non-interest-bearing legal-tender notes to finance the construction of roads all over the country. It was estimated that this would give jobs to 4 million workmen. Under another of his measures, Congress was to authorize state and local governments to issue non-interest-bearing bonds against the credit of the United States up to one-half of the assessed valuation of property, the proceeds to be spent for the relief of the unemployed. When presented at the Treasury, the bonds would be instantly honored in legal-tender notes.

When Coxey's "army" reached Washington and deployed at the foot of the Capitol to deliver its petition, it was speedily dispersed by the police, and Coxey and his aides were arrested for walking on the grass. The bills never came to a vote, for relief for the unemployed was not yet considered to be a matter for Federal concern. Reflecting the general opinion, *The Chicago Record,* a relatively liberal newspaper, wrote on March 30, 1894: "The continual turning of the people to Washington for aid, of which the Coxey army is merely a caricature, is pathetic and portentious. The country is sick just to the extent that its people try to lean on the government instead of standing upright on their own feet." But more thoughtful observers felt that the movement, grotesque as it was, had a deeper meaning and was "a manifestation of the prevailing unrest and dissatisfaction among the laboring classes."[7]

The Wilson-Gorman Tariff. After the repeal of the Sherman Act, the Cleveland administration turned its attention to tariff reform. Both Cleveland and the tariff-reform group believed that the principal reason for the Democratic victories in 1890 and 1892 was the widespread public dissatisfaction with the McKinley Tariff. In 1894, therefore, Representative Wilson, chairman of the House Ways and Means Committee, introduced a bill to accomplish a general reduction of the tariff and the elimination of duties on raw materials. In the course of its consideration, a third objective was added—the introduction of an income tax as a permanent feature of the Federal revenue system.

The Wilson bill was quickly passed by the House, 204 to 140. But in the Senate, under the leadership of Senator Gorman of Maryland, a small group of Democrats joined the Republicans in amending the bill 633 times. The emasculated version was then passed 39 to 34 in July, 1894.

The Congressional leaders who had managed the original Wilson bill reluctantly accepted the Wilson-Gorman bill as the best that could be

[7] Quoted in Ray Stannard Baker, *American Chronicle,* p. 19.

obtained under trying circumstances. Nevertheless, Cleveland, opposed as always to compromise, condemned the bill in the sharpest language. Denouncing the Democrats who had prevented the passage of a thorough tariff-reform measure, he quixotically called upon the House not to accept the Senate's bowdlerized version. For a time it appeared that the last vestige of party harmony had been destroyed. However, administration leaders in Congress successfully quieted the violent reaction to the President's sensational indictment and the Wilson-Gorman bill finally passed the House, 182 to 106, and became law without Cleveland's signature.

Income Tax of 1894. While the Act eliminated the reciprocity clause of the McKinley bill, repealed the bounty on sugar, and restored the duty on raw sugar, its most important feature was the income tax clause. It was added to the original bill over the combined protests of both Chairman Wilson and President Cleveland, who believed that it would tend to cloud the fundamental issue and endanger the success of tariff reform. As a matter of fact, it proved to be the most popular section of the entire act.

The termination of the Civil War income tax in 1872 had never settled the issue. In the twenty years thereafter, 66 separate bills were introduced to establish a peacetime Federal income tax of one sort or another. In every case, they were introduced by Western or Southern congressmen and died in committee. They were examples of the same agrarian ferment that caused the demands for increases in the currency supply. Western and Southern farmers thought that the regressive tax system, existing in both the Federal and the state governments, placed a disproportionate share of the tax burden on agriculture. They contended that the financial and industrial interests had saddled the farmer with an excessive tax load and, through conservative money policies, had denied to him the hope of increasing farm prices.

Urban industrial workers shared the farmer's enthusiasm for an income tax, but the upper-income groups were violently opposed. David A. Wells, who at one time appeared sympathetic to the income tax, wrote a magazine article in March, 1880, which he entitled "The Communism of a Discriminating Income Tax." The most influential newspapers, including the *New York Times*, the *New York Tribune*, and the Philadelphia *Public Ledger*, opposed the tax, with only the Chicago *Times* and the New York *World* supporting it.

In the debate on the tariff bill as a whole, the conservatives concentrated their attack on the income tax. Senator Hill denounced it as "an assault on states' rights," and both he and Representative Cockran declared that it would deprive a large group of citizens of a feeling of responsibility for the conduct of government. According to Representative Walker, the tax "would take from the wealth of the thrifty and enterprising and give to the shiftless and the sluggard." But the most oft-repeated and devious argument was that the income tax would ultimately be shifted to the poor.

The opposition of the conservatives only made the proponents more determined. Then, too, circumstances were never better for the enactment of the measure. The Treasury was in need of additional revenue, and the Wilson tariff bill would reimpose a duty on sugar which would bear most heavily on the poor. It was contended that the income tax would provide the additional revenue and that, in all fairness, it should be imposed to counterbalance the regressive sugar duty. The argument proved effective, for the income tax remained in the bill as passed.[8]

The tax was to be levied for five years beginning January 1, 1895, on both corporations and individuals. Since it applied to all "gains, profits, and income derived from any kind of property, rents, interest, dividends, or salaries, or from any profession, trade, employment, or vocation," inheritances and gifts were taxed as income. The tax was based on the income of the preceding calendar year and was due on July 1. The rate was a flat 2 per cent on incomes over $4,000 and applied to both resident and nonresident citizens, but it did not apply to municipal and state employees or to income from Federal securities, and income from dividends was not taxed on the theory that it had already been taxed as corporate income.

The income tax was estimated to yield about $75 million a year, but it never really went into effect, for its constitutionality was immediately attacked in the courts. In two famous hearings in the case of *Pollock v. Farmers' Loan and Trust Company* (1895), the Supreme Court, after considerable hesitation and by a vote of 5 to 4, held the entire income tax unconstitutional. In the original hearings, four questions were raised for the Court's decision: was the tax on income from real estate a direct tax within the meaning of the Constitution, was the tax on income from personal property a direct tax, did the tax violate the constitutional requirement that all taxes must be uniform, and was a tax on interest from municipal government securities constitutional? The Attorney General based his case on precedent. He cited the Hylton case of 1797 and *Springer v. United States* (1881). The plaintiff's case was argued long and learnedly by Joseph Choate, but its most effective weapon was the atmosphere of the day. It was a time when the Populist party was at its height, when the silver controversy was embroiled in emotionalism, when the Court had just decided that Eugene V. Debs had violated the law in the railroad strike of 1894—when, in short, conservatives were frightened by the

[8] See Allen Nevins, *Grover Cleveland*.

exaggerated shadow of radicalism. Choate used this fear to great advantage, pleading with the Court to save the nation from an essentially socialistic law.

The decision in the first *Pollock v. Farmers' Loan and Trust Company* case was indecisive. It held that a tax on income from either real estate or municipal bonds was a direct tax and thus unconstitutional unless levied among the states in accordance with population. But on the crucial question of whether the entire income tax section was unconstitutional, the Court divided 4 to 4, one justice not being in attendance. In the second *Pollock v. Farmers' Loan and Trust Company* case, Chief Justice Fuller held in a 5-to-4 decision that the tax on income from land was a tax on the land itself and therefore a direct tax, that taxes on income from personal property were also direct, and that all the income tax sections of the law were inseparable and were therefore inoperative and void. Thus, the earlier decision of the Supreme Court in 1881, sustaining the constitutionality of the Civil War income tax, was completely reversed. Populist sentiment was outraged by this decision, and progressives began to talk about the desirability of amending the Constitution to remove the supposed inhibition. But almost twenty years had to pass before this movement achieved its purposes.

It is impossible to evaluate the actual and potential effects of the Wilson-Gorman Act on government revenue. It was passed during a depression, when customs revenues would in any case have been relatively low; it was in effect for only three years before being replaced by a new, heavily protectionist measure; and its principal source of revenue, the income tax, produced only $77,000 before being declared unconstitutional.

Fiscal Administrative Reform. During Cleveland's second administration Congress reexamined on a much more comprehensive scale the problem of reforming Treasury operations. A Joint Committee on Executive Departments, commonly known as the Dockery-Cockrell Committee, was appointed in March, 1893. Unlike the Cockrell Committee, it was provided with a substantial appropriation which enabled it to engage a group of eminent experts (J. W. Reinhart, C. W. Haskins, and E. W. Sells) and a capable staff to assist it in its work. Over the next two years this committee published a series of reports with drafts of bills providing for a great many changes in the fiscal and administrative operations of the Treasury and other departments. Many of these bills were speedily enacted, but probably the most important among them was the Dockery Act of 1894, providing for a greater centralization of accounting functions and for a single audit of accounts in place of the ancient and cumbersome system of triplicate audits. The offices of First and Second Comptroller of the Treasury and Commissioner of Customs were abolished, leaving only the Comptroller and the Assistant Comptroller. At the same time the titles of the auditors were changed. Instead of First Auditor, Second Auditor, and so on, an auditor was created for each department. The Comptroller of the Treasury was given advisory and judicial functions, and provision was made for every requisition to be sent to the proper auditor before it was paid.

The Dockery Act, by eliminating excess offices, by instituting preliminary examination of requisitions, by providing for centralized auditing, and by simplifying the accounts, introduced order into that part of the Treasury's operations. But it did nothing to correct the indefensible lack of system in the control of appropriations, especially of deficiencies.

CHAPTER 20: FINANCES OF THE GILDED AGE:
THE TRIUMPH OF INDUSTRIALISM

As the depression became worse, the Treasury gold reserve reached a critical stage. European confidence in American securities continued to decline, resulting in almost constant gold exports. The depression reduced the private economy's need for currency and caused a government deficit, accelerating the endless chain of redemption and reissue of paper money. By January, 1894, the gold reserve had sunk to $66 million.

The gold standard could be maintained only by stopping the drain on the Treasury gold reserve or by devising a means for replenishing it continuously. The problem required one or more of the following: a readjustment of American prices to bring them more into line with international prices, a rebirth of European confidence in American securities, a revival of business activity at home, the retirement of a large part of the paper currency, or the elimination of the Treasury deficit. Manifestly, none of these could be brought about quickly. In the meanwhile, therefore, the administration had to choose between abandoning the gold standard and replenishing its reserve by borrowing gold from private holders. The first choice was not even considered by the Cleveland administration.

Selling Bonds to Replenish the Gold Reserve. Secretary Carlisle first attempted to alleviate the Treasury's difficulties by recommending that Congress adopt temporary excise taxes to supply revenue until collections came in under the recently enacted income tax. He also asked Congress for authority to sell short-term obligations for gold at the current market rate of interest. But Congress refused his requests, hoping to force the Treasury to redeem paper money in silver instead of gold. In answer, Carlisle declared that the Treasury would pay out gold as long as it had any in its possession. The statement was interpreted to mean that gold payments might be abandoned, and instead of bolstering confidence as intended, it increased what was already a severe case of the jitters and generally diminished faith in the future of the American dollar.

Although no help could be expected from Congress, the Resumption Act of 1875 was still in force. While it specifically authorized the Secretary to sell bonds for gold in order to expedite the resumption of specie payments, Carlisle interpreted this to include the right to sell bonds to maintain specie payments. Unfortunately, the only existing authorizations for borrowing were those under the refunding acts of 1870–1871, allowing only long-term issues at high interest rates. It was illogical for the Treasury to borrow for ten- and thirty-year terms to meet a temporary emergency and to pay 4 and 5 per cent interest when the market rate was only 2 to 3 per cent. But there was no other alternative. Therefore, in January, 1894, Carlisle offered $50 million of 10-year 5 per cent bonds at a price of 117. The inflationists, caught unawares, denied that the Secretary had the power to sell bonds under the Resumption Act, and the Knights of Labor applied for an injunction enjoining the sale, but the suit was immediately dismissed.

Carlisle was much more chagrined by the attitude of the New York bankers. Never forgetting the Secretary's inflationist record, they regarded the bond sale with complete indifference. This was most embarrassing not only because of the need for gold to replenish the reserve, but also because the Treasury was facing a deficit of $70 million. As Secretary Chase had done thirty-three years before, Carlisle journeyed to New York and convinced at least four of the leading bankers—Stillman, Woodward, Stuart, and King—that the Treasury was within a hair's breadth of abandoning gold payments. They assumed personal responsibility for the issue and peddled it from bank to bank, disposing of it on the last day before the subscription period expired. By the sale of this issue the gold reserve was temporarily restored to $107 million.

Meanwhile, Representative Bland introduced a bill to coin the profits on the purchase of silver. The silverites took the position that 412½ grains of silver 9/10 fine equaled one dollar and that silver was worth $1.292 per ounce. Under the Sherman Act, notes were issued only up to the market price of silver, which averaged 92 cents, yielding the government a theoretical profit of more than $50 million. Congress passed the "seigniorage" bill in March, 1894, 168 to 129 in the House and 44 to 31 in the Senate. Although Cleveland vetoed it, it had the effect of further depressing business confidence.

With every decline in confidence, exports and private hoarding of gold increased, and by November, 1894, the Treasury gold reserve was down to $55 million. Carlisle again offered $50 million of 10-year 5's, but this time he had less difficulty, for they were all taken by J. P. Morgan and Co. at 117.077 on an "all-or-none" basis.

Congress's Continued Refusal to Cooperate. During 1894 the Treasury borrowed to replenish its gold stock and to cover operating deficits. Borrowing for the first purpose did not increase the government's net debt, since it correspondingly increased the Treasury's cash reserve. But it did increase interest charges, since the cash surplus did not earn interest to offset the charges on the newly issued government bonds. On the other hand, borrowing to cover operating deficits increased both the net debt and the Treasury's interest payments. Between 1893 and 1896 the Treasury sold $262.3 million of new bonds, of which some $107 million went to cover operating deficits and the balance, to replenish the gold stock.

Carlisle's two bond sales enabled him to meet the deficits but did nothing to solve the basic monetary difficulty. As soon as the bonds were sold, the endless chain resumed its pressure. Therefore, in January, 1895, Cleveland appealed to Congress for authority to cancel greenbacks and Treasury notes of 1890 as they were redeemed and to sell 3 per cent government bonds specifically payable in gold. Cleveland believed that his plan would stop the drain on gold by restoring confidence in American money and by eliminating the paper-money issues which were being presented for redemption in gold. The plan would also save the government needless expense, for it would no longer be necessary to borrow to replenish the gold reserve, and interest rates on loans to cover deficits would be reduced.

Representative Springer introduced a bill incorporating Cleveland's proposals, but it met with violent opposition.[1] The silver bloc contended that Cleveland's plan would contract the money supply by eliminating $350 million of greenbacks and $150 million of Treasury notes of 1890.

J. P. Morgan and the Third Bond Sale. While the Springer bill was being debated, the gold reserve continued to decline, and by the last of January it was only $45 million. At the suggestion of August Belmont, the investment banker, Assistant Secretary Curtis discussed the crisis with J. P. Morgan on January 31. In these discussions, Morgan offered to raise gold abroad in order to replenish the reserve if the Treasury would agree to make a private contract with him. The legal obstacles were quickly disposed of, it being decided among Curtis, Carlisle, and Attorney General Olney that the Treasury had the power to purchase gold under an unrepealed law passed during the Civil War when the free-gold market was operating.

Carlisle was reluctant to enter into a private agreement, for he knew that public criticism of such action would be unbounded. Instead, he decided to advertise for the sale of bonds for gold as he had done in the two preceding crises. But Morgan insisted that another general bond offering would end in a fiasco, and after persuading Carlisle to postpone his advertisement for a few days, he made arrangements to see the President personally. On February 5 he explained his proposal to Cleveland, who agreed to think it over while awaiting the House's action on the Springer bill. When the Springer bill was defeated in the House on February 7, the

---

[1] The Atlanta *Constitution* editorialized, "Outside the hotbeds of goldbuggery and Shylockism, the people of this country do not care how soon gold payments are suspended." The Topeka *State Capital* wrote, "Wheat is now worth but 50 cents a bushel. . . . If the President's suggestion shall be enacted into law, we may look to see it come down to 25 cents a bushel."

crisis reached its height. With Congress demonstrating its unwillingness to aid the administration, Cleveland was confronted with a Hobson's choice. If he refused Morgan's offer, gold payments would have to cease. If he accepted the proposal, public criticism would engulf him. With his usual moral courage and despite his lack of enthusiasm for the banker's plan, he chose to accept it.[2]

Under the contract between the Treasury and the Morgan syndicate, the government bought 3½ million ounces of gold amounting to $65.1 million. At least half was to be obtained from Europe in amounts not to exceed 300,000 ounces per month. The bankers also agreed to exert all their power to prevent gold exports during the six months of the contract. In exchange for the gold, the bankers received $62.3 million of 30-year 4 per cent bonds payable in coin. The price of the bonds was therefore 104.5, and the actual yield 3.75 per cent. Although the bankers offered to take 3 per cent bonds at par if they were specifically payable in gold instead of coin, Congress, 167 to 120, refused to grant the authority, thereby increasing the cost of the loan to the government by about $16 million. The syndicate did exceptionally well with the bonds. Offered to the public at 112¼, they were oversubscribed six times in New York and ten times in London. Shortly after the loan was floated, the price of the bonds on the open market was 123.

The bankers proposed to stop the outflow of gold by selling whatever drafts were needed to pay European claims. But instead of redeeming the drafts in London with gold, they proposed to use their credits in the London money market.[3]

There were two weaknesses in the Morgan plan. First, it could not work if an abnormally high demand for funds against New York continued. The bankers hoped that the increase in the Treasury gold reserve would restore European confidence and reduce the liquidation of American securities and the demand for funds against New York. This hope was at first justified. Foreign investment in American securities again became very large, and the pound sterling receded from the gold export point, effectively stopping the outflow of gold. However, this was only half the battle. It was equally necessary that American crops supply great amounts for export. This did not take place. Speculation set in, prices increased,

[2] The dramatic story of the Cleveland-Morgan negotiations has been exceptionally well told in James A. Barnes, *John G. Carlisle;* Lewis Corey, *The House of Morgan;* Frederick Lewis Allen, *The Great Pierpont Morgan;* and Allen Nevins, *Grover Cleveland.*

[3] An American owing funds to a European could buy drafts from an American banker. The European creditor, in turn, could cash the drafts against credits in the accounts of the American bankers. It was an early example, in a limited fashion, of the exchange controls which were to become so popular in the twentieth century. This one, however, was a private rather than a government attempt at control.

and it seemed likely that an unfavorable balance of payments would re-appear and gold exports would be resumed. In addition, upward pressure was exerted on the pound when, in the latter part of 1895, the money market became uneasy over Cleveland's belligerent defense of the Monroe Doctrine in connection with the Venezuela boundary dispute.

The second weakness in Morgan's plan lay in the fact that it could not work if anyone with close European banking connections refused to co-operate. With this possibility in mind, Morgan had included in his syndi-cate every banking house with important European connections, 61 in all. Each member had agreed not to draw gold from the Treasury during the six months in which the contract was to be in force. As the price of the pound rose in the money market, the syndicate agreed to sell drafts at $4.90, but it refused to ship gold even though the pound had passed the gold export point. For six months the bankers successfully prevented gold exports, but finally an American import house entered the market and offered pounds at $4.89, a point below the bankers' price. The bid, of course, took over the market. The import house sold sterling, shipping gold to cover the drafts. In the last half of 1895, $65 million in gold was shipped abroad. In the final analysis, the Morgan plan was therefore a failure, for in January, 1896, the Treasury gold reserve again sank to $50 million.

The Fourth Bond Sale. Since substantial losses were sustained in foreign-exchange operations, Morgan's profits on the third bond sale were not exorbitant.[4] However, he made no attempt to explain the intricacies of his financial dealings with the government. Others were not so taciturn and subjected both Cleveland and Morgan to the most critical publicity, claim-ing that Cleveland had "mortgaged the United States" and Morgan had taken advantage of his country's plight to drive a Shylock's bargain.[5] The New York *World*, the leading Democratic newspaper, was especially critical and demanded that the Treasury offer its bonds for public sub-scription if monetary difficulties reoccurred.

But for a while it appeared as though the furor was a tempest in a teapot, for the monetary crisis seemed to have passed. Business was showing signs of recovery and needed more currency to carry on its transactions, thus reducing the redundancy of the money supply. However, the improve-ment was short-lived. Cleveland's continued pugnacious attitude in the Venezuelan dispute frightened foreign investors, and liquidation of American securities again began on a mammoth scale.

When the gold reserve sank to $50 million in January, 1896, Morgan

[4] Allen, *op. cit.*, p. 124; N. S. B. Gras and Henrietta Larson, *Casebook in American Business History*, p. 560.

[5] See Alexander D. Noyes, *Forty Years of American Finance* (p. 234), for a critical comment by a conservative commentator.

began to form a new syndicate to provide $100 million to $200 million in gold on the same terms as before. But the Treasury by-passed the bankers, offering $100 million of 4 per cent bonds for public subscription. The response demonstrated conclusively that the public had complete confidence in the government's credit. There were 4,640 subscriptions with aggregate bids of $688 million ranging from 110.7 to 120. The average bid was 111⅛, and the proceeds, $111 million. In another respect, however, the bond issue was a failure, for it did not increase the gold reserve materially. The bonds were sold for gold, and the public obtained the gold by presenting paper money for redemption at the Treasury. In brief, the Treasury was buying back its own gold and was converting its paper-money issues into long-term debt. The proceedings were made even more irrational by the fact that cash was becoming scarce. Wholly illogical practices developed, for citizens, in their eagerness to purchase government bonds, began to bid a premium for both gold and legal tenders. Some bankers even began to import gold from abroad at a premium in order to obtain a share of the bond issue, but at the same time gold was being exported to cover the liquidation of American securities by European investors.

It became evident that the government's embarrassment was caused neither by public fear of imminent government bankruptcy nor by public distrust of profligate government spending, but by the extremely clumsy nature of the country's monetary system, the obstinate refusal of the strongly intrenched inflationists in Congress to permit any modification of that system, and the administration's desperate determination to maintain the gold standard at any cost. Such determination was admirable from a traditional and moral point of view, but considering the prevailing economic conditions, it seemed doomed to failure.[6]

To maintain the gold standard, the Cleveland administration had to impose a strait jacket on the economy. Paper money was gradually drained into the Treasury, and gold was exported or hoarded. As a result, bank reserves contracted and the monetary funds necessary for an expansion of business activity were not available. In brief, the monetary policy succeeded in maintaining the *de facto* gold standard but at a cost of limiting the expansion of the economy. Whether or not this policy could be continued indefinitely was open to serious question.

Monetary Issues in the Campaign of 1896. Cleveland's monetary policies alienated the majority of his party, and in the West and in the South the inflationists took over control. As the 1896 political conventions approached, it was a foregone conclusion that the Democratic platform

---

[6] Even among the bankers, the prevailing view was extremely pessimistic. Jacob Schiff thought, "It can only be a question of time before we are on a silver standard." (Cyrus Adler, *Jacob H. Schiff*, Vol. I, p. 262.)

would favor bimetallism. The only thing in doubt was the Presidential nominee.

A month before the Democratic convention, the Republicans met, and led by the erstwhile businessman Mark Hanna, they nominated William McKinley of Ohio. McKinley had an excellent reputation among protectionists, but his record on monetary issues aroused little enthusiasm among sound-money groups. He had voted for the Bland bill in 1877, the Bland-Allison Act, and the Sherman Silver Act. However, Hanna was a sound-money man through and through, and the Republican platform declared:

We are unalterably opposed to every measure calculated to debase our currency or impair the credit of our country. We are, therefore, opposed to the free coinage of silver except by international agreement and until such agreement can be obtained, the existing gold standard must be preserved.

Since there was no possibility of achieving international bimetallism, the plank was a complete endorsement of the gold coin standard. The advocates of silver were repudiated, and they withdrew from the convention.

In July, when the Democrats met in Chicago in an atmosphere charged with emotion, the silver steam roller quickly disposed of the Eastern sound-money group. Senator Hill and ex-Secretary of the Navy William C. Whitney made a valiant effort in support of the gold standard, but they were unsuccessful. At the climax of the debate on the money plank, William Jennings Bryan made the concluding address for the silverites. For years he had prepared for this opportunity, and when it came, it did not find him wanting. In a masterpiece of oratorical pyrotechnics, he began:

This is not a contest between persons. The humblest citizen in all the land, when clad in the armour of a righteous cause, is stronger than all the hosts of error. I come to speak to you in defence of a cause as holy as the cause of liberty—the cause of humanity.

Subtly, he impressed upon the delegates the conflict between the agrarians and industrialists,

The man who is employed for wages is as much a business man as his employer; the attorney in a country town is as much a business man as the corporation counsel in a great metropolis . . . ; the farmer who goes forth in the morning and toils all day . . . and who by the application of brain and muscle to the natural resources of the country creates wealth, is as much a business man as the man who goes upon the board of trade and bets upon the price of grain.

Skillfully combining persuasion and defiance, Bryan held his listeners spell-bound as he portrayed the silver advocates as strong men whose patience had finally broken down under constant provocation.

We are fighting in the defense of our homes. We have petitioned, and our petitions have been scorned; we have entreated, and our entreaties have been disregarded; we have begged, and they have mocked when our calamity came. We beg no longer; we entreat no more; we petition no more. We defy them.

Resurrecting the ghosts of Jefferson, Jackson, and Benton, the historical champions of agrarianism, he rang the changes on the productiveness of the farm as compared with the sterility of the city. He appealed to the Anglophobe by calling silver the "issue of 1776 over again." Gradually leading his audience to a peak of emotionalism, he closed with the famous passage,

Having behind us the producing masses of this nation and the world, supported by the commercial interests, the labouring interests, and the toilers everywhere, we will answer their demand for a gold standard by saying to them: You shall not press down upon the brow of labour this crown of thorns, you shall not crucify mankind upon a cross of gold.

Bryan's speech served its purposes magnificently. It did not matter that it was singularly lacking in economic profundities or that it was completely emotional. It gave silver a spokesman, and it gave the convention a nominee.

Crushing Defeat of the Silverites. In the ensuing campaign, the tariff issue receded into the background and free silver became dominant. As the "Advance Agent of Prosperity" and the progenitor of the "Full Dinner Pail," McKinley conducted his campaign conservatively. Hanna raised a large campaign fund and distributed more than 100 million pamphlets in a variety of languages. Conservatives on all sides—Democrats as well as Republicans—joined in the campaign against silver. The sound-money Democrats organized the National Democratic party and nominated John M. Palmer for President. Clergymen querulously referred to Bryan as "a mouthing, slobbering demagogue." Employers told their workers that they would close their plants if Bryan were elected. The *New York Tribune* declared that the Bryan campaign took the name of the Lord in vain and was based on theft, false witness, and covetousness. With more insight, the *Nation*, speaking for the conservatives, observed, "Probably no man in civil life has succeeded in inspiring so much terror, without taking life, as Bryan."

While McKinley conducted a "front-porch campaign" and had the assistance of almost all the nation's press, Bryan campaigned almost singlehandedly. He traveled throughout the country, on some days delivering as many as 36 speeches. But they were all essentially the same, and in time they lost their effectiveness. During the campaign the Treasury's gold reserve sank below $100 million, but the bankers quickly supplied enough to restore it. Near the close of the campaign, the price of wheat started to rise, and there was a general belief that business was recovering. Although this belief was premature, it hurt Bryan's prospects, and in November McKinley won a complete victory in the Electoral College, 271 to 176, but the popular vote was much closer—7 million to 6.5 million.

On the day after the election the New York *World* gave thanks for the verdict. "Not since the fall of Richmond have patriotic Americans had such cause for rejoicing. . . . Then the integrity of the Union was secured. Now its honor is preserved. It is a triumph of morality and patriotism." A writer in the Socialist *Arena* presented a more sophisticated analysis: "The real meaning of this campaign lies far deeper than any question of one metal or two for a monetary base. It is a question of entrusting Federal power to men in hearty sympathy with the great common people or to men in sympathy with Wall Street." As the champion of agrarianism, Bryan was an obstacle to the progress of the industrial and financial way of life, and with his defeat, the movement toward domination of American society by business, which had been going on since the Civil War, reached its fruition.[7]

The Dingley Tariff. Although the presidential campaign of 1896 had been fought over the currency issue, McKinley's chief interest continued to be the protective tariff. Disregarding for the moment the nation's monetary morass, his administration, to the disgust of the sound-money adherents, turned its primary attention to undoing the slight damage done to protectionism by the Wilson-Gorman Tariff. Its determination was strengthened by the continued Treasury deficit and the need for new revenue.

The resultant Dingley Tariff of July, 1897, was the highest tariff in the history of the country up to that time. Its average rate on dutiable imports in 1899 was 52 per cent compared with 40 per cent in 1896 under the Wilson-Gorman Act and 49.5 per cent in 1893 under the McKinley Tariff. The new tariff increased the duty on raw sugar, since revenue was badly needed and the infant beet-sugar industry demanded protection. In addition, it restored the duties on wool (removed by the 1894 tariff) and raised those on woolen goods, silks, linen and other textiles, and on the finer types of manufactured iron and steel (but not on steel rails and pig iron).

The most interesting feature of the Dingley Tariff was its reciprocity provision. Like the McKinley Tariff, it authorized the President to remove certain commodities from the free list. But it also authorized him to

[7] The bizarre aspects of the Bryan campaign have tended to monopolize public interest, and myths have been created tending to obscure its much more fundamental, if less sensational, social and economic aspects. (See, for example, James A. Barnes, "Myths of the Bryan Campaign," *Mississippi Valley Historical Review*, Vol. XXXIV, No. 3, December, 1947.)

reduce duties on a small list of commodities, and most important of all, he was given the power for two years to make treaties reducing duties up to 20 per cent. Such treaties were to be effective for five years and required the consent of the House as well as the Senate. It was the declared intention of the Republican party so to direct the treaties "as to open our markets on favorable terms for what we do not ourselves produce in return for free foreign markets." With such a unilateral idea in mind, it was not strange that none of the treaties made under the President's limited power was ratified.

The Dingley Act introduced the concept of "United States value" for appraising imported goods. Defined as the wholesale price (after deducting duties and transport costs) of similar merchandise offered for sale in the United States, United States value was to be used only when all methods of appraisal failed.

Financing the Spanish-American War. Under McKinley, American imperialism entered its heyday, and by the turn of the century the United States was emerging from her century-old isolationist shell and was becoming a factor in world politics and world finance. After many years of negotiation a treaty of annexation with Hawaii was ratified in July, 1898. In the meanwhile, the United States intervened on the side of Cuba against Spain, finally in 1898 becoming fully embroiled in war. By the peace treaty the Philippines were acquired for $20 million, Puerto Rico and Guam were annexed, and a protectorate over Cuba was assumed. Americans became deeply interested in political and economic developments in China and took part militarily in the Boxer insurrection in 1900. They also became involved financially and sentimentally in the Boer War, which broke out at about the same time.

Financially, the Spanish-American War was, as Theodore Roosevelt described it, "that splendid little war." It lasted only from April to August, 1898, and cost approximately $250 million, although its aftermaths in Cuba and the Philippines and in pension claims cost many times that amount.

Representative Dingley, chairman of the Ways and Means Committee, proposed to finance the war by loans and assorted excise taxes. Representatives from the South and the West countered with proposals for a 3 per cent income tax on all incomes over $2,000, the coinage of $42 million from the seigniorage on silver, and a $150 million greenback issue. In the end, a compromise was reached, imposing miscellaneous excises—stamp taxes on legal papers, cosmetics, drugs, chewing gum, playing cards, and pullman tickets; license taxes on bankers and brokers; and amusement taxes on admissions to theaters and other places of entertainment—imposing a stock-transfer tax, doubling tobacco and beer taxes, and levying an inheritance tax applicable to all estates of over $10,000, except those inherited by spouses, at rates ranging from ¾ of 1 per cent to 15 per cent.

In addition, Congress authorized the coinage of 1.5 million silver dollars and the issue of $100 million in 3 per cent certificates of indebtedness and $400 million of 10–20-year 3 per cent bonds. Bonds were issued in denominations as low as $20, and a total of $1.4 billion was subscribed. However, only $200 million was allotted. The number of subscribers was so large and subscriptions were offered so rapidly that the bonds could probably have been sold at a premium if they had been offered for competitive bidding.

TABLE 30. FEDERAL RECEIPTS, EXPENDITURES, AND DEBT, 1897–1899
(In millions of dollars)

	1897	1898	1899
Receipts:			
Customs..................	$ 176.6	$ 149.6	$ 206.1
Internal revenue..........	146.7	170.9	273.4
Other revenue............	24.5	84.8	36.4
Totals................	$ 347.7	$ 405.3	$ 516.0
Expenditures:			
Civil....................	$ 23.7	$ 24.0	$ 24.7
Foreign..................	2.1	2.5	22.6*
War.....................	35.3	71.2	213.7
Navy....................	34.6	58.8	63.9
River and harbor..........	13.7	20.8	16.1
Pensions.................	141.1	147.5	139.4
Indians..................	13.0	11.0	12.8
Interest..................	37.8	37.6	39.9
Other....................	64.6	70.0	71.9
Totals................	$ 365.8	$ 443.4	$ 605.1
Deficit...................	$ 18.1	$ 38.0	$ 89.1
Gross debt...............	1,817.7	1,796.5	1,991.9
Interest-bearing debt.........	847.4	847.4	1,046.0

SOURCE: *Annual Reports of the Secretary of the Treasury*, 1897–1899.

* $20 million to Spain for payment of ceded lands.

The bond sale also demonstrated that, with the revival of business activity, the Treasury's monetary difficulties had disappeared. Well over half the subscriptions, $125.2 million, were paid by check. But of cash payments $28.7 million were in gold; $25.3 million, in greenbacks; and $13.9 million, in silver certificates.

While the total costs of the war were covered chiefly by the $200 million loan, tax revenue in 1899 was $160 million higher than before the war, largely because of the Dingley Tariff, the wartime excise taxes, and the recovery in business. In 1898 the Union Pacific and Kansas Pacific Railroads paid $64 million in settlement of a total debt of about $70 million, and in the following year the Central Pacific settled its estimated $58.8 million debt by paying the government 20 notes of $2.9 million each. The last of these notes was paid off in 1909, bringing to a close the episode of Federal investment in the transcontinental railroads. Considering that without government help the railroads would not have been built until a much later period, the Federal experience with railroad finance turned out much more satisfactorily than the most sanguine observers had thought possible.

Premature Attempt to Establish the Gold Standard. Despite McKinley's lack of enthusiasm, the sound-money interests were determined to exercise the mandate of the 1896 election by establishing the gold standard and reforming the national banking system at the earliest possible time.

For many years, Comptrollers of the Currency and Secretaries of the Treasury had recommended sweeping changes in the National Bank Act, and by the eighties these recommendations were being echoed by bankers all over the country. The most important of the suggested reforms were designed to increase the elasticity or, more accurately, to diminish the inverse elasticity of the national-bank currency.

The need for an elastic bank currency was probably overemphasized, since state banks were by this time far more important than national banks, and it was estimated that over 90 per cent of the nation's business was transacted by check. Nevertheless, in the country areas where currency was used much more heavily, the national-bank note was very important. The country banks, in fact, issued more than 72 per cent of all bank notes, even though they had a far smaller amount of the total mediums of exchange. Moreover, the belief that there was not enough money in circulation was most prominent in the country areas. Conservative spokesmen, while opposed to cheap money, were anxious to appease the agrarian malcontents by suggesting methods to increase bank currency. In 1894 a convention of bankers recommended allowing national banks to issue notes secured by general assets. At about the same time Secretary Carlisle proposed the repeal of all laws requiring the deposit of bonds as security, the issue of national-bank notes up to 75 per cent of a bank's capital, a safety fund to be provided by taxation, and suspension of the 10 per cent tax on state-bank issues. At various other times it was suggested that the tax on national-bank circulation be lowered, that outstanding government bonds be refunded, and that the minimum capital requirement for national banks be reduced.

In January, 1897, the Indianapolis Board of Trade called a national convention of businessmen, representing boards of trade, chambers of commerce, and other similar bodies, to consider the question of monetary reform. The convention appointed a "monetary commission" to report a plan for the establishment of a gold standard and the improvement of the monetary system. The commission consisted of 11 members, including ex-Senator Edmunds, the author of the Resumption Act; ex-Secretary of the Treasury Fairchild; and Professor J. Lawrence Laughlin of Chicago University. Dr. H. Parker Willis, who was to be an active participant in the framing of the Federal Reserve Act twenty years later, was the research assistant. As a result of the commission's study, a bill to establish the gold standard was introduced in the House in January, 1898. The report, accompanying the bill cited the defects in the monetary system: the fiat money which represented a forced loan and lacked adequate provision for redemption; the national-bank notes secured by government bonds that were costly and difficult to obtain; the circulation of different forms of currency having different qualities of legal tender and receivability for government dues; the circulation of silver dollars whose face value was less than their bullion value; the impossibility of expanding the currency to meet the needs for seasonal increases, population growth, and commercial expansion; the unequal geographic distribution of loanable funds; the unjustified geographic variations in interest rates; and the confusion of the fiscal and monetary functions of the Treasury. The commission proposed to correct these weaknesses by adopting a *de jure* gold standard, retiring the greenbacks, changing the security for national-bank notes from government bonds to general assets, and separating the fiscal and monetary functions of the Treasury.

Congress took no action on the bill, and the commission spent the next two years in a campaign of public education. Numerous changes in the original bill were made to satisfy the critics who, while subscribing to the gold standard, were not yet ready for the more advanced features of the program, especially the proposal for altering the security of the national-bank note. While the monetary commission bill was being debated, a free-silver bill was defeated in the House, 182 to 132, ending the free-silver movement until the depression of the 1930's rekindled interest in inflation.

Effect of Business Recovery on Currency and Fiscal Operations. Fortunately for the reform movement, economic conditions began to improve in 1897 and received a great impetus in 1898 and 1899 from the Spanish-American War and the Boer War.[8] Business activity increased; international price levels, especially in farm commodities, recovered; European investors regained confidence in American securities; the balance of pay-

[8] The Spanish-American War increased government spending by more than 50 per cent. The British war with the Boers proved surprisingly prolonged and cost more than $1 million a day, a large part of which was spent in the United States.

TABLE 31. CHANGES IN CURRENCY AND PRICES, 1890–1899 (JULY 1)

	1890	1892	1894	1896	1898	1899
	In millions of dollars					
United States notes:						
In circulation	$334.7	$309.6	$266.6	$224.2	$284.6	$308.4
In Treasury	12.0	37.1	80.1	122.4	62.1	38.3
National-bank notes:						
In circulation	181.6	167.2	200.2	215.2	223.0	237.8
In Treasury	4.4	5.5	6.6	10.8	4.9	3.5
Subsidiary silver:						
In circulation	54.0	63.3	58.5	60.2	64.1	69.1
In Treasury	22.8	14.2	17.7	15.8	12.1	5.8
Silver dollars:						
In circulation	56.3	56.8	52.6	52.1	58.5	61.5
In Treasury	323.8	434.2	495.4	499.6	502.9	502.2
Silver certificates:						
(including Treasury notes of 1890)						
In circulation	297.6	424.9	461.7	425.7	488.4	494.7
In Treasury	4.0	8.4	28.1	46.6	11.3	4.9
Gold coin:						
In circulation	374.3	408.6	496.0	454.9	658.0	679.7
In Treasury	321.3	255.7	131.3	144.7	203.6	283.8
Gold certificates:						
In circulation	130.8	141.1	66.3	42.2	35.8	32.7
In Treasury	26.7	15.5	.....	0.6	1.6	1.6
Other currency in circulation	.....	29.8	58.9	31.9	25.6	20.3
	In dollars					
Per capita money in circulation	$22.82	$24.44	$24.28	$21.10	$24.66	$25.00
Price of No. 2 wheat bushel in Chicago	0.89	0.79	0.55	0.64	1.08	
	Index numbers					
Wholesale prices (United States 1860 = 100)	92.2	85.6	78.6	76.3	79.5	85.6
Wholesale prices (Great Britain 1860 = 100)	72.5	68.9	63.6	61.4	64.4	68.8

SOURCE: *Annual Reports of the Secretary of the Treasury*, 1898, 1899; U.S. Census Bureau, *Historical Statistics of the United States*, 1949; Clough and Cole, *Economic History of Europe*; *Annual Report of the Director of the Mint*, 1898.

ments became favorable; gold production increased; and in 1900 a Treasury surplus reappeared and a large percentage of government dues were again paid in gold.

As prosperity returned, larger amounts of money were needed to transact business. Payrolls and profits swelled, and the national income, estimated at $10.7 billion in 1889, rose to $16.2 billion in 1900. Domestic savings increased substantially, enabling the United States to become an important lender in the world money market and reducing the pressure imposed on her gold stock by the net liquidation of foreign holdings.[9] The new prosperity also exerted an upward pressure on domestic prices. At the same time, farm production was stabilized, and farm prices began to rise. In 1898 the average price of spring wheat in Chicago passed $1 a bushel for the first time in fifteen years. After thirty years of secular decline, an upward trend began of almost the same length, increasing the demand for currency and tending to make it less redundant.[10] As business recovered, the demand for currency increased and the stock of money which had piled up in the Treasury began to enter circulation. Between 1896 and 1899 money in circulation increased from $21.10 to $25 per capita while the Treasury's cash holdings remained practically the same.

Coincidental with the need for increased supplies of money came discoveries of new gold mines and new processes for refining the metal. World gold production increased from 5.7 million ounces in 1890 to 9.8 million in 1896 and 13.9 million in 1898. In addition, beginning in August, 1897, gold began to be imported. Consequently by 1898 the estimated stock of gold in the United States was more than 40 per cent greater than in 1896. Thus, there was brought into existence an adequate amount of gold to act as a base for expanding the money supply, eliminating one of the most potent arguments of the silver advocates.

From a fiscal standpoint, prospects for establishing the gold standard also were more encouraging. The Treasury deficit ended in 1900, eliminating the need for borrowing in the money market. Then, too, the increased gold production made possible larger payments of government dues in gold, and by April, 1898, 52.7 per cent of customs duties were paid in gold.

In short, for the first time since the Civil War economic conditions were on a solid enough basis to make possible the adoption of a gold standard.

[9] The Boer War experience typified the change that was occurring. In 1899 British investors began to liquidate American holdings, money tightened, and the call rate in New York rose to 186 per cent. But the economy rode out the storm. Funds were provided not only for the domestic market but for loans to Britain as well.

[10] The historical evidence of the period 1873 to 1900 seems to demonstrate that, in the absence of flourishing business activity and heavy spending, additional supplies of currency did not raise prices. On the other hand, rising prices resulted from expanded business activity and spending and caused an increase in money in circulation and an expansion of credit.

CHAPTER 21: THE PROGRESSIVE ERA: MONETARY AND BANKING REFORMS

At the opening of the twentieth century the United States was in the midst of one of the most important transitional periods in her social, economic, and political evolution. It was an age of optimism and faith in the future. But each segment of society had its own interpretation of what the future would bring. Industrialists expected to dominate the markets of the world. Financiers were confident that New York City would soon replace London as the principal international money market. Farmers took on new hope as relative prosperity appeared in agriculture. Workers believed that the eight-hour day and the trade agreement would soon be universal. Imperialists were absorbed in the "white man's burden" in the Far East and the development of South American markets under "dollar diplomacy." Government functionaries saw themselves advancing steadily in importance in the economic and social scene.

Though not equaling the original expectations, the economic achievements of this era were substantial, especially during the years 1900 to 1905. According to the estimates of Professor Kuznets, per capita national income in constant prices in the decade 1899 to 1908 averaged 14.2 per cent more than in the previous decade, but in 1904 to 1913 it was only 9.6 per cent higher than in the previous ten years.

The years up to 1904 were also featured by vast consolidations of business enterprise and great expansion in trade-union membership. By 1904 it was estimated that 40 per cent of the total capital invested in manufacturing was controlled by trusts of one sort or other, and between 1899 and 1904 trade-union membership grew from 604,000 to 2,072,000. However, after 1904 the consolidation movement slowed down, while labor unions had difficulty in holding their own.

As the economy grew and became more complicated, more regulatory and other services by government were demanded. But even if these demands had not developed, the Federal government would still have been impelled to widen its sphere of activities. The United States was obtaining a "place in the sun," as imperialistic advocates expressed it, and the expansion of her colonial power and her influence in world affairs magnified the importance of the Federal government in the public eye and caused a greater activity on its part. Moreover, the philosophy of government and the management of Federal affairs had changed fundamentally. Whereas the post-Civil War Presidents believed in minimum Federal activity, the Presidents of the new era—Theodore Roosevelt, Taft, and Wilson—favored Federal economic intervention. They were not only conscious of the problems presented by the increasing influence of finance capitalism and by the struggle of organized labor for a better status, but they were aware of the national character of these problems and the inability of state and local governments to deal with them adequately. These men were therefore included among the so-called "progressives."

On the whole, Roosevelt's progressivism was not very deep or consistent, and he did not fulfill much of his "square deal" economic program, which embraced "trust busting," strengthening the Interstate Commerce Commission, and tariff reform. But he was singularly effective in launching broad programs of conservation of natural resources and reclamation of Western farm lands. Being a nationalist and expansionist, he was most effective in the international sphere. He made the Panama Canal a reality, gave a broader meaning to the Monroe Doctrine, initiated the so-called "dollar diplomacy," and relentlessly pressed for a big navy.

On the other hand, the administration of Taft, Roosevelt's chosen successor, achieved a reputation for conservatism but actually accelerated the expansion of Federal powers and adopted a number of progressive measures: a Federal corporation tax, an income tax amendment, and a postal savings system. It created a National Monetary Commission and a Tariff Board, while Taft himself pressed vigorously for an executive budget and greater efficiency in Federal administration.

Woodrow Wilson, with his program of the "New Freedom," brought to fruition the expansion of powers initiated by his two predecessors, while extending the boundaries of social progressivism still further. Wilson brought about the first real tariff reform since 1846, as well as more stringent antitrust legislation, fundamental banking and monetary reform, and the enactment of a graduated income tax.

The vast increase in Federal powers was accompanied by a less picturesque, but even broader, accentuation of state and local activity. Under the guidance of experts and with new methods of public management, municipal and state governments became the laboratories for experiments which later were carried over into the Federal administration. Systems of centralized administrative control, budgeting, independent auditing, accounting, and the use of the government corporation, so important in Federal management in later times, were first developed on the state level. Thus, the trend was not so much toward the centralization of government in Washington as it was toward an ever-widening area of government powers in general.

This expansion of activities was achieved only by tremendous increases in the expenditures of all governments, Federal, state, and city. Especially on the Federal level, the government progressively expanded its long-accepted functions and entered fields of activity and spending which had been regarded with distrust by previous administrations.

The Currency Act of 1900. In March, 1900, Congress passed the Currency Act of 1900, otherwise known as the Gold Standard Act. Embodying most of the Indianapolis Monetary Commission's recommendations, it fundamentally changed the monetary and banking system as follows:

1. It established a monometallic gold standard with a dollar of 25.8 grains of gold, nine-tenth fine, and directed the Secretary of the Treasury to maintain all forms of money in parity with this standard.

2. It directed the Secretary of the Treasury to set aside a fund of $150 million in gold coin and bullion to be used to redeem greenbacks and Treasury notes of 1890. If the gold reserve fell below $150 million, the redeemed notes were to be retained in the fund to make up the difference. If it fell below $100 million, the Secretary was to discontinue issuing gold certificates and to sell for gold enough 3 per cent one-year gold bonds to raise the reserve to its legal minimum.

3. The Treasury notes of 1890 were to be withdrawn from circulation and replaced with silver dollars, and the issue of certificates of deposits was discontinued.

4. The minimum capital for a national bank was reduced to $25,000 for cities with less than 3,000 population.

5. National-bank notes could be issued up to the full par value of deposited bonds, instead of 90 per cent as previously.

6. The Treasury was authorized to refund the outstanding 5's of 1904, 4's of 1907, and 3's of 1908 into 30-year 2 per cent bonds (consols of 1930). The value of the refundable bonds was calculated to maturity on a basis to yield 2¼ per cent, and the difference between this capitalized value and par was to be paid to the owner in cash. To increase the inducement to refund, the tax on circulation secured by the new 2 per cent bonds was reduced to ¼ of 1 per cent semiannually, while the tax on notes secured by the old bonds remained at ½ of 1 per cent.

Effects of the Act on Gold and Silver Circulation. The Act strengthened the gold standard and facilitated the gold redemption of paper money in at least four main ways: by segregating the gold reserve from the Treasury's cash balance and preventing its use to cover budgetary deficits; by increasing the reserve from $100 million to $150 million; by directing its replenishment through the sale of short-term gold obligations; and by sterilizing the greenbacks in times of their increased presentation for redemption in gold. The Act was singularly successful in accomplishing these objectives. Of course, this would not have been possible had not economic conditions been favorable. However, with greater business activity and a large inflow of gold, the Treasury reserve increased to well over $200 million, far in excess of the requirements.

The Currency Act also improved the silver circulation. Treasury notes of 1890 were rapidly retired and by 1910 amounted to less than $4 million, compared with a peak circulation of $141 million in 1893. Most of the notes were redeemed in silver dollars, reducing the Treasury's silver-bullion stock. At the same time the growth of population and the rise of business activity increased the circulation of subsidiary silver and silver certificates so greatly that the bullion purchased under the Sherman Act was exhausted, and by 1905 the Treasury's accumulated silver dollars were not in excess of the amount that could be disposed of in the regular transaction of government business.

Effects of the Act on the Volume of Banking Currency. The banking provisions of the Currency Act were enormously successful in accomplishing their main purpose, the expansion of national-bank-note circulation. The substantial reduction in the circulation tax and the privilege of issuing notes against the full par value of deposited bonds made it profitable once again for the banks to issue notes, and they began to purchase government bonds in the open market and to issue notes against them. By 1905 they held over 50 per cent of the Federal net debt; by 1907, almost 70 per cent; and in 1914, almost 75 per cent. National-bank circulation more than doubled in eight years, from $265 million in 1900 to $614 million in 1908. At the same time, the refunding provisions offered the banks a capital profit which they were quick to accept, and by 1905 over 98 per cent of the securities behind bank notes were 2 per cent consols of 1930.

Because the banks constantly purchased the old bonds in the market and exchanged them for new consols, the government was able, by

TABLE 32.   RESULTS OF REFUNDING OPERATIONS, 1900–1903
(In millions of dollars)

	3%	4%	5%	Total
Amount refunded into 2% consols.............	$119.3	$351.6	$72.1	$542.9
Interest saved on old bonds to maturity........	27.3	89.9	13.1	130.2
Less interest paid on new bonds to maturity of old bonds.................................	18.2	44.9	5.2	68.3
Less premium paid on old bonds..............	6.2	36.4	6.9	49.5
Plus premium received for new bonds..........	0.4	1.5	.....	1.9
Net profit.................................	3.2	10.0	1.0	14.2

SOURCE: *Annual Report of the Secretary of the Treasury*, 1904, p. 19.

December 31, 1903, to refund $500 million of the $839 million of refundable obligations outstanding in 1900. The Secretary of the Treasury claimed a $14.2 million profit for the government on the conversion.

Actually, far from providing a profit, the refunding in the long run cost the Treasury considerable extra money, as it compelled the government, despite the realization of substantial surpluses, to keep outstanding a large debt on which interest had to be paid. With a total surplus of $277.5 million from 1900 to 1907, only $151.2 million of the interest-bearing debt was paid off, and even on this heavy premiums were paid.[1] But this extra cost was entered upon designedly as an aid to the maintenance of national-bank-note circulation.

TABLE 33. NATIONAL-BANK OPERATIONS, 1890–1914
(In millions of dollars)

Year	No. of banks	Loans	Investments	Capital	National-bank notes in circulation	Individual deposits	U.S. government deposits
1890	3,484	$1,934	$ 311	$ 642	$126	$1,522	$ 31
1895	3,715	2,017	447	658	179	1,736	13
1897	3,610	1,978	484	632	197	1,771	16
1900	3,732	2,624	775	622	265	2,458	99
1903	4,939	3,415	1,025	744	359	3,201	147
1905	5,668	3,899	1,205	792	446	3,784	75
1908	6,778	4,528	1,520	912	614	4,314	182
1910	7,145	5,430	1,576	990	676	5,287	55
1912	7,372	5,954	1,823	1,034	707	5,826	59
1914	7,525	6,430	1,870	1,058	723	6,269	67

SOURCE: Annual Report of the Comptroller of the Currency, 1914; Federal Reserve Board, Banking and Monetary Statistics, p. 20.

Effect of the Currency Act on National Banking. The Currency Act of 1900 also contributed to a marked increase in the number of national banks. The return of profitable note issue, the reduction of capital requirements, and the general improvement of economic conditions resulted in the formation of 3,046 national banks between 1900 and 1908, almost doubling the number in existence in 1900. It was debatable whether this increase was entirely beneficial, for almost two-thirds of all the new banks were capitalized at less than $50,000, and banks with small capitalization were the most vulnerable to failure. In 1905, for example, 23

[1] Premiums paid by the Treasury under the Currency Act and in open-market purchases were $74.0 million in 1900 to 1904 and $1.6 million in 1906 to 1907.

national banks failed. Of these 6 were capitalized at $25,000, 6 at $50,000, 5 between $50,000 and $100,000, 3 between $100,000 and $200,000, and 3 at $300,000.

For obvious economic reasons, most of the increase in the number of banks occurred in the South and in the West. Between 1900 and 1908, 1,784 banks were organized west of the Mississippi River and south of the Mason-Dixon line. The enormous increase in the number of country banks accentuated the pyramiding of reserves which characterized the national banking system. And since country banks still transacted most of their business in cash, the increase in their number also accentuated inelasticity by giving further impetus to the issue of national-bank notes. In 1908, for example, country banks accounted for 55 per cent of the aggregate national banking capital and surplus, 48 per cent of total loans and discounts, and 64 per cent of the total bank-note circulation.

Further Revival of State Banks. Although national banking experienced a new burst of activity in the first decade of the new century, its relative importance in the whole banking structure continued to decline. State commercial banks, which had surpassed the national banks in number in 1892, continued to grow faster both in number and in the size of their business. And a new type of banking organization, the trust company, had the most spectacular growth of all.

TABLE 34. BANK DEPOSITS, 1900 AND 1908
(In millions of dollars)

Section	1900			1908		
	National banks	State banks	Trust companies	National banks	State banks	Trust companies
New England........	$ 312.3	$ 8.9	$ 163.9	$ 402.7	$ 11.3	$ 315.6
Eastern states........	1,073.6	341.3	859.4	1,758.8	534.8	1,403.9
Southern states.......	201.6	150.4	0.3	434.5	447.0	8.8
Middle West.........	651.8	561.2	4.7	1,193.3	1,358.5	129.6
Western states........	142.8	84.9	....	332.0	237.7	9.1
Pacific states.........	75.9	118.2	....	252.0	328.5*	
Islands..............	....	1.8	....	1.2	19.3	
Totals...........	$2,458.1	$1,266.7	$1,028.2	$4,374.5	$2,937.1	$1,867.0

SOURCE: *Annual Report of the Comptroller of the Currency*, 1908, p. 41.

* Includes trust companies.

In 1890 state-bank deposits were equal to a little more than 33⅓ per cent of national-bank deposits; by 1908 they were equal to almost 70 per cent. Most of this increase occurred in the West and South, where state-bank deposits actually surpassed national-bank deposits. In the more populous East, the growth of state commercial banks was comparatively small, but the expansion of trust companies was more than sufficient to place the national banks in a subordinate position. Between 1894 and 1904 the trust companies in New York City increased from 27 to 47, while national banks declined from 47 to 41. The relative growth of deposits was even more striking. Trust-company deposits increased more than 3½ times from $260 million to $875 million, while national-bank deposits only doubled from $550 million to $1.1 billion.

Table 34 demonstrates that deposits in national banks still exceeded those in state banks and trust companies in 1900. But by 1908 this was no longer true, and it was evident that the national banking system had failed to fulfill almost all the great hopes originally held for it. The state banks had not been displaced as had been hoped, and the nation still had 49 different types of banking regulation. Although a uniform currency had been produced, it was inelastic and it had failed to become the universal currency of the country. Even in 1908, after a number of years of ex-

TABLE 35. OPERATIONS OF STATE BANKS AND TRUST COMPANIES*
(In millions of dollars)
State Banks

Year	Number	Real estate loans	Other loans	Other assets	Capital and surplus	Deposits
1890	2,101	$ 34.3	$ 547.2	$ 289.3	$262.4	$ 553.1
1895	3,774	44.3	648.5	454.7	351.4	712.4
1897	3,857	50.0	619.8	468.3	330.9	723.6
1900	4,369	61.0	969.3	729.5	366.9	1,266.7
1905	7,794	123.4	1,760.7	1,306.8	597.4	2,365.2
1908	11,220	188.4	2,218.2	1,626.0	806.1	2,937.1
1910	12,166	472.4	1,903.1	1,319.6	689.1	2,727.9
1912	13,381	572.9	1,943.5	1,381.4	730.4	2,920.0
1914	14,512	539.4	2,340.4	1,473.9	768.2	3,226.8

Trust Companies

Year	Number	Real estate loans	Loans on securities	Other loans	Other assets	Capital and surplus	Deposits
1904	585	$110.0	$ 655.3	$ 382.3	$1,232.7	$ 567.5	$1,600.3
1908	842	153.7	821.3	404.4	1,486.1	694.4	1,867.0
1912	1,410	526.5	1,280.0	900.4	2,400.5	975.7	3,674.6
1914	1,564	565.5	1,213.9	1,122.4	2,587.7	1,032.6	3,939.8

SOURCE: *Annual Reports of the Comptroller of the Currency*, 1908, 1914.

* Includes only those states reporting to the Comptroller of the Currency and is, therefore, incomplete.

pansion, national-bank notes represented only 20 per cent of the total circulation. Nor had the plan for a constant and inexhaustible market for government bonds turned out beneficially, for when the government's deficit was replaced by a surplus, it was forced to maintain its debt and surrender its freedom of action in fiscal operations. Finally, the national banking system had not succeeded in protecting the community from bank failures, although unquestionably, taken as a whole, national banks were safer than state banks. From 1863 to 1907, 8,853 national banks were chartered. Of these 449 failed, but 80 per cent of the claims of creditors were satisfied, and the total money loss was approximately $50 million. In the same period there were almost 2,000 failures among state banks with losses impossible to estimate, but certainly far in excess of $100 million.

Whatever safety had been given to the banking system by the National Bank Act was progressively diminished by the developments after 1900. The easing of capital requirements invited inefficient management and encouraged the formation of smaller and weaker banks. The lax regulation of state banks and trust companies created a demand for less rigid national-bank regulation, and state commercial banks and trust companies increased their real estate loans and security investments at the expense of their commercial loans, thus impairing their liquidity in an era when there was no central bank to which illiquid assets could be shifted.

The Postal Savings System. In June, 1910, the Federal government, after many years of agitation by progressive forces, established a postal savings system designed as a depository for the savings of the low-income groups. A board of trustees, consisting of the Postmaster General, the Secretary of the Treasury, and the Attorney General, was created and authorized to designate specific post offices as postal savings offices. Interest at 2 per cent per annum was to be paid on deposits. Of the postal savings funds, 5 per cent was to be deposited with the Treasurer of the United States as a reserve. The remainder could be deposited with national or state banks if secured by public obligations and if at least 2¼ per cent interest was paid. The Board of Trustees was also empowered to invest up to 30 per cent of the total funds in United States bonds.

The Postal Savings Act was passed when Congress was beginning to think seriously about establishing a central bank and eliminating the bond-secured circulation. But the 2 per cent consols of 1930 presented a serious problem. Since their only advantage was to act as security against bank notes and since there was no market for them among individual citizens, the national banks had to be relieved of them before the bond-secured currency could be eliminated. It was thought by some supporters of central banking that the postal savings system could buy the 2 per cents from the national banks. However, this was not necessary, for when the Federal Reserve Act was passed, it did not provide for complete and immediate elimination of national-bank notes. In any case, the postal savings system did not immediately become the roaring success which its sponsors had envisaged. By 1914 it had acquired only $5.9 million of Federal bonds. Total deposits in 6,717 depositories were $41 million, representing 388,511 different depositors. Between 1913 and 1914 deposits increased about $10 million in contrast to a $200 million increase in private savings bank deposits.

New York City Develops into an International Money Market. During the first decade of the twentieth century, the great rise in national income and the extraordinary growth of banks, trust companies, and other financial institutions enabled the United States to prepare to step out of her role of consistent borrower and enter the ranks of the principal lending nations.[2] The opportunity came with the Boer War. To meet the costs of this vastly under-estimated African campaign, Great Britain not only had to stop all her foreign lending, thus prompting her customary borrowers to turn to the United States for accommodations, but eventually she herself had to borrow. The American bankers made the most of their opportunity. In 1889 they sold $2.2 million of Chinese securities to finance the construction of the Hankow-Canton Railroad. In 1900 the National Park Bank negotiated a $10 million loan for Sweden, Germany borrowed $20 million through Kuhn, Loeb and Co., $10 million was loaned to various continental cities, and the National City Bank floated a $25 million loan for Russian railroads. In March, 1900, Great Britain began to tap the New York money market, and by 1902 she had borrowed $227 million, $223 million being placed by Morgan syndicates in four different loans all of which were oversubscribed.

Optimists prophesied that New York would soon usurp London's position as the world's money market, and as long as Europeans were engaged in wars, this possibility was not far-fetched. However, when the Boer War ended, England again assumed her preeminent position, and by 1903

[2] In the twenty years after the Civil War, the continuous expansion of industry and the construction of railroads absorbed all of America's domestic savings and in addition required continuous borrowing in Europe. American industrialists and investment bankers made international investments only occasionally and only on a small scale. Morgan, Dabney and Company took part in a small Peruvian loan in the sixties, and in 1879 Morgan sold $3 million of a Quebec loan. After the Spanish-American War American bankers sold a number of loans for Mexico. By 1898 industrialists had directly invested some $350 million in Central and South America and the West Indies, and total American foreign investments were only $685 million. Since foreign investments in the United States aggregated $3.4 billion, the United States was a net debtor for $2.7 billion. (Cleona Lewis, *America's Stake in International Investments*, p. 445.)

she had repurchased most of the British and German bonds sold in the United States during the period of her imperial embarrassment.

The Russo-Japanese War in 1904–1905 gave international lending by the United States a new lease on life. Kuhn Loeb and Co. placed $130 million of Japanese loans on very favorable investment terms. But the end of the Manchurian War temporarily brought to a close the abortive rise of the American investment banker as an international lender. By 1909 American overseas investments had increased to $2.5 billion, but foreign investments in the United States had increased to $6.4 billion, leaving the United States a net debtor for $3.9 billion.

Treasury Attempts to Regulate the Money Market. Freed of the vexatious problem of maintaining the gold standard against the demand of the in-flationists, the Treasury, under Secretaries Shaw and Cortelyou, turned its attention to the positive contributions which it could make toward alleviating panics and producing a greater degree of stability in the money market.

When Shaw assumed office in 1902, the Independent Treasury system was still in existence, although its original prohibition against using the banks as public depositories and against accepting anything but specie or Treasury notes in payment of government dues had been partially re-moved or fundamentally modified. Beginning with the Civil War, the Treasury was permitted to make deposits in national banks under speci-fied conditions, and greenbacks and national-bank notes were made re-ceivable for all government dues except customs. Later, silver certificates and Treasury notes of 1890 were made receivable for government dues.

Along with the legislative modifications of the system, a change in philosophy took place. The agrarian groups which had been whole-heartedly opposed to soft money disappeared. At the same time the Inde-pendent Treasury system became one of the issues in the developing struggle between business and government, for the modern businessman regarded the Jacksonian separation of government from banking as an unwarranted sabotaging of business by government.

Actually, the Treasury could not remain aloof from the banks. Each time it collected customs duties or taxes, bank reserves were contracted. Each time the Treasury paid out funds, bank reserves were expanded. As the operations of the Federal government increased, the shock on the banking system increased to a like degree. Describing the situation as it existed in 1910, Professor Wildman wrote:

On August 4, the treasury drew pension checks amounting to $14,970,000. . . . About half of this sum was drawn upon the assistant treasurer at New York. . . . In a few days . . . an equivalent amount of money is transferred from the subtreasury to the banks whose combined reserves . . . are increased $7 million. Without any alteration in the aggregate wealth of the country or even of New York City the lending power of the New York banks is raised about $28 million.

To reverse the illustration let us suppose that the collection of duties at . . . New York in a given week reaches . . . $10 million. This amount of money is drawn from local banks and trust companies and locked up in the sub-Treasury. In as far as the effect on reserves and lending power is concerned, it might quite as well have been sunk in New York harbor. The rate for call loans rises, stocks fall or commercial paper . . . remains unsold and the production and exchange of goods may be curtailed.[3]

But even if the Treasury had been able to remain aloof from the banks, it would not have been permitted to do so by its more modern managers, who conceived it to be their responsibility to regulate the money market. In his report for 1906 Secretary Shaw asserted that it was the government's duty to protect the people against financial panics just as it protected them from yellow fever. But the tools which the government could use to regulate the money market were very crude. It issued and redeemed notes, transferred funds to move crops, and maintained a gold reserve. It could therefore exert some influence over the total amount of money and over the discount rate by contracting and expanding currency, by increasing and decreasing its gold reserve, and by shifting funds between the banks and the subtreasuries.

Shaw almost immediately expanded these functions. To offset the seasonal demand for funds in the spring and in the fall, he withdrew government deposits in the winter and summer, held them as a cash reserve, and redeposited them as stringency developed in the money market. In 1906, for example, he drew down $60 million and held it for redeposit.

He not only continued to use the national banks as depositories but allowed banks to collect government moneys and used bank warrants to pay its obligations. In addition, he announced that depository banks need not maintain the legal reserve requirement against government deposits. To help banks import gold, he agreed to make deposits with them while gold was in transit. By thus eliminating interest losses, he lowered the gold import point. In 1902 he contributed, probably beyond his legal authority, to an expansion of bank-note currency. Under the terms of the National Bank Act, the government could deposit funds in any national bank, but the Secretary was directed to require security "by the deposit of United States bonds *and* otherwise." Sensing an imminent shortage of reserves, Shaw informed the banks that he would accept selected state and municipal obligations as security against government deposits provided the released United States bonds were used as a base for the

[3] "The Independent Treasury and the Banks," *Annals of the American Academy*, November, 1910.

issue of additional bank-note circulation. In 1904 he added railroad bonds, and in 1907 Congress removed any doubts as to the legality of Shaw's actions by specifically providing that bonds other than Federal obligations could be used as security for deposits.

Shaw was active in other ways in attempting to regulate the money market. He and his successor Cortelyou anticipated the payment of interest on government bonds, and in order to put money back into circulation, they purchased bonds in the open market at. premiums, Shaw paying as high as 38 points. Together with the Comptrollers of the Currency, they constantly clamored for improvements in the currency. To give added elasticity to national-bank notes, they suggested that banks be allowed to increase the maximum amount of currency which they could retire each month. To correct the tendency of bank reserves to concentrate in New York, Cortelyou suggested that the country be divided into zones with the reserves of the banks in each zone retained in the zone itself, thus presaging the plan set up a few years later under the Federal Reserve Act. Congress heeded some of the Treasury's recommendations, and in 1907 permitted national banks to retire up to $9 million of bank notes per month, but no serious consideration was given to the more important recommendations dealing with the basic weakness of the system.

If Shaw intended to expand the currency, he was vastly successful. National-bank-note circulation, stimulated by the Currency Act of 1900 and the Secretary's activities, constantly expanded. Holdings of bonds, other than those of the United States, as security against deposits also increased from approximately $20 million in 1902 to $150 million in 1908. But if the goal was to stabilize the money market, the Treasury was not successful, for the conditions which aggravated panics were inherent in the national banking system.

Panic of 1907. The panic of 1907 was exclusively banking. It could not, as in 1873, be blamed upon an overly large amount of irredeemable greenbacks or, as in 1893, upon a redundant silver currency. For some time there had been an unhealthy increase in speculative activity. Large amounts of capital funds were concentrated in New York City, some estimates putting the amount at $500 million of foreign funds and $300 million of domestic.[4] As was customary, out-of-town banks were redepositing their reserves with New York banks, the Secretary of the Treasury estimating that about 20 per cent of total bank reserves were redeposited.

By late summer, there were numerous evidences that the money market was teetering on its high pedestal. New issues of railroad securities were

[4] Alexander D. Noyes, *Forty Years of American Finance*, pp. 355–356. Chapter 15 contains an excellent account of the panic.

not being easily disposed of, copper stocks and other securities were overvalued by conservative standards, and building construction was beginning to slacken. In August, bank loans reached a peak, and reserves in New York City banks were close to the legal minimum, but higher than at the same date in 1906 and 1905. Interest rates began to tighten, and the Secretary of the Treasury began to deposit $28 million of government funds around the country to facilitate the movement of crops.

In mid-October, the panic broke out. After a decline in the price of copper stocks, there was a run on the Mercantile National Bank. This quickly spread to the trust companies which were heavily involved in copper pools. On October 22 the Knickerbocker Trust Company, holding $50 million of deposits for 17,000 depositors, closed its doors. For many days, runs continued on the Trust Company of America and the Lincoln Trust Company. Meanwhile, the banks, like their depositors, sought to turn their assets into cash. Loans began to contract, and the call-money rate rose to 125 per cent. It was estimated that almost $300 million of currency disappeared completely from the outbreak of the panic in late October to the time when it began to subside in December, and bank reserves in New York fell from a surplus of $11 million to a deficit of $54 million.

The banks tried to lessen the shortage of currency induced by the private hoarding of cash. Clearinghouse certificates were introduced on October 26, but on a much larger scale than in any previous panic. The maximum amount outstanding in New York was $88.4 million as compared with $38.3 million during the panic of 1893. Clearinghouses throughout the country did the same with the result that $238 million of such certificates were issued in the United States as against $69 million during 1893. To retain their fast-dwindling reserves, the members of the New York Clearing House agreed to suspend cash payments. Immediately cash went to a premium in terms of checks, $100 in cash being worth $104 in checks in New York City. Business houses began to settle their accounts in emergency currency or scrip, and it seemed likely that, unless the hysterical rush for liquidity could be stopped, economic transactions would return to the barter state.

Meanwhile the Treasury tried to stem the panic by pouring money into the banks. Between August and December government deposits in the banks were increased by approximately $80 million, reducing Treasury cash to a dangerous minimum. In addition, Cortelyou proposed to increase the base for an expansion of national-bank notes by selling the banks $50 million of 2 per cent bonds and $100 million of 3 per cent certificates. To prevent further curtailment of bank reserves, the Treasury planned to leave 90 per cent of the bond proceeds and 75 per cent of the certificate proceeds on deposit with the banks. But this plan would have at least partially cut the already desperately small bank reserves. Consequently, when the obligations were finally offered in mid-November, only $24.6 million of the bonds and $15.4 million of the certificates were placed.

There were some bright spots in the general economic picture, and these asserted themselves before long. American crops were good and European crops were poor, resulting in an upward tendency in the balance of trade. Furthermore, the premium on cash offered attractive possibilities for profit to those who were fortunate enough to have currency and who were intrepid enough to take a slight risk. Hence, there,was pressure on the pound sterling, and it fell to $4.80, far below the normal gold import point of $4.84. In November and December a net of $104 million of gold was imported, and in January, 1908, after the disappearance of the premium on cash, an additional $9 million arrived. The cash that was poured in from the Treasury and from abroad ended the shortage of currency and stopped the panic.

Aldrich-Vreeland Act and the National Monetary Commission. With its periodic money panics and the continual strains which it exerted on the gold supply, the United States was clearly disrupting international financial affairs. The panic of 1907 was the last straw. A European banker epitomized the impatience of bankers and monetary experts, both in Europe and in the United States, with the inefficiencies of the American banking structure by bluntly declaring that the United States was "a great financial nuisance." Banking opinion turned more and more to plans for central banking and methods for increasing the elasticity of the currency. As early as 1906 the American Bankers Association and the New York Chamber of Commerce, echoing the recommendations of the Indianapolis Monetary Commission, proposed that national banks be permitted to issue notes secured by general assets. In his report of 1907 Comptroller of the Currency Ridgely proposed "the establishment by the government of a central bank of issue and reserve" to correct the inelasticity of the currency and the immobility of reserves and to "provide machinery for conducting Treasury operations in their relations to the banks with the least disturbance."

In May, 1908, with the experience of the panic still fresh in mind, Congress took the first steps toward correcting the patent weaknesses in American banking. It enacted the Aldrich-Vreeland bill, with the following provisions:

1. National banks at least 10 in number with at least $5 million in capital and surplus could form a National Currency Association.

2. Through the Currency Association, a bank with outstanding circulating notes equal to at least 40 per cent of its capital could apply to the Comptroller

of the Currency for emergency currency to be issued against 90 per cent of the market value of certain specified state or city bonds and up to 75 per cent of the cash value of other securities or commercial paper. But total emergency currency was limited to $500 million and was to be taxed progressively, beginning at 5 per cent per annum in the first month and increasing 1 per cent per month up to 10 per cent.

3. National banks were required to pay interest on government deposits at a rate to be determined by the Secretary of the Treasury. (The rate was set at 1 per cent in 1908 and at 2 per cent in 1913.)

4. The Act was to expire June 30, 1914.

5. A Monetary Commission of nine senators and nine congressmen was established to make a comprehensive study of the necessary and desirable changes in the money and the banking system.

Under the chairmanship of Senator Nelson Aldrich, the National Monetary Commission immediately began upon the labors which were eventually to be of great importance in the writing of the Federal Reserve Act. With the aid of experts the commission made an array of studies of banking and currency problems, eventually publishing them in more than twenty volumes.

The Struggle over the Federal Reserve Act. The Aldrich-Vreeland Act was an emergency measure to prevent currency famine until the Monetary Commission could prepare a plan for a central bank. But the first detailed plan of central banking came in 1910 when Paul M. Warburg of Kuhn, Loeb and Co., who for years had advocated central banking, made public his plan for a "United Reserve Bank."[5] Then at the end of 1911 Senator Aldrich began to publicize the plans of the National Monetary Commission. Early in 1912 he introduced a bill to establish a National Reserve Association. Although it was never adopted, many of its features later became embodied in the Federal Reserve Act. Briefly, it proposed to establish a national reserve association and 15 regional associations. Control was to be exercised completely by private bankers, although bank membership in the reserve associations was voluntary. Bank notes were to be issued against general assets and government bonds. There were also provisions for central rediscounting of commercial paper, reserves against deposits, and reserves against note issues.

There were three main reasons why the proposal for a central bank along the lines of the Aldrich bill could not be adopted: agrarians objected heatedly to the election of directors and the issue of private cur-

[5] As early as November, 1906, a committee of the Chamber of Commerce of the State of New York issued a report recommending the creation of a central bank, and a committee of the American Bankers Association recommended a somewhat similar plan at about the same time. (Charles A. Conant, *A History of Modern Banks of Issue*, pp. 437–440.)

rency by the banks; the investigation of the money trust by the Pujo Committee was going on in Washington, and its more or less sensational disclosures heightened the distrust of "Wall Street;" and the Democrats, who controlled Congress, had persistently resolved in their conventions against a central bank controlled by bankers and a currency not issued by the Federal government. Although this was a throwback to the Jacksonian "antimonopoly" cry, it was sufficient to doom the Aldrich bill.

Despite the failure of the Aldrich bill, the demand for a central bank steadily claimed new converts, and its supporters became more and more articulate. Secretary of the Treasury MacVeagh introduced his 1912 report with a sweeping denunciation of the snaillike pace of banking reform. "As long as the financial system created by our Federal laws remains unchanged and unreformed," MacVeagh said, "the government will be exclusively responsible for the commercial, industrial and social disasters which flow from panics." Declaring that "a panic is as unnecessary and as avoidable as an epidemic of smallpox," he warned the public that the nation would suffer from them "only so long as we refuse to apply the simple preventives which he who runs may read."

If MacVeagh hoped that President Wilson was both a runner and a reader, he was not disappointed, for shortly after his election, Wilson began to study a tentative plan for currency and banking reform prepared by the House Banking and Currency Committee. After he had made some important suggestions, a bill incorporating most of the features of the committee's plan was drafted, principally by Carter Glass, chairman of the committee, and Dr. H. Parker Willis, its expert. The bill proposed to organize a number of regional Federal Reserve banks with power to hold the reserves of individual member banks, to act as fiscal agents for the Treasury, to issue notes backed by gold and liquid assets, to establish unified rediscounting, and to buy and sell government obligations in the open market. All national banks were to be compelled to belong to the system, and a central board with supervisory powers was to be created. In addition, the bill provided for the establishment of a par collection system and for the retirement of national-bank notes. It gave private bankers minority representation on the Federal Reserve Board, and vested the power of note issue exclusively with the Federal Reserve banks, with no guarantee by the Federal government.

Although the Glass bill did not go so far in the direction of private control as the Aldrich bill, the agrarians opposed it completely, demanding that the powers of the bankers be clipped by removing bank representatives from the Board and making note issue the exclusive responsibility of the government.

Wilson called a special session of Congress for early April, 1913, to deal with the problems of banking reform and tariff reduction. While the Senate debated the tariff, the Glass bill was introduced in the House. In the Senate shortly thereafter, Robert Owen of Oklahoma introduced a bill more in accord with the views of the group of agrarians for whom Secretary of State Bryan was the chief spokesman. It denied the bankers representation on the governing board and provided for a greater expansion of money and credit.

President Wilson supported the elimination of the bankers from the Board, and he also insisted that for the sake of expediency Federal Reserve notes be considered an obligation of the United States government. The amendments suggested by the President served to appease the Bryan wing, but they antagonized most of the bankers, who began to criticize the bill as committing the United States to socialism and fiat money. Meanwhile, the more radical group among the agrarians was also marshaling its forces to oppose the Glass bill. Claiming that it had Bryan's support, it proposed to make a bona fide laborer, a bona fide farmer, and all ex-Presidents members of the Board. In addition, it concocted a scheme for the issue of three kinds of legal-tender currency: $200 million to be available for loans to corn, cotton, and wheat growers; $300 million to be available to general commerce; and $200 million to be issued for public works in the states and their subdivisions. Bryan would have no part of the proposal, and its importance as a potential threat rapidly faded. Thereafter, the Glass bill had clear sailing, and it passed the House, 287 (239 Democrats and 48 Republicans) to 85 (3 Democrats and 82 Republicans). In the Senate the Owen bill was passed in December, 1913, 54 to 34.

The agrarians and inflationists in both Houses preferred the Owen bill, but the bankers were not pleased with either bill. They thought that government participation was on too great a scale. They objected to the issue of what they persistently and erroneously called "Treasury notes," and they believed that a reserve system would break down the correspondent relationships between city and country banks. Commenting on the House bill, the American Bankers Association said:

If the government can appropriate one-tenth of a bank's capital, they may appropriate one-tenth next year and so on until the capital is all transferred to the government bank. If they can fix the compensation at 5 per cent this year, they may make it 4 per cent next year—a very simple and easy process whereby the entire capital of the banks may be transferred to the government.[6]

These criticisms, however, were exaggerated and made little impression on Congress.

Most of the differences of opinion between the Senate and the House

[6] H. Parker Willis, *The Federal Reserve System*, p. 403.

were settled by the conference committee in favor of the more conservative views of the House.[7] Chief among these were the elimination of a pseudo deposit insurance provision, the prohibition of the use of Federal Reserve notes as member bank reserves, and the practical establishment of a par collection system. The report of the conference committee was quickly passed, and the bill was signed by the President on December 23, 1913. In August, 1914, the Federal Reserve Board took office, and on November 16 the Secretary of the Treasury announced that the Federal Reserve System was open for business. Widely divergent reactions greeted the enactment of the law. The *Commercial and Financial Chronicle* wrote, "The practical considerations possibly standing in the way of successful establishment of the system over-shadow everything else." The American Bankers Association was convinced that the Act was inherently bad. "For those who do not believe in socialism," it stated, "it is very hard to accept and ratify this proposed action on the part of the government."[8] The Comptroller of the Currency, on the other hand, was naïvely enthusiastic. "Under the operation of this law," he wrote in 1914, "such financial and commercial crises or 'panics' as this country experienced in 1873, 1893, and again in 1907 . . . seem to be mathematically impossible."

Provisions of the Federal Reserve Act. The provisions of the Federal Reserve Act, or more technically, "An act to provide for the establishment of Federal Reserve banks, to furnish an elastic currency, to afford means of rediscounting commercial paper, to establish a more effective supervision of banking, and for other purposes," were as follows:

1. The country was divided into not less than eight or more than twelve districts as determined by a majority vote of a committee composed of the Secretary of the Treasury, the Secretary of Agriculture, and the Comptroller of the Currency.

2. A Federal Reserve Board, with headquarters in Washington, was set up to supervise the entire system. It was to consist of seven members, including the Secretary of the Treasury, the Comptroller of the Currency, and five members appointed by the President for a term of ten years. At least two members of the Board were to have had banking or financial experience.

3. National banks were compelled and state banks were allowed to become members.

[7] The complicated legislative proceedings involved in the passage of the Federal Reserve Act later caused a series of acrimonious debates over the true authorship of the Act. The plethora of written material on the subject makes it abundantly clear that, although the Glass bill formed its backbone, the final measure was the work, not of one person, but of more than a score of individuals, including academic experts, political leaders, and some bankers. See the works of McAdoo, Glass, Laughlin, Warburg, and Willis listed in the bibliography.

[8] *Commercial and Financial Chronicle*, Oct. 18, 1913.

4. A Federal Reserve bank, with a capital of at least $4 million, was established in each district.

5. All member banks were required to purchase district bank stock equal to 6 per cent of their capital and surplus, 3 per cent to be paid within six months and the remainder to be subject to call. A dividend of 6 per cent cumulative was to be paid on each share of stock. If a bank's capital increased, it was to purchase additional stock, and vice versa.

6. Each district bank was headed by nine directors: three Class A, representing bankers; three Class B, representing business, commerce, or agriculture; and three Class C, representing the public at large. No Class B director could be an officer, director, or employee of a bank. Class C directors were subject to the same restriction, and in addition, they could not be stockholders in any bank. Class A and B directors were elected by the member banks, and Class C directors were appointed by the Federal Reserve Board. For the purpose of electing directors, the member banks of each district were divided into three groups according to the size of their capital, each group electing two directors.

7. District bank earnings in excess of 6 per cent were to be divided equally between the Federal government and the surplus fund of the district bank. But when the surplus equaled 40 per cent of the paid-in capital, all excess earnings were to be paid to the government as a franchise tax. The amounts received by the government were to be used to reduce the Federal debt or to increase the reserve fund supporting the greenbacks.

8. Every district bank was permitted to issue Federal Reserve notes secured by 100 per cent commercial paper and a reserve of 40 per cent in gold or gold certificates, including a 5 per cent redemption fund.

9. If the reserve against notes was not maintained, a graduated tax was to be levied, reaching a maximum of 1.5 per cent on 2.5 per cent or more by which the reserve fell below 32.5 per cent.

10. Each district bank was required to maintain in lawful money a reserve of 35 per cent against deposits. "Lawful money" was defined as gold and silver coin, greenbacks, gold certificates, silver certificates, and Treasury notes of 1890.

11. Each district bank was permitted to rediscount commercial paper for member banks, such paper to be for a term of ninety days or, in the case of agricultural obligations, six months.

12. Each district bank was permitted to buy and sell government obligations under rules and regulations of the Federal Reserve Board.

13. District banks were permitted to deal in gold coin or bullion, to maintain foreign bank accounts, to establish branches, and to act as fiscal agents for the government.

14. Member banks were classified as reserve city, city, or country banks and were required to maintain the following reserves against demand deposits: 18 per cent for reserve city banks, 15 per cent for city banks, and 12 per cent for country banks. On time deposits all banks were to maintain a reserve of 5 per cent. One-third of the reserves had to be maintained in the bank's own

vaults; seven-eighteenths, six-fifteenths, and five-twelfths had to be deposited with the district bank, and the remainder could be deposited in the district bank or maintained in the bank's vaults.

15. A Federal Advisory Council of one member from each of the 12 districts was formed to make recommendations on banking and credit policies and to discuss general business conditions.

16. A system for clearing checks without cost to the payee or the payor was set up, and any bank could become a member of this par collection system without being a member of the Reserve System itself.

17. After 1915 any bank could apply to sell its government bonds and eliminate its national-bank circulation, and the district banks were to be authorized by the Board to purchase at par up to $25 million of 2 per cent United States bonds in any one year and to issue notes against them or to convert them into bonds not bearing the circulation privilege.

18. District banks were prohibited from paying out any notes but their own.

19. National banks were permitted to make five-year loans on farm real estate mortgages.

20. The Federal Reserve Board was given administrative and advisory powers, including the right to examine reserve banks and member banks, to call for reports and statements, to suspend reserve requirements during emergencies, to permit district banks to rediscount for one another, to supervise the issue and retirement of Federal Reserve notes, to classify reserve and central reserve cities, to suspend and remove officers, and to suspend district banks.

21. The Aldrich-Vreeland Act, which was to expire on June 30, 1914, was extended to June 30, 1915, and the tax on emergency currency was lowered to a rate beginning at 3 per cent and gradually increasing to 6 per cent.

Early Operations of the Federal Reserve System. The Federal Reserve Act was weak in that it did not create a central bank such as existed in Europe or had operated in the United States eighty years before. The System did not have the power, despite the fond hopes of its most optimistic founders, to prevent financial crises or bank failures. On the other hand, it was a vastly better system than had existed at any time since the Second Bank of the United States, for it corrected the more glaring weaknesses of the national banking system, including inelasticity of currency, pyramiding of reserves, and expensive and inefficient check clearance. In addition, it supplied what was lacking under the national banking and Independent Treasury systems: centralized control over the discount rate and the gold stock, a reservoir of credit to which banks could turn in emergencies, and a fiscal agent to link the Treasury with the banking system.

In attempting to correct the inelasticity of the currency, the creators of the Federal Reserve Act were motivated by a sincere belief in the "real-bills" doctrine. But they also believed in the gold standard and accordingly, required the maintenance of a gold reserve, in addition to the 100 per cent commercial-paper security. Although it was hoped that the inelastic national-bank notes could be quickly eliminated from the currency system, this was not finally accomplished until 1935.

To prevent bank reserves from accumulating in the reserve cities, member banks were required to keep them within the confines of their reserve districts. Although some experts, including Warburg, thought that there were too many districts and that funds would still concentrate in New York, the immobility of reserves was corrected. At the same time the new reserve requirements had the effect of creating a much greater potential credit expansion than was possible under the National Bank Act. The Comptroller of the Currency in 1914 estimated that, on the basis of existing deposits, the reserve required under the National Bank Act was slightly above 20 per cent while the reserve required under the Federal Reserve Act was less than 14 per cent. Thus, about one-third of the legal reserves required under the old system became excess reserves under the new system and could be used to expand credit.

Before the Federal Reserve Act, discount rates had been affected to some extent by Treasury deposits and withdrawals from the banks, but this control had been very crude. The new system improved the control of the discount rate, but in creating an almost powerless Reserve Board and in diffusing authority among 12 different district banks, it still left much to be desired. It was originally expected that the rediscount rate would be the chief instrument of control over the money market, but in time it was learned that raising the rate was without effect in periods of speculative boom and that lowering the rate was ineffective if nobody wished to borrow.

Other instruments of credit control were at first either ignored or regarded with indifference. Reserve requirements were rigid and could not be manipulated in an attempt to control credit expansion or contraction. Open-market operations (the purchase and sale of earning assets by the district banks) were not regarded as of major importance. The function of fiscal agent for the government was even less important in the early years, for it was not until the beginning of 1916 that Secretary McAdoo began to transfer government funds from the subtreasuries to the district banks. Even then, the transfers were made only within the 12 district cities, and it was not until 1921 that the last subtreasury was finally closed. The influence which a strong central bank could exert, and which was later to be of great importance under the term "moral suasion," could not be exercised unless membership was large. However, banks did not join the System with enthusiasm, for they thought that their earning possibilities would be greatly diminished by the clearing facilities offered by the Federal Reserve banks. By the end of 1914 only 42.6 per cent of the country's commercial banking resources were controlled by member banks, and at the end of 1916 only 37 state banks had joined the System.

Despite the fact that the Federal Reserve System was not organized to control the money market, its effects on the economy even in its early operation were substantial. In addition to correcting the defects in the national banking system, it allowed national banks for the first time in their history to make real estate loans to farmers. The banks immediately took advantage of the privilege, and by June, 1916, they had loaned $45.7 million on farm mortgages.

Federal Farm Loan Act. But loans to farmers under the Federal Reserve Act were still too restricted in scope, and in July, 1916, the Federal government, continuously widening its sphere of influence, passed the Federal Farm Loan Act, which went much further in making agricultural credit available.

A Federal Farm Loan Bureau was created under the direction of the Federal Farm Loan Board. Twelve districts were established, and in each of these a Federal land bank was formed with a minimum capital of $750,000 and the power to sell additional debentures. The capital stock was offered to the public with the understanding that the Treasury would purchase any unsubscribed stock and waive dividends on its subscription. The land banks were to loan money on first mortgages through National Farm Loan Associations. No loan was to be for less than $100 or more than $10,000 ($25,000 in 1923) and not in excess of 50 per cent of the appraised value of the mortgaged land or 20 per cent of the value of permanent improvements. Interest was not to exceed 6 per cent, and loans were to be amortized in five to forty years at the option of the borrower. Whenever any loan association obtained a loan for a member, it was required to subscribe for capital stock in the land bank to the amount of 5 per cent of such loan. Thus, the Treasury's holdings were gradually reduced from $8.9 million to $326,000 in 1929.

The Federal land banks changed farm credit drastically. First of all, they increased the amount of capital funds flowing into agricultural regions, thereby reducing interest rates on farm mortgages. Second, they quickly assumed a large proportion of the total farm mortgage debt—14.6 per cent in 1924 and 19.1 per cent in 1927. Whether these developments were beneficial to the farmer in the long run is debatable. The easier credit terms offered through the loan banks tended to encourage borrowing by the farmer and thus tended to increase total farm mortgage debt. Yet this can be exaggerated, for most of the loans (76.5 per cent in a typical year) were used to replace old mortgages and to pay off old loans.

Chapter 22: THE PROGRESSIVE ERA: FISCAL POLICY

The previous chapter was concerned with monetary and banking reform in the first years of the new century. This chapter is intended to explain how the rise in Federal power manifested itself in the expansion of Federal expenditures, the reorganization of the revenue system, and the improvement of fiscal administration.

Principal Increases in Federal Expenditures. During the three years immediately succeeding the Spanish-American War Federal expenditures declined about 20 per cent from the wartime peak. But then they rebounded, and by 1914 they not only were double the expenditures of the middle 1890's but were also in excess of the highest expenditures of the war period. This extraordinary increase resulted from six main developments: enlargement of Federal responsibility for conservation of natural resources and improvement of agriculture; expansion of Federal regulation of business, protection of labor, and social welfare; increases in the Navy; liberalization of veterans' pension laws; extension of public works for the improvement of rivers and harbors; and construction of the Panama Canal.

Conservation and Aids to Agriculture. Probably the most important accomplishment of the Theodore Roosevelt administration was the effective beginning of conservation. Over a period of years, much of the country's natural resources had been acquired by private individuals at very low prices and were being ruthlessly wasted. The situation was particularly alarming in the nation's timberlands, for between the close of the Civil War and 1900, government-owned timberlands dropped from 80 to 20 per cent of the total. Some steps for the preservation of the publicly owned forests had been taken a few years earlier. In 1891 Congress authorized the President to set aside as national parks any government lands containing forests. Harrison and later Cleveland set aside some 45 million acres of land despite strenuous opposition from private interests. However, the personnel charged with the duty of administering the lands was too small to be efficient.

It was under Theodore Roosevelt that the program was really put under way, and before the end of his administration, he set aside some 148 million acres. President Taft continued the program, and by 1910, there were 149 national forests containing 193 million acres. The Forestry Serv-

Table 36. Federal Receipts, Expenditures, and Debt, 1900–1914

(In millions of dollars)

	1900	1901	1902	1903	1904	1905	1906	1907	1908	1909	1910	1911	1912	1913	1914
Receipts:															
Customs	$ 233.2	$ 238.6	$ 254.4	$ 284.5	$ 261.3	$ 261.8	$ 300.3	$ 332.2	$ 286.1	$ 300.7	$ 333.7	$ 314.5	$ 311.3	$ 318.9	$ 292.3
Corporation excise and income tax											21.0	33.5	28.6	35.0	71.4
Other excises	295.3	307.2	271.9	230.8	232.9	234.1	249.2	269.7	251.7	246.2	269.0	289.0	293.0	309.4	308.7
Public-land sales	2.8	3.0	4.1	8.9	7.5	4.9	4.9	7.9	9.7	7.7	6.4	5.7	5.4	2.9	2.6
Premiums on bond sales				1.5	0.5		0.5	1.5							
Panama Canal						0.4	0.4	1.2	1.1	0.7	3.2	1.8	3.0	4.1	0.7
Miscellaneous	35.9	38.9	32.1	36.2	38.9	43.1	39.8	53.4	53.2	49.0	42.3	57.3	51.3	53.8	59.0
Totals	$ 567.2	$ 587.7	$ 562.5	$ 561.9	$ 541.1	$ 544.3	$ 595.0	$ 665.9	$ 601.9	$ 604.3	$ 675.5	$ 701.8	$ 692.6	$ 724.1	$ 734.7
Expenditures:															
Legislative and Executive	$ 10.2	$ 11.4	$ 11.5	$ 12.6	$ 12.2	$ 12.2	$ 11.7	$ 12.2	$ 14.2	$ 14.2	$ 14.1	$ 14.0	$ 13.6	$ 13.9	$ 14.1
War	119.0	128.0	99.8	102.1	95.0	101.8	94.5	101.5	109.7	129.0	129.2	128.7	115.6	121.1	127.4
Navy	56.4	61.0	68.3	83.1	103.6	118.3	111.2	97.8	118.7	116.3	124.0	120.7	136.4	134.1	140.6
Interior	10.2	18.7	13.3	11.7	14.0	15.8	19.1	26.1	25.5	24.9	22.0	23.1	24.0	22.4	22.7
Post office	8.8	6.5	4.0	4.9	8.7	17.3	15.0	10.1	15.3	21.6	10.1	1.8	3.0	3.2	2.2
Agriculture	3.6	4.0	4.6	5.3	5.6	6.5	7.6	10.5	13.5	16.3	17.0	17.7	19.5	20.5	22.2
Commerce	0.2	0.2	0.2	9.3	10.6	10.9	10.5	11.0	14.9	14.3	19.2	18.5	14.5	11.3	11.0
Labor														3.3	3.8
Justice	6.4	6.7	6.8	7.9	8.1	8.3	8.6	9.4	9.1	9.1	9.6	9.5	9.7	10.4	10.2
Treasury	52.7	61.3	57.8	57.7	60.7	54.4	53.1	55.7	64.2	61.7	66.1	66.4	65.9	62.1	60.1
Pensions	140.9	139.3	138.5	138.4	142.6	141.8	141.0	139.3	153.9	161.7	160.7	158.0	153.6	175.1	173.4
District of Columbia	7.1	8.7	9.4	8.6	9.4	11.7	11.5	11.4	12.2	14.8	11.7	12.3	13.0	12.8	12.8
Rivers and harbors	18.7	19.5	14.9	19.6	22.5	22.8	25.9	23.3	30.2	34.4	29.0	33.6	35.5	41.5	48.3
Panama Canal					50.2	3.9	19.4	27.2	38.1	31.4	33.9	37.1	35.3	41.7	34.8
Indian affairs	10.2	10.9	10.0	12.9	10.4	14.2	14.2	15.2	14.6	15.7	18.5	20.9	20.1	20.3	20.2
Interest	40.2	32.3	29.1	28.6	24.6	24.6	24.3	24.5	21.4	21.8	21.3	21.3	22.6	22.9	22.9
Premiums	33.1	14.7	14.0	10.9	1.3		1.4	0.2							
Other	3.4	1.3	3.0	3.4	4.4	2.8	2.5	3.7	3.7	6.8	7.2	7.5	7.1	7.9	8.5
Totals	$ 520.8	$ 524.6	$ 485.2	$ 517.0	$ 583.7	$ 567.3	$ 570.2	$ 579.1	$ 659.2	$ 693.7	$ 693.6	$ 691.2	$ 689.9	$ 724.5	$ 735.1
Surplus (+) or deficit (−)	$ +46.4	$ +63.1	$ +77.2	$ +44.9	$ −42.6	$ −23.0	$ +24.8	$ +86.7	$ −57.3	$ −89.4	$ −18.1	$ +10.6	$ +2.7	$ −0.4	$ −0.4
Gross debt	2,137.0	2,143.3	2,158.6	2,202.5	2,264.0	2,274.6	2,337.2	2,457.2	2,626.8	2,639.5	2,652.7	2,765.6	2,868.4	2,916.2	2,912.5
Interest-bearing debt	1,023.5	987.1	931.1	914.5	895.2	895.2	895.2	894.8	897.5	913.3	913.3	915.4	963.8	965.7	968.0

Source: *Annual Reports of the Secretary of the Treasury*, 1900–1914.

ice was greatly expanded, and in 1906 it was made a separate division in the Department of Agriculture. Its expenditures increased rapidly from $1.1 million in 1906 to over $4 million a year by 1910.

Simultaneously, the Federal government expanded its program for the improvement of agriculture. Grants-in-aid to states for agricultural experiment stations, originally initiated in 1887, were increased in 1906 from $15,000 to $30,000 a year for each state. In 1908 Congress doubled the grants-in-aid for the support of agricultural colleges, which had been fixed at $25,000 annually for each state under the second Morrill Act of 1890. In 1906 an ambitious program was put under way, with an annual expenditure first of $1 million and later of $2.5 million, to stop the spread of the boll weevil which was systematically devastating Southern cotton crops. In 1914 the grant-in-aid programs for agricultural colleges and experiment stations were supplemented by the Smith-Lever Act, which provided Federal grants "to aid in diffusing among the people useful and practical information on subjects relating to agriculture." The grants, which were fixed at $10,000 for each state with additional amounts in proportion to rural population, had to be matched by an equal state appropriation. The matching requirement was an important innovation, which in later years established a pattern for the numerous Federal grant-in-aid programs that were introduced in various fields of government activity.[1]

Under the impact of those several conservation and agricultural development programs, the annual expenditures of the Department of Agriculture increased sixfold from 3.6 million in 1900 to $22.2 million in 1914.

The most important development in the conservation movement occurred in 1902 when Congress passed the Reclamation Act. More familiarly known as the Newlands Act, this law provided that the proceeds from the sale of public lands in 16 semiarid and arid states and territories be set aside as a revolving fund to be used for the construction of dams and the irrigation of lands in these areas. Construction costs were to be repaid by the owners of the irrigated lands in equal annual installments, not exceeding ten. In 1914, the period of repayment was extended to twenty years and in 1926, to forty years.

By 1910 the reclamation fund had accumulated almost $70 million, but in the same period, the Federal government had advanced $54.5 million for construction costs. With a balance of less than $16 million, it became clear that repayments would not come in fast enough to carry on further construction at maximum efficiency, and Congress authorized a loan of $20 million to the fund. This loan was subsequently repaid, and in the interim it enabled construction to continue at an annual rate of about $8 million.

[1] James A. Maxwell, *The Fiscal Impact of Federalism*, p. 77.

The entire reclamation program was administered through the Bureau of Reclamation established in the Department of the Interior in 1902. Since most of the program was in the long run self-supporting, its actual cost to the Treasury was small. Yet the program was immensely beneficial to the farmers, for in time more than 1,000 square miles of the most arid lands were irrigated. Reclamation also provided invaluable experience for the later launching of a broad program of water-power development through the construction of huge dams at Federal expense.[2]

Regulation and Promotion of Business and Protection of Labor. It had long been realized that the regulation of business, made necessary by its increasingly interstate nature and the increasing complexities of the industrial system, had to be carried on on the Federal as well as the state level. The establishment of the Interstate Commerce Commission in 1887 and the enactment of the Sherman Anti-Trust Act in 1890 were the first manifestations of this consciousness. But it remained for the administrations and Congress of this period to give it a broader effect by such measures as the Hepburn, Clayton, and Federal Trade Commission Acts.

Equally important and altogether novel extensions of government regulation of business came in 1906 with the Pure Food and Drug Act and a law providing for the inspection by the Department of Agriculture of all meats shipped in interstate commerce. These acts were passed under pressure from the President, who became aroused over the revolting conditions in the Chicago stockyards and the evils in the production and advertising of drugs as portrayed in Upton Sinclair's *The Jungle* and in *Collier's* magazine. The cost of meat and stockyard inspection during its first year of operation was $1.6 million, but by 1909 it was more than $4 million.[3]

Along with its "policing" functions, the Federal government developed new administrative devices for the promotion of domestic and foreign commerce. In 1903 an independent Department of Commerce and Labor was given cabinet status, and the Bureau of Labor Statistics, the Census Service, the Immigration Bureau, the Steamboat Inspection Service, the Light House Establishment, and the Fish Commission were transferred

[2] In line with his conservation and reclamation program, Theodore Roosevelt laid a foundation for public ownership of water-power sites by vetoing, in 1903, a bill giving a private citizen the right to construct a dam and power station at Muscle Shoals, Alabama. He thus prepared the way for another Roosevelt to sign a bill authorizing a Federally chartered power project in the same area thirty years later. (Henry Pringle, *Theodore Roosevelt*, p. 431.)

[3] An attempt by the Progressive bloc in the Senate to levy the costs of meat inspection on the packers failed. The debate on the bill was extremely bitter and was typical of the continuous battle which raged during the Progressive Era between the spokesmen for business and those who wished to extend government regulation. (Claude G. Bowers, *Beveridge and the Progressive Era*, pp. 223–283.)

from the Departments of Treasury and Interior to the newly created Department. In addition, new functions were added, including a Bureau of Corporations, with power to investigate corporate operations. Whereas, in 1900, the various divisions taken together spent $5 million, the new Department spent $9.3 million in 1903, and by 1913 its annual expenditures were over $14 million. In the latter year the Department was split into a Department of Commerce and a Department of Labor. The Department of Commerce was primarily an informational and promotional organization rather than an operating agency, but it led in later times to the creation of special agencies lending direct financial assistance to business. The Department of Labor, which included the Bureau of Labor Statistics, the Immigration Service, the Conciliation Service, the newly established Children's Bureau, and several others, was, like the Department of Commerce, an informational and regulatory, rather than a subsidy- or benefits-dispensing agency.

Expansion of Federal Social Services. The Roosevelt administration was the first to engage in expenditures for the relief of individual citizens on a significant scale. In striking contrast to Cleveland's veto of appropriations to provide seeds for flooded areas, the administration spent $3 million for disaster relief in the Philippine Islands in 1903 and $2 million for the relief of sufferers in the San Francisco earthquake of 1906. During the Taft administration, lesser sums were spent for relief in areas of the South and the West which had been badly hit by cyclones, and in the Wilson administration relief was given to victims of floods in the Middle West.

Further expanding government activities in social service, the different Federal health services, which had been scattered among the various departments, were consolidated in 1912 into the Public Health Service under the Department of the Treasury. The seven administrative divisions of the Service, including the Scientific Research Division, the Hygienic Laboratory, and the Marine Hospitals, accounted for expenditures of $1.7 million in 1912 and $2.4 million in 1916. But like all Federal labor and social services, it was not to become really important until later. Eventually, it was to carry on comprehensive programs for grants-in-aid to states over the whole field of public-health activity.

Expenditures for National Defense and Veterans' Pensions. Because of the constant expansion of America's international interests and the jingoistic tendencies of President Theodore Roosevelt, Navy expenditures more than doubled in less than eight years and increased fourfold compared with the middle nineties. In 1903, $26.3 million was spent for ship construction compared with $15.2 million in 1901. Once begun, these expenditures did not recede, and during the Wilson administration new ship construction exceeded $30 million a year. More ships demanded more men, and the payroll of the Navy jumped from about $13 million at the turn of the century to almost $40 million at the end of the era.

The expenditures for the Army, excluding river and harbor improvements and the Panama Canal, increased only moderately. The increases which did occur were confined almost completely to increased contributions to the state militia. Federal contributions to militia support had been initiated in 1808 with an annual appropriation of $200,000. They were not increased until 1886, when they were doubled. Thereafter, they were raised successively until in 1908 they amounted to $4 million and in 1914 to $7 million a year. However, despite the size of its financial contributions, the Federal government was not yet able to obtain any authoritative control over the National Guard.

Concurrently with the expansion of the Navy and the National Guard, veterans' pension laws were constantly liberalized, and payments, which had declined from the 1893 high, again began to increase, reaching $175.1 million in 1913. Service pensions were extended in 1902 and 1908 to cover veterans of the Indian campaigns of 1817 to 1858, veterans of the Mexican War, veterans of the Texas border disturbances of 1855 to 1860, and the widows of such veterans. Civil War pensions were gradually extended and increased. In 1904 an Executive Order made old age and disability synonymous, by providing that all veterans of the Civil War of sixty-two years of age or over were to be granted pensions of $6 to $12 per month. In February, 1907, Civil War pensions were increased to between $12 and $20 a month and in 1912 to between $13 and $30 a month. Meanwhile, disability pensions to veterans of the Spanish-American War also increased gradually.

Public-works Expenditures. Public-works expenditures more than doubled during the Progressive Era, illustrating once again the expansion of the government's role in the economy. From $40 million in 1900, they increased to $88 million in 1908 and to over $100 million in 1914. There was a substantial increase in expenditures for river and harbor improvements, which, under the Treasury's accounting system, were included in the War Department. In 1902 expenditures for this form of public works were only $14.9 million, but from then on they rose year by year until in 1914, they totaled almost $50 million, rivaling and finally exceeding the Panama Canal as a Federal capital investment.

The Panama Canal, however, was the most famous government investment of the time. It was not only an astonishing engineering feat but a significant illustration of the rapidly broadening influence of the Federal government, especially of the Executive branch. In the negotiations leading to the acquisition of a right of way for the canal, Roosevelt moved with lightninglike rapidity. Disregarding Congress, he helped Panama obtain her independence from the Republic of Colombia, began the construction of the Canal, and confronted Congress with a *fait accompli.*

There was nothing new about the idea of a canal to connect the Atlantic and Pacific Oceans, but it took time to master the international and other difficulties that stood in the way of its consummation. The idea was first suggested in 1826 at the Congress of American Republics. Then in 1850 a railroad was constructed across the Isthmus of Panama, chiefly by American citizens. After the Civil War, seemingly interminable diplomatic negotiations were carried on with Nicaragua, Colombia, and Great Britain over a proposed canal. In the meanwhile, in 1878, a French company obtained a concession to construct a canal across Panama. The project met with little success, but it impelled the United States to take action, and in 1902 Congress authorized the President to acquire the rights and properties of the French company at a cost not to exceed $40 million. He was also authorized to acquire from Colombia a strip of land at least six miles in width across the Isthmus and to proceed with the construction of a canal. But if Colombian land could not be bought at a reasonable price and within a reasonable time, the President was instructed to acquire the necessary strip through Nicaragua. To cover the costs, the Secretary of the Treasury was authorized to borrow from time to time $130 million by the sale of 2 per cent bonds.

After seven months of negotiation, the United States and Colombia signed a treaty providing for the payment by the United States of $10 million in cash and an annuity of $250,000 for the lease of a strip of land 6 miles wide. But the Colombian Senate, convinced that it could obtain a better price, refused to ratify. The action was extremely rash. The French company, having long since abandoned hopes of ever completing construction and fearing that its entire investment would be lost, began to encourage agitators in Panama to revolt for independence. Although Secretary of State Hay refused to give the revolutionists any encouragement, Roosevelt dispatched four warships to the Isthmus, instructing their commanders "to prevent the landing of any armed force." In less than a week, a revolution had occurred, the new Republic of Panama had been formed, and a treaty had been signed with the United States. When Congress met in December, 1902, it was confronted with an accomplished fact. The President had demonstrated the power of the Executive, and the Senate had no choice but to ratify the treaty.

In the treaty, the United States guaranteed the independence of Panama and agreed to pay her a lump sum of $10 million and an annual rental of $250,000 beginning in 1913 (increased to $430,000 a year in 1940). In return, the United States received a perpetual grant of a strip of land 10 miles wide across the Isthmus. Temporarily, the Republic of Colombia received nothing, but in 1909 she was offered $2.5 million, which she refused as insignificant. Eventually, in 1921 a settlement was reached. Colombia received preferential treatment in the use of the canal and $25 million in five annual installments beginning in 1923. Cynical observers were not slow in pointing out that the settlement represented a tremendous boon to American oil interests, which had been finding it difficult to operate in the oil-rich, but indignant, Republic of Colombia.

The land having been obtained, it remained only to buy out the French company. This was accomplished in 1904 for $40 million. Who actually received this money remains a mystery. It was deposited with J. P. Morgan and Co. for transmittal to the stockholders but disappeared in the confused accounts of the bankrupt French corporation. As a part of this transaction, the government came into possession of the Panama Railroad Company and continued to operate it under the corporate form, the first Federal wholly owned "government corporation."

The technical aspects of the $50 million payment offered an illuminating sidelight on the progress which the United States had made as a financial power. Only a decade previously, the international payment of this amount of money would have disrupted the entire economy, but in 1904 no specie left the country and the transactions created no disturbance. Panama reinvested its share ($10 million) in this country, and the French claims were transferred through the foreign-exchange market without any gold shipment.

When the canal opened in 1914, it had cost $398.4 million—$377.3 million for the right of way and construction, $6.2 million for fortifications, and $14.9 million for interest. Of the total outlay, 65 per cent was financed from ordinary revenue and 35 per cent ($134.6 million) by loans. Originally, in 1907 and 1908, the Treasury had sought to place the canal loans with the banks and accordingly issued $84.6 million of 2 per cent 10–30 bonds, selling them at an average price of 103.4. But beginning in 1911, in response to popular demand, it issued 3 per cent 50-year bonds without the circulation privilege, selling $50 million of them at an average price of 102.6. Despite these fresh loans, the Treasury was able to reduce the interest-bearing debt from $1 billion in 1900 to $968 million in 1914. At the same time, annual debt charges dropped from $40.2 million to less than $22 million, mainly as a result of the reconversion under the Act of 1900.

Payne-Aldrich Tariff of 1909. The fundamental changes which occurred in the economy during the Progressive Era placed the protective tariff increasingly on the defensive. Rightly or wrongly, the urban populations blamed the tariff for the current rise in prices. The expansion of American manufactures caused farsighted industrialists to think that high tariffs would limit the ability of foreign countries to buy their goods. Middle

Western political leaders strongly opposed the protective tariff, because they considered it one of the chief props of monopoly. Finally, the growth of Federal expenditures made the tariff inadequate from a revenue standpoint.

In the Republican convention of 1908 the champions of protectionism lost some ground, for the tariff plank did not pay the traditional homage to the high-tariff policy. On the other hand, it seemed to commit the Republican party to tariff reform, declaring, "In all protective legislation the true principle of protection is best maintained by the imposition of such duties as will equal the difference between the cost of production at home and abroad, together with a reasonable profit to American industries."

After the election of 1908, Congressman Payne, interpreting the "true principle" to mean lower tariffs, introduced a bill to reduce rates in general. But it was soon made evident that, although protectionism might have become a less virile doctrine, it was by no means dead. The Senate, under the leadership of Nelson Aldrich, amended the House bill 847 times. The measure which emerged from the conference committee was similar to the Dingley Tariff, but it was adopted after heated debate (195 to 183 in the House and 47 to 31 in the Senate) and signed somewhat apologetically by President Taft in August, 1909. The Payne-Aldrich Tariff repealed the reciprocity clause of the Dingley Act. Instead, it authorized the President, if he thought that the United States was being discriminated against by given countries, to apply to them maximum duties, 25 per cent ad valorem higher than the set rates which were declared to be minimum duties. In the administration of the tariff, Taft imposed only minimum duties, and although the new tariff had abolished the reciprocity clause, he negotiated a treaty with Canada in 1910 and obtained Congress's approval after much travail, only to have it rejected at the last moment by the Canadian Parliament. The Act also created a Tariff Board to investigate the comparative costs of production domestically and internationally. The Tariff Board made useful investigations, but it was unpopular with Congress, being looked upon as an encroachment by the President. In 1912, largely because Taft had vetoed tariff-reduction bills in 1911 and 1912, Congress, under pressure from the Democrats, who controlled the House, refused to appropriate funds for the Board, thus forcing it to discontinue operation.

Corporation Excise Tax and Income Tax. The most important development arising from the Payne-Aldrich Act was not concerned with tariff rates, but with a renewal of the campaign for the imposition of an income tax. With customs and excises insufficient to finance rising Federal expenditures, direct taxes had to be provided. In his original bill, Congressman Payne included an inheritance tax. But the Democrats, led by Congressman Cordell Hull of Tennessee, and the Progressive Republicans, led by Senators Cummins of Iowa and La Follette of Wisconsin, attempted to add an income tax. They stressed the ability-to-pay principle of taxation, while Aldrich, Lodge, and Elihu Root, speaking for the conservatives, argued that the income tax was socialistic, inequitable, unnecessary, easily evaded, and dangerous to the welfare of the workingman because it would tend to deprive him of the protection afforded by the tariff.

The debate went on interminably, delaying the enactment of the tariff bill. Finally in June, President Taft sent the Senate a message recalling that the income tax had been declared unconstitutional by the Supreme Court and questioning whether anything had happened in the interim to change judicial opinion. He suggested a compromise involving the submission of an income tax amendment to the Constitution and the imposition, in the meanwhile, of only a tax on corporate net income. This compromise was accepted, with the tax fixed at 1 per cent and made applicable only to net incomes over $5,000. To avoid constitutional difficulties, the tax was called an excise on the privilege of doing business and not on incomes as such, and in 1911 the Supreme Court in the case of *Flint v. Stone Tracy Company* held that the tax was an excise and, therefore, constitutional.[4] Immediate receipts from the tax were small, ranging from $21.0 million in the fiscal year 1910 to $34.8 million in the fiscal year 1912.

In accordance with the Taft compromise, a constitutional amendment was introduced, giving Congress the power to tax incomes "from whatever source derived, without apportionment among the several states, and without regard to any census or enumeration." Senator Aldrich and other conservative leaders, who were not in any way sympathetic to the proposal, did not oppose the bill, believing that it would never be ratified. In this they were completely mistaken, for after being passed in July, 1909, 77 to 0 in the Senate and 318 to 14 in the House, the income tax amendment was adopted by one state after another, and in February, 1913, it became a part of the Constitution.

Underwood Tariff. Greatly disappointed by the Payne-Aldrich Act, tariff reformers and free traders took new hope with the inauguration of a Democratic administration in 1913. President Wilson was committed, both by party platform and by personal inclination, to a sweeping reduction in tariff rates, and he gave his strongest support to the free-trade

[4] In the years 1909 to 1912 inclusive, 1.1 million returns were filed under the corporation tax. Approximately 20 per cent showed a taxable income, and the average net income per year was $3.3 billion. (*Annual Reports of the Commissioner of Internal Revenue.*)

leaders. A tariff-reduction bill had already been prepared in the outgoing Congress by Chairman Underwood of the Ways and Means Committee, and this became the basis of a new bill. It was speedily passed by the House, 281 to 139, in May, 1913, but it appeared for a time that it might be emasculated in the Senate just as had been done twenty years before during Cleveland's administration. However, Wilson had the advantage of being able to use political patronage, for the Democrats were just returning to office after a sixteen-year absence. He did not hesitate to do so, and the Underwood Tariff with some slight amendments passed the Senate, 44 to 37, in September, 1913.

Although the Underwood Tariff did not satisfy extreme free traders, it established the lowest rates since those imposed by the Tariff Act of 1857, and it was to be more than thirty years before equally low rates would again be effective. The average rate was reduced from 40 to 29 per cent, and most schedules were put on an ad valorem basis.[5] There were no reciprocity features in the Underwood Tariff, and the Payne-Aldrich provision for maximum and minimum duties was repealed. Although the Republicans argued strenuously for another tariff board, none was created. But in 1916 a tariff commission was formed with powers to investigate the fiscal and industrial effects of customs duties, the relation between raw materials and finished goods, the effect of export bounties, the volume of imports compared with domestic production, and the effects of foreign competition and dumping. The commission was able and nonpartisan. But it was a purely research organization. It published a number of excellent studies, but these had no effect on either Congressional or administrative action.

The Income Tax Law. It was estimated that the Underwood Tariff would lower customs revenue by approximately $70 million, and since Federal receipts and expenditures were at best about equal, it was considered imperative to find new sources of taxation. Fortunately, the income tax amendment had been ratified shortly before inauguration, giving the administration an ideal medium through which to replace lost revenue. An amendment was therefore attached to the Underwood Tariff and eventually became the income tax law. Written by Cordell Hull, it replaced the corporation excise with a 1 per cent tax on corporate net incomes earned after March 1, 1913, without any exemptions. It also imposed a "normal tax" of 1 per cent on personal incomes of over $3,000 for a single person and $4,000 for a married couple. In addition, individual

---

[5] The average duty on manufactured woolens was reduced from 56 to 18½ per cent. Steel rails, raw wool, iron ore, and agricultural implements were placed on the free list, and raw sugar was to be admitted free after 1916. The latter provision, however, was repealed before the effective date because of revenue requirements.

incomes were subject to surtaxes ranging from 1 per cent on incomes of $20,000 to 6 per cent on over $500,000. There was no exemption for dependents, and all persons or corporations paying rent, interest, or salaries in excess of $3,000 were required to deduct from it 1 per cent and pay it to the Bureau of Internal Revenue. It was estimated that, through such withholding, at least two-thirds of the tax would be collected at the source. It was little realized at the time that vesting the Federal government with the power to levy an income tax without any limitations gave it such dominance over the fiscal resources of the country that it was to be exceedingly difficult for the states to maintain their fiscal independence. Nor was it realized that the income tax would make it possible to obtain for public purposes 25 per cent or more of the total national income.

TABLE 37.   INCOME-TAX COLLECTIONS AND RETURNS, 1914

	Collections (Millions)
Normal tax	$12.7
Surtax and income bracket:	
1%, $ 20,000–$ 50,000	2.9
2%, 50,000– 75,000	1.6
3%, 75,000– 100,000	1.3
4%, 100,000– 250,000	3.8
5%, 250,000– 500,000	2.3
6%, over $500,000	3.4
Total	$28.3

Income Bracket	No. of Returns
$ 2,500–$ 3,333	79,426
3,333– 5,000	114,484
5,000– 10,000	101,718
10,000– 20,000	38,795
20,000– 30,000	10,981
30,000– 50,000	6,980
50,000– 100,000	3,616
100,000– 200,000	1,096
200,000– 500,000	367
500,000– 1,000,000	91
$1,000,000 and over	44
Total	357,598

SOURCE: *Annual Report of the Commissioner of Internal Revenue*, 1914, pp. 20–21.

At first, the tax was poorly enforced, evasions were widespread, and the collections moderate. In the first full fiscal year of its existence, 1913–1914, it produced $28.3 million from individual incomes and $32.4 million from corporate incomes, while an additional $10.7 million was collected on the old corporation excise.

Since customs revenue fell slightly in 1914, a beginning was made in the direction of more progressive taxation, but it was merely a beginning, since income taxes applied to a relatively small number of individuals and were imposed at relatively low rates.

Fiscal Administrative Reforms. With the great expansion of the Federal government, it became more important than ever to correct the long-standing unbusinesslike methods in fiscal and administrative operations. The public was no longer indifferent to waste, and on all levels of government it demanded "economy and efficiency." Realizing this, President Theodore Roosevelt, without waiting for Congressional authorization, in June, 1905, appointed an interdepartmental committee "to investigate the business methods and practices of the Executive Departments and to report plans for their improvement." During the succeeding three years this committee, known as the "Keep Committee" because it was headed by C. H. Keep, Assistant Secretary of the Treasury, submitted a number of reports to the departmental heads recommending procedural changes. Only a few of these were published, but a number were acted upon by the departments themselves. Several dealt with accounting and disbursement methods, and one of the most outstanding was a plan prepared by Herbert D. Brown, later head of the U.S. Bureau of Efficiency, for an actuarial system for the retirement of Federal employees. The relative sparsity of positive action arising from the Keep Committee was caused by inadequate Congressional appropriations. Only $5,000 was made available to the committee for the employment of outside experts, although the President had asked for $25,000.

Meanwhile, in order to stamp out the vicious departmental practice of expending an entire appropriation before the end of the year in expectation of a deficiency grant, Congress inserted in its General Deficiency Appropriation Act of 1905 a provision known as the "Anti-Deficiency Act." In succeeding appropriation acts, Congress supplemented it by other broad provisions. Taken together, these provisions prohibited any department or agency from expending in any one fiscal year more than its Congressional appropriation; required each department, before the beginning of the fiscal year, to apportion all appropriations, with certain specified exceptions, in monthly or other allotments; permitted the waiving or modification of such allotments only in the case of extraordinary emergencies and only by a full explanation in writing to Congress; required the departments to include in their estimates the entire year's appropriations and permitted supplemental estimates only when such were necessitated by additional legislation or "when deemed imperatively necessary for the public service"; and punished violations of the law by removal from office, imprisonment, and fine.

The requirements were well designed, but they lacked the requisite central executive control to make them effective. Congress itself lacked the machinery with which to check on the completeness of the estimates, the proper segregation of the appropriations into allotments, adherence to these allotments, and so on. As long as the administration of the plan was left to the individual departments, its enforcement was not well ensured. Actually, the antideficiency law remained a dead letter for many years, and it was not enforced until the Executive Budget System and the General Accounting Office were established and fully developed.[6]

While Congress was attempting to check deficiency appropriations, the Treasury endeavored to correct other unbusinesslike practices ingrown in its own operations. One of these concerned the closing of accounts for funds which had been lost through embezzlement or accident or were otherwise unavailable,[7] and another was the adoption in 1907 of the double-entry system of bookkeeping.

Unsuccessful Attempts to Introduce a Budget System. The most fundamental weakness in the fiscal operations of the government was the lack of a centralized executive budget system or of any budget system at all. Under the existing arrangement each department formulated its own estimates of appropriations. These were then transmitted without modification to Congress, where they were acted upon without relation to one another in a pell-mell fashion. No one in or out of Congress ever knew how much money would be actually spent during the year, how much might be spent under appropriations previously enacted, and whether or not the revenues for the year would be sufficient to cover the expenditures.

Many Treasury officials deprecated the absence of a budget system, but Secretary Cortelyou was the first to bring up the subject in an exhaustive way. In his report for 1908 he pointed out that, excluding payments of interest on the government debt, Federal expenditures had increased from $135 million in 1878 to $638 million in 1908. In the light of this enormous increase, he urged Congress to institute a system somewhat similar to the one which was finally adopted in the Budget and Accounting Act of 1921.

[6] See D. T. Selko, *The Federal Financial System*, pp. 97–98; W. F. Willoughby, *The Problem of a National Budget*, Chap. 8.

[7] Since no money could be paid out of the Treasury except by Congressional appropriation, the Treasurer was forced to carry an account called "Unavailable Funds" which amounted to many millions of dollars and included the so-called "loan" to the states made in 1837. Treasurer after Treasurer appealed to Congress to close this account, and finally in 1910 Congress complied. For the first time in seventy years, the Treasury's books failed to carry as assets $28.1 million which had long since disappeared into thin air.

Treasury officials did not stop with their demands for a budget system. They were far ahead of their time in their concepts of budgeting practice. Treasurer Treat, for example, in his report for 1905 denied categorically the value of a consistently balanced budget. Secretary Cortelyou suggested a double budget to separate expenditures for capital outlays from those for current operation. Because this proposal has been repeatedly suggested but never adopted and is still being discussed today, Cortelyou's presentation is especially interesting. At the time, as during most of Federal financial history, the proceeds of bonds, regardless of how used, were not counted as receipts, but all the money which was paid out for acquisition of capital assets as well as for current expense was included in expenditures. Thus, expenditures for public works such as the Panama Canal were treated on the same basis as payments to the state of Delaware for expenditures in the War of 1812. This unbusinesslike method of accounting for expenditures gave an inaccurate picture of the government's fiscal situation, for payments for public works created large apparent deficits even though they increased the government's physical capital. In 1908, for example, the deficit was $58.1 million, but as Cortelyou explained, "Of total expenditures, the sum of $88.7 million was expended on public works, including $38 million on the Panama Canal and $30 million on rivers and harbors." Calling attention to the fact that the separation of capital expenditures from operating ones was common practice in many European nations, Cortelyou suggested that when bonds were sold "to meet the cost of an important public work, like the Panama Canal, such expenditures be placed in a separate account or the proceeds of the bonds sold be included in the receipts." It will be noted that Cortelyou spoke of "receipts," not "revenues." Manifestly, the bond moneys would still need to be separated from tax funds and other current revenues. Had Cortelyou's suggestions been adopted by carrying extraordinary expenditures to a separate account, there would have been a surplus of current receipts amounting to over $30 million. In concluding his statement, Cortelyou "commended to the serious consideration of the Congress whether a careful study should not be made of the entire subject of the budget, with a view not to niggardly economies, but to applying the money of the taxpayers in the most efficient and beneficial manner to those objects of expenditure which are most desirable."

However, President Theodore Roosevelt was not much interested in budgetary reform or administrative techniques. It remained for President Taft to take up the cudgels. Realizing the complexity of the subject, he requested Congress in 1910 to give him authority to appoint a "President's Commission on Economy and Efficiency" to make the most comprehensive technical inquiry into the problem of efficient administration and budgeting that had ever been made in this country. Congress gave him the authority and provided altogether $260,000 for the commission over the three years of its existence. As chairman the President appointed Dr. F. A. Cleveland, then director of the New York Bureau of Municipal Research, the leading contemporary research organization in the art of public administration. During its existence the commission published a number of reports, but the one on the "Need for a National Budget," submitted to Congress in June, 1912, was most notable. After first tracing the history and critically analyzing the existing practices of the Executive and Congress with respect to the preparation of the estimates and enactment of appropriation and revenue bills, it made constructive recommendations for an all-embracing budget and presented a *pro forma* budget for the fiscal year 1912–1913, organized in accordance with the recommended plan.

The commission recommended that the President be given the responsibility for the preparation and execution of the budget and Congress be given merely the authority to revise and enact the budget. It concluded that only through an "executive budget system" could "responsible" and "responsive" government be achieved. President Taft fully agreed with the recommendations and took the unprecedented action of requesting the departments and other agencies, while preparing their estimates for Congress, to prepare another set in accordance with the instructions of the commission.

Congress deeply resented the President's attempt to usurp what it regarded as its traditional prerogative in matters of finance. It inserted in one of the appropriation bills a clause prohibiting the departments from preparing estimates other than those prescribed by law. President Taft, however, felt confident that under the Constitution he had the right to demand of his executive agencies any information he deemed necessary. He proceeded with his plan and in due time transmitted to Congress the commission's report, together with his recommended form of budget. However, there was a general notion that Taft would not be reelected. Under the circumstances, Congress ignored the report completely, and in 1912 when the President requested an appropriation of $250,000 for the commission, it granted only $75,000. Despite the lack of Congressional support, the President's action and the commission's report were most effective in bringing the issue before the country and in developing the main outlines for its solution.

President Wilson did not pursue any of the recommendations of President Taft's commission, nor did he offer any proposals or institute any major reform of his own in this field. The new administration allowed the Commission on Economy and Efficiency to go out of existence, leaving only a feeble substitute for it, in the form of a Division of Efficiency in the United States Civil Service Commission. This division was to develop and install a system of efficiency ratings for Federal employees. A small appropriation was provided, and Herbert D. Brown, formerly of the staff of the Commission on Economy and Efficiency, was appointed its chief. Later, in 1916, this division, renamed the United States Bureau of Efficiency, was given broader powers to carry on investigations of the operations of the departments and to make reports directly to Congress. But it was never provided with sufficient funds to do effective work.

PART III

SINCE WORLD WAR I

Chapter 23: FINANCING WORLD WAR I

America's part in World War I, lasting for only nineteen months, cost approximately ten times as much as four years of the Civil War. Yet it was financed much more efficiently, partly because of the lessons which had been learned in the Civil War, but much more because of the expansion of the economy and the changes that had taken place in social and political institutions over the previous half century.

The Civil War was fought in an agrarian age, and manpower rather than technology was emphasized. But the great expansion of industrialism between the Civil War and the world war made it possible to use more technological means of warfare. Hence, in the Civil War more than 13 per cent of the total population was in the armed forces at one time or another, but in the world war only 5 per cent was so involved and a larger percentage was engaged in the production of munitions. In addition, the locale of the conflict was completely different. All of the Civil War was fought within the national boundaries of the United States, whereas in the world war the United States was a supply depot for the fighting, which took place in the rest of the world. Finally, the social, economic, and political advancement of the country made for a new system of war finance. The rise in productivity and in national income together with the greater political consciousness of the middle classes and labor made possible the largest proportional tax increases in American history. Moreover, the Treasury did not have to resort to greenbacks as in 1862, but because of the existence of a semicentral bank, it accomplished much the same inflation of the money supply by the more subtle means of selling bonds to the commercial banks. The advancement of America's position in the international money market also made the Treasury's path much smoother, for the United States was no longer dependent on European money markets. Instead, she was supplying her former creditors with funds, and there was much less danger of a complete abandonment of specie payments.

Although World War I was not a total war, it was much more so than the Civil War. For the first time in this country's history the central government found it necessary to insert controls throughout the economy. At the same time, there was a generally increased demand for government assistance. Consequently, one of the most important effects of World War I was the great enhancement of the Federal government's influence in the economy. As Secretary Houston described it in 1920:

The first impulse of many was to turn to the Government, and especially to the Treasury, as the sole instrumentality for full economic salvation. This disposition, well developed before the war, was reinforced during hostilities by practices of the Government which became necessary for the successful prosecution of the war. It is this disposition, rather than self-aggrandizing efforts of Federal departments to extend their functions, which is the main explanation of mounting Federal budgets and of centralizing tendencies frequently criticized.

The evolution of America's international position, both politically and economically, which took place during the war was quite as important as the expansion of centralized government. Politically, the war catapulted the nation into the midst of international problems. Financially, the United States changed from a mature debtor to a mature creditor almost overnight. Yet although the war demonstrated that American insularity was a dangerous delusion, it was to require another world war to make this truth generally accepted. In the interim the policy of the United States was featured by a plethora of inconsistencies.

The war also revolutionized the American banking system. Pioneer central banking, as represented by the Federal Reserve System, was not permitted to develop gradually but was projected at once into a most trying situation, thereby losing any opportunity it might have had of achieving political and economic independence. As its policies became completely dominated by the exigencies of war finance, it became an adjunct of the Treasury. Thus, the Jacksonian traditions of separation of government and banking mildly embodied in some of the features of the Federal Reserve Act were once and for all smashed beyond repair.

First Impact of the War on the American Economy. The financing of the world war may be conveniently divided into four periods: the near-panic and depression that followed the outbreak of the war and continued until mid-1915, the prosperity period of neutrality, the preparedness phase which began in 1916, and the period of active warfare from April, 1917, to November, 1918.

In the early summer of 1914 events in Europe moved with precipitate haste. On June 28, the Archduke Franz Ferdinand was assassinated, and by the end of July, the whole of central Europe was marching to war. Panic-stricken investors offered their securities at any price, and selling was so great that on July 31 the London Stock Exchange closed for the first time in history. Liquidation was not confined to the European exchanges but rapidly spread to New York. At the time, foreign holdings of American securities and short-term credits were estimated at about $6 billion, while American investors held less than $1 billion of foreign securities. After allowing for direct investments, the United States was a net debtor for at least $3.5 billion. Fearing that the United States would soon abandon the gold standard, Europeans dumped their securities in New York, creating a large demand for sterling exchange and driving the pound far beyond the gold export point. Exports of gold were extraordinarily heavy, totaling more than $150 million between June and November, 1914. Yet even more gold would have been exported but for a lack of shipping space and a fear that cargoes would be sunk. Consequently, the demand for pounds became so great that they eventually reached the phenomenal price of $7.

The great wave of liquidation placed tremendous pressure on the money market and on stock prices, while the gold exports reduced bank reserves. The New York City banks soon found themselves with a reserve deficit of more than $17 million. Since the Federal Reserve System had not yet opened and the Board had not yet taken office, responsibility for alleviating the tension devolved upon the Treasury and upon the bankers who were willing to cooperate. The challenge was accepted with alacrity, and action came quickly enough to avert a money market panic. The first move came on Friday, July 31, 1914, when the Board of Governors of the New York Stock Exchange decided to follow London's example and not open. Stock trading immediately shifted to an outlaw market, which continued to operate until the exchange reopened in April, 1915.

On August 2 Secretary McAdoo arranged with the clearinghouses for an informal embargo on gold, and through the agency of the Federal Reserve Board, the banks were persuaded to raise a pool of $100 million to depress the price of sterling exchange. By October the pound was back to normal. Concurrently, a banking syndicate raised a pool of $52 million to help New York City meet some maturing short-term notes which were held in England and France. Next McAdoo, under the Aldrich-Vreeland Act, divided the country into 44 districts, formed national currency associations in each district, and issued emergency currency to the national banks on the security of commercial paper. Between August 1 and October 30, the Secretary issued $369.5 million of emergency currency, all of which was redeemed by the middle of 1915, the maximum outstanding at any one time being $363.6 million. While McAdoo issued emergency currency, the bankers cooperated by issuing the ubiquitous clearinghouse certificates. In New York $109.2 million of these were issued, but only $57.6 million were put into circulation.

To give the banks more reserves, the Treasury deposited part of its cash with the national banks, $3.4 million being deposited between August 1 and October 31 in New York City. As the money stringency abated, excess bank reserves began to appear, and McAdoo assumed that banks were hoarding funds. Late in September he tried to force them to make loans by threatening to withdraw government deposits. This threat was of no avail, for banks were not hoarding intentionally. A business recession had set in, and it was impossible for the banks to find borrowers.

The Federal government felt the effects of the recession immediately. Revenues from customs and internal taxes declined sharply, and in order to avert an operating deficit, Congress passed the Emergency Revenue Act of October 22, 1914. It increased the rate on beer and wine and imposed special excises on toilet articles, chewing gum, telegraph and telephone messages, and freight charges; special license taxes on tobacco manufacturers and dealers, bankers, brokers, and amusement places; and stamp taxes on legal transactions. The Act, which was expected to produce $100 million, was to expire on December 31, 1915, but at that time a further and much sharper decline in customs revenue as well as a rise in expenditures caused Congress to extend its life to December 31, 1916. Despite the tax increase, there was a slight deficit in the fiscal year 1914 and a much larger one in 1915. However, the Federal government continued to expand its activities, and it was in the midst of making plans for the relief of the large number of unemployed when suddenly in June, 1915, conditions were reversed and the most sensational boom in American history began.

The Neutrality Period. By the end of 1914 it was obvious that, if Europe had to rely exclusively on its own limited wealth, it would not be able to prosecute a war on the mammoth scale contemplated. Food production had been curtailed by shortages of manpower, manufactured articles of war were being constantly destroyed, and ships were being regularly sunk. But in the fight for survival, food, steel, ammunition, ships, and armor plate were vitally necessary. Therefore, in December, 1914, both belligerent groups turned to the United States to obtain them at any cost.

TABLE 38. VOLUME OF FOREIGN TRADE, INCLUDING SILVER, 1914–1917
(In millions of dollars)

Calendar year	Exports	Imports	Balance
1914*	$ 1,091	$ 822	$ 269
1915	3,608	1,813	1,795
1916	5,554	2,424	3,130
1917	6,318	3,005	3,313
Totals.........	$16,572	$8,064	$8,507

SOURCE: *Statistical Abstract of the United States*, 1949.

* Second half of year.

In a short time, a large part of America's productive resources was channeled into war production. American exports increased sixfold as Europe pleaded for more war goods. Plants engaged in war production began to expand their operations, unemployment disappeared, and the real gross national product increased by almost 20 per cent in three years.

The enormous increase in exports was not offset by a commensurate increase in imports. This tendency became further accentuated during the succeeding periods of preparation for and actual participation in the war. As a result, the net export balance between 1914 and 1917 was almost as great as the aggregate of all the previous American favorable balances of trade.

In the four years of neutrality, preparedness, and part of the war, the United States took over a creditor position which Great Britain had needed centuries to achieve. A net debtor at the beginning of the war, for $3 billion to $4 billion, the United States was a net creditor for over $5 billion by 1917. But Europeans were much more impressed by this revolution in international finance than were the Americans. No American comment described the situation as well as an editorial in the *Manchester Guardian:*

European financiers would be well advised to face the fact that the war has radically transformed the relations between the United States and Europe. . . . The United States . . . by the end of this war will have wiped out most of its debt to foreign investors. It will have a currency of unimpeachable magnitude. The American bankers will have acquired the experience they have hitherto lacked in the international money market and all this strengthened financial fabric will rest upon an economic fabric which the war will have much expanded. It can hardly be doubted that under these circumstances, New York will enter the lists for the financial leadership of the world.[1]

To settle the $8 billion balance due to American individuals and corporations, foreign nations liquidated approximately half their American securities. Shipping and other services accounted for approximately $1 billion, and payments in gold covered another billion. The remainder was paid for by the sale of approximately $2.7 billion of bonds to the American public. Beginning in October, 1914, with a small French loan, Europe offered 273 issues for public subscription before the end of 1917. Most of these were by Great Britain and France and were sold through banking syndicates organized by J. P. Morgan and Co. The most famous was the Anglo-French loan of October, 1915, for $500 million of 5-year 5 per cent bonds, sold to the Morgan syndicate at 96 and immediately resold to the public at 98.

The gold imports were the largest in history, and as early as November, 1915, they raised the gold stock of the United States to over $2 billion, the largest amount ever possessed by any nation. These huge imports greatly expanded banking reserves, making it possible to finance great increases in business activity at exceptionally low interest rates. Total

[1] Quoted in the *Annual Report of the Secretary of the Treasury,* 1916.

commercial bank loans rose 38 per cent (from $13.1 billion in June, 1914, to $18.1 billion in 1917). In the same period bank deposits increased 50 per cent (from $17.3 billion to $25.9 billion).

The banking system encouraged rather than discouraged the great inflation of credit. In September, 1916, the Federal Reserve Bank of New York lowered its rediscount rate to 3 per cent from the 4 per cent rate maintained throughout the 1915 recession. In the same month an additional impetus was given to credit expansion by amending the Federal Reserve Act to permit member banks to secure "advances" from the district banks on 15-day promissory notes secured by government obligations or eligible paper.

Preparedness Period. As the war progressed, the program of domestic reform embodied in the "New Freedom" was abandoned, and attention turned more and more to international affairs. Eventually, it became apparent that the United States would have to abandon her role of a neutral supplying goods to maintain hostilities and become a belligerent supplying resources to attain a quick and decisive victory.

American commerce, engaged in supplying war materials to European countries, was caught between the opposed interests of the belligerents. Great Britain confiscated war cargoes being shipped to neutral countries, and Germany began an intensive submarine campaign to prevent goods from being landed in the British Isles. Throughout the early period, President Wilson followed a policy of neutrality and isolation, but in December, 1915, he urged Congress to increase the country's preparedness by raising the appropriations for the Army and the Navy. At the same time Secretary McAdoo suggested that Congress cover the proposed increases in expenditures by reducing income tax exemptions for married and single persons to $3,000 and $2,000, beginning the surtax at $10,000 instead of $20,000, and imposing excise taxes on gasoline and automobiles.

At first Congress was indifferent, but in the summer of 1916 after the publication of the British blacklist, the failure of an American peace mission, and a threatened resumption of a more severe submarine campaign by Germany, it passed legislation increasing the armed forces and establishing a Council of National Defense. This was followed on September 8, 1916, by a general increase in taxes. The income tax exemptions of $4,000 and $3,000 remained unchanged, but the normal tax was doubled to 2 per cent, and the maximum surtax was stepped up from 6 to 13 per cent. The rate of the corporation tax was also doubled to 2 per cent, and Congress imposed a special tax of 12.5 per cent on the net profits of munitions manufacturers. In addition, a graduated estate tax was imposed, beginning at 1 per cent on the first $50,000 to 10 per cent on amounts in excess of $5 million. This was the fourth time in the country's history that an inheritance tax was imposed by the Federal government. This time, the states, which almost universally levied inheritance taxes, expressed concern over the utilization of the tax by the Federal government. But the presumption was that this tax, as the previous ones, would last only for the duration of the emergency.

On March 3, 1917, another emergency revenue act increased the estate tax to a range of 1½ to 15 per cent and imposed an 8 per cent excess-profits tax on all business income—individual and partnership as well as corporate—in excess of 8 per cent of invested capital after deducting $5,000. In addition, the Act authorized the Treasury to borrow up to $300 million by the sale of certificates of indebtedness. McAdoo immediately took advantage of this authority and sold $50 million of certificates to the Federal Reserve banks in anticipation of taxes. Thus, even before the United States entered the war, inflationary methods of financing were being used.

The Problem of War Finance. All the foregoing revenue enactments suddenly became inadequate, for Congress was called into special session on April 2, 1917, and declared war against Germany on April 6. The declaration of war found the nation fairly well prepared economically but un-prepared financially. To wage war on the scale required by modern conditions, the government had to acquire huge amounts of goods and services and spend huge amounts of money for them. In doing this, it had to siphon off consumer income and put a clamp on unessential production and consumption. In brief, the private economy had to be prevented from competing against the government in the market place. It was not a time for "business as usual," but unfortunately, that slogan was descriptive of the public attitude. To some extent the Treasury was aware of the problem. Early in the war, Secretary McAdoo warned the public,

Business must be readjusted to the war-making functions of the nation. What is of superlative importance in the readjustment is that our people shall be impressed with the necessity of economizing in everything which constitutes a drain upon available supplies, materials, and resources of the country. So far as I have been able to observe, the American people are not sufficiently aroused to the necessity of economy in this really serious time.[2]

In facing the concrete problems of war financing, McAdoo had little historical experience to guide him. In prior moments of leisure, he had studied the history of Civil War financing, but the lessons had been negative, teaching him only what not to do.[3] The questions which he had to answer without the assistance of Chase's experience were: How much would the war cost? To what extent should the government tax, and to what extent should it borrow? In borrowing, what methods should be

[2] *Annual Report of the Secretary of the Treasury*, 1917.
[3] William Gibbs McAdoo. *Crowded Years*, p. 373.

used and what rate of interest should be set? The intricate economic effects of financing a major war had hardly been probed in 1917, and in answering the above questions, McAdoo seems to have paid little attention to the long-run effects of wartime fiscal policy, for at all times he considered the immediate money costs as the primary problem. In trying to keep them down, he sometimes resorted to policies which had deplorable economic effects.

McAdoo estimated the outlays for the first full fiscal year of the war (1917–1918) at $8.5 billion, but as matters developed, this was a considerable underestimate. Having calculated the cost, he had to decide how much to raise from taxes and how much from borrowing and then determine how much of the borrowing should be from individuals, corporations, savings banks, and other noncommercial bank investors and how much from the commercial and Federal Reserve banks. Paper-money issues, such as those of the Civil War, were not considered by anyone.

From an economic point of view, taxation offered the greatest advantages. If the government took spending power away from individuals and corporations through taxes, it would tend to reduce competition for scarce goods and the upward pressure on prices. But an overemphasis on taxation might weaken incentives to produce or might undermine political morale. Borrowing funds, ordinarily spent on consumption and capital goods, from nonbank investors would also tend to reduce the upward pressure on the price level, but it would require an active bond-selling campaign and a high interest rate, and even then it was not certain just how much money could be obtained. Borrowing from the banks offered the easiest method, but because it increased the total money supply, it would stimulate competition for goods and tend to raise prices.

McAdoo initially planned to finance at least 50 per cent of the war costs from taxation. His theory was supported by many leading economists, who thought that high taxes not only would lessen the pressures of inflation but would also place the major financial burden of war on those who were best able to bear it. As early as December, 1916, Professor O. M. W. Sprague vigorously attacked borrowing, asserting that it was both inflationary and inequitable. He recommended paying for the war "mainly, if not entirely," through taxation applied especially to consumer goods and to nonessential goods, services, and occupations.[4] Professor E. R. A. Seligman, on the other hand, asserted that "war taxes should never be stretched beyond the point where they begin to lessen the social output, to hamper the transfer of pre-war to war production, or to press unduly on desirable consumption."[5]

Most of the banking and financial experts did not support McAdoo's

[4] *American Economic Review*, March, 1917.
[5] *Annals of the American Academy of Political and Social Science*, Vol. LXXV, January, 1918.

original idea. Alexander D. Noyes, financial editor of the *New York Post*, conceded that high taxes would keep down prices, but he belittled the significance of the theory, for "the man whose means of buying necessities is cut off will scarcely be in a better position than the man who, with an unchanged income, has to pay more for them."[6] In answering an inquiry by the Treasury, J. P. Morgan wrote,

It is exceedingly important that investors of all size should not be discouraged, as they easily may be, by a scale of taxation which is felt by them to bear unjustly upon the investing class of the country. . . . I would suggest also that the amount of money which can be . . . actually spent . . . during that year should be ascertained with some approach to accuracy. And that a proportion not exceeding 20 per cent of this amount should be considered as the sum to be obtained by taxation.[7]

Eventually, McAdoo was persuaded that his goal was too high and that a tax burden sufficient to cover 50 per cent of the war costs "would be excessive, and perhaps destructive to some extent of the capitalized energy which keeps the wheels turning."[8] Consequently, he finally decided on 33⅓ per cent as the amount which should be raised by taxation. But the enactment of new tax laws and the collection of new revenue were bound to take time. In the interim, the need for money was stupendous, and the only way of securing it quickly was by borrowing.

Wartime Borrowing. After a study of national income statistics and "a lot of figures relating to bank deposits," McAdoo relied on a "hunch" and decided to make the first wartime bond issue $3 billion.[9] The question of the interest rate caused him a great deal of concern, and the bankers offered him little help. Almost universally they insisted that the Treasury should not borrow more than $1 billion, and they urged rates as high as 5½ per cent. Only Paul M. Warburg thought that as much as $2.5 billion could be borrowed on long-term obligations. But McAdoo stuck to his original plan, and on April 24 Congress passed the First Liberty Loan Act, authorizing the Treasury to borrow up to $5 billion at 3.5 per cent and to sell up to $2 billion of certificates of indebtedness in anticipation of loans. The bonds were to be convertible into any issues which might later be offered at a higher interest rate. Furthermore, they were exempt from all taxes except estate and inheritance.

On April 24, in anticipation of the sale of Liberty bonds, McAdoo sold $268 million of 3 per cent certificates to the commercial banks through the Federal Reserve System. In May and June, he sold three more batches of $200 million each to the banks. This policy of selling short-

[6] *Ibid.*

[7] McAdoo, *op. cit.*, p. 383.

[8] *Ibid.*, p. 384.

[9] *Ibid.*, p. 382.

term issues to the commercial banks in anticipation of bond sales and taxes was to be followed throughout the war. It offered a simple but dangerously inflationary method of financing. Perhaps, in the absence of alternatives, the first sale of short-term obligations to the banks was necessary, but at later periods, it should have been forsaken in favor of more determined sales—even at higher interest rates—to nonbank investors.

On May 14, the Treasury offered the First Liberty Loan of 1917 for public subscription. Despite the bankers' skepticism, it was decided to sell $2 billion of 3½ per cent bonds, callable in fifteen and maturing in thirty years. The bond campaign was conducted in a manner reminiscent of Jay Cooke. As McAdoo expressed it, "We went direct to the people; and that means to everybody—to businessmen, workmen, farmers, bankers, millionaires, schoolteachers, laborers. We capitalized the profound impulse called patriotism."[10] Anybody who could make a small down payment could buy a bond in denominations of $50 or more and pay the balance in installments extending over months. The loan met with success, and subscriptions totaling more than $3 billion were received, a larger amount than had been sold in the entire Civil War. But the Treasury did not take advantage of the oversubscription, placing only the $2 billion originally offered. By the time the date arrived for the payment of the first installment on the subscriptions, the bank-held certificates were $868 million, and over 40 per cent of the proceeds of the First Liberty Loan had to be used for refunding them.

The success of the First Liberty Loan convinced McAdoo of the wisdom of offering interest rates below the market level. In later years, he wrote, "Think of the enormous additional burden that the people would have been forced to carry if I had issued bonds at an increase of even one half of one per cent in the rate of interest!"[11] No doubt this verdict was substantially accurate as far as it went. But there were considerations in addition to money costs which should have been taken into account. In its anxiety to sell bonds at low interest rates, the Treasury urged individuals to buy bonds by borrowing from the banks, and this policy of "borrow and buy" unquestionably had an inflationary effect on the money supply and on prices. Moreover, when bond subscriptions showed signs of lagging, the Treasury called on the banks to fill the breach, with the result that Liberty Loan subscriptions did not come exclusively from nonbank investors.

The proceeds of the First Liberty Loan were exhausted by August, 1917, and the Treasury again sold certificates to the banks. Between August and November six issues, totaling $2.3 billion, were sold, about 88 per cent going to the commercial banks. On some of these issues, the

[10] *Ibid.*, p. 378.
[11] *Ibid.*, p. 381.

interest rate was as high as 4 per cent. Meanwhile, in September Congress authorized the Treasury to borrow an additional $7.5 billion in long-term obligations and an additional $2 billion of certificates. On October 1, 1917, the Treasury offered the Second Liberty Loan for $3 billion in 10–25-year bonds, with interest at 4 per cent, ½ per cent higher than the first loan. These bonds were also convertible if higher interest rate bonds were offered at any future date. But the tax features were not so attractive as in the first loan, for bond interest on principal exceeding $5,000 was subject to the surtax as well as the estate tax. Nevertheless, subscriptions totaled $4.6 billion, an oversubscription of $1.6 billion, of which the Treasury accepted half, allotting $3.8 billion. Certificates of indebtedness, which were maturing and had to be funded, absorbed 61 per cent of the loan.

In December, 1917, the Treasury began a concerted effort to tap low incomes by offering war savings stamps in denominations of 25 cents and higher. Later, war savings certificates in denominations of $25 and higher were issued. They ran uniformly to January, 1923 and paid 4 per cent if held to maturity. The sale of these obligations was surprisingly large, considering the relatively unattractive nature of their interest rate. In fact, by February the Treasury was issuing certificates of indebtedness at 4½ per cent. About 60 per cent of these were taken by the banks.

In April, 1918, Congress increased the authorization for Liberty Loans to $12 billion and extended the authority for certificates of indebtedness to $8 billion. McAdoo offered the Third Liberty Loan of $3 billion shortly thereafter at 4¼ per cent interest, although banking opinion still insisted that the rate was too low. The new issue was callable in ten years, and it had the same tax features as the second loan. But three new features were added: the bonds were not convertible, they were receivable in payment of estate taxes, and for the first time, an attempt was made to support the government-bond market by empowering the Secretary to purchase 5 per cent of each outstanding issue, except the 3½ per cents. The issue was again oversubscribed, this time up to $4.2 billion, and the Treasury accepted all subscriptions. The outstanding certificates of indebtedness, mostly bank-held, equaled about 62 per cent of the proceeds. Thus, an increasing proportion of each new bond issue had already been anticipated by the sale of short-term obligations to the commercial banks.

When the fiscal year ended in June, 1918, it became evident that war expenditures had been underestimated. Instead of $8.5 billion, the first full year of war cost $12.7 billion, of which only $3.7 billion, or 29 per cent, was covered by ordinary revenues. The government was spending at a rate of about $35 million a day, and a fourth loan was necessary. In July, 1918, Congress increased the loan authorization to $20 billion, and in September, McAdoo offered the Fourth Liberty Loan of $6 billion of 15–20-year bonds at 4¼ per cent interest. To offset this low rate, interest on individual holdings up to $30,000 of bonds was exempt from surtaxes and excess-profits taxes until two years after the war.[12] The extraordinary prosperity developed during the war was amply demonstrated by the fact that $7 billion, all of which was allotted, was subscribed in 22.8 million different subscriptions, 84 per cent for less than $100. Money wages had risen to unprecedented heights. Not only was there full employment, but millions of people were being added to the labor force. Profits were high, and so were farm incomes. As individual and corporate savings grew, they flowed in a heavy stream into war bonds. Nevertheless, a great amount of the proceeds of the loans continued to be used to refund short-term obligations, and the dangerous "borrow and buy" practice was growing with the full encouragement of the government. Actual hostilities ended on November 11, 1918, but extraordinary expenditures continued. Total expenditures in the fiscal year 1919 exceeded $18.5 billion, 50 per cent more than in 1917–1918. Since Congress was slow in raising more taxes, the proceeds of the Fourth Liberty Loan were soon exhausted, and the Treasury again resorted to short-term loans.

TABLE 39. LIBERTY AND VICTORY LOANS, 1917–1919
(In billions of dollars)

	Authorized (billions)	Subscribed (billions)	Issued (billions)	Rate (per cent)	Term
First Liberty*.........	$ 5.0	$ 3.0	$ 2.0	3½	15–30's
Second Liberty†.......	7.5	4.6	3.8	4	10–25's
Third Liberty†........	12.0	4.2	4.2	4¼	10's
Fourth Liberty‡........	20.0	7.0	7.0	4¼	15–20's
Victory Loan*.........	7.0	5.2	4.5	4¾ and 3¾	3–4's
Totals.............	$51.5	$24.0	$21.5		

SOURCE: *Annual Report of the Secretary of the Treasury*, 1917–1919.

* Exempt from normal and surtax.
† Income from principal of more than $5,000 subject to surtax.
‡ Income from principal of more than $30,000 subject to surtax.

In March, 1919, a postwar Victory Loan was offered to refund maturing certificates and to provide the Treasury with current funds. Congress authorized $7 billion of 1- to 5-year notes payable in gold and made a momentous change in debt administration by giving the Secretary the

[12] In addition, a holder of $30,000 of the Fourth Liberty Loan received an exemption from surtaxes and excess-profits taxes on the interest received after Jan. 1, 1918, on an aggregate of $45,000 of Second and Third Liberty bonds.

power to fix terms and rates. In April Secretary Carter Glass, who had succeeded McAdoo in December, 1918, offered $4.5 billion of 3- to 4-year 4¾ per cent notes, exempt from all taxes except estate, inheritance, and normal income taxes. They were convertible into 3¾ per cent notes, which were exempt from the normal income tax as well as the surtax.

Altogether, from April, 1917, to October, 1919, the Treasury sold $21.5 billion of long-term bonds and, including reissues, $32.7 billion of certificates of indebtedness. Of the total certificates, $18.7 billion was sold in anticipation of loans, $6.1 billion in anticipation of taxes, and $8 billion were special issues. On October 31, 1919, $3.7 billion were still outstanding.

The gross debt at its highest point on August 31, 1919, was $26.6 billion. At that time, the Treasury's cash balance was $1.1 billion, leaving a net debt of $25.5 billion. Of the total debt, $19.1 billion represented Liberty bonds and Victory notes. These were distributed in 78.7 million pieces, of which almost 40 million were for $50 or less. It was reliably estimated that 30 per cent of the Liberty bonds were owned by persons with incomes of $2,000 or less.

TABLE 40.   DISTRIBUTION OF DEBT, JUNE 30, 1919
(In millions of dollars)

By Maturities		By Ownership	
5 years	$ 7,093	Federal agencies	$ 158
5–10 years	3,959	Reserve banks	292
10–20 years	6,881	Member banks	3,803
Over 20 years	6,348	All other commercial banks	1,340
Total marketable	$24,281	All other	19,670
		Total	$25,263

SOURCE: *Annual Report of the Secretary of the Treasury*, 1919.

The Treasury followed a confused policy in its loan operations. It attempted to reduce consumer purchasing power through the sale of Liberty bonds, war savings certificates, and thrift stamps. But at the same time it increased total purchasing power by encouraging individuals to buy bonds with money borrowed from the banks. Fearing that its loans might not be successful and desiring to keep service charges on the debt at a minimum, it relied too heavily on short-term obligations and on sales to the banks. As a result, commercial bank holdings of government obligations increased, demand deposits rose, consumer spending increased, and an upward pressure was exerted on prices. It is debatable whether higher interest rates would have dissuaded entrepreneurs from investing in nonessential activities or would have persuaded nonbank investors to buy more government bonds. But the Treasury never allowed the issue to come to a test, and it survived to plague the money market in the postwar era as well as in World War II and its aftermath.

Expansion of Credit. The Treasury's cheap-money policy required an enormous expansion of credit, and since the Federal Reserve System was obligated to support the Treasury's plans of war finance, it continued its prewar policy of making reserves easily available to the banks. With the help of various amendments to the Federal Reserve Act, it created a pool of credit which enabled the banks to buy government obligations and to make loans to individuals purchasing government bonds, making it possible for the Treasury to finance the war easily but dangerously.

TABLE 41. BANKING OPERATIONS, JUNE, 1916 TO JUNE, 1919
(In millions of dollars)

	1916	1917	1918	1919
Total deposits.......................	$21,926	$26,171	$29,505	$34,429
Member bank.....................	11,133	13,397	18,981	22,833
Nonmember bank...................	10,221	11,667	8,732	9,655
Federal Reserve....................	512	1,107	1,792	1,941
Total loans.........................	15,768	18,185	20,073	22,363
Member bank.....................	7,964	9,370	13,233	15,414
Nonmember bank...................	7,804	8,815	6,840	6,949
Total investments....................	4,643	5,678	7,307	9,397
Member bank.....................	2,351	3,083	5,274	6,827
Nonmember bank...................	2,292	2,595	2,033	2,570
Total investment in governments........	806	1,667	3,451	5,447
Member bank.....................	703	1,065	2,465	3,803
Nonmember bank...................	48	480	747	1,344
Federal Reserve....................	55	122	239	300
Federal Reserve note circulation........	155	492	1,661	2,501
National-bank circulation..............	716	691	691	639
Reserve ratio of district banks..........	83	70.9	57.4	50.6

SOURCE: Federal Reserve Board, *Banking and Monetary Statistics.*

Throughout 1917, member-bank loans, investments, and deposits increased steadily, and member banks, with the full encouragement of the Federal Reserve, began to borrow from the district banks to replenish their reserves. The rediscount rate at New York was kept at 3 per cent, and advances on promissory notes secured by government obligations were made at rates below the coupon rate of the security. With easy credit, rediscounting increased from $28.6 milion at the end of 1916 to $197 million in June, 1917, and Federal Reserve deposits expanded from $623 million to $1.1 billion, while Federal Reserve note circulation rose from $265 million to $492 million. As liabilities increased, the reserve ratio (the ratio of reserves to the net liability of the district banks) dropped from 81.1 to 70.9 per cent. This was substantially in excess of legal requirements; nevertheless, it was decided to expand reserves even further. On June 21, 1917, the Federal Reserve Act was fundamentally amended. Reserve requirements for member banks were reduced to 7, 10, and 13 per cent for country banks, city banks, and reserve city banks, respectively, and all reserves were required to be deposited in the district banks. In addition, no reserves were required against government deposits, and the security against Federal Reserve notes was changed to at least 40 per cent in gold and the remainder in commercial paper instead of 100 per cent as previously. By this amendment the reserve ratio was increased to over 78 per cent, the excess reserves of the member banks were greatly expanded, and the possibilities for multiple credit expansion were once again enormous.

In the meanwhile, however, another threat to monetary expansion appeared, for gold exports began as soon as the United States entered the war. By July they were substantial, and in the next three months almost $100 million was exported. The gold stock decreased about $70 million, contracting the base of the entire monetary and credit structure. To control gold exports, Congress passed the Espionage Act of June 15, 1917, authorizing the President to prohibit the export of any commodity. In September an embargo was imposed on coin, bullion, and currency. To close the last loophole, the Trading with the Enemy Act of October 6, 1917, authorized the President to restrict transactions in foreign exchange and gold. Thereafter, gold could not be exported except under license from the Federal Reserve Board, and between September, 1917, and January, 1919, licenses were granted for the export of only $45.5 million. Although payments in gold continued to be maintained domestically, the embargo on gold exports took the United States off a true gold standard for the fourth time in history.

War financing was not solely responsible for the wartime expansion of bank credit. Total bank loans increased by approximately $6.6 billion. About $1 billion represented loans on bonds under the "borrow and buy" policy, but the remainder represented business loans, a large share of which was unessential to the prosecution of the war. It was not until very late in the war that the government took steps to eliminate nonessential private borrowing. In the early part of 1918 the Federal Reserve Board created an informal Capital Issues Committee which received statutory status in April, 1918. Its function was to investigate and pass upon new security issues, but it was not too successful, since borrowers were not legally obligated to submit securities for investigation or to abide by the committee's decisions. Up to the armistice, the committee passed upon $26 billion of new issues, only 14 per cent of which involved new construction or equipment.

Despite the enormous impetus given to credit expansion by the government fiscal and banking policy, the supply of capital funds quickly evaporated, and in the absence of adequate controls, rates of interest increased in spite of the Treasury's desire to maintain cheap money. Rates on government obligations increased from 3 (the rate on the early certificates) to 4¾ per cent (the rate on the Victory notes). Market interest rates, of course, followed a similar pattern. Between 1914 and 1918 the call-loan rate increased from 3.43 to 5.29 per cent, while 60- to 90-day commercial paper rose from 4.79 to 5.88 per cent.

The Silver Problem. In addition to the critical problem of financing the war, the Treasury had to deal with the ubiquitous silver issue. The war increased the demand for silver for industrial uses, inflating its price far beyond its peacetime normal. In 1919 it reached $1.3825 an ounce. Since $1.382 of subsidiary coin contained 1 ounce of silver, the price was almost high enough to make it profitable to melt coins and sell them in the bullion market. Hence, the United States was within an ace of again witnessing the annoying, but interesting, spectacle that had occurred during the Civil War, when the subsidiary silver coinage disappeared from circulation. Fortunately, the price of silver stopped rising, and a crisis was averted.

The same demand which almost precipitated a domestic coinage crisis created a scarcity of silver in Great Britain. In order to increase the supply, Congress passed the Pittman Act of 1918, authorizing the melting down and sale of 350 million silver dollars at $1 an ounce. To fill the resulting void in the currency, the Treasury was instructed to issue Federal Reserve bank notes. To protect the silver interests, provision was made for the eventual repurchase of enough raw silver at $1 an ounce to replace the number of silver dollars sold during the war. Under the Pittman Act, 260 million silver dollars were melted down and sold.

Wartime Taxation. Shortly after the declaration of war and the emergency revenue law of March, 1917, McAdoo recommended another increase in taxation to raise $1.8 billion of additional money in the fiscal year 1918. He proposed to lower income tax exemptions drastically, to increase maximum surtax rates from 13 to 40 per cent, to apply surtaxes at $3,000 instead of $20,000, to impose a special tax on incomes earned in 1916, and to extend the list of special excises.

In May, Chairman Kitchen of the Ways and Means Committee introduced a bill embodying most of McAdoo's suggestions. It was passed quickly by the House, but in the Senate, the Republican leaders Lodge and Penrose attempted to scale down the proposed rates so as to produce only an additional $1¼ billion. The debate dragged on throughout the summer, and it was not until October 3, 1917, almost six months after the country's entry into war, that the bill was finally passed. It (1) raised the normal tax on individual incomes from 2 to 4 per cent and the maximum surtaxes from 13 to 63 per cent (thus making the maximum combined normal and surtax rate 67 per cent); (2) started the surtaxes at $5,000 instead of $20,000 and lowered personal exemptions to $1,000 for single and $2,000 for married persons with an additional $200 for each dependent; (3) raised the corporate income tax from 2 to 6 per cent; (4) increased the estate tax to a range of 2 to 25 per cent; (5) substituted a new excess-profits tax at progressive rates of 20 to 60 per cent for the earlier one and reduced the munitions tax from 12½ to 10 per cent (the new tax was calculated on profits in excess of the average net earnings in 1911 to 1913, with a deduction of $6,000 plus 7 to 9 per cent of capital); (6) increased taxes on alcoholic beverages and tobacco and extended the list, and increased the rates of the special excises on transportation, admissions, etc.; and (7) increased postal rates. The Act also imposed a tax on undistributed profits, but this was never enforced and was repealed in 1918.

The rates of the October, 1917, Act were regarded by many persons as confiscatory. Professor Seligman characterized them as "the highwater mark thus far reached in the history of taxation," observing that "never before, in the annals of civilization, has an attempt been made to take as much as two-thirds of a man's income by taxation."[13] Yet this record was to be exceeded during the same war and much more substantially during World War II.

In his annual report of December, 1917, McAdoo raised his estimates for the then current fiscal year to $18.7 billion, including $6 billion for Allied loans. Yet he did not advise further tax increases, fearing that they would deter war production and interfere with his efforts to borrow at low costs. He wrote:

It is my earnest conviction that the general economy of the country should be permitted to readjust itself to the new revenue laws before consideration should be given to the imposition of additional tax burdens. If a situation should develop where the government could not sell convertible and partly tax-exempt bonds upon a 4 per cent basis, it would become necessary to seriously consider further revenue legislation.

The administration continued cool to new tax measures until May, 1918, when it realized that the war would be longer and even more expensive than originally expected. By that time expenditures were in excess of $50 million a day. Therefore, President Wilson, on May 27, delivered a special message to Congress appealing for more reliance on taxation and less on loans. In June, McAdoo estimated expenditures for the fiscal year 1919 at $24 billion and recommended that one-third, or $8 billion, be raised through taxes. He suggested a "real war-profits tax" superimposed on the

[13] E. R. A. Seligman, *Essays in Taxation*, p. 694.

excess-profits tax, a substantial increase in normal tax rates, and heavy taxes on luxuries. Since 1918 was an election year, Congress was reluctant to increase taxes, but in September a tax bill was introduced in the House. Before it could be enacted, the armistice was signed, and McAdoo immediately suggested that the measure be revised downward to provide only $6 billion of revenue in 1919 and $4 billion in 1920. Even with the scaling down, the rates were still raised considerably above those of the October, 1917, Act.

TABLE 42. FEDERAL RECEIPTS, EXPENDITURES, AND DEBT, 1915–1919
(In millions of dollars)

	1915	1916	1917	1918	1919
Receipts:					
Customs..................	$ 209.8	$ 213.2	$ 226.0	$ 182.8	$ 183.4
Income and profits.........	80.2	124.9	387.4	2,852.3	2,600.8
Estate.....................	....	....	6.1	47.5	82.0
Capital stock..............	....	....	10.5	25.0	28.8
Excise taxes:					
Spirits................	144.6	158.7	192.1	317.6	365.2
Fermented liquor.........	79.3	88.8	91.9	126.3	117.8
Tobacco................	80.0	88.1	103.2	156.2	206.0
Manufacturers'...........	....	....	....	36.6	75.6
Sales, stamps, and playing cards................	24.1	43.0	9.7	23.2	49.7
Transportation..........	....	....	....	64.4	219.9
Telephone and telegraph and insurance..........	....	....	....	12.8	32.4
Occupation, admissions, and dues..............	....	6.9	5.2	31.4	59.7
Other revenue............	79.9	58.9	92.2	304.3	633.1
Totals.................	$ 697.9	$ 782.5	$1,124.3	$ 4,180.4	$ 4,654.4
Expenditures*..............	$ 760.6	$ 740.9	$2,086.1	$13,791.9	$18,952.1
Surplus (+) or deficit (−)*...	−62.7	+41.6	−961.8	−9,611.5	−14,297.7
Gross debt†................	1,191.3	1,225.1	2,975.6	12,243.6	25,482.0
Interest-bearing debt.........	969.8	971.6	2,712.5	11,985.9	25,234.5

SOURCE: *Annual Report of the Secretary of the Treasury*, 1915–1919, 1950.

* For explanation of differences between figures given here and those of the historical series, see p. 3 and Appendix 1.

† Figures for the gross debt beginning 1915 are taken from the 1950 Treasury report and differ from the earlier series mainly in that they do not include gold and silver certificates.

Although the bill became law on February 24, 1919, it was known as the Revenue Act of 1918. It (1) raised the normal tax to 6 to 12 per cent on 1918 individual incomes and 4 to 8 per cent on 1919 incomes; (2) retained exemptions of $2,000 and $1,000 with $200 for each dependent; (3) raised surtaxes to a maximum of 65 per cent, bringing the maximum combined normal rate and surtax to 77 per cent; (4) increased the corporation tax to 12 per cent in 1918 and to 10 per cent thereafter on net income in excess of $2,000; (5) increased excess-profits tax rates for 1918 to 30 to 65 per cent and to 20 to 40 per cent thereafter on net income over 8 per cent of invested captial after a deduction of $3,000.

Actual tax collections under the two historic measures of October, 1917, and February, 1919, rose to $3.9 billion in fiscal 1918 and $4.1 billion in fiscal 1919. Although, in the main, these gains in revenue resulted from increased levies, the wartime inflation of incomes was a contributing factor. But large as it was, the gain in revenues lagged behind the increase in expenditures. The ratio of revenues to expenditures, which had been 60.4 per cent in 1917, dropped to 33.8 per cent in 1918 and to 26 per cent in the fiscal year 1919. The main revenue supports came from individual and corporate income and profits taxes. Excise taxes were increased to a lesser extent, and for the first time in the history of war financing, tariff rates were not raised. In brief, the wartime revenue policies gave a decided impetus to progressive and direct taxation.

Cost of the War. Although it is impossible to estimate the aggregate costs of World War I to the United States, since some of them extended far into the future, it is possible to estimate them for the actual period of conflict and the succeeding year of liquidation. Professor Seligman, after allowing for ordinary peacetime expenditures, estimated the costs from April 5, 1917, to July 1, 1919, at $32.7 billion, including $9.4 billion of Allied war loans. He calculated that 31 per cent of the war costs were paid from taxation. In 1920 Secretary Houston, after deducting from total expenditures of $38.8 billion estimated peacetime expenditures of $3.8 billion and miscellaneous revenue of $1.6 billion attributable to the war, estimated total war expenditures from April 6, 1917, to June 30, 1920, at $33.4 billion.

All the regular departments, because of either the assumption of emergency functions or payment of higher compensation, had to spend more money. In the Treasury Department, the main additions were war insurance losses, military family allowances, expenses for loan campaigns, and losses on silver under the Pittman Act. Increases in agricultural expenditures were due to an increase in personnel and a campaign to expand farm production. Expenses for the independent offices rose because of the creation of various administrative groups, such as the Council of National Defense, the War Industries Board, the Shipping Board, the Emergency Fleet Corporation, the Railroad Administration, the Food and Fuel Administration, the Grain Corporation, the Housing Corporation, and the War Finance Corporation.

Among the most substantial war costs were approximately $9.5 billion of loans to the Allied powers, authorized by Congress in the various

Liberty Loan Acts. In payment, the United States received certificates of indebtedness almost all of which were payable on demand in gold coin with interest at 5 per cent. The proceeds were spent entirely in the United States for American goods and services. Since they were financed for the most part through credit inflation and since they reduced the domestic supply of goods, they contributed in two ways to price inflation. However, their greatest importance was in assisting materially to win the war. Unfortunately, they were to become the subject for long negotiation and intense feeling after the war was over.

TABLE 43. FEDERAL EXPENDITURES, 1915–1919
(In millions of dollars)

	1915	1916	1917	1918	1919
War	$128.4	$134.3	$ 412.5	$ 5,672.9	$ 9,240.2
Navy	142.7	155.9	258.2	1,370.4	2,019.1
Legislature, Executive, etc	32.0	31.3	33.3	49.7	73.5
Interior	29.1	24.8	29.2	35.3	29.1
Commerce and labor	15.3	14.9	15.5	19.2	29.0
Treasury	71.1	73.7	84.9	181.8	289.9
Agriculture	29.1	28.0	29.6	46.8	36.9
Independent bureaus	5.7	7.2	22.7	1,135.8	2,723.5
Rivers and harbors	46.8	32.5	30.5	29.6	33.1
Panama Canal	29.2	17.5	19.3	20.8	12.3
Pensions	164.4	159.3	160.3	181.1	221.6
Purchase of foreign obligations	......	......	885.0	4,739.4	3,477.9
Interest	22.9	22.9	24.7	197.5	615.9
Miscellaneous	43.7	38.5	80.2	111.3	150.4
Totals	$760.6	$740.9	$2,086.1	$13,791.9	$18,952.1

SOURCE: *Annual Report of the Secretary of the Treasury*, 1915–1919.

Economic Controls. Although this country was not so hard pressed for strategic raw materials as were Germany and the Allied Powers, she was nevertheless pressed considerably and, like them, had to institute controls over the use of steel, lumber, wool, and a multitude of other scarce supplies. To organize the war effort effectively, controls had to be applied to almost every aspect of economic life.

The War Industries Board was organized with powers to establish priorities in the use of scarce materials and services, to commandeer and allocate them, to prohibit their nonessential use, and to order the use of substitutes. The Board's controls were extended to almost the entire field of production, transportation, distribution, employment, and credit. Other agencies were created for the exercise of specialized controls—the Food and Fuel Administration, the War Trade Board, the War Labor Board, etc. Eventually, almost no manufacturing contract could be executed or building erected without some form of assent from the War Administration.

The railway system was nationalized for the duration of the war with the government paying all expenses (far exceeding railway revenue) and undertakinig to pay owners a fair return and, upon returning the railways after the war, to compensate them for any damage to the property. The Shipping Board was created to build transports, and the Emergency Fleet Corporation to operate them.

To expedite war production, the "cost plus" system of compensation—a wide departure from the peacetime price system—was adopted. By removing from the operators all incentives to economize, it greatly and unnecessarily increased the costs of the war to the government.

The War Finance Corporation was set up to make advances to banks making loans to enterprises essential to the war effort or, in exceptional cases, to make such advances directly to such enterprises. The corporation could also make loans to savings banks and other financial institutions where such loans were necessary to sustain their operations and could not be obtained through commercial channels. The capital of the corporation, $500 million, was subscribed wholly by the government, and during the war it made loans totaling $67.7 million. Fifteen years later it served as a pattern for the creation of the Reconstruction Finance Corporation.

No direct controls were established over the prices of consumer goods, but these were potently influenced by indirect methods, applied largely at the point of marketing of raw materials. Thus, the Food Administration, under Hoover's direction, by entering into agreements with farmers and major buyers and processers of farm products regarding prices and markups, rolled back or held down the prices of most staple food products. In some cases the government intervened directly, purchasing an entire crop and then selling it to processers or exporters at agreed upon prices. This was done with wheat and sugar, with the aid of a special fund of $150 million. Two subsidiary organizations were set up by the Food Administration for such intervention—the United States Grain Corporation and the Sugar Stabilization Board. Much profiteering was eliminated in this way.[14]

Although no rationing of civilian consumer goods was established, appeals were made to citizens voluntarily to cut their consumption of sugar, butter, and other foods in short supply.

These various direct and indirect economic controls were of revolutionary nature. They not only helped to win the war but made the government's fiscal policies much more effective. Moreover, the institution of these broad controls, even though done only to meet an emergency,

[14] See Herbert Hoover, "Memoirs of Public Life," *Collier's*, Sept. 1, 1951.

made a deep imprint on the country's economic thinking which no subsequent return to traditionalism could altogether wipe out.

Impact of the War on the National Income. On the assumption that war expenditures approximated $33 billion from April, 1917, to July 1, 1919, they represented approximately 20 per cent of the total gross national product and, at their highest point, approximately 25 per cent. This enormous spending had a stimulative effect on the national income and the gross national product, but some of the addition was illusory, being the result of inflated prices. In terms of goods and services, that is, in constant prices, the increase was far less impressive.[15]

Unlike World War II, war production was not completely superimposed on peacetime production. Therefore, consumers paid a substantial part of the war costs, for while spending about the same amount of dollars as in peacetime, they did not obtain so great a quantity or so good a quality of goods and services. Professor J. M. Clark estimated that of the $32 billion expended for war purposes, $13 billion came from increased production and $19 billion from consumer retrenchment.[16]

Because of the inadequacy of the data, it is difficult to reach a definite conclusion concerning the effect of the war on income distribution. Real salaries in 1916 to 1919 fell from the level of 1912 to 1915, and real wages remained practically stationary after 1916. Business profits were atypically high in 1916 but declined during the years of actual belligerency. Because of much greater reliance on progressive taxation, the entrepreneurial groups fared much worse than in the Civil War. On the other hand, agricultural income rose continuously.

In terms of income distribution by size, the share received by the upper-income group declined, whereas that of the low-income group increased because of heavier employment and larger payments to agriculture. As the government increased its indebtedness, individual savings rose sharply, from an average rate of about $4 billion in 1914 to $6.8 billion in 1916, $9.6 billion in 1917, and $11.5 billion in 1918. From this high level, they declined to $10.8 billion in 1919, $9 billion in 1920, and $2.3 billion in 1921.

[15] Gross national product in current dollars increased from $36.3 billion in 1914 to $75.2 billion in 1919. In terms of 1914 dollars, the increase was from $36.3 billion in 1914 to $43.7 billion in 1917. Thereafter, it declined to $41.8 billion in 1919. (Simon Kuznets, *National Product in Wartime*, pp. 128, 134.) Prices rose sharply from 100 in the summer, 1915 (June, 1914 = 100) to 122 in the summer, 1916, and 180 in the summer, 1917. Then they were temporarily stabilized only to rise again in 1919. Average hourly earnings in selected industries rose from 101 in 1915 (1914 = 100) to 109 in 1916, 123 in 1917, and 151 in 1918.

[16] J. M. Clark, *The Costs of the World War to the American People.*

Chapter 24: THE PROSPEROUS TWENTIES: FISCAL PROBLEMS

At the end of the war, the country's capacity for Federal regulation was temporarily satisfied, and there was a general desire to return to the state and local management characteristic of the prewar years. The twenties were, therefore, years of interregnum when "normalcy" was one of the watchwords of the day and "taking the government out of business" was one of the most important goals.

In the first postwar election, the reaction against centralized government resulted in a decisive defeat for the Wilson administration, even though it had quietly buried the New Freedom long before and even though it seemed to share the general desire to return to peacetime "normalcy" as quickly as possible. During its last days in office, it recommended cutting expenditures, reorganizing the tax structure to stimulate business activity, and retiring the debt as quickly as possible.

The Harding and Coolidge administrations followed the same goals, but with much greater enthusiasm. They believed sincerely in minimum government interference with business. President Harding was convinced that the pressing need of the United States was "not nostrums but normalcy; not revolution but restoration," and President Coolidge believed that "the business of America is business." Under the circumstances, policies friendly to business were emphasized, while assistance to farmer and labor groups was avoided. Vigorous deflationary action was not taken. Expenditures which interfered with business were cut, while those which aided business were increased. Taxes were reduced sharply. A comfortable, rather than a ruthless, debt-retirement policy was instituted, and the monetary authorities tended to follow easy-money policies, even at the risk of encouraging speculation. The resultant philosophy was not *laissez faire* but neomercantilism, designed not so much to enhance the power of the state as to advance the interests of a certain group of articulate businessmen.

Economic Pattern of the Period. During the first few months after the armistice there was a transition to peacetime conditions during which prices fell slightly and business was dull. However, by the spring of 1919 reconversion had been completed, and a postwar price and credit inflation began. Possibly the most important propelling factor was the vast European demand for American goods. The American export balance, $400 million in January, 1919, had passed $625 million by June. More than 60 per cent of this balance was financed by government relief measures of one type or another. In addition to the European demand, a backlog of domestic demand acted as a tonic. Business activity expanded, and investment spending reached 20 per cent of the gross national product. At the beginning of 1920 the cost of living was twice as high as it had been in 1913 and almost 20 per cent higher than in the spring of 1919. But the gross national product in 1920 was $85 billion, compared with $38.5 billion in 1914 and $77.9 billion in 1919.

By early spring of 1920 there were signs that business activity had reached its peak. The export trade was definitely declining, for the government had abruptly ceased its policy of extending credits to Europe and private finance was unable or unwilling to take over. The decline gathered speed, and by the summer of 1920 a full rout was under way.

Recovery did not begin until mid-1921, but in the eight years thereafter "good times" were the rule, with only short interruptions in 1924 and 1927. Gross national product, which had dropped to $69.9 billion in 1922, rebounded to $81.6 billion in 1923 and reached $99.4 billion in 1929. Productivity increased about 3 per cent per year, but the wholesale price level showed little change from 1923 to 1929. Excess purchasing power found its way into speculative channels, and real estate and security values became extraordinarily inflated. In later years it became fashionable to pin the responsibility for the boom on the government's fiscal and monetary policies. While these charges had some justification, the real causes lay elsewhere.

Reduction of Wartime Ependitures. The demand for a return to the pre-1916 expenditure pattern asserted itself as soon as the war ended, but it was a few months after Armistice Day before it was satisfied. Up to January, 1919, the United States was spending approximately $2 billion a month. But thereafter expenditures declined impressively. By the summer they were below $1 billion a month and by November, below $400 million. For the full fiscal year 1920 total expenditures were $6.1 billion, one-third the 1919 figure.

It was the desire of the Wilson administration to cut expenditures even more in order to retire as much of the national debt as possible. But the return to peacetime conditions required vast outlays for reconstruction. In 1920 the Federal government spent $350 million to support declining wheat prices, $680 million in returning the railroads to private management, and $100 million for European food relief. The rising cost of living necessitated a general increase in the compensation of government employees, and a newly inaugurated system of Federal aid to states for highways took $20 million a year with larger outlays to come. The retrench-

TABLE 44.   FEDERAL EXPENDITURES, 1920–1929

(In millions of dollars)

	1920	1921	1922	1923	1924	1925	1926	1927	1928	1929
Legislative, Executive, Judicial, and District of Columbia	$503.6[a]	62.1	$58.8	$62.1	$62.0	$71.7	$74.6	$82.5	$84.1	$87.4
State	13.6	8.5	10.4	14.2	14.2	15.9	16.0	16.5	11.6	13.4
Interior	28.2	48.8	47.6	48.5	47.9	48.2	47.6	31.0	32.3	34.2
Post office	38.4	134.0	67.8	32.8	12.8	23.3	39.5	27.3	32.1	137.7
Agriculture	66.6	120.6	144.0	126.6	143.7	159.7	155.8	156.3	161.8	171.7
Commerce	35.8	25.9	21.2	20.7	21.5	25.9	29.1	31.0	34.3	40.5
Labor	6.1	7.0	6.2	6.5	7.0	8.7	8.6	9.8	9.8	11.4
Treasury	214.6	438.2[b]	175.7	129.6	118.4	135.4	134.1	144.6	199.3	199.5
Tax refunds	45.9	54.0	87.7	157.6	159.3	182.5	201.3	136.2	166.7	213.0
Independent offices[e]	1,237.5	864.0	348.0	511.0	400.4	−174.2[g]	416.0	383.3	440.5	459.0
Military establishments	1,050.2	505.8	355.1	299.7	265.5	268.6	278.8	286.9	308.1	329.7
Navy establishments	632.7	649.9	458.8	322.5	324.1	326.4	311.6	322.6	322.2	366.2
Rivers and harbors	49.9	58.8	43.3	51.4	75.6	79.4	69.9	66.9	78.4	83.4
Panama Canal	9.5	16.2	3.7	4.6	7.5	10.0	9.6	8.2	11.7	10.5
Indian affairs	40.5	41.5	38.5	45.1	46.8	38.8	48.4	36.8	38.7	37.2
Pensions	213.3	260.6	252.6	265.9	229.6	219.9	208.7	232.0	228.7	229.5
Interest	1,024.0	996.7	989.5	1,055.1	938.7	882.0	831.5	787.8	731.9	679.0
Adjusted service fund						100.0	120.0	116.0	111.7	111.8
Shipping board	469.1	92.9	86.1	78.3	57.7	41.4	23.9	13.3	33.8	16.1
Other special accounts[d]									58.8	70.9
Miscellaneous	462.3[c]	11.2	0.7	12.4	13.8	0.4[f]	5.3[f]	8.1[f]	0.7	
Totals	$6,141.7	$4,468.7	$3,195.7	$3,244.7	$2,946.4	$2,464.2	$3,030.4	$2,897.1	$3,107.0	$3,302.0
Statutory debt retirement	$ 78.7	$ 427.1	$ 422.7	$ 402.9	$ 458.0	$ 466.5	$ 487.4	$ 519.6	$ 540.3	$ 549.6
Totals	$6,220.4	$4,895.8	$3,618.4	$3,647.6	$3,404.4	$2,930.7	$3,517.8	$3,416.7	$3,647.6	$3,851.6

SOURCE: *Annual Report of the Secretary of the Treasury,* 1920–1929. Debt retirement figures, *Annual Report,* 1930.

[a] $350.0 million for wheat-guarantee fund.

[b] Increases for government life insurance and enforcement of prohibition.

[c] In 1920 and 1921 the largest items ($1 billion and $0.7 billion) were for compensation to railroads; in subsequent years to the Veterans' Bureau (upward of $400 million a year, excluding adjusted service certificate fund payments).

[d] Trust funds.

[e] $421.3 million for purchase of foreign obligations and $12 million for control of private telegraph and telephone companies.

[f] Premium on bond purchases.

[g] Excess of capital repayments by War Finance Corporation over expenditures for independent offices.

ment which did occur was confined almost exclusively to defense and wartime activities. Wartime economic controls were abandoned almost as soon as the war was over, expenditures for independent bureaus being cut by over $1 billion in fiscal 1920, as the Food and Fuel Administration, the Bureau of Industrial Housing and Transportation, the War Finance Corporation, the Emergency Shipping Fund, the Federal Employment Offices, and other regulatory and service bureaus went out of existence.

A change in emphasis in fiscal policy took place in March, 1921, when Andrew W. Mellon became Secretary of the Treasury. A private financier of distinction who had quitely amassed one of the largest fortunes in America, Mellon brought to his new task the same persistence and conservatism which characterized his private operations. He planned to cut expenditures, but unlike Houston, his Democratic predecessor, he regarded tax reduction rather than debt retirement as the primary goal of fiscal policy.

Total expenditures dropped from $6.2 billion in the fiscal year 1920 to $4.9 billion in 1921, and hovered around $3.5 billion during the remaining twenties,[1] or about five times the prewar figure. Thus, the administration did not succeed in reducing expenditures as drastically as it had hoped.

Although theoretically opposed to further expansion of centralized government, the public inconsistently demanded increased services on the Federal level whenever they could not be obtained readily on the state and local level. Expenditures for peacetime services therefore increased, and total spending was reduced to $3.5 billion a year and kept at about that level only because expenditures for military and international activities and interest on the debt declined.

The public not only opposed proposals for compulsory military training, but demanded a reduction in the regular army. The resultant cuts in Army expenditures were only slightly offset by increases in Federal contributions to the National Guard and by larger expenditures for the Air Force.[2]

As a result of the Washington disarmament agreement of 1923, a part of the Navy was scrapped and its operations curtailed. But under the London treaty in 1929 the Navy began to expand, although not enough to satisfy the demands of the advocates of a "strong navy." Over $10 million was spent in increasing the Navy, pay and subsistence were raised

[1] Occasionally, expenditures were considerably lower, but the reductions were largely illusory. In 1925, for example, total expenditures were only $3 billion, but this was because $499 million received in the liquidation of the War Finance Corporation was deducted from expenditures rather than added to receipts.

[2] In 1915 contributions to the National Guard were $4.8 million, approximately one-third the total cost. In 1929 they were $33.2 million, about three-quarters of the total cost. Air Force expenditures were $11.3 million in 1924 and $23.5 million in 1929.

$7 million, repairs and construction of yards and docks rose $8.5 million, and an added $6 million was spent on naval aeronautics. Interest payments decreased, with the reduction in the debt, from over $1 billion to less than $700 million.

Expenditures for Veterans. Demands for veterans' bonuses sprang up immediately after the war on the state as well as Federal level. Between 1919 to 1924, 20 states granted almost $400 million of such bonuses, and 3 established loan funds aggregating approximately $100 million.[3] But the Federal government at first was able to resist similar proposals on the ground that bonuses would require increased taxation. Every budget message foretold a sizable deficit, yet every fiscal year ended with a sizable surplus. These forecasts of deficits which never materialized put a damper on the bonus campaign, but in 1922 Congress did pass a bonus bill, the aggregate cost of which was estimated at $4 billion. President Harding promptly vetoed it. He called it class legislation, asserted that the government was already spending over $500 million a year for the veterans,[4] and pointed to the "strained" condition of the Treasury.

Finally, in 1924 Congress passed, over President Coolidge's veto, a compromise program (the Adjusted Compensation Act). It provided for the issue to veterans of bonus certificates maturing in twenty years or at prior death. The amounts of the certificates varied with length of service in the armed forces but could not exceed $625. A reserve was established into which the Treasury paid approximately $100 million a year which was invested in Federal 4 per cent bonds. Holders of the certificates could borrow up to 90 per cent of the reserve with interest at 6 per cent. No actual cash expenditures were made from this reserve except in payment of death claims or in making loans. The Adjusted Compensation Fund was therefore a trust fund, similar to the later Social Security and Railroad Retirement Funds. Its net effect was to create a discrepancy between budget expenditures and cash expenditures.

Expenditures to Encourage Business. Expenditures for the encouragement of business were substantial throughout the "normalcy" period. Under Secretary Hoover's direction, the Department of Commerce took on new importance and became in essence an agency for publicizing and advancing American business. Its expenditures grew from $21.2 million in 1922 to $40.5 million in 1929, with $4.9 million representing subsidies for commercial aeronautics. But even greater subsidies were paid to the merchant marine. In 1920 Congress, confronted with the problem of dis-

[3] Benjamin U. Ratchford, *American State Debts*, pp. 320, 332.
[4] Most of the expenditures of the Veterans' Bureau were for disabled veterans, but the dishonesty in the organization became one of the most sordid scandals of the Harding administration.

posing of a government-owned fleet far in excess of peacetime needs, passed the Merchant Marine Act, declaring that

. . . it was necessary for the national defense and for the proper growth of its foreign and domestic commerce that the United States shall have a merchant marine of the best equipped and most suitable types of vessels sufficient to carry the greater portion of its commerce and serve as a naval or military auxiliary in time of war, ultimately to be owned and operated privately by citizens of the United States.

A Shipping Board was created to operate the government fleet until responsible private purchasers could be found. It was also authorized to establish a $25 million construction fund to be loaned to help private companies build new ships. The Board sold 1,164 ships between June, 1921, and June, 1928, at an average price of $18 a ton.[5] Meanwhile, in response to the demands of the private companies and the Shipping Board, Congress, in 1928, passed the Jones-White bill authorizing the Postmaster General to grant mail contracts to noncoastal shippers. Payments were graduated according to the size and speed of the ships, with a maximum of $12 per nautical mile. Under these contracts, subsidies of $9 million were paid in the fiscal year 1929.

Expenditures for Public Works and the Expansion of Grants-in-Aid. Federal construction activity, suspended during the war, was resumed and soon carried on at high speed. An extensive program of new building construction was started, and large outlays were voted for rivers and harbors and for flood control in the Mississippi Valley and at Muscle Shoals. As a result, total public-works expenditures grew from $223 million in 1924 to $294 million in 1929. Although these capital outlays were small in comparison with the huge private and state and municipal construction expenditures of the time (estimated at $7.8 billion and $2.2 billion, respectively, for 1929),[6] they nevertheless contributed to the business boom of the period.

Occasionally, responsible officials made ineffective attempts to correlate the government's public-works program with the business cycle. Beginning in 1923 Secretary Hoover urged Congress to use Federal expenditures for public works as a stabilizing factor in the national economy, and in 1928 Representative Jones introduced a bill to set up a prosperity reserve to be held for public works. This was defeated, and government construction continued to be planned without regard to the business cycle.

In addition to the large expenditures made for its own construction, the

[5] The Dollar Line paid $14 million for 17 passenger liners which had cost the government $92.5 million.

[6] *Survey of Current Business*, July, 1947, Supplement.

Federal government increased considerably its subsidies for state and local highway construction, originated in 1916. These were expanded from $20 million a year in 1920 to over $90 million. At the same time, the grants for vocational education established in 1917 were increased and the grant-in-aid system was extended into other fields of state and local activity, such as vocational rehabilitation, maternal- and child-health care, forest-fire prevention, and forestry. On the other hand, grants for venereal-disease control, inaugurated in 1918, were terminated, only to be resumed years later. Total grants-in-aid, which in 1914 amounted to only $8 million and in 1920, $34 million, exceeded $100 million by 1925.[7] There were two main reasons for this stupendous expansion: (1) public recognition that many so-called state and local functions were vested with national interest and hence warranted partial Federal support and direction and (2) the superior ability of the Federal government in raising revenue. Then, too, through Federal grants-in-aid, new pressure groups, who had set up their headquarters in Washington during the war, were afforded an opportunity to establish their programs for the expansion of particular state and local services in the 48 states simultaneously instead of more slowly and laboriously through separate endeavors in each state.

Each grant program carried a specific annual appropriation, apportioned by formula among the states according to needs. For example, state population, area, and rural free delivery road mileage each determined one-third of the apportionment of highway aid. Most grant programs required the state to match the Federal contribution. They also required state compliance to certain standards fixed by Federal law or regulation and thus involved Federal administrative supervision. The grant system therefore introduced into the country's dual system of government a totally new element of intergovernment cooperation never anticipated by the framers of the Constitution.

With Federal expenditures stabilized at around $3.5 billion and national income rising with the expansion of private, state, and municipal activity, the ratio of Federal expenditures to national income declined from 8 per cent in 1920 to 4 per cent in 1929.

The Postwar Controversy over Tax Revision. While expenditures declined, revenues in 1920 reached a record high of $6.7 billion, $2 billion more than in 1919. The increase was caused by the inflationary price and income rise, which swelled receipts from income taxes; the gradual recon-

[7] In 1929 the grants for highways amounted to $84 million, agricultural experiment stations, $3.8 million; agricultural extension, $7.1 million; land grant colleges, $2.5 million; forest aids, $1.1 million; vocational education, $6.8 million; vocational rehabilitation, $0.7 million; and maternal and child health care, $0.7 million (Council of State Governments, *Federal Grants-in-Aid*, pp. 32, 218; *Annual Report of the Secretary of the Treasury*, 1945, p. 711).

struction of Europe, which caused an increase in trade and a concomitant increase in customs duties; collections under the last wartime revenue act; and the reorganization of the Internal Revenue Bureau, which for the first time found itself able to cope with the multiplicity of tax returns and the complexities of the income tax law.[8] Every type of revenue but one —that from alcoholic-beverage taxes—increased. Following the ratification, by the end of 1918, of the constitutional amendment prohibiting the sale of liquor, collections of liquor taxes became altogether insignificant after 1920.

As soon as revenues exceeded expenditures, a heated debate began over the disposition of the Treasury surplus. It could be used to reduce the debt, to increase expenditures, or to cut tax rates. No one believed in maintaining the wartime tax level indefinitely, but opinions differed as to how quickly reductions were to be made, some favoring a high tax level until the debt was substantially reduced and some insisting on an immediate lowering of rates.

In the immediate postwar years, Secretaries Glass and Houston wanted to use the surpluses to retire the national debt as fast as possible. They opposed any increases in expenditures or reductions in revenue, although they did favor reorganizing the tax structure. As early as November, 1919, Glass proposed the immediate repeal of the excess-profits tax, and in his report for 1920, Houston proposed that Congress repeal the excess-profits tax and adopt a tax on undistributed corporate profits as a partial substitute. Insisting that high surtax rates tended to restrict industrial development by driving the wealthier taxpayers into tax-free securities, he recommended that the rates be reduced to a maximum of 20 per cent on that portion of income which was saved and reinvested in property or business while continuing at a maximum of 65 per cent on incomes "spent or wasted or invested in tax-free securities." To prevent a decline in revenue, Houston proposed to increase normal tax rates and add new taxes on certain "luxuries," largely consumed by the lower-income groups. His plan would have given tax reduction to the upper-income brackets at the expense of higher taxes on the lower-income groups. However, he did oppose as "altogether inexpedient" a general sales tax which was the pet project of conservative business organizations.

In some quarters, the administration attitude was denounced as "unjust, uneconomic, and deceitful." Opposition took one of two forms: demands for increased expenditures, such as the veterans' bonus, or equally

[8] During the war the number of tax returns increased from 400,000 to 20 million a year, but it was not until 1919 that a self-contained income tax division was set up. The increase of its personnel from 2,672 in 1919 to 4,317 in 1920 helped the Bureau to collect over $1 billion, which should have been paid during the war. (*Annual Report of the Commissioner of Internal Revenue*, 1920.)

vehement demands for sweeping tax reductions. Senator Copeland of New York declared that it was "legalized larceny to take money from the people when there might be a still further reduction in taxation." The National Association of Manufacturers contended that "relief . . . from an undue tax burden is not a privilege but a right. A continuing surplus of revenue justifies a steady demand for relief until revenue is reduced to the reasonable requirements of the government."[9]

The Tax Reduction of 1921. The rationale for a program of drastic tax reduction was eventually provided by Secretary Mellon, but on first assuming office, he approached the subject cautiously. In his first report in 1921, he iterated Houston's belief that surtaxes were excessive and were driving wealth into tax-exempt securities. Expecting expenditures to be cut drastically, he recommended that Congress reduce the internal revenues from the current level of $4.6 billion to $3 billion by repealing the excess-profits tax, reducing the corporate income tax to $2\frac{1}{2}$ per cent, cutting the maximum personal income surtax from 65 to 32 per cent, reducing certain luxury taxes, and imposing new stamp taxes.

By this time, the feasibility of tax reduction had been accepted, and the burning question was which groups were to receive the largest reductions. The Democrats and the dissident Republicans of the Middle West, espousing the principle of taxation according to ability to pay, favored reductions in the lower brackets, while the administration wanted to do most of the cutting in the upper brackets on the ground that such a policy would encourage risk taking, business expansion, and employment. The first postwar tax reduction—the Revenue Act of 1921—was a compromise between these two points of view. Estimated to reduce taxes by $835 million in the fiscal year 1923 (half the amount recommended by the Treasury), the Act raised the exemption for the head of a family from $2,000 to $2,500 and for dependents from $200 to $400, reduced the normal tax from 6 to 12 per cent to 4 to 8 per cent, raised the minimum at which surtaxes began from $5,000 to $6,000 and reduced their maximum rate from 65 to 50 per cent, repealed the excess-profits tax, raised the corporate tax from 10 to $12\frac{1}{2}$ per cent, and abolished a few luxury taxes.

The Mellon Plan and the Tax Reduction of 1924. In 1924 Mellon began to give publicity to a forceful and comprehensive statement of the case for tax reduction, especially in the upper-income brackets. Although he did not support the extremists who opposed all debt reduction, he undoubtedly considered tax reduction more important. To Mellon, "taxation is not a means of confiscating wealth, but of raising necessary reve-

[9] Henry G. Hendricks, *The Federal Debt, 1919–1930*, p. 192; S. Ratner, *American Taxation*, p. 404.

nues." He recommended reductions "not to relieve the rich but because the higher tax rates have already passed the point where they can be collected." Convinced that upper-income groups were seeking to invest in tax-exempt securities, he said, "If a man has an income of $100,000, and is asked to invest money in some constructive project, the new project must return to him $1.75 for every $1 he would receive from investing the same money in tax-exempt securities."[10]

In answer to accusations that he favored "soaking the poor" and aiding the rich, Mellon said,

A reduction in the lower brackets means no increase in taxable income . . . a reduction in the surtax, however, increases the amount of capital which is put into productive enterprises, stimulates business, and makes more certain that there will be more $5,000 jobs to go around.

Mellon also thought it would be better to reduce income taxes before excise taxes.

Assuming we left the high surtaxes untouched and abolished the automobile taxes, the government would lose $130 million of revenue. . . . Suppose, however, we reversed the procedure and reduced the surtaxes to a figure which would indicate a loss of $130 million. The effect would be to stimulate the creation of additional taxable incomes and therefore the collection of substantially as much revenue under lower rates of surtax as under the existing rates. In a year or so the revenue would be restored, there would again be a surplus of $130 million a year, and the automobile taxes could also be eliminated.[11]

According to Mellon's economic philosophy, all savings would be automatically invested in a way which would increase productivity and jobs. He therefore recommended that Congress cut the surtax in half to a maximum of 25 per cent, reduce the normal tax to 3 to 6 per cent, repeal various excises, and allow a 25 per cent reduction in the normal tax on earned income.

Congress again rejected Mellon's recommendations. By the Revenue Act of 1924, the surtax began at $10,000 and its maximum rate was reduced to 40 per cent, a 25 per cent reduction was allowed in the normal tax on earned income up to $10,000, and normal tax rates were reduced to 2 to 6 per cent. Some of the most objectionable wartime excises—those on candy, soft drinks, low-cost admissions, cheap jewelry, etc.—were either repealed or reduced. But Congress increased the estate tax, imposed

[10] Some authorities questioned whether tax-exempts actually had as important an effect as the Treasury assumed. (Charles O. Hardy, "Taxation and Tax-exempt Securities," *Proceedings of the National Tax Association*, 1925, p. 222.)

[11] *Annual Report of the Secretary of the Treasury*, 1924; Andrew W. Mellon, *Taxation: The People's Business*, pp. 11, 71, 120; Philip Love, *Andrew W. Mellon*, p. 154.

a gift tax, and made provision for the publication of the names and tax payments of individuals with large incomes.

Tax Reductions of 1926 and 1928. The administration objected strenuously to the type of reductions in the 1924 Act, and in 1926 Mellon again recommended sharper cuts in the upper brackets. This time he urged Congress to lower the maximum surtax to 20 per cent and to repeal the gift tax, the estate tax, and the publicity clause. In the Revenue Act of 1926, Congress finally followed most of Mellon's suggestions. It reduced the maximum surtax to 20 per cent, repealed the gift tax, and reduced the estate tax maximum rate to 20 per cent and raised the exemption to $100,000. Exemptions under the personal income tax were raised to $1,500 for single persons and $3,500 for married couples. The normal tax was reduced to 1½ to 5 per cent, and the 25 per cent earned-income credit was made applicable to incomes up to $20,000 for both normal and surtax. The corporation capital-stock tax was repealed, but the corporate income tax rate was increased from 12½ to 13½ per cent. The excise list was further cut. The Act also did away with some of the duplication of Federal and state inheritance levies by allowing taxpayers a credit for payments of state inheritance taxes up to 80 per cent of the Federal tax. The primary purpose of this change was to bring about greater uniformity in state inheritance taxation.

Mellon hinted that, if business continued to boom, he would recommend additional tax relief. In 1927 he did suggest some further cuts, but he did not press them, demonstrating that the Treasury was reasonably satisfied.[12] Thereupon Congress took up the cudgels. In 1928 it made the credit for earned income applicable to incomes up to $30,000 a year, reduced the corporation tax from 13½ to 12 per cent, and swept away nearly all the remaining wartime excises.

In summary, within four years from its presentation, the Mellon plan for drastic tax reductions, especially on higher incomes, was adopted almost in toto, while reductions on middle and lower incomes were carried beyond his recommendations. The normal rates of the individual income tax were reduced from 6 to 12 per cent to 1½ to 5 per cent, and the corporation tax was reduced from 13½ to 12 per cent. At the same time, in a return toward protectionism, Congress raised the tariff, which, as a revenue producer, had long since dropped to a secondary place. Despite the general reduction in income taxes and the increase in customs,

[12] In November, 1927, Undersecretary Ogden Mills told a group of bankers, "Rather from accident than from design, our Federal tax system is, on the whole, a well-balanced and equitable one. By that I mean that direct taxes . . . and indirect taxes . . . are fairly well apportioned. As a consequence, there is a reasonable distribution of the burden in accordance with ability to pay." (*Annual Report of the Secretary of the Treasury*, 1928.)

TABLE 45. FEDERAL RECEIPTS, EXPENDITURES, AND DEBT, 1920–1929
(In millions of dollars)

	1920	1921	1922	1923	1924	1925	1926	1927	1928	1929
Receipts:										
Customs	$ 323	$ 308	$ 356	$ 562	$ 546	$ 458	$ 579	$ 606	$ 569	$ 602
Individual income	*	*	*	*	*	845	879	912	883	1,095
Corporate income including excess profits	*	*	*	*	*	916	1,095	1,308	1,292	1,236
Total income	$3,957	$3,228	$2,087	$1,691	$1,842	$1,762	$1,974	$2,220	$2,175	$2,331
Capital stock	$ 93	$ 82	$ 81	$ 82	$ 87	$ 90	$ 97	$ 9	$ 9	$ 9
Estate and gift	104†	154†	139†	127†	103	109	119	100	60	62
Liquors	140	83	46	30	28	26	26	21	15	13
Tobacco	296	255	271	309	326	345	371	376	396	434
Stamp, stock transfers, etc.	84	73	59	65	63	49	54	38	49	64
Manufacturers' excises	268	229	174	185	201	141	150	67	52	6
Soft drinks	57	59	34	10	10					
Telegraph, etc.	28	28	29	30	35					
Transportation	262	273	170							
Insurance	18	19	11							
Admissions and clubs	82	96	80	77	86	40	34	28	28	17
Oleomargarine	4	3	2	2	3	3	3	3	3	4
Other internal revenue	15	14	16	13	14	20	7	3	3	2
Foreign debts—interest	3.8	31.1	27.7	201.3	160.7	160.1	160.1	160.4	161.1	160.3
Foreign debts—principal	71.0	83.7	49.1	31.6	61.0	23.2	34.1	45.7	47.8	38.8
Other revenue and nonrevenue§	899.8	580.2	461.1	425.1	323.0	286.1	297.7	343.3	469.0	294.3
Totals	$6,705	$5,585	$4,104	$3,847	$3,884	$3,608	$3,908	$4,024	$4,038	$4,036
Expenditures‡	$6,220	$4,496	$3,618	$3,648	$3,404	$2,931	$3,518	$3,417	$3,647	$3,852
Surplus‡	484	689	485	199	480	677	391	607	391	184
Gross debt	24,299	23,977	22,963	22,350	21,251	20,516	19,643	18,512	17,604	16,931
Interest-bearing debt	24,063	23,739	22,710	22,007	20,981	20,211	19,384	18,253	17,318	17,639

SOURCE: *Annual Report of the Secretary of the Treasury*, 1920–1929, 1950.

* Separate figures for the individual income, corporate income, and excess-profits taxes not available.   † Estate tax only.

‡ The above figures of expenditures and surpluses given in the Annual Reports of the Secretary of the Treasury differ especially widely from those published in the historical series in the Treasury reports. The total of the surpluses, 1920 to 1929, given above, is $4.7 billion compared with $3.8 billion for those in the historical series. See p. 3 for a general explanation of the divergence between the individual reports and the historical series. The expenditure totals include statutory debt retirement; surplus is after such retirement.

§ Sale of surplus war supplies, repayments by government corporations of the Treasury's capital subscriptions, Panama Canal, District of Columbia, and trust fund receipts, miscellaneous departmental revenues, etc.

the trend toward direct taxation, which had begun before the war, was not reversed in any major way. Individual and corporate income taxes continued to produce almost as great a percentage of total tax revenues as they had done at the peak of the war and much greater than before the war. Excise taxation had gained three new minor recruits—the admissions, stock-transfer and playing-cards stamp taxes—but had lost the mighty liquor tax.

It likewise appeared that the Federal tax policy increased, rather than decreased, the proportion of the total income tax revenue paid by the upper-income brackets.

TABLE 46. DISTRIBUTION OF TAX RECEIPTS, 1910–1929

Period	Average annual tax receipts (millions)	Income and profits (per cent)	Customs (per cent)	Misc. internal revenue (per cent)
1910–1916	$ 654.4	8.6	43.5	47.9
1917–1921	3,906.8	65.7	6.3	28.0
1922–1925	3,308.5	55.6	15.2	29.2
1926–1929	3,450.7	63.2	17.1	19.8

SOURCE: *Annual Report of the Secretary of the Treasury*, 1929.

TABLE 47. PERCENTAGE OF TOTAL INCOME TAX PAID BY VARIOUS INCOME GROUPS, 1920–1929

Income	1920	1925	1929
Under $5,000................	15.43	1.89	0.45
$ 5,000–$ 10,000.............	9.11	2.61	0.95
10,000– 25,000.............	16.02	10.10	5.98
25,000– 100,000.............	29.58	36.56	27.42
Over $100,000...............	29.86	48.84	65.20

SOURCE: Internal Revenue Office, *Statistics of Income*.

The Problems of Debt Management. At its peak, on August 21, 1919, the Federal gross debt was $26.6 billion, or almost ten times greater than the previous high of 1866. In absolute terms, the debt seemed incredibly large, but relative to national output, it was probably not any larger than the debt at the end of the Civil War. Moreover, the entire debt was owed domestically, whereas in the post-Civil War period, a large percentage was owed to foreigners. Approximately $9.2 billion, or 35 per cent, of the $26.3 billion of interest-bearing debt was in short-term obligations, that is, maturing within five years. Interest payments amounted to a little over $1 billion in 1920, and were about the size of the total Federal budget in the prewar years and only slightly less than the total prewar debt. But in proportion to national income they were lower than the charges on the Civil War debt.

Because of the decisions that had to be made, debt management was the most intricate of all the postwar fiscal problems. The Treasury had to decide how rapidly to retire the debt, what methods to use in refunding the short-term debt, and what interest to pay on new security issues. In arriving at the answers to these questions, the Treasury recognized that all aspects of fiscal policy were interrelated and had an impact on the money market. But it paid little attention to the influence which debt management exerted on the distribution of income and aggregate size of income and to the effects of debt repayment on savings, consumption, and investment.

Refunding Operations under Houston. The large amount of outstanding short-term obligations posed the most immediate problem, for as they matured, they had to be either repaid or refunded. The first alternative was definitely limited, for the large cash balance which had been raised by the Victory Loan was soon exhausted, and the revenue surplus, though substantial, was never large enough to make possible the retirement of the aggregate annual debt maturities. Furthermore, while debt maturities occurred continuously throughout the year, collections were concentrated on quarterly tax-payment dates and were relatively low at other times. To even out this periodic disparity between revenue flow and debt payments, the Treasury continuously sold new securities and was therefore always vulnerable to the vagaries of the money market.

In carrying out his refunding operations, Houston offered 9- to 12-month certificates of indebtedness. At first, they sold well at interest rates of 4¼ and 4¾ per cent and together with the use of the cash balance and the revenue surplus placed the Treasury in a comfortable position to meet its maturities. This was most fortunate, for the sale of certificates became increasingly difficult once the postwar credit and price inflation began to roar upward. Private loans increased, capital funds became scarce, and interest rates rose sharply. In March, 1920, the Treasury offered certificates at the comparatively low rate of 4¾ per cent, but only $201.4 million was taken. Despite this disappointing response by the public, Houston made no attempt to control the interest rate on governments by selling securities to the Federal Reserve banks. Under the circumstances, he had no alternative but to offer higher interest rates, and during the remainder of the postwar boom he sold certificates at rates as high as 6 per cent. Even then, the offerings were not overly successful, but after the inflated credit balloon blew up in the spring of 1920, capital funds were obtainable at lower rates and debt management became easier.

Mellon's Debt-refunding Policy. Under Secretary Mellon, the government's refunding policy became more varied. In April, 1921, Mellon announced that he expected to reduce the short-term debt, which at that time amounted to $7.6 billion, by about $1 billion within two years. The remainder would be refunded not only with monthly offerings of certificates, but also with 3- to 5-year treasury notes in order to distribute it more evenly over the period 1923 to 1928. During the next eight years, refunding operations encountered no difficulties. Certificates of indebtedness and treasury notes were consistently oversubscribed, even though the rate of interest had been reduced to 2¾ per cent as early as 1924.

In 1929 Congress authorized a third form of short-term obligation, the treasury bill. It sold at a discount instead of at a fixed interest rate and ran from 60 to 91 days. It was expected that bills would procure money for the government at lower cost than certificates, since their extremely short duration would afford banking institutions and corporations a convenient means of investing temporarily unused balances. They would also invite keener competition among lenders and would command a price which reflected the condition of the money market more accurately. The bill proved to possess most of these advantages and eventually added greatly to the flexibility and smoothness of Treasury financing.

In summary, the twenties were productive of great refinements in Treasury financing. New instruments of temporary borrowing were devised, ensuring utmost elasticity of operations. A great permanent gain which was to prove its worth during the trials of the depression and World War II was also accomplished when Congress conceded that debt management was a highly technical problem belonging in the field of administration. For the first time in history it gave the Treasury complete discretion to determine the forms, maturities, distribution, and interest rates of the debt, confining its own activities with respect thereto to the establishment or approval of basic procedures. Debt management as affecting these four phases of debt structure was for the first time in this country refined to the point of an art.

The Appeal to the Small Investor and the Flotation of Refunding Bonds. During the twenties the Treasury continued its efforts to tap the resources of the small saver. In 1921 the Treasury renovated the savings certificates (formerly the war savings certificates) by offering them at 4½ per cent if held to maturity (in five years) or 3½ per cent if redeemed before maturity. A sales campaign was organized in every city, town, and hamlet. While it was extremely successful, private borrowers protested that the certificates were sold at a relatively high interest rate and discouraged public investment in nongovernment securities. Therefore, the Treasury gradually deemphasized its thrift campaign, stopping the issuance of savings certificates in 1924 and redeeming the last of them in 1929. It was not until the depression of the thirties that a similar security was again offered.

Although the withdrawal of the small-denomination certificates crippled efforts to appeal to the very small investor, the Treasury still made an effort to attract the savings of the middle group. In time, it brought out five long-term refunding bond issues, each of which was oversubscribed. In making allotments, the Treasury favored smaller investors by filling a larger percentage of their subscriptions.

The first refunding bonds were issued in 1922 at 4¼ per cent, callable in 25 and maturing in 30 years. The offering of $500 million was oversubscribed, and $764 million was finally allotted on a graduated scale. Subscribers for over $1 million received 10 per cent of their subscriptions, those for $500,000 received 15 per cent, and so on, until the subscriber for $10,000 received 40 per cent. In 1924, 20-30's were offered at 4 per cent. The authorization was for $200 million, but the Secretary was given the power to allot additional bonds if payment were tended in 4¼ per cent Liberty bonds, treasury notes, or certificates of indebtedness. Once again the oversubscription was enormous, but only $1 billion was allotted, and the large subscriptions were cut heavily.

By June 30, 1925, the short-term debt was down to $6.3 billion. During the next year, it was reduced further to $4.7 billion partially by the sale of a third long-term issue for $500 million of 20–30-year bonds. Because the interest rate was only 3.75 per cent, the oversubscription was not so large as on prior issues, but once again the large subscribers were allotted a smaller percentage of their total subscriptions.

In 1927 the Treasury began its most complicated refunding operation, calling the 4 and 4¼ per cent Second Liberty Loan bonds. In June it sold for cash $249.6 million of 3⅜ per cent 16–20-year bonds and exchanged for Liberties $245.3 million of the 16–20-year bonds and $1.4 billion of 3.5 per cent treasury notes. In 1928 the remainder of the Second Liberty Loan ($1.2 billion) was refunded with 3⅛ per cent certificates. In addition, $1.2 billion of the 4¼ per cent Third Liberty Loan was refunded with 3⅜ per cent 12–15-year bonds and treasury notes and certificates. These colossal operations, carried out in an easy-money market, not only spread maturities more conveniently but saved considerable sums in future interest charges.

No major refunding operations were undertaken in 1929, for the speculative mania, which by this time had seized the country, began to affect Treasury borrowing. In order to compete with the stock market, the Treasury had to raise its interest rates, eventually offering certificates at 5⅛ per cent. But the situation was not alarming, for the refunding operations of the previous years had eliminated the embarrassments of an excessive short-term debt. By June 30, 1930, short-term debt comprised only 29 per cent of the total interest-bearing debt, compared with 35 per cent in 1919 (see Table 48).

TABLE 48.   INTEREST-BEARING DEBT, 1919–1930
(In millions of dollars)

	Aug. 31, 1919	June 30, 1925	June 30, 1930
Prewar..............................	$ 883	$ 765	$ 773*
First Liberty 3½'s....................	1,410	1,410	1,392
First Liberty 4's†....................	165	5	5
First Liberty 4¼'s†...................	409	536	536
Second Liberty 4's...................	688	21	
Second Liberty 4¼'s†.................	2,879	3,083	
Third Liberty.......................	3,954	2,886	
Fourth Liberty......................	6,714	6,325	6,268
Victory notes.......................	4,114		
Certificates of indebtedness............	4,201	579	1,264
War savings certificates...............	932	386	
Treasury bonds of 1947–1952...........		764	759
Treasury bonds of 1944–1954...........		1,047	1,037
Treasury notes......................		2,404	2,390
Treasury bills.......................			156
Treasury bonds of 1946–1956...........			489
Treasury bonds of 1943–1947...........			493
Treasury bonds of 1940–1943...........			359
Totals............................	$26,349	$20,211	$15,922

SOURCE: *Annual Report of the Secretary of the Treasury*, 1926, 1930.

* Increase was due to additional issues of postal savings bonds.
† Issued under conversion privilege of First and Second Liberty Loans.

Debt Retirement. How much of the debt was to be retired and how quickly retirement could be accomplished was dependent in a large measure on the intensity of the demand for tax reduction. Obviously those who wanted maximum tax reduction would not favor rapid debt repayment. Conversely those advocating rapid debt repayment would not favor sweeping tax reduction. In time, the issue was also colored by new concepts of credit control, it being held that rapid debt repayment would contract the money supply and hamper the freedom of open-market operations by reducing the volume of government securities. However, this reasoning was too obscure for the layman and was confined to a few academic experts.

The Treasury tended to follow a compromise policy. It decided to repay $500 million of the debt annually from ordinary receipts and to regard the surplus as a source of tax relief. Mellon's annual report for

1924, which explained the administration's fiscal policy, for the most part followed orthodox thinking. But it also rationalized his preference for tax reduction over debt reduction and included some novel ideas which, in the next decade, were to shock the traditionally minded. On the one hand, he declared, "The nation which does not follow a policy of paying its debts but allows them to accumulate may be compared to an individual who follows a similar course. It is a sign of debility and denotes the absence of essential vigor and foresight." On the other hand, he recognized that a nation's domestic debt differed from a private debt and denied that the war debts could be passed on to future generations, for "while this liability may be handed down to the next generation, equivalent assets in the form of Government securities would also be handed down, and that generation, viewed as a whole, would be neither richer nor poorer." Recognizing that debt repayment was a process of redistributing national assets, Mellon said,

If every citizen had subscribed to the government war securities in the proportion of his tax payments to total tax collections, the process of financing the war in part by loans would have been a useless expense because in that event the Government would return to each individual in debt payments just the amount it collects from him in taxes. . . . There is one group who hold Government war obligations in excess of the amount which they will ultimately pay in taxes for debt redemptions as contrasted with another group who will pay in taxes an amount greater than their holdings of Government obligations. . . . The problem of the public debt, then, is largely a question of how rapidly the distribution may be effected.

There were available six sources of debt reduction: statutory appropriations to the sinking fund, government bonds accepted in payment of tax obligations, the accumulated cash balance in the general fund, the revenue surpluses not absorbed by tax relief, the repayment by the foreign governments of their debts in United States obligations, and miscellaneous specified receipts.

The Victory Loan Act of 1919 established a sinking fund for the retirement of the debt. Payments into this fund were fixed at $2\frac{1}{2}$ per cent cumulative on the debt outstanding on July 1, 1920 ($19.6 billion) less the amount of foreign-government obligations held by the United States on that date ($9.4 billion). It was calculated that the sum involved ($10.1 billion) would be amortized at that rate in twenty-five years.

Under the terms of the Third Liberty Loan, government bonds bearing more than 4 per cent interest were acceptable at par in payment of estate taxes. Therefore, whenever prices of government bonds fell below par, executors of estates found it advantageous to pay taxes in bonds. Similarly, interest and principal on the Allied loans were usually paid in government bonds at par, and the repayments of such principal had to be applied to the retirement of Liberty bonds. Receipts from the franchise tax on Federal Reserve banks were also used for debt retirement, since they were allocated by law for that purpose.

Reductions in the cash balance were an important source of debt reduction only during the first year or so after the war when the balance had been artificially swelled by wartime financial necessities and over-borrowing. They were a source for a reduction of the gross debt only and left the net debt unchanged.

TABLE 49. SOURCES OF DEBT RETIREMENT, 1920–1930
(In millions of dollars)

Year	Appropriations to sinking fund	Foreign repayments	Misc.*	Total from ordinary receipts	Surplus receipts	Decrease in general fund balance	Total debt reduction	Gross debt at end of fiscal year
1920	....	$ 72.7	$ 6.0	$ 78.7	$ 212.5	$ 894.0	$1,185.2	$24,299.3
1921	$ 261.1	73.9	92.0†	427.1	86.7	−192.0	321.9	23,977.5
1922	276.0	64.8	81.8	422.7	313.8	277.6	1,014.1	22,963.4
1923	284.0	100.9	18.0	402.9	309.7	−98.8	613.7	22,349.7
1924	296.0	149.4	12.6	458.0	505.4	135.5	1,098.9	21,250.8
1925	306.3	159.2	1.0	466.5	250.5	17.6	734.6	20,516.2
1926	317.1	169.7	0.7	487.4	377.8	7.8	873.0	19,643.2
1927	333.5	179.3	6.8	519.6	635.8	−24.1	1,131.3	18,511.9
1928	354.7	181.8	3.7	540.3	398.8	−31.5	907.6	17,604.3
1929	370.3	176.2	3.1	549.6	184.8	−61.2	673.2	16,931.1
1930	388.4	160.9	4.7	553.9	183.8	8.1	745.8	16,185.3
Totals..	$3,187.4	$1,488.8	$230.4	$4,906.7	$3,459.6	$ 933.0	$9,299.2	

SOURCE: *Annual Report of the Secretary of the Treasury*, 1930.

* Includes bond receipts from estate taxes, franchise taxes, gifts, and forfeitures.
† Includes $4.8 million written off on account of fractional currency estimated as lost.

Surpluses of revenue supplied on the average more than $300 million a year for debt reduction throughout the entire 1920 to 1930 period. Altogether, by these six methods, the debt was reduced $9.3 billion between 1919 and 1930, or at an average rate of $850 million a year. This was a reduction of 37 per cent compared with the 23 per cent reduction over a corresponding period after the Civil War. It was impressive, but it could have been larger with highly salutary results if Mellon and Congress had not subordinated debt reduction to tax reduction.

In achieving a more favorable debt distribution by liquidating the debt held by the commercial banks, Mellon made little headway. Before he came into office, the total investments of the Federal Reserve banks and the commercial banks in government securities had been reduced from

$5.4 billion to $3.6 billion, or by 33⅓ per cent. After that, the trend was reversed, bank holdings increasing to $4.4 billion in 1922, $5.0 billion in 1925, and $5.5 billion in 1929, or to more than they had been at the end of the war. However, the Treasury did retire a large part of the bonds available as security for national-bank circulation. In 1925 the historic bonds which were sold to the Morgan syndicate and to the public during the silver crisis of 1895 and 1896 were redeemed. After their retirement, the only remaining bonds with the circulation privilege were the consols of 1930, the Panamas of 1916 to 1936, and the Panamas of 1918 to 1938, totaling only $674.6 million.

Viewed in retrospect, Federal fiscal policy was undoubtedly mistakenly conceived. Taxes were reduced much too sharply and too rapidly at all income levels, releasing substantial portions of income for added spending, thereby accentuating inflationary pressures and tendencies toward speculation. The rate at which debt was to be retired was set much too low. The average annual retirement was only about 4½ per cent of the average annual debt, and about half of this was due to fortuitous circumstances rather than planned action. Instead of seeking merely to achieve budgetary balance inclusive of a small debt amortization, the administration and Congressional budgeteers should have sought to achieve an overbalanced budget regularly yielding annual surpluses of a billion dollars or more. Such a fiscal policy would have contributed to greater economic stability in the long run.

But although great mistakes were made, it seems unjustifiable to pin primary, and almost sole, responsibility for the great debacle of the twenties on the Treasury. The speculative inflation was the result of the operation of the private, much more than the public, economy. Even at the height of the boom, Federal expenditures amounted to less than 4 per cent of the gross national product, and state and local expenditures amounted to only 8 per cent. Even though their effect on the economy was greater than indicated by their relative size, since they were highly concentrated and operated on particularly sensitive parts of private income production, distribution, and expenditures, they were secondary in importance.[13]

The Complexity of Federal Accounts. The increasing complexity of the government made it more and more difficult to obtain a clear impression of its fiscal affairs. Some budget transactions, such as veterans' bonus payments, were made on an accrual basis and involved no immediate cash payments. But they were accounted for in the same way as cash transactions, with the result that the cash position of the Treasury and its effects

[13] While Federal debt declined, private debt increased by $100 billion and state and local debt by $10 billion, offsetting severalfold the Federal reduction.

on the money stream were never clearly revealed. In addition, tax refunds, which averaged over $160 million annually, or approximately 5 per cent of current income and outgo, were treated as expenditures instead of being deducted from receipts, with the result that both expenditures and receipts were correspondingly exaggerated.

The operations of government business enterprise were a source of even greater confusion. The Postal Service was operated as a separate entity, having its own income and expenditures and represented in the general fund total only by its deficits or surpluses. Other enterprises, such as the Reclamation Service, the Alaska Railroad, and the Inland Waterways Corporation, were operated as subsidiaries of the Interior and War Departments. Still others, like the Housing Corporation, were among the independent bureaus, maintained like regular departments from the general tax revenue. Moreover, they were not operated under consistent budget and accounting classifications. Tolls and profits from the Panama Canal were listed among the miscellaneous receipts, and receipts of the Housing Corporation were deducted from expenditures. In like manner, expenditures were scattered among various departments. For example, most of the expenditures for the Panama Canal were included in the War Department, but some were listed under the State Department.

Finally, no consistent form of business organization was followed. The largest enterprises, those formed before the war, obtained their operating funds from ordinary appropriations and were therefore entirely dependent upon Congress. During the war the government-owned corporation was invented and soon became the standard form of organization. Usually financed by stock issues purchased by the Treasury and existing as more or less autonomous institutions, government-owned corporations had independent incomes not subject to the appropriation process.[14]

Although none of the business enterprises of the government were designed to make a profit, some of them consistently did so. The Panama Canal, which had been constructed for defense and for facilitating trade, earned over $10 million annually, and the Housing Corporation also showed a small profit. However, the Post Office almost always lost

[14] The War Finance Corporation afforded a good illustration of early government corporations. When it was formed, the Treasury bought its $500 million stock issue, listing the purchase price as an ordinary expenditure. At the end of the war, the Corporation prepared to liquidate, but in 1920 Congress passed a joint resolution over the President's veto reestablishing it as a temporary farm credit agency to assist in financing exports. In December, 1924, when the corporation actually began liquidation, its loans totaled $689.7 million, of which $649.1 million had already been repaid. By the end of the decade, the Treasury had been repaid its $500 million original investment and a profit of $64 million, which was estimated as equal to the interest cost on the original advance. All these payments were listed by the Treasury as deductions from current expenditures rather than as receipts.

money,[15] as did the Alaska Railroad, the Inland Waterways Corporation, and the Merchant Fleet Corporation.

Establishment of the Budget System. In general, "normalcy" was unfortunately inept. Nevertheless, it was during its reign that a budget system was finally established. Postwar conditions were exceedingly propitious for the revival of the budget proposal. Demands for immediate reduction in taxation and expenditures could be intelligently accomplished only if government needs could be accurately determined. Moreover, now that most Federal revenue was derived from direct taxes, millions of taxpayers were keenly interested in keeping government expenditures and income in balance.

Curiously enough, the initiative for the establishment of a budget system in the postwar era came from Congress, even though it meant surrendering to the President the prerogative of initial approval of the appropriations of the administrative departments.

In July, 1919, James W. Good, chairman of the House Appropriations Committee, succeeded in creating a "Select Committee on the Budget" with himself as chairman. This committee, with the technical assistance of the Institute for Government Research (later the Brookings Institution), held extensive hearings and prepared a bill providing for an executive budget system. Following the theory that the budget was an administrative as well as fiscal tool, the bill, which was passed by the House in October, 1919, with only three dissenting votes, vested responsibility for the preparation of the budget solely in the President and provided for the establishment in his office of a Bureau of the Budget to give him technical assistance.

In the meanwhile, the Senate passed a rival bill, introduced by Medill McCormick, which established a Budget Bureau in the Treasury Department and made the Secretary responsible for the preparation of the budget. McCormick contended that the Secretary, unlike the President, would be able to devote his entire time to budgetary and fiscal policy and management, especially if relieved of some of his routine functions. In addition to establishing a budget system, the McCormick bill provided for a Comptroller General who would take over the existing functions of the Comptroller of the Treasury. He was to prevent disbursements made in violation of a law and to act as an independent source of information to Congress as well as a check on the Executive. To assure the independence of the office, the Comptroller and the Assistant Comptroller were removable only by impeachment by Congress.

Though not expressing a preference between the House and Senate

[15] In the 94 years, 1837 to 1930, the Post Office turned over surpluses to the Treasury only during 7: 1914, 1915, 1917 to 1920, and 1922.

bills, President Wilson, in his annual message of December, 1919, endorsed the budget concept and expressed a hope that it would become law before the end of the session. He urged that "the burden of preparing the budget must . . . rest upon the Executive," that "the budget so prepared should be submitted to and approved or amended by a single committee of each House," and that "no single appropriation should be made by the Congress, except such as may have been included in the budget prepared by the Executive or added by the particular committee of Congress charged with the budget legislation."

The conference committee reached an agreement in May, 1920, placing the Budget Bureau under the Secretary of the Treasury and creating the office of Comptroller General. The compromise bill passed both Houses, but President Wilson unexpectedly vetoed it, believing that it unconstitutionally curtailed the powers of the President by prohibiting him from removing the Comptroller General from office. After the change in the Presidency in March, 1921, Congress repassed the bill with only one important change. The Secretary of the Treasury was given no authority over the Director of the Budget, even though the Bureau was placed in the Treasury Department. President Harding signed the bill, known as the "Budget and Accounting Act of 1921," in June, 1921. Its principal provisions were as follows:

1. The President was to transmit to Congress at the beginning of each session a budget containing estimates of expenditures and receipts for the ensuing fiscal year, information on the Treasury's condition during the current and previous year, and recommendations of appropriate tax increases or reductions to deal with an impending deficit or surplus.

2. The President might transmit to Congress supplemental estimates for appropriations with explanations as to why they had not been included in the original budget.

3. The Bureau of the Budget was created to prepare the budget, to make studies of the departments and establishments in the interest of greater economy and efficiency, and to furnish to Congressional committees such aid as they might request. Its Director and Assistant Director were to be appointed by the President to serve at his pleasure.

4. The head of each deparment or establishment was to appoint a budget officer to prepare and transmit to the Bureau estimates of regular, supplemental, or deficiency appropriations.

5. The offices of the Comptroller and Assistant Comptroller of the Treasury were abolished, and the offices of the Comptroller General and the Assistant Comptroller General were created. Both were to be appointed by the President with the approval of the Senate for a term of fifteen years and could be removed only by impeachment or by joint resolution of Congress.

6. The Comptroller General was to investigate all matters relating to the

receipt and disbursement of public funds and to report to Congress every expenditure or contract made in violation of the law.

7. A General Accounting Office, under the Comptroller General, was created to assume all the powers formerly exercised by the Comptroller of the Treasury and the six auditors therein, as well as certain duties of the Division of Bookkeeping and Warrants.

First Ten Years of the Budget System. The Budget Bureau was organized in 1921 with General Charles G. Dawes as its first director. Both he and General H. M. Lord, who succeeded him a year later, conceived their task, not without good reason, as a militant campaign against departmental wastes and insularity. However, the Bureau's staff was so small that its ability to penetrate the morass of departmental routine was limited. Furthermore, the departments resisted interference, and the Bureau's success was therefore dependent upon the constant vigilance of the President. As General Dawes wrote, "The minute he [the President] relaxes his attitude of attention, . . . there will be felt the natural pull . . . towards the old system of complete independence and decentralization."[16]

Under the circumstances, the budget system during the first decade of its operation accomplished few of the objectives set by its framers. It produced a unified picture of the financial condition of the Treasury by presenting expenditures and revenues in comparative form with the resulting operating surplus or deficit. But in other respects it was only an expenditure program, failing to provide effective centralized execution.

The President avoided specific commitments regarding revenue and borrowing policies, leaving them to be dealt with by the Secretary of the Treasury. Since his recommendations did not possess the same prestige as the President's, the revenue committees of Congress continued to dominate the planning of taxation measures. But their procedures were not in the least improved by the adoption of the budget. The appropriation requests and revenue requirements of the government continued to be considered by two separate committees in each House. Therefore, the two sides of the budget were not planned jointly as they should have been. Moreover, the evil of extensive deficiency appropriations was not eliminated.

The designers of the budget system planned to combat the practice of deficiency appropriations by establishing a contingency fund, by authorizing intradepartmental transfers of appropriations, by making lump-sum appropriations to permit the application of unexpended portions for unexpected needs, and by establishing centrally supervised work programs and quarterly allotments of appropriations, including authority for the

[16] Charles G. Dawes, *The First Year of the Budget of the United States*, p. 136.

Budget Bureau to withhold portions of appropriations not deemed necessary for the accomplishment of the purpose set. None of these solutions was adopted. Congress feared that a contingency reserve would be an invitation to the Executive to spend it, and it believed that appropriation transfers would result in irresponsible expenditures. At first, it was not inclined to pass appropriations in lump sums, but later, particularly after the passage of the 1923 Classification Act, which divided the services into grades with designated salary ranges, lump-sum appropriations began to be made to cover personnel service expenditures in each unit. Quarterly allotments and work programs could not be instituted because the Bureau's staff was too small to determine competently whether or not a portion of an appropriation should be spent and because the departments were unwilling to accept such a system of control.

The Office of Comptroller General also failed to live up to original expectations. Starting largely with the staff taken over from the Treasury, it audited accounts in much the same manner as was done before and became bogged down in extensive routine work. It also engaged in detailed pre-audits, thereby destroying much of its usefulness as an agency for independent post-audit and information and advice to Congress. Having pre-audited the accounts or promulgated rules to be followed in disbursements, it was scarcely free to post-audit the same accounts.

Chapter 25: THE PROSPEROUS TWENTIES: MONETARY AND INTERNATIONAL FINANCIAL POLICIES

The problems associated with the credit and banking system, international finance and the tariff, like those in the fiscal field, were deeply affected by the governmental philosophy of "normalcy." Believing in minimum interference with business, the administration made no significant attempt to strengthen the banking system or to make the control of the credit structure more effective. In the international field, there was no realization that the world at large, far from recovering its balance after World War I, was getting more dislocated every day and was preparing for an even greater calamity. Both the government and the people at large were indifferent to the concerns of the world, regarding them as separate from American interests. In a futile effort to return to the legend of economic isolation, the United States increased her tariff. Yet, at the same time American bankers were lending money in all the international money markets and American experts were tackling the knotty problem of German reparations. In brief, the twenties were characterized by a naïve belief that America could have its cake and eat it too.

The Treasury and the Money Market. Whether intended or not, every major decision by the government on expenditure, tax, or debt policy influenced the money market. Of the several fiscal agencies of the executive and legislative departments—the Treasury, the Bureau of the Budget, and the Congressional fiscal committees—the Treasury was most cognizant of the interrelationship between fiscal policy and the supply of capital funds, money rates, and the price level. In his annual report for 1925, Secretary Mellon wrote:

Whether [the repayment of public debt] has any effect upon savings and the short and long time interest rate depends in some measure upon how the taxes are collected and upon the type of securities retired. . . . If a large proportion of the taxes with which debt retirements are met is collected from persons who would normally save the amounts paid in taxes, the volume of investment funds will not be materially affected. . . . On the other hand, whenever tax collections result in a reduction of personal expenditures the result is a net increase in the supply of capital with a consequent reduction in general interest rates. . . . When the government pays off the short-term debt, . . . a large proportion of which is held by financial institutions, it releases bank credit for other uses, and money rates tend to decline.

But the theory that fiscal policy should be framed primarily with the view of controlling the operations of the private economy had not yet been evolved. By and large, therefore, the Treasury favored easy-money conditions, because they tended to reduce the interest rate on the Federal debt. However, it did not make this its major objective, and it had no intention of controlling the money market deliberately, preferring to follow, rather than lead, in fixing the interest rates on its new borrowings.

The policy of noninterference with the market was adopted during the postwar period of credit inflation. As the market interest rate rose, investors sold their government bonds because other investments were more tempting. As a result, the 4's fell to 81.70 and the 3½'s, in spite of their attractive tax features, declined to 89.90. Some congressmen demanded that the Treasury take action to stop the disastrous decline in bond prices. It was suggested that all the outstanding bonds be made acceptable as security against the issue of national-bank notes or that they be converted into interest-bearing currency. Realizing that either action would give a further impetus to credit and price inflation, Secretary Houston refused to adopt the suggestions. He also refused to refund the war loans with higher interest obligations or to use the Treasury's facilities to support the price of the outstanding bonds. He repeated with enthusiastic approval a statement originally made by Secretary McAdoo:

The only sound and sure way to protect the market price of government bonds is to teach the people to save. Any attempt to peg the price of liberty bonds at par would be unwise and subject to legitimate criticism as turning the government's long term 20 or 30 year bonds into demand obligations. The only way in which that could be done would be for the government to stand ready to redeem them at par at any time.

Since this view prevailed also with the succeeding Secretaries, the rate on new government borrowing conformed to the market rate, being high when money was tight, as in 1921 and 1929, and low when money became easier. But the pattern displayed some irrationality. Thus, at the height of the speculative craze in 1929, the rate on certificates of indebtedness was higher than the yield on a standard list of common stocks.

Federal Reserve Policy, 1919 to 1924. During the twenties there were few changes in the structure of the Federal Reserve System. In 1919 a change was made in the distribution of all district bank earnings. All earnings in excess of 6 per cent were payable into the surplus until it equaled the paid-in capital. Thereafter, 10 per cent of surplus earnings was to be paid into the surplus fund and 90 per cent to the Federal government as a franchise tax. In 1923 the farm bloc in Congress finally succeeded in adding a representative of agriculture to the Board, increasing its membership to eight. At the same time, agricultural borrowing was made easier by making nine-months agricultural paper eligible for rediscount. Although these amendments were of no particular significance, many changes of great importance took place in the System's operations and in the aims and views of its managers. There was a gradual shift from the original theories on which the System was based, and in time the Board developed new instruments of credit control, emancipated itself from domination by the Treasury, and worked out a set of principles to guide it in regulating the money market.

For a time after the war, the Reserve banks continued to subordinate themselves to the Treasury. In March, 1919, they agreed to maintain their low rediscount rates (four per cent in New York) in order not to interfere with the sale of the relatively low-rate Victory notes. Private bankers guided themselves accordingly and loaned funds freely. Once business activity picked up, it was fed by bank loans, and a spiral of credit and price inflation developed. Member banks began to borrow from the Reserve banks in order to replenish their reserves. As a result, the ratio of reserves to deposit and note liabilities declined from 50.6 per cent in June, 1919, to 40.6 per cent, or almost to the legal minimum, in March, 1920. During the same period, currency in circulation increased from $46.42 to $51.36 per capita, and the turnover of demand deposits rose from 35 to 35.4.

The Reserve Board was aware of the dangers in the situation, for as early as June, 1919, it expressed concern over the existing speculative tendencies, but it said, "While ordinarily this could be corrected by an advance in discount rates, it is not practicable to apply this check at this time because of Government financing." Instead of increasing the rediscount rate, the Board asked the individual bankers of the nation to grant only those loans which were for essential and productive purposes. This policy of moral suasion was ineffective in dissuading people from borrowing, and the inflation continued to mount. In September, 1919, the Board, in answer to criticisms, declared that the sensational increases in the price level were due to increased business activity and not to an excessive volume of currency. It accepted the theory that the increase in currency was caused by rising prices, rather than vice versa. Nevertheless, the New York Reserve Bank began to take steps to discourage further credit expansion, thus divorcing itself from Treasury policies. It raised its rediscount rate to 4¾ per cent in November, 1919, 6 per cent in January, 1920, and 7 per cent in June. These increases did not have a decisive effect. Member bank demand deposits did reach their highest point ($26.1 billion) in December, 1919, but total loans did not reach a peak ($19.9 billion) until November, 1920, and Federal Reserve note circulation expanded until December, 1920, at which time total currency in circulation established a record at $51.29 per capita. The wholesale price index reached its highest point in May, 1920, five months after the peak of demand deposits, six months after the first increase in the rediscount rate, and seven months before the peak of money in circulation.

Although recession began in mid-1920, the Federal Reserve authorities pursued deflationary policies well into 1921, partly because they thought the liquidation had not been completed and partly because they feared that gold would be exported if rates were lowered. But in the summer and early fall of 1921, the New York Bank lowered its rediscount rate to 4½ per cent.

It was during the depression of 1920 that the Federal Reserve banks began to develop open-market operations. However, this strategy, which later became such an important instrument of credit control, was not originally adopted for that purpose, but rather to replenish the earning assets of the district banks. As the depression developed, bank loans declined and at the same time there was a constant inflow of gold. Consequently, member banks were able to repay their past borrowings, and rediscounts declined from $2.7 billion in 1920 to $618 million in 1922. When a further reduction in the rediscount rate to 4 per cent in June, 1922, did not encourage new bank borrowings, the district banks began to buy government obligations in the open market with their excess funds. Between October, 1921, and May, 1922, total holdings of government obligations by the Federal Reserve banks increased from $191 million to $603 million.

At first, each district bank carried on its own open-market operations as it deemed fit, but this was a disorderly and ineffectual arrangement. When it became evident that changes in the rediscount rate were not so effective as originally thought, open-market operations began to be considered as a major instrument of control, and under the leadership of Governor Strong of the New York Bank, an Open Market Investment Committee was formed in April, 1923, to coordinate the operations of all the district banks. Although it had no legal status or mandatory powers, it did tend to guide buying and selling operations.

With the recovery of business activity, the Federal Reserve banks reversed their expansion policies to some extent. They attempted to neutralize the effects of gold imports by selling government obligations to the member banks. As a result of this early sterilization operation, Reserve bank holdings of government securities declined between May, 1922, and June, 1923, by over $500 million, or more than the total gold imports.

As business approached what was considered a normal condition and as the Treasury relaxed its controls over the money market, the Board took advantage of its first opportunity to formulate theories of credit control. In its report for 1923, it concluded that it could not base its policy on the price index, for "price fluctuations proceed from a great variety of causes most of which lie outside the range of influence of the credit system." It also rejected the reserve ratio as a satisfactory guide, because it had significance only if the whole world was on a gold standard. The ideal objective, according to the Board, was "the constant exercise of a steadying influence on credit conditions." Accordingly, it believed that, although business should not be encouraged by too easy credit conditions in a period of rapid expansion or speculation, cheaper credit should be made available when industry was in the process of recovering after a period of reaction.

In the years between 1923 and 1929, the Board found it difficult to act in accordance with its theories. In the first place, the Board occupied a subordinate rather than a dominant position in the management of credit, for each of the 12 district banks wielded more influence, and the New York Bank was vastly more powerful. Furthermore, the Treasury, whether it wished to or not, continued to exert an important influence over the money market. With so many different decision makers, it was impossible for the System to follow a consistent policy. Then, too, there was no agreement on the aims of credit management. Many members of the Federal Reserve Board wanted to regulate the quality as well as the quantity of credit. On the other hand, the managers of the New York Bank believed that it was impossible to exert qualitative control. In addition, the Board was constantly besieged by demands that it make stabilization of prices its primary goal. Finally, and probably of most importance, the Board had to choose between the interests of business and the interests of stock-market speculation. If it followed a policy of credit contraction, both business activity and stock speculation would be equally discouraged. As the twenties progressed, this conflict loomed more and more important, but it was generally resolved in favor of encouraging business activity, and the monetary authorities tended to follow an easy-money policy even though it encouraged speculation and did not accord completely with the theories of credit management developed in 1923.

Easy-money Policy, 1924 to 1928. When a slight business recession developed in 1924, the Board, in accordance with its previously declared objectives, definitely began to follow an easy-money policy. Although the Board insisted that business conditions were the determining factor, it was charged that the decision was made in order to discourage imports of foreign capital and thereby help Great Britain and Germany to return to the gold standard. The stock market did not influence the policy, although security speculation was already a familiar aspect of the economic scene.

The Federal Reserve banks began their attempt to expand credit as early as December, 1923, when they began to buy government securities in the open market. They continued to buy until November, 1924, increasing their holdings from $84 million to $582 million. In addition, the New York Bank lowered its rediscount rate from 4 to 3 per cent in June and August, 1924. Whether it was so intended or not, the easy-money policy did help Great Britain to restore the gold standard. Gold imports began to decline in 1924, and gold was exported throughout 1925. Moreover, in 1925 the Federal Reserve Bank of New York established a credit of $200 million for the Bank of England.

As soon as economic recovery occurred, the Federal Reserve authorities reversed their policies. Between November, 1924, and March, 1925, they sold $260 million of government securities to mop up excess bank reserves, and in February, 1925, the New York rediscount rate was increased to 3½ per cent.

In its 1925 report the Federal Reserve Board began to take notice of stockmarket speculation. It noted a rapid increase in security loans, but it decided against taking any action that would increase the cost of credit to commerce and industry. Instead, it admonished the member banks to borrow only for temporary and seasonal business needs, not for security speculation.

The temporary tightening of business conditions in 1927 gave a new stimulus to the easy-money philosophy and resulted in a new attempt to encourage credit expansion. Rediscount rates were again lowered to 3½ per cent, and the Reserve banks began to buy bonds. Between May and November they purchased $270 million, increasing their holdings to over $600 million, the largest amount on record. Loans by member banks began to increase, and the policy was bitterly criticized, especially by such authorities as H. Parker Willis and B. M. Anderson.[1] There was also a difference of opinion among the monetary managers themselves. The Chicago Federal Reserve Bank was reluctant to reduce its rediscount rate, but the Federal Reserve Board ordered it to do so, in spite of the fact that some of its own members were opposed to the reduction.

Meanwhile, attempts were being made to force the Board to adopt price stabilization as its primary objective. In 1926, Representative Strong introduced a bill providing that "all of the powers of the Federal Reserve System be used for promoting stability in the price level." After extensive hearings, the bill was amended to provide that "stabilization of prices and of business conditions" was to be "the primary objective of credit policy." The Board opposed the Strong bill and breathed more easily when it was

---

[1] H. Parker Willis, *The Federal Reserve System;* Benjamin M. Anderson, *Economics and the Public Welfare.*

defeated, but the issue was not settled. Similar bills were to be introduced regularly during the depression of the thirties.

Attempts to Curb Speculation in 1928 and 1929. By 1928 the Federal Reserve Board was confronted with a Hobson's choice. On the one hand, conservative economists, pointing to the phenomenal rise in stock prices, called on the Board to take action to curb speculation. On the other hand, those who favored easy money argued that a change in policy would cause a business decline and endanger the gold standard in Europe. The Reserve authorities chose to restrict credit, hoping to bring speculation to a halt. In the first six months of 1928, rediscount rates were increased from $3\frac{1}{2}$ to 5 per cent, and holdings of government securities were reduced from $617 million to $235 million. Little selling took place during the rest of the year, but in the first half of 1929, holdings were further reduced to $145 million. These tactics discouraged stock-market speculation only temporarily, for as the Reserve banks mopped up excess reserves, the member banks increased them by rediscounting. Brokers' loans continued to mount, and by the latter half of 1928 stock prices were climbing into the stratosphere. Conservatives accused the Board of aiding the speculative excesses. But the Board indignantly denied the charge, contending that the heavy borrowing by member banks was not for speculation, but to cover gold exports, which were very heavy at the time. The Board also contended that brokers' loans were being fed, not by Reserve credit, but by private funds (the so-called "loans for the account of others") over which it had no control.[2]

Although there was much truth to the Board's contention that quantitative controls were being made ineffective, they should have been continued. But in February, 1929, when the New York Bank proposed another increase in rediscount rates, the Board refused to give its approval. Instead, it resorted to moral suasion; in the famous circular of February, 1929, it said: "The Federal Reserve Act does not, in the opinion of the Federal Reserve Board, contemplate the use of the resources of the Federal Reserve Banks for the creation or extension of speculative credit. A member bank is not within its reasonable claims for rediscount facilities . . . when it borrows either for the purpose of making speculative loans or for the purpose of maintaining speculative loans." Although this statement was clearly a call for restrictive action by the district banks against stock market loans, universal cooperation was not forthcoming. The Chicago Bank applied pressure on its member banks, but the New York Bank took no action. On the contrary, one of its directors, Charles E. Mitchell, an-

[2] For a defense of the System, see *The Annual Report of the Secretary of the Treasury*, 1928, and the *Annual Report of the Federal Reserve Board*, 1928.

nounced that the National City Bank, of which he was president, was willing to loan up to $25 million in the call-money market.[3] The New York Bank did not refuse to cooperate because it wished to encourage further speculation, but because it disagreed with the tactics. It favored continued increases in the rediscount rate, or quantitative rather than qualitative controls. In May the Board made a determined effort to make the moral-suasion policy effective. It sent the New York Bank a list of member banks holding a large volume of collateral loans, and it requested that appropriate action be taken. The New York Bank refused, and moral suasion collapsed.

Since qualitative credit control was impossible, the Board returned half-heartedly to quantitative controls. In August, it approved an increase in the New York rediscount rate to 6 per cent, but at the same time it agreed to a lowering of the buying rate on acceptances from $5\frac{1}{4}$ to $5\frac{1}{8}$ per cent. By this inconsistent policy, one action nullified the other, for member banks immediately shifted to the sale of acceptances instead of rediscounting commercial paper.

Meanwhile, business activity began to decline in midsummer, and while the average price of stocks continued to go up, this was due more to selective increases than to any generalized movement. Finally in September, prices of even the "blue chips" reached their peaks, and from then until the great collapse in October, the market was listless.

Failure to Reform the Banking System. Throughout the twenties, despite the high hopes that had been held for it, the Federal Reserve System was not able to eliminate the basic weaknesses of commercial banking inherited from prewar times. First of all, bank failures continued at a shocking rate throughout the prosperity period.

From both an absolute and a relative point of view, failures were much more numerous among state banks than among national banks and among nonmember than among member banks. Whereas there were $2\frac{1}{2}$ times as many state banks as national banks, their failures were $6\frac{1}{2}$ times greater and the deposits tied up in their suspensions were $3\frac{1}{2}$ times as large. It was also evident that member banks were safer than nonmember banks. Although the number of nonmember banks was only twice as large as the number of member banks, failures were 4.8 times greater and accounted for 2.3 times as much in deposits.

During this period as before, failures were most frequent among small banks, 88.4 per cent of the failures occurring among banks with a capital

[3] Comments on Mitchell's action illustrate the confusion that existed even in the best minds in regard to Reserve policy and tactics. (*Bankers Magazine*, April, 1929, and the *Monthly Letter* of the National City Bank, April, 1929. See also the illuminating comments of A. C. Miller, Senate Banking and Currency Committee, *Hearings on the Banking Act of 1935*, p. 763.)

of less than $100,000. The smaller banks being concentrated in the agricultural areas of the West and in the South, where considerable distress prevailed even during prosperity, it was not surprising that 94 per cent of the total failures occurred in the South, Middle West, and West. Smaller communities also suffered more heavily from bank failures than the metropolitan districts. Towns of less than 2,500 population experienced 80 per cent of the total suspensions, with approximately half of these in towns of less than 500 population. Suspensions in cities of over 25,000 population comprised only 5 per cent of the total. Since banking continued to be regarded as a type of business which should be open to competition, it was simple to obtain a charter in most states, and in spite of a general tendency for the number of banks to decline, there were still too many banks for safety. Iowa, which had the most bank failures, had one bank for every 1,400 people, while New Jersey, with the least failures, had one bank for every 7,500.

TABLE 50.   COMMERCIAL-BANK SUSPENSIONS, 1921–1929

Year	Number				Deposits (millions)		
	Total	National	State member	Non-member	Member	Non-member	Estimated loss to depositors
1921	505	52	19	434	$ 38.2	$ 134.1	$ 60
1922	366	49	13	304	27.3	63.9	38
1923	646	90	32	524	46.8	102.8	62
1924	775	122	38	615	78.5	131.6	79
1925	618	118	28	472	65.5	102.1	61
1926	976	123	35	818	67.5	192.9	83
1927	669	91	31	547	63.4	135.8	61
1928	498	57	16	425	46.7	95.6	44
1929	659	64	17	578	58.1	172.6	77
Totals.....	5,712	766	229	4,717	$492.0	$1,131.4	$565

SOURCE: Federal Reserve Board, *Banking and Monetary Statistics*, p. 283.

To summarize, bank failures were most prominent among state and nonmember banks which were least regulated and had the smallest capital; in agricultural communities, where prices and farm values collapsed after 1920 and where phenomenal prosperity was never enjoyed; in the smaller towns in which, with the advent of the automobile, local shops were brought into closer competition with the stores in the larger urban centers; and in those areas, usually agricultural and sparsely populated, where there were too many banks and where diversification of investment was impossible.

In general, membership in the Federal Reserve System was confined to the national banks and the large state banks. In 1921, only 33 per cent of all commercial banks controlling 71 per cent of the total commercial banking resources were members, and in 1929, 37 per cent of the commercial banks controlling 76 per cent of the resources were members. While the relative proportion of member banks increased, their absolute number did not, for all during the decade the total number of commercial banks declined steadily. The numerous bank failures eliminated many of the weaker banks. In addition, mergers were very common, especially after 1926. Furthermore, there was a gradual increase in branch banking, from 547 banks operating 1,455 branches in 1920 to 763 banks with 3,349 branches in 1929.

Although consolidation encouraged the growth of the Reserve System, the original Federal Reserve Act did not encourage consolidation, for it failed to revise the provision in the National Bank Act prohibiting new national banks from operating branches. For many years, the Comptroller of the Currency unsuccessfully recommended a change in the law. Finally, in February, 1927, Congress passed the McFadden Branch Banking Act, authorizing the national banks to establish branches within the corporate limits of the places in which they were located, provided state law permitted branch banking. Since 22 states prohibited branch banking, the Act did little toward establishing it. On the whole, the McFadden Act was weak, for it was not designed to revise the banking structure but to give the national banks some of the dubious advantages possessed by the state banks. Its branch-banking section was wholesome, but its other features enlarged the power of the national banks to make real estate loans, relaxed the limitation on the amount which could be loaned to a single borrower, and allowed the national banks to purchase investment securities.

Shift from Commercial Loans to Less Liquid Assets. In addition to the decline in the number of commercial banks, the following tendencies in banking were apparent during the twenties: (1) a decline in the relative importance of commercial loans, (2) an impressive increase in real estate loans, (3) an increase in the volume of investments, (4) an increase in the ratio of deposits to capital, and (5) a greater increase in time than demand deposits. It was evident that the entire banking system was becoming more and more rigid and less liquid. It was also evident that the Federal Reserve System no longer conformed to the "real bills" doctrine on which it was founded, for while member-bank commercial loans remained about the same from 1921 to 1929, their security loans increased 121 per cent, real estate loans 178 per cent, and investments, 67 per cent.

There were many reasons for the shift from commercial loans to less liquid assets. Wartime financing stimulated security issues and made the public familiar with them. Therefore, business turned more and more to security markets rather than to banks for capital funds. In addition, busi-

TABLE 51. COMMERCIAL-BANK OPERATIONS, 1921–1929
(Dollar figures in millions)

	1921		1925		1929	
	National	All other	National	All other	National	All other
Number.............	8,154	21,057	8,072	19,186	7,536	16,436
Loans (other than real estate).............	$11,962.6	$11,460.8	$11,929.5	$14,462.3	$13,388.1	$16,642.7
Loans (real estate)....	280.2	1,989.1	744.6	1,023.0	1,413.0	3,124.6
Investments..........	4,025.1	4,410.2	5,916.3	5,888.7	6,651.0	6,534.2
Total assets..........	20,517.9	22,555.5	24,350.9	27,699.9	27,440.2	33,136.0
Capital..............	1,273.9	1,590.1	1,369.4	1,716.5	1,627.4	2,098.1
Demand deposits.....	8,695.9	8,558.6	10,427.5	8,542.2	10,504.3	13,527.7
Time deposits........	3,641.6	5,798.2	5,924.7	6,082.3	8,317.1	10,308.8

SOURCE: *Annual Report of the Comptroller of the Currency*, 1921, 1925, 1929.

TABLE 52. LOANS AND INVESTMENTS OF MEMBER BANKS, 1921–1929

	1921		1925		1929	
	Amount (millions)	Per cent	Amount (millions)	Per cent	Amount (millions)	Per cent
Total loans and investments.........	$24,121	100	$29,518	100	$35,710	100
Total loans on securities...........	4,400	18	6,718	23	9,759	27
Total loans on real estate...........	1,135	5	2,338	8	3,164	9
All other loans..................	12,584	52	11,599	39	12,735	36
Investments.....................	6,002	25	8,863	30	10,052	28

SOURCE: Federal Reserve Board, *Banking and Monetary Statistics*, pp. 76, 79.

ness profits were growing along with the general economy, and as they grew, businesses were able to provide increasing proportions of their capital requirements from them. The boom in real estate and in the stock market made lending in those fields highly profitable to banks, and the more rapid increase in deposits than in loans left the banks no alternative but to invest an increasing portion of their deposits in government bonds. The effect of these trends was to make the banking structure much less elastic. As subsequent developments showed, when a serious economic crisis appeared, the banking system no longer underwent a short, but paralyzing, period of deflation. Instead, it went through a prolonged liquidation attended by groups of disastrous failures.

Expansion of Agricultural Credit. Throughout the twenties the Federal government continued to expand the facilities for agricultural credit first created under the Federal Farm Loan Act of 1916. Immediately after the war, the War Finance Corporation was reactivated to aid agricultural exports and to make loans to banks which extended credits to farmers. In March, 1923, Congress passed the Agricultural Intermediate Credit Act establishing 12 Federal Intermediate Credit banks in the same cities in which the Federal land banks, created under the Act of 1916, were operating. Each of these banks was to offer credit of six months to three years (as contrasted to the five- to forty-year loans on mortgages offered by land banks). They were capitalized at $5 million and could raise additional funds through the sale of securities. Although credits could not be extended directly to farmers, the banks could make loans to the various financial agencies that did lend money to farmers. Extension of loans under the Intermediate Credit system proceeded at a very slow pace, and in 1929 rediscounts amounted to only $50 million. Meanwhile, the banks, which had been set up under the Farm Loan Act, were having a critical time. In 1927 one land bank was in the hands of a receiver, two others were about to join it, and numerous others were on the verge of disaster. Evidently, the attempts by the Federal government to provide credit for farmers had only limited success, but they did tend to redistribute capital funds by bringing Federal moneys raised in other sections of the country into the farm regions. After 1929, the government turned to a new program of agricultural assistance. In addition to providing credit facilities, it decided to make an attempt to help stabilize farm prices. By the Agricultural Marketing Act of 1929, a Federal Farm Board was authorized to make loans out of a $500 million revolving fund to agricultural cooperatives to assist them in marketing crops. The plan was never successful, for with the coming of the depression and the subsequent extreme decline in farm prices, most of the revolving fund was quickly lost. But it did accelerate the organization of cooperatives in agriculture.

Monetary Policies of the Twenties in Retrospect. Since the depression of the 1930's, virulent criticism has been poured on the Federal Reserve Board for following an easy-money policy and for its failure to take strong steps to check the speculative inflation of the twenties. These criticisms underestimate the dilemma which the Board faced, namely, the problem of encouraging business activity and at the same time discouraging speculation. Critics also tend to exaggerate the effectiveness of monetary controls. Except for short intervals, the System failed whenever it attempted to restrict credit. Increases in the rediscount rate discouraged speculation only until speculators became accustomed to the new rate. Each time securities were sold in the open market, the strategy was largely nullified because banks replenished their reserves by borrowing from the district banks rather than by contracting their loans. Nor did the Board possess the power to regulate effectively the quantity or quality of credit. It could not control loans for the account of others, and it had no control over reserve requirements, margin requirements, or Treasury fiscal policy.

Although there is little justification for pinning chief responsibility for the disaster of 1929 on the Federal Reserve System, it nevertheless committed very serious errors. But these errors, like most in the politically ineffectual twenties, were of ommission rather than commission. Attempts to stifle credit expansion were made too belatedly in 1920 and in 1929, and no vigorous effort was made to urge Congress to enact badly needed banking reform.

The Treasury was also at fault, not only in its failure to retire as much of the bank-held debt as possible, but also in its persistent encouragement of the stock market. The White House chant, "Brokers' loans are not too high," was deplorable coming as it did when the Reserve System was attempting to curb speculation. But the administration's failure to exert controls over money and credit was characteristic of its whole philosophy, for it consistently denied the existence of any serious problems and it did not believe that its functions included listening for any rumblings below the surface of the economy. This, rather than any single specific fiscal or monetary policy, was the tragedy of the decade.

Funding the Allied Loans. In its treatment of the loans to the Allies and of the tariff problem, the philosophy of normalcy revealed its greatest and most tragic shortsightedness, for here the consequences were world-wide.

During the year and a half following the Armistice, the United States loaned various foreign governments, primarily for relief and rehabilitation, $2.8 billion in addition to the $7.3 billion in loans made during the war. These new loans were made under the acts of July, 1918, empowering the War and Navy Departments to sell to foreign governments surplus war materials on credit; February, 1919, appropriating $100 million to the American Relief Administration for relief of nonenemy European populations; and March, 1920, authorizing the United States Grain Corporation to sell 5 million barrels of flour for cash or credit.

The question as to whether the foreign governments could pay their obligations arose almost immediately after the war. It was understood by both the United States and the debtor nations that immediate payment was impossible, and the intention was to fund the short-term certificates of indebtedness into long-term bonds at some time in the near future.

At first, payments on interest were met, partly from the resources of the foreign government itself, but mostly from the proceeds of new American loans. Once these loans stopped, interest payments also stopped. The foreign governments hoped that the debts would be greatly reduced or completely canceled by the United States, but they received no encouragement from the Treasury Department, although even at this early date, sophisticates were skeptical as to the feasibility of payment. The Treasury did recognize that the chaotic condition of the foreign-exchange market made international payments difficult. Therefore, in September, 1919, Secretary Glass announced that interest payments would be deferred until arrangements could be made for funding the debts. In the following few years, desultory negotiations took place, mostly with Great Britain. In sparring for concessions, the British argued that the American loans, the inter-Allied loans, and German reparations should be treated as inseparable. However, the United States refused to consider the American loans as in any way connected with other loans or reparations growing out of the war.

TABLE 53. STATUS OF ALLIED LOANS, NOV. 15, 1920
(In millions of dollars)

	Credits established	Cash advanced	Repayments	Net advances
Liberty Loans..............	$ 9,710.5	$9,580.8*	$114.5	$ 9,466.3
Sale of surplus.............	563.0	....	......	563.0
Relief administration........	84.0	....	......	84.0
Totals..................	$10,357.5	$9,580.8	$114.5	$10,113.3

SOURCE: *Annual Report of the Secretary of the Treasury*, 1920, p. 54.

* Approximately $7.3 billion before Nov. 30, 1918.

When it became apparent that informal negotiations were accomplishing nothing, Congress, in February, 1922, created a World War Foreign Debt Commission, comprised of the Secretaries of the Treasury, State, and Commerce; one senator; and one congressman. The Commission was given power "to refund or convert, and to extend the time of payment of the principal or the interest, or both, of any obligation of any foreign Government . . . held by the United States." But bonds offered in payment could not mature later than June 15, 1947, and could not be for less than 4¼ per cent annually. This Act was impractical, and in February, 1923, after a long and bitter debate, Congress amended it. Shortly afterward, a settlement was reached with Great Britain, which owed $4.6 billion of the $12.1 billion principal and interest owed by all foreign governments. Britain agreed to pay $4.6 billion of principal over the next sixty-two years with interest at 3 per cent until 1932 and 3½ per cent thereafter. She had the right to defer half the interest payments during the first five years, and any obligations of the United States issued after

April 6, 1917, were to be accepted at par in payment of interest. Between 1923 and 1926, 13 agreements were signed, providing for the eventual payment of $11.5 billion of principal and $10.6 billion of interest. Of the principal, $1.7 billion represented accumulated interest and $9.8 billion, funded principal. Interest rates varied from an average of 0.3 per cent in the settlement with Greece to 3.3 per cent in most of the others. The average annual rate for all agreements was 2.1 per cent.

Foreign Private Loans. The administration assumed without qualification that the intergovernmental debts would be paid in full, and only time was to prove the fallacy of this assumption. In the interim, debt payments were regarded as a lucrative source of funds for the retirement of the Federal debt. As the debtor nations met their obligations, often with United States bonds selling at a discount, the administration took steps to protect its creditor position by preventing American investment bankers from making loans to foreign countries which had failed to make an adjustment of their debts to the United States. In his annual report of 1925, the Secretary of the Treasury wrote:

It is now customary for American bankers intending to . . . grant credits to foreign governments to consult the State Department before final action is taken. Upon receipt of advice from the bankers the State Department confers with the Commerce and Treasury Departments and then notifies the bankers of the attitude of the Government, whether or not objection to the financing is interposed. In failing to raise any objection, however, the Government does not pass upon the merits of the financing in any way.

Competition for international loans was intense among some groups of bankers, and gradually during the decade, international borrowing in the New York money market picked up, $623 million of foreign securities being sold to the American public in 1921, $969 million in 1924, and $1.3 billion in 1927. Thereafter, offerings of foreign securities tapered off to some extent, but still they amounted to $905 million in 1930. These colossal international loans contributed to the domestic business boom, especially since a large part of the funds was spent for goods in this country.

Whereas fifty years earlier American prosperity had depended upon the ability of the United States to float loans in Europe and to purchase European goods, now it appeared that American prosperity was dependent to a great extent upon loans to Europeans and on the purchases of American products generated thereby. This was not a stable foundation for prosperity in view of the financial weakness of foreign countries and America's muddled international financial and tariff policies. Huge interest payments were due on government and private debts while the balance of trade continued to be unfavorable for the debtor countries. The resulting heavy demand for dollars depressed foreign currencies and compelled foreign governments to introduce artificial exchange rates and restrictions on foreign trade. Thus, conditions were being prepared for a great world crash which would engulf the United States even more than any other country, since no other nation enjoyed greater prosperity or was more involved internationally.

Fordney-McCumber Tariff. In making the United States a mature creditor nation, the war largely eliminated the remaining economic justification for protective tariffs. Yet, paradoxically, by stimulating American nationalism and isolationism, it strengthened, temporarily at least, the forces of protectionism.

Early in the postwar period, the protectionists in Congress prepared to replace the relatively low rates of the Underwood Tariff with more robust duties. President Wilson opposed this move. In a message to Congress in December, 1919, he emphasized the changing nature of America's international position, stressing the fact that Europe could pay her debts only in gold, credit, or goods. He pointed out that the first two alternatives were limited and therefore foreign countries could buy our exports only by selling their own goods. "Whatever," he concluded, "may have been our views during the period of growth of American business concerning tariff legislation, we must now adjust our own economic life to a changed condition growing out of the fact that American business is full grown and that America is the greatest capitalist in the world."

Instead of heeding this advice, Congress passed an emergency tariff act, preparatory to adopting the more permanent Fordney-McCumber Act of September, 1922, which raised the average tariff rate to the highest in history. The vote in the House on the Fordney Act was 292 to 131, with only seven Republicans opposing the bill and only seven Democrats supporting it. In the Senate, the vote was equally one-sided, 48 to 25. In many respects, this tariff was an anachronism, for it brought back an economic nationalism of the type that had thrived in 1816. It emphasized self-sufficiency, protection for war-born industries, and assistance for agriculture. In other respects, the Act was a logical link in the chain of tariff by negotiation which had been inaugurated crudely by the McKinley Act of 1890. The President was given the power to raise or lower tariff rates whenever the rates were found not to equalize the differences in the costs of foreign and domestic production, to impose additional duties on imports which were supported by government bounties, and to impose an embargo on goods from any country discriminating against the commerce of the United States. The Tariff Commission was given the administrative duty to investigate and advise the President regarding the rates which would accomplish the equalization. It was thus restored to the function first established in the Taft administration.

The "flexible plan" of tariff administration worked out badly. Neither the Harding nor the Coolidge administration had any intention of lowering tariff rates, and the Tariff Commission took its cue from them. Between September, 1922, and December, 1928, there were 500 applications for rate changes—300 for increases and 200 for reductions. Approximately 100 of these were investigated. The President increased duties in 24, reduced duties in 2 (live bobwhite quail and paintbrush handles), sent back 13 for more information, and suspended 10 without recommendation. The remainder were still under consideration at the time the Hawley-Smoot Tariff was passed in 1930.

CHAPTER 26: STATE AND LOCAL FINANCE, 1900 TO 1930[1]

The expansion of government activity which characterized the new century expressed itself even more on the state level than on the Federal. Moreover, the technological revolution wrought in transportation and industry by the invention of the automobile called for government services beyond the capacity of local governments. The public, therefore, turned more to their state governments, and the states became more important service and fiscal agencies than they had ever been before.

Expansion of State Expenditures and Revenues. During the first three decades of the twentieth century, Federal expenditures increased sixfold and local expenditures sevenfold, but state expenditures increased fifteenfold. The contrast was especially marked after World War I, when state expenditures almost tripled, Federal expenditures became stabilized, and local expenditures increased by only 50 per cent.

The most rapid increase in state expenditures was for roads, which rose from practically nothing to more than a billion dollars a year. Prior to 1900, except for the brief period 1830 to 1850, state governments left this field to local governments—the towns and the counties. But the advent of motor transportation changed this. Existing roads had to be completely reconstructed, and new hard-surface highways connecting the urban centers had to be built. The job was beyond the administrative and fiscal capacities of the localities, and major highways had to be planned, financed, built, and maintained entirely by the states. Even in the case of feeder roads, the states had to provide financial aid and administrative supervision, and later they had to assume responsibility for the application of Federal aid.[2]

State expenditures for education rose from less than $50 million in 1902 to more than $600 million in 1932. The greater part of these expenditures represented state aid to local school districts, which increased from $30 million to $400 million, one-fourth of total local school expenditures. As

[1] For a consecutive development of state and local finance, see Chaps. 5 (1775 to 1800), 12 (1800 to 1860), 17 (1860 to 1900), and 28 to 30 (1930 to 1950).

[2] New Jersey, in 1891, was the pioneer in the movement. New York established aid to towns for road construction and maintenance in 1898. In 1906 to 1908 it established a state highway system and a state highway commission. During the 1920's it created a state department of public works uniting the care of canals, highways, and public buildings.

secondary education became universal, the number of young people wishing to enter college multiplied. Since many of them lacked the means with which to pay the substantial tuition fees charged by private institutions, they sought admission to state-supported institutions, and to accommodate them the states had to expand considerably the facilities of these institutions. State expenditures for higher education increased accordingly from approximately $15 million in 1902 to $200 million in 1932.[3]

TABLE 54. STATE AND LOCAL EXPENDITURES, 1902–1932
(In millions of dollars)

	State			Local		
	1902	1913	1932	1902	1913	1932
Expenditures (excluding debt retirement)............................	$182	$378	$2,734	$888	$1,460	$6,501
Operation.........................	115	229	1,058	667	936	4,476
General control..................	26	40	124	138	171	*
Public safety.....................	7	25	87	90	156	*
Highways........................	5	14	214	112	143	*
Health, welfare, and correction.....	56	93	354	84	134	*
Education........................	16	50	188	220	281	*
Recreation.......................	1	2	72	13	22	*
Miscellaneous....................	4	5	18	10	29	*
Aid to other governments.......,....	54	87	764	......	......	65
Capital outlays....................	2	48	775	166	394	1,281
Interest..........................	10	14	114	57	121	610
Contributions to trust funds and enterprises..........................	*	*	23	......	9	69
Per capita expenditures (dollars)......	$2.30	$3.89	$21.80	$11.22	$15.02	$52.07

SOURCE: U.S. Bureau of the Census, *Historical Review of State and Local Government Finances*.

* Not available.

With the improvement of transportation facilities, many social-welfare functions, which in the horse-and-buggy days had had to be performed on a local basis, were taken over by the states. Existing institutions were expanded, and new ones were established for the care of special categories, such as epileptics, crippled children, and the tuberculous. Many states established pensions for the aged and for widowed mothers, either paying

[3] The figures for state and particularly municipal financial operations are given mostly for the years 1902, 1913, 1932 because financial operations are comprehensively reported by the Census Bureau only for these years and no other compilations of them are available.

the entire cost or, where such programs were locally administered, furnishing state aid.

A number of states developed parks, public beaches, and other recreational facilities.[4] Even in the field of police administration, the states had to assume responsibility, for state highways had to be patrolled and the improvement of transportation had made crime a state-wide, rather than a local, business.

TABLE 55. STATE-TAX COLLECTIONS, 1902–1930
(In millions of dollars)

Tax	1902	1915	1922	1930
Property..............................	$ 82	$ 186	$ 348	$ 345
Income (individual and corporation)	*	2	98	233
Death and gift........................	*	29	66	183
Motor vehicles.......................	*	15	165	851
Alcoholic beverages....................	*	21		
Other................................	74	115	271	495
Totals............................	$ 156	$ 368	$ 947	$ 2,108
Per capita (dollars)	$1.97	$3.66	$8.61	$17.12

SOURCE: U.S. Bureau of the Census, *Historical Review of State and Local Government Finances.*

* Not available.

Between 1900 and 1930 a revolution occurred in state tax systems. New taxes were added to meet the vast increases in expenditures, and some old taxes were reduced or eliminated. The automobile opened an enormous area for state taxation. Motor-vehicle license taxes were imposed early in the century, and Oregon adopted the first gasoline tax in 1919. By 1925 motor taxes had become the most productive sources of state revenue, and in 1930 the gasoline tax provided almost 25 per cent and motor-vehicle taxes almost 20 per cent of total state tax collections. Yet the combined collections under automobile taxes were estimated at less than half the cost of the nation's streets and highways.[5]

Another innovation came in 1911 when Wisconsin adopted the first efficient state income tax. By 1930, 20 states were imposing state income taxes, and their aggregate yield comprised 20 per cent of the total state revenue.

The sales tax and the gross receipts tax were also first adopted during

[4] New York State pioneered in this work. With the aid of publicly approved bond issues of $2.5 million for the improvement of the Interstate Palisades Park in 1910 and of $25 million in 1916 and 1924 for parks, a vast chain of parks was developed throughout the state.

[5] A. G. Buehler, *Public Finance,* 2d ed., p. 650.

this period, West Virginia being the pioneer in 1921. However, returns were almost insignificant, and the tax was not to become important until the depression of the 1930's.

Meanwhile, in a number of states the general property tax was reorganized either by exempting all intangible personal property and in a few cases all tangibles or else by converting it into a classified property tax, that is, by assessing or taxing tangible personalty at lower rates than realty. To compensate the localities for the resulting loss of revenue, the states offered to them shares of the proceeds of certain of their newly imposed taxes, particularly the corporation franchise and personal income taxes.

Expansion of Municipal Expenditures and Revenues. The expansion of municipal activity and expenditures proceeded at an accelerated rate during the years 1900 to 1914, was temporarily halted by World War I, and then reached its peak during the prosperous 1920's.

In rural as well as urban areas more and better schools were built. As high-school attendance was made mandatory, school enrollment and school expenditures rose sharply. County governments expanded their social-welfare functions, assumed responsibility for the control of public health and sanitation, built and operated hospitals, and took on many other new functions. All municipalities had to motorize and otherwise reequip at considerable cost their police, fire, street-cleaning, and other forces. In a few cities the area of public ownership was extended to include the operation of street railways and rapid-transit systems, and many ventured into the ownership and operation of electric-light and gas plants, docks and ferries, toll bridges, markets, auditoriums, and even cemeteries. Many of these enterprises were operated at a deficit, thus increasing the budgetary problems of the cities. In 1915, Professor Plehn, reviewing the growth of municipal expenditures over the decade 1902 to 1913, wrote,

Much of the work done by cities . . . is cooperative or semi-socialistic. That is to say, the cities provide for the individual citizens things which they might —and for a long time did—provide for themselves, or which might be provided by private enterprise. The big motor-driven street sweeper has taken the place of the primitive rule "let every man sweep in front of his own door."[6]

The greatest expansion of municipal activities and expenditures took place in metropolitan areas. The wider diffusion of population and greater congestion of traffic (incident to growth of motor transportation) created new problems demanding attention not only from the central city but also from its surrounding suburbs. The central cities had to build at staggering capital costs underground electric railways and superbridges or install high-powered ferries, widen their streets and boulevards, build new and

[6] Carl C. Plehn, *Government Finance in the United States*, p. 85.

larger hospitals, and establish health centers. In many cases the problems of metropolitan areas were taken care of by the creation of special authorities having special taxing and borrowing powers. In several areas these authorities built and operated parks and parkways, rapid-transit lines, under-river tunnels, huge water supplies, sewerage systems, and other facilities serving the entire metropolitan population.

The yield of the local property tax increased sharply. The rate rose to 3 per cent or more of the assessed valuations, while the valuations themselves, reflecting higher property values as well as new building construction, increased several fold.[7] Property owners insisted that the burden of the tax was too great, and in order to alleviate it and also to help the localities to finance their increased expenditures, most states increased their aids to the localities. Several, as already indicated, also abandoned their own levies on real estate, turning to other taxes as a substitute.

The total sums distributed to the localities in the form of specific aids and shared taxes increased from $58 million in 1902, or 7 per cent of the total local revenue, to $915 million, or 14 per cent, in 1932. State and local revenue systems became closely interlocked.

In many fields, state financing was more effective than local financing and was being substituted therefor. A centralizing trend toward state financing appeared in each state. Compared with Federal and local revenues, state revenue still was third in size, but it was closing the gap. Qualitatively, it was superior to local revenue systems, being more varied, equitable, and elastic. This qualitative superiority manifested itself during this period in the introduction of shared taxes and in the considerable expansion of state aid. It was to manifest itself even more emphatically in succeeding years.

Growth of State and Local Debt. The states rushed into debt about as rapidly as they had in the 1830's. The people swept aside existing constitutional restrictions either by voting constitutional exceptions or by voting favorably in all bond-issue referendums. State gross debts increased from $270 million in 1902 to $2.9 billion in 1932, with the greatest increases occurring in the 1920's.[8]

[7] In New York City from 1900 to 1930, as against an increase in population from 3.4 million to 6.9 million, assessed valuations of real estate increased from $3.2 billion to $18.2 billion while the tax rate increased from 2.14 to 2.7 per cent.

[8] In New York State the following bond issues were approved by constitutional amendments: in 1905, $50 million for highways; in 1923, $45 million for a soldiers' bonus; in 1925, $100 million for institutions and various other purposes and $300 million for grade-crossing elimination. By bond referendums: in 1903 to 1915, an aggregate of $150 million for the enlargement of the barge canal; in 1912, a second $50 million for highways; in 1910 to 1924, an aggregate of $27.5 million for state parks; and in 1923, $50 million for state institutions. State indebtedness increased from $8.6 million in 1900 to $273 million in 1930.

Local governments also borrowed heavily. Their gross debts grew from $1.9 billion to $16.7 billion, or about nine times, with a similar concentration of increases in the 1920's. The largest increases were in the debts of school districts, special districts (metropolitan authorities and suburban improvement districts), and counties. In the cities increases were especially notable in debts for public-ownership enterprises: water supplies, toll bridges, rapid-transit systems, docks, and ferries.[9]

TABLE 56. STATE AND LOCAL GROSS DEBTS, 1902–1932
(In millions of dollars)

	1902	1913	1932
Total..................	$2,194	$4,498	$19,573
State..................	270	423	2,907
Local..................	1,924	4,075	16,680
County...............	205	393	2,775
City.................	1,612	3,447	9,909
Township.............	57	80	433
School district.........	46	119	2,170
Special district.........	5	36	1,393

SOURCE: U.S. Bureau of the Census, *Historical Review of State and Local Government Finances.*

State Administrative and Fiscal Reorganization. With the increase in the cost of state government came an insistence on more responsible, efficient, and economical state administration. For years state management was dominated by the party "boss," who operated behind the scene and was responsible to no one. The government was "invisible," as Elihu Root once put it, and it was corrupt, inefficient, and wasteful.

The movement for reorganization of state government took two different forms. One program continued to stress the development of centralized executive leadership which had begun in the late nineteenth century. The other plan looked to the improvement of the existing system of government by independently elected commissions or boards. It clung to the traditional American distrust of executive leadership and to the illusion that decentralization of administration and direct election of all administrative officials by the people ensured popular control.

The first plan was followed in New York, California, Minnesota, and Illinois. As early as 1910 in his annual message Governor Hughes of New York recommended that responsibility be "centered in the governor, who should appoint a cabinet of administrative heads accountable to him and

[9] New York City's net debt increased from $250 million in 1900 to $1.6 billion in 1930. More than half of the latter sum was for debt incurred for public-ownership enterprises. Rapid transit alone was responsible for a debt of more than $400 million.

charged with the duties now devolved upon elective state officers." A resolution to amend the constitution to give effect to this plan was introduced in the legislature but failed to pass. Governor Sulzer took up the proposal and appointed a Department of Efficiency and Economy in 1913 to develop plans for such an administrative reorganization of the state government. In the meanwhile, in 1915, a constitutional convention was held which concerned itself particularly with the question of state administrative reorganization and leaned heavily on the New York Bureau of Municipal Research for technical assistance. The constitution submitted to the people provided for centralization of responsibility in the executive, an executive budget system, and other far-reaching reforms. Although the constitution was not approved by the people, its most important proposals were finally adopted in the form of separate constitutional amendments in 1925 and 1927. They were extremely important, since they served as models for a number of other states. The governor was given the power to appoint and remove the heads of all administrative agencies, except the departments of the attorney general, audit and control, and education; 150 agencies were consolidated into 18 departments; the governor was required to prepare and submit annually to the legislature "a budget containing a complete plan of the proposed expenditures and estimated revenues," together with appropriation bills and measures of taxation, if any; the legislature could not "alter an appropriation bill submitted by the Governor except to strike out or reduce items therein" but it could add thereto items of appropriation "provided that such additions are stated separately and distinctly from the original items of the bill and refer each to a single object or purpose."

Several states were not ready to proceed with the plan of centralizing administrative and budgetary responsibility in the governor. Instead they experimented with the alternative or compromise plan of "government by commission." In 1911 under the progressive leadership of Governor Hiram Johnson, California established a State Board of Control with large powers of both audit and approval. In 1912 the board prepared a budget for the legislature which represented the first attempt to handle appropriations intelligently. In 1911 Wisconsin created a State Board of Public Affairs to take charge of the finances of the State and to promote methods of economy and efficiency. The Wisconsin example was followed in 1912 by the establishment in New Jersey and Massachusetts of a State Commission on Economy and Efficiency and the inauguration, a few years later, of a centralized budget procedure. Everywhere, administrative reorganization and centralized budgeting became the motto of the day.

Local Administrative and Fiscal Reorganization. In the cities during these three decades major improvements in the methods of assessment of real property were introduced, increasing the productivity of the property tax and helping to make it more equitable. In St. Paul, W. A. Sommers, former assessor and engineer, using the front foot as a unit of measurement for city lots, developed depth tables for purposes of valuation and also rules for determining corner influence, irregular lots, and the like. In 1896 in accordance with these scientific rules, he made a complete reassessment of property. A few years later in New York City, Lawson Purdy, chairman of the tax commission, introduced land-value maps for valuation purposes and similarly systematized the assessments of taxable real estate. From that time on the movement spread to other cities. At the same time systems of administrative review of assessments by special boards were developed in New Jersey, New York City, and elsewhere, thus speeding up the process of review and reducing the expense to apellants.

The movement toward home rule and greater executive power, begun in the 1880's and 1890's, continued to thrive. In addition to the "strong-mayor" form of government, cities developed the commission form, under which all administrative as well as legislative powers were vested in a single board of elected commissioners, and the city-manager form, under which an expert in municipal administration was hired by a small city council to administer most of the services through appointed department heads. The commission form of government, initiated in Galveston, Texas, in 1901, spread to some 400 municipalities in the next fifteen years, including such fairly large cities as Buffalo, Newark, New Orleans, St. Paul, and Portland. The city-manager form of government was instituted in Staunton, Virginia, in 1908 and achieved national importance in 1914 following its establishment in Dayton, Ohio, and in a number of smaller cities.

These structural reorganizations in local government were generally accompanied by basic improvements in the procedures of government, including management of local finances. The financial structures were simplified and made more amenable to budgetary control. Methods of appropriating funds, accounting and controlling expenditures, revenue collections, and other operations were improved, and the authority for the preparation of the budget was centralized in the mayor, the city commission, the city manager, or the board of estimate. The system of the executive budget, centralized accounting, and independent auditing was thus developed in both theory and practice on the municipal level before it was thought of either by the states or by the national authority. As part of the same trend, cities developed systems of classification of positions, standardization of salaries, and centralized purchasing which at a later date were carried over into state and national governmental practice.

Constructive state administrative supervision over municipal finance was also first initiated during this period. Wyoming led the way with the enactment in 1890 of a law establishing state supervision over municipal accounts, audits, and reports. New York began in 1905 to prepare and install model accounting systems in local governments. But the outstanding leadership was probably supplied by Massachusetts. In 1906 it required the municipalities to submit to the State Bureau of Statistics a statement of their expenditures, revenues, and debt operation. This was followed in 1910 by a law giving the State Bureau the responsibility for improving the accounting and auditing methods of the cities which were found to be defective. In 1913 two additional important laws were passed: one required the establishment of a budget system in every city except Boston, which was provided for separately; the other revised completely the existing municipal borrowing practices in order to eliminate such abuses of municipal credit as borrowing for current purposes, excessive borrowing in anticipation of tax collections, diversion of trust funds, and mismanagement of sinking funds. Similar developments took place during this period in other states. By 1930 nearly all states maintained some form of state administrative supervision over municipal finance. Thus, municipal governments were being gradually redeemed from the shameful condition into which they had sunk during the preceding half a century, while state and local fiscal administrations were being brought together into a new type of constructive cooperative relationship.

Since state and local expenditures and revenues by the end of the 1920's were double the size of Federal expenditures and revenues and since state and local debts were greater than the Federal debt, it seemed that the decentralization of financial operations characteristic of peacetime periods had been fully reestablished. But this was an illusion, for the new decentralization could not possibly last long. It had been achieved by an enormous expansion of state and local activity, and in the process state and local governments had strained their resources to the utmost. Furthermore, decentralization was taking place in spite of indubitably superior Federal fiscal powers and in spite of powerful social and economic forces of a centralizing nature. The expansion of Federal aid to states—still moderate in nature, but potentially almost limitless—and the continued large Federal surpluses vividly evidenced the shaky foundations of the new decentralization. Yet not even the keenest contemporary observers foresaw the impending revolution in the relationship of Federal to state-local finance.

Chapter 27: THE GLOOMY YEARS

Prosperity began to fade in early 1929, although the public did not begin to realize it until after the sensational stock-market crash in October. As early as April, businessmen began to reduce their commitments, and in midsummer business activity began to decline. But there was no devastating panic in the money market or paralyzing liquidation in commercial banking. Optimists were therefore led to believe that, if a business recession occurred, it would not be any worse than those of 1924 and 1927. However, by mid-1930 even official circles lost their optimism as it became undeniable that a depression of more than usual severity had begun.

Instead of a short panic, the 1930's featured a deflation and liquidation that became increasingly severe as time passed. National income dropped from $83.3 billion in 1929 to $68.9 billion in 1930 and $40.0 billion in 1932. The Federal Reserve index of industrial production fell from 110 in 1929 to 91 in 1930 and 58 in 1932. Unemployment was estimated at 3½ million in 1930 and 15 million in 1933. The wholesale price index declined from 95.3 in 1929 to 86.4 in 1930 and 64.8 in 1932.

Herbert Hoover had the misfortune of being President when the storm broke. A successful businessman and an accomplished administrator, he lacked political acumen and an understanding of public feeling. He could not arouse enthusiasm for his administration or reinstill a spirit of confidence in the soundness of the economy. His was the first administration to use the powers of the Federal government as a means of recovering from the depression, and he himself tried desperately to turn the economic tide. Nevertheless, the public experienced a revulsion of feeling against the "Great Engineer" and constantly and unjustly denounced him as a "do-nothing" President. As a result, the Republican party lost control of Congress in the elections of 1930. The Hoover administration spent its last two years at constant loggerheads with the Democratically controlled Congress, and the Federal government was badly handicapped in its efforts to solve the problems of the depression.

According to the official biographers of the Hoover administration, the depression was comprised of five major breakdowns. After each one, Hoover succeeded in laying the groundwork for recovery. But his efforts were always defeated by factors beyond his control. The stock-market crash ushered in the first phase of the depression. It represented a reaction from the preceding boom which had been caused chiefly by the easy-money policy of the Federal Reserve System. The second phase occurred in the spring of 1931, following the breakdown of the European economy. In September, recovery was again cut short when Great Britain went off the gold standard. In June, 1932, the low point of the depression was reached, and recovery would have been assured but the obstructionist tactics pursued by the Democratic Congress destroyed public confidence. Finally, the catastrophic banking collapse of February-March, 1933, was caused by a public fear that President-elect Roosevelt would resort to currency manipulation and inflationary tactics as soon as he took office.[1] However, this is scarcely an adequate account.

In his prescriptions for recovery during the greater part of his administration, Hoover stressed reliance on private initiative and the restoration of public confidence. He used traditional, rather than new and experimental, methods, emphasizing "patient constructive action," "saving," and the "American system," rather than "bureaucracy and state control."[2]

At first, he sought to restimulate confidence by denying the existence of the depression and by calling on businessmen to maintain production and high wage rates. But by the end of 1930 it became apparent that moral suasion was having little effect. Accordingly, the administration widened its efforts and made them more direct. It emphasized a balanced budget, a moderate increase in public-works expenditures, and large tax increases. It tried to expand credit by using monetary and banking controls. It attempted to stabilize international finance. And it made direct loans to corporations and state and local governments.

Increased Expenditures for Public Works. Although the Hoover administration believed in economy and a balanced budget, it was forced by the exigencies of the depression gradually to overcome its inhibitions against Federal spending. With Congressional approval, it expanded and accelerated Federal construction and increased its grants to states for highways.

When the depression broke out, the government had just begun to put into execution a huge building program approved by Congress in 1926 and 1928. Calling for the construction of $300 million of buildings in Washington and elsewhere to house the various activities of the government, the work was under the direction of the Supervising Architect and was to take ten years. The maximum expenditure in any one year was limited to $35 million, but unexpended balances could be carried over and spent in subsequent years. In March, 1930, and again in February, 1931, Congress, at the administration's recommendation, passed

[1] William Starr Myers and Walter H. Newton, *The Hoover Administration*, pp. 7–21.
[2] See Hoover's Indianapolis speech of June, 1931, *The New York Times*, June 16, 1931.

the Keyes-Elliott Acts appropriating an additional $330 million for Federal buildings in order to aid employment. The maximum annual outlay, not counting unexpended balances from previous years, was raised to $65 million. The program embraced 817 projects and was to be completed by 1937. With this as a nucleus, the Office of the Supervising Architect spent $60 million in the fiscal year 1930, $110 million in 1932, and $127 million in 1933. Since the administration followed a pay-as-you go method of financing capital expenditures and was committed to a balanced budget, this represented a substantial increase in expenditures.

Expenditures for the improvement of rivers and harbors were raised to more than $100 million a year, and construction was begun in 1930 on the Colorado River Dam (intermittently known as the Hoover Dam and the Boulder Dam). Designed primarily to provide irrigation as far west as the Imperial Valley in California, the dam was to be a self-liquidating project, for it was to generate and sell power to private companies at rates which would cover operating costs and pay off construction costs plus interest within fifty years. In the interim, however, funds for its construction had to be raised by Congressional appropriation, not from revenue of the Reclamation Bureau, and by mid-1933 more than $50 million had been expended.

TABLE 57. ESTIMATED EXPENDITURES FOR PUBLIC WORKS, 1930–1933
(In millions of dollars)

Year	Annual report of the Secretary*	Myers and Newton†	Temporary National Economic Committee‡	Federal Employment Stabilization Board§
1930	$ 411.8	$ 412.4	$ 445.0	$ 338.7
1931	548.5	574.9	540.0	489.6
1932	633.3	670.3	590.0	556.1
1933‖	712.6	727.8	524.0	368.6
Totals...	$2,306.2	$2,385.4	$2,099.0	$1,753.0

* Includes rivers and harbors, road construction, naval construction, Supervising Architect, forts and fortifications, forest service, lighthouses, and Reclamation Bureau.
† *The Hoover Administration*, p. 157.
‡ *TNEC Hearings*, Part 9, "Savings and Investment," p. 4064.
§ New construction, repairs, and alterations. (Arthur D. Gayer, *Public Works in Prosperity and Depression*, p. 73.)
‖ Two-thirds of the fiscal year.

At the same time, under the Emergency Construction Appropriation Act of December 20, 1930, and the Emergency Relief and Construction Act of July 21, 1932, Federal grants to states for highway construction were increased from $85.9 million in the fiscal year 1930 to $172.3 million in 1933.

Since some groups among the public clamored for larger increases in public-works expenditures, Hoover appointed a committee to examine the question. This committee, composed of Colonel Leonard P. Ayers, Matthew Woll, James R. Garfield, Jacob H. Hollander, and others, reported that, whatever the cause of the depression, the common-sense remedy was to balance the budget. "It did not appear reasonable," the committee wrote, "to believe that a construction program could greatly hasten recovery."[3] The President echoed the committee's report. He especially denounced proposals for "non-productive works," insisting that they would increase public expenditures, weaken government credit, and result in a net increase in unemployment. "It will serve no good purpose, and will fool no one," he said, "to try to cover appearances by resorting to a so-called 'extraordinary budget.' That device . . . means a breach of faith to holders of all government securities."[4] Yet, according to the most conservative estimates, the average annual expenditures for public works during the Hoover administration were twice as large as those of the prosperity years.

The Veterans' Bonus. Concerned over growing unemployment among their members, the American Legion and other veterans' organizations started agitation in 1930 for the immediate payment of the adjusted service certificates or at least for an increase in their loan value. President Hoover opposed this demand, but in February, 1931, Congress passed a law over his veto, directing the Treasury to loan to applying veterans up to 50 per cent of the face value of their certificates at interest of 4½ per cent. To make these loans, the Treasury sold $1.1 billion of government securities in the Adjusted Service Fund during the fiscal years 1931 and 1932. While the loans did not affect the budget, since they were made from payments accounted for in past budgets, they did increase the government's cash outlay and added to the purchasing power of the population.

The veterans' organizations continued to demand the immediate payment of the full face value of the bonus, and in May, 1932, an enlarged replica of Coxey's army of 1893, the "bonus army," arrived in Washington to make the demand more impressive. In the meanwhile, Representative Patman of Texas introduced a bill authorizing $2.4 billion of greenbacks to be used to pay off the remainder of the face value of the certificates. The bill passed the House on June 15 by a vote of 209 to 176 but was almost immediately defeated in the Senate, 62 to 18, temporarily ending the issue.

[3] Myers and Newton, *op. cit.*, p. 156.
[4] *Ibid.*, p. 211.

Relief and Public Works. As unemployment increased, it was apparent that the cost of relief was bound to be far in excess of the resources of the state and local governments. They therefore began to bring pressure on the Federal government to come to their aid. In February, 1931, President Hoover promised to provide them with assistance but only if all their facilities proved inadequate. Meanwhile, he opposed any form of "Federal dole," direct or indirect, as being foreign to the "philosophy and creed of our people." In June, 1931, he asserted that there were two groups of ideas for dealing with the depression: "The first is whether we shall go on with our American system which holds that the major purpose of the state is to protect the people. . . . The other is that we shall, directly or indirectly, regiment the population into a bureaucracy to serve the state. . . ." In his annual message of December, 1931, he said, "The Federal government must not encroach upon nor permit local communities to abandon that precious possession of local initiative and responsibility." But local governments saw nothing precious about their responsibility; they appealed to the states, and the states appealed to Washington.

In spite of administration objections, the Costigan-LaFollette bill, providing $375 million for grants-in-aid to states for relief, was introduced in February, 1932. It was defeated in the Senate, but in July Congress passed the Wagner-Garner bill, allocating $2.3 billion on the basis of population to the states for use in public works and relief and authorizing loans to individuals, corporations, and local governments through the Reconstruction Finance Corporation (described on page 371, below). The President vetoed the bill, calling it a pork barrel containing too many "nonproductive public works." But he objected most of all to the loan section, insisting that it would put the Federal government into private business, that the states and municipalities would dump their financial problems on the Federal government, that it would be impracticable and would establish a huge bureaucracy, that it would saddle the RFC with all the doubtful loans in the United States, and that it would require the RFC to sell more than $3 billion of additional securities. He suggested a compromise which Congress promptly adopted and which became law ten days after the veto of the Garner bill. By this Act (the Emergency Relief and Construction Act of July, 1932), the RFC was authorized to make loans up to $300 million to such states as were absolutely unable to finance the relief of distress. The loans were to be repaid annually beginning in 1935 with interest at 3 per cent and were reminiscent of the 1837 loan to the states. However, Congress converted them into gifts in 1934. The Act also authorized the RFC to make loans to states and municipalities up to $1½ billion to finance self-liquidating public works, appropriated $322 million for public works which were not required to

TABLE 58.   FEDERAL EXPENDITURES, 1930–1933
(In millions of dollars)

	1930	1931	1932	1933
Legislative, Executive, Judicial, etc........	$ 67.2	$ 84.7	$ 99.4	$ 82.1
Treasury*............................	194.5	204.6	287.7	266.9
War................................	346.1	354.1	351.4	320.0
Navy...............................	375.4	354.1	357.8	349.7
Interior.............................	38.2	37.9	55.4	51.4
Agriculture..........................	177.3	296.9	319.0	251.0
Commerce...........................	57.1	61.4	52.7	46.0
Labor...............................	10.6	12.2	14.7	13.6
Veterans' Administration...............	433.3	554.7	626.6	600.3
Other independent offices†.............	48.2	52.0	52.8	45.2
Rivers and harbors....................	107.9	124.3	116.8	118.1
Post office (deficit)	91.7	145.6	202.9	117.4
Tax refunds.........................	152.7	91.8	101.0	68.3
Panama Canal........................	11.3	9.9	10.2	11.4
Pensions............................	219.0	234.1	232.5	235.0
Indian affairs........................	31.7	33.6	36.0	28.0
Adjusted Service Fund.................	112.1	232.9	188.6	107.6
Agricultural Marketing Fund...........	148.6	191.5	136.5	−5.3
Other special accounts‡................	139.7	103.1	746.6	1,441.0
Interest.............................	658.6	610.8	599.7	689.2
Adjustments.........................	9.1	−10.3	5.7	5.1
Totals............................	$3,440.3	$3,779.9	$4,594.0	$4,845.0§
Statutory debt retirement..............	$ 553.9	$ 440.1	$ 412.6	$ 461.6
Totals............................	$3,994.2	$4,220.0	$5,006.6	$5,306.6§

SOURCE: *Annual Reports of the Secretary of the Treasury, 1930–1933.*

* Includes besides regular Treasury functions, the construction and maintenance of public buildings, Coast Guard, Public Health Service, etc.

† Excludes RFC, Federal land banks, and Shipping Board.

‡ Includes RFC $500 million in 1932 and $1.3 billion in 1923, Federal land banks $125 million in 1932, Shipping Board $52 million in 1932 and $29 million in 1933, $35 million for distribution of wheat and cotton for relief in 1933, and Civil Service Retirement Fund, $21 million in 1932 and 1933.

§ This total is based on the old accounting system. Under a new system introduced in 1933 and carried back to 1932 in the historical series certain trust fund and special agency expenditures are excluded. See Table 69 for different totals for 1933.

be self-liquidating,[5] and authorized the Federal Reserve banks to make loans to individuals if accommodation could not be obtained through ordinary channels. Only $859,000 of such loans was made in 1932. But regular grants-in-aid increased from $102 million in 1930 to $157 million

[5] Including $120 million for Federal-aid highway system, $16 million for national forests and Indian reservations, $30 million for rivers and harbors, $15½ million for flood control, $10 million for Hoover Dam, $10 million for yards and docks, $15 million for Army posts, $5.1 million for the Department of Commerce.

in 1932, the largest increase being for highways. At the same time an emergency grant-in-aid program for relief and public works was inaugurated. It involved an annual outlay of $341 million in 1933.[6]

The Relief and Construction Act closed a chapter in American financial history by writing finis to the doctrine that welfare payments to individuals were outside the scope of the Federal government. The Hoover administration continued to pay lip service to the dictum that "though the people support the government, the government should not support the people," but it began to have a hollow sound, and when private charity, municipal government, and state resources proved unable to cope with the problem of relief, the President had no choice but to retreat from his oft-expressed opposition to Federal aid.

While expanding its expenditures for public works considerably, the Hoover administration also sought to reduce unessential expenditures. It kept down the expenditures of the War and Navy departments and attempted to effect economies in the operation of the veterans' services, which were notorious for their inefficiency and waste. Under an Act of July 3, 1930, the Veterans' Bureau, the Bureau of Pensions of the Interior Department, the National Home for Disabled Volunteer Soldiers, as well as certain units in the War Department were consolidated in one Veterans' Administration. How much economy was effected thereby was uncertain, inasmuch as at the same time some of the services and benefits for the veterans were greatly expanded. The administration's most comprehensive program of economy was developed during its last year in office, but only part of this program was enacted into law, and its effect was not realized until the administration went out of office.

From Surpluses to Deficits. In the early years of the depression, the administration was deceived in regard to the real state of Federal finances by the exceedingly cumbersome and inelastic nature of the Federal revenue system. Since it consisted to a large extent of personal and corporate income taxes assessed on incomes earned in the preceding calendar year, the revenue did not immediately reflect changes in business conditions. Thus the depression which began in the calendar year 1929 did not affect personal and corporate incomes until the calendar year 1930 and did not affect Federal revenue until the calendar year 1931. After it became evident that revenues were declining, it took a whole year to change the revenue laws and another year before the changes were even partly effective. Hence, the administration's attempts to balance the budget by increasing the revenue, although started in 1931, did not produce any results until 1933.

The administration planned its budgetary operations late in 1929 for

[6] Council of State Governments, *Federal Grants-in-Aid*, pp. 31–32.

the fiscal year 1931 in an atmosphere of optimism. The surplus in 1929 had been $185 million, and the Treasury expected that it would be even larger in fiscal 1930 because of the unusually high incomes of 1929. Indeed, in his budget message of December, President Hoover recommended a temporary cut in personal and corporate income taxes of some $160 million applicable on 1929 income tax returns, that is, on taxes due March 15, 1930. He estimated that, even with the reduction, there would be a $60 million surplus in 1931. Congress cheerfully adopted the President's recommendation before the month was over. The resulting measure, known as the Revenue Act of 1929, reduced the normal rate of the income tax and the corporate income tax rate by another 1 per cent, but only for one year.

As expected, the fiscal year 1930 ended with another large surplus, $184 million, for revenue collections were not as yet affected by the depression. However, by December, 1930, President Hoover had to change his forecasts for the fiscal year 1931 from a surplus to a deficit of $180 million. Under the circumstances, he could not recommend a repetition of the temporary tax reduction, and even with reinstated tax rates, he could promise a balanced budget in the fiscal year 1932 only if Congress refrained from increasing expenditures. Congress concurred, allowing the Revenue Act of 1929 to expire and the individual and corporate income taxes to go back to the rates of the 1928 Revenue Act.

In his budget message of December, 1931, the President reported a disastrous outlook for the fiscal year 1932. Receipts from personal and corporate income taxes were declining steadily, largely because of losses on the sale of capital assets. Customs revenue was falling off as foreign trade was coming to a standstill. Even the tobacco tax was declining, and there would be a default on Allied debt payments. In addition, expenditures would be slightly higher than anticipated. Instead of being neatly balanced as expected, the budget would show a $2.1 billion deficit —a sum which seemed staggering in a period of peacetime operation.

Faced with what he considered a fiscal emergency, President Hoover recommended that Congress reinstate, with a few alterations, the tax rates of the Revenue Act of 1924. According to his estimates, revenue would be increased by $390 million immediately and by $920 million more in the fiscal year 1933. Together with recommended economies of $370 million, this would eliminate the deficit in 1933 and provide enough revenue by 1934 to balance the budget, including statutory debt retirement. Thereafter, the increased taxes could be gradually repealed. The President concluded his message with renewed emphasis on the need for budgetary balance to reestablish confidence in the financial integrity of the government and to restore national prosperity.

What exactly was meant by a balanced budget was never clearly explained by the administration. Sometimes it appeared to mean that expenditures should equal receipts over a period of years, at other times that they be equal from year to year. Sometimes it seemed to mean that all expenditures—capital as well as current—be covered by current receipts, at other times that only current expenditures be so covered.[7] There was also disagreement as to whether the budget should be considered balanced on the basis of expenditures which included debt retirement or expenditures which did not. In the latter case, the deficit would appear much smaller.

Revenue Act of 1932. In January, 1932, the Treasury recommended (1) raising the normal rates of the personal income tax, (2) increasing the maximum surtax to 40 per cent on incomes in excess of $500,000, (3) lowering personal exemptions, (4) increasing the corporation income tax slightly, (5) reintroducing a number of miscellaneous wartime taxes, (6) increasing the maximum rate of the estate tax from 20 to 25 per cent, (7) imposing a gasoline tax, and (8) raising the postal rates so as to eliminate the $150 million postal deficit.

In the meanwhile, considerable sentiment developed among important business groups in favor of a manufacturers' sales tax instead of the miscellaneous excises and some of the proposed increases in income tax levies. The Treasury, though readily admitting certain advantages in the sales tax, at first opposed its introduction on the ground that it would entail too much additional work. However, the House Ways and Means Committee, in February, submitted a bill embodying a 2¼ per cent sales tax, estimated to yield approximately $600 million. It contained liberal exemptions for agricultural products and avoided pyramiding by exempting sales among manufacturers. While incorporating many of the other features of the Treasury program, the bill raised the rate of the corporation income tax to 13 per cent, made the new income tax rates applicable to 1932 rather than 1931 incomes, and raised the maximum rate of the estate tax to 40 per cent. It was estimated that the entire bill would produce $1.1 billion of additional revenue.

By the time the committee had reported its bill, Ogden Mills had replaced Mellon as Secretary of the Treasury. Shortly before, the Canadian

[7] In his annual report for 1931 Secretary Mellon declared that the maintenance of the public credit required that "over a period of years revenues must be equal to expenditures." Shortly thereafter, Undersecretary of the Treasury Mills said, "The principle of a balanced budget must never be abandoned, and when emergency conditions upset the balance, every effort must be made to restore it at the earliest opportunity." President Hoover included capital expenditures in his concept of a balanced budget, while Mills defined a balanced budget to mean "that current receipts will be adequate to cover current expenditures, and that borrowing will not be resorted to to pay the ordinary running expenses of the government."

sales tax had been thoroughly investigated by two tax experts of the Treasury, Professor Thomas Adams and E. C. Alvord, and Mills now definitely favored it. He therefore dropped the Treasury's original recommendations in favor of the House committee's measure, dissenting only from the proposed maximum 40 per cent estate tax rate.

When the House took up the committee's bill, a group of independent Republicans and Democrats, led by Fiorello H. LaGuardia, denounced the sales tax as regressive and succeeded in passing a substitute measure which omitted the sales tax but included many more manufacturers' and other excises on luxury goods, such as candy, chewing gum, cosmetics, jewelry, furs, and sporting goods. The measure also increased normal rates and surtaxes of the individual income tax and the corporation income tax, and it subjected income from dividends to the normal income tax, disregarding the complaint that this was double taxation of stockholders. Finally, it provided for a further tightening of the estate tax and for the reimposition of a gift tax. In general, it was designed to bear much more heavily on the high- and middle-income groups and much less heavily on the low-income groups than the original Treasury proposal or original House bill. The Treasury opposed the bill, contending that it would have an adverse effect on business and that it would not raise the necessary $1.1 billion of additional revenue.

Immediately after the House action, President Hoover sent a special message to Congress in which he estimated that annual savings of $250 million could be accomplished by placing government employees on a five-day week at reduced salaries and by giving the Executive Department broad powers to reorganize the government. Incessant wrangling between the Executive and the majority of Congress followed the President's message. The House insisted that the recommendations were too vague; the administration insisted that Congress was not interested in economy. The House wanted to cut government salaries; the administration wanted a furlough plan. Finally, the House passed a bill providing for an estimated $30 million of cuts.

At this point, amicable relations between Hoover and the Democratic Congress broke down completely. In May the President vetoed a tariff bill which would have stripped him of many of his powers over tariff administration. In the same month he denounced the House for failing to adopt his recommendations on taxes and economy and called upon the Senate to cut expenditures by more than $300 million and to balance the budget promptly so that business confidence might be restored. Finally, in June, 1932, the Senate passed a revenue bill which differed from the House measure only by making the income and estate tax rates even more progressive and retaining the existing exemption of dividends from the normal rate of the income tax. Hoover was dis-

TABLE 59. FEDERAL RECEIPTS, EXPENDITURES, AND DEBT, 1930–1933
(In millions of dollars)

	1930	1931	1932	1933
Receipts:				
Customs*.......................	$ 587.0	$ 378.4	$ 327.8	$ 250.8
Individual income...............	1,146.8	833.6	427.2	352.6
Corporate income...............	1,263.4	1,026.4	629.6	394.2
Estate and gift.................	64.8	48.1	47.4	34.3
Liquors.......................	11.7	10.4	8.7	43.2
Tobacco......................	450.3	444.3	398.6	402.7
Stamp, stock transfer, etc.........	77.7	47.0	32.2	57.3
Manufacturers' excises..........	2.7	0.1	....	243.6
Soft drinks.....................	....	....	....	4.2
Telephone, telegraph, etc.........	....	....	....	22.1
Checks, drafts, etc..............	....	....	....	40.8
Admissions and clubs............	16.8	14.3	11.1	22.2
Oleomargarine.................	3.9	2.7	1.7	1.3
Other taxes...................	2.0	1.3	1.2	1.3
Total tax receipts.............	$ 3,627.1	$ 2,806.6	$ 1,885.5	$ 1,870.6
Foreign debts—interest............	141.9	184.5	....	67.2
Foreign debts—principal...........	97.6	51.6	....	31.6
Miscellaneous, departmental, etc.....	182.5	146.7	116.7	125.8
Adjustments....................	−0.8	0.2	3.5	15.5
Total general and special fund receipts....................	$ 4,048.3	$ 3,189.6	$ 2,005.7	$ 2,079.7
Trust fund receipts...............	129.6	127.6	115.5	158.7
Totals......................	$ 4,177.9	$ 3,317.2	$ 2,121.2	$ 2,238.4†
Expenditures, including statutory debt retirement.....................	$ 3,994.2	$ 4,220.0	$ 5,006.6	$ 5,306.6†
Surplus (+) or deficit (−) after debt retirement.....................	$ +183.8	$ −902.7	$ −2,885.4	$ −3,068.2‡
Surplus (+) or deficit (−) before debt retirement...................	+737.7	−462.6	−2,472.8	−2,606.6
Gross debt......................	$16,185.3	$16,801.3	$ 19,487.0	$ 22,538.7
Interest-bearing debt..............	15,921.9	16,519.6	19,161.3	22,157.6

SOURCE: *Annual Report of the Secretary of the Treasury*, 1930–1933.

* Beginning with 1932, tonnage duties were reported in miscellaneous receipts.

† These tables are based on the old accounting system. Under a new system introduced in 1933 and carried back to 1932 in the historical series, certain trust fund and special agency receipts and expenditures are excluded. See Table 69 for different totals for 1933.

‡ *Annual Report of the Secretary of the Treasury*, 1933, p. 298; includes $3,063.2 million in general and special funds and $5 million in trust funds.

appointed with the result, since he preferred the sales tax. Nevertheless, he signed the bill, declaring, "While many of the taxes are not as I desired, the bill will effect the great major purpose of assurance to the country and the world of the determination of the American people to maintain their finances and their currency on a sound basis."[8]

The Act provided for the largest peacetime tax increase in history. It reduced exemptions from $3,500 and $1,500 to $2,500 and $1,000, raised the normal tax on 1932 incomes from 1½ to 5 per cent to 4 to 8 per cent, imposed surtaxes of 1 per cent on incomes of $6,000 to 55 per cent on incomes of $1 million or more, eliminated the earned-income credit, lowered the estate tax exemption from $100,000 to $50,000, raised the maximum rate from 20 to 45 per cent and did not extend the credit for state inheritance taxes to the additional rates, imposed a gift tax at rates of ¾ to 33½ per cent after exemptions of $50,000 in the aggregate and $5,000 per year to any one individual, raised the corporate tax from 12 to 13¾ per cent, and introduced a variety of manufacturers' and other excise taxes including a 1 cent gasoline tax. The Act practically restored the high income tax rates of the Act of 1921.

The administration's demand for economy still remained unattended, but in June Congress passed a measure cutting Federal spending by $134 million. It adopted the President's furlough scheme of putting government employees on a five-day week with an 8¼ per cent cut in salaries but gave him only a part of the reorganization powers he had requested.

Although on paper Congress had balanced the budget, it soon became evident that revenue would fall far short of expectations. In December, 1932, Mills estimated that receipts would be almost $500 million less than expected, but the actual returns were even more disappointing, for while the bill was being debated, there was heavy buying of goods in anticipation of the new excises, and the national income continued to decline with the result that higher tax rates enabled the Treasury only to hold its own.

Challenge to the Balanced-budget Doctrine. The general public, especially business leaders, believed wholeheartedly in a balanced budget, but they were just as vague in defining a balanced budget as were the politicians. Alfred P. Sloan believed that Congress should cut expenditures to the bone, balance the budget, and go home. Winthrop Aldrich and Bernard Baruch maintained that government revenue should be high enough to cover operating expenses and the interest on the debt but that capital outlays and loans could be financed by borrowing. Eugene

[8] For a fuller discussion of the controversies attending this enactment see Roy G. Blakey and Gladys C. Blakey, "Revenue Act of 1932," *American Economic Review*, December, 1932.

Grace thought that "taxes must come down, the burden of government costs must be lightened, and the budget must be balanced."[9]

Dissent from the faith in a balanced budget came from a small group of unorthodox economists and social commentators and an occasional businessman or banker. In 1931 John Maynard Keynes ridiculed the pursuit of economy and balanced budgets, saying, "If the theory which underlies all this is to be accepted, the end will be that no one can be employed except those happy few who grow their own potatoes."[10] Advocating increased government spending as the only sure road to recovery, Keynes observed that bringing up the bogy of inflation as an objection was like warning a patient who is wasting away from emaciation of the dangers of excessive corpulence.

In the December, 1932, issue of *Scribner's*, Stuart Chase carried the argument further, saying,

Government is the one employer in a time of tragic deflation which can carry its force. . . . No private business can afford to do so. The government is the one hope of maintaining purchasing power. It can, if it must, borrow and inflate. . . . That such action connotes risk is manifest, but emergencies require drastic remedies. . . . Prosperity can never be restored by spending less, but only by spending more.

Marriner S. Eccles told a Senate committee that the concept of a balanced budget was archaic. He denied that it was "necessary to conserve government credit to the point of providing a starvation existence for milions of our people." He also denied that an unbalanced budget undermined confidence and insisted that new taxes would merely reduce the buying power of the people and lead to more deflation.[11]

Changes in Size and Composition of the Debt. The depression made the problems of debt management much more complicated than they had been in prosperity, for in addition to refunding maturing short-term obligations, the Treasury had to borrow to cover operating deficits. In meeting these problems, the Treasury relied extensively on both long-term and short-term issues.

[9] *The New York Times*, Jan. 19, 1932.
[10] Dudley Dillard, *The Economics of John Maynard Keynes*, p. 312.
[11] Virgil Jordan developed this same point of view in a more sardonic manner, saying, "The idea that taxpayers actually save anything by public economy during a period of general deflation is a delusion. Those who so ardently urge a balancing of budgets and curtailment of public expenditures during depressions are gluttons for punishment. . . . What the end of the process is no one can say, although some of the whirling dervishes of deflation and the experts of the castor-oil school of economics assure us that ultimately we arrive at some mysterious automatic equilibrium point." (New York University, *Current Problems in Public Finance*, Commerce Clearing House, 1933.)

To provide more freedom in debt management, Congress in March, 1931, increased the Treasury's borrowing power under the Second Liberty Loan Act from $20 billion to $28 billion. Under this authorization, the Treasury immediately issued $594.2 million of 10–12-year bonds. In June it issued $821.4 million of 15-18's, and in September $800.4 million of 20-24's, making a total of $2.2 billion of long-term issues during the Hoover administration. In addition, the Treasury issued $3.0 billion of short terms between June, 1930, and March, 1933. Some of the new issues were used for refunding, and the gross debt increased $4.7 billion between June, 1930, and March, 1933.

TABLE 60.   FEDERAL DEBT, 1929–1933
(In millions of dollars)

	June, 1929	June, 1930	June, 1931	June, 1932	Mar. 1, 1933
Treasury bills................	....	$ 156	$ 445	$ 616	$ 641
Certificates of indebtedness......	$ 1,640	1,264	1,802	2,726	2,013
Treasury notes................	2,254	1,626	452	1,261	3,352
Prewar debt..................	770	773	776	790	806
Treasury bonds...............	11,354	11,339	12,754	13,460	13,424
Special issues................	620	764	291	309	348
Non-interest-bearing...........	293	264	282	326	350
Gross debt...................	$16,931	$16,185	$16,801	$19,487	$20,935

SOURCE: *Annual Report of the Secretary of the Treasury*, 1929–1933.

Fluctuations in Government Credit. The administration's anxiety to balance the budget was based upon a fear that an increase in government debt would undermine the government's credit. And in early 1932 the government's credit actually did weaken. Numerous bank failures at that time caused the market to be flooded with bonds, and prices declined, some Treasury issues sinking to 83. But as the excess supply was gradually eliminated, government-bond prices rallied. Thereafter, the Treasury found it possible to borrow at successively lower rates, for the demand for funds in the private economy constantly decreased and excess bank reserves constantly increased, forcing the banks to invest in government securities. The average yield on government bonds declined from 4.26 per cent in January, 1932, to 3.42 per cent in March, 1933, and the yield on certificates from 2.48 to 1.34 per cent during the same time.

The administration assumed that the basic cause of the inactive state of business was lack of confidence, which was evidenced by a tendency on the part of the public to hoard. As this tendency became stronger in 1932, the administration organized a psychological campaign, under the direction of Colonel Frank Knox, to counteract it and also attempted to attract hoarded savings by offering so-called "baby bonds," 1-year certificates of low denomination, bearing interest at 2 per cent. Since the Postal Savings System was paying the same rate and since the Treasury later offered 1-year certificates at 3¾ per cent, the bonds met with little success. On the other hand, the psychological campaign, which seemed less rational, was a considerable success.

TABLE 61. BANK HOLDINGS AND AVERAGE YIELDS ON GOVERNMENT SECURITIES, 1930–1933
(Dollar figures in millions)

	Dec., 1929	Dec., 1930	June, 1931	Dec., 1931	June, 1932	Dec., 1932
National banks..............	$2,609	$2,649	$3,251	$3,171	$3,347	$3,755
State member banks.........	1,254	1,476	2,092	2,148	2,281	2,784
All other commercial banks..	*	*	671	*	589	*
Federal Reserve banks.......	446	644	609	777	1,697	1,854
Mutual savings banks........	*	*	648	*	678	*
Yield on government bonds...	3.36%	3.22%	3.13%	3.93%	3.76%	3.35%
Yield on certificates.........	3.03%	1.48%	0.55%	2.41%	0.34%	0.04%
Average rate on new bills....	3.3 %	1.7 %	0.63%	3.25%	0.41%	0.09%

SOURCE: Federal Reserve Board, *Banking and Monetary Statistics*, 1943; *Banking Studies*, 1948.
* Not available.

Federal Reserve Attempts to Expand Credit. As soon as the stock-market crash occurred, the Federal Reserve banks reversed their policy of restricting the flow of credit to the member banks and tried to encourage expansion. The New York Bank reduced its rediscount rate to 4½ per cent in November, 2½ per cent in June, 1930, and 1½ in May, 1931. The Reserve banks also expanded member bank reserves by buying $150 million of government bonds in October, 1929. During the succeeding year through an Open Market Policy Conference established in March, 1930, and consisting of the 12 district governors, they bought an additional $300 million, increasing Reserve holdings to $600 million by October, 1930. A second bond-buying campaign started in June, 1931, raising total Reserve holdings to $777 million by the end of the year.

The easy-money policy did not succeed in expanding the use of credit, for there was a general desire for liquidity on the part of domestic citizens and foreign investors. Domestic hoarding was evidenced by an increase in money in circulation from $4.7 billion in January, 1931, to $5.5 billion in October, and foreign liquidation resulted in heavy gold exports. The reduction in the rediscount rate did not persuade entrepreneurs to borrow, and commercial bank loans declined steadily. At the same time, the reserves which were poured into the banks by the Federal Reserve's open-market purchases were not used to expand credit but to satisfy the foreign demand for gold and the domestic demand for currency.

Under the impact of withdrawals of currency, the Federal Reserve ratio declined from 77.5 per cent in September, 1931, to 62.6 per cent in October. The Reserve authorities were faced with a dilemma: Should an attempt be made to protect the reserve ratio at the expense of trying to encourage business borrowing, or should the policy of pouring reserves into the money market be continued regardless of what happened to the reserve ratio? It was decided to maintain the reserve ratio, and the rediscount rate in New York was increased to 3½ per cent in October, 1931. In the following months there was little increase in money in circulation, and there was some net import of gold. Consequently, the reserve ratio rose to 67.4 per cent in February, 1932, and the Federal Reserve banks returned to an easy-money policy, reducing the New York rediscount rate to 3 per cent and to 2½ per cent in June. Unfortunately, this maneuver was no more successful than the previous ones.

Attempts to Expand the Currency: The Glass-Steagall Act. Meanwhile, a new difficulty appeared. Under the Federal Reserve Act, Federal Reserve notes had to be backed by at least 40 per cent in gold with the remainder secured by commercial paper. But with the decline in business activity, the supply of commercial paper diminished and notes had to be backed increasingly with gold. In February, 1932, the commercial-paper holdings of the Reserve banks amounted to only $990 million, or 37 per cent of the $2.7 billion of outstanding notes. The remaining 63 per cent was in gold. The constant decline in commercial paper and the increasing use of gold as security for note issues constituted a serious threat to continued expansion of the currency, especially as gold exports had resumed and were running at the rate of $50 million a month. To avert the danger, it was decided to free the excess gold backing of the notes, and in late February, 1932, Congress passed the Glass-Steagall Act, authorizing the Federal Reserve banks to use government obligations as well as commercial paper as collateral for note issues. The authorization was to expire in March, 1933, but it was extended from time to time and made permanent in June, 1945. The Act, by making possible continuous buying of government obligations without fear of contracting the currency supply, removed one of the potential restrictions on Federal Reserve credit control. In addition, it authorized, with certain qualifications, socalled "lombard loans" (advances to member banks on their promissory notes secured by any assets satisfactory to the Reserve banks).

The Glass-Steagall Act ushered in the third and most ambitious open-market operation. The New York Bank alone bought government obligations at the rate of $25 million, and later $100 million, a week. In March, 1932, Reserve holdings of governments increased from $740 million to $872 million; in April, to $1.2 billion; and by July, to $1.8 billion. However, the open-market campaign once again failed to stimulate business borrowing. Instead, the proceeds were used to reduce rediscounts by about $400 million, to cover $300 million of gold exports, to raise money in circulation by $125 million, and to increase excess reserves by $160 million.

Congressional Inflationary Proposals. As it became increasingly evident that Federal Reserve policy was not succeeding in bringing prosperity around the corner, inflationists in Congress demanded more radical measures. During the Seventy-second Congress, they introduced more than fifty inflation bills. Although these included such old stand-bys as free silver and greenbacks as well as the Frazier-Sinclair bill to set up a land bank similar to those of colonial days, some inflationists had become more sophisiticated. Greatly impressed by Professor Irving Fisher's "commodity dollar," a refined version of the quantity theory of money, they introduced in the spring of 1932 the Goldsborough bill, authorizing and directing the Federal Reserve System "to take all available steps to raise the present deflated wholesale commodity level of prices as speedily as possible to the level existing before the present deflation, and afterwards to use all available means to maintain such wholesale commodity level of prices." Unlike the measures introduced during the secular price decline of the latter nineteenth century, the Goldsborough bill did not propose to raise prices by coining more silver or by issuing more greenbacks. It proposed to raise and stabilize prices by broadening the Federal Reserve Board's open-market operations and by authorizing the Board to raise or lower the official price of gold, or, in other words, to devalue or revalue the dollar. Subsequently, the bill was somewhat modified, and when it passed the House in May (289 to 60), it charged the Federal Reserve System and the Secretary of the Treasury "with the duty of making effective . . . by the control of the volume of credit and currency" a policy of restoration and maintenance of the "average purchasing power of the dollar as ascertained by the Department of Labor in the wholesale commodity markets for the period covering the years 1921 to 1929, inclusive." Conservative forces in the Senate succeeded in shunting aside the Goldsborough bill. Instead, they attached to the Home Loan Bank Act of July, 1932, the Glass-Borah amendment, making all Federal bonds of 3⅜ per cent or less eligible as security for national-bank notes for a period of three years, thus making possible an increase of $900 million in the volume of currency. However, since there was no demand for additional currency, the national banks did not take advantage of the privilege to the full extent and issued only $200 million of new notes.

Commercial Banking Developments, 1930 to 1932. Commercial banking operations during these three and a half years were featured by a vast increase in the number of suspensions, an even greater contraction in the number of banks, a gradual but steady decline in deposits and commercial

TABLE 62.   COMMERCIAL-BANK SUSPENSIONS, 1930–1932

	1930	1931	1932
Total suspensions	1,350	2,293	1,453
Member banks	188	516	331
Nonmember banks	1,162	1,777	1,122
As a percentage of total banks	6%	10%	8%
Total deposits (millions)	$837	$1,690	$706
Member banks	$373	.$ 733	$269
Nonmember banks	$464	$ 957	$437
Estimated loss to depositors (millions)	$237	$ 391	$168

SOURCE: Federal Reserve Board, *Banking and Monetary Statistics.*

TABLE 63.   BANKING OPERATIONS, 1930–1932
(Dollar figures in millions)

	Dec. 31, 1929	June 30, 1931	June 30, 1932	Dec. 29, 1932	Per cent decline
All commercial banks:					
Number	24,026	21,309	18,449	17,802	27
Loans	$35,966	$29,166	$21,806	$20,081	44
Investments	13,501	15,687	14,285	15,002	+12
Total deposits	50,994	46,974	35,484	35,957	30
Time deposits	19,192	18,691	14,049	13,631	29
United States securities	4,950	6,014	6,217	6,800	+37
Member banks:					
Number	8,522	7,782	6,980	6,816	20
Loans	$26,150	$21,816	$16,587	$15,204	42
Open-market paper	582	885	658	723	+24
On securities	10,148	8,334	5,570	5,205	49
Real estate	3,191	3,218	2,894	2,862	10
Other*	11,515	8,922	6,892	5,970	47
Investments	9,784	12,106	11,414	12,265	+25
Deposits	37,981	36,123	27,836	28,690	25
Total assets	48,108	44,837	35,856	36,245	25
Mutual savings bank deposits	8,838	9,928	9,927	9,929	+12
Postal savings deposits	159	342	780	897	+464

SOURCE: Federal Reserve Board, *Banking and Monetary Statistics.*

* Not including interbank loans.

loans, an increase in the amount of investments especially in United States securities, and a vast increase in the desire for liquidity as evidenced by a phenomenal rise in savings bank deposits.

As had been demonstrated during the prosperity era, the Federal Reserve System had not eliminated bank failures. However, during the depression following 1929, unlike previous major business recessions, bank failures occurred in clusters rather than being concentrated in the panic phase of the cycle. Therefore, the Federal Reserve System seems to have made banking less susceptible to sudden and drastic deflation. While total bank suspensions were tragically high for the whole banking structure, failures continued to be much higher among nonmember banks, small banks, and banks in agricultural communities. Nonmember banks accounted for 80 per cent of total failures and 57 per cent of total deposits; 85 per cent of total suspensions were in the nation's five agricultural sections, and the first large bank failure in a large city did not occur until December, 1930, when the Bank of the United States suspended in New York City.

Although bank failures totaled 5,096 during these years of depression, the number of banks declined by 6,224, the difference representing bank mergers or consolidations.

Establishment of the Reconstruction Finance Corporation and Other Lending Institutions. The depression of the thirties differed from previous major depressions in that liquidation and deflation became increasingly worse as time wore on. Whereas in the first eighteen months of depression loans declined by 20 per cent, in the second they declined 30 per cent, and bank suspensions in 1931 were almost twice as large as in 1930. The extreme deflation made it impossible for banks to liquidate their assets except at huge losses. Yet they had to liquidate in order to meet withdrawals of deposits. Under the circumstances, the Federal government for the first time in history took steps to protect the banks against the losses of forced liquidation. Following the typical Hoover pattern, the first attempt was to appeal to private initiative. In September, 1931, the President proposed to the Federal Reserve Advisory Council that the banks form a pool to discount frozen assets for the weaker banks. Then in October a more formal organization, the National Credit Corporation, was created to make loans to needy banks against acceptable assets. Capital was to be raised by having the banks subscribe 2 per cent of their net deposits. The corporation opened in late October, 1931, but it could not cope with the banking crisis, and during its entire career it made loans of less than $150 million.

In his annual message of December, 1931, Hoover recommended the establishment of "an emergency Reconstruction Corporation," along the lines of the War Finance Corporation, to make loans to financial institutions which were in difficulties. He said, "It may not be necessary to use such an instrumentality very extensively. The very existence of such a bulwark will strengthen confidence." He did not abandon his faith in the adequacy of private, voluntary measures of assistance but considered that the government corporation's functions "would not overlap those of the National Credit Corporation." Congress acted promptly, creating the Reconstruction Finance Corporation in January, 1932. Its capital stock of $500 million was to be fully subscribed by the United States, and in addition, it could sell $1.5 billion of debentures. By amendment, under the Emergency Relief and Construction Act of July, 1932, its borrowing power was further increased to $3.3 billion. The corporation was authorized to make "fully and adequately secured" loans to banks and insurance companies, temporary loans to railroads which could not obtain funds upon reasonable terms from banks or from the general public, and, by the Emergency Relief and Construction Act of 1932, loans to states and to farmers. The corporation's lending powers were to expire in January, 1933, but they were extended from time to time by presidential order and by subsequent amendments.

Up to March, 1933, the RFC authorized $2.9 billion of loans. It actually loaned $2.2 billion, of which $1.8 billion was still outstanding ($669 million to banks, $361 million to public agencies, $302 million in agricultural credit, $296 million to railroads, $115 million for housing, $63 million to insurance companies, and $19 million to miscellaneous loans).[12]

About 40 per cent of the RFC's first-year loans were made in the quarter ending June, 1932. Most of them were to institutions located in small communities. For example, 70 per cent of the first 5,000 banks to obtain loans were in towns of less than 5,000 population, and only 5.3 per cent were in cities of over 1 million.

In its early operation the RFC undoubtedly prevented the bankruptcy of many railroads and saved many banks, but it did not eliminate failures completely. The emphasis on "full and adequate security" was a mistake. However, the Democratic Congress, despite the opposition of the administration, insisted upon inserting in the law a provision which was far worse. In amending the Act in July, 1932, it directed the corporation to report to the President and Congress the names of borrowers together with the amounts and the rate of interest. The Clerk of the House took this to mean that the information was to be made public. Thus, the public was apprised of every bank which was in a critical financial condition with the result that the condition of these banks often became further aggravated. Furthermore, the law prohibited any loan made "for the purpose of initiating, setting on foot, or financing any enterprise not initiated, set on

[12] *Quarterly Reports of the Reconstruction Finance Corporation.*

foot, or undertaken prior to the adoption of this act." In other words, the law was really for relief rather than reconstruction. As such, its contribution to economic recovery was necessarily limited.

In the same message of December, 1931, the President recommended a general reform of the banking structure. In January, 1932, he added more detail, proposing (1) to require all commercial banks to belong to the Federal Reserve System, (2) to create a system of uniform inspection for all commercial banks, (3) to separate commercial banks from their security affiliates, (4) to exclude long-term credits from demand deposit banks, (5) to separate savings from demand deposit institutions, (6) to permit national banks to engage in state-wide branch banking, and (7) to create a system of mortgage discount banks. Senator Glass introduced a bill containing most of the President's recommendations, but it was immediately criticized by a great number of bankers and failed to pass, although it unquestionably would have added great strength to the banking system. By refusing to pass it, Congress made it necessary to adopt the reforms piecemeal over a long period of time, and some provisions still remain to be adopted.

The Hoover administration attempted in other ways to protect capital institutions and prevent further deflation. It established the Home Loan Bank system in July, 1932, with a capital of $125 million provided by the RFC. Twelve banks were established with authority to rediscount first mortgages for lending institutions, such as savings banks, building and loan associations, and insurance companies. Rediscounts were limited to 60 per cent of the value of the mortgage, but they were not to apply to mortgages for more than fifteen or less than eight years or in excess of 40 per cent of the property value, or on homes valued at more than $20,000. With all these qualifications, it was apparent that the Home Loan Banks could not offer much relief to the distressed homeowner, and by March, 1933, only $9 million of rediscounts was outstanding. However, they afforded an important precedent for a much more comprehensive system of loans to homeowners established in the next administration.

The Hoover administration also attempted to provide greater credit facilities for agriculture. In 1932, at the height of deflation, the Treasury was authorized to invest an additional $125 million in the capital of the Federal land banks. By the Emergency Relief and Construction Act, the RFC was directed to make $200 million available to the Secretary of Agriculture for direct emergency loans to farmers. Finally, the RFC was to provide capital for an Agricultural Credit Corporation which could make direct short-term loans to farmers. By April, 1933, over $100 million of such loans were outstanding.

In all its attempts to shore up the economic structure, except in the case of agriculture, the Hoover administration gave financial assistance only to institutions and then only against excellent assets. The net result was that little relief was given to the real sore spots of deflation and the large funds made available by the Federal government were hardly tapped.

International Financial Problems. In the early thirties three significant events took place in America's international economic relations: the decline in American foreign investments, the passage of the Hawley-Smoot tariff bill, and the Hoover moratorium on international debt payments. Neither of the first two was a·fundamental factor in causing the American depression, but each was an intensifying factor. When new foreign loans fell from $905 million in 1930 to $229 million in 1931, foreign purchases which were financed from these loans fell off correspondingly and lowered the demand for goods. In like manner, the Hawley-Smoot Tariff intensified the depression, for besides contributing directly to the decline of international trade, it contributed indirectly by accelerating the trend toward economic nationalism.

When the administration took up the tariff, it had no intention of raising rates generally. It sought to raise rates merely on farm products and reform the flexible provisions. But the die-hard protectionists, led by Senator Smoot of Utah and Congressman Hawley of Oregon, thought otherwise. After more than a year of consideration and despite vociferous protests and threats of retaliation from foreign countries, Congress enacted in June, 1930, sweeping increases, raising rates to the highest in history. Changes were made in 1,125 items, 34 per cent of those listed as dutiable; 890 were increases and 235 were decreases, the most important increases being on agricultural products and textiles.[13]

The Hawley-Smoot Tariff also made some important changes in the flexible provision. Whereas the Fordney-McCumber Act had vested responsibility for instituting investigations on changes in cost of production in the President alone, the Hawley-Smoot Act permitted the Tariff Commission to make investigations on its own motion or at the request of any interested party. The commission could then specify rate changes for the President's approval up to 50 per cent of the statutory rate. This change offered an enormous possibility for improvement in the tariff administration and was the factor which caused Hoover to sign the bill. But it left unchanged the principle of equalization of foreign and domestic costs. Actually, the operation of the flexible provision under the new act was little better than it had been under the Fordney-McCumber Act. Ten of the commission's investigations resulted in increases of

[13] The average tariff rate on agricultural products was 19.86 per cent in 1922, 33.62 per cent in 1930. The average rate on wool and woolen manufactures increased from 49.54 to 59.83 per cent. The average rate on metals rose from 33.71 to 35.01 per cent. (Frank Taussig, "The Tariff of 1930," *Quarterly Journal of Economics,* November, 1930.)

rates, 20 in decreases, 25 in no change, and in four cases the President sent the report back for more information.

The cessation of American capital exports and the effects of the Hawley-Smoot Tariff broke down the European economy which had been in precarious condition ever since the end of the war. In May, 1931, the Kredit Anstalt, the largest bank in Austria, announced that it was in difficulties. The Austrian government appealed to Western Europe for a loan, which was made by Great Britain. Subsequently, the breakdown spread to Germany, and the German government announced that it could no longer meet its international obligations. It was evident that, for the moment at least, payments on international debts could not be made.

On June 20, 1931, having previously consulted with the leaders of both parties in Congress, President Hoover issued a statement offering a moratorium on all international payments due to the United States during the fiscal year 1932 provided that the other important creditor nations would take similar action. General agreement to the plan was not obtained until July 6. Meanwhile, a scramble for liquidity began, and Great Britain, who had made long-term loans, was pressed for payment by her short-term creditors. In September, 1931, she abandoned the gold standard. At the same time, the United States began to lose gold as foreign investors liquidated their American securities. In the summer of 1931 earmarking of gold increased, and in October $337.7 million was exported, by far the largest amount on record. Despite this pressure, the stability of the dollar was never threatened. Unlike previous emergencies such as had occurred in the 1890's and in 1914, the American gold stock could not be endangered by European runs, for even at its lowest point, the United States possessed more than 36 per cent of the world's monetary gold stock.

Ineffectiveness of the Hoover Policies. The Hoover administration adopted many measures designed to turn the tide of the depression. But most of them lacked boldness and were adopted too late to be effective. The adherence to the doctrine of a balanced budget at all costs was its gravest error. However, at that time the doctrine was entertained generally, and it began to be abandoned only in the next administration, when its futility in a deflationary period had become more clearly and more painfully apparent. Even though the doctrine could not be followed literally, it led the Hoover administration to recommend tax increases which tended to prevent economic expansion, and it kept the administration from adopting more vigorous spending and lending policies. Those which were adopted—always with profuse apologies—did tend to increase the national income (see Table 64), but they were too small to offset the decline in private and municipal spending and investment and were important chiefly as precedents for the bolder approach of the succeeding administration.

The results of the easy-money policies were equally disappointing. They did not increase bank lending, for easy money was also cautious money and entrepreneurs for the most part were interested in neither expanding nor borrowing.

TABLE 64.   NET INCOME-INCREASING GOVERNMENT EXPENDITURES, 1930–1932

Calendar year	Federal (millions)	State and local (millions)	Total (millions)	Federal by fiscal year (millions)	Gross national product by calendar year (billions)
1930	$ 249.0	$844.5	$1,093.5	$−535.7	$90.9
1931	1,749.9	596.9	2,346.8	1,302.0	75.9
1932	1,822.3	353.2	2,175.5	1,880.2	58.3

SOURCE: H. H. Villard, *Deficit Spending and the National Income*, pp. 287, 293, 323; *Survey of Current Business*, July, 1950.

Campaign of 1932. The presidential campaign of 1932 began at a most unpropitious moment. The economy was at its lowest point. International trade was almost at a standstill. Many European nations had abandoned the gold standard, and the trend was more and more in the direction of exchange controls and trade restrictions. The problem of international debts was in a state of suspended animation. Domestically, the Reconstruction Finance Corporation had just begun operations, but the banking structure was very precarious. Hoarding of currency was rampant, and the administration lived in daily fear of the breakdown of the gold standard. Politically, the machinery of government was bogged down in petty wrangling, and faith in the President was shattered irreparably. It became certain that the person who obtained the Democratic nomination was assured of the Presidency.

President Hoover was renominated by the Republican party on a platform which extolled his administration, laid the severity of the American depression on the European doorstep, and viewed "with profound dismay" the ineptitude of the Democratic Congress. More specifically, the platform emphasized many of the principles laid down in the Republican platform of 1896. It favored the "extension of the general Republican principle of tariff protection," the principle of a balanced budget, the maintenance of the gold standard, and an international conference on money. It also promised farm relief with control of acreage, but without burdensome bureaucracy. It called for general reorganization of the government, various welfare projects, and the tightening of credit to discourage wholesale speculation in securities.

The Democratic party nominated Governor Franklin D. Roosevelt on a platform which was far from radical. It advocated

. . . drastic reduction of governmental expenditures by abolishing useless commissions and offices . . . to accomplish a saving of not less than 25 per cent . . . maintenance of the national credit by a Federal budget annually balanced . . . a sound currency to be preserved at all hazards and an international monetary conference . . . a competitive tariff for revenue . . . extension of Federal credit to the states to provide unemployment relief wherever the diminishing resources of the states make it impossible for them to provide for the needy . . . unemployment and old-age insurance under state laws . . . enactment of every constitutional measure that will aid the farmers to receive prices in excess of cost.

It demanded banking reform along the lines of the Glass bill, opposed cancellation of debts owed by foreign nations, and denounced various policies and tactics of the Republican administration, such as the Hawley-Smoot Tariff, the State Department's informal control over foreign investments, the "extravagance" of the Farm Board, and the "utterances of high public officials designed to influence stock exchange prices."

Basically, there was little difference between the two platforms. The Democratic party supported Federal aid to states where necessary, but this principle had been endorsed by Hoover when he signed the Emergency Relief and Construction Act. The Republican platform supported the gold standard, while the Democratic platform was for "sound currency." There were a difference of opinion on the tariff and a mutual conviction that the other party was incompetent. But in the course of the campaign it became clear that the two candidates differed sharply in their interpretation of the economic crisis and in the spirit of their remedial approach.

Roosevelt surrounded himself with a group of academic experts, inspiredly dubbed the "Brain Trust." The leader of this group, Raymond Moley, did much to persuade Roosevelt that the economic crisis was domestic in nature and required domestic remedies. On the other hand, Hoover was more strongly convinced than ever that the depression was of European origin. Roosevelt also emphasized the need for change. In one of his campaign speeches he said, "The country needs, and, unless I mistake its temper, the country demands bold, persistent experimentation." He was not averse philosophically to extending the power of the Federal government. Furthermore, he believed that "our basic trouble was an insufficient distribution of buying power," and he promised a "New Deal" containing vast social reforms. Hoover disagreed with this whole point of view. He distrusted experimentation, and he was philosophically opposed to extending the power of the Federal government.

Even long after he had in practice resorted to government action, he clung to his faith in the omnipotence of individual initiative and he did not believe that pouring money into the hands of consumers was an open sesame to economic prosperity. These differences between the two candidates were esoteric, and their importance became apparent only with the passage of time. In the meanwhile, the public emphasized differences in personality and, becoming convinced that the alleged inactivity of Hoover would be replaced by energetic action by Roosevelt, voted Roosevelt into office.

Post-election Problems. The disadvantages of the American political system were thrown into sharp relief by the events that occurred between Roosevelt's election and his inauguration. During those four months, the nation was plagued by international, fiscal, and banking crises, but there was no governmental machinery which could take effective action.

Under the Hoover moratorium, payment on international debts again became due in December, 1932, but the European nations, with the British government taking the initiative, requested a renegotiation of the whole debt question. In a letter to Roosevelt suggesting that the President-elect stop in Washington to discuss the request, Hoover wrote, "I do not favor cancellation in any form . . . we should be receptive to proposals . . . of tangible compensation in other forms than direct payment in expansion of markets for the products of our labor and our farms." Although Roosevelt agreed to confer, he insisted that responsibility for the problem rested with the incumbent administration and that existing diplomatic channels afforded the most convenient avenue for negotiation. After the conference, Hoover and Roosevelt issued separate statements, but both agreed that the loans were extended originally with the understanding that they would be paid off, that all international debts should be considered separately, and that Congress alone had power to alter the agreements. Their only concession to the debtors was a recommendation that the question of capacity to pay should be considered. When the time for payment arrived, Great Britain, Italy, and a few small nations met the installment, but France and most of the other debtors did not.

One of the most awkward effects of the delay between election and inauguration was that Hoover was required to submit a budget which would not begin to operate until he was out of office for three months. In this budget Hoover recommended reductions in Federal pay and veterans' benefits and reorganization of the government and the Veterans' Administration. If these cuts were adopted, he estimated that expenditures would be $3.3 billion in 1933-1934 compared with $4.8

billion in 1932–1933. He estimated receipts at $2.9 billion compared with $2.2 billion in fiscal 1933. The revenue gain would mostly come from a recommended 2¼ per cent manufacturers' sales tax, estimated to yield $355 million. The Democratic leaders also expressed a desire for a balanced budget, but they were cold to the Hoover plan and specifically rejected the sales tax. Nevertheless, Hoover continued to urge his program, saying "The Congress has already established a sales tax as the basis of one-quarter of the whole public revenue. To extend this form of taxation is neither new nor revolutionary." However, the Democratic leaders decided to wait until after March 4 to take action. Consequently, Hoover's budgetary motions were much ado about nothing.

Banking Collapse of February, 1933. The greatest problem of the transitional period was the increasing instability and final collapse of the entire banking system. Bank suspensions increased substantially as early as the late spring and early summer of 1932.[14] President Hoover placed the responsibility for the increase on Congress's failure to balance the budget, the publication of information on RFC loans, and the failure of the Democratic platform to support the gold standard unequivocally. But these were aggravating, rather than fundamental, factors. The root of the difficulty was in the banking system itself. The RFC had neither prevented bank failures nor revived the public's confidence in the banks. There was therefore a general desire for liquidity among the banks as well as among individuals, and as Jacob Viner expressed it, "Banking failures were survived only by those banks which were most quick and expert in converting themselves into safety deposit institutions." The desire for liquidity produced a vicious circle, for it resulted in bank failures which intensified the desire for liquidity, resulting in more failures. Since there was not enough cash to make simultaneous conversion possible, the endless round could only end in complete collapse of the banking structure.

The first event in the banking debacle occurred on October 31, 1932, when the lieutenant governor of Nevada proclaimed a twelve-day banking holiday. Then on February 4, 1933, Louisiana declared a holiday to commemorate the anniversary of the severance of diplomatic relations with Germany. These holidays served to convince the public that the banking structure was on its last legs. By this time, too, the press was reporting in great detail that the President-elect was in favor of "reflating" the dollar, and many of the influential leaders of the Democratic party were stating openly that the United States should inflate the money

---

[14] Bank suspensions declined from 342 in January to 46 in March, but there were 82 in May, 132 in July, 242 in January, 1933, and 154 in February. (*Annual Reports of the Federal Reserve Board.*)

supply either by abandoning the gold standard or by adopting a managed currency. As a result, the character of the liquidation changed fundamentally. Instead of redeeming their assets for currency, the public now demanded gold, and runs developed on the Federal Reserve banks as well as on the individual commercial banks. Beginning in February, the gold stock, the member bank deposits, and the reserve ratio of the Reserve banks declined alarmingly under the pressure of gold exports and increased hoarding.

TABLE 65.   FEDERAL RESERVE OPERATIONS, FEBRUARY TO MARCH, 1933
(Dollar figures in millions)

	Deposits	Federal Reserve notes	Total cash reserve	Reserve ratio per cent	Money in circulation	Gold stock in Treasury and Reserve banks
Feb. 1......	$2,540	$2,730	$3,457	65.6	$5,652	$3,477
Feb. 8......	2,500	2,773	3,442	65.3	5,705	3,459
Feb. 15.....	2,376	2,891	3,387	64.4	5,854	3,418
Feb. 21.....	2,399	3,000	3,305	61.2	5,988	3,345
Feb. 28.....	2,236	3,417	3,126	55.3	6,545	3,159
Mar. 1......	2,157	3,580	3,067	53.5	6,719	3,105
Mar. 2......	2,178	3,769	2,997	50.4	6,960	3,041
Mar. 3......	2,094	4,103	2,810	45.3	7,414	2,861
Mar. 4......	2,053	4,165	2,802	45.1	7,485	2,853

SOURCE: *Federal Reserve Bulletin*, April, 1933.

When the Michigan banking system collapsed on February 14, 1933, President Hoover wrote to Roosevelt, suggesting "the desirability of clarifying the public mind on certain essentials which will give renewed confidence." His message set forth the conservative viewpoint admirably. In part he said:

The facts about this last interruption are simple. . . . With the election there came the natural and inevitable hesitation. . . . But a number of very discouraging things have happened on top of this natural hesitation. The breakdown in balancing the budget; . . . the proposals for inflation of the currency . . . ; the publication of the RFC loans and the bank runs, hoarding, and bank failures from this cause; increase in unemployment due to imports from depreciated currency countries; failure of the Congress to enact banking and other vital legislation; proposals to abrogate constitutional responsibility by the Congress, with all the chatter about dictatorship. It would steady the country greatly, if there could be prompt assurance that there will be no tampering or inflation of the currency; that the budget will be unquestionably balanced, even if further taxation is necessary; that the Government credit will be maintained by refusal to exhaust it in the issue of securities.

This was a most extraordinary letter, for, as Hoover himself wrote to Senator Reed,

I realize that if these declarations be made by the President-elect, he will have ratified the whole major program of the Republican Administration; that is, it means the abandonment of 90 per cent of the so-called new deal. But unless this is done, they run a grave danger of precipitating a complete financial debacle.[15]

In short, through the vagaries of the political system, a repudiated administration confronted an incoming administration with a choice of either abandoning its program or causing a complete breakdown of the national economy.

Because of an almost inconceivable mixup, Roosevelt's reply was delayed for almost two weeks. It stated among other things:

The real trouble is that on present values very few financial institutions anywhere in the country are actually able to pay off their deposits in full, and the knowledge of this fact is widely held. Bankers with the narrower viewpoint have urged me to make a general statement, but even they seriously doubt if it would have a definite effect.[16]

The banking panic gathered speed daily. During the week ending March 1, over $200 million in gold was withdrawn from the Federal Reserve banks, and during the next few days another $200 million was withdrawn, bringing the gold reserve down almost to the legal minimum. Meanwhile, more governors declared bank holidays, and President Hoover suggested to the Federal Reserve Board the possibility of a Federal guarantee of bank deposits. The Board countered with a recommendation that the President proclaim a general bank holiday. Exactly what took place in the last days of the Hoover administration is vague. Myers and Newton insist that Roosevelt told Hoover that he did not favor closing the banks. Moley insists that Hoover said he would do nothing.[17] Regardless of which view is correct, the crisis approached its inevitable conclusion. At 4:20 on the morning of March 4 Governor Lehman was persuaded to issue a proclamation closing the New York banks, which were being pressed hard by withdrawals by foreign and domestic banks. On the morning of Inauguration Day, therefore, almost all the commercial banks in the country were already closed, and the New Deal had the opportunity of making the most dramatic entrance in American political history.

[15] Myers and Newton, *op. cit.* pp. 339*ff.*
[16] *Ibid.*, p. 345.
[17] Raymond Moley, *After Seven Years*, p. 144.

Chapter 28: THE NEW DEAL: MONETARY, BANKING, AND TARIFF POLICIES

The New Deal covered a period of over seven years, from March, 1933, to June, 1940, when the commencement of war preparations lifted the economy out of its subnormal state, terminated all government concerns with recovery, and ended social and economic reforms for the time being.

The New Deal was not so much a revolution as the culmination of trends long in the process of development, for in its early phases, at least, it continued on a broader scale the antidepression policies inaugurated by Hoover. It strove for economy and a balanced budget, proceeded with plans for government reorganization, expanded the credit agencies inherited from the Hoover administration, and reformed the banking system along the lines of the Glass bill which had been unsuccessfully introduced long before. New departures were made in the TVA, NRA, AAA, and SEC. However, the Hoover administration had started the construction of the Boulder Dam, and just before it left office it was making attempts to cut farm acreage and was considering proposals to control the securities markets.

The economic difficulties which changed the course of the Hoover administration and caused it to enter into broader fields than were originally contemplated continued to be felt in the Roosevelt administration with the result that there was not one New Deal, but two or even three. Action was continually improvised. No hard-and-fast program or consistent strategy or abstract philosophy ever gained the upper hand. The first New Deal, March, 1933, to mid-1935, emphasized recovery more than reform. The dominant goal was to increase prices. Under the influence of Moley and, to a lesser extent, Berle, Baruch, Tugwell, Wallace, Hugh Johnson, and others, attempts at "economic planning," such as the NRA and the AAA, were made. But above all, the emphasis was on monetary techniques—the abandonment of the gold standard, the Warren gold-buying program, and the devaluation of the dollar. All these programs assumed that the American depression was domestic in nature, and they were pursued regardless of their adverse international implications.

The second New Deal, mid-1935 to the depression of 1937, shifted the emphasis from recovery to social and economic reform. It catered particularly to labor and antagonized most of the business group. It abandoned economic nationalism and moved gradually toward fiscal, rather than monetary, controls. The third New Deal, mid-1937 to June, 1940, was characterized by renewed emphasis on recovery, and definite allegiance was given to new doctrines of fiscal policy. The phrase "balanced budget" was replaced by "deficit financing," and the desire for economy was supplanted by a desire for full employment.

Reopening of the Banks and Suspension of the Gold Standard. The banking crisis was the most immediate problem facing the Roosevelt administration. As early as the morning of Inauguration Day, the new Secretary of the Treasury William H. Woodin attacked the problem in conference with the outgoing Treasury officials, including ex-Secretary Mills and Undersecretary Arthur A. Ballantine. By Monday, March 6, the Treasury was ready with a plan of action. Rejecting the proposal to nationalize the banks, which had extensive Congressional and public support, the administration decided to keep the banks closed until the public could be convinced that the banking system was safe. The plan was to abandon the gold standard, to issue an appeal for confidence, and to make a tremendous gesture toward economy. In addition, the RFC was to give financial assistance to the weaker banks, and the Federal Reserve System was to make advances to nonmember as well as to member banks.

On March 6 the President, under the authority of the wartime Trading with the Enemy Act, issued an Executive Order closing all banks until March 9 and prohibiting them from exporting, earmarking, paying out, or allowing the withdrawal of specie. On March 9 Congress, meeting in special session, passed the Emergency Banking bill to help reopen most of the closed banks. It approved the action of March 6 and gave the President wide powers over specie transactions; authorized the Secretary of the Treasury to require the transfer of all gold and gold certificates to the Treasury of the United States; authorized banks to issue 6 per cent cumulative, nonassessable preferred stock eligible for RFC subscription; revived Federal Reserve bank notes, allowing them to be issued against government bonds, commercial paper, or bankers' acceptances; authorized the Comptroller of the Currency to appoint conservators to reopen or liquidate closed banks; and permitted the Reserve banks for one year to make loans secured by satisfactory assets at 1 per cent above the established rediscount rate. On March 10 the United States was taken off the gold standard by an Executive Order prohibiting the export of gold coin, bullion, or certificates except under license issued by the Secretary of the Treasury. To prevent speculation, banks were not permitted to engage in transactions in foreign exchange unless "undertaken for legitimate and normal business requirements."

In an effort to revive the public's confidence in the banking structure, the President delivered his first "fireside chat" on March 12. A number of people, including Arthur A. Ballantine, contributed to this speech which was a psychological masterpiece as well as an exposition of elementary banking principles. After explaining what had been done and announcing that, beginning the next day, the banks would be gradually reopened, the President said, "It needs no prophet to tell you that when the people find that they can get their money . . . the phantom of fear will soon be laid. . . . I can assure you that it is safer to keep your money in a reopened bank than under the mattress." He did not promise that every bank would be reopened or that individual losses would not be suffered, but he pointed out that a sound banking system could be created only if it was recognized that

. . . there is an element in the readjustment of our financial system more important than currency, more important than gold, and that is the confidence of the people. Confidence and courage are the essentials of success in carrying out our plan. You people must have faith; you must not be stampeded by rumors or guesses.

The handling of the banking crisis was one of the brightest pages in the New Deal's history. Confidence was restored by the President's air of optimism. Federal Reserve bank notes of $25 million were immediately put into circulation, and by December, 1933, they exceeded $200 million. But as the emergency receded, they were gradually retired. The RFC purchased $1.3 billion of bank stock, and the Federal Reserve banks, exercising a power given to them by an Act of March 24, made direct loans to nonmember banks and trust companies. When the banks began to reopen, runs did not resume. On the contrary, bank deposits began to increase.

Effects of the Suspension of the Gold Standard. Meanwhile, the administration proceeded to take the nation further away from the gold standard. By the Executive Orders of April 5, 20, and 28, an embargo was placed on all international transactions in gold except under license issued by the Secretary of the Treasury. No person or institution, except a Federal Reserve bank, was permitted to hold gold or gold certificates except up to $100 for use in the arts or gold coins having a special value to collectors. By joint resolution on June 5, Congress voided the "gold clause" in government bonds and private obligations. Thus, for the first time in American history the gold standard was abandoned deliberately, rather than under compulsion.

The administration believed that any attempt to raise prices under a gold standard would defeat itself by causing gold exports and deflationary pressure on prices. It reasoned that it could maintain the gold standard with its international parity of exchange and a deflated domestic price level or it could abandon the gold standard, allow the international value of the dollar to find its own level, and institute monetary controls to raise and stabilize domestic prices. It chose the latter alternative, hoping that the dollar would depreciate rapidly in foreign exchange.

Orthodox monetary theorists, including Professors Edwin W. Kemmerer, Benjamin M. Anderson, and Walter E. Spahr, immediately denounced the administration's actions. Denying categorically that the gold standard had contributed to deflation and depression, they questioned both the advisability and the possibility of restoring prices to a preexisting level. Insisting that the gold standard was the best objective monetary standard, they asserted that its permanent suspension would leave the country with an unsound domestic inconvertible paper currency which would tend to depreciate in value, resulting in price inflation and uncertainty. According to them, the abrogation of the gold clause was a violation of contract and therefore dishonorable, and they regretted that, after the election, Roosevelt had not joined Hoover in a "bipartisan declaration of the ringing Grover Cleveland type." The conservatives were on solid ground in questioning the ethics of the abrogation of the gold clause, for the Supreme Court in February, 1935, held that Congress had exceeded its powers in suspending the gold clause. However, this was an academic decision, since the Court also decided that bondholders were not entitled to redress because they had not been able to demonstrate an actual money loss.

TABLE 66. PRICES, JUNE, 1932 TO MAY, 1933

	Whole-sale*	23 basic† commodities	Farm products*	Primary products‡
June, 1932..............	100	100	100	100
January, 1933...........	95.5	95.4	93.2	97.5
February, 1933..........	93.6	94.0	89.5	96.3
March, 1933.............	94.2	100.6	93.7	100.0
April, 1933.............	94.5	102.0	97.4	111.3
May, 1933.............	98.1	124.5	109.9	135.0

* Bureau of Labor Statistics, Vol. 37, p. 450.
† Guarantee Trust Co. of New York, *Guarantee Survey*, Dec. 26, 1933, p. 20.
‡ Mills, *Prices in Recession and Recovery*, p. 214.

The effect of the suspension of the gold standard on price levels, interest rates, and the banking structure was not easy to evaluate. Immediately after suspension, the dollar did begin to depreciate, cable drafts falling from $3.42 to the pound in April to $4.35 in July. But some prices rose more than proportionately. Thus, between April 20 and June

10, the price of gold rose 23.2 per cent in the London free-gold market, while the prices of 17 commodities important in international trade rose 45 per cent. It is impossible to tell how much of this rise was due to going off gold and how much to other causes, such as the increase in public confidence and the establishment of the NRA and the AAA. That it was a factor is unquestionable, since international prices rose more rapidly than domestic.

The abandonment of the gold standard made it possible for the United States to follow a cheap-money policy more consistently although not with any more recuperative effects. It also aided materially in rehabilitating the banking structure, for it removed an important element in bank runs and it increased the gold reserves of the Federal Reserve System from $2.7 billion on March 8 to $3.3 billion on April 5 and the reserve ratio from 45.6 to 59.7 per cent.

Thomas Inflation Amendment. The reflationary activities of the administration were not wide-sweeping enough to satisfy the inflationists in Congress. Toward the end of the Hoover administration, Senator Wheeler of Montana had introduced a bill for free silver, but it was defeated 56 to 18. Then in the Seventy-third Congress Wheeler added a free-silver amendment to the Agricultural Adjustment Act. Although it was again defeated, the vote was much closer, demonstrating that inflationary sentiment was gaining. When Senator Elmer Thomas of Oklahoma introduced an omnibus inflation amendment to the AAA, the President's political advisers were positive that they could not defeat it. Therefore, a compromise was arranged. The inflationists agreed to make their proposals discretionary, rather than mandatory, and the administration agreed to support the amendment, which was passed by the Senate 64 to 21 and by the House 307 to 86. The bill was signed by the President on May 12, 1933.[1]

The Thomas amendment authorized the Federal Reserve banks to purchase up to $3 billion of government securities directly from the Treasury. If the banks refused to purchase the securities, or if the purchases did not increase the general price level, or if the President judged that additional measures were required, he was authorized to direct the Secretary of the Treasury to issue up to $3 billion in greenbacks to be used only to buy government obligations and to be retired at the rate of 4 per cent annually. In order to give them full standing, all money was made legal tender. The President was also permitted to reduce the weight of the gold or silver dollar or both by any amount up to 50 per

[1] When the President decided to accept the Thomas amendment, Lewis Douglas, the Budget Director, is reported to have said, "Well, this is the end of Western civilization." (Raymond Moley, *After Seven Years*, p. 160.)

cent, to restore bimetallism by providing for unlimited coinage of gold and silver at a fixed ratio, and to accept, during the next six months, up to $200 million of silver valued at 50 cents an ounce in payment of interest and principal on international debts. Finally, the Federal Reserve Board was authorized, with the approval of the Secretary of the Treasury, to require the Reserve banks to take action to prevent undue credit expansion. By a vote of at least five members, the Board could also change reserve requirements during periods of emergency.

If the administration and the Federal Reserve Board had availed themselves of all their powers under the amendment, they could have expanded the currency by about $10 billion, or by more than twice the existing amount in circulation. However, only two provisions in the amendment were used: the gold dollar was devalued, and European nations paid about $11.4 million in silver on their debt installments due in 1933. The implications of the Thomas amendment were therefore more important than its practical effects. It demonstrated that faith in the quantity theory of money and in the omnipotence of monetary controls was still strong, it continued the trend toward greater centralized control over banking, and it advanced the power of the Treasury over Federal Reserve operations.

The International Monetary Conference. By the spring of 1933 international finance was in a state of chaos. Whether necessary or not, the traditional gold standard had been wrecked, and stabilization of international exchange had disappeared. International trade was crippled by towering tariff walls and asphyxiating quotas, exchange controls, and quasi-barter agreements of all sorts. The problem of international debts had not been solved but was in a state of quiescence, contributing enormously to the general economic uncertainty.

It was to solve these problems that the International Monetary Conference was called in London in June, 1933. However, the Conference was doomed to failure, for broad agreement among the nations on economic policy was not possible. The United States was experimenting with economic nationalism and was not willing to discuss currency stabilization or international debts—the questions in which the foreign nations were most interested. Under the circumstances, there was no common meeting ground. Moreover, the American delegation itself was confused in its aims. Secretary of State Hull, who headed the delegation, wanted to reduce international tariffs. He was supported by James M. Cox, ex-Presidential candidate and newspaper publisher, and Representative McReynolds of Tennessee. On the other hand, Senators Pittman of Nevada and Couzens of Michigan were high-tariff men. On money issues Couzens was for soft money, and Pittman was determined that, if the Conference did nothing else, it would agree to do something for silver. The views of the sixth member of the delegation, Ralph W. Morrison, a wealthy Texan, were completely unknown.

The Conference was getting nowhere when Roosevelt decided to send Moley over to act as liaison agent. The selection was most unfortunate, for Moley was the personification of economic nationalism and it was immediately concluded that the President had completely repudiated Hull and all that he represented. When Moley arrived in London, Great Britain and the gold-standard countries asked him to present for the President's approval a declaration stating that the international gold standard would ultimately be reestablished and that in the interim each nation would pledge itself to adopt measures to limit speculation in exchange. It was expected that the declaration was too innocuous to arouse opposition, but Roosevelt refused to accept it, having been persuaded to abandon any thought of international stabilization in favor of monetary experiments to restore the domestic price level. In reply to Moley's cable, he declared,

Let me be frank in saying that the United States seeks the kind of dollar which a generation hence will have the same purchasing and debt-paying power as the dollar value we hope to attain in the near future. That objective means more to the good of other nations than a fixed ratio for a month or two in terms of the pound or franc.

The Roosevelt message gave the *coup de grace* to the International Monetary Conference and eliminated the last small hope of bringing order out of international monetary disruption. In fact, it gave new impetus to economic nationalism and competitive exchange depreciation. But even if Roosevelt had approved the declaration, it is questionable if the Conference would have produced anything worth while. In its six weeks of existence, its only accomplishment was an agreement among the principal silver-producing nations not to dump the metal on the market. The United States, producing less than 20 per cent of the world output, agreed to buy 24.4 million ounces of silver annually, while the other nations agreed to purchase 11.6 million ounces.

Warren Gold-buying Program. The increase in prices which had been so heartwarming to the inflationists in the spring of 1933 was reversed during the summer. The speculative impulse, which helped to carry prices up, began to peter out, and the general excitement accompanying the feverish activity of the early New Deal began to cool off. With the decline in prices and in business activity, the administration decided to try to raise the general price level by raising the price of gold, that is, by devaluating the gold dollar. President Roosevelt announced the adoption of the new plan in a fireside chat on October 22. After declaring that the administration's policy was to restore commodity prices and maintain a dollar with a stable purchasing and debt-paying power, he said,

I am going to establish a government market for gold in the United States. . . . I am authorizing the Reconstruction Finance Corporation to buy gold newly mined in the United States at prices to be determined from time to time after consultation with the Secretary of the Treasury and the President. Whenever necessary, we shall also buy or sell gold in the world market. . . . We are thus continuing to move towards a managed currency.[2]

The theoretical basis for the gold-purchase program was the quantity theory of money. According to Professor Warren of Cornell, the leading exponent of the program, an increase in the price of gold would expand the gold supply and the amount of money in circulation by making it more profitable to mine gold and by making it possible to issue more currency against a given quantity of gold.

Starting on October 25 at a price of $31.36 an ounce, slightly higher than the London free-gold market, gold was gradually raised to $35 an ounce by December.[3] While the increase in the price of gold created more dollars in the Treasury, there was no accompanying plan for pouring the new dollars into the economy. Furthermore, the plan had a most unfortunate effect on business psychology. The business group frankly confessed that it did not understand the theory and that it could not carry on its operations, especially in international trade, in terms of a dollar which changed from day to day by government proclamation. As confidence ebbed, business activity ebbed. Therefore, general prices did not rise. In fact, the BLS wholesale price index declined from 71.2 in October to 70.8 in December, and farm prices dropped from 55.7 to 55.5.

Gold Reserve Act of 1934. By January, 1934, it was apparent that gold purchases at advanced prices had not increased the general price level. Therefore, the program was abandoned, and on January 30 Congress stabilized the dollar by passing the Gold Reserve Act. With its passage, most of the New Deal attempts to raise prices by monetary manipulation came to a halt.

The Gold Reserve Act placed the United States on a gold-bullion standard internationally and on an irredeemable paper standard domestically. The Act required the Federal Reserve banks to deliver their gold

[2] The power to buy gold was taken from an unrepealed act of 1862, which had enabled the government to purchase gold during the Civil War suspension of specie payments. Ironically, the same power had been used by Cleveland in buying gold from the Morgan syndicate to maintain the gold standard.

[3] The price was not fixed according to any scientific plan, but on occasion it was determined by magic numbers. (Henry Morgenthau, Jr., "The Morgenthau Diaries," *Collier's*, September to November, 1947.)

to the Treasury in exchange for gold certificates in denominations of $100,000 and higher. All monetary gold was to be converted into gold bullion, and minting of gold coins was prohibited except for accounts of foreign countries. Redemption of paper money in gold was not permitted domestically, but gold in bullion form could be obtained in settlement of international balances. The Secretary of the Treasury was empowered to buy and sell gold at rates and upon terms that he deemed advisable in the public interest. He was also authorized to prescribe the conditions under which gold might be acquired, held, and transported. The Thomas amendment was amended to give the President the power to devalue the dollar to between 50 and 60 per cent of its former' gold value. This power was to expire in two years, but it was renewed from time to time, finally being repealed as of June 30, 1943, by act of Congress on April 16, 1943.

Immediately after the passage of the Act, President Roosevelt, by proclamation, devalued the dollar to 59.06 per cent of its former value, and Secretary of the Treasury Morgenthau announced that he would buy and sell gold at $35 an ounce minus or plus $\frac{1}{4}$ of 1 per cent handling charge. The new dollar contained $15\frac{5}{21}$ grains of gold, $\frac{9}{10}$ fine (13.714+ pure), compared with the old dollar of 25.8 grains, $\frac{9}{10}$ fine (23.22 pure).[4]

The devaluation resulted in a profit of $2.8 billion for the Treasury. Of this sum, $2 billion was placed in a fund (the Stabilization Fund) to stabilize the dollar in international exchange, $645 million was used to retire the national-bank notes, $139 million was placed in a fund for industrial loans by the Federal Reserve banks, $24 million was used to cover devaluation losses incurred by the Philippine Islands under the gold exchange standard, $2 million was set aside for losses due to converting gold coins into bullion, and the remainder was unassigned.

Increased Support to Silver. In any scheme for raising prices by the use of monetary techniques, it was impossible to leave silver out of the picture. Optimistic conservatives believed that the issues of bimetallism, the limping standard, and free silver had all been disposed of by the election of 1896, but the agrarians and the silverites continued to raise the old arguments. In addition, Senator Pittman reasoned that an increase in the price of silver would enhance the international purchasing power of China, which was on a silver standard. However, China produced no silver and had to purchase it on the international market. If the price of silver increased and the price of Chinese exported goods remained the same, "doing something for silver" would injure China severely by pre-

[4] Holders of gold obligations insisted that they had suffered not 41, but a 69 per cent loss. They argued that they were entitled to $35 in paper money for each $20.67 stated in their contracts. For example, in the case of a $10,000 bond, they demanded $16,931.25 in paper money. However, the Supreme Court denied the plea. (See above, p. 385.)

venting her from obtaining silver and eventually driving her to a paper standard.

When the administration made price restoration its goal, the friends of silver had their great opportunity, and they made the most of it. Under the authority of the pact signed at the London Conference, the President in December, 1933, ordered the purchase of newly mined domestic silver up to 24.4 million ounces at $1.29 an ounce less a 50 per cent seigniorage, making the net price to the producer 64½ cents. The Treasury was to issue silver dollars against these purchases, and by the Gold Reserve Act, it was authorized to issue certificates instead of "cartwheels." The limping standard of the Bland-Allison days was back again in all its glory, for the average market price of silver during 1934 was 43 cents, giving the silver producers a subsidy of more than 20 cents an ounce.

At the beginning of 1934, silverites introduced bills to restore the system in existence under the Sherman Act of 1890. A House bill, introduced by Martin Dies of Texas, directed the Treasury to purchase 50 million ounces of silver monthly until the market price reached $1.29 an ounce or the price level was restored to the 1926 level. The administration prevented its passage, but only at the expense of a compromise, the Silver Purchase Act of June, 1934, which authorized and directed the Secretary of the Treasury to buy silver at home and abroad until the silver stock equaled 25 per cent of the nation's metallic reserves or until the price reached $1.29 per ounce. However, no purchase of existing silver might be for more than 50 cents an ounce. The Act was not the work of a few silver congressmen, for it passed the House, 263 to 77, and the Senate, 54 to 25. In April, 1935, the effective price of newly mined domestic silver was raised by Presidential order to 77.57 cents an ounce, and during the fiscal year 1935 the Treasury bought 438 million ounces of silver at a cost of $232 million. This was estimated as equal to 12 times as much silver as was produced in the United States and 2.2 times as much as was produced in the world during the same period.

In December, 1937, the administration incensed the silver bloc by restoring the seigniorage to 50 per cent, reducing the effective price to 64½ cents. When attempts to persuade the Secretary to pursue a more aggressive silver policy failed, the silver bloc passed a new silver bill in July, 1939, ordering the Treasury to buy all the newly mined domestic silver that was offered at an effective price of 71.11 cents an ounce.

In the fiscal years 1935 to 1940 silver purchases varied from 227 million ounces in 1937 to 610 million ounces in 1936 at a cost ranging from $122 million to $395 million. The average number of ounces purchased per year was 393 million, and the average cost was $212 million.

As in the past, the new silver policy did not raise either the general price level or the price of silver. In 1934 before the policy was inaugurated, the average market price of silver was 43 cents an ounce, and it was still the same in 1939. Nor had the policy met the announced objective of eventually having one-quarter of the monetary stock in silver. Continued flight to the dollar by frightened Europeans brought in large gold stocks. As a result, the ratio of silver to gold in 1939 was about the same as in 1934. Finally, the silver policy did not help China or the other silver nations. On the contrary, they were drained of their silver when the United States offered premium prices for it. In short, the only achievement of the silver program was that foreign and domestic silver producers received a subsidy, and although the program gave some stimulus to employment and to American exports, its costs were stupendous.

International Cooperation for Currency Stabilization. As has been already noted, in 1934 the administration abandoned the use of monetary policy to raise prices. Immediately after the passage of the Gold Reserve Act, it embarked upon the program of international stabilization which it had repudiated previously at the London Conference. It maintained that there was no inconsistency in its policy, as its refusal to stabilize prematurely had helped to restore the domestic price level and had now made it possible to promote international stability. This reasoning seemed too neat. It implied that economic nationalism was confined to monetary matters and had successfully achieved its ends. Actually, it had also embraced tariff policy, and it had failed to bring recovery. A more likely explanation for the reversal of policy was that the administration had come to believe that economic nationalism had failed. It was significant that at this time the nationalists among the President's advisers—Moley, Peek, and others—were being gradually superseded by the internationalists —Hull, Wallace, and others.

Regardless of the reason, the administration not only stabilized the dollar but also adopted the Hull reciprocal trade agreements plan. However, international cooperation at stabilization did not occur until 1936. Then in September, 1936, France abandoned the gold standard and devalued the franc. Immediately thereafter, the Tripartite Accord was signed by Great Britain, France, and the United States. While the accord was shrouded in mystery, the Treasury made it plain that the signers pledged their allegiance "to foster those conditions which safeguard peace and will best contribute to the restoration of order in international economic relations . . . to continue to use appropriate available resources so as to avoid as far as possible any disturbance of the basis of international exchange." The three nations attached "the greatest importance to action being taken to relax progressivley the present system of quotas and exchange controls with a view to their abolition." They also trusted that "no country will attempt to obtain an unreasonable competitive exchange advantage." Each of the nations continued its own stabilization fund and agreed to sell gold to the others at a price fixed on a twenty-four-hour basis. The American Stabilization Fund bought foreign currencies or gold whenever the price of the dollar tended to increase internationally. But it never held foreign currencies for more than twenty-four hours, converting them into gold every day.

The Tripartite agreement was useful in smoothing out short-term fluctuations in exchange rates but was helpless against persistent changes of fundamental economic origin. It could operate only as long as the central banks were willing or able to export gold. By the time the agreement came to an end in 1939, the United States almost had a corner on the world's gold supply. Nevertheless, the agreement did represent a step in the direction of international monetary cooperation. And from a business point of view, the Stabilization Fund was enormously successful, for between 1934 and 1940 its earnings after expenses were $21.5 million.

Other New Deal Monetary Measures. The profit on devaluation made possible a long-contemplated reform in the currency system—the retirement of the national-bank notes. In the spring of 1935 two issues of bonds were outstanding which were eligible as security against national-bank notes: the 2 per cent consols of 1930 and the 2 per cent Panama Canal bonds, aggregating $674.6 million. The Borah amendment of 1932 had extended the circulation privilege, but it was due to expire in July, 1935.

Using $645 million of the devaluation profit, the Treasury redeemed the consols of 1930 on July 1 and the Panama Canal bonds on August 1, 1935. In order to prevent an increase in member bank reserves, payments for the bonds were made only when national banks actually retired their currency by depositing lawful money with the Treasury. The Treasury then assumed the obligation of the national-bank notes. It redeemed about $246 million during the fiscal year 1935, the remainder becoming part of the non-interest-bearing public debt.

The gradual retirement of the national-bank notes not only eliminated a concentrated headache which had existed since 1863 but, together with the substantial retirement of the Federal Reserve bank notes, it put a stop to the issue of money by private commercial banks. This was done without any reduction in the amount of money in circulation. On the contrary, money in circulation increased about 46 per cent between 1934 and 1940 because of growing desire for security on the part of the public, the great amount of hoarding of American dollars among foreign citizens, the continued use of government bonds as partial security against Federal Reserve notes, and the silver program. Yet despite a more than 50 per cent increase in currency and demand deposits in the latter thirties, the price level rose from 74.9 only to 77.1, for the velocity of money was much lower than at any previous time, the turnover of all commercial bank deposits declining from 29.9 in 1929 to 16.0 in 1934 and 12.9 in 1940.

TABLE 67. CHANGES IN MONEY CIRCULATION, 1934–1940
(In millions of dollars)

Year	National-bank notes	Federal Reserve bank notes	Federal Reserve notes	Total money in circulation
1934	$901.9	$141.6	$3,068.4	$5,373.5
1935	704.3	81.5	3,222.9	5,567.1
1936	366.1	52.0	4,002.2	6,241.2
1937	268.9	37.6	4,168.8	6,447.1
1938	217.4	30.1	4,114.3	6,460.9
1939	186.5	25.6	4,483.6	7,046.7
1940	165.2	22.4	5,163.3	7,847.5

SOURCE: *Annual Report of the Secretary of the Treasury*, 1940.

Several factors combined at this time to bring into the United States a flood of gold. The government's deliberate policy of placing a high value on gold, the natural effects of America's position as the world's largest creditor, the consistently favorable balance of trade, and, most important of all, the flight to the dollar by uneasy Europeans caused net gold imports of $15.9 billion in the seven years from 1934 to 1940. Most of this inflow could not be digested by the economic system, and it merely increased the excess reserves of the commercial banks, creating a base for some future inflation. Alarmed by this situation, the Treasury in December, 1936, announced that it would prevent gold imports from increasing bank reserves. Henceforth, gold acquisitions would be segregated in an inactive account, no gold certificates would be issued against new gold deposits, and new government obligations would be sold to the banks in amounts equal to net gold acquisitions. Thus, the Treasury would increase its gross debt and its interest charges in order to "sterilize" gold. At the same time, the Federal Reserve Board was cooperating by using other theoretically deflationary credit devices.

The sterilization policy had little effect on the economy. It was instituted to prevent the use of bank funds to feed an inflationary spiral in the event of a substantial expansion of economic activity. It was a well-advised, farsighted, and cautious program, but no boom appeared.

Instead, a recession developed in 1937, causing the Treasury to curtail its sterilization activities. In February, 1938, it announced that it would place in the inactive account only such new gold as exceeded $100 million a quarter. Then in April, 1938, as part of the so-called "lend-spend" program of economic expansion, it announced that sterilization would be discontinued and $1.4 billion would be desterilized. The Treasury was attempting to expand credit by pumping reserves into the banking system. But once again attempts at expansion only increased excess reserves, reviving the widespread uneasiness which had prevailed previously.

Centralization of Banking: the Acts of 1933 and 1935. During the latter thirties the banking structure became inseparably connected with government monetary and fiscal policy, and the Federal Reserve System and the Treasury were operated in tandem. During the prosperity era there was some plausibility to the contention that the banking system could act independently of the Treasury. However, during the Hoover years, the contention seemed unrealistic, and at the height of the great depression it became obvious that independent central banking was a thing of the past, if it had ever existed.

As has been already noted, the administration's monetary policies had important effects on banking reserves. The devaluation of the dollar increased the gold supply, debt management was used to eliminate the private issue of currency, the silver policy increased currency and banking reserves, and the Treasury's sterilization policy neutralized the effects of the constant inflow of gold. Therefore, the Federal Reserve System had to cooperate with the Treasury or the economic policies of the country would have become a shambles.

In order to achieve the greatest possible cooperation and to increase and make more effective the controls over money, banking, and credit, the administration tried to make the Reserve System more centralized and the commercial banking system more unified. It was fairly successful in attaining the first objective, but not the second.

The first step in the trend toward further centralization of the banking structure was the Banking Act of June 16, 1933. As originally introduced by Senator Glass, it resembled the unsuccessful attempts made during the Hoover administration to reform the banking system. However, the provisions for separation of savings and commercial banking and for compulsory membership in the Reserve System had been dropped, and in the House, Representative Steagall, despite administration objections, had added a provision for insuring bank deposits.

The Act was designed to strengthen the commercial banks, weaken the connection between speculation and banking, and give added powers to the Federal Reserve System. Specifically, it (1) established a Federal Deposit Insurance Corporation, open to all commercial banks, with a capital of $289 million, $150 million subscribed by the Treasury and the remainder representing one-half of the surplus of the Federal Reserve banks; (2) prohibited interest on demand deposits; (3) raised the minimum capital requirement for national banks to $50,000; (4) permitted state-wide branch banking for national banks where allowed state banks by state law; (5) required separation of security affiliates from commercial banks; (6) empowered the Reserve Board to suspend a member bank from the use of Reserve credit if it made undue use of credit for speculative purposes; (7) authorized the Board to limit the amount of security loans made by member banks; (8) authorized 90-day direct loans to member banks, such loans to be payable on demand if the bank increased its outstanding security loans after being warned; (9) made mutual savings and Morris Plan banks eligible for Reserve membership; (10) increased the term of office of Reserve Board members from ten to twelve years; (11) created an open-market committee of one member from each Reserve bank; and (12) eliminated the franchise tax on Reserve bank earnings.

Of all the provisions in the Banking Act, the Federal Deposit Insurance Corporation was most discussed. Critics pointed out that state deposit insurance had never worked and that the system was not insurance, but an arrangement by which the strong banks upheld the weak banks very much in the manner of the old New York safety fund system. These criticisms had some foundation, but the FDIC was a tonic to the jaded psychology of the American public, for it did much to remove the public's distrust of the banking system.

The Act had other provisions which were more important than deposit insurance. It gave the Federal Reserve Board the opportunity to use qualitative credit controls, and by extending the lombard loan provision, it practically eliminated the "real-bills" doctrine from Reserve bank operation. Unfortunately, it failed to require all banks to become members of the Reserve System, and it did nothing positive to encourage branch banking. All in all, the Act was an improvement in banking, but it fell short of the reforms suggested by Hoover at the time when the Glass bill was first introduced.

In June, 1934, the Reserve banks were given the power to make loans to individuals, and in the same month, under the provisions of the Securities Exchange Act, the Board was given authority to regulate margin requirements in security transactions. But the real effort to extend centralized control over banking came in early 1935 with the introduction of a bill expressing the views of Marriner Eccles, governor of the Federal Reserve Board. Eccles was a pre-Keynesian proponent of the

"New Economics"—cyclical budgets, centralized credit and monetary controls, and close cooperation between the Treasury and the central bank. Never backward in expressing his views, he took an active part in framing legislation to give the Reserve Board more power.

The Eccles bill was sharply debated by the monetary conservatives, the monetary managers, and the inflationists. The original Eccles bill frankly stated that its objective was to facilitate monetary management. It made the President's power of appointment and removal of members of the Federal Reserve Board practically unlimited, set up an open-market committee independent of the Board, broadened the power of the Board over rediscounts, and gave it mandatory power over reserve requirements. To give the Reserve System more power, all nonmember banks protected by the FDIC had to become member banks by July, 1937, or forfeit their insurance protection. The bill also liberalized real estate loans and lombard loans and empowered the Reserve banks to issue Federal Reserve notes secured by all the assets of the issuing bank.

The inflationists objected to the bill because it did not make price stabilization the primary goal, and they sponsored the Goldsborough amendment which contemplated stabilizing prices at the 1921 to 1929 level by authorizing the Treasury and the Reserve Board to alter the price of gold. The amendment was defeated 128 to 122. The conservatives objected to the bill because they believed that it would make the Board political in character and would eliminate what was left of the original theory of liquidity. With the help of Senator Glass, they were successful in modifying the bill substantially before it was passed in August, 1935.

The provisions of the Banking Act of 1935 were as follows: (1) state nonmember banks having $1 million or more of deposits were required to become members of the Reserve System by July, 1942, or forfeit their insurance benefits; (2) the old Federal Reserve Board was dissolved and replaced by a Board of Governors composed of seven members appointed by the President for fourteen years; (3) the Secretary of the Treasury and the Comptroller of the Currency were not eligible for membership on the Board; (4) no special qualifications were prescribed for membership, but no member serving a full term was eligible for reappointment; (5) the chief officer of each Federal Reserve bank was designated as president, and his appointment by each board of directors had to be approved by the Board of Governors of the System; (6) an open-market committee composed of the Board of Governors and five representatives of the Reserve banks was created; (7) any district bank could make advances to a member on four-months paper bearing interest at least ½ of 1 per cent above the regular rediscount rate; (8) the Board could set reserve requirements anywhere within the range of 7 to 14 per cent for country banks, 10 to 20 per cent for city banks, and 13 to 26 per cent for Reserve city banks; (9) Reserve banks were prohibited from buying securities directly from the Treasury; (10) each Reserve bank was required to restate its rediscount rate every two weeks, and approval of the rate had to be obtained from the Board; (11) national banks could make ten-year loans on real estate up to 60 per cent of appraised value; (12) double liability was eliminated on all national-bank stock; (13) cumulative voting was required in national banks; (14) the Board was authorized to regulate the rate of interest paid by member banks on time deposits; (15) amounts due from other banks could be deducted from gross demand deposits in calculating reserves.

The Banking Act of 1935 was unquestionably the longest step in the direction of central banking taken by the United States since the passage of the Federal Reserve Act and perhaps in its entire history. It greatly broadened the Board's powers over reserve requirements, rediscount rates, open-market operations, and the appointments of heads of district banks. On the other hand, however, it did not go so far as the exponents of monetary management wanted: it repealed the provision of the Thomas amendment allowing the Federal Reserve banks to buy securities directly from the Treasury, and because of the opposition of some small banks, it failed to make membership in the Federal Reserve System universal.

Federal Reserve Policy, 1933 to 1939. Despite the fact that the Reserve Board's powers over credit were enormously enhanced during the latter thirties, the trend of events during 1933 to 1939 merely added new evidence that monetary and credit policy could not encourage entrepreneurs to borrow and could not expand the use of credit. No one was more cognizant of this than the monetary managers themselves. Late in the period, Eccles stated flatly that monetary policy by itself could not cure a slump and placed increasing emphasis on fiscal policy. As Professor John H. Williams aptly expressed it, "One of the most striking facts about the development of fiscal policy in the last decade is that, while it grew out of monetary policy and was designed to supplement and strengthen it, fiscal policy has ended up by threatening to supplant monetary policy altogether."[5]

Except for a temporary deviation between July, 1936, and April, 1937, the Board maintained a consistent easy-money policy. It was hoped that expanding excess reserves and reduced rediscount rates would encourage borrowing and lending. In 1934 the New York rate was reduced to 1½ per cent, where it remained until 1937. Similarly Reserve hold-

[5] John H. Williams, "The Implications of Fiscal Policy for Monetary Policy and the Banking System," *American Economic Review*, Supplement, March, 1942.

ings of government securities were increased from $1.8 billion in March, 1933, to $2.4 billion in October. At the same time excess reserves were also increased by huge gold imports from Europe, and by July, 1936, they were up to $3 billion compared with $379 million in April, 1933.

With the building up of excess reserves, it was feared that a dangerous inflation might result, and in fact, some prices were rising. Yet the economy as a whole still exhibited deflation: the national income was relatively low, unemployment was high, and commercial bank loans were no higher than they had been in June, 1933. Nevertheless, the Treasury and the Federal Reserve Board took steps to tighten the money market. In July, 1936, reserve requirements were raised to 10½, 15, and 19½ per cent; in March, 1937, to 12¼, 17½, and 22¾ per cent; and finally in May, 1937, to the maximum level of 14, 20, and 26 per cent.

When a sharp business recession began in the spring of 1937, many commentators attributed it to the tightening of credit by the Reserve authorities. But Chairman Eccles insisted that monetary action had not caused the slump and would not rectify it. Nevertheless, the Board returned to its easy-money policy. It persuaded the Treasury to release $300 million of its inactive gold. The Reserve banks bought large blocks of government bonds, increasing their holdings from $2.4 billion in March, 1937, to $2.6 billion in November. Rediscount rates were reduced in August and September, 1937, the New York rate being lowered to 1 per cent. In April, 1938, reserve requirements were reduced to 12, 17½, and 22¾ per cent. Having made these changes to expand reserves and encourage credit, the Board returned to its policy of watchful waiting, making no other changes until the outbreak of war in Europe in 1939. But the policy of pouring funds into the banking system in the hope that they would overflow into private business did not succeed any better than prior attempts. Instead, excess reserves increased steadily, exceeding $1 billion in October, 1937; $2 billion in April, 1938; $5 billion in September, 1939; and almost $7 billion in October, 1940. While building up their excess reserves, the member banks also paid off their indebtedness to the district banks. Bills discounted at the Reserve banks declined from $191 million in June, 1933, to $2 million (the all-time low) in June, 1940. Bills bought in the open market declined steadily until by 1940 the Reserve banks had none at all.

In the meanwhile, proposals for price stabilization through monetary action were again presented, and in March, 1939, the Board of Governors replied with an exhaustive statement. It declared that the proposals were neither practicable nor beneficial, because experience showed that prices could not be controlled by changes in the amount and cost of money, the Board's control over the amount of money was not complete and could not be made so, a steady average of prices would not necessarily result in lasting prosperity, nor would it be so important to the people as a fair relationship between prices. Denying that there was any cause-and-effect relationship between the quantity of money and the price level, the Board cited the fact that, from 1926 to 1938, money in circulation increased from $3.6 billion to $5.7 billion and demand deposits, from $22 to $26 billion. Yet prices were 23 per cent lower in 1938 than in 1926. The Board concluded,

There have been times when the amount of money and prices have changed together; but usually they have not. When they have moved together this may have been due to the fact that it takes more money to do the same amount of business when prices are high than when they are low.

In analyzing its powers of credit control, the Board said,

If the Reserve System . . . should buy Government bonds and . . . pay out Federal Reserve notes for them, this currency would come right back to the Reserve banks and would serve no useful purpose. . . . It cannot make the people borrow, and it cannot make the public spend.

Commercial Bank Operation, 1933 to 1939. During the late thirties the trends in commercial banking which had been occurring over a long period of years reached a climax. To a marked degree the banks became mere recipients and transferers of deposits and investors in government

TABLE 68.   COMMERCIAL BANKING OPERATIONS, 1933–1939
(Dollar figures in millions)

	1933	1934	1935	1936	1937	1938	1939
Member banks:							
Number..............	5,606	6,375	6,410	6,400	6,357	6,338	6,330
Total loans............	$12,858	$12,523	$11,928	$12,542	$14,285	$12,938	$13,141
Security.............	4,704	4,598	4,098	4,209	4,365	3,316	1,467
Real estate..........	2,372	2,357	2,277	2,340	2,505	2,613	2,828
Total investments.......	11,928	14,652	16,857	19,717	18,454	17,783	19,462
United States securities	6,887	9,413	11,430	13,672	12,689	12,343	13,777
Total deposits (except interbank).............	23,272	26,657	29,545	34,098	35,439	34,745	38,027
No. of suspensions......	1,275	1	4	1	6	2	7
Nonmember banks:							
Number..............	8,343	8,978	9,068	8,843	8,619	8,399	8,201
Total loans............	$ 3,491	$ 3,177	$ 2,981	$ 3,017	$ 3,147	$ 3,115	$ 3,282
Total investments.......	2,080	2,390	2,822	3,264	3,586	3,273	3,482
United States securities	589	895	1,287	1,598	1,874	1,699	1,923
Total deposits (except interbank).............	5,196	5,527	6,117	6,929	7,326	7,007	7,530
No. of suspensions......	2,725	56	30	43	53	52	35

SOURCE: Federal Reserve Board, *Banking and Monetary Statistics.*

bonds. As Table 68 shows, investments, which had been growing relatively during the twenties and during the early part of the depression, finally passed loans in importance. This trend was general throughout the commercial banking system but was most prominent among the member banks, where investments in government securities alone were larger than loans by June, 1936. Relying for the greater part of their earnings on government bonds, commercial banks became more dependent upon the Treasury than upon the Federal Reserve. Being such large holders of government securities, they had to do everything in their power to support the price of governments. Consequently, they became a certain market for government-bond sales.

New Deal Tariff Program. The administration's gradual shift from economic nationalism to economic internationalism was illustrated by the change in its monetary policies and, even more so, by the adoption of the Reciprocal Trade Agreements Act. During the New Deal's first year, the President was authorized under the NIRA to impose fees or quotas on the importation of goods which endangered the continued effectiveness of NRA codes. Under the AAA, compensatory tariffs were imposed on imported goods processed from basic farm products. In March, 1934, however, the administration prepared to fulfill its campaign pledges on the tariff. In a message to Congress, the President asked for authority to enter into executive commercial agreements with foreign nations for the reciprocal reduction of tariffs and other trade barriers. He pointed out that in 1933 the world's international trade was only 70 per cent of the 1929 level in volume and only 35 per cent in money value. But exports by the United States were only 52 per cent by volume and 32 per cent by value and imports only 66 and 33 per cent of the 1929 level.

Protectionists retorted that the importance of foreign trade to the American economy was greatly exaggerated, since it amounted in 1929 to only about 6 per cent of the national income. They feared that, if the President's recommendations were adopted, imports would increase, injuring domestic industry and obstructing economic recovery. They also charged that the request of the President meant an unconstitutional extension of executive power. After lengthy debate, however, the Trade Agreements Act was adopted in June, 1934, authorizing the President, whenever he found that any existing duties or other import restrictions of the United States or any foreign country were unduly burdening the foreign trade of the United States, to enter into trade agreements with foreign governments without the advice and the consent of the Senate. Duties could be raised or lowered by not more than 50 per cent of the rates in effect under the Tariff of 1930. However, reasonable notice of intention to negotiate had to be given to any interested party. In addition, no article could be transferred between the dutiable and the free list. Finally, the authority to make treaties was limited to three years, but subsequently, Congress renewed it until 1945.

Between 1934 and 1940, 23 trade agreements were negotiated, effecting over 1,000 reductions in the rates of the Hawley-Smoot Tariff. Between 1933 and 1938, when the European war was not yet a factor, exports to trade-agreement countries increased 100 per cent compared with a 44 per cent increase in imports; by contrast, exports to other countries increased only 50 per cent and imports only 9 per cent. The ratio of total imports to exports with trade-agreement nations increased from 97 per cent in 1933 to 105 per cent in 1936 but then fell to 66 per cent. On the other hand, the ratio of imports to exports with non-trade-agreement countries was 80 per cent in 1933, 86 per cent in 1936, and 58 per cent in 1938.

Failure to Solve the Allied Debt Problem. The shift to economic internationalism, was not sufficiently broad to accomplish any satisfactory solution to the problem of international debts, for public opinion was not in a mood to agree to any proposal except full payment by the debtor nations. After the fiasco of December, 1932, the incoming administration carried on informal negotiations with the British ambassador, and in April, 1933, conversations were held with Prime Minister MacDonald, but nothing developed. However, Great Britain made a token payment of $10 million in silver on June 15, 1933. At the same time, other nations paid an additional $1.4 million in silver. Only $9 million was paid on the $153 million due on December 15, 1933, and from then on all payments ceased except those from Finland.

The breakdown of negotiations and the cessation of debt payments were caused by inability to agree on fundamental premises. In reporting to Congress on the debt situation in 1934, President Roosevelt stressed America's willingness to negotiate fairly with the debtors, but he also stressed that the debts represented money borrowed from the people of the United States and therefore had to be covered by taxes. Congress was doubly committed to this view, and in April, 1934, it passed the Johnson Act making it unlawful to sell in the United States the securities of any nation or political subdivision thereof while such government was in default on its obligations to the United States. By November, 1940, foreign governments had paid a total of $2.8 billion, but $13.5 billion of indebtedness was still outstanding, of which $11.5 billion represented principal and $2.0 billion accrued interest.

CHAPTER 29: THE NEW DEAL: FISCAL POLICIES

As monetary controls failed to prove an open sesame to prosperity, the Roosevelt administration, gradually and apparently after much soul searching, shifted more and more to the use of fiscal policy, particularly to spending policy.

The New Deal's spending, taxing, and borrowing policies, like its monetary and banking policies, were characterized by a spirit of experimentation. But whereas the monetary and banking programs were heavily weighted from the outset with the objective of business recovery, fiscal policy was at first designed merely to relieve distress and achieve social reform, and only later was invested with the purpose of achieving recovery. The New Deal's spending program benefited the low-income groups primarily, the tax program became increasingly progressive, and the borrowing program, which initially relied on bank loans, increasingly emphasized the absorption of idle savings in the hands of individuals.[1] Thus debt management provided the banks with income which they otherwise would not have been able to earn, and Federal credit, which was strong, was substituted for state, municipal, and private credit, which was weak.

The New Deal's Early "Economy" Approach. In the beginning the Roosevelt administration was pledged to economy and fiscal orthodoxy. Indeed, during the campaign Roosevelt was more outspoken than Hoover in his promises to cut expenditures. Like Hoover, he thought that a balanced budget was indispensable to the preservation of public credit and the achievement of recovery.

Less than a week after his inauguration, on March 10, Roosevelt asked Congress for "authority to effect drastic economies in government." "For three long years," he said, "the Federal Government has been on the road toward bankruptcy." In language reminiscent of some of Gladstone's speeches of the mid-nineteenth century he asserted, "Too often in recent history liberal governments have been wrecked on rocks of loose fiscal policy." He promised that, if the necessary authority were given to him, "there is reasonable prospect that within a year the in-

---

[1] Between 1933 and 1935 the banks absorbed 92 per cent of the gross debt increase but only 26 per cent of the 1935 to 1937 increase and 30 per cent of the 1937 to 1940 increase.

come of the Government will be sufficient to cover the expenditures of the Government."

Congress responded by enacting, on March 20, 1933, the Economy Act, entitling it "An Act to Maintain the Credit of the United States Government." Largely written by Director of the Budget Lewis W. Douglas, the administration's outstanding advocate of economy, it authorized the President to reduce salaries in proportion to the decline in the cost of living since the first six months of 1928 and to make additional adjustments every six months thereafter. But reductions were limited to a maximum of 15 per cent in any six-month period. The President was also permitted to revise and reduce veterans' pensions. The possible savings were estimated at almost three-quarters of a billion dollars. On March 28, 1933, the President issued an Executive Order reducing salaries 15 per cent, and on June 30 he reduced veterans' pensions 10 per cent. On July 3, 1933, and again on January 9, 1934, he extended these reductions for another six months. However, on March 28, 1934, Congress, over the President's veto, restored 95 per cent of the pay cuts as of June 30, 1934, bringing almost to naught the budgetary savings from this source.

Shift from Economy to Heavy Spending. In the meanwhile, the problems of unemployment and declining farm income forced the administration to increase expenditures and defer the balancing of the budget to the future. It did this with great reluctance. However, the alternative of tolerating starvation among the people was much more dangerous. Furthermore, upon the advice of some of its economists, the administration claimed that, in addition to its ethical justification, government spending raised consumer purchasing power and "primed the pump." Once pump priming had been accomplished, business would proceed under its own power. Each year the administration stressed the temporary nature of emergency spending, predicting its termination within the near future. Unfortunately, the anticipated business recovery did not materialize, and the administration had to continue emergency expenditures, piling up new deficits from year to year.

Being unable to balance the budget in the orthodox sense, the New Deal recast its fiscal thinking and began to interpret a balanced budget as one in which only ordinary expenditures were covered by revenues, expenditures for relief and recovery being financed by borrowing. The two classes of expenditures were carefully segregated, thus introducing the so-called "double budget," which conservatives condemned, asserting that it presented a deceptive picture of government finances.

Although the New Deal's spending policies were pursued reluctantly, they were most disturbing to businessmen, and in a short time, most of this group lost its faith in the New Deal. On its part the administration seemed anxious to accentuate the growing rift. It made no attempt to prevent the erstwhile captains and kings from departing, and many of its most influential members missed no opportunity to cast epithets at the business group. The political advantage thus obtained was dearly bought, for while the administration prayed for a revival of business initiative, it helped to undermine public confidence in the soundness of the business system.

The administration's preoccupation with budget balancing during this period was well illustrated by the annual budget messages. In January, 1934, the President estimated a deficit of $7.3 billion for the then current year and $2 billion for the fiscal year 1935. But he offered some encouragement to conservatives by forecasting a balanced budget in the fiscal year 1936.

In his message of January, 1935, the President, admitting that his previous year's forecast had been too optimistic, now estimated a deficit of $4.3 billion for 1935 and $3.9 billion for fiscal 1936. Still pursuing the objective of a balanced budget, he recommended in June, 1935, a program for increased taxation. In his budget message of January, 1936, the President again asserted that a balanced budget was in sight, but he was again oversanguine. Nevertheless, in the next budget message, he proclaimed the 1938 budget to be in balance. "Employment is increasing," he reported. "Industrial production, factory payrolls, and farm prices have steadily risen. These gains make it possible to reduce for the fiscal year 1938 many expenditures of the Federal government which the depression made necessary."

For a while it really seemed as if the long-awaited business recovery was being achieved, and with it the administration moved closer to a balanced budget. However, one of the factors which contributed to the improvement in business conditions in 1936 and early 1937 was the prepayment of the veterans' bonus. With the termination of this artificial prop, the simultaneous reduction in Federal spending, and the introduction of social security taxes, consumer demand fell off considerably, and business conditions took a turn for the worse.

Abandonment of the Goal of the Balanced Budget. The business recession of 1937 gave a new turn to the administration's fiscal thinking. As Secretary Morgenthau explained it, "The early New Dealers from Roosevelt down, were looking forward to a balanced budget. . . . But in the course of time new theories, based in part on the reasoning of John Maynard Keynes . . . had come into vogue." According to Morgenthau the leading government spokesmen for the Keynesian thesis were Leon Henderson, Lauchlin Currie, Thomas Corcoran, and Ben Cohen. Un-

TABLE 69. FEDERAL RECEIPTS, EXPENDITURES, AND DEBT 1933–1940
(In millions of dollars)

	1933	1934	1935	1936	1937	1938	1939	1940
Receipts:								
Customs.........	$ 250.8	$ 313.4	$ 343.4	$ 386.8	$ 486.4	$ 359.2	$ 318.8	$ 348.6
Individual income	352.6	419.5	527.1	674.4	1,091.7	1,286.3	1,028.8	982.0
Corporate income	394.2	397.5	572.1	738.5	1,056.9	1,299.9	1,122.5	1,120.6
Excess profits....	....	2.6	6.6	14.5	25.1	36.6	27.1	18.5
Capital stock and dividends......	....	130.4	92.5	95.3	137.5	139.4	127.2	132.7
Estate and gifts..	34.3	113.1	212.1	378.8	305.5	416.9	360.7	360.1
Liquors..........	43.2	259.0	410.8	505.3	593.9	567.7	587.6	624.1
Tobacco.........	402.7	424.7	458.8	500.8	551.9	567.8	579.8	608.1
Stamps, stock transfers, etc...	57.3	66.6	43.0	69.0	69.9	46.3	41.1	38.6
Manufacturers' excises.........	243.6	385.3	342.2	382.7	450.6	417.2	397.0	447.2
Other excises.....	91.9	101.7	90.1	72.5	85.2	123.3	150.1	157.3
Agricultural adjustment, etc...	....	371.4	526.2	67.6				
Social security....	....	....	....	....	265.5	593.2	631.0	711.5
Carriers and their employees.....	....	....	....	....	0.3	149.5	109.4	122.0
Adjustment to daily Treasury statement (unrevised)........	− 15.5	− 31.0	− 4.0	+ 13.4	− 36.9	+ 30.5	− 1.2	− 19.7
Total taxes..	$1,855.1	$2,954.1	$3,621.0	$3,899.7	$5,083.4	$6,033.5	$5,480.0	$5,651.7
Foreign debts—principal.......	31.6	0.4	0.1	0.1	0.1	0.1	0.1	0.1
Foreign debts—interest........	67.2	20.0	0.6	0.5	0.5	0.5	0.4	0.3
Other revenue and nonrevenue....	125.8	141.1	178.8	215.7	209.8	207.6	187.3	272.7
Total........	$2,079.7	$3,115.6	$3,800.5	$4,116.0	$5,293.8	$6,241.7	$5,667.8	$5,924.8
Less: Appropriations to Federal old-age and survivors insurance trust fund.....	....	....	....	....	265.0	387.0	503.0	537.7
Total receipts	$2,079.7	$3,115.6	$3,800.5	$4,116.0	$5,028.8	$5,854.7	$5,164.8	$5,387.1
Expenditures:								
Relief..........	$ 350.2	$1,844.9	$2,267.0	$2,291.7	$2,375.9	$1,869.0	$2,601.6	$1,906.4
Social security....	....	....	....	27.8	166.9	271.5	320.3	356.5
Public works.....	442.4	698.0	883.4	729.7	1,023.9	782.9	991.8	947.5
Agriculture.......	209.0	779.9	1,076.3	938.0	976.4	860.5	1,235.4	1,567.4
National defense.	651.2	540.3	709.9	911.6	935.1	1,027.8	1,162.5	1,558.8
Pensions.........	863.2	557.0	607.1	2,351.4*	1,137.3*	582.0	557.1	556.7
Civil departments	356.0	302.8	335.7	342.4	365.9	401.2	488.7	594.9
Interest..........	689.4	756.6	820.9	749.4	866.4	926.3	940.5	1,040.9
Tax refunds......	70.3	63.9	76.5	54.3	55.9	99.7	67.9	91.1
Loan and security agencies........	72.9	229.5	134.3	125.3	162.6	139.1	99.7	90.7
Postal deficit.....	117.4	52.0	64.0	86.0	41.9	44.3	41.2	40.9
Transfers to trust accounts.......	21.3	21.1	21.0	40.7	46.7	219.7	182.2	207.9
Panama Canal..	12.7	9.9	9.0	11.5	11.9	11.4	9.8	25.0

TABLE 69. FEDERAL RECEIPTS, EXPENDITURES, AND DEBT 1933–1940. *(Continued)*

	1933	1934	1935	1936	1937	1938	1939	1940
Other expenditures	7.7	155.3†	4.9	5.9	10.5	3.6	8.3	13.5
Totals (net)....	$3,863.5	$6,011.1	$7,009.9	$8,665.6	$8,177.4	$7,238.8	$8,707.3	$8,998.2
Debt retirement..	461.6	359.9	573.6	403.2	104.0	65.5	58.2	129.2
Totals (gross)..	$4,325.1	$6,370.9	$7,583.4	$9,068.9	$8,281.4	$7,304.3	$8,765.3	$9,127.4
Deficits (net)‡....	1,783.8	2,895.5	3,209.4	4,549.7	3,148.6	1,384.2	3,542.3	3,611.1
Deficits (gross)§..	2,245.5	3,255.4	3,783.0	4,952.9	3,252.5	1,449.2	3,600.5	3,740.2

SOURCE: *Annual Report of the Secretary of the Treasury*, 1940, pp. 628, 632, 644, 652, 664.

* Including $1,773.5 for veterans' bonus in 1936 and $556.7 in 1937.
† Including $149.5 for FDIC.
‡ Before statutory debt retirement.
§ After statutory debt retirement.

doubtedly, Marriner Eccles was also influential, as were numerous anonymous economists. Of the men who were very close to the President, Harry Hopkins and James Roosevelt advocated a new spending program. Morgenthau, Garner, and Hull, on the other hand, argued that the best way to stop the recession was to cut spending. "The President listened to one group, then to another," Morgenthau recalled, "and could not decide which course to follow."[2] But something had to be done, for the decline in business activity was the most precipitate in history.

According to the more extreme Keynesians, the existing business depression differed from all previous depressions in that it was not temporary. The American economy was said to have attained a state of "maturity," that is, to have lost its capacity for further growth and for maintenance of full employment. It was said that the opportunities for vast new private investment had dried up and a permanent insufficiency of new investment outlets had developed. The only way to avoid permanent stagnation was to have the government engage in continuous deficit spending in amounts sufficient to compensate for the deficiency of private spending and investment. In other words, in order to maintain full employment, the government budget would have to be kept permanently unbalanced and the public debt would have to be increased continually.

According to another group, interpreting Keynes more mildly, the deficiency in private investment was only temporary and could be offset by temporary government deficit spending for public works. But deficit spending would have to be large enough to have the requisite compensatory effect. These economists believed in a cyclical fiscal policy, involving deficit financing and debt increase in depression and surplus financing and debt reduction in prosperity.

[2] Henry Morgenthau, Jr., "The Morgenthau Diaries," *Collier's*, Sept. 24, Oct. 4, 1947.

Both of the foregoing theories were referred to by their exponents as the "compensatory fiscal policy," and the boundaries between them were by no means clear. Both differed basically from the pump-priming doctrine of the early New Deal, and at the moment both were agreed on one point—that public-works expenditures should be renewed on a substantial scale and that deficit financing should be continued.

At the time of his budget message of January, 1938, Roosevelt was not yet prepared to adopt the newly suggested "compensatory" course. His expenditure estimates for 1939 were $539 million below 1938, although he reserved the right to ask for additional appropriations at a later date. As the economic situation showed a further deterioration, the President decided on the new approach. On April 14 he recommended to Congress an antideflation program of increased spending and lending for public works, calling for additional appropriations of more than $3 billion. Expressing the new philosophy, he asserted, "Today's purchasing power . . . is not sufficient to drive the economic system at higher speed. Responsibility of government requires us . . . to supplement the normal processes and . . . to make sure that the addition is adequate. We must start again on a long steady upward incline in national income." At the same time, Marriner Eccles, who had long since become convinced that fiscal and monetary policy could not be treated separately, testified before the Senate Banking and Currency Committee on the so-called "spend-lend" bill. Said Eccles:

One of three alternatives faces this country, either an unforeseen and unforeseeable very large outlet for investment must develop . . . , a very considerable increase must be brought about in the proportion of the national income that goes into consumption, or the government must provide an outlet for idle funds through deficit financing. . . . Unless some or all of these developments take place, we cannot escape continuous depression. . . . It is only as adequate outlays are provided for our savings that the national income can rise to a satisfactory level, and it is only as the national income increases that tax revenue adequate to balance the budget can be achieved.

Congress did not adopt the "spend-lend" bill in total, but the spending program was resumed and magnified, and in his budget message of January, 1939, the President moved even further toward the "new economics." Omitting all mention of eventually balancing the budget, he stressed the interrelationship between fiscal policy and national income and treated government fiscal policy as a prime stabilizing factor in the national economy. He argued that the level of national income was affected by the rate of government expenditure, and he attributed the partial recovery of the national income since 1932 to the government's deficit spending.

Roosevelt gave a new meaning to his earlier distinction between ordinary and extraordinary expenditures, identifying the former with an operating budget and the latter with an investment budget. Influenced by the reconstitution of the Swedish budget along those lines, he recommended the establishment of a separate budget for self-liquidating projects, a thought originally advanced by Secretary Cortelyou in 1908. Echoing Cortelyou's argument that operating deficits often represented the acquisition of valuable assets, Roosevelt said, "The greater part of the budgetary deficits that have been incurred have gone for permanent, tangible additions to our national wealth. The balance has been an investment in the conservation of our human resources, and I do not regard a penny of it wasted." As evidence, he presented the figures given in Table 70:

TABLE 70. DEFICITS AND NET ADDITIONS TO WEALTH, 1931–1938
(In millions of dollars)

	1931	1932	1933	1934	1935	1936	1937	1938
Deficit (before debt retirement)	$481	$2,529	$1,784	$2,895	$3,210	$4,550	$3,148	$1,384
Outlays for durable improvements and recoverable loans	684	1,372	662	1,838	1,625	1,875	2,198	1,742

SOURCE: *President's Budget Message*, 1939–1940.

The administration's fiscal policy was now dominated by the principle of compensatory deficit financing. But this principle was never too well defined. To some members of the administration's advisory staff, it meant continuous deficit financing, but to the President, it seemed to mean cyclical deficit financing. In his budget message of January, 1940, he charged that the pre-1933 fiscal policy, which "tried to keep expenditures as low as possible in the face of a shrinking national income, came near to bankrupting both our people and our government." The President attributed the rise in the national income from $42 billion in 1932 to $72 billion in 1937 to the policy of "borrowing idle funds to put idle men and idle factories to work," while putting "purchasing power in the hands of those who urgently needed it." In his opinion the cause of the recession of 1937 was "over-optimism which led the government to curtail its net expenditures too abruptly, and business to expand production and to raise prices too sharply for consumers' purchasing power to keep pace." He cited the marked improvement in the national income since 1938 as the direct result of prompt fiscal action, and he recommended for the future "a gradual tapering off, rather than an abrupt cessation of the deficit."

In summary, the New Deal twice changed its spending policy. After pursuing the goal of budget balancing, it shifted in the spring of 1933 to large deficit spending. At the same time, it changed in part from the consolidated budget to a double budget by showing ordinary and extraordinary expenditures in separate subtotals. The second shift, in 1938, was toward much freer and deliberate "compensatory" deficit spending. The consolidated budget was fully restored by abandoning the distinction between ordinary and extraordinary expenditures. The proposal to set up a separate capital budget was never executed.

On the whole, the New Deal's deficit spending, whether reluctant or deliberate, helped to tide the economy over the critical period of the depression. It saved millions of workers, farmers, and small businessmen from destitution and saved society from moral and economic disintegration. But it would have been much more successful had it been carried on more consistently and with greater regard for business psychology and sensibilities. As it was, it did not succeed in bringing about complete economic recovery, and it tended to perpetuate itself.

TABLE 71.   ESTIMATED NET INCOME-INCREASING EXPENDITURES BY
GOVERNMENT, 1933–1939
(In millions of dollars)

Year	Federal government	State and local government	Total
1933	$1,825.5	$ −338.2	$1,487.3
1934	3,302.9	179.4	3,482.3
1935	3,042.6	152.3	3,194.9
1936	3,942.5	115.9	4,058.4
1937	833.5	−32.5	801.0
1938	2,434.0	265.4	2,699.4
1939	3,651.0	1.5	3,652.5

SOURCE: Henry H. Villard, *Deficit Spending and the National Income*, pp. 287, 293, 323.

Expenditures for Relief. The largest New Deal expenditures were for relief and work relief. The Federal relief program began in earnest in May, 1933, when the Federal Emergency Relief Administration (FERA) was created. Instead of loans to the states, as under the Emergency Relief and Construction Act of 1932, the FERA appropriated $500 million for distribution to the states as grants, half at the discretion of the Relief Administrator and the other half on the basis of $1 for every $3 spent for relief by the state and local governments.

Theoretically, FERA grants were to be expended by the states as they saw fit with minimum Federal regulation. But increasingly, Relief Administrator Harry Hopkins directed the expenditures. In October, 1933, all unexpended balances were transferred to the discretionary management of the Administrator, and later when appropriations were increased to $3.3 billion, the requirement of state or local matching of Federal grants was dropped. No fixed formula was followed in the apportionment of funds. Too often political pressure and the bargaining ability of the governor as well as sheer accident determined the share received by a state.

Altogether FERA spent $3.1 billion during the approximately three years of its existence. Most of its disbursements went for direct relief in cash and in kind. At the height of the program in January, 1935, relief families were receiving $30.45 a month, and the Federal government was supplying 74 per cent of total relief funds. Thus, relief became a Federal function, whereas less than a year before it had been considered a state function and a year prior to that, a local function.

TABLE 72. EXPENDITURES FOR RELIEF AND WORK RELIEF, 1933–1940
(In millions of dollars)

	1933	1934	1935	1936	1937	1938	1939	1940	Total
RFC.........	$298.1	$ 0.5	$ −0.9	$ −1.3	$ −13.3	$ −0.3	....	....	$ 282.8
FERA........	37.9	707.4	1,821.0	495.6	12.4	4.4	$ 1.7	$ 0.5	3,080.9
CWA........	....	805.1	11.3	0.7	0.3	0.2	0.2	....	817.8
WPA........	....	....	....	1,228.1	1,830.8	1,421.3	2,161.5	1,477.5	8,119.3
NYA........	....	....	....	35.5	65.6	51.2	78.1	94.6	325.0
CCC........	14.2	331.9	435.5	486.3	385.8	326.4	290.4	283.2	2,553.8
Other........	....	....	....	46.8	94.3	65.7	69.8	50.4	326.9
Totals......	$350.2	$1,844.9	$2,267.0	$2,291.7	$2,375.9	$1,869.0	$2,601.6	$1,906.4	$15,506.7

SOURCE: *Annual Report of the Secretary of the Treasury*, 1940, p. 26.

The administration considered that direct relief weakened morale and it did not lend itself well to Federal financing. From the beginning, FERA was regarded as a temporary device to be used until a public-works program could begin to roll. But public works were disappointingly slow in getting started. Moreover, for every dollar spent, direct relief could take care of far more unemployed than work relief. Therefore, there was a constant conflict within the administration between those who supported work relief and those who supported the more economical direct relief. Harry Hopkins was the chief supporter of the work-relief program, and he dissuaded the President from returning to direct relief. Instead, a Civil Works Administration was created in November, 1933.

The CWA program operated directly through the Federal government, rather than through grants-in-aid to the states. It was a "make-work" program and was greatly limited in its effectiveness, because it was not permitted to engage in any work enhancing the value of private property or competing with private industry. The CWA terminated officially in May, 1934, and was out of business by the end of 1935.

By the end of 1934 it was estimated that 5 million households, or 18 million people, were on Federal relief, leading many to fear that the nation was on its way to adopting a permanent "dole." President Roosevelt apparently shared this fear, for in his annual message of 1935 he said, "The Federal government must and shall quit this business of relief." He proposed that the Federal government confine itself to giving work to employables and that state and local governments reassume the task of taking care of unemployables. The result was the passage of the Emergency Relief and Appropriation Act in April, 1935, appropriating $4.9 billion for a Works Progress Administration. The WPA, as it came to be called, was a compromise between relief and public works. Direct relief cost about $33.66 per family per month, public works cost $206, and WPA cost $80 per month per employed person.

Of all the relief agencies, the WPA became the butt of the most criticism. Its work was derisively labeled "boondoggling," and it was commonly charged with preventing the reemployment of the unemployed and with being honeycombed with politics. However, the criticisms were directed more at the administration of work relief than at its principle, were largely political and partisan in nature, and were grossly exaggerated. The WPA gave jobs to an average of 2.2 million per year from 1936 to 1940, and its administration cost only about 4 per cent of the amount spent. But many of its projects were wasteful, for they had to be geared to the abilities of the unemployed and they were not permitted to compete with private enterprise or to spend adequate amounts for materials. Then, too, the original intention of giving the unemployables back to state care did not work out, as many states refused to take over the unemployable, compelling the Federal government to retain them on its rolls.

Public Works. The expansion of a national public-works program began when the National Industrial Recovery Act became law in June, 1933. Under Title II a fund of $3.3 billion was set up for the Public Works Administration, the entire amount to be allotted by June, 1935. The PWA could allocate for Federal projects $1.3 billion, of which $400 million was earmarked for highways, $50 million for roads in national parks, $15 million for subsistence homesteads, and $238 million for the construction of naval vessels. It could give an outright grant to the states on non-Federal projects equal to 30 per cent of the cost of labor and materials.[3] The remaining 70 per cent was to be in the form of a loan at 4 per cent. In addition, the PWA could make loans, but not grants,

[3] Under later acts, the grant was increased to 45 per cent.

for private construction. In time, the PWA's funds were increased by additional appropriations under the Emergency Appropriation Act of June, 1934, the Emergency Relief Appropriation Act of April, 1935, and the Public Works Administration Appropriation Act of 1938.

TABLE 73. PUBLIC WORKS EXPENDITURES, 1933–1940
(In millions of dollars)

	1933	1934	1935	1936	1937	1938	1939	1940	Total
Rivers and harbors.........	$118.4	$150.7	$203.0	$223.7	$ 235.0	$198.6	$193.0	$212.9	$1,535.3
Public roads....	171.3	267.9	317.4	243.9	350.6	236.6	204.5	176.4	1,968.6
Public buildings.	127.4	87.8	67.4	79.7	88.9	91.5	66.3	75.0	684.1
Reclamation....	25.2	24.7	40.9	64.0	58.7	65.4	79.3	96.4	454.5
PWA*...........	......	155.9	218.5	69.5	248.8	148.7	407.9	347.7	1,597.0
TVA...........	......	11.0	36.1	48.8	42.0	42.0	40.8	39.1	260.0
Totals.......	$442.4	$698.0	$883.4	$729.7	$1,023.9	$782.9	$991.8	$947.5	$6,499.6

SOURCE: *Annual Report of the Secretary of the Treasury*, 1940, p. 28.

* Less repayment of loans.

TABLE 74. ESTIMATED EXPENDITURES FOR PUBLIC AND PRIVATE
CONSTRUCTION, 1930–1940
(In millions of dollars)

Year	Public construction financed by Federal funds (including work relief)	Public construction financed by state and local funds	Private construction	Total
1930	$ 307	$2,469	$5,941	$8,717
1932	460	1,334	1,767	3,561
1935	1,234	616	1,605	3,455
1940	2,281	1,143	3,985	7,409

SOURCE: National Resources Planning Board, *Development of Resources and Stabilization of Employment in the United States*, Part I, p. 17.

From the beginning, the public-works program was hotly debated. Some authorities doubted the government's ability to find sufficient capital works on which to spend the contemplated sums quickly enough to help recovery. Secretary of the Interior Ickes, who was appointed administrator, believed in a slow but sure policy which would prevent graft and waste. On the other hand, Relief Administrator Hopkins clamored for quick spending as an aid to recovery. When the PWA failed to produce quick results, Hopkins's less formidable WPA program described above was put under way to bridge the gap.

The contribution which public works made toward recovery must not be exaggerated. Since private construction and state and local public works declined substantially, the Federal program merely offset these declines to some extent.

Veterans' Bonus, Social Security, and Welfare Grants to States. It took veterans' organizations three years under the New Deal to win Congressional approval for full prepayment of the bonus. The administration opposed it to the very end as special legislation which would divert public funds from broader and more important and equitable uses. In 1933 and 1934 veterans' bonus bills were defeated in the Senate; in May, 1935, the Patman bill to issue greenbacks in prepayment of the adjusted service certificates was passed by Congress, but President Roosevelt vetoed it. Finally, in January, 1936, a milder measure was passed over the President's veto, providing for the payment of the bonus in baby bonds, cashable immediately or maturing in 1945 with interest at 3 per cent annually. By the end of November, 73.3 per cent of the bonds had been cashed, and during the fiscal year 1936, the Treasury paid out $1.8 billion of bonus money with an additional $0.5 billion in 1937. It was estimated by the American Legion that about 34.5 per cent of the bonus money went to pay debts due to merchants and retailers, 19 per cent went into investments and savings, and 15.5 per cent was spent for consumer goods. Thus, the bonus payment gave the consumer-goods economy a slight and temporary stimulant.

For some years agitation had been carried on by social reformers for the establishment of unemployment insurance and old-age assistance on the state level. This movement was not wholly successful, for in 1934 only 29 states had old-age assistance programs and only one had an unemployment insurance plan. Since state governments had always been the innovators in extending government activity, it seemed unlikely that social insurance would be adopted on a large scale. Yet the depression of the thirties and the advent of an imaginative administration opened the way to the achievement of these goals on a Federal level.

Under the Social Security Act, approved August 14, 1935, the Federal government established old-age insurance; a basis for state unemployment insurance; and grants to states for old-age assistance, aid to the blind, aid to dependent and crippled children, various public-health services, and the administration of state unemployment-insurance and employment offices.

The unemployment-compensation section of the Social Security Act imposed a tax on employers of eight or more employees at 3 per cent on their payrolls (lower rate, in 1936 and 1937). If a state enacted an unemployment-compensation law which conformed to Federal minimum requirements, employers could offset their state contributions up to 90 per cent of the Federal tax, but all moneys collected under state law had to be paid into a trust fund held by the Treasury of the United States. The state could draw the money out as needed to pay unemployment insurance benefits. Subject to the foregoing requirements, each state was free to establish such rates of benefits and terms of payment as it deemed best. The Federal government, from its share of the payroll tax, 0.3 per cent of the payrolls, made grants to states for the administrative expenses of their unemployment-compensation systems and employment offices and also for its own supervisory expenses.

The old-age-insurance section of the Act provided a nationally administered contributory old-age benefit to all employees other than domestics, farm employees, and employees of government and non-profit-making institutions. In 1939 this Act was amended to provide benefits to the survivors of the insured, and the system was renamed "Old Age and Survivorship Insurance." Employers and employees were each taxed 1 per cent on each employee's salary or wages up to $3,000 a year. Originally, it was contemplated that contributions would be stepped up ½ per cent every three years, beginning 1940, until a maximum of 3 per cent was reached in 1949, but the increase was deferred each time it was due. Benefits, in the form of an annuity, were paid at age sixty-five and were calculated from a formula based on the amount of the worker's average earnings up to $3,000 a year together with the length of time he had been employed in an insured employment. Average payments, being based only on a few years of contribution, were exceedingly small at first, and old-age assistance was expected to take care of the aged workers in the interim.

Federal grants for old-age assistance were made for one-half of the first $30 of assistance. By subsequent amendments, this was increased until in 1948 it equaled three-fourths of the first $20 plus one-half of the next $30.

Simultaneously with the Social Security Act, an act was passed establishing a National Railroad Retirement System financed by a 3½ per cent contribution from employees and a like contribution from the railroads.

Grants to the states were expanded during this period at a startling rate and over a wide range of social-welfare, educational, and developmental functions. Some of this expansion was only temporary. Thus, the grants for emergency purposes, such as relief and certain types of public works, after reaching approximately $300 million during the fiscal year 1933 and increasing further to $2 billion in 1935, dropped back to $300 million by 1940. But a very considerable proportion of the expansion was permanent in nature. The expenditures for regular grants increased from $130 million in 1933 to $288 million in 1937, and to $574 million in 1940. These increases represented not only an amplification of the older grant programs, but an extension into new fields of state and local activity.[4] The largest resulted from the social security enactments of 1935.

The Expansion of the RFC, Housing, and the Merchant Marine. Under the Roosevelt administration, the activities of the RFC were greatly extended to include loans to newly established public financial institutions, as well as to existing public agencies and private financial and other businesses. Among the RFC's loans for public self-liquidating and private limited dividend projects were $73 million for the San Francisco Golden Gate Bridge, $208.5 billion for a 240-mile aqueduct from Arizona to Southern California, $22.8 million for a power line from Boulder Dam to Los Angeles, $8.1 million for the construction of Knickerbocker Village in New York City, $5.1 million for causeways and other improvements at Jones Beach, Long Island, $35 million for the Harrisburg-Pittsburgh highway, $3.5 million for a bridge at Puget Sound, and $2.2 million for a bridge across the Mississippi at Greenville, Mississippi. A school authority loan was made when Chicago was unable to pay $22.3 million of back pay to her school teachers. The loan was secured by a mortgage on real estate in the Loop district which the Federal government had ceded to the state of Illinois in 1818 for the support of the public schools.

From a business standpoint, the RFC was a success. Its operating expenses were less than 1 per cent of total loans, and despite the fact that its loans were increasingly offered against shaky security, it accumulated a reserve of $200 million which it estimated as adequate to cover all losses. Its chief losses were from loans of less than $50,000 to small businesses. These represented 83 per cent of total business loans, and by 1939, 543 were in default and 46 had already been foreclosed. The railroad loans, which seemed almost hopeless at the time they were made, held their own. The loans to banks were almost all paid off by 1939, the only large loss being an estimated $5 million on the famous $90 million loan to General Dawes's Central Republic Bank and Trust Company of Chicago.

[4] The largest increases were for old-age assistance, from $25 million in 1936, its first year of operation, to $228 million in 1940, and for aid to dependent children, from $2.5 million to $45 million, and aid to the blind, from $1.3 million to $6.2 million. Public-health grants, which amounted to less than $1 million before 1936, jumped to $23 million by 1940. Those for unemployment-compensation administration starting at $2 million in 1936 grew to $58 million by 1940, and those for employment services which began at $600,000 in 1934 increased to over $3 million by 1940. The older grant programs increased less spectacularly from 1933 to 1940—highways, from $104 million to $153 million, agricultural experiment stations, extension, forest aid and land grant colleges, from $17 million to $32 million, vocational education from $8 million to $19 million, and vocational rehabilitation from $1 million to $2 million (Council of State Governments, *Federal Grants-in-Aid*, p. 32).

In attacking the problem of defaulting residential mortgages, the Roosevelt administration, unlike the Hoover administration, offered relief to individual homeowners at the bottom of the structure rather than to financial institutions at the top. The Home Owners' Loan Corporation was created in June, 1933, with authority to assume the mortgages of distressed homeowners who could not obtain accommodation from any other source. Lending by the HOLC ceased on June 13, 1936, by which time over a million loans totaling $3.1 billion had been made.

TABLE 75. RFC LOANS, JANUARY, 1932 TO FEBRUARY, 1939
(In millions of dollars)

	Authori-zations	Can-celed	Dis-bursed	Repaid	Balance out-standing
Agriculture......................	$ 2,584.6	$ 982.5	$ 1,446.3	$1,415.0	$ 31.3
To open banks..................	1,334.7	196.4	1,138.2	1,060.6	77.6
To depositors in closed banks.......	1,331.8	327.5	983.7	920.6	63.1
For bank capital..................	1,349.2	169.6	1,146.6	562.6	584.0
For self-liquidating projects........	954.1	44.7	741.7	457.8	283.9
To business enterprise............	390.8	86.0	160.6	49.7	110.9
To drainage, levee, and irrigation districts......................	142.8	20.5	85.6	3.2	82.4
To railroads.....................	1,248.3	307.6	826.8	346.5	480.3
To mortgage-loan companies........	608.6	103.6	418.7	298.0	120.6
To insurance companies...........	138.9	13.3	125.2	95.4	29.8
To building and loan associations....	154.2	29.0	118.2	116.3	2.0
To public-school authorities.......	24.6	1.3	22.5	22.3	0.1
Catastrophe rehabilitation loans.....	16.8	4.1	12.0	9.5	2.5
To state funds for insurance of deposits.......................	13.1	....	13.1	13.1	
For mining, milling, and smelting businesses....................	12.7	7.4	4.2	1.5	2.6
For other purposes...............	0.7	....	0.6	0.5	0.1
Totals by directors.............	$10,306.0	$2,293.6	$ 7,243.9	$5,372.6	$1,871.3
Allocations at direction of Congress.	2,900.6	0.1	2,801.1	2,753.4	47.7
Grand totals..................	$13,206.6	$2,293.6	$10,045.0	$8,126.0	$1,919.0

SOURCE: Reconstruction Finance Corporation, *Seven Year Report*, 1939, p. 22.

In June, 1934, when it was estimated that 13 million houses were badly in need of repairs and that there was a shortage of 1¾ million houses, effective assistance was rendered to small property owners and indirectly to the construction industry by the National Housing Act, which set up a Federal Housing Administration to insure loans for the purchase or modernization of houses. The FHA insured mortgages made by private lenders up to $16,000 if the mortgage was not in excess of 80 per cent of appraised value and was to be amortized over a period of 20 years or less.

In order to encourage the building of low-cost housing, the PWA was authorized to make loans to limited dividend corporations, but construction under this system was very slow. As a result, the Housing Division of the PWA decided to build and operate its own low-rent projects. Then in 1934 a separate Housing Authority was set up, and between 1934 and 1940, it expended $136 million on emergency housing and slum-clearance work.

Early in the New Deal an investigating committee under Senator Black of Alabama concluded that the government's mail contract system had not strengthened the merchant marine. After a long dispute between those who favored a government-operated merchant marine and those who were satisfied with the existing system, a direct subsidy bill was passed in 1936.

The new subsidy law continued to emphasize the development of a privately owned merchant marine capable of serving as a naval auxiliary in time of war. All existing mail contracts were to be terminated by June 30, 1937, and replaced by straight subsidies to cover the difference between American and foreign construction and operating costs. A United States Maritime Commission was created with powers to estimate differential costs, administer the subsidies, and build and operate ships. The "scientific subsidy" resembled the policy urged on Congress by James G. Blaine fifty years previously. The Maritime Commission expended a total of $122.7 million in the years 1933 to 1940, but $98.7 million was spent in 1940 alone. Although it was a far more efficient and, on the whole, a less costly policy than the previous one, it still left much to be desired from a financial and economic point of view.

Aids to Agriculture. Federal expenditures for agriculture took five different forms: the extension of credit, payment of subsidies, aid to tenants, farm modernization, and the normal operations of the Department of Agriculture. Credit was advanced either directly or through the various agricultural credit agencies, which had been previously organized and were now expanded greatly.

The largest expenditures were for subsidies to raise agricultural prices by curtailing production. Under the Agricultural Adjustment Act and the Soil Conservation and the second AAA Acts, which succeeded it in 1936 and 1938, Congress appropriated close to $1 billion annually for the disposition of crop surpluses. Payments of 60 cents per hundred pounds were also made to domestic cane-sugar and beet-sugar producers under the Sugar Act of 1937.

The Resettlement Administration was created in April, 1935, to help farm tenants to obtain their own farms. In addition, the Department of Agriculture continued its program of education, warfare against plant and animal disease, forest preservation, meat inspection, enforcement of the Food and Drug Act, care of the forests, and other activities originally begun at the turn of the century.

In general, the trend of agricultural expenditures illustrated the endeavor on the part of agrarians to neutralize what they considered the evil effects of the competitive system. Unable to use the techniques of the businessman, the farmer appealed to the Federal government for security, and subsidy payments gradually increased while the use of Federal farm credit declined.

TABLE 76. FEDERAL EXPENDITURES FOR AGRICULTURE, 1933–1940
(In millions of dollars)

Year	Farm credit	AAA	Farm security	Rural electrification	Dept. of Agriculture	Total
1933	$ 131.1	....	....	....	$ 77.9	$ 209.0
1934	415.6	$ 291.9	$ 2.4	....	70.0	779.9
1935	202.4	792.8	5.4	....	75.5	1,076.3
1936	38.8	632.0	138.0	$ 1.4	127.8	938.0
1937	73.6	527.5	209.7	8.9	156.6	976.4
1938	71.1	456.0	183.2	15.2	135.0	860.5
1939	46.5	786.7	210.3	37.8	154.2	1,235.4
1940	35.0	1,139.7	200.3	38.0	154.3	1,567.4
Totals..	$1,014.1	$4,626.7	$949.3	$101.3	$951.4	$7,642.7

SOURCE: *Annual Report of the Secretary of the Treasury*, 1940, p. 29.

Period of Relative Passivity in Tax Policy. The New Deal's taxing policies evolved much more slowly than its spending policies. But when they finally took shape, they contained as many improvisations as the spending policies and in some respects were even more radical in nature.

The development of the tax policy may be divided into three periods. From 1933 to mid-1935 was a period of relative passivity. From 1935 to 1938 taxation was used for such nonfiscal purposes as the equalization of the distribution of wealth, the equalization of the competitive positions of small and big business, and the conversion of supposedly idle corporate savings into active consumer purchasing power. From 1938 to 1940 there was a return to fiscal objectives and to more orthodox approaches.

During its first year, the New Deal administration had the advantage of the higher revenue yields produced by the 1932 Revenue Act. It made only a few moves to secure additional revenue, and nearly all of these were made as a part of other legislation. The Agricultural Adjustment Act of May, 1933, authorized the Secretary of Agriculture to impose taxes on the processing of basic farm commodities at rates to equal the difference between the current average price of each commodity and its fair exchange value, *i.e.* its price during the so-called "parity" period, 1909 to 1914. For example, the Secretary imposed a tax of 30 cents a bushel on wheat processing. Basically, it was a tax on consumption for the farmers' benefit, since it increased wholesale and retail prices more or less correspondingly. It was challenged in the courts and was declared unconstitutional by the Supreme Court in *United States v. Butler* in January, 1936, on the ground that it was not a tax for the general welfare and that Congress had no right to regulate agriculture.

The National Industrial Recovery Act of June 16, 1933, imposed new taxes to provide revenue to service the debt of $3.3 billion incurred to finance public-works expenditures. It was stipulated that these taxes were to be repealed automatically as soon as the budget was balanced or as soon as prohibition was repealed and a liquor tax was introduced. The taxes in question were imposed chiefly on corporations. They included a 5 per cent excess-profits tax on profits in excess of 12½ per cent of the adjusted declared value of the capital stock, a 5 per cent withholding tax on dividends paid to individuals, and a tax of $1 on every $1,000 of the declared value of the capital stock.

In January, 1934, with the repeal of prohibition the taxes imposed under the NRA were automatically repealed, but the Revenue Act of May 10, 1934, reimposed the additional corporate taxes. In addition, consolidated returns were prohibited for all corporations except railroads; an undistributed profits tax was levied on personal holding companies; excise taxes were changed slightly; the rates on individual incomes, estates, and gifts were made slightly more progressive (the normal tax was made a flat 4 per cent, and the maximum surtax was raised to 59 per cent); the 10 per cent credit for earned income was restored; and the capital-gains tax was revised with the rate made more dependent on the length of time the asset had been held.

The "Soak-the-Rich" Program. When the administration's effort to balance the budget failed, pressure for increased taxes was brought to bear by some congressmen, who wanted to increase revenue; by "share-the-wealth" groups; and by some New Dealers, who urged tax revision as a means of achieving economic recovery.

President Roosevelt was impressed by these demands, and in June, 1935, he sent a message to Congress, recommending a broad revision of the existing tax system. He declared, "Our revenue laws have operated in many ways to the advantage of the few, and they have done little to prevent an unjust concentration of wealth and economic power." He contended that the accumulation of great wealth created "social unrest" and should be prevented by "very high taxes." He recommended increases in the personal income tax rates in the higher brackets, an inheritance tax (in addition to the existing estate tax) on very large legacies, a graduated corporate income tax, and a constitutional amendment permitting the Federal government to tax income from state and municipal securities. The President's tax program was clearly designed to correct social and economic inequality rather than to raise additional revenue. Some of its features, such as the proposed superinheritance tax, were of questionable practicality. Businessmen throughout the country instantly labeled the proposals the "soak-the-rich" program and interpreted the message as final evidence of the administration's antibusiness bias.

The revenue bill which was finally enacted into law on August 30, 1935, was much less one-sided than the President's plan. Congress did not stop with heavier taxation on large incomes but increased rates in the middle brackets. Surtaxes on incomes of over $50,000 were increased. The maximum surtax was raised from 59 to 75 per cent, and the maximum estate tax rate, from 60 to 70 per cent. The principle of a graduated corporation income tax was adopted, but in a form scarcely resembling the President's proposal, the rate being raised from $13\frac{3}{4}$ per cent to a range of $12\frac{1}{2}$ to 15 per cent. On the other hand, the excess-profits tax and the capital-stock tax were increased, and a tax on intercorporate dividends was imposed. Members of the so-called progressive bloc were unsuccessful in their attempts to reduce the personal income tax exemptions, and no action was taken on the proposed constitutional amendment affecting tax-exempt bonds.

Even in this mild form, the Revenue Law of 1935 marked a definite and final rift between the administration and business. Roy W. Howard, owner of the Scripps-Howard chain of newspapers, addressed a public letter to the President on August 26, 1935, saying,

Any experienced reporter will tell you that throughout the country many businessmen who once gave you sincere support are now not merely hostile, they are frightened. Many of these men whose patriotism and sense of public service will compare with that of any men in political life, have become convinced and sincerely believe that you fathered a tax bill that aims at revenge rather than revenue—revenge on business; that the administration has sidestepped broadening the tax base to the extent necessary to approximate the needs of the situation; that there can be no real recovery until the fears of business have been allayed through the granting of a breathing spell to industry.

To this letter President Roosevelt replied on September 2:

The tax program of which you speak is based upon a broad and just social and economic purpose . . . not to destroy wealth, but to create broader range of opportunity . . . to lay the burdens of Government where they can best be carried. . . . Congress declined to broaden the tax base because it was recognized that the tax base had already been broadened to a very considerable extent. . . . In 1929 consumers' taxes represented only 30 per cent of the national revenue. Today they are 60 per cent. . . . This Administration came into power pledged to a very considerable legislative program. . . . This basic program has now reached substantial completion and the "breathing spell" of which you speak is here.[5]

In the meanwhile, in 1936 and 1937, the unemployment insurance, old-age social security, and the railroad retirement taxes took effect. Although progressive business leadership accepted the new levies as desirable in the long run, it was concerned as to their immediate effects, since they increased costs and therefore acted to deter business activity.

Undistributed Profits Tax. The budget was put completely out of balance in January, 1936, when the Supreme Court declared the AAA processing tax unconstitutional and Congress prepaid the veterans' bonus. However, the President had no intention of abandoning his program of social reform or his belief in the need for a balanced budget. To supply the needed revenue, he recommended in a supplemental budget message in March, 1936, the repeal of all corporation taxes and their replacement by an undistributed profits tax.

The President maintained that corporations were retaining a substantial portion of their profits in order to save their large stockholders from paying high surtaxes on dividends. Using Treasury estimates, he asserted that, during the calendar year 1936, some $4.5 billion of corporate profits would be retained by corporations, causing a $1.3 billion loss of revenue. He therefore proposed a graduated undistributed profit tax to "yield approximately the same amount of revenue as would be yielded if corporate profits were distributed and taxed in the hands of stockholders." The President's proposal also had an economic purpose, namely, to take away from management and corporation directors the power to retain and reinvest stockholders' funds. He wished to force corporations to pay out all their profits to stockholders so that the latter could decide for themselves whether to reinvest a part of their dividends in the same corporations or to invest them in other corporations or to spend them all on consumer goods and services. By this time, too, the President and some of his Keynesian advisers were determined to impose punitive taxes on savings and to use tax and expenditure programs as a means of increasing purchasing power by transferring private funds from the upper-income groups who saved to the lower-income groups who consumed.

Businessmen were completely shocked by the proposal, since they re-

[5] For a fuller discussion of the controversies over the 1935 Act see Studenski and others, *Taxation and Public Policy*, pp. 167–170; and of those involved in the succeeding revenue laws of the 1935 to 1940 period, see Roy G. Blakey and Gladys C. Blakey's articles in the 1935 to 1940 numbers of the *American Economic Review*.

garded the practice of "plowing back earnings" as one of the main sources of the strength of American enterprise. They viewed the proposal as an attack on the American system and as a flagrant misuse of the power of taxation. They were amply supported in this notion by orthodox professional economic opinion.

Notwithstanding these protests, Congress in June, 1936, enacted an undistributed corporate profits tax with rates of 7 to 27 per cent, reduced the corporate income tax to 8 per cent in the lower brackets, and subjected corporate dividends received by individuals to the normal tax as well as to the surtax, thus inaugurating what soon became known as double taxation of stockholders' income.

During the fiscal year 1937, revenue collections from personal and corporate income taxes were so disappointing that an investigation was immediately undertaken. The Treasury discovered widespread tax evasion. Personal holding companies were set up in foreign countries where taxes were low and corporation laws lax. Domestic personal holding companies were formed, transforming individual income into corporate income, subject to the lower corporate tax rates. Yachts and country estates were incorporated, enabling taxpayers to deduct their maintenance costs as business expenses. Multiple trusts were created, making possible the splitting of income into many parts and avoidance of the higher surtaxes. On June 1, 1937, Congress passed a new revenue law, closing some of these existing loopholes. This was a purely administrative law and was the first entirely fiscal revenue measure since the beginning of the New Deal. It was also the first tax measure in two years which did not stir up great animosities among businessmen.

Breathing Spell in Tax Policy. The business community blamed the business recession of 1937 in part on the undistributed profits tax and called upon the administration to give some tax relief. When the President made no tax recommendations in his budget message of January, 1938, Congress took matters in its own hands. It passed a bill in May without the President's signature, sharply reducing the rates of the undistributed profits tax, making it applicable only to corporations with incomes of over $25,000 and only for the year 1938, making capital gains subject to ordinary taxes or to a flat rate of 30 per cent, raising the corporate income tax rate to $12\frac{1}{2}$ to 19 per cent dependent on the proportion of retained earnings, and repealing various excise taxes.

When business conditions failed to improve, Secretary Morgenthau and Undersecretary Hanes urged the President to remove "deterrents to business incentives" from the existing tax system, and Congress, in spite of the President's objections, repealed the last of the undistributed profits tax on June 29, 1939.

This action was soon followed by a moderation of social security financing. Originally, the plan called for the accumulation of an actuarial reserve from which payments could be made as they came due. The reserve, estimated eventually to reach $47 billion, was to be invested in 3 per cent government bonds. Critics of the plan held that the reserve would be merely a paper account containing only the government's IOU's. When current payments exceeded the current revenues of the fund, it would be necessary to draw on the reserve, and the government would have to go into the open market and sell its bonds just as if the reserve had not existed. The accumulation of the reserve would also create investment problems and act as a constant temptation to profligate spending. Influenced by this reasoning, Congress abandoned the reserve plan in August, 1939, freezing the tax rate at 1 per cent for the next three years and providing merely for a contingency reserve equal to three times the annual expenditure for benefits. At the same time benefits were liberalized.

During the same year Congress, in response to a special message from the President, passed the Public Salary Tax Act. The Act made state and municipal salaries taxable under the Federal income tax and also permitted nondiscriminatory state taxation of Federal salaries. The way for this enactment had been paved by several notable decisions rendered by the Supreme Court in 1937 and 1938 (*Helvering v. Gerhardt* and *Graves v. N.Y. ex rel. O'Keefe*) declaring nondiscriminatory intergovernmental taxation of public salaries to be constitutional, thus completely reversing earlier decisions. The Act also terminated the exemption of Federal judicial salaries from the Federal income tax. Federal judges had enjoyed this exemption under previous statutes and interpretations of the constitutional provision that salaries of judges shall not be diminished during their continuance in office. Because of the increasing size of the public payrolls and the inevitable lowering of personal exemptions in the future, the gain in both Federal and state revenue from the removal of these exemptions, though not very large immediately, was bound to become considerable in time. But even more important was its moral effect. The removal of these exemptions greatly strengthened the fabric of both Federal and state income taxes, for the private citizens who had to pay these taxes (and were uninitiated in the niceties of legalistic doctrines) could never understand why public employees should have been exempted from these taxes.

The President in the same message of January, 1939, had also asked immediate legislation subjecting interest on state and municipal bonds to nondiscriminatory Federal taxation and permitting nondiscriminatory state taxation of interest on Federal bonds. New evidence was furnished by the Treasury that wealthy individuals were escaping the high surtaxes of the Federal income tax by investing in state and municipal bonds. The resulting losses in Federal revenue and inequities in the application of the tax were shown to be considerable. But here the doctrine of reciprocal immunity proved much more strongly intrenched. State and municipal governments vigorously opposed the proposed change, claiming that it would increase considerably their costs of borrowing, and the general public was confused about the issue. Under the circumstances, the proposal made little headway in Congress.

On the whole, the New Deal tax philosophy emphasized nonfiscal objectives; that is, it sought to correct economic inequality and to influence the operation of the economy by breaking down concentration of economic power and by converting savings into spending. With the exception of the early AAA processing taxes, which were ill-advised, and the social security taxes, which were regressive, it avoided taxes on consumer buying power partly because of a fear that such taxes would aggravate the depression and partly for reasons of distributive justice. This policy was justified, but on the other hand, in seeking to augment progressive taxes and reduce savings, the New Deal somewhat inconsistently showed no interest in tapping the considerable taxpaying capacity of the middle-income groups (the $6,000 to $100,000 brackets) even though a considerable portion of those incomes was being saved.

New Deal Debt Operations. Over the eight fiscal years 1933 through 1940 budgetary deficits aggregated $26.3 billion or, exclusive of statutory debt retirement, $24.1 billion. In addition, because of the larger scope of expenditures, the cash balance in the general fund increased $1.5 billion. Consequently, it was necessary to raise $25.6 billion. Of this, $2.1 billion came from devaluation and from the seigniorage on silver, while $23.5 billion came from fresh borrowing. In addition to providing these new funds, the Treasury had to refund maturing obligations into new issues, and it took advantage of the callable feature in some of the long-term issues by replacing them with lower interest-bearing obligations. In these operations, the Treasury relied much more on long-term callable issues (five years or more) than on short-term issues. Thus, the proportion of long-term obligations in the total public-held interest-bearing debt increased from 65 to 80 per cent.

The most important innovation in the technique of debt management was the appearance of United States savings bonds which were similar in nature to the war savings certificates of World War I. Authorized by the Act of February 4, 1935, they were first placed on sale on March 1, 1935, and sold at a discount price of $75 for each $100 of maturity value. Single ownership was limited to $10,000. If held to maturity (ten years), they yielded about 2.9 per cent annually. However, they were redeemable after sixty days and were therefore demand obligations which could be classified as short-term debts. If the bonds were so classified, the proportion of the long-term debt in the total public-held interest-bearing debt increased from 65 to only 71 per cent.

Another significant change in the Treasury's debt operations was the great increase in the government's borrowing from its own trust funds. Between 1933 and 1940 the holdings of trust funds increased from $323 million to $4.8 billion, or from 1.5 to 11.5 per cent of the total interest-bearing debt. Borrowing from the trust funds was accomplished through special issues bearing a fixed rate of interest, rather than through purchase of existing bonds in the open market.

TABLE 77. CHANGES IN THE FEDERAL DEBT, JUNE 30, 1933–1940
(In millions of dollars)

	1933	1935	1937	1939	1940
Interest-bearing:					
Prewar and postal savings bonds	$ 806	$ 855	$ 198	$ 196	$ 196
Liberty bonds	8,201	1,335			
Treasury bonds	5,216	12,684	19,936	25,218	26,555
United States savings bonds	....	62	800	1,868	2,905
Adjusted service bonds, 1945	....	....	389	283	261
Total long-term bonds	$14,224	$14,936	$21,323	$27,565	$29,917
Treasury notes	$ 4,548	$10,023	$10,617	$ 7,243	$ 6,383
Treasury bills	954	2,053	2,303	1,308	1,302
Certificates of indebtedness	2,108				
Total short-term	$ 7,611	$12,076	$12,920	$ 8,551	$ 7,685
Total public issues	$21,835	$27,012	$34,242	$36,116	$37,602
Special issues:					
Government life-insurance fund	....	....	$ 500	$ 500	$ 500
Treasury notes	$ 231	$ 478	708	1,983	2,553
Certificates of indebtedness	92	156	350	1,287	1,721
Total special issues	$ 323	$ 633	$ 1,558	$ 3,770	$ 4,775
Total interest-bearing debt	$22,158	$27,645	$35,800	$39,886	$42,376
Matured debt	$ 66	$ 231	$ 119	$ 142	$ 205
Non-interest-bearing debt	315	825	506	411	386
Total gross debt	$22,539	$28,701	$36,425	$40,440	$42,968
Guaranteed obligations	....	$ 4,123	$ 4,665	$ 5,451	$ 5,529

SOURCE: *Annual Report of the Secretary of the Treasury*, 1940, pp. 51, 75.

The Treasury relied on bills to remove the disturbances in its fiscal operations caused by top-heavy tax collections on quarterly dates. Occasionally, the bills were issued for 182 or 273 days, but in most instances for 91 days. The refunding of bills was not so complicated as the refunding of notes into new notes or bonds. But the largest refunding operations were those undertaken in connection with the remaining

Liberty bonds. In October, 1933, there remained outstanding $6.3 billion of the Fourth Liberty Loan. Over the next two years $800 million was paid off, $4.4 billion was exchanged for 2¾ to 3¾ per cent bonds, and $1 billion for 1½ and 2½ per cent notes. Conditions in the money market continued to be highly favorable, and in 1935 the last $1.9 billion of the First Liberty Loan was refunded into 2⅞ per cent bonds and 1⅝ per cent notes. The annual interest savings on these operations was $111 million.

Changes in Method of Debt Authorization. During the great borrowing operations of the depression, Congress completely relinquished its control over debt management. In February, 1935, Congress amended the Second Liberty Loan Act, imposing a maximum limit of $25 billion on outstanding bonds and $20 billion on short-term issues, but allowing the Treasury to reissue them once they had been retired. In July, 1939, the Secretary of the Treasury was given additional discretionary power when Congress increased the debt limit to $45 billion and removed the restrictions on the type of obligations which could be issued. From this time on, the Treasury was in control of debt management, Congress merely stipulating the statutory debt maximum and influencing debt policy indirectly through its exclusive power over the appropriation of money. The new arrangement promised to be far more efficient, for there was no good reason to hobble the Treasury after Congress appropriated funds and the departments spent them.

During the later thirties, too, the operation of the sinking fund became of only academic importance. In the beginning of the decade, Congress, concerned over government credit, provided under the Emergency Relief and Construction Act of 1932 and the National Industrial Recovery Act of 1933 that a sum equal to 2½ per cent of the expenditures for Federal public works be appropriated annually for the sinking fund. But since the Treasury was operating with a large deficit, these provisions would not affect the net amount of the public debt but would only change its composition. Moneys for the sinking fund were raised by the sale of new obligations and were used to retire old obligations, the whole performance being nothing more nor less than a refunding operation. Recognizing this, the Treasury, beginning in 1937, did not use the entire sinking-fund appropriation to retire obligations but carried the unused portion over to the next year, continuing this procedure in each year thereafter.

Decline in Interest Rates. As the government debt increased, conservatives continually sounded alarms, forecasting steady increases in interest rates and inevitable price inflation. These predictions might have had some validity for the more distant future, but not for the immediate situation, for as long as industry had large unused productive capacity, there could be no runaway inflation. In its early years, the New Deal administration itself believed that the public credit could not sustain continuous budgetary deficits and increases in the public debt. But in practice this also proved incorrect. The public credit did not collapse under the burden of increased public debt. On the contrary, government credit grew stronger, interest rates on new government borrowing declined steadily, and the Treasury found it increasingly easy to finance its operations. Between 1933 and 1940 the computed annual interest rate on Treasury bonds fell from 3.8 to 2.9 per cent, and the average rate on the entire government interest-bearing debt declined from 3.3 to 2.6 per cent. Moreover, the Treasury found it possible to sell its obligations at a premium. In June, 1935, 3 per cent bonds were sold for cash at a price of 103.6, the average bid on 2⅞ per cent bonds was 101.6, and 1⅛ per cent notes were exchanged for maturing obligations at a price of 101.

TABLE 78.   OWNERSHIP OF DIRECT AND GUARANTEED GOVERNMENT SECURITIES,
JUNE 30, 1933–1940
(In billions of dollars)

	1933	1934	1935	1936	1937	1938	1939	1940
Federal trust funds........	$ 0.7	$ 1.4	$ 2.0	$ 2.3	$ 3.6	$ 4.8	$ 5.9	$ 7.1
Federal Reserve banks.....	2.0	2.4	2.4	2.4	2.5	2.6	2.6	2.5
Commercial banks........	7.5	10.3	12.7	15.3	14.6	14.0	15.7	16.6
Mutual savings banks.....	0.7	1.0	1.5	2.1	2.4	2.7	3.0	3.1
Insurance companies......	1.0	1.5	2.6	3.9	5.0	5.5	5.9	6.5
Other investors...........	10.3	10.5	10.5	11.7	12.4	11.9	12.3	12.2
Total securities........	$22.2	$27.2	$31.8	$37.7	$40.5	$41.4	$45.3	$47.9*

SOURCE: Federal Reserve Board, *Banking and Monetary Statistics*, 1941, p. 512.

* Total interest-bearing direct debt was $42.4 billion and guaranteed debt was $5.5 billion.

The yields on government securities, reflecting changes in the market price of obligations, also drifted downward. On March 3, 1933, the yield on long-term governments was 3.42 per cent. On June 30, 1940, it was 2.39 per cent. Indeed, at times short-term obligations gave a negative yield, since they could be used as rights in purchasing long-term obligations at lower than market prices. However, there were five temporary upswings in the yields: at the time of the bank holiday, during the gold-buying period at the end of 1933, in the summer of 1934 because of a crisis in central Europe, in March, 1937, when reserve requirements were increased, and at the outbreak of war in September, 1939. In each of these cases, the countersecular trend lasted for less than three months.

The principal cause of the decline of interest rates was the fact that excess reserves in the commercial banks were constantly increasing. Not being able to find borrowers, commercial banks bought a large part of the increased public debt. In addition, insurance companies and savings banks tapped the savings of individuals, and in the absence of other investment outlets, they bought government obligations.

Of the total increase in debt, commercial-bank and Reserve bank holdings accounted for 37 per cent; the trust funds, 25 per cent; insurance companies, 21 per cent; and the savings banks, 9 per cent. Commercial banks held the largest percentage of the total debt: 34 per cent on June 30, 1933, and 35 per cent on June 30, 1940. The holdings of noninstitutional investors declined from over 46 per cent in 1933 to only 25 per cent in 1940. On the other hand, the holdings of savings banks and insurance companies increased from 8 to over 20 per cent, and trust-fund ownership rose from 3 to 15 per cent. Federal Reserve holdings declined from 8 to 4 per cent.

There was also some anxiety at first regarding the future burdens of interest payments and debt repayment. But this fear gradually vanished as the emergency expenditures shifted from relief to public works and as an increasing portion of the new debt was represented by newly created, socially useful public improvements. The administration was persuaded by some of its economic advisers that government borrowing increased the national income, thus creating the means with which to pay debt charges. At the same time a foothold was obtained for the new theory that an internally held debt was of no consequence, because though it represented a debt for the nation as a whole, it also represented a credit for the citizens who comprised the nation. While the latter part of this contention was logically indisputable, the conclusion that a domestically held debt was harmless because "we owe it to ourselves" was false. The existence of a large domestic debt has profound economic and political consequences, arising from the type of its distribution.[6] The contention tended to minimize the main problem of debt management, that of achieving a most advantageous distribution of the debt.

Attempts at Reorganization of Executive Departments. The Roosevelt administration inherited the problem of reorganization of the executive departments tackled unsuccessfully by the Republican administrations in the early 1920's and again by Hoover. Under the Act of June 30, 1932, the President was empowered to "transfer the whole or any part" of any executive department or independent agency "and/or the functions

[6] Even if the domestic debt was distributed in exactly the same manner as taxes, an obviously unrealizable situation, it would still have substantial economic and political effects.

thereof" to the jurisdiction of any other executive department or independent agency and "to designate and fix the name and functions of any consolidated activity or executive agency and the title, powers and duties of its executive head." Action was to be by Executive Orders, which were to become effective within sixty days, unless vetoed by Congress. As soon as Congress reconvened in December, 1932, President Hoover issued several Executive Orders, reorganizing the executive branch, but since in the meanwhile a new President had been elected, Congress disapproved these orders.

On March 3, 1933, Congress amended the enabling act of 1932 authorizing the President not merely to transfer but also to abolish functions of any executive agency. It also removed the Congressional veto power over Executive Orders, but it retained the provision that the orders could become effective only within sixty days. It limited the authority to two years, abolished the Bureau of Efficiency, and transferred its records to the Bureau of the Budget.

Under this authority, the President unified the several existing farm credit agencies into one Farm Credit Administration in 1933, consolidated a number of minor agencies having to do with parks, buildings, and certain other properties in one Office of National Parks, Buildings and Reservation, and established a new Division of Disbursements in the Treasury in 1934, and transferred the functions of the United States Shipping Board and Merchant Fleet Corporation to the United States Maritime Commission in 1936. An important change in the allocation of fiscal functions was made in 1933 when the authority to make, waive, and modify apportionments of appropriations was transferred from the heads of departments and independent agencies to the Director of the Budget, thus strengthening considerably his power to prevent deficiencies. A few other less important changes were made before the President's power expired in March, 1935.

In the meanwhile, as a result of the creation of numerous emergency agencies, the executive organization had become even more sprawling. Recognizing the necessity for a more systematic reorganization, Congress, in February, 1936, set up a committee under the chairmanship of Senator Byrd "to investigate the executive agencies of the government." This committee engaged the Brookings Institution to conduct a survey. This was followed in March, 1936, by the appointment by the President of his own "Committee on Administrative Management" comprised of three experts in public administration.

The two groups issued separate reports within a year. These differed widely in their recommendations, especially in regard to fiscal management. The Congressional group sought to strengthen the General Accounting Office, while the President's committee recommended abolishing the Office, transferring its functions to the Treasury, and creating a new General Auditing Office to advise Congress. It maintained that pre-audit was an executive function which should be located in the Treasury, and that only post-audit should be vested in an independent agency responsible to Congress. The Committee also proposed substantial reorganization of the independent agencies by Executive Order while the congressional group opposed such reorganization.[7]

The net effect of these surveys and discussions was the enactment in 1939 of the Reorganization Act, establishing the Executive Department, shifting thereto the Bureau of the Budget from its nominal position in the Treasury, and renewing the President's authority to effect reorganization of executive departments by Executive Order. The Executive Order effecting the transfer broadened considerably the power of the Bureau, specifically directing it to assist the President in the formulation of his "fiscal program," a term for the first time introduced into law, implying an interrelated use of governmental spending, taxing, and borrowing for the achievement of specific objectives. The Bureau's authority over the execution of the Budget, particularly over the segregation of lump sum appropriations, was greatly strengthened, the aim being to constitute the Bureau into the President's prime instrument of administrative management. The Budget Bureau was divided into five divisions: (1) estimates, (2) fiscal policy, (3) administrative management, (4) statistical standards, and (5) legislative reference, and its staff was greatly enlarged.[8]

The Treasury was also reorganized considerably by Executive Orders. Thus, in 1940 the offices of accounts and deposits, public debt, and treasurer were consolidated in one Fiscal Service under the direction of a permanent Fiscal Assistant Secretary.

State and Local Finance during the Depression. The outbreak of the depression severely upset the finances of state and local governments. Their revenues declined sharply, and their credit began to give way. To maintain budgetary balance, as required by law or by long-established practice, and to save their credit, state and local governments suspended capital outlays, sought new revenue sources, cut services, and reduced personnel and pay rates. The states were in a better position to find new revenues than were the localities, and they were also less entangled in debt. Accordingly, they succeeded sooner in reestablishing their finances on a firm foundation.

[7] Lewis Meriam and Laurence F. Schmeckebier, *Reorganization of the National Government;* U.S. President's Committee on Administrative Management, *Report.*
[8] Norman M. Pearson, "The Budget Bureau: From Routine Business to General Staff," *Public Administration Review,* Vol. 3, No. 2, Spring, 1943.

The states sustained their greatest revenue losses in personal and corporate income and inheritance tax yields.[9] By contrast, motor-fuel and vehicle taxes and gross-receipts business taxes held up fairly well. A few states had accumulated during the last years of the boom substantial surpluses (in New York, over $100 million) which helped them to meet their first budgetary deficits. But these surpluses were soon exhausted. By 1932 and 1933, every state tried to increase its revenue either by increasing existing tax rates or by imposing new taxes. Among the latter, the general sales tax and the cigarette tax became favorites. One or two states adopted the pari-mutuel tax and, rather surprisingly in a period of depression, found it to be a substantial revenue producer. All such rate increases or new taxes were voted as temporary measures but were renewed each year as the depression continued. The repeal of prohibition in the fall of 1932 also helped state revenue, as it made possible the reimposition of liquor taxes or the realization of substantial profits from the operation of state liquor monopolies. By 1937, state revenue had not only been rebuilt to its former level but even raised above it.[10]

Since state debts were relatively moderate and mostly long term, they caused little trouble. Temporarily, loans became unobtainable, but once revenue systems were repaired and expanded, states were able to resume borrowing. New borrowings were mostly for relief expenditures and were not immoderate, and since money rates had declined, these new loans were incurred at interest rates which did not bear heavily upon state budgets. Despite an increase in total net long-term state debt from $2 billion in 1932 to $2.6 billion in 1940, interest charges remained practically unchanged at approximately $117 million a year. Having increased considerably their revenue resources and also improved their credit, the states were able to increase their assistance to the local governments, which were in dire need of help.

Municipal revenues declined gradually, reaching their lowest point in 1933, but unlike state revenues, they did not lend themselves to quick repair. Collections from the property tax—the only tax source of the localities—fell off sharply as thousands of property owners, having become unemployed or having lost their tenants, became delinquent on their taxes.[11] Thousands of properties had to be sold for taxes or, in de-

[9] In New York State, tax collections (state share) dropped from $260 million in the fiscal year 1930 to $202 million in the fiscal year 1932. The yield of the personal income tax dropped from $40 million in 1930 to $20 million in 1931, that of the corporation franchise net income tax from $40 million in 1931 to $20 million in 1933, and that of the inheritance tax from $50 million in 1930 to $34 million in 1933.

[10] Thus, in New York State, state tax revenue in 1937 was $344 million, 30 per cent above the peak of the boom period.

[11] A study by the U.S. Bureau of the Census (*Current Tax Delinquency*, 1934) showed that in the fiscal year ending June 30, 1933, $909 million of property taxes was

fault of buyers, taken over by the localities and held indefinitely. Assessed valuations also shrank considerably as the assessors were compelled by irate property owners, often armed with court orders, to reduce their assessments. Property owners were generally able to demonstrate in review proceedings that their assessments were above the current depressed market values of their properties.[12]

As municipal revenue declined, municipal credit suffered a catastrophic blow. Municipal debts had been greatly overextended during the boom period, and many of them were for short terms. For years it had been a general practice of the municipalities to borrow regularly in anticipation of tax collections. Now as their tax collections suddenly fell off, they found themselves unable to pay their immediately maturing obligations. Ordinarily the banks would have given them new credit, but now the banks themselves needed all the money they could muster to meet the demands of their depositors. As the banks insisted on payment, hundreds of municipalities defaulted on their obligations, and this, in turn, brought on a panic in the municipal-bond market. New York City bonds sold at 30 per cent discount in 1933, and its finances were placed for a period of four years under a practical receivership under the so-called "bankers' agreement." Some municipalities failed to pay not only their obligations to bondholders but even their current bills and payrolls. Not a few paid their employees in scrip which, while received at par for taxes, circulated at a discount.

Eventually in the second half of the thirties, the financial condition of most municipalities improved. Moratoriums on mortgage foreclosures granted by state law together with the extension of credit to property owners at low rates by Federal lending agencies helped property owners to liquidate their tax arrears and to pay their taxes currently. A revival of home construction under FHA loans added new properties to the assessment rolls and increased property tax revenues. At the same time, the expenditure load of the local governments was lightened by the establishment of Federal old-age assistance and expansion of Federal public-works expenditures for their benefit as well as by the increased state aids for relief, old-age pensions, schools, and other purposes.

---

uncollected and delinquent. The average delinquency was 20 per cent of the levy, and the range was from 6 per cent in Massachusetts to 40 per cent in Michigan. Delinquency was most extensive in large urban areas, since real estate there had particularly overexpanded during the boom period and now experienced a particularly great crash.

[12] In New York City the assessed valuations dropped from $19.6 billion in 1932 to $16.6 billion in 1934, and they remained at about the latter figure throughout the remainder of the 1930's. The tax collections declined from $478 million in 1931 to $433 million in 1933. In the country as a whole assessed values shrank from $163 billion in 1932 to $141 billion in 1937.

Some of the larger cities were granted power by state legislatures to impose special nonproperty taxes of a temporary nature for the financing of relief. Thus, New York City was permitted in 1935 to levy a general sales tax, a gross-receipts business tax, a tax on the gross receipts of utilities, and a cigarette tax, obtaining from these sources approximately $70 million a year. Philadelphia in 1939 imposed the first municipal income tax. These were revolutionary innovations, for it had never been thought that municipalities could successfully administer any but property taxes.

Municipalities also derived considerable aid from loans extended to them at low interest rates by Federal lending agencies and in some states (Massachusetts, Minnesota, and North Carolina) by the state governments. In some states, state governments took over the servicing of specific highway and other bond issues, reducing municipal burdens to that extent. On June 30, 1940, the total local bond issues thus being serviced by states aggregated $403 million and the annual charge borne by the states on account of the localities amounted to $20 million.

As a result of all these developments, most of the municipalities paid off or successfully funded all their short-term obligations by 1937, thereby reestablishing their credit. Prices of municipal bonds recovered, and many municipalities were able to refinance portions of their debts at lower interest rates as well as to resume borrowing for new capital improvements. However, they borrowed more cautiously, and many did not borrow at all, reducing their debts instead.

The entire local net debt was just about the same in 1940 as in 1932, but its structure had altered. The net debts of special districts had increased from $1.6 billion to $2.5 billion, just about equal to the reduction effected in the city, county, township, and school district debts.[13] The special districts were concentrated mainly in metropolitan regions. They were suburban sanitary and other improvement districts or else metropolitan authorities, such as the Port of New York Authority, the New York Triborough Bridge Authority, the Chicago Sanitary District, or the Metropolitan Water District of Southern California. A large proportion of these district debts—35 per cent—was of the "revenue bond" type, that is, non-tax-supported. Since the new borrowings were at lower interest rates, the annual expenditures for interest, despite the unchanged amount of the principal, were one-third lower in 1940 than in 1932.

By 1940-1941, state and local finance were in greatly altered relative positions. Both were submerged by the great expansion of Federal finance. But within this over-all submergence, state finance made gains

[13] City debts amounted to $8.8 billion in 1932 and $8.7 billion in 1940. County debts decreased from $2.4 billion to $2 billion, township from $344 million to $274 million, and school-district debts from $2 billion to $1.7 billion.

while local finance lost ground. State revenue systems were enhanced by increases in tax rates and by the addition of new taxes which, to all intents and purposes, had become permanent. On the other hand, local revenue systems, except in a few places, remained unchanged. Both state and local governments became substantially dependent on Federal aid, and local government became more than ever dependent on state aid. In short, the depression had increased the centralization of fiscal powers in the Federal government relative to the states and in the state governments relative to the localities.

TABLE 79. STATE AND LOCAL FINANCE, SELECTED YEARS, 1930–1942
(In millions of dollars)

	State			Local	
	1930	1933	1940	1 932	1942
Tax revenues (excluding unemployment compensation)	$2,108	$1,724	$3,313	$ 4,468	$ 4,597
Property.	345	285	260	4,353	4,273
Personal income. . . . . }	233	64	206		
Corporation income. . . . . }		57	155		
General sales and gross receipts. .	1	16	499		
Alcoholic beverage and license. . . .	. . . . . .	10	255		
Tobacco.	12	20	97		
Motor vehicle and fuel.	851	821	1,226		
Inheritance.	183	127	113		
Other.	482	325	502	115	324
	1930	1932	1940	1932	1942
Expenditures (excluding debt retirement)	. . . . . .	$2,734	$5,114	$ 6,501	$ 6,315
Operation.	*	1,058	1,745	4,476	5,301
Capital outlays.	✦	775	725	1,281	402
Interest.	*	114	117	610	405
Aid to other governments.	*	764	1,627	65	48
Contributions to unemployment compensation and retirement funds.	*	23	900	69	159
Per capita expenditures (dollars). . . .	*	21.90	39.28	52.07	46.89
Debt, total net.	*	2,361	2,732	15,216	14,603

SOURCE: U.S. Bureau of the Census, *Historical Review of State and Local Finances, Governmental Debt in 1950*, pp. 13, 14, 20, 33. The Tax Foundation, *Facts and Figures on Government Finance, 1950–51*, pp. 89, 140.

* Not available.

Chapter 30: FINANCING WORLD WAR II

The financing of World War II was a repeat performance of the financing of World War I, but on a much larger scale. In World War II half the average annual production was used to prosecute the war compared with 25 per cent in 1917–1918. However, the costs of World War II were paid entirely out of increased production which, because of a great expansion in labor force and plant capacity, was twice as high as in 1939, whereas the costs of the other war had to be met in part by curtailing civilian consumption.

World War II required much more complicated and sophisticated financing. In the organization of this financing, the lessons of the other war and of the depression of the 1930's were heeded. Nevertheless, some of the same mistakes were made, particularly by Congress.

Controls over the economy (price ceilings, rationing, priorities, etc.) were instituted much more quickly than in World War I, but they were not exerted equally in all segments of the economy. Although 46 per cent of total war costs, the highest percentage in the history of American war finance, was covered by taxes, this was not so much as was possible or desirable. In its loan operations the Treasury relied much too heavily on bank financing. In World War II 40 per cent of the increased government debt was absorbed by the banks, compared with 17 per cent in World War I. Repeating the mistakes of Chase and McAdoo, the Treasury followed an extreme easy-money policy, and put too much emphasis on low interest rates. In addition, it not only instituted a policy of controlling long-term market interest rates, but it attempted to maintain a differential between long- and short-term rates. However, it did avoid the deplorable "borrow and buy" policy of 1917, and it was much more successful in tapping the potential spending power of the vast mass of consumers.

Supplying the Democracies and Arming for Defense. When the war broke out in September, 1939, the United States had the potential power to supply vast quantities of arms and materials of war. Emerging from a severe and prolonged depression, she had vast unused plant capacity, a labor reserve of 8 million unemployed, and a huge reservoir of idle capital funds. Politically, however, the majority of the people, as in 1914, wanted to keep out of the war. Reflecting this sentiment, the President issued a formal declaration of neutrality on September 5, 1939, proclaiming an embargo on arms and munitions to all belligerents. However, Roosevelt, unlike Wilson in 1914, was not at all interested in "neutrality in thought as well as in action." He hoped to assist the democracies and win time to strengthen America's military power, and he considered the existing neutrality legislation "most vitally dangerous to American neutrality, American security, and American peace." Therefore, he called Congress into special session and recommended that the neutrality acts of 1935 and 1937 be amended to allow belligerents to purchase American war materials in the United States provided they paid cash and carried the commodities away in their own ships. Although it met with bitter opposition, the "cash-and-carry" plan was enacted in November, 1939, by substantial majorities in both houses.

During the so-called "phony war" of late 1939 and early 1940, there was little demand for American war material. However, demand increased in the spring of 1940 when the *Wehrmacht* went into action against the low countries and invaded France. What was more important, many Americans began to realize the true state of affairs, and instead of waiting two years as in 1914 to 1916, the United States began its preparedness campaign less than a year after the outbreak of war.

In the midst of the invasion of France, President Roosevelt, on May 16, 1940, requested Congress immediately to appropriate an additional $896 million for the armed forces and $286 million for contract obligations. After dramatically outlining the speed with which military operations could be carried out against the United States from Europe, the President emphasized the need to put Army and Navy construction on a twenty-four-hour shift and to provide 50,000 airplanes per year. At the end of May, the President appointed a National Defense Advisory Commission to expedite and coordinate the production and distribution of the nation's resources. On June 20 a selective service bill was introduced and was eventually passed in September. On July 2, Congress voted $5 billion for the Army and Navy, 2½ times as much as had been expended in the fiscal year 1940, and authorized the Treasury to issue $4 billion of national defense obligations over and above the existing $45 billion debt limit. In July a system of export controls was inaugurated, and in August by Executive agreement, 50 overage destroyers were traded to Great Britain for donations of naval and air bases in Newfoundland and Bermuda and ninety-nine-year leases on bases in the Caribbean area.

Revenue Acts of 1940 and 1941. In the seventeen months from July 1, 1940, when the defense program really began, to December 1, 1941 expenditures totaled $21.7 billion, far in excess of anything previously spent by the New Deal. National defense accounted for $12.7 billion, or about

59 per cent, and tended to increase continuously—from a monthly rate of $199 million in July, 1940, to $1.4 billion in November, 1941.

There were two theories on how to meet these increased costs. Some experts argued for a continuation of deficit financing as long as the national income was below the point necessary for full employment. Others insisted on a strong tax program to prevent price inflation. The administration tended at first to follow a compromise policy. In the budget message of January, 1940, the President requested Congress to impose taxes sufficient to cover emergency defense expenditures but to "avoid taxes which decrease consumer buying power." Congress, proceeding slowly, enacted a revenue act in June, 1940. The base of the income tax was broadened by lowering exemptions from $2,500 and $1,000 to $2,000 and $800, surtaxes were increased in the $6,000 to $100,000 bracket, the corporation tax was increased to a maximum of 19 per cent; and income, capital-stock, gift, estate, and excess-profits taxes were all increased 10 per cent. These so-called "defense taxes" were to be in effect for five years, and their proceeds were to be used to retire obligations issued to finance national defense. In addition, excise taxes were increased, in most cases by 10 per cent, but in the case of cigarettes, 8 per cent, and on gasoline, 50 per cent. A proposal for an excess-profits tax, favored by the President and sponsored by Senator LaFollette, was not adopted. However, at Roosevelt's insistence, Congress later set to work upon such a measure, and in October in the Second Revenue Act of 1940, it imposed an excess-profits tax of 25 to 50 per cent and increased the normal corporation tax to 24 per cent on incomes in excess of $25,000.

In his budget message of January, 1941, President Roosevelt estimated deficits of $6.2 billion for 1941 and $9.2 billion for 1942. Yet the defense program had only begun. He recommended increased taxes, but he objected to "a tax policy which restricts general consumption as long as unused capacity is available and as long as idle labor can be employed." At the same time, Secretary Morgenthau urged Congress to raise at least two-thirds of the costs of defense from taxes. He said, "If, in an attempt to protect the incomes of our people, we hold down taxes and as a result the cost of living rises, we shall have taxed them just as fully . . . and we shall have the inflated costs of defense to pay later from taxes." He recommended a drastic reduction in ordinary expenditures, a more stringent excess-profits tax, closing the loopholes allowed in community property states, and abolishing the tax exemption on state and local securities. Despite the administration's appeals, Congress proceeded with its "business-as-usual" program. In August it passed a bill appropriating $320 million for highway construction and another bill to prevent the government from disposing of its stocks of cotton and wheat. President Roosevelt vetoed both bills.

Finally, on September 20, 1941, the third defense tax bill was enacted. It reduced exemptions to $1,500 and $750, raised income tax rates to 10 to 77 per cent and corporate taxes to 31 per cent, increased excess-profits and estate and gift taxes, and made permanent the temporary excise taxes on a host of goods, including perfume, playing cards, jewelry, furs, communications, and musical instruments. It was estimated that the Act would produce $3.5 billion, but President Roosevelt denounced it as wholly inadequate. There was an immediate rebuttal from Congressional leaders, and it became apparent that a decided coolness already existed between the President and Congress on fiscal matters.

First Signs of Inflation under the Pressure of Increased Deficits. During the seventeen months of the defense program, receipts were only $11.7 billion, covering only 54 per cent of expenditures and leaving a deficit of $10 billion.

In the absence of adequate taxes, the Treasury depended mostly upon the banking system, which possessed ample resources to finance the greatly increased but not yet staggering deficit. In July, 1940, the excess reserves of the member banks were almost $7 billion, and the reserve ratio of the district banks was 89 per cent. During the remainder of the year, commercial banks increased their holdings of government securities by $1.2 billion, holdings of member banks alone increasing by $1.1 billion. Nevertheless, reserves were not reduced appreciably, for gold imports continued to be very large.

Many experts were disturbed by the inflationary potential of such vast quantities of bank credit. The situation was made worse by the fact that the member banks were practically out of debt to the Reserve banks. If economic activity became accelerated, the member banks could make extensive loans on the basis of their excess reserves, and in addition, they could acquire more reserves by discounting with the Reserve banks. Therefore, the possibility of a colossal increase in demand deposits was omnipresent.

As early as December, 1940, the Federal Reserve Board of Governors pointed out to Congress the incalculably dangerous potentialities of the volume of demand deposits, currency in circulation, and excess bank reserves. It recommended that Congress immediately expand the Board's powers over reserve requirements, eliminate various potential sources of excess reserves such as the power to devalue the dollar and the greenback provision of the Thomas amendment, sterilize gold imports, limit as far as possible the sale of new government bonds to the banks, and pay for a larger proportion of expenditures from taxes as the national income increased.

Secretary Morgenthau and Secretary of Commerce Jesse Jones disagreed with the Board, the latter declaring, "I want to see as much bank credit as possible." On the other hand, Marriner Eccles and a group of experts, including Gerhard Colm and Alvin Hansen, recommended that the government borrow only as long as unemployment continued. Once full employment was reached, heavily progressive taxation should be instituted, and finally when inflation became substantial, merciless taxation should be employed on the broadest possible front. The Board's recommendations were not adopted, and in September it took the only action within its powers, raising reserve requirements as of November 1 to the maximum of 26, 20, and 14 per cent.

Events soon demonstrated that the Board's alarm had a substantial foundation. By mid-1941 there was a scarcity of strategic materials. The government's spending program was stimulating business activity and consumer spending, and the price level was shooting upward. Wholesale prices were at 92 per cent of the 1926 level, 22 per cent higher than in 1939. The index of 28 basic commodities was 55 per cent above 1939. Maximum prices had been set on 12 of these by the Division of Price Stabilization, and on August 9 the President, in order to discourage installment buying, authorized the Board of Governors to regulate the terms and conditions under which consumer credit could be extended.

Despite the evidence of inflation, the Treasury financed almost half its defense deficit by selling securities to the commercial banks. Under the impact of this inadvisable inflationary financing, demand deposits increased from $50 billion to $60 billion and government deposits in commercial banks increased by almost $1 billion. Yet excess reserves, owing to the continuing inflow of gold, declined only to $3.4 billion. Offsetting the bank financing to some extent, the Treasury on May 1, 1941, began to offer savings bonds (Series E, F, and G) in denominations of $25 to $1,000 to siphon off the purchasing power of the lower-income brackets. By December, 1941, cumulative sales of these bonds were $2.5 billion, and redemptions were only $14 million.

Lend Lease. Meanwhile, the British were finding it more and more difficult to raise the money required by "cash-and-carry." Their gold stock was flowing across the Atlantic, and 60 per cent of their holdings in American common stocks had already been sold. In addition, they were liquidating their direct investments, including the major part of the American Viscose Company, and they were borrowing against their American equities, the RFC loaning $40 million to Brown and Williamson, wholly owned subsidiary of the British tobacco trust.

It appeared that, in a short time, Britain would be devoid of means to finance further purchases. On the ground that the defense of Britain was also the defense of America, President Roosevelt in January, 1941, urged

Congress to adopt legislation making it possible for the British to obtain on credit "every ounce and every ton of munitions and supplies that we can possibly spare."

On March 11, 1941, Congress passed the "Lend-Lease Act," empowering the President to authorize heads of departments or agencies to "sell, transfer title to, exchange, lease, lend, or otherwise dispose of" any article of defense to "the government of any country whose defense the President deems vital to the defense of the United States" without regard to the terms of any existing legislation. An initial appropriation of $7 billion was made, and it was provided that up to $1.3 billion of articles could be disposed of from existing government property.

Exports, which had been declining, increased immediately after the passage of lend-lease, giving an additional stimulus to the American economy.

TABLE 80. FOREIGN TRADE IN SELECTED MONTHS, 1939 AND 1941
(In millions of dollars)

	Exports	Imports
August, 1939.............	250	176
January, 1941.............	325	229
March, 1941.............	357	268
June, 1941...............	330	280
August, 1941.............	460	283

SOURCE: *Federal Reserve Bulletin*, January, 1942, p. 63.

Altogether during the war Congress appropriated $63.8 billion for lend-lease ($27.9 billion directly and $35.9 through the War and Navy Departments), $50.7 billion of lend-lease was actually furnished, and the United States received $7.8 billion in reverse lend-lease, making $42.9 billion of net advances, or more than 4½ times as much as had been advanced to the associated powers in World War I.

Treasury Policy of War Finance. By Pearl Harbor Day, the Treasury had already formulated a policy of war finance. The paramount goal, of course, was to win the war, and all the nation's financial resources were mobilized to that end. This tended to produce money, credit, and price inflation, and although the Treasury put more emphasis on taxation than in any previous war, and although it set up the mechanics for borrowing excess purchasing power from consumers in all income brackets, these efforts were not aggressive enough to offset completely the enormous inflationary pressures created by total war.

In mobilizing the nation's financial resources, the already close alliance between the Treasury and the Federal Reserve System was cemented more firmly. The banking authorities announced that member banks would at all times be supplied with enough reserves to provide the Treasury with whatever funds it needed. Moreover, these funds would be provided at the lowest possible interest rate, for the Treasury was convinced that the wisest policy was a cheap-money policy. The Reserve authorities were sceptical, but they were overruled. To keep the interest rate as low as possible and to dissuade potential investors from holding back in the hope that interest rates would rise, it was decided to stabilize the yields on government securities by guaranteeing a fixed price for them. In April, 1942, the Reserve banks announced that they would stabilize the short-term market by buying or selling unlimited quantities of Treasury bills at ⅜ of 1 per cent. They went even further and sought to put rigidity into the entire government-bond market. Bonds were to be pegged at a yield of 2½ per cent by open-market operations, and the same would be done for certificates and Treasury notes. The wide disparity between the short- and the long-term interest rate caused the banks to shift more and more from short-term obligations to bonds. There was little danger for the banks in playing this "pattern of rates," for government obligations, under the price-pegging commitment, were equivalent to interest-bearing cash. Consequently, purchases of bonds by the banks were higher than they would ordinarily have been, and purchases by nonbank investors tended to be smaller. Furthermore, the Reserve banks were regularly called upon to buy the short-term obligations which the banks were unloading because of the greater investment attractiveness of bonds. Thus, the whole process increased demand deposits and the volume of currency, providing the fuel to feed inflation.

There were other features of Treasury policy which tended to inflate currency and demand deposits. The rediscount rate was reduced to 1 per cent, and a preferential rate of ½ of 1 per cent was offered on advances secured by government obligations maturing in one year or less. This was not so important as it had been in World War I, because member banks could raise their reserves at any time by selling part of their portfolio of governments—a process that was much less expensive and more appealing than rediscounting. The government also allowed banks to pay for new issues of securities by crediting the Treasury with a deposit in a so-called "war loan account" which was exempt from reserve requirements and assessments for deposit insurance and, therefore, increased demand deposits by an amount equal to 100 per cent of their value.

Soon after the war began, price inflation developed on a dangerous scale, for titanic government expenditures greatly increased business activity, shortages developed in labor and raw materials, consumer incomes expanded, and the money supply increased. Controls were gradually instituted, and the government took steps to prevent the private economy from competing with war production. On January 16, 1942, an Executive Order established the War Production Board to coordinate production, establish priorities, and facilitate the supplying of the armed forces. In February, 1942, automobile production was stopped completely. Later, the production of radios and refrigerators was also eliminated. On January 30 Congress passed the Emergency Price Control Act, although it took some time before regulations could be set up. By then, the wholesale price index was at 96.5 per cent of the 1926 level, but farm prices were at 101.9. At a much later date, March, 1942, a system of point rationing was instituted, and rollback and differential surpluses were put into effect a little later. All these measures were important and effective in holding a lid on the cost of living, but they could not prevent eventual increases unless accompanied by policies which dealt with fundamental causes in a vigorous manner.

Knowing full well McAdoo's experiences in financing World War I, why did the Treasury again pursue tactics which were certain to expand money and credit and thus help to inflate the price level? Its motives were exactly the same as McAdoo's in 1917. It desired to finance the war at as low an interest cost as possible, and therefore it kept excess bank reserves at a high level. Morgenthau was much more successful in accomplishing a "cheap war" than McAdoo had been. Because the government pegged the bond market and because savings were enormously high, borrowing was done at consistently low interest rates, the average rate on the $257 billion debt of 1945 being only 1.94 per cent as compared with 2.53 per cent on the $45 billion debt of 1939 and 4.2 per cent on the $25 billion debt of 1919.

By 1943, when it became evident that cheap money and bank financing possessed as many disadvantages as advantages, the Treasury made long-term issues ineligible for bank investment. This was only partially successful, for the banks began to engage in so-called "roll-over operations"; that is, they dumped their short terms and bought bonds which were eligible for bank investment from insurance companies, savings institutions, corporations, and other nonbank investors at premium prices. The nonbank investors then took the proceeds and purchased new issues of government bonds.

Cost of the War. From July 1, 1940, to June 30, 1946, the Federal government spent $387 billion, of which 95 per cent ($360 billion) was for defense and war. The $100 billion spent in 1945 was more than ten times the highest prewar annual expenditure. The most startling feature of this war spending was that it was accomplished entirely by increasing production without reduction in total private consumption. There was some reduction in the consumption of durable goods, but this was offset by increased consumption of nondurable goods. The whole population was better fed and clothed than it had been during peacetime.

During the first three years contracts were awarded to industry on exceedingly liberal terms, but when in 1943 it appeared that excessive profits were being earned thereunder, Congress provided for the renegotiation of all contracts and the recapture of all overpayments. This was a startling innovation in the handling of war expenditures and it saved the government considerable sums. In 1944 and 1945 alone, the recoveries by the Treasury exceeded $2 billion a year.

TABLE 81.   FEDERAL EXPENDITURES, 1941–1946
(In billions of dollars)

	1941	1942	1943	1944	1945	1946
National defense..................	$ 6.3	$26.0	$72.1	$87.0	$90.0	$48.5
War Department..............	3.7	14.1	42.3	49.2	50.3	27.8
Navy Department.............	2.3	8.6	20.9	26.5	30.0	15.2
U.S. Maritime Commission.....	0.1	0.9	2.8	3.8	3.2	0.7
War Shipping Administration....	.....	0.1	1.1	1.9	2.0	1.4
Other........................	0.3	2.3	5.1	5.5	4.4	3.5
Veterans' benefits................	0.6	0.6	0.6	0.7	2.1	4.3
Social security and railroad retirement*.......................	0.6	0.7	0.7	0.8	0.8	0.8
Public works....................	0.7	0.7	0.5	0.4	0.3	0.4
Aid to agriculture................	0.9	1.2	1.2	0.9	0.8	1.0
Work relief.....................	1.6	1.1	0.3			
Interest on debt.................	1.1	1.3	1.8	2.6	3.6	4.7
Tax refunds.....................	0.1	0.1	0.1	0.3	1.7	3.0
International finance..............	.....	.....	.....	.....	......	0.8
Government corporations........	1.1	1.9	1.5	1.8	......	−1.3
Other.........................	0.8	0.8	0.8	0.9	1.1	1.4
Totals†.....................	$13.8	$34.3	$79.7	$95.6	$100.4	$63.7

SOURCE: *Annual Report of the Secretary of the Treasury*, 1947, pp. 306–307.

* Excluding appropriations to the old-age and survivorship insurance fund.
† Excluding debt retirement.

While war expenditures increased to amounts which seemed humanly impossible, Federal disbursements for ordinary activities were reduced, but not so much as was desirable considering that a condition of overemployment and inflation existed. Furthermore, as soon as the war was over in Europe, Federal expenditures began to increase too soon for the best interests of the economy.

One of the major differences between the two world wars was the great increase in government financing of new plant and equipment. During World War II expenditures for industrial facilities totaled about $25 billion, of which two-thirds were financed directly by the Federal government. On the other hand, the Federal government financed only one-tenth of the $6 billion expansion that occurred in World War I. Through the Defense Plant Corporation, a subsidiary of the RFC, the Federal government invested some $7 billion in commercial plants many of which might not have been constructed ordinarily. As a result, the DPC owned more than 10 per cent of the nation's plant capacity on June 30, 1945, when it was dissolved. In addition to its direct investments, the Federal government guaranteed loans to businesses and made advances on war contracts.[1]

TABLE 82.   WAR EXPENDITURES, 1941–1945
(In billions of dollars)

	1941	1942	1943	1944	1945
Munitions (including ships).................	$2.3	$12.7	$42.3	$55.6	$53.8
War construction and war plants............	2.2	7.6	12.7	4.6	2.2
Pay, subsistence, and other nonmunitions.....	2.2	8.0	20.1	29.5	33.0
Totals...................................	$6.7	$28.3	$75.1	$89.7	$89.0

SOURCE: *President's Budget Message*, 1945–1946.

Revenue Act of 1942. The conflict, begun in 1940, between the administration and Congress over tax policy continued throughout the war. As expenditures doubled and redoubled, the administration called for ever higher taxes, but Congress never adopted the recommendations in full. It passed three revenue acts, two of them of a broad and sweeping nature, but on the whole its tax legislation was inadequate, overly complicated, and inexcusably opportunistic. As a result, only 46 per cent of the total war costs was covered by taxation. Although this was better than the 33 per cent raised in World War I, it was nevertheless disappointing, especially when viewed in the light of the enormous increase in the people's income.

In his first budget message after the declaration of war, President Roosevelt estimated expenditures for the fiscal year 1943 at $58.9 billion and receipts at $23.5 billion. Hoping to cover half the cost of the war through taxes, he recommended that Congress impose new levies to raise an additional $7 billion. In March Secretary Morgenthau again stressed the need for additional taxes and recommended a general increase in income taxes with collection at the source, a maximum excess-profits tax of 75 per cent, general increases in the estate and gift taxes, new excise taxes, and the elimination of various loopholes such as the community property arrangements maintained in some states.

[1] See Douglas R. Fuller, *Government Financing of Private Enterprises;* Gerald T. White, "Financing Industrial Expansion for War," *Journal of Economic History,* Vol. IX, No. 2, November, 1949.

In a momentous anti-inflation message of April, 1942, the President reiterated the need for immediate broad increases in taxation and urged Congress to adopt a universal price ceiling, stabilization of wages, a 100 per cent tax on excess profits and a limitation on individual incomes to $25,000 after taxes, a ceiling on farm prices at parity, rationing of scarce items, strict limits on credit, and a forced savings plan, unless bond buying increased vastly.

Meanwhile, many experts and business groups were calling for a general sales tax to cut consumer spending, but Morgenthau opposed it. Instead, he recommended in May, 1942, a general broadening of the tax base by again reducing exemptions. Congress worked on the tax bill all through the summer. By then, it was clear that Federal expenditures would be far in excess of the President's original estimates, and the Treasury called for even higher taxes than it had originally recommended. In addition to everything else, Morgenthau suggested a graduated tax on spending, partially refundable after the war. To the Ways and Means Committee, this tax appeared to be completely incomprehensible and was therefore immediately rejected.

Congress passed a tax bill on October 21, 1942. It lowered exemptions to $1,200 and $500, enlarging tremendously the number of income tax payers; imposed a 5 per cent victory tax (partly refundable at a later date); and repealed the earned-income credit. It raised personal income tax rates from 10 to 77 to 19 to 88 per cent, the corporate rate from 31 to 40 per cent, the excess-profits tax from a maximum of 60 to a maximum of 90 per cent, and increased substantially the rates of the estate tax and of various excises.

Revenue Act of 1943. In November, 1942, the national debt passed $100 billion. The government was spending $6 billion a month with revenues running at less than $2 billion a month. In his budget message of January, 1943, the President estimated expenditures at over $100 billion for 1944. To raise half of these estimated expenditures from taxes, he proposed that $16 billion of additional taxes be provided. When Congress caught its breath, Senator George, chairman of the Finance Committee, declared that Congress could not raise more than an additional $6 billion. Most other congressmen thought that even this was impossible, and higher excise taxes on luxury goods, including spirits, furs, jewelry, cosmetics, and luggage, were the only tax increases in 1943.[2]

In the meanwhile, a most fundamental recasting of the personal income

---

[2] The conflict between the President and Congress was made more intense in March when the President issued an Executive Order restricting salaries to $25,000 a year after taxes. Congress promptly rescinded the order by attaching a rider to the so-called Disney Act, which was passed to increase the debt limit to $210 billion. This was further raised to $275 billion in 1946.

tax on a "current payment" and withholding basis came under consideration. From the inception of the income tax, payments were made beginning in March on incomes earned in the previous year. From the individual's standpoint this method was considered a source of great hardship, especially when income taxes were comparatively high. From the
Treasury's standpoint collections were always a year behind income.
Various plans were suggested for changing tax payments to a current
basis, but Beardsley Ruml's proposal for a withholding tax on current
income with no tax liability for the previous year's income received the
widest publicity. All through the early spring the debate on pay-as-you-go
continued, but the Ruml plan was twice defeated. Then in June, 1943, a
compromise bill was passed, providing a 20 per cent withholding tax after
July 1, 1943, with partial abatement of one year's tax, graduated according
to the size of the individual income. The withholding system tremendously facilitated the collection of the personal income tax and increased
its yield. The Act of 1943 also raised the rates of luxury taxes from 10 to
20 per cent and the tax on spirits from $6 to $9 a gallon. This and the
Revenue Act of 1942 were the most momentous tax measures of the entire
war.

Revenue Act of 1944. Many congressmen, viewing taxation as a purely
fiscal matter and paying little attention to the effects of tax rates on spending power, believed that pay-as-you-go reduced the need for revenue.
However, the administration continued to press for additional taxes, although the Treasury reduced its recommendations to $10.5 billion, one-
fifth of which would be refundable after the war. It was estimated that,
even if this proposal was adopted, consumers would still have $7 billion
of excess purchasing power which, if spent instead of saved, would cause
further price increases. It was this so-called "inflationary gap" which
bothered economists and Treasury officials. Professor Frank Graham,
speaking for 85 economists, pronounced the Treasury program insufficient, and Marriner Eccles proposed a tax plan to provide $13 billion, but
the economists' criticism was ignored and the Eccles proposal was labeled
fantastic. In like manner, the Ways and Means Committee killed a suggestion for a 5 to 10 per cent general sales tax offered by E. C. Alvord, tax
expert for the Chamber of Commerce. The Treasury continued to the end
of the war to oppose the imposition of a general sales tax because of its
regressive nature.

Finally, in mid-November the Ways and Means Committee submitted
a new tax bill to provide $2.2 billion of additional revenue. In a long
report, the Committee said:

The conclusion of the Committee was that maintenance by the Government
of the proper psychology, and freedom from fear on the part of every consumer, is considerably more important than the absorption of current excess

buying power through additional taxes. . . . The Committee is firmly convinced that the proper psychology can be maintained only by strict economy in government expenditures, through effective price control, rationing, and wage control.

While a tax bill was being considered in the Senate, President Roosevelt delivered his budget message of January, 1944. Estimating expenditures for the fiscal year 1945 at $98.0 billion and the deficit at 59 per cent of total expenditures, he recommended the earliest possible enactment of additional tax legislation, saying:

Nothing has occurred to indicate that the administration's tax program is more than a minimum. Let us face the fact—the failure thus far to enact an adequate fiscal program has aggravated the difficulties of maintaining economic stabilization. The time to impose high taxes is now, when incomes are high and goods are scarce. The time to relax some war-time taxes will come when goods are again plentiful. . . . In view of these facts, I must urge upon the Congress the need for additional revenue beyond that provided in the bill now pending before the Senate.

TABLE 83.   CHANGES IN FEDERAL INDIVIDUAL AND CORPORATE INCOME, DEATH, AND EXCISE TAXES, 1940–1944

	1940	1941	1942	1943	1944
Individual income tax:					
Exemption.........	$2,000 and $800	$1,500 and $750	$1,200 and $500	*	$1,000 and $500
Dependency allowance............	$400	*	$350	*	$500
Victory tax..........	....	....	5%‡	3%‡	Repealed
Normal tax..........	4%	*	6%	*	3%
Surtax.............	4–75%	6–77%	13–82%§	*	20–91%§
Minimum starts at..	$4,000	0	*	*	*
Maximum starts at..	$5,000,000	*	$200,000	*	*
Corporation:					
Normal tax........	14.85–24%	15–24%	*	*	*
Surtax............	....	6–7%	10–16%	*	*
Excess profits.......	25–50%	35–60%	90%	95%	*
Estate tax...........	2–70%	3–77%	*	*	*
Exemption.........	$40,000	*	$60,000‖	*	*
Gift tax.............	1½–52½%	2¼–57¾%	*	*	*
Exemption.........	$40,000+	*	$30,000+	*	*
	$4,000 annually		$3,000 annually		
Spirits...............	$3 per gal.	$4	$6	$9	*
Automobile parts......	2½%	5%	*	*	*
Luxury goods........	....	10%	*	20%	*

SOURCE: *Annual Report of the Secretary of the Treasury*, 1944, p. 458.

* No change.
† Imposed on profits in excess of 1936–1939 average earnings or in excess of stated percentages of invested capital. After 1942 postwar credits were allowed.
‡ Imposed on personal net income over $624 less certain credits.
§ Total effective income tax rate limited to a maximum of 90 per cent.
‖ Eliminated previous $40,000 life-insurance exemption.

But the Senate did not find itself able to increase taxes. Senator George declared, "We have about reached the bottom of the barrel as far as existing taxes are concerned."[3]

The Individual Income Tax Act of 1944, which came out of the conference committee and was presented to the President, repealed the victory tax, lowered exemptions, and raised income tax rates generally. In addition, it froze social security taxes at the rates originally established. It made no changes in the estate, gift, and corporation taxes and allowed liberal allowances for depletion in extractive industries. The President promptly vetoed the bill as "wholly ineffective and providing relief not for the needy, but for the greedy." It was the first time in history that a President had vetoed a tax bill, and Congress was furious. It promptly passed the bill (February 25, 1944) over the veto by overwhelming majorities. Although the Act yielded considerably more revenue than had at first been estimated, it did not accomplish all that could be desired. However, it was the last tax act of the war. In the ensuing months it was not possible to persuade Congress to pass additional legislation, and by January, 1945, when it appeared that expenditures would begin to fall, the administration stopped recommending tax increases.

Easing the Tax Burden. As soon as the war in Europe was over, congressional tax leaders began to propose an easing of the tax burden. Senator George supported a proposal for increasing the specific exemption under the excess-profits tax and reducing personal income taxes by 1946. In July, a bill was passed increasing the excess-profits exemption as of January 1, 1946. However, this Act was never effective, for the war with Japan ended on August 14, 1945, with a resultant drop in expenditures, and both the Truman administration, which took office on April 12, 1945, and Congress moved for a broad cut in taxes. Secretary Vinson succeeded Morgenthau on July 23, 1945, and on October 1 he announced his support of complete repeal of the excess-profits tax, a general reduction in excise taxes, and elimination of the 3 per cent normal tax. He thought that tax reduction should not exceed $5 billion and should be given primarily to the lower income groups. The Republicans proposed a 20 per cent across-the-board reduction but with little hope of obtaining it.

The proponents of tax reduction were, on the whole, well satisfied with the Revenue Act of August 11, 1945, which made reductions estimated at $5.9 billion. The excess-profits tax was repealed as of January 1, 1946. Corporate rates were reduced to 38 per cent. The personal income tax rate in each surtax bracket was reduced 3 per cent, and an additional over-all reduction of 5 per cent was allowed in the total tax.

[3] *The New York Times*, Jan. 14, 1944.

Summary of Wartime Revenue. Total net receipts from all sources rose from $7.6 billion in 1941 to a peak of $46.5 billion in 1945. In the six years, 1941 through 1946, the tax yield was $155.8 billion. By far the largest share came from individual and corporate income taxes, with individual taxes assuming supremacy after 1944. Hence, World War II, like its predecessor, gave significant impetus to direct taxation. During the depression years, income taxes supplied less than 30 per cent of the revenue, in the late thirties they supplied little more than 40 per cent, but in 1944 they supplied 76 per cent, and in 1946 they still returned 70 per cent. On the other hand, miscellaneous internal revenue, which supplied almost 50 per cent in 1936, declined to 14 per cent in 1945, and customs became altogether insignificant. Tax collections had not apparently encountered the point of diminishing returns, for increased rates, with a constantly rising national income, continued to produce heavier and heavier revenues.

TABLE 84.   FEDERAL REVENUES, EXPENDITURES, AND DEFICITS, 1941–1946
(In billions of dollars)

	1941	1942	1943	1944	1945	1946
Expenditures......................	$13.8	$34.3	$79.7	$95.6	$100.4	$63.7
Revenues:						
Corporate income and excess profits	$ 2.1	$ 4.7	$ 9.7	$14.8	$ 16.0	$12.6
Individual income...............	1.4	3.3	6.6	18.3	19.0	18.7
Estate and gift.................	0.4	0.4	0.4	0.5	0.6	0.7
Capital stock..................	0.2	0.3	0.3	0.4	0.4	0.4
Liquor........................	0.8	1.0	1.4	1.6	2.3	2.5
Tobacco.......................	0.7	0.8	0.9	1.0	0.9	1.2
Gasoline.......................	0.3	0.4	0.3	0.3	0.4	0.4
Other manufacturers' excises.....	0.3	0.4	0.3	0.3	0.4	0.5
Retail taxes on luxuries.........	....	0.1	0.2	0.2	0.4	0.5
Transportation, telephone, etc.....	0.2	0.4	0.7	1.1	1.4	1.5
Employment taxes...............	0.9	1.2	1.5	1.8	1.8	1.7
Customs......................	0.4	0.4	0.3	0.4	0.4	0.4
Miscellaneous..................	0.5	0.3	0.9	3.3	3.5	3.5
Adjusted to Daily Statement.....	....	....	−0.2	1.6	0.1	−0.4
Totals......................	$ 8.3	$13.7	$23.4	$45.4	$ 47.7	$44.2
Less appropriations to OASI fund...	0.7	0.9	1.1	1.3	1.3	1.2
Net budget receipts.............	$ 7.6	$12.8	$22.3	$44.1	$ 46.5	$43.0
Deficit........................	$ 6.2	$21.5	$57.4	$51.5	$ 53.9	$20.7

SOURCE: *Annual Report of the Secretary of the Treasury*, 1947, pp. 304–305, 307.

Although liquor and tobacco taxes continued to lead the field of excise taxation, they were now joined by a great many more excises, some of which, like the transportation tax or the retail sales taxes on luxury goods, had also become prolific revenue producers. Receipts from the excess-profits tax became colossal, increasing from $166 million in 1941 to $6.7 billion in 1946. After 1943 they accounted for more than half of the corporation income tax receipts.

Besides stimulating direct taxation, World War II made the tax system much more progressive. The effective income tax rate on the lowest taxable income ($500 to $1,000) was only 2.97 per cent, whereas the effective rate on an income of $1 million was 64.75 per cent.

TABLE 85. INCOME TAX RETURNS, 1944

Income	No. of returns (thousands)	Adjusted gross income (billions)	Total tax (billions)	Effective tax rates (per cent)	Per cent of total tax
Under $500	3,452	$ 0.9			
$ 500–$ 2,000	20,154	25.7	$1.8	2– 9	11.1
2,000– 3,000	11,302	28.0	2.7	9–10	16.6
3,000– 5,000	9,736	36.2	4.3	11–14	26.5
5,000– 10,000	1,834	11.7	2.0	15–21	12.4
10,000– 25,000	495	7.3	2.0	22–34	12.4
25,000– 100,000	129	5.3	2.4	38–58	14.8
$100,000 and over	8	1.5	1.0	61–76	6.2

SOURCE: Bureau of Internal Revenue, *Statistics of Income*, 1944, pp. 15, 96.

Borrowing Operations. From 1941 to 1946 Treasury operations in the money market were considerably in excess of $125 billion per year, for the Treasury not only financed the increase in the gross debt but refunded maturing short-term debt and 11 callable bond issues, aggregating $9.9 billion. The gross debt increased from $43.0 billion on June 30, 1940, to $269.4 billion on June 30, 1946 (the per capita being approximately $2,000 compared with $240 in 1919 and $75 in 1865). At its highest point on February 28, 1946, the gross debt was $279.8 billion. For the first time in history the public debt exceeded the total private debt. It also exceeded the annual national income, equaling, in 1946, 180 per cent of the national income compared with 41 per cent in 1919 and 50 per cent in 1865. Payments of interest rose to 3.5 per cent of the national income compared with 2 per cent after World War I and 2.6 per cent after the Civil War. Furthermore, government securities came to represent 43 per cent of the liquid assets of nonbank investors compared with 24 per cent in 1939. All this meant that henceforth the management of the public debt was going to be a potent instrument in influencing the entire economy.

The Treasury directed a large part of its borrowing activities toward attracting excess spending power away from consumers, especially from those who would ordinarily spend all their incomes. In order to make government securities attractive, the Treasury tailored its offerings to fit the requirements of different individuals and groups. Instead of providing one type of long-term security, as in World War I, it offered three different types of savings bonds as well as the usual long-term bonds. In addition, it offered short-term obligations to corporations and those in the upper-income brackets who for one reason or another desired to invest funds for short periods. Certificates of indebtedness, which had not been used since 1934, were again issued beginning in June, 1942. Treasury bills, unknown during World War I, were offered weekly, at first at $100 million a week, but gradually increasing to $1.3 billion a week in 1946. They usually ran for 91 days, but at times were for only 71 days. The use of treasury notes gradually increased, and as early as July, 1941, tax savings notes, acceptable at par and accrued interest, were sold.

TABLE 86.   FEDERAL DEBT, JUNE 30, 1941–1946
(In billions of dollars)

	1941	1942	1943	1944	1945	Feb., 1946	1946
Treasury bills......................	$ 1.6	$ 2.5	$ 11.9	$ 14.7	$ 17.0	$ 17.0	$ 17.0
Certificates of indebtedness...........		3.1	16.6	28.8	34.1	41.4	34.8
Treasury notes.....................	5.7	6.7	9.2	17.4	23.5	19.6	18.3
Treasury bonds....................	30.2	38.1	57.5	79.2	106.4	121.6	119.3
Other bonds.......................	0.2	0.2	0.2	0.2	0.2	0.2	0.2
Total marketable.................	$37.7	$50.6	$ 95.3	$140.4	$181.3	$199.8	$189.6
Savings notes.....................		$ 3.0	$ 7.5	$ 9.6	$ 10.1	$ 8.0	$ 6.7
Savings bonds.....................	$ 4.3	10.2	21.3	34.6	45.6	48.7	49.0
Adjusted service bonds..............	0.2	0.2	0.2	0.2			
Depository funds...................		0.1	0.2	0.5	0.5	0.5	0.4
Special issues to government funds.....	6.1	7.9	10.9	14.3	18.8	20.9	22.3
Total interest-bearing debt........	$48.4	$72.0	$135.4	$199.5	$256.4	$277.9	$268.1
Non-interest-bearing debt............	0.6	0.5	1.3	1.5	2.3	1.3	1.3
Gross debt.....................	$49.0	$72.4	$136.7	$201.0	$258.7	$279.2	$269.4

SOURCE: *Annual Report of the Secretary of the Treasury*, 1946, pp. 40, 457–458.

The policy of adapting securities to individual needs was remarkably successful, for it enabled the Treasury to obtain about 45 per cent of the total funds which individuals had available for investment. It also made inevitable a large amount of short-term securities, and by 1945 they comprised approximately 30 per cent of the interest-bearing debt. In addition, the nonmarketable debt was actually short term in nature, bringing the total to over 50 per cent of the interest-bearing debt. In previous years, this would have been an almost insuperable obstacle to orderly debt management, but the development of fiscal and monetary controls since World War I had lessened the disadvantages of a short-term debt considerably.

The tremendous increase in the reserves of social insurance and other government trust funds (civil service, national-service life insurance, etc.) from $4.8 billion in 1940 to $22 billion in 1946 afforded a ready source for the internal absorption of a substantial portion of the Federal debt within the government itself, reducing to that extent the amount needed to be borrowed from the public. This feature of war financing was entirely new.

The Eight War Loan Campaigns. Following traditional procedures, the Treasury sold $11.6 billion of long-term bonds up to November, 1942. During the same period, sales of savings bonds totaled $9.2 billion, and redemptions amounted to $246 million, leaving $11.4 billion outstanding in December, 1942. Recognizing that bond sales to individuals removed spendable income as effectively as taxation, the Treasury began, in November, 1942, to campaign for bond sales.

Altogether, it carried on seven wartime loan campaigns and one Victory Loan. They were the most commendable activity in Treasury war financing and, from any viewpoint, the largest bond-selling campaigns in history. More people purchased bonds than in any previous loan drive, Secretary Vinson estimating the total number of owners at 85 million in 1946.[4] The number of selling agents—6 million—was the largest ever engaged in the bond-selling business; the total amount sold—$156.9 billion—was almost five times as much as the total cost of the entire World War I and almost twice as large as the total national income in 1929.

In carrying on the war loans, the Treasury tried to restrict bank participation, but it was not wholly successful. In the first two drives, the amounts which the commercial banks could purchase were limited. Thereafter, they were excluded completely from direct participation. Moreover, commercial banks were requested to refrain from making loans for speculative purposes, and nonbank investors were requested not to sell securities for the sole purpose of acquiring new securities. The purpose of these regulations was to prevent the "free ride" and the "roll over" operation. The "free ride" had some similarity to the "borrow and buy" plan of World War I. Under it, private investors purchased government bonds on margin in the expectation of realizing a profit from later increases in the market price. Data are not available to show the increase

[4] Henry C. Murphy (*The National Debt in War and Transition*, p. 198) asserts that 85 million was probably too low an estimate of buyers and much too high an estimate of holders.

in bank loans for the purchase of government securities during the first three loan drives, but it was estimated at $1.1 billion. In the last five drives it was $6.7 billion.

The war loan drives had one other great weakness—the failure of individual subscriptions to equal expectations. In each drive, they barely achieved their goal or fell short of it, whereas other nonbank investors (corporations, insurance companies, and savings banks) far exceeded their goal in every case.[5] Individual subscriptions were also concentrated in savings bonds, and many of these were redeemed soon after purchase.

TABLE 87. SALES AND REDEMPTIONS OF E, F, AND G BONDS
(In millions of dollars)

	E	F	G	Total
Cumulative sales to June 30, 1945.......	$35,791.5	$2,771.3	$10,720.0	$49,282.8
Cumulative redemptions to June 30, 1945.	6,694.4	166.9	421.3	7,282.6
Sales in fiscal 1946....................	7,172.7	440.1	2,465.4	10,078.2
Redemptions in fiscal 1946.............	5,911.7	149.1	347.7	6,408.5

SOURCE: *Annual Report of the Secretary of the Treasury*, 1945, p. 58; 1946, p. 518.

Distribution of the Debt. Who owns the debt is much more important than its size, for if the debt were divided among the citizens in proportion to their tax liability, each individual would be paying to himself the interest on his bonds and the whole debt would lose all meaning and could be canceled. On the other hand, once the debt is distributed in different proportions from taxes, it involves a burden on taxpayers for the benefit of bondholders. There are no available data on the distribution of the debt by income groups. However, some insight into the problem can be gleaned from an analysis of savings bond sales and redemptions by denominations. Between 1942 and 1945, $24.5 billion of savings bonds was sold in denominations of $10 to $100. Of these $7.6 billion was redeemed by June, 1945, leaving a net of $16.9 billion. Since this represented only about 35 per cent of the total outstanding savings bonds and about 6 per cent of the total debt, the lower-income group did not own so large a share of the debt as might have been desired in the interest of a most favorable debt distribution, although a larger share than in any previous war. Nor was the proportion of bond holdings by commercial banks held down as much as desirable, for it remained exactly the same in 1946 as it had been in 1941, and since the aggregate debt had greatly expanded, this meant a vast increase in deposits and checkbook money.

[5] See the breakdown of the goals and sales in each war loan drive as given in the *Annual Report of the Secretary of the Treasury*, 1946.

TABLE 88. ABSORPTION OF THE FEDERAL INTEREST-BEARING DEBT, JUNE, 1941–1946
(Dollar figures in billions)

	Owned in 1940	1941	1942	1943	1944	1945	1946	Owned in 1946
Individuals.............	$ 9.7	$ 1.2	$ 7.0	$12.4	$14.8	$13.4	$ 4.4	$ 62.9
Other nonbank........	19.6	2.4	7.9	19.8	22.9	19.7	5.2	97.5
Commercial banks.....	16.1	3.6	6.4	26.2	16.2	15.8	0.2	84.4
Federal Reserve banks.	2.5	−0.3	0.5	4.6	7.7	6.9	2.0	23.8
Totals..............	$47.9	$ 6.9	$21.8	$63.0	$61.6	$55.7	$11.8	$268.6
Per cent owned by:								
Individuals.........	20%	20%	24%	22%	22%	23%	23%	
Other nonbank......	41%	40%	39%	36%	36%	36%	37%	
Commercial banks...	39%	40%	38%	43%	41%	41%	40%	

SOURCE: *Annual Report of the Secretary of the Treasury*, 1946, pp. 58, 60.

Impact of the War on Banking and Money in Circulation. As a result of government war finance, total deposits of all commercial banks doubled between 1941 and 1946. Investments in government securities almost quadrupled, whereas other investments increased only slightly. Agricultural loans remained almost constant, but ordinary commercial, industrial, consumer, and real estate loans declined as the government expanded and strengthened its controls. The only bank lending which showed an increase was that which contributed to the financing of the war. War production loans, guaranteed by government agencies, increased constantly, and at their peak in June, 1944, they represented about 28 per cent of the total loans of the insured commercial banks. Currency in circulation increased along with bank deposits. From $9.6 billion in 1941, it rose rapidly to $22.5 billion by 1944 and $28.2 billion in 1946. Therefore, by 1946, the total money supply was $171.1 billion.

The Treasury defended the enormous increase in money as necessary for the increased business activity caused by the financing of the war. Secretary Morgenthau did not consider the amount of money in circulation in 1945 as "excessive," and he "did not believe that it harbored an inflationary hazard." Yet the total money supply was equal to well over half the gross national product, and it was far in excess of the goods that were available for purchase. Its inflationary pressure was restrained only by the decline in the velocity of money. Had the annual rate of turnover remained at the 1939 level, the gross national product would have been about 25 per cent higher than it actually was, and all the difference would have represented inflated price levels rather than additional goods and services.

As commercial bank deposits expanded, reserves began to diminish. At the same time district bank reserves declined as a result of heavier government deposits and large exports of gold ($951.7 million in 1944 and 1945). Under the circumstances, the Treasury and the Reserve Board took steps to conserve and increase available bank credit. Twice, when stringencies developed in the money markets of New York and Chicago, reserve requirements for those cities were reduced. Consumer credit was further restricted, and security transactions on margin were eliminated altogether. Nevertheless, the reserves of the district banks gradually approached the 40 per cent minimum, and on June 12, 1945, Congress, by amendment to the Federal Reserve Act, reduced the reserve requirement against Federal Reserve notes and deposits to 25 per cent. In addition, it repealed the Federal Reserve System's right to issue Federal Reserve bank notes and the President's power to issue $3 billion in greenbacks. It also made permanent the authorization to use government obligations as security against Federal Reserve notes.

TABLE 89.   CHANGES IN BANK OPERATIONS, 1941–1946
(In billions of dollars)

	December, 1941	June, 1942	June 1943	June 1944	June 1945	June 1946
All commercial banks:						
Number...............	14,277	14,228	14,073	14,000	14,000	14,026
Total deposits...........	$71.2	$72.3	$96.1	$116.1	$136.6	$142.9
United States deposits.....	1.9	1.8	8.0	19.5	24.4	13.4
Total loans.............	21.7	20.3	17.7	21.0	23.7	27.1
United States obligations...	21.8	26.4	52.5	68.4	84.1	84.5
Other investments....:....	7.2	7.0	6.5	6.3	6.8	7.8
Member banks:						
Total deposits...........	61.7	63.4	84.0	101.3	118.4	122.5
Total loans.............	18.0	16.9	14.8	18.1	20.6	23.3
United States obligations...	19.5	24.1	47.0	60.3	73.2	72.3
Other investment........	6.0	5.8	5.4	5.2	5.6	6.5
Excess reserves...........	3.1	2.6	1.2	1.4	1.5	1.1
Federal Reserve banks:						
Total deposits...........	14.7	14.0	14.0	15.4	17.2	18.2
Note circulation..........	8.2	9.4	13.9	18.9	23.0	24.2
Reserve ratio (per cent) ...	90.8	89.3	73.8	55.4	44.9	42.7
Annual rate of deposit turn-over..................	19.4	18.4	17.4	17.3	16.1	16.7

SOURCE: *Federal Reserve Bulletins.*

War finance not only increased the total stock of money but it also changed the structure of American banking. Before the war, big business in banking was concentrated in New York and Chicago, but the war added new production centers, and other areas obtained their share of banking leviathans. In 1939 there were 81 banks with deposits of over

$100 million; 25 were in New York and Chicago. In 1946 there were 180 banks in the $100 million group, but only 34 were in the central Reserve cities. There ·was also a greater rate of growth among smaller banks; 71 per cent of the banks with deposits of less than $1 million grew in size 300 per cent or more between 1939 and 1945, but only 30 per cent of the $5 to $50 million group and 22 per cent of the $50 million or more group had such a high rate of growth.[6]

Impact of War Finance on the Income Flow. Between July 1, 1940, and June 30, 1946, total spending equaled $1,042 billion, of which the Federal government spent $387 billion, or a little more than one-third. During the year 1945 alone, it accounted for almost half the aggregate spending of $214 billion. This was proportionately twice as high as the rate in World War I, for in the fiscal year 1919, Federal expenditures accounted for $19 billion out of $75 billion, or a little less than one-quarter. The vast increase of spending caused by the war economy, generated a corresponding increase in national income and in gross national product. Since every dollar borrowed represented a credit to someone else, Federal spending and the steady increase in Federal debt augmented the liquid assets of the other segments of the economy: individuals, banks, and state and local governments.[7]

The Federal deficits totaled $211 billion, which was exactly equal to the increase in savings of individuals, corporations, and state and local governments. In addition, there was approximately $6 billion of increases in bank credit due to larger supplies of monetary gold and silver and to slightly expanded bank loans. Thus, liquid assets in all sectors except the Federal government rose by $217 billion between the beginning and the end of the war. The owners of these assets, by deciding between savings and spending, had it within their power to determine how far price inflation would go. On the other hand, the Federal government could attempt to restrain price inflation only by retaining its controls over the economy and maintaining a high tax level until such time as the supply of goods for the consumer market could be increased. Whether or not an increase in total production was possible in the face of effective economic controls became the most hotly debated issue of the early postwar years.

State and Local Finance during World War II. At the beginning of World War II, fear was expressed by some state and local officials that the war would create great financial difficulties for their governments. Actually, these fears proved unfounded. Expenditures had to be kept low in order

[6] Federal Reserve Board, *Federal Reserve Policy*, Postwar Economic Studies, No. 8.
[7] See the *Annual Report of the Secretary of the Treasury*, 1946, for the detailed breakdown of the effect of government war financing on the gross income flow.

to release labor and materials for war needs, and while costs of operation were increased by rising prices and wage rates, these increases were absorbed in the economies attained through reductions of personnel, through deferment of repairs and capital outlays, and through savings in interest costs incident to reductions in debt. State expenditures, exclusive of debt retirements and Federal grants, increased imperceptibly from $3.6 billion in 1941 to $3.8 billion in 1945, while local expenditures, exclusive of Federal and state grants, first dropped from $4.8 billion in 1941 to $4.4 billion in 1943 and then climbed back to $4.9 billion in 1945.[8]

State revenues, being relatively flexible, reflected the inflationary wartime increases in personal and corporate incomes, expanding from $3.6 billion in 1941 to $4.3 billion in 1945. States, such as New York and California, which derived large portions of their revenue from personal and corporate income taxes enjoyed especially large gains in revenues and large annual surpluses. They husbanded these surpluses as carefully as possible, accumulating them in reserves for financing capital outlays after the war or for meeting possible future budgetary deficits.

Local tax revenues, being based on the property tax, stayed about the same throughout the war ($4.7 billion in 1941 and $4.9 billion in 1945). Together with Federal aid and state assistance, these revenues were ample to cover wartime needs, but they did not produce any substantial surpluses.

Both state and local net long-term debts were substantially reduced— the former from $2.6 billion in 1940 to $1.8 billion in 1945 and the latter from $14.6 billion to $12.3 billion. Among the local debts, only those of special districts were not reduced, but these were to a substantial degree for revenue-producing projects and some of them were closely connected with the war effort.

[8] The Tax Foundation, *Facts and Figures on Government Finance, 1950–1951*, p. 52.

CHAPTER 31: DEFLATION OR INFLATION: PEACE OR WAR

The vast changes which the depression and World War II wrought in the economic and social structure resulted in a postwar period fraught with uncertainty, insecurity, and indecision.

The five years 1946 through 1950 were characterized by continuous inflationary pressures, but the experiences of the depression could not be forgotten. Living in constant fear of unemployment and the threat of deflation, the people and the administration sublimated the American dream and made the quest for security the paramount objective of their economic policy. Inflationary government policies, such as continued heavy Federal spending, price supports, housing loans, tax reduction, and an easy-money policy, commanded popularity and were followed by the administration. At the same time, the constant infusion of rigidities into the economy in the form of government and monopolistic private price and wage supports gave support to scepticism regarding the economy's ability to maintain a continuous high rate of growth.

Internationally, the postwar years were even more heavily clouded by uncertainty and insecurity. The hopes for one world had not materialized. Instead, the war had accentuated the cleavage between the capitalist and the communist worlds. Nevertheless, the public and the administration ardently wished to believe that peace had been reestablished and normal life had once again become possible. As the "iron curtain" enclosed a larger and larger area of Europe and Asia and as the "cold war" became increasingly serious, there was a desire to escape from reality. Despite pleas from military leaders and internationalists, the public was not enthusiastic about making the sacrifices necessary for vigorous measures of national defense and for continuous financial assistance to friendly nations. Governmental policies during this period reflected the state of public opinion and were inconsistent and often self-defeating. The outbreak of the Korean War in June, 1950, brought the true state of international affairs painfully to the public mind and put an end to governmental indecision regarding the financial and economic measures to be pursued, while at the same time making it clear that continuous inflation was going to be the real threat.

Political and Economic Setting. Politically, the first few years after World War II were colored by President Truman's Fair Deal, a revival

459

in a less spectacular form of the New Deal. The Fair Deal was imbued with profarmerism and prolaborism, but unlike the New Deal, it did not bear the stamp of intellectualism. Never arousing much enthusiasm, it succeeded neither in creating the conviction that it was a crusade for social reform nor in planting the impression that it had a set of deep political convictions.

Economically, the period could be divided into four subperiods: (1) a short period of reconversion from a war to a peacetime economy, (2) a period of uncontrolled inflation, (3) a mild recession, and (4) a period of renewed economic expansion and inflation.

At the end of the war many economists, trained in the "mature economy" theory evolved during the depression of the thirties, prophesied a slow and difficult reconversion and the recurrence of severe unemployment which could be cured only by continuous substantial government spending.[1] These forecasts proved incorrect, for reconversion was accomplished in 1945-1946 more rapidly than anyone had dared to hope. The Federal Reserve index of industrial production, after dropping from 225 on V-E Day to 186 on V-J Day, declined gradually to 152 in February, 1946. Thereafter, it rose steadily, reaching 182 by the end of 1946 and 195 by October, 1948. The slight business recession in mid-1948 brought the index down to 161 in July, 1949, but this was followed by a sharp recovery to 200 in June, 1950. Employment, after dropping from a wartime peak of 65 million to 52 million in February, 1946, passed 60 million in June, 1947. During the recession it declined to 57 million but reached a peacetime high of 62 million in June, 1950. Gross national product, after declining slightly from $215.2 billion in 1945 to $212.6 billion in 1946, rose to $235.7 billion in 1947 and $262.4 billion in 1948. It dropped slightly to $257.4 billion in 1949 but reached an annual rate of $275 billion in June, 1950.

Private investment spending, which increased from $10.7 billion in 1945 to $45.0 billion in 1948, was far in excess of forecasts. Together with a less spectacular increase in consumption expenditures, it exerted an inflationary pressure which gradually came into the open when controls were removed.[2] The cost-of-living index, after increasing slightly from 129 in June, 1945, to 133.3 in June, 1946, rose to a peak of 174.5 in August, 1948. In the next six months it declined to 166.5, but with heavy incomes,

---

[1] See National Planning Association, *National Budgets for Full Employment,* Washington, March, 1945; Morris Livingston, Arthur Smithies, and Jacob Mosak, "Forecasting Post War Demands," *Econometrica,* January, 1945; R. A. Musgrave, "Alternative Budget Policies for Full Employment," *Am. Ec. Rev.,* June, 1945; Jacob Mosak, "National Budgets and National Policy," *ibid.,* March, 1946.

[2] Rationing was largely abandoned in November, 1945. Price controls were modified in June, 1946, and eliminated completely in November.

a large backlog of liquid assets, and an increase in the turnover of money, a second postwar price inflation began, carrying the cost of living to 170.2 in June, 1950. Wholesale prices followed the same trend, increasing from 105.8 in June, 1945, to 112.9 in June, 1946, and 169.5 in August, 1948; declining to 151.2 in December, 1949; and advancing to 157.3 in June, 1950.

Since most of the postwar period was characterized by price and credit inflation, deflationary fiscal and monetary policies were called for. But the administration and Congress, partly by design and partly because of unavoidable conditions, followed policies which contributed to inflation. Federal spending was maintained at a high level. Federal taxes were drastically reduced. Interest rates were kept low, and credit was made easily available.

Continuation of Large Federal Expenditures. Federal expenditures after 1946 dropped to 40 per cent of the wartime peak but were still 4.6 times greater than the five-year prewar average. In this respect, they followed the usual postwar pattern, but in other respects there were sharp differences. Instead of representing a small fraction, Federal spending averaged 17 per cent of the national income, and instead of declining year by year, it showed a substantial rise in the late forties.

Military expenditures were reduced gradually from $48.2 billion in 1946 to $11.1 billion in 1948.[3] As the international situation grew more intense, they rose to $12.4 billion in 1950. Appropriations were $14.5 billion, but it took time to translate them into expenditures. At $12.4 billion they were about ten times prewar expenditures and 30 per cent of total current expenditures. While the size of the military force was reduced gradually from 3.8 million in 1946 to 1½ million in 1950, about 46 per cent of total military expenditures went for pay and maintenance of personnel, 30 per cent for operation and maintenance of equipment and for military public works, 10 per cent for aircraft procurement, 4 per cent for other procurement, 6 per cent for research and development, and 2½ per cent for stockpiling. This was a very different distribution from that which prevailed during the war (Table 82).

Veterans' benefits, under the GI Bill of Rights, were maintained on a scale considerably more ambitious than after any previous war. Of approximately $7 billion a year, $2½ billion was paid for education and on-the-job training. In 1948 at the height of the program 2 million vet-

[3] Although many commentators insisted that disarmament was too drastic, the reduction in defense expenditures was considerably less than after previous wars. Between 1945 and 1949, the reduction was to one-eighth of the peak compared with reductions to one-thirteenth and one-seventeenth after the Civil War and World War I.

erans were enrolled in such activities. In addition, the Veterans' Administration paid $2 billion in pensions, $500 million for medical care, and $500 million for unemployment compensation.

Unlike previous postwar periods, interest payments on the public debt were relatively small. Because of the unprecedented low interest rate at which the debt had increased, they aggregated only $5 billion a year, or approximately 12½ per cent of total expenditures.

Expenditures for international finance and aid accounted for 10 to 15 per cent of annual expenditures. Most of these were in goods and services or in credits with which goods and services could be purchased from American business and represented an intensely inflationary pressure on the American economy.

On July 31, 1945, Congress passed the Bretton Woods Agreements Act, authorizing the United States to join the International Monetary Fund and the International Bank for Reconstruction and Development. The purposes of the Fund were to stabilize international currencies and to eliminate restrictions on foreign-exchange transactions. The Bank was designed to guarantee private loans or to make direct loans to war-torn or economically backward areas. The United States' subscription to the Fund was $2¾ billion and to the Bank, $3.2 billion. However, only 20 per cent of the Bank quota was payable immediately. The subscription to the Fund was paid partly in gold ($687.5 million), partly in cash ($280.5 milion), and partly in non-negotiable, non-interest-bearing notes ($1.8 billion). Only $950 million of this subscription appeared as an expenditure in the Treasury's accounts, the remainder being transferred from the Exchange Stabilization Fund.

By the Anglo-American loan agreement, ratified by Congress in July, 1946, a line of credit for $3¾ billion, effective until December 31, 1951, was established in the United States for Great Britain. All amounts borrowed against the credit were to be repaid in 50 annual installments, beginning in 1952, at interest of 2 per cent annually. However, interest would be waived in any year in which the International Monetary Fund certified that the real value of British exports and invisible items was less than the average real value of British imports during 1936 to 1938. For its part, Britain agreed to pay $650 million in settlement of lend-lease and other wartime obligations, to unfreeze the sterling balances of the creditor nations, and to relax exchange controls.

Throughout the early postwar period, European nations were drained of their gold and dollar reserves in spite of various measures of assistance such as the sale of surplus materials, United Nations Relief and Rehabilitation, loans by the Export-Import Bank, and the special credit for the United Kingdom. Between June 30, 1945, and June 30, 1947, Europe suffered a net loss of over $2 billion in her gold and dollar reserves and therefore began to impose drastic exchange restrictions.

In June, 1947, Secretary of State Marshall, in an address at Harvard University, proposed a three- to four-year program of American assistance toward European rehabilitation. In the ensuing six months, 16

TABLE 90. FEDERAL RECEIPTS, EXPENDITURES, AND DEBT, 1946–1950
(In billions of dollars)

	1946	1947	1948	1949	1950
Receipts	$ 40.0	$ 40.0	$ 42.2	$ 38.2	$ 37.0
Expenditures	$ 60.7	$ 39.3	$ 33.8	$ 40.1	$ 40.2
National defense	$ 48.2	$ 15.3	$ 11.1	$ 12.2	$ 12.4
Army	27.8	6.9	6.0	5.4	4.1
Navy	15.2	5.0	4.2	4.4	4.1
Air Force	....	....	....	1.7	3.5
Armed Forces Leave Act	....	2.0	0.3		
Other	5.2	1.4	0.7	0.6	0.7
International finance	1.5	6.4	4.4	6.0	4.7
UNRRA	0.7	1.5	0.3		
Bretton Woods	0.2	1.4			
Export-import bank	0.6	0.9	0.5		
Credit to United Kingdom	....	2.1	1.7		
Greek-Turkish assistance	....	......	0.2	0.3	0.1
Government relief	....	0.5	0.9	1.3	0.8
ECA	....	......	0.1	4.0	3.5
Other	....	......	0.8	0.4	0.2
Interest on public debt	4.7	5.0	5.2	5.3	5.8
Veterans' Administration	4.3	7.3	6.5	6.9	6.5
Total for or on account of war	$ 58.7	$ 34.0	$ 27.2	$ 30.0	$ 29.4
Aid to agriculture	$ −0.2	$ 1.2	$ 0.8	$ 2.7	$ 3.0
Social security program	0.8	1.1	1.6	1.7	2.0
Public works*	0.4	0.7	1.1	1.5	1.6
Miscellaneous†	1.1	2.4	2.9	3.8	4.3
Surplus (+) or deficit (−)	$ −20.7	$ +0.8	$ +8.4	$ −1.8	$ −3.1
Gross debt	269.4	258.3	252.3	252.8	257.4

SOURCE: *Annual Report of the Secretary of the Treasury*, 1950, pp. 480–481, 491.

* Includes FWA, forest roads, rivers and harbors, reclamation, and TVA.
† Includes civil expenditures, Panama Canal (except War Department), postal deficiency, etc.

European nations surveyed their economic needs and estimated that they would want approximately $20 billion to balance their international accounts from April, 1948, to June, 1952, when it was expected that rehabilitation would be completed. It was proposed that of the $20 billion the United States provide $17 billion in loans and gifts. In a special message in December, 1947, President Truman urged Congress to adopt what had by this time become known as the Marshall Plan. In March, 1948, Congress passed the Economic Cooperation Act, and in June it appropriated $4 billion for the European Recovery Program and $2 billion for other types of international relief.

The magnitude of American assistance in supplying foreign nations with goods may be realized from the fact that from July, 1945, through December, 1949, foreign nations imported from the United States $74.6 billion of goods and services, while exporting only $40.1 billion. Of the $34.5 billion deficit, they covered only $6.3 billion by reducing their dollar and gold balances, receiving $24.7 billion in net United States government aid.[4]

Only $5 billion to $10 billion a year was spent for purposes of strictly peacetime origin. Among these the largest single item was agricultural aid. From $1.2 billion in 1947, it rose, as foreign demand for American agricultural products subsided, to $3 billion in 1950. Of the $2.7 billion spent in 1949, $1.6 billion went for farm price support[5] (60 per cent of which went to one-eighth of the farmers).[6] In addition, $300 million was spent for rural electrification, $250 million for conservation, $100 million for farm housing, and $125 million for removing surplus commodities and the administration of the Sugar Act.

The two other large expenditures of nonwar nature were for social security, which increased from $800 million in the fiscal year 1946 to $2 billion in 1950, and for public works, which increased from $400 million to $1.6 billion. Interspersed with these and other civil expenditures were grants-in-aid to states, which rose from $750 million in 1946 to $2 billion in 1950.

Introduction of a Cash Budget. The influence of Federal finance on the economy is exerted most immediately through the Treasury's cash transactions with the public. Any excess of Treasury cash receipts over cash payments reduces the disposable income of the population and tends to depress private employment, while any excess of Treasury payments over receipts tends to have the opposite effect. Traditional budget accounts do not give an accurate picture of all the Federal government's cash transactions with the public and therefore do not reflect the impact of Federal finance on the economy. Since budget accounts deal only

[4] *Annual Report of the Secretary of the Treasury*, 1949; *Federal Reserve Bulletin*, April, 1950.

[5] As of Jan. 1, 1950, the Commodity Credit Corporation had purchased or made loans on $1.8 billion of farm products. Its inventory included 3.7 million bales of cotton, 159.7 million bushels of wheat, 78.1 million pounds of dried eggs, 51.4 million pounds of wool, 100.1 million pounds of butter, and 100.8 million bushels of corn.

[6] *President's Budget Message*, 1947–1948.

with general and special fund receipts and disbursements, they omit the cash transactions of the trust funds (old age, railroad retirement, unemployment, etc.) with the public, but they include transfer payments between the general fund and the trust funds even though these have little effect on the public. In addition, some of the disbursements in the budget accounts, for example, interest on savings bonds, are mere accruals and involve no actual cash payments. The divergence between the budget accounts and the cash transactions with the public first became important in the middle thirties. It grew wider as the size of the trust funds increased. The exclusion of trust-fund transactions from the budget accounts in 1933, instead of alleviating, accentuated the confusion.

TABLE 91.   COMPARISON OF BUDGET ACCOUNTS AND CASH TRANSACTIONS WITH THE PUBLIC
(In billions of dollars)

	1943	1944	1945	1946	1947	1948	1949	1950
Budget accounts:								
Receipts....................	$ 22.2	$ 43.9	$ 44.8	$ 40.0	$ 40.0	$ 42.2	$ 38.2	$ 37.0
Expenditures..............	79.6	95.3	98.7	60.7	39.3	33.8	40.1	40.2
Surplus (+) or deficit (−)......	$−57.4	$−51.4	$−53.9	$−20.7	$+0.8	$+8.4	$−1.8	$−3.1
Cash transactions with the public:								
Cash budget receipts...........	$ 22.1	$ 43.9	$ 45.5	38.9	$ 39.9	$ 41.8	$ 38.1	$ 36.9
Cash trust-account receipts.......	3.0	3.9	4.7	4.9	3.7	3.6	3.5	4.0
Total cash receipts...........	$ 25.2	$ 47.9	$ 50.2	43.8	$ 43.6	$ 45.4	$ 41.6	$ 41.0
Cash budget expenditures.........	$ 78.4	$ 93.8	$ 96.0	$ 57.4	$ 33.2	$ 32.5	$ 37.5	$ 37.0
Cash trust-account payments......	0.5	0.1	−0.8	4.3	3.3	2.9	3.3	6.9
Exchange Stabilization Fund payments........................	......	......	......	......	1.0	0.6	0.1	−0.2
Clearing-account payments........	......	......	......	......	−0.6	0.5	−0.4	−0.5
Total cash expenditures........	$ 78.9	$ 94.0	$ 95.2	61.7	$ 36.9	$ 36.5	$ 40.6	$ 43.2
Excess of cash receipts over cash expenditures (+) or payments over receipts (−).............	$−53.7	$−46.1	$−44.9	$−17.9	$+6.7	$+8.9	$+1.1	$−2.2

SOURCE: U.S. Treasury Bulletin, March, 1951, pp. 1, 12.

The need for annual or more frequent statements of cash transactions with the public became clear during World War II when it was realized that the inflationary effects of increased governmental fiscal operations were determined by the excess of governmental cash payments to the public and not by the excess of budgetary expenditures over budgetary receipts. Since the government economic and fiscal policy could not be formulated most efficiently by reference to budget accounts, the Treasury started to prepare more comprehensive cash accounts.

Table 91 shows the difference between budget accounts and cash accounts. It will be noted that for 1947 the budget accounts showed a surplus of only $0.8 billion, but the surplus of Treasury cash receipts over cash payments was $6.7 billion. In other words, the Treasury's fiscal operations during that year were much more deflationary than indicated by budget accounts. For 1949 the budget showed a deficit of $1.8 billion, but since cash accounts showed a deficit of only $1.1 billion, the inflationary influence of government finances was somewhat smaller than suggested by the budget accounts.

The Full Employment Act and the Introduction of Economic Planning. Near the end of World War II, there was a widespread belief that the chief economic problem after V-J Day would be deflation, depression, and mass unemployment. It was a freely accepted theory that leadership in preventing this development would have to come from the Federal government.

To facilitate the exercise of this leadership, Senator Murray of Montana introduced, in January, 1945, a full-employment bill which asserted that every American "able and willing to work . . . has the right to a . . . job." The bill declared that "to the extent that continuing full employment cannot otherwise be achieved, it is the . . . responsibility of the Federal Government to provide such volume of Federal investment and expenditures as may be needed to assure continuing full employment." Each year the President was to transmit to Congress "a National Production and Employment Budget," in which he was to estimate the size of the labor force, the gross national product, and the level of gross national product necessary to provide full employment. If a deficit between the actual and required gross product was forecast, the President was to recommend increased Federal spending, but if estimated gross product exceeded the volume necessary for full employment, he was to recommend a general program for preventing inflationary dislocations.

The Murray bill represented the culmination of a trend toward regarding the Federal budget as an instrument to regulate the economy rather than as a purely fiscal device. Since it was a most ambitious step in the direction of compensatory fiscal policy, opposition quickly developed. It was argued that the bill would destroy initiative, undermine confidence, and lead to inflation; that the gross national product could not be forecast accurately; and that the whole concept of the bill was incompatible with the principles of a free society. The bill was therefore considerably modified during the Congressional debates, and in its final form, the Employment Act declared,

It is the continuing policy and responsibility of the Federal Government to use all practicable means consistent with its needs and obligations . . . to utilize all its . . . resources for the purpose of creating and maintaining, in a manner calculated to foster and promote free competitive enterprise . . . conditions under which there will be afforded useful employment.

The President was to submit to Congress an economic report setting forth an analysis of the nation's economic condition and recommending a program to carry out the declared policy of the Act. A Council of Economic Advisers, composed of three members, was created in the Executive Office of the President, to advise the President in preparing the Economic Report; to gather, analyze, and interpret information concerning economic developments and trends; to appraise the Federal government's activities in order to determine to what extent they were contributing to promoting maximum employment; and to recommend economic policies to promote free competitive enterprise, to avoid economic fluctuations, and to maintain employment. In addition, the Act established a Joint Committee on the Economic Report, composed of seven senators and seven congressmen, to review for Congress the President's Economic Report and its recommendations and to make its own recommendations in light thereof.

The Full Employment Act, in its original form, called for the preparation of a so-called "Nation's Economic Budget," the concept of which was developed originally by the Budget Bureau during World War II. The Council of Economic Advisers, set up under the Act, undertook the regular semiannual preparation of this "economic budget," showing the current changes in the rate of the gross national income and expenditures received and disbursed by each one of the four sections of the national economy—consumers, business, the international account, and the government. The Council used this economic budget as a basis for the formulation of economic policies. Soon after its organization, the Council split on the question of its participation in policy decisions. Chairman Edwin G. Nourse, who regarded the Council as a purely advisory nonpartisan body, independent of the Administration, resigned on October 18, 1949, and was replaced by Leon H. Keyserling, who favored participation by the Council in administrative decisions and its appearance before Congress on behalf of the administration.

Unsuccessful Attempts to Cut Expenditures. While it was the consensus of opinion that the Federal government was spending too much money, there was little general agreement as to which items in the budget could best be reduced.

The Truman administration insisted that "in a period of high prosperity it is not sound policy to operate at a deficit,"[7] but its hopes of achieving an overbalanced budget relied much more heavily on tax increases than on expenditure reductions. It refused to delay the inauguration of social programs or to modify existing programs despite conservative disapproval, and it had apparently abandoned the New Deal's earlier con-

[7] *President's Budget Message, 1949–1950.*

cept of cyclical compensatory public-works spending in favor of a belief that a permanently high plateau of public works was necessary to
prevent deflation.[8]

The administration's strongest economy moves were taken in connection with defense spending. In his budget message for 1949-1950
President Truman said, "The principal objective we should have in mind
in planning for our national defense is to build a foundation of military
strength which can be sustained for a period of years without excessive
strain on our productive resources, and which will permit rapid expansion
should the need arise." With this in mind, the administration followed
a middle-of-the-road policy, imposing a $15 billion budget ceiling on
defense spending, while the military establishment submitted a preliminary budget estimate of $30 billion and some of the economy group
urged a $12 billion limit.

Congress for its part played with the idea of economy but never actually put into practice any concrete reductions. The Legislative Reorganization Act of August, 1946, created a joint Congressional committee
to consider the President's budget message and to recommend a legislative budget. This joint Committee on the Legislative Budget made its
first report in February, 1947, on the President's budget for the fiscal
year 1948. It emphasized the following principles: the elimination of
government functions which might be desirable but not imperative, a
return wherever possible to prewar levels of appropriations, and the reduction of government employees by at least 500,000. With due consideration to these principles, the committee estimated expenditures at
$31.5 billion, $6 billion less than the President's estimate. However, the
committee did not specify where these cuts were to be made, and while
the House voted to accept the legislative budget, the Senate voted to limit
expenditure cuts to 4½ billion. The conference committee appointed
to iron out the differences never reached an agreement, and the actual
Congressional appropriations departed even further from the committee's
report. By the most liberal estimate, Congress appropriated $3 billion
less than estimated in the President's budget and by the most conservative estimates $1.0 billion less.[9]

Again in 1948, the Legislative Budget Committee voted to reduce the

[8] Reflecting this philosophy, President Truman said in his *Economic Report* of
January, 1947: "We should attempt to stabilize public-works construction according
to our long-term needs. Increasing regularization of public-works expenditures at all
levels of governmental activity over a long period will offer an assurance of a demand for capital, of a market for materials and equipment, and of a field for employment, which will assist in stabilizing that segment of the business world."

[9] Actual expenditures were $33.8 billion compared with the President's estimate of
$37.5 billion and the committee's estimate of $31.5 billion.

President's budget for 1949 by $2.5 billion without giving a specific identification of where cuts were to be made.[10]

The most articulate criticism of Federal spending came from two groups: those who opposed government spending on traditional grounds and those who, though not opposing Federal spending per se, urged heavy cuts as a means of reducing inflationary pressures.

The drastic economizers—Senator Byrd, the National Association of Manufacturers, the Chamber of Commerce of the United States, etc.— believed that the budget could be reduced to $25 billion or $30 billion within a two-year period. In December, 1947, the NAM proposed a $30 billion budget for 1949, including $9 billion for defense, $6½ billion for veterans, $5 billion for interest, $2½ billion for social welfare and agriculture, $1 billion for transportation and communication, $1 billion for general government, $1 billion for natural resources, and $4 billion for contingencies including international affairs.[11] Even as late as December, 1949, Senator Byrd still insisted that, after allowing for increases in foreign aid and interest charges, at least $6 billion could be cut out of the forthcoming budget: $2.2 billion out of national defense and $4.1 billion out of veterans' services, social welfare, and general government.[12] Yet the hopes of those who, like Senator Byrd, thought in terms of "the old rule of balanced budgets, reduced debt, and reduction in taxes" were somewhat dampened by the international situation. When the Senate in February, 1947, voted to cut $4.5 billion from the Truman budget for 1947-1948, it explained its failure to cut more by saying that extreme cuts "would give other nations opportunity for further intransigence."[13]

Marriner Eccles and Senator Paul Douglas were the chief spokesmen for the point of view that expenditures should be reduced to combat inflation. In November, 1947, Eccles, without specifying the possible economies, urged "the most rigid government economy" which would produce "the largest possible surplus."[14] In January, 1950, Senator Douglas suggested cutting $2.8 billion from the proposed $42.4 billion budget by cutting $500 million from national defense, eliminating the $800 million provided for the National Mortgage Association, cutting $700 million from the Federal payrolls through a reduction of personnel and reduction of vacations, doing away with $150 million of silver and other subsidies, and saving $200 million through the consolidation of certain agencies. In addition, he pointed to the possibilities of large savings

[10] Expenditures were actually $40.1 billion compared with the President's estimate of $39.7 billion.

[11] *The New York Times*, Oct. 9, 1947; Oct. 19, 1947; Dec. 5, 1947.

[12] *New York Herald-Tribune*, Dec. 9, 1949.

[13] *The New York Times*, Feb. 20, 1947.

[14] Testimony before the Joint Committee on the Economic Report.

through the postponement to a more suitable time of a number of river and harbor and other public-works projects.

Campaign for Tax Reduction. At the end of the war all classes of society looked forward to speedy tax reduction such as had occurred in the decades following the Civil War and World War I. To some extent, these hopes were satisfied, for there were relatively sharp reductions in 1945 and 1948. However, as it became clear that government expenditures would increase rather than decrease, the public reluctantly became reconciled to the fact that further tax reductions were simply not in the cards. This was the only postwar period in the country's history not characterized by sustained tax reductions.

In many respects, the controversy over tax reduction was similar to that which had occurred after World War I. Immediately after the war, there was a hard core of opinion opposing all tax reduction. In time this opposition softened, tax reduction became inevitable, and the conflict shifted to the question of which economic groups were to receive the major share of the reduction.

From V-J Day on, conservatives urged tax reduction for corporations and for the upper-income brackets. They asserted that the wartime rates had passed the point of diminishing returns and were destroying initiative and preventing the private investment necessary for economic growth. As soon as a Treasury surplus appeared, the campaign went into high gear. The United States Chamber of Commerce denounced "the present high corporate tax rates as a severe handicap upon industrial and commercial operations" and called for their reduction below 25 per cent. It also criticized the capital-gains tax as "a direct and unwise restriction upon the private enterprise system" and recommended reducing the rate to 12½ per cent.[15] President Shreve of the Chamber contended that tax reduction was more urgent than further debt reduction, for "present taxes are a brake on production, kill initiative, and deny incentive."[16] The National Association of Manufacturers outlined a program for a $6 billion tax cut. It included reductions in personal income rates to a range of 12 to 50 per cent, returning estate and gift taxes to the states, adopting the community property arrangement for the Federal income tax, and other minor revisions. The House Republican Tax Study Committee, under Representative Knutson, denounced "reckless spending of the people's money" and called for a 20 per cent across-the-board tax reduction.[17]

Meanwhile, the CIO, insisting that the wartime tax measures bore

[15] *The New York Times,* June 17, 1947.
[16] *The New York Times,* July 15, 1947.
[17] *The New York Times,* July 25, 1946.

most heavily on the low-income taxpayers, supported tax reductions which would increase purchasing power in the hands of consumers rather than reductions which would increase funds in the hands of potential investors. Denying that tax reduction for the low-income groups was inflationary and insisting that more of the tax burden be shifted to corporations, the CIO recommended increasing personal exemptions to $2,500 for married persons and $1,250 for single persons; eliminating excise taxes, except those which were regulatory in nature; closing loopholes by eliminating tax-exempt securities, by requiring joint returns, and by strengthening estate and gift taxes; and placing a tax upon undistributed profits and upon excess profits.[18]

Middle-of-the-roaders like the Committee for Economic Development argued against immediate tax reduction, but in a short time they shifted to an "early revision of the tax laws to provide a $6 billion tax reduction."[19] The Truman administration, however, continued to oppose further tax cuts, the President asserting in his budget message of January, 1947: "As long as business, employment, and national income continue high, we should maintain tax revenues at levels that will not only meet current expenditures but also leave a surplus for retirement of the public debt. There is no justification now for tax reduction."

As soon as the eightieth Congress was organized under Republican control in January, 1947, Representative Knutson introduced a bill reducing personal income taxes $10\frac{1}{2}$ to 20 per cent and allowing a special exemption of $500 for taxpayers over sixty-five. It was estimated that the bill would cut revenue by $3.3 billion a year, and the administration immediately objected, (1) because under current economic conditions it was "sound policy to achieve a substantial surplus" and (2) because "the bill would give too little reduction to lower incomes and relatively too much to higher incomes."[20] Thus, a fissure, which was to constantly widen, appeared in the administration's anti-tax-reduction armor.

Instead of being impressed by the administration's anti-inflationary argument, the House passed a bill which went even further than the original Knutson proposals, reducing tax rates $10\frac{1}{2}$ to 30 per cent and reducing revenue by almost $4 billion. The proponents of the measure insisted that it would encourage incentive, increase investment, and raise production. The reasoning was somewhat dubious, since increased investment spending would have an inflationary effect and the opportunities for increased production, under existing full resource employment, were limited. Nevertheless, in May the Senate, 52 to 34, passed a similar bill,

[18] Senate Committee on Finance, *Hearings on Individual Income Tax Reduction,* 1947, pp. 237ff.; 1948, pp. 388ff.

[19] *The New York Times,* Nov. 13, 1947.

[20] *Annual Report of the Secretary of the Treasury,* 1947.

but with somewhat lower reductions in the middle-income brackets. In early June both Houses agreed on a compromise, but on June 16 President Truman vetoed the bill, saying:

This bill represents the wrong kind of tax reduction, at the wrong time. . . . Ample evidence points to the continuation of inflationary pressures. Tax reduction now would increase them. . . . An adjustment of the tax system should provide fair and equitable relief. . . . H.R. 1 reduced taxes in the high income brackets to a grossly disproportionate extent. . . . A good tax reduction bill would give a greater proportion of relief to the low income groups.

In one respect, the Truman message contained a major inconsistency, for though he was on solid ground in contending that tax reduction was inflationary, tax reduction in the lower-income brackets would be more inflationary than in the upper-income brackets.

Representative Knutson charged that the veto was "cold-blooded politics" and promptly reintroduced his tax bill, but with reductions effective as of January 1, 1948, instead of July, 1947. The bill passed the House, 302 to 112, and the Senate, 60 to 32, but on July 18, the President again exercised his veto. Although the House repassed the reduction, 299 to 108, the Senate failed to override.

Tax Reduction of 1948. Temporarily, tax reduction remained in abeyance while Congress was not in session. But in November a Special Tax Study Committee, headed by Roswell Magill, recommended general reductions "with due regard for the cost of living of those in the lower income groups and for the needs of the balance of the economy." By the time Congress met in mid-November, the administration was forecasting a $7 billion surplus for fiscal 1948. But Representative Knutson asserted that it would be closer to $10 billion, and on that basis he introduced a bill cutting income tax rates 10 to 30 per cent, increasing the exemption from $500 to $600, providing double exemptions for the blind and for persons over sixty-five, and incorporating a type of community-property arrangement in Federal estate and income taxation. By this time the administration was well aware of the general desire for tax reduction, and in his annual message of January 7, 1948, President Truman, after announcing his opposition to any net reduction in Federal revenue, recommended tax revision similar in some respects to the program previously outlined by the CIO. He suggested a cost-of-living tax credit of $40 per capita, and since this would reduce revenue by $3.2 billion, he proposed an offsetting increase in the corporation income tax. At the same time, the Treasury leveled a barrage of criticism against the Knutson bill, asserting that it would reduce revenue by over $7 billion.

Both the Congressional bill and the President's proposal were presented at the height of the inflationary spiral, and neither was well advised. The Knutson bill by reducing the budgetary surplus would have made it almost impossible for the Treasury to follow an intelligent antiinflationary fiscal policy. But if it lived up to the expectations of its supporters, it would have increased investment spending and eventually augmented the supply of goods. Therefore, its long-run effect was deflationary. The President's program, on the other hand, would have maintained the Treasury surplus, but it would have increased the most inflationary type of dollars—those in the hands of consumers in the lower brackets.

TABLE 92. FEDERAL RECEIPTS, 1946–1950
(In billions of dollars)

	1946	1947	1948	1949	1950
Individual income tax	$18.7	$19.3	$21.0	$18.1	$17.2
Corporate income and excess-profits taxes*	12.6	9.7	10.2	11.6	10.9
Employment taxes	1.7	2.0	2.4	2.5	2.9
Estate and gift	0.7	0.8	0.9	0.8	0.7
Capital stock	0.4				
Liquor	2.5	.2.5	2.3	2.2	2.2
Tobacco	1.2	1.2	1.3	1.3	1.3
Gasoline	0.4	0.4	0.5	0.5	0.5
Other manufacturers' excises	0.6	1.0	1.1	1.2	1.3
Retail taxes on luxuries	0.5	0.5	0.5	0.4	0.4
Transportation, telephone, etc	1.6	1.6	1.7	1.8	1.8
Customs	0.4	0.5	0.4	0.4	0.4
Renegotiation of war contracts	1.1	0.3	0.2	0.1	
Surplus property	0.5	2.9	1.9	0.6	
Other	1.9	1.5	1.7	1.4	1.4
Total budget receipts	$44.2	$44.5	$46.1	$42.8	$41.3
Less appropriations to Federal old-age and survivors' trust fund	$ 1.2	$ 1.5	$ 1.6	$ 1.7	$ 2.1
Less refund of receipts	3.0	3.0	2.3	2.8	2.2
Net receipts	$40.0	$40.0	$42.2	$38.2	$37.0

SOURCE: *Annual Report of the Secretary of Treasury, 1946–1950.*

* For the excess-profits tax after 1946 only back collections.

The President's proposals and various administration attempts[21] to modify or change the Knutson bill were given short shrift, and in February the House, 297 to 120, passed the bill. However, the Senate passed a much more moderate bill, reducing revenue by an estimated $4.7

[21] For example, Congressman Doughton proposed to limit the income tax cut to 5 to 15 per cent, and the Rayburn amendment sought to increase the exemption to $700 and add an excess-profits tax.

billion and differing from the House bill in providing cuts of only 5 to 12.6 per cent. In early April the House accepted the Senate version.

Meanwhile, agricultural prices declined sharply, and the "cold war" became more intense. Under the circumstances, the administration began to waver between fears of inflation and deflation and between the needs of defense and the attractiveness of tax reduction. Nevertheless, President Truman promptly vetoed the tax reduction, calling it "inequitable" and a "gamble with the dangers of further inflation" and insisting that "it would endanger the soundness of our national finances at a time when our responsibilities are great in an unsettled world." Paying no attention to the President's admonition, Congress immediately repassed the bill, 311 to 88 in the House and 77 to 10 in the Senate. As a result of the tax cut and the slight recession, Federal receipts fell off from $42.2 billion in 1948 to $38.2 billion in 1949.

Need for More Revenue and the Collapse of the 1950 Tax-reduction Program. The President was severely criticized for vetoing the 1948 tax-reduction bill. Some critics suggested that he should have accepted the bill on the assumption that, if a balanced budget was not maintained or if defense needs increased, he could always ask for added taxes. This point of view was unrealistic, for by 1949 the budget was unbalanced and uneasiness concerning American defenses was widespread. Yet when the President asked for added taxes, he was met with indifference. In his annual message of January 5, 1949, he recommended that Congress increase the corporate income tax, increase the personal income tax in the middle and upper brackets, and revise the gift and estate taxes to produce an additional $4 billion of revenue. But the prevalent Congressional opinion was that deflation was now the real threat. Tax increases were therefore "temporarily delayed," and reduction in spending became the widely recommended method of budget balancing.

In October, 1949, the President said, "We've got to find money to run the government, and that's all there is to it." But Chairman Doughton of the Ways and Means Committee was not certain that the public would stand for more taxes without an effort being made to cut expenditures. Senator George, chairman of the Finance Committee, thought, "The way to meet the deficit is, first, to reduce spendings, and, second, readjust taxes to encourage production and stimulate business."[22]

Again in January, 1950, President Truman asked for tax reorganization and increases to yield an additional $1 billion. Pointing to an estimated $5.1 billion deficit for the fiscal year 1950, he blamed it on the "shortsighted tax reduction enacted by the Eighthieth Congress." He recom-

[22] *New York Herald-Tribune*, Oct. 21, 1949.

mended the reduction of retail excise taxes and those on transportation and communication. As offsets, he urged Congress to close some existing loopholes in the tax laws, such as "excessive depletion exemptions, . . . abuse of the tax exemption accorded educational and charitable organizations," and "undertaxation" of life insurance companies. In addition, he asked for $1 billion in additional revenue from changes in the estate, gift, and corporate income taxes. On February 3, Secretary Snyder presented specific proposals to the Ways and Means Committee. They included 50 per cent cuts in most retail excise taxes and lesser cuts in taxes on transportation and communication, increased estate and gift taxes, a special tax on television sets, and an increase in the maximum corporation tax from 38 to 42 per cent. The Ways and Means Committee quickly voted to reduce excise taxes and to close tax loopholes, but it was not until mid-June, after a threat of a Presidential veto, that it voted to raise the corporation tax by eliminating graduated rates and imposing a 21 per cent rate on the first $25,000 of net income and a surtax of 20 per cent on all additional earnings. The House passed the bill on June 29, but before the Senate could consider it, the Korean War had broken out. Not only was action on tax reorganization suspended, but Congress, finally and reluctantly, turned its attention to the consideration of stringent tax increases.

Weak and Unsustained Debt Reduction. The Federal gross debt reached its all-time high in February, 1946, at $279.2 billion. Thereafter, by reducing the general fund balance, which had been built up by the sale of the Victory Loan, the gross debt was reduced to $269.4 billion in June, 1946. Constituting 60 per cent of the nation's combined private and public debt as compared with 23 per cent in 1939 and less than 20 per cent in the 1920's, the Federal debt was the most important single factor in the economy.

The majority of economic opinion looked upon debt reduction as the government's most powerful anti-inflationary weapon. Yet at no time during this period did the administration or Congress set any definite annual rate of debt retirement as a goal. The amount actually retired was largely determined by accident, since it depended upon the surpluses resulting from the annual clash of expenditure and tax policies and on the effects of economic conditions on tax collections.

Under the circumstances, debt reduction lasted only for two years, 1946 to 1948, and even then, while the gross debt was reduced from $269.4 billion to $252.3 billion, more than half the reduction ($9.3 billion) was accomplished by reducing the general fund balance, that is, by liquidating deposits in war loan accounts. This type of debt retirement in itself had neither important deflationary nor important inflationary effects.

Most of the debt reduction which was accomplished took place in short-term obligations which declined from 28 to 20 per cent of the total debt. At the same time, the volume of refunding amounted to about $50 billion annually, or more than the total refunding operations of all other borrowers during the previous 25 years.

TABLE 93. FEDERAL-DEBT OPERATIONS, JUNE 30, 1945–1950
(In billions of dollars)

	1945	1946	1947	1948	1949	1950
Bills..................................	$ 17.0	$ 17.0	$ 15.8	$ 13.8	$ 11.5	$ 13.5
Certificates..........................	34.1	34.8	25.3	22.6	29.4	18.4
Notes................................	23.5	18.3	8.1	11.4	3.6	20.4
Treasury bonds.......................	106.5	119.4	119.3	112.5	110.4	102.8
Other bonds..........................	0.2	0.2	0.2	0.2	0.2	0.2
Total marketable....................	$181.3	$189.6	$168.7	$160.3	$155.1	$155.3
United States savings bonds..............	$ 45.6	$ 49.0	$ 51.4	$ 53.3	$ 56.3	$ 57.5
Savings notes........................	10.1	6.7	5.6	4.4	4.9	8.5
Armed forces leave bonds...............	......	......	1.8	0.6	0.4	0.3
Treasury bonds, investment series........	......	......	......	1.0	1.0	1.0
Other bonds.........................	0.5	0.4	0.3	0.3	0.4	0.3
Total nonmarketable.................	$ 56.2	$ 56.2	$ 59.0	$ 59.5	$ 62.8	$ 67.5
Special issues.......................	18.8	22.3	27.4	30.2	32.8	32.4
Total interest-bearing...............	$256.4	$268.1	$255.1	$250.1	$250.8	$255.2
Matured debt.........................	$ 0.3	$ 0.4	$ 0.2	$ 0.3	$ 0.2	$ 0.3
Non-interest-bearing..................	2.0	0.9	2.9	1.9	1.8	1.8
Total gross debt.....................	$258.7	$269.4	$258.3	$252.3	$252.8	$257.4
General fund balance..................	24.7	14.2	3.3	4.9	3.5	5.5
Net debt............................	$234.0	$255.2	$255.0	$247.4	$249.3	$251.9
Guaranteed obligations................	$ 0.4	$ 0.5	$ 0.1	$ 0.1		
Change in gross public debt during year....	+57.7	+10.7	−11.1	−6.0	+ .5	+4.6
Due to surplus or deficit...............	+53.9	+20.7	−0.8	−8.4	+1.8	+3.1
Due to net trust fund, etc., receipts (+) or expenditures (−).................	−0.8	+0.5	+0.6	+0.8	+0.1	−0.6
Due to changes in general fund balance...	+4.5	−10.5	−10.9	+1.6	−1.5	+2.0

SOURCE: *Annual Report of the Secretary of the Treasury,* 1950, pp. 492–493, 555.

Besides the constant replacement of short-term bills, certificates, and notes, the Treasury redeemed or refunded $6.9 billion of long-term bonds in the fiscal year 1948, $2.1 billion in 1949, and $7.7 billion in 1950.[23] The amount redeemed for cash was relatively small, usually less than 15 per cent, although in the case of the 2¾'s of 1948, 21 per cent were so redeemed. In refunding long-term obligations, the Treasury re-

[23] The maturing obligations included the 4¼'s of 1947 to 1952 issued in 1922, the 3⅛'s issued in 1934, and various 1¾ to 2¾ per cent issues.

lied exclusively on notes and certificates.[24] While this saved large amounts in net interest charges, it tended to increase outstanding short-term securities and perpetuated Treasury control over interest rates and over the price of government obligations.

Maintenance of Low Interest Rates. The Treasury's debt-management program had three principal objectives: to reduce the amount of the debt, to maintain government credit and keep debt costs low, and to widen the distribution of Federal securities. Of the three objectives, the Treasury considered the second to be the most important,[25] and it sought to achieve this aim by maintaining control over interest rates and by stabilizing government security prices at a low yield. It insisted that, if the interest rate was not controlled, interest charges on the debt would rise, the already enormous Federal expenditures would increase even further, refunding operations would become more difficult, financial institutions and other investors in governments would suffer serious losses, and panic selling would result.[26] At first, the Treasury had the complete cooperation of the Federal Reserve authorities, for the money managers were no more eager than the Treasury to risk a collapse of the government-bond market.

With the Treasury in control, only slight increases in the interest rate were permitted, and those only gradually. The first increase came in July, 1947, when the wartime bill rate of ⅜ of 1 per cent ceased to be maintained.[27] The rate on certificates, however, continued to be controlled, although it was allowed to rise gradually from ⅞ of 1 per cent to 1⅛ per cent after August, 1947. The second easing of controls occurred in December when the Open Market Committee lowered its support price on bonds, promising only to maintain them at par.[28] In August, 1948, the Treasury stated that certificates would be issued at 1¼ per cent.

After the peak of inflation had been reached in the summer of 1948 and private loans had begun to contract, the banks used their excess re-

[24] For example, the $4.4 billion of 2 to 3⅛ per cent bonds callable in December, 1949, were almost all exchanged for 1⅜ per cent notes, and 91 per cent of maturing 2 per cent bonds were exchanged for 1¼ per cent certificates in December, 1948.

[25] The Treasury was greatly impressed by the experience of the twenties when Liberties fell to 84. (*Annual Report of the Secretary of the Treasury*, 1949.)

[26] See address of Undersecretary Wiggins, *Annual Report of the Secretary of the Treasury*, 1948.

[27] To help the Treasury offset the rise in interest costs caused by this easing of controls, the Board of Governors levied on the Reserve banks for 1947 an interest charge, payable to the Treasury, on Federal Reserve notes equal to 90 per cent of their earnings, or $54 million.

[28] Throughout 1947 and 1948, the Federal Reserve System continued to maintain the yield on bonds at 2½ per cent. Although its portfolio showed no change over the whole period, its transactions in governments totaled almost $80 billion.

serves to buy governments. But the price of governments did not rise substantially, for the Federal Reserve was supplying them freely in accordance with its stated policy of maintaining stable prices. However, on June 28, 1949, the stabilization policy was abandoned, and the Open Market Committee, after consultation with the Treasury, announced:

With a view to increasing the supply of funds available in the market . . . it will be the policy to direct purchases, sales, and exchanges of Government securities by the Federal Reserve Banks with primary regard to the general business and credit situation. The policy of maintaining orderly conditions in the Government security market, and the confidence of investors in Government bonds will be continued. Under present conditions the maintenance of a relatively fixed pattern of rates has the undesirable effect of absorbing reserves at a time when the availability of credit should be increased.

In brief, the announcement meant that the Reserve System was committing itself to an aggressively easy-money policy instead of maintaining a stable and relatively low interest rate as it had done all through the hyperinflation.

The Treasury was signally successful in maintaining the price of government obligations at a low yield. For even though large amounts of low-interest short-term obligations were being retired and savings bonds with their 2.9 per cent rate were increasing, the computed annual interest charge increased by only $230 million and the computed annual interest rate rose from 1.995 to 2.199 per cent between June, 1946, and June, 1950.

In spite of its success, the whole policy was highly controversial. The Treasury contended that "it contributed to the underlying strength of the country's financial system and eased reconversion . . . in marked contrast to the situation after the First World War, when the severe decline in the prices of Government securities contributed to the business collapse."[29] It was also asserted that low interest rates benefited the taxpayer by making possible a lower level of government expenditures and stimulated the economy generally by enabling consumers and producers to obtain more durable goods for each dollar. Chairman McCabe of the Board of Governors also defended the policy, saying, "I am convinced that we could not have abandoned our support position during this period without damaging repercussions on our entire financial mechanism as well as seriously adverse effects on the economy generally."[30] Opponents of the policy insisted that it was inflationary, since it encouraged borrowing and weakened the System's instruments of credit control by preventing effective use of the rediscount rate and anti-in-

[29] *Annual Report of the Secretary of the Treasury*, 1949, p. 15.

[30] "Statement before the Banking and Currency Committee, May 11, 1949," *Federal Reserve Bulletin*, May, 1949.

flationary open market operations. Among the most articulate critics of the easy-money policy was Marriner Eccles, who had defended the price-support program in the immediate postwar years but who had gradually drifted away from the Treasury point of view, finally resigning as chairman of the Board of Governors in January, 1948. In December, 1949, Eccles said, "In making a cheap money policy for the Treasury, we cannot avoid making it for everybody. All monetary and credit restraints are gone under such conditions; the Federal Reserve becomes simply an engine of inflation."[31]

Those who disagreed with the Treasury's policy conceded that releasing control over the interest rate would result in substantial liquidation by investors, but they proposed to prevent this by refunding the debt into consols at a higher coupon rate.[32] The resulting increase in interest charges would not be so large as expected, since taxes would mop up a large portion, and it was believed that, if artificially low interest rates were eliminated, inflation would not be so great.[33]

In point of fact, the Treasury had the bear by the tail. Undoubtedly, the control of interest rates vitiated anti-inflationary monetary controls. However, if controls were released, it was not certain that bond refunding could be handled quickly enough to prevent panic in the government-bond market.

The Distribution of the Debt. The Treasury had indifferent success in widening the distribution of the debt and reducing the amount held by banks. In June, 1946, commercial banks held 31 per cent of the national debt, representing 71 per cent of their earning assets, and Federal Reserve banks held 9 per cent of the debt. Mutual savings banks had about 64 per cent and life insurance companies about 22 per cent of their total assets invested in Federal obligations. By June, 1948, the percentage held by the commercial and Federal Reserve banks had been reduced, but since the reduction had been accomplished mostly by the use of the war loan accounts, its anti-inflationary effects were not great.

The distribution of the debt among the different income brackets seemed to be getting worse rather than better. From 1946 on, redemptions of $10 to $50 bonds far exceeded sales, whereas the opposite was true of the higher denomination bonds.

[31] See also *Report of the Subcommittee on Monetary, Credit, and Fiscal Policies of the Joint Committee on the Economic Report* (Douglas Report), 1950, pp. 26ff.

[32] See Henry Simonds, "On Debt Policy," *Journal of Political Economy*, December, 1944; and B. M. Anderson, "Inflation, Interest Rates, and Public Debt Management," *Commercial and Financial Chronicle*, May 29, 1947.

[33] See Lester Chandler, "Federal Reserve Policy and the Federal Debt," *American Economic Review*, Vol. 39, No. 2, March, 1949; and the rebuttal by Peter Bernstein, *ibid.*, December, 1949.

TABLE 94. CHANGES IN FEDERAL DEBT DISTRIBUTION, 1946–1950

	In billions of dollars									Per cent		
	June, 1946	Dec., 1946	June, 1947	Dec., 1947	June, 1948	Dec., 1948	June, 1949	Dec., 1949	June, 1950	June, 1946	June, 1948	June, 1950
Commercial banks	$ 84.4	$ 74.5	$ 70.0	$ 68.7	$ 64.6	$ 62.5	$ 63.0	$ 67.0	$ 65.6	31	26	26
Federal Reserve banks	23.8	23.4	21.9	22.6	21.4	23.3	19.3	18.9	18.3	9	8	7
Total bank held	$108.2	$ 97.9	$ 91.9	$ 91.3	$ 86.0	$ 85.8	$ 82.4	$ 85.9	$ 83.9	40	34	33
Individuals	$ 64.1	$ 64.9	$ 67.1	$ 66.6	$ 67.0	$ 67.6	$ 68.9	$ 69.5	$ 67.2	24	27	26
Insurance companies	25.3	25.3	25.0	24.3	23.2	21.5	20.9	20.5	20.1	9	9	8
Savings banks	11.5	11.8	12.1	12.0	12.0	11.5	11.6	11.4	11.6	4	5	4
Other private	25.3	22.4	22.3	21.2	20.7	21.4	22.7	22.6	28.5	9	8	11
State and local governments	6.5	6.3	7.1	7.3	7.8	7.9	8.0	8.1	8.2	3	3	3
United States government trust accounts	29.1	30.9	32.8	34.4	35.7	37.3	38.3	39.3	37.8	11	14	15
Totals	$269.9	$259.5	$258.4	$257.0	$252.4	$252.9	$252.8	$257.2	$257.4			

SOURCE: *Federal Reserve Bulletin*, June, 1950, p. 716; January, 1951, p. 72.

Expansion of Bank Credit. Since public debt at the end of the war exceeded the aggregate private debt, the government deliberately gave prior consideration to the requirements of public-debt management over the requirements of private-debt management. Low interest rates in private credit were made ancillary to low interest rates in public credit. They were also favored at first for the purpose of stimulating reconversion and mitigating the supposed threat of deflation. However, deflation did not materialize. Instead, gross private domestic investment in 1946 was $28.7 billion, and by 1948 it was $42.7 billion, four times as much as in 1939. While a large portion of this increased investment spending was financed from retained earnings, bank loans increased $15.4 billion between June, 1946, and December, 1948. This was the largest expansion on record and more than offset the deflationary effects of the Federal cash surplus.

As credit inflation developed and it became desirable to apply restraints on the expansion of private credit, the Treasury's easy-money policy prevented the Federal Reserve System from resorting to its usual monetary controls to check expansion in the total money supply. It could not mop up excess reserves by selling securities to the banks, for that would depress bond prices. Increases in the rediscount rate had become meaningless, for as long as the Federal Reserve supported short-term obligations, it would be illogical for banks to rediscount. Reserve requirements could not be raised effectively, for in most cases they had already reached their legal maximum.

Recognizing the reality of credit inflation, the Reserve Board, in June, 1946, asked Congress to expand its powers in order to enable it to prevent credit expansion and at the same time to cooperate with the Treasury in controlling interest rates. To strengthen the position of short-term obligations, it asked for authority (1) to place a maximum on the amount of long-term marketable securities held by the banks; (2) to set secondary reserve requirements in the form of short-term governments, vault cash, or deposits with the Reserve banks; and (3) to increase reserve requirements by 100 per cent. The proposals were immediately attacked by leading bankers and monetary conservatives and were given little consideration by Congress. Nevertheless, Eccles continued to raise the issue all through the rising price trend of 1947, and McCabe, who replaced him as chairman, continued to request sweeping powers.

Meanwhile, the Board appealed to the banks not to use their excess reserves to expand loans and discounts, and in January, 1948, it increased the rediscount rate to 1¼ per cent and in August, 1948, to 1½ per cent. As in 1919, the "moral suasion" policy did not prevent credit expansion, and the change in rediscount rates was not effective.

At the height of the inflationary spiral, Congress granted some of the

TABLE 95. BANKING OPERATIONS, 1946–1950
(Dollar figures in billions)

	June, 1946	June, 1947	Dec., 1947	June, 1948	Dec., 1948	June, 1949	Dec., 1949	June, 1950
All commercial banks:								
Number................................	14,026	14,183	14,181	14,187	14,171	14,150	14,156	14,144
Total deposits.......................	$142.9	$135.9	$144.1	$138.1	$142.8	$137.5	$145.2	$143.8
United States deposits..............	13.4	1.4	1.5	2.2	2.5	2.3	3.2	3.8
Total loans...........................	27.1	33.7	38.1	39.9	42.5	41.0	43.0	44.8
United States obligations...........	84.5	70.5	69.2	64.8	62.6	63.2	67.0	65.8
Other investments...................	7.8	8.5	9.0	9.2	9.2	9.5	10.2	11.2
Member banks:								
Total deposits.......................	122.5	115.4	122.5	117.5	121.4	117.0	123.9	122.7
Total loans...........................	23.3	28.7	32.6	33.9	36.1	34.5	36.2	37.7
United States obligations...........	72.3	59.2	57.9	54.1	52.2	53.1	56.9	55.8
Other investments...................	6.5	6.9	7.3	7.4	7.4	7.7	8.4	9.3
Excess reserves......................	1.1	0.7	1.5	0.7	1.2	0.9	1.0	0.4
Federal Reserve banks:								
Total deposits.......................	18.2	17.7	19.7	20.2	22.8	19.2	18.9	18.3
Total Federal Reserve notes in circulation.	24.2	24.2	24.8	23.8	24.2	23.4	23.5	22.9
Reserve ratio (per cent)............	42.7%	47.8%	48.3%	50.7%	48.9%	54.5%	54.7%	55.7%
Annual rate of deposit turnover*.....	16.7	17.9	20.0	19.1	21.0	18.7	20.0	20.2

SOURCE: *Federal Reserve Bulletin.*

* In leading cities except New York.

Board's requests. The anti-inflation bill of August, 1948, restored the Board's power to regulate consumer credit and authorized an increase in reserve requirements by 4 percentage points for demand and 1½ percentage points for time deposits.[34] Reserve requirements were increased to 26, 22, and 16 per cent as of September, and excess reserves declined to less than $700 million. However, by the fall it was evident that prices were temporarily declining, and in the spring of 1949, after total deposits and currency had declined by $3.5 billion, the Board became aggressively "cheap-money" minded. It modified consumer credit controls and lowered margin requirements in March. In May it began to lower reserve requirements, bringing them down to 22, 18, and 12 per cent by December. In June, as already described, it terminated its policy of keeping government bonds at par.

Even though it was following an easy-money policy, the Board, as insurance against another inflationary upsurge, continued to urge Congress to broaden its powers, specifically asking for a renewal of its powers over consumer credit and the right to increase reserve requirements by 10 per cent and set them not only for member banks, but for all insured commercial banks. Once again, however, the suggestions aroused vigorous opposition among bankers and were not considered by Congress. Subsequently, prices again began to advance, and when the Korean War broke out in June, 1950, bank loans and consumer credit were at their all-time highs. Private domestic investment was running at the rate of $47.9 billion. As "scare buying" became prominent, the Federal Reserve was powerless to staunch the flow of credit.

State and Local Finance after the War. After the war, state and local finance expanded considerably as the early fear of a supposedly impending deflation was dissipated, giving way to a spirit of optimism. Businessmen and consumers demanded more and better public services and facilities, and these could now be furnished, since all restrictions on the use of labor and materials had been lifted. The expansion of state and local finance, however, was not altogether unrestrained. It was held back by international uncertainties, the high prices which had to be paid for labor and materials, and the continuance of high Federal taxes. In the face of high Federal tax burdens, neither the states nor the local governments could raise tax rates or introduce new taxes in the fullest required measure.

In four years 1945 to 1949, state expenditures, exclusive of Federal grants and contributions to the unemployment-compensation fund, more than doubled, increasing from $3.8 billion to $8.8 billion. The increase was due not only to increased activity but also to the increased pay which had to be granted to state employees because of rising living costs as well

[34] These powers were to expire June 30, 1949.

as to the higher prices which had to be paid for materials and construction. The largest increase was in state capital outlays which, including Federal grants, grew sevenfold from $267 million to $1.8 billion. The highways and the institutional plants of the states had deteriorated and become inadequate during the depression and war years, and they had to be rehabilitated and expanded. Operating expenditures and grants to localities doubled. But interest payments and provisions for debt retirement remained the same, and the contributions to the unemployment-compensation fund decreased slightly.

State revenues increased almost as rapidly as state expenditures—from $4.3 billion in 1945 to $7.9 billion in 1950. These increases resulted from higher yields under existing tax rates rather than from new taxes or increases in rates. The largest increases were in the yields of taxes which were peculiarly affected by the inflationary rise in personal incomes, business profits, and consumer spending, namely, the personal and corporate income taxes, the general sales tax, and the motor-fuel tax. State net long-term debt, largely as a result of loans for veterans' bonuses, increased 2½ times, from $1.8 billion to $4.4 billion, and together with the increase in local debt offset to a great extent the reduction in the Federal debt, which took place at the same time.

Local expenditures, exclusive of state grants, increased less rapidly than state expenditures, from $4.9 billion in 1945 to $9 billion in 1949. The details of this increase are not available, but from debt figures it is clear that the greatest rise was in capital outlays financed by borrowing.

Local revenues grew not only less rapidly than state revenues but also less rapidly than the local expenditures, increasing in five years from $4.9 billion to $8.0 billion, or only 60 per cent. The most significant development in local revenue during this period was a broader adoption by municipalities of nonproperty taxes, such as general sales, amusement, hotel, business gross-receipts taxes, and the like, as an auxiliary revenue. The proportion of this nonproperty tax revenue in the total increased during the five-year period from 7 to 12 per cent; in New York City, it increased from 12 to 30 per cent.

Local net long-term debts also increased less rapidly than state debts—from $13.3 billion in 1945 to $15.5 billion in 1950. The largest increases were in school district debts, which more than doubled.[35]

The centralization of fiscal powers in the Federal and, to a lesser degree, in the state governments which had been going on for some decades, as described in previous chapters, became further accentuated. The relative positions of the Federal to state and of the state to the local tax revenues became completely and apparently permanently reversed or

[35] The increases were as follows: county debts from $1.4 to $1.5 billion, city from $7.0 to $8.3 billion, school districts from $1.2 to $2.5 billion, and special districts from $2.6 to $3 billion. Township debts remained small, less than $300 million.

altered. Instead of the traditional pattern of Federal tax revenues being approximately one-third, they now amounted to two-thirds. State revenues, which had always been much smaller than the aggregate local revenues, now equaled them.

TABLE 96. STATE AND LOCAL FINANCE, 1940–1950
(In millions of dollars)

	State			Local		
	1940	1945	1950*	1942	1945	1950
Total tax revenue (excluding unemployment compensation)	$3,313	$4,307	$ 7,939	$ 4,632	$ 4,888	$ 8,002
Property	260	276	305	4,273	4,526	7,056
Personal income	206	357	743	27	26	64
Corporation income	155	453	578	3	5	7
General sales and gross receipts	499	776	1,679	133	156	484
Alcoholic beverages and license	255	370	498			
Tobacco	97	145	421			
Motor vehicles and fuel	1,226	1,091	2,297			
Inheritance	113	132	170			
Other	502	708	1,248	197	175	390
Unemployment compensation	844	1,254	1,028			

	1940	1945	1950	1942		
Total expenditures (excluding debt retirement)	$5,114	$5,775	$12,907	$ 6,315	†	†
Operation	1,745	2,253	5,457	5,301	†	†
Capital outlays	725	267	2,112	402	†	†
Interest	117	80	88	405	†	†
Aid to other governments	1,627	1,838	4,011	45	†	†
Contributions to unemployment compensation and retirement funds	900	1,336	1,239	159	†	†
Provision for debt retirement	307	223	275	781	†	†
Per capita expenditures	$39.07	$43.00	$86.79	$47.10	†	†

	1940	1945	1950	1940	1945	1950
Debt (net long term)	$2,611	$1,809	$ 4,361	$14,571	$12,308	$15,484

SOURCE: The Tax Foundation, *Facts and Figures on Government Finance, 1950–1951*, pp. 89, 140, 175, 190; U.S. Bureau of the Census, *Governmental Debts, 1950*, p. 5; *Governmental Revenue, 1950*, p. 8.

* Estimated.
† Not available.

Government spending also became more centralized, although not to the same degree or so clearly as government revenue. Whereas Federal functions expanded more rapidly than state, and state functions more rapidly than local, thus manifesting centralization of expenditures, on the other hand Federal and state grants also increased considerably, representing largely a compromise between centralization and decentralization. The advantages and disadvantages of the grants-in-aid began to be actively discussed. In several states, assistances to the localities were reorganized on a more equitable and economically sound basis, and need for a fundamental reordering by the Federal government of its grants so as to involve less administrative regulations was urged.[36]

TABLE 97.   PERCENTAGE DISTRIBUTION OF FEDERAL, STATE, AND LOCAL TAX RECEIPTS FOR
. SELECTED YEARS, 1915–1950

Year	Federal	State	Local
1915	30.1	18.1	51.8
1927	36.9	17.8	45.4
1932	22.2	23.1	54.7
1940	38.7	26.0	35.3
1944	82.1	8.3	9.6
1946	78.2	10.6	11.1
1950	68.6	15.5	15.8

SOURCE: The Tax Foundation, *Facts and Figures on Government Finance, 1950–1951*, p. 110.

Federal Legislative and Administrative Reorganization. The tremendous increase in Federal expenditures over the prewar level gave considerable impetus to a long-standing public demand for the improvement of Federal fiscal procedures and the administrative machinery. The outcome was the passage by Congress in 1946 of the LaFollette-Monroney Congressional Reorganization Act and in July, 1947, of an act creating the "United States Commission on Organization of the Executive Branch of the Government," better known as the "Hoover Commission."

The Congressional Reorganization Act simplified the organization of the Congressional committees and provided each committee and each member of the Senate with technical experts. It provided for the creation of a Joint Committee on the Legislative Budget (comprised of the memberships of the two appropriation committees and two revenue committees of the two Houses) which was to review the President's recommended budget policy and make its own budget recommendations to Congress. The Act also limited permanent appropriations and forbade the reappropriation of unobligated balances.

The fiscal provisions of the Congressional Reorganization Act proved disappointing. The Joint Committee on the Budget, although aiming at an exceedingly worthy object—coordinated consideration by Congress of the expenditure and revenue sides of the budget—was much too large to act effectively. Without having had time to study the facts, it became involved in a budgetary issue. As a result, it could make no specific

[36] Paul Studenski, "Federal Grants-in-Aid." *National Tax Journal*, September, 1949.

recommendations, but only set arbitrary ceilings for total appropriations. Its first two performances ended in complete fiasco. Then in 1949 Congress suspended the operation of this part of the Reorganization Act, and during the immediately succeeding period made no attempt to bring together the Joint Committee on the Budget. The old practice of considering appropriations and revenue measures apart from each other by different committees was continued (see page 468).

The Hoover Commission was created "to promote economy, efficiency, and improved service in . . . the executive branch of the government" by limiting expenditures and by eliminating duplication and overlapping of services. In its reports the Commission pointed out that the Federal government had developed into the most gigantic business on earth, employing over 2 million civil employees in 1,800 different bureaus. But it concluded that the government was "paying heavily for a lack of order, a lack of clear lines of authority and responsibility, and a lack of effective organization in the executive branch." While the Commission made no official estimate of the money that could be saved by administrative reforms, some sources placed it at $3 billion to $4 billion.[37]

The Hoover Commission's recommendations included (1) regrouping the major executive agencies according to major purposes, thereby pruning the 65 major departments, agencies, boards, etc., to 20; (2) giving the President more authority by giving him the right to organize his own staff and by instituting strong staff-and-line management throughout the executive branch; (3) reforming the budget and accounting processes on a performance, instead of an agency, basis; (4) separating operating from capital outlays; (5) improving government personnel by instituting an active recruiting campaign, by increasing salaries, and by avoiding some of the stultifying effects of civil service; (6) coordinating in a National Monetary and Credit Council the 30 agencies actively engaged in extending and guaranteeing credit; and (7) eliminating, by consolidation or liquidation, 30 of the 100 business enterprises in which the government had an interest and replacing the government obligations owned by these enterprises with non-interest-bearing notes.

In addition, the Hoover Commission made many specific recommendations, including (1) reorganizing the Veterans' Administration to eliminate conflicting lines of authority, excessive units, excessive number of staff officers, high turnover, and generally inefficient service; (2) expanding the Commerce Department to include the ICC, the Maritime Commission, the Coast Guard, etc.; (3) making the Treasury Department a real department of finance by transferring to it the FDIC, the RFC, and

[37] For the exhaustive recommendations of the Commission, see U.S. Commission on Organization of the Executive Branch of the Government, *Reports* 1 to 20; and Frank Gervasi, *Big Government*.

part of the General Accounting Office and by transferring narcotics and secret service to the Justice Department, Coast Guard to the Commerce Department, and the office of Comptroller of the Currency to the Federal Reserve; (4) creating an Office of General Services to manage supplies and records and to operate and maintain public buildings; (5) eliminating political appointments in the post office, decentralizing its administrative structure, and reconstructing it as a business enterprise to eliminate part of its $300 million annual loss; (6) transferring all land activities to the Department of Agriculture and all water development to the Interior Department; and (7) creating a new Department of Social Security and Education.

The administration immediately began to submit to Congress reorganization plans which conformed in the main to the recommendations of the Hoover Commission. Up to June 30, 1950, Congress had passed laws strengthening the management of the State Department, unifying the Armed Services, providing a long-range program for the improvement of the post office, creating a General Service Administration, and reforming the administration of personnel. In addition, various reorganization plans were still pending. At the same time, the Budget Bureau presented the 1950 budget in the form of a performance budget, and the Treasury Department had instituted management reforms estimated to produce a $56 million saving. Most of these reforms were accomplished by consolidation, improvements in methods, and further mechanization.[38]

It was a grave error to take comfort from what had been accomplished under the Hoover Commission's recommendations. The achievement in the direction of economy and efficiency was at best mediocre. Yet the need for economy and efficiency in the Federal administrative machinery was probably never greater. With the outbreak of the Korean War, the world seemed doomed to waste its substance in a long series of armed conflicts between communism and capitalism, with the United States carrying the major burden for the Western powers. At the beginning of the fiscal year 1951 the Federal government faced the prospect of a $50 billion budget with a strong possibility of $70 billion by fiscal 1952. Constant unbalanced budgets and heavy private investment and consumer spending augured unmitigated inflationary pressures on credit, the money supply, and the cost of living, all of which were rapidly approaching the highest points in history. To keep inflation within bounds, taxes were raised and government controls were increasingly contemplated, but there was little evidence of a comprehensive effort to reduce non-essential expenditures or to create a completely efficient and up-to-date administrative machinery in the government's general operations.

[38] See *Annual Report of the Secretary of the Treasury*, 1949, pp. 35ff.

BIBLIOGRAPHY

An asterisk (*) designates the most helpful sources.

GENERAL DOCUMENTARY AND STATISTICAL SOURCES

*ANDREWS, ABRAHAM PIATT: *Statistics for the United States, 1867–1909*, Publications of the National Monetary Commission, Vol. XXI, No. 1, Government Printing Office, Washington, 1910.

*BAYLEY, RAFAEL A.: *The National Loans of the United States, from July 4, 1776 to June 30, 1880*, Government Printing Office, Washington, 1881.

Council of State Governments, Committee on Grants-in-Aid: *Federal Grants-in-Aid*, 1949.

*DEKNIGHT, WILLIAM F.: *History of the Currency of the Country and of the Loans of the United States from the Earliest Period to June 30, 1896*, Government Printing Office, Washington, 1897.

DUNBAR, CHARLES F.: *Laws of the U.S. Relating to Currency, Finance and Banking*, Ginn & Company, Boston, 1891.

*GALLATIN, ALBERT: *The Writings of Albert Gallatin*, edited by Henry Adams, J. B. Lippincott Company, Philadelphia, 1879.

*HAMILTON, ALEXANDER: *Papers on Public Credit, Commerce, and Finance*, edited by Samuel McKee, Jr., Columbia University Press, New York, 1934.

*HUNTINGTON, ANDREW T., and ROBERT J. MAWHINNEY: *Laws of the United States Concerning Money, Banking and Loans, 1778–1909*, Publications of the National Monetary Commission, Vol. II, Government Printing Office, Washington, 1910.

*POWELL, FRED W.: *Control of Federal Expenditures: A Documentary History, 1775–1794*, The Brookings Institution, Washington, 1939.

*Reconstruction Finance Corporation: *Seven Year Report to the President and the Congress of the U.S.*, Government Printing Office, Washington, 1939.

*RICHARDSON, JAMES D. (comp.): *A Compilation of the Messages and Papers of the Presidents, 1789–1897*, Government Printing Office, Washington, 1896–1899.

*ROOSEVELT, FRANKLIN D.: *The Public Papers and Addresses of Franklin D. Roosevelt, with a Special Introduction and Explanatory Notes by President Roosevelt* (Samuel I. Rosenman, ed.), Random House, New York, 1938.

Tax Foundation: *Facts and Figures on Government Finance, 1950–1951*, New York, 1951.

WILBUR, RAY C., and ARTHUR M. HYDE: *The Hoover Policies*, Charles Scribner's Sons, New York, 1937. (A Documentary Collection.)

U.S. Government Publications

*Board of Governors of the Federal Reserve System: *Annual Reports*, 1914–1950.
*————: *Banking and Monetary Statistics*, 1943.
————: *Banking Studies*, 1948.
*————: *Federal Reserve Bulletin*, 1914–1950.
*Bureau of the Budget: *The Budget of the U.S. Government*, 1921–1951.
*Census Bureau: *Historical Review of State and Local Government Finances*, 1948.
*————: *Historical Statistics of the U.S., 1789–1945*, 1949.
————: *Statistical Abstract, 1950*.

*Commission on Organization of the Executive Branch of the Government, *Reports* 1–20, Government Printing Office, Washington, 1949.

*Comptroller of the Currency, *Annual Report*, 1864–1949.

*Congress: *American State Papers, Finance, 1789–1828*, Washington, 1832–1861.

*Congress, House Committees on Banking and Currency and Senate Committee on Finance: *Hearings and Reports* on revenue and banking legislation, occasional publications.

*Congress, Joint Committee on the Economic Report, *Reports*, 1948–1950.

Department of the Interior: *Report on Federal Reclamation to the Secretary of the Interior*, by John W. Haw and F. E. Schmitt, Dec. 1, 1934, Government Printing Office, Washington, 1935.

Internal Revenue Office: *Annual Report of the Commissioner*, 1864–1949.

*————: *Statistics of Income*, 1916–1949.

National Resources Planning Board: *Development of Resources and Stabilization of Employment in the United States*, January, 1941.

President: *Economic Report of the President*, 1947–1950, semiannually.

*Treasury Department: *Annual Report of the Secretary*, 1800–1950.

*————: *Combined Statement of Receipts, Expenditures, and Balances of the U.S. Government, Annual Reports*, 1871–1950.

*————: *Federal Tax Rates, 1913 to 1940, Annual Report of the Secretary of the Treasury*, 1941.

*————: *Federal Tax Rates, 1939 through 1944, Annual Report of the Secretary of the Treasury*, 1944.

————: *History of Public Buildings under the Control of the Treasury Department*, Government Printing Office, Washington, 1900.

————: Special Committee on Intergovernmental Fiscal Relations: *Federal, State, and Local Fiscal Relations*, Sen. Doc. 69, 1943.

————: *Statement of Appropriations and Expenditures, Rivers and Harbors, Forts, Arsenals, Armories, and Other Public Works from March 4, 1789 to June 30, 1882*, Government Printing Office, Washington, 1882.

————: *Treasury Bulletin*, 1939–1950.

Works Projects Administration: *Construction Expenditures and Employment, 1925–1936*, Government Printing Office, Washington, 1937.

GENERAL WORKS

*ANDERSON, BENJAMIN M.: *Economics and the Public Welfare; Financial and Economic History of the United States, 1914–1946*, D. Van Nostrand Company, Inc., New York, 1949.

BEALE, HOWARD K.: *The Critical Year: A Study of Andrew Johnson and Reconstruction*, Chapt. 10, Harcourt, Brace and Company, Inc., New York, 1930.

*BOLLES, ALBERT S.: *The Financial History of the United States, from 1774 to 1789*, D. Appleton & Company, Inc., New York, 1879.

————: *The Financial History of the United States, from 1789 to 1860*, D. Appleton & Company, Inc., New York, 1885.

————: *The Financial History of the United States, from 1861 to 1885*, D. Appleton & Company, Inc., New York, 1886.

*DEWEY, DAVIS R.: *Financial History of the United States*, Longmans, Green & Co., Inc., New York, 1934.

DUNBAR, CHARLES F.: *Economic Essays*, The Macmillan Company, New York, 1904.

*The Economist: *The New Deal; An Analysis and Appraisal*, by the editors of *The Economist* (London), Alfred A. Knopf, Inc., New York, 1937.

FRASER, HUGH R.: *Democracy in the Making; The Jackson-Tyler Era*, Bobbs-Merrill Company, Indianapolis, 1938.

GRAYSON, THEODORE J.: *Leaders and Periods of American Finance*, John Wiley & Sons, Inc., New York, 1932.

*HACKER, LOUIS M.: *A Short History of the New Deal*, F. S. Crofts & Co., New York, 1934.

HAWK, EMORY Q.: *Economic History of the South*, Chapt. 14, Prentice-Hall, Inc., New York, 1934.

*LINDLEY, ERNEST K.: *Half Way with Roosevelt*, The Viking Press, Inc., New York, 1936.

————: *The Roosevelt Revolution, First Phase*, The Viking Press, Inc., New York, 1933.

*MAI, CHIEN TSENG: *The Fiscal Policies of Albert Gallatin*, privately printed, New York, 1930.

McGRANE, REGINALD C.: *The Panic of 1837; Some Financial Problems of the Jacksonian Era*, University of Chicago Press, Chicago, 1924.

MITCHELL, BROADUS: *Depression Decade; From New Era Through New Deal, 1929–1941*, Rinehart & Company, Inc., New York, 1947.

*MITCHELL, WESLEY C.: *Business Cycles and Their Causes*, University of California Press, Berkeley, 1941.

*MOLEY, RAYMOND: *After Seven Years*, Harper & Brothers, New York, 1939.

*MYERS, WILLIAM S., and WALTER H. NEWTON: *The Hoover Administration; A Documentated Narrative*. Charles Scribner's Sons, New York, 1936.

*NOYES, ALEXANDER D.: *Forty Years of American Finance, 1865–1907*, G. P. Putnam's Sons, New York, 1909.

————: *The War Period of American Finance, 1908–1925*, G. P. Putnam's Sons, New York, 1926.

SCHULTZ, W. J., and M. R. CAINE: *Financial Development of the United States*, Prentice-Hall, Inc., New York, 1937.

*SCHLESINGER, ARTHUR M., JR.: *The Age of Jackson*, Little, Brown & Company, Boston, 1945.

SOULE, GEORGE H.: *Prosperity Decade; From War to Depression: 1917–1929*, Rinehart & Company, Inc., New York, 1947.

STUDENSKI, PAUL (ed.): "Government Finance in the Modern Economy," *Annals of the American Academy of Political and Social Science*, January, 1936.

VAN VLECK, GEORGE W.: *The Panic of 1857; An Analytical Study*, Columbia University Press, New York, 1943.

FEDERAL FINANCE

General

*ADAMS, HENRY C.: *Public Debts; An Essay in the Science of Finance*, D. Appleton & Company, Inc., New York, 1887.

*BITTERMANN, HENRY J.: *State and Federal Grants-in-Aid*, Mentzer, Bush & Company, Chicago, 1938.

BLAKEY, ROY G., and GLADYS C. BLAKEY: *The Federal Income Tax*, Longmans, Green & Co., Inc., New York, 1940.

BROWNE, VINCENT J.: *The Control of the Public Budget*, Public Affairs Press, Washington, 1949.

Committee on Public Debt Policy: *Our National Debt*, Harcourt, Brace and Company, Inc., New York, 1949.

*Council of State Governments: *Federal Grants-in-Aid*, Chicago, 1949.

*GLASSON, WILLIAM H.: *Federal Military Pensions in the United States,* Oxford University Press, New York, 1918.

GOSS, JOHN D.: *A History of Tariff Administration in the United States, from Colonial Times to the McKinley Administrative Bill,* Columbia University Press, New York, 1897.

*HOWE, FREDERIC C.: *Taxation and Taxes in the United States under the Internal Revenue System, 1791–1895,* The Thomas Y. Crowell Company, New York, 1896.

*LARKIN, JOHN D.: *The President's Control of the Tariff,* Harvard University Press, Cambridge, Mass., 1936.

*LEWIS, CLEONA, assisted by Karl T. Schlotterbeck: *America's Stake in International Investments,* The Brookings Institution, Washington, 1938.

LOVE, ROBERT A.: *Federal Financing; A Study of the Methods Employed by the Treasury in Its Borrowing Operations,* Columbia University Press, New York, 1931.

*MAXWELL, JAMES A.: *The Fiscal Impact of Federalism in the United States,* Harvard University Press, Cambridge, Mass., 1946.

*MEEKER, ROYAL: *History of Shipping Subsidies,* Publications of the American Economic Association, 3d series, Vol. VI, No. 3, The Macmillan Company, New York, 1905.

POOLE, KENYON E.: *Fiscal Policies and the American Economy,* Prentice-Hall, Inc., New York, 1951.

*RATNER, SIDNEY: *American Taxation, Its History as a Social Force in Democracy,* W. W. Norton & Company, New York, 1942.

ROSS, EDWARD A.: *Sinking Funds,* Publications of the American Economic Association, Vol. VII, 1892.

SELIGMAN, EDWIN R. A.: *Essays in Taxation,* The Macmillan Company, New York, 1925.

———: *The Income Tax; A Study of the History, Theory and Practice of Income Taxation at Home and Abroad,* The Macmillan Company, New York, 1914.

*SELKO, DANIEL T.: *The Federal Financial System,* The Brookings Institution, Washington, D.C., 1940.

*SMITH, RALPH E.: *Customs Valuation in the United States; A Study in Tariff Administration,* University of Chicago Press, Chicago, 1947.

*STANWOOD, EDWARD: *American Tariff Controversies in the Nineteenth Century,* Houghton, Mifflin Company, Boston, 1903.

*TAUSSIG, FRANK W.: *The Tariff History of the United States,* 8th ed., G. P. Putnam's Sons, New York, 1931.

U.S. Tariff Commission: *The Tariff and Its History,* Government Printing Office, Washington, D.C., 1934.

*WILMERDING, LUCIUS: *The Spending Power; A History of the Efforts of Congress to Control Expenditures,* Yale University Press, New Haven, Conn., 1943.

*ZEIS, PAUL M.: *American Shipping Policy,* Princeton University Press, Princeton, N.J., 1938.

1789–1900

ADAMS, HENRY C.: *Taxation in the United States, 1789–1816,* Johns Hopkins Press, Baltimore, 1884.

BOURNE, EDWARD G.: *The History of the Surplus Revenue of 1837 . . . Its Origin, Its Distribution . . . and the Uses to Which It Was Applied,* G. P. Putnam's Sons, New York, 1888.

*BULLOCK, CHARLES J.: *The Finances of the United States from 1775 to 1789 with Special Reference to the Budget,* Madison, Wis., 1895.

COULTER, E. MERTON: *The Confederate States of America,* Chap. 7, Louisiana State University Press, Baton Rouge, La., 1950.

*FISH, CARL R.: *The American Civil War; An Interpretation,* edited by William E. Smith, Chap. 15, Longmans, Green & Co., Inc., New York, 1937.

*HILL, WILLIAM: *The First Stages of the Tariff Policy of the United States,* Publications of the American Economic Association, Vol. 8, No. 6, Baltimore, 1893.

*JENKS, LELAND H.: *The Migration of British Capital to 1875,* Alfred A. Knopf, Inc., New York, 1927.

RICHARDSON, WILLIAM A.: *Practical Information Concerning the Public Debt of the U.S.,* W. H. and O. H. Morrison, Washington, 1873.

*SCHWAB, JOHN C.: *The Confederate States of America, 1861–1865; A Financial and Industrial History of the South during the Civil War,* Charles Scribner's Sons, New York, 1901.

SHAW, ALBERT (ed.): *The National Revenues; A Collection of Papers by American Economists,* A. C. McClurg & Company, Chicago, 1888.

SHERMAN, JOHN: *Speeches and Reports on Finance and Taxation,* D. Appleton & Company, Inc., New York, 1879.

SMITH, ERNEST A.: *The History of the Confederate Treasury,* Press of Harrisburg Publishing Co., Harrisburg, Pa., 1901.

SMITH, HARRY E.: *The United States Federal Internal Tax History, from 1861–1871,* Houghton Mifflin Company, Boston, 1914.

SUMNER, WILLIAM G.: *The Financier and the Finances of the American Revolution,* Dodd, Mead & Company, Inc., New York, 1891.

TARBELL, IDA M.: *The Tariff in Our Times,* The Macmillan Company, New York, 1911.

1900–1920

*American Academy of Political and Social Science: "Financing the War," *The Annals,* Vol. LXXV, Philadelphia, 1918.

BOGART, ERNEST L.: *Direct and Indirect Costs of the Great World War,* Oxford University Press, New York, 1919.

The Brookings Institution: *The Bureau of Internal Revenue, The Bureau of Pensions, The General Land Office, The Office of the Comptroller of Currency, The Office of the Supervising Architect, The Tariff Commission,* Washington, 1919–1926.

CLARK, JOHN M.: *The Costs of the World War to the American People,* Yale University Press, New Haven, Conn., 1931.

*CLEVELAND, FREDERICK A., and ARTHUR E. BUCK: *The Budget and Responsible Government,* The Macmillan Company, New York, 1920.

*HOLLANDER, JACOB H.: *War Borrowing; A Study of Treasury Certificates of Indebtedness of the United States,* The Macmillan Company, New York, 1919.

SAMUELSON, PAUL A., and EVERETT E. HAGEN: *After the War, 1918–1920, Military and Economic Demobilization of the United States,* Government Printing Office, Washington, 1943.

U.S. President's Commission on Economy and Efficiency: *The Need for a National Budget,* Government Printing Office, Washington, 1912.

U.S. President's Committee on Administrative Management: *Report,* Washington, 1937.

WILLOUGHBY, WILLIAM F.: *Government Organization in Wartime and After; A*

Survey of the Federal Civil Agencies Created for the Prosecution of the War, D. Appleton & Company, Inc., New York, 1919.

*————: *The Problem of A National Budget*, D. Appleton & Company, Inc., New York, 1918.

1920–1930

*BENSON, GEORGE C. S.: *Financial Control and Integration; A Study in Administration with Especial Reference to the Comptroller-general of the United States*, Harper & Brothers, New York, 1934.

*BUCK, ARTHUR E.: *Public Budgeting*, Harper & Brothers, New York, 1929.

*————: *The Budget in Governments of To-day*, The Macmillan Company, New York, 1934.

DAWES, CHARLES G.: *The First Year of the Budget of the United States*, Harper & Brothers, New York, 1923.

*HENDRICKS, HENRY G.: *The Federal Debt, 1919–1930; A Chapter in American Public Finance*, Mimeoform Press, Washington, D.C., 1933.

MADDEN, JOHN T., MARCUS NADLER, and HARRY C. SAUVAIN: *America's Experience as a Creditor Nation*, Prentice-Hall, Inc., New York, 1937.

*MELLON, ANDREW W.: *Taxation: The People's Business*, The Macmillan Company, New York, 1924.

*MOULTON, HAROLD G., and LEO PASVOLSKY: *War Debts and World Prosperity*, The Brookings Institution, Washington, D.C., 1934.

————: *World War Debt Settlements*, The Macmillan Company, New York, 1926.

*National Industrial Conference Board: *The Cost of Government in the U.S., 1926–1935*, New York, 1936.

————: *The International Financial Position of the United States*, New York, 1929.

WILLOUGHBY, WILLIAM F.: *Financial Condition and Operations of the National Government, 1921–1930*, The Brookings Institution, Washington, 1931.

————: *The Legal Status and Functions of the General Accounting Office of the National Government*, Johns Hopkins Press, Baltimore, 1927.

————: *The National Budget System, with Suggestions for Its Improvement*, Johns Hopkins Press, Baltimore, 1927.

WITHERS, WILLIAM, *The Retirement of National Debts; The Theory and History since the World War*, Columbia University Press, New York, 1932.

1930–1950

BAILEY, STEPHEN K.: *Congress Makes a Law: The Story behind the Employment Act of 1946*, Columbia University Press, New York, 1950.

*BENSON, GEORGE C. S.: *The New Centralization, A Study of Intergovernmental Relationships in the United States*, Rinehart & Company, Inc., New York, 1941.

BURNS, EVELINE: *The American Social Security System*, Houghton Mifflin Company, Boston, 1949.

ECCLES, MARRINER S.: *Economic Balance and a Balanced Budget*, edited by Rudolph L. Weissman, Harper and Brothers, New York, 1940.

FULLER, DOUGLAS R.: *Government Financing of Private Enterprise*, Stanford University Press, Stanford University, Calif., 1947.

GALBRAITH, JOHN K.: *The Economic Effects of the Federal Public Works Expenditures, 1933–1938*, Government Printing Office, Washington, 1940.

*GAYER, ARTHUR D.: *Public Works in Prosperity and Depression*, National Bureau of Economic Research, Inc., New York, 1935.

GERVASI, FRANK: *Big Government: The Meaning and Purpose of the Hoover Commission Report*, McGraw-Hill Book Company, Inc., New York, 1949.

*HOWARD, DONALD S.: *The W.P.A. and Federal Relief Policy*, Russell Sage Foundation, New York, 1943.

MERIAM, LEWIS, and LAURENCE F. SCHMECKEBIER: *Reorganization of the National Government*, The Brookings Institution, Washington, 1939.

*MURPHY, HENRY C.: *The National Debt in War and Transition*, McGraw-Hill Book Company, Inc., New York, 1950.

*National Industrial Conference Board: *The World War Veterans and the Federal Treasury*, New York, 1932.

STEWART, PAUL W., and RUFUS E. TUCKER: *The National Debt and Government Credit; Factual Findings*, The Twentieth Century Fund, Inc., New York, 1937.

U.S. Tariff Commission: *Operation of the Trade Agreements Program, June 1934 to April 1948*, Government Printing Office, Washington, 1948.

CURRENCY AND BANKING

General

ANDERSON, THOMAS J., JR.: *Federal and State Control of Banking*, Bankers Publishing Company, Cambridge, Mass., 1934.

*BULLOCK, CHARLES J.: *Essays on the Monetary History of the United States*, The Macmillan Company, New York, 1900.

*CAROTHERS, NEIL: *Fractional Money*, John Wiley & Sons, Inc., New York, 1930.

CONANT, CHARLES A.: *A History of Modern Banks of Issue*, G. P. Putnam's Sons, New York, 1927.

DUNBAR, CHARLES E.: *The Theory and History of Banking*, G. P. Putnam's Sons, New York, 1929.

ELIOT, CLARA: *The Farmer's Campaign for Credit*, Appleton-Century-Crofts, Inc., New York, 1927.

EVANS, GEORGE G.: *Illustrated History of the United States Mint, with Short Historical Sketches & Illustrations of the Branch Mints and Assay Offices, and a Complete Description of American Coinage from the Earliest to the Present Time*, G. G. Evans, Philadelphia, 1897.

*HELDERMAN, LEONARD C.: *National & State Banks; A Study of Their Origins*, Houghton Mifflin Company, Boston, 1931.

*HEPBURN, ALONZO B.: *History of Coinage and Currency in the United States and the Perennial Contest for Sound Money*, The Macmillan Company, New York, 1924.

HOGGSON, NOBEL F.: *Epochs in American Banking*, The John Day Company, New York, 1929.

*KINLEY, DAVIS: *The Independent Treasury of the United States and Its Relations to the Banks of the Country*, Publications of the National Monetary Commission, Vol. VII, No. 2, Government Printing Office, Washington, 1910.

*KNOX, JOHN J.: *A History of Banking in the United States*, B. Rhodes & Co., New York, 1900.

————: *History of Treasury Notes*, Charles Scribner's Sons, New York, 1884.

LANIER, HENRY W.: *A Century of Banking in New York, 1822–1922*, Doubleday & Company, Inc., New York, 1922.

LAUGHLIN, JAMES L.: *The History of Bimetallism in the United States*, D. Appleton & Company, Inc., New York, 1900.

*MINTS, LLOYD W.: *A History of Banking Theory in Great Britain and the United States*, University of Chicago Press, Chicago, 1945.

MYERS, MARGARET G.: *The New York Money Market*, Columbia University Press, New York, 1931–1932.

SCROGGS, WILLIAM O.: *A Century of Banking Progress*, Doubleday & Company, Inc., New York, 1924.

*SPARKS, EARL S.: *History and Theory of Agricultural Credit in the United States*, The Thomas Y. Crowell Company, New York, 1932.

SUMNER, WILLIAM G.: *A History of American Currency*, Henry Holt and Company, Inc., New York, 1874.

TAUS, ESTHER R.: *Central Banking Functions of the United States Treasury*, 1789–1941, Columbia University Press, New York, 1943.

WATSON, DAVIS K.: *History of American Coinage*, G. P. Putnam's Sons, New York, 1899.

WESTERFIELD, RAY B.: *Our Silver Debacle*, The Ronald Press Company, New York, 1936.

WHITE, HORACE: *Money and Banking*, revised and enlarged by Charles S. Tippetts and Lewis A. Froman, Ginn & Company, Boston, 1935.

*WILDMAN, MURRAY S.: *Money Inflation in the United States*, G. P. Putnam's Sons, New York, 1905.

Colonial

*DAVIS, ANDREW M.: *Currency and Banking in the Province of the Massachusetts Bay*, Publications of the American Economic Association, 3d series, Vol. I, No. 4; Vol. II, No. 2, The Macmillan Company, New York, 1901.

*LESTER, RICHARD A.: *Monetary Experiments; Early American and Recent Scandinavian*, Princeton University Press, Princeton, N.J., 1939.

*NETTELS, CURTIS P.: *The Money Supply of the American Colonies before 1720*, University of Wisconsin Press, Madison, Wis., 1934.

PHILLIPS, HENRY: *Historical Sketches of the Paper Currency of the American Colonies, Prior to the Adoption of the Federal Constitution*, W. E. Woodward, Roxbury, Mass., 1865–1866.

WEBSTER, PELATIAH: *Political Essays on the Nature and Operation of Money, Public Finances, and Other Essays*, Joseph Crukshank, Philadelphia, 1791.

WEEDEN, WILLIAM B.: *Indian Money as a Factor in New England Civilization*, Johns Hopkins Press, Baltimore, 1884.

1776–1860

*CATTERALL, RALPH C. H.: *The Second Bank of the United States*, University of Chicago Press, Chicago, 1903.

CHADDOCK, ROBERT E.: *The Safety Fund Banking System in New York, 1829–1866*, Publications of the National Monetary Commission, Vol. IV, No. 2, Government Printing Office, Washington, 1910.

*CLARKE, MATTHEW ST. CLAIR, and D. A. HALL (comp.): *Legislative and Documentary History of the Bank of the United States: Including the Original Bank of North America*, Gales and Seaton, Washington, 1832.

DEWEY, DAVIS R.: *The Second Bank of the United States*, Publications of the National Monetary Commission, Vol. IV, No. 1, Government Printing Office, Washington, 1910.

———: *State Banking before the Civil War*, National Monetary Commission, Vol. IV, No. 2, Government Printing Office, Washington, 1910.

GIBBONS, JAMES S.: *The Banks of New York, Their Dealers, the Clearing House and the Panic of 1857*, D. Appleton & Company, Inc., New York, 1859.

GOUGE, WILLIAM M.: *A Short History of Paper Money and Banking in the United States, Including an Account of Provincial and Continental Paper Money*, T. W. Ustick, Philadelphia, 1833.

*HOLDSWORTH, JOHN T.: *The First Bank of the United States*, Publications of the National Monetary Commission, Vol. IV, No. 1, Government Printing Office, Washington, 1911.

*KNOX, JOHN J.: *United States Notes; A History of the Various Issues of Paper Money by the Government of the United States*, Charles Scribner's Sons, New York, 1884.

*LEWIS, LAWRENCE: *A History of the Bank of North America*, J. B. Lippincott Company, Philadelphia, 1882.

LINDERMAN, HENRY R.: *Money and Legal Tender in the United States*, G. P. Putnam's Sons, New York, 1877.

*MADELEINE, SISTER M. GRACE: *Monetary and Banking Theories of Jacksonian Democracy*, Dolphin Press, Philadelphia, 1943.

MILLER, HARRY E.: *Banking Theories in the United States before 1860*, Harvard University Press, Cambridge, Mass., 1927.

*MITCHELL, WESLEY C.: *Gold, Prices, and Wages under the Greenback Standard*, University of California Press, Berkeley, Calif., 1908.

————: *A History of the Greenbacks, with Special Reference to the Economic Consequences of Their Issue: 1862–1865*, University of Chicago Press, Chicago, 1903.

RAGUET, CONDY: *A Treatise on Currency & Banking*, Grigg & Elliot, Philadelphia, 1839.

SPAULDING, ELBRIDGE G.: *History of Legal Tender Paper Money Issued during the "Great Rebellion,"* Buffalo, 1875.

*WHITNEY, D. R.: *The Suffolk Bank*, privately printed, Cambridge, Mass., 1878.

1860–1900

BARRETT, DON CARLOS: *The Greenbacks and Resumption of Specie Payments, 1862–1879*, Harvard University Press, Cambridge, Mass., 1931.

BLAKE, GEORGE H.: *United States Paper Money: A Reference List of Paper Money, including Fractional Currency, Issued since 1861*, Wynkopp, Hallenback, Crawford Co., New York, 1908.

DAVIS, ANDREW M.: *The Origin of the National Banking System*, Publications of the National Monetary Commission, Vol. V, No. 1, Government Printing Office, Washington, 1910–1911.

KANE, THOMAS P.: *The Romance and Tragedy of Banking; Problems and Incidents of Governmental Supervision of National Banks*, Bankers Publishing Company, Cambridge, Mass., 1923.

LAUCK, WILLIAM J.: *The Causes of the Panic of 1893*, Houghton Mifflin Company, Boston, 1907.

*Monetary Convention of Indianapolis: *Report of the Monetary Commission of the Indianapolis Convention of Boards of Trade, Chambers of Commerce, Commercial Clubs, and Similar Bodies of the United States*, University of Chicago Press, Chicago, 1898.

NOYES, ALEXANDER D.: *History of the National-bank Currency*, Publications of National Monetary Commission, Vol. V, No. 2, Government Printing Office, Washington, 1910.

*SPRAGUE, OLIVER M. W.: *History of Crises under the National Banking System*, Publications of the National Monetary Commission, Vol. V, No. 3, Government Printing Office, Washington, 1911.

SWANSON, WILLIAM W.: *The Establishment of the National Banking System*, The Jackson Press, Chicago, 1910.

*TAUSSIG, FRANK W.: *The Silver Situation in the United States.* Publications of the American Economic Association, Vol. VII, No. 1, Press of Guggenheimer, Weil & Co., Baltimore, 1892.

WALKER, F. A.: *The Relation of Changes in the Volume of Currency to Prosperity*, American Economic Association, Vol. I, 1896.

*WHITE, TRUMBULL (ed.): *Silver and Gold; or, Both Sides of the Shield*, Publisher's Union, Chicago, 1895.

1900–1950

*BARNETT, GEORGE E.: *State Banks and Trust Companies since the Passage of the National-bank Act*, Publications of the National Monetary Commission, Vol. VII, No. 1, Government Printing Office, Washington, 1911.

*Board of Governors of the Federal Reserve System: *Banking Studies*, 1948.

———: *Federal Reserve Policy*, 1947.

*BURGESS, W. RANDOLPH: *The Reserve Banks and the Money Market*, Harper & Brothers, New York, 1946.

CARTINHOUR, GAINES T.: *Branch, Group and Chain Banking*, The Macmillan Company, New York, 1931.

CLARK, LAWRENCE E.: *Central Banking under the Federal Reserve System with Special Consideration of the Federal Reserve Bank of New York*, The Macmillian Company, New York, 1935.

COLT, CHARLES C., and N. S. KEITH: *28 Days; A History of the Banking Crisis*, Greenberg: Publisher, Inc., New York, 1933.

*CRAWFORD, ARTHUR W.: *Monetary Management under the New Deal; The Evolution of a Managed Currency System—Its Problems and Results*, American Council on Public Affairs, Washington, 1940.

EVEREST, ALLAN S.: *Morgenthau, the New Deal, and Silver*, Columbia University Press, New York, 1950.

GAYER, ARTHUR D.: *Monetary Policy and Economic Stabilization; A Study of the Gold Standard*, The Macmillan Company, New York, 1937.

*GLASS, CARTER: *An Adventure in Constructive Finance*, Doubleday and Company, Inc., New York, 1927.

*GOLDENWEISER, EMANUEL A.: *Federal Reserve System in Operation*, McGraw-Hill Book Company, Inc., New York, 1925.

———: *American Monetary Policy*, McGraw-Hill Book Company, Inc., New York, 1951.

*GOLDSCHMIDT, RAIMUND W.: *The Changing Structure of American Banking*, George Routledge & Sons, Ltd., London, 1933.

HARDING, WILLIAM P. G.: *The Formative Period of the Federal Reserve System*, Houghton Mifflin Company, Boston, 1925.

*HARDY, CHARLES O.: *Credit Policies of the Federal Reserve System*, The Brookings Institution, Washington, 1932.

*HARRIS, SEYMOUR E.: *Twenty Years of Federal Reserve Policy, Including an Extended Discussion of the Monetary Crisis, 1927–1933*, Harvard University Press, Cambridge, Mass., 1933.

*JOHNSON, G. GRIFFITHS: *The Treasury and Monetary Policy, 1933–1938*, Harvard University Press, Cambridge, Mass., 1939.

JOHNSON, JOSEPH F.: *Money and Currency in Relation to Industry, Prices and the Rate of Interest*, Ginn & Company, Boston, 1905.

KEMMERER, EDWIN W.: *The ABC of the Federal Reserve System; Why the Federal Reserve Systems Was Called into Being, the Main Features of Its Organization, and How It Works*, Princeton University Press, Princeton, N. J., 1938.

LAUGHLIN, JAMES L.: *The Federal Reserve Act, Its Origins and Problems*, The Macmillan Company, New York, 1933.

*NADLER, MARCUS, and JULES I. BOGEN: *The Banking Crisis; The End of an Epoch*, Mead & Company, Inc., New York, 1933.

*National Industrial Conference Board: *The Banking Situation in the United States*, New York, 1932.

O'CONNOR, JAMES F. T.: *The Banking Crisis and Recovery under the Roosevelt Administration*, Callaghan & Co., Chicago, 1938.

PARIS, JAMES D.: *Monetary Policies of the United States, 1932–1938*, Columbia University Press, New York, 1938.

*PASVOLSKY, LEO: *Current Monetary Issues*, The Brookings Institution, Washington, 1933.

*PHILLIPS, CHESTER A., T. F. McMANUS, and R. W. NELSON: *Banking and the Business Cycle; A Study of the Great Depression in the United States*, The Macmillan Company, New York, 1937.

SPAHR, WALTER E.: *An Appraisal of the Monetary Policies of Our Federal Government, 1933–1938*, Economists' National Committee on Monetary Policy, New York, 1938.

TIPPETTS, CHARLES: *State Banks and the Federal Reserve System*, D. Van Nostrand Company, Inc., New York, 1929.

WARBURG, PAUL M.: *The Federal Reserve System, Its Origin and Growth*, The Macmillan Company, New York, 1930.

WEISSMAN, RUDOLPH L.: *The New Federal Reserve System; The Board Assumes Control*, Harper & Brothers, New York, 1936.

WHITNEY, CAROLINE: *Experiments in Credit Control; The Federal Reserve System*, Columbia University Press, New York, 1934.

WILLIS, H. PARKER: *The Federal Reserve System; Legislation, Organization, and Operation*, The Ronald Press Company, New York, 1923.

STATE AND LOCAL FINANCE

BIDWELL, FREDERICK D.: *Taxation in New York State*, J. B. Lyon Co., Albany, 1918.

BOGART, ERNEST L.: *Financial History of Ohio*, University of Illinois Press, Urbana, Ill., 1912.

BUCK, ARTHUR E.: *Municipal Finance*, The Macmillan Company, New York, 1926.

BULLOCK, CHARLES J.: *Historical Sketch of the Finances of Massachusetts*, Publications of the American Economic Association, 3d series, Vol. VIII, No. 2, May, 1907.

*DOUGLAS, CHARLES H. J.: *The Financial History of Massachusetts, From the Organization of the Massachusetts Bay Colony to the American Revolution*, Columbia University Press, New York, 1892.

DURAND, EDWARD D.: *The Finances of New York City*, The Macmillan Company, New York, 1898.

HANNA, HUGH S.: *Financial History of Maryland, 1789–1848*, Johns Hopkins Press, Baltimore, 1907.

HOLLANDER, JACOB H.: *Financial History of Baltimore*, Johns Hopkins Press, Baltimore, 1899.

HUSE, CHARLES P.: *The Financial History of Boston, 1822–1908*, Harvard University Press, Cambridge, Mass., 1916.

KILPATRICK, WYLIE: *State Supervision of Local Finance*, Public Administration Service, Chicago, 1941.

McGRANE, REGINALD C.: *Foreign Bondholders and American State Debts*, The Macmillan Company, New York, 1935.

*NEVINS, ALLAN: *The American States during and after the Revolution, 1775–1789*, Chap. 11, The Macmillan Company, New York, 1927.

New York State Constitutional Convention Committee: *Reports, Vol. X, Problems Relating to Taxation and Finance*, Borland Printing Co., Inc., New York, 1938.

PLEHN, CARL C.: *Government Finance in the United States*, A. C. McClurg & Company, Chicago, 1915.

*RATCHFORD, BENJAMIN U.: *American State Debts*, Duke University Press, Durham, N.C., 1941.

*RIPLEY, WILLIAM Z.: *The Financial History of Virginia, 1609–1776*, Columbia College, New York, 1893.

SCOTT, WILLIAM A.: *The Repudiation of State Debts*, The Thomas Y. Crowell Company, New York, 1893.

*SOWERS, DON C.: *The Financial History of New York State from 1789 to 1912*, Columbia University Press, New York, 1914.

STOKES, H. K.: *Finances and Financial Administration of Providence*, Johns Hopkins University, Baltimore, 1903.

STUDENSKI, PAUL: *The Government of Metropolitan Areas in the United States*, National Municipal League, New York, 1930.

*————: *Public Borrowing*, National Municipal League, New York, 1930.

SUNDELSON, J. W.: *Budgetary Methods in National and State Governments*, New York State Tax Commission, Albany, 1938.

VAN DE WOESTYNE, ROYAL S.: *State Control of Local Finance in Massachusetts*, Harvard University Press, Cambridge, Mass., 1935.

WORTHINGTON, T. K.: *Historical Sketch of the Finances of Pennsylvania*, Publications of the American Economic Association, Vol. II, No. 2, 1887.

BIOGRAPHIES

1776–1860

*ADAMS, HENRY: *The Life of Albert Gallatin*, J. B. Lippincott Company, Philadelphia, 1880.

*BASSETT, JOHN S.: *The Life of Andrew Jackson*, The Macmillan Company, New York, 1925.

BENTON, THOMAS HART: *Thirty Years View: Or, a History of the Working of the American Government for Thirty Years, from 1820 to 1850*, D. Appleton & Company, Inc., New York, 1874.

*BRANT, IRVING: *James Madison: Father of the Constitution*, Bobbs-Merrill Company, Indianapolis, 1950.

CAREY, ROBERT L.: *Daniel Webster as an Economist*, Columbia University Press, New York, 1929.

COIT, MARGARET L.: *John C. Calhoun: American Portrait*, Houghton Mifflin Company, Boston, 1950.

JAMES, MARQUIS: *Andrew Jackson, Portrait of a President*, Bobbs-Merrill Company, Indianapolis, 1937.

KONKLE, BURTON A.: *Thomas Willing and the First American Financial System*, University of Pennsylvania Press, Philadelphia, 1937.

LIPSKY, GEORGE A.: *John Quincy Adams; His Theory and Ideas,* The Thomas Y. Crowell Company, New York, 1950.

LODGE, HENRY CABOT: *Daniel Webster,* Houghton Mifflin Company, Boston, 1883.

LYNCH, DENIS T.: *An Epoch and a Man, Martin Van Buren and His Times,* Liveright Publishing Corp., New York, 1929.

*OBERHOLTZER, ELLIS P.: *Robert Morris, Patriot and Financier,* The Macmillan Company, New York, 1903.

*ROOSEVELT, THEODORE: *Life of Thomas Hart Benton,* Houghton Mifflin Company, Boston, 1914.

*SCHACHNER, NATHAN: *Alexander Hamilton,* Appleton-Century-Crofts, Inc., New York, 1946.

*SCHURZ, CARL: *Life of Henry Clay,* Houghton Mifflin Company, Boston, 1915.

*SHEPARD, EDWIN M.: *Martin Van Buren,* Houghton Mifflin Company, Boston, 1916.

*STEVENS, JOHN A.: *Albert Gallatin,* Houghton Mifflin Company, Boston, 1911.

*SUMNER, WILLIAM G.: *Andrew Jackson,* Houghton Mifflin Company, Boston, 1910.

SWISHER, CARL B.: *Roger B. Taney,* The Macmillan Company, New York, 1935.

VAN DEUSEN, GLYNDON G.: *The Life of Henry Clay,* Little, Brown & Company, Boston, 1937.

WILTSE, CHARLES M.: *John C. Calhoun,* 3 vols., Bobbs-Merrill Co., Indianapolis, Ind., 1944–1951.

YOUNG, ELEANOR: *Forgotten Patriot: Robert Morris,* The Macmillan Company, New York, 1950.

1860–1900

*BARNES, JAMES A.: *John G. Carlisle, Financial Statesman,* Dodd, Mead & Company, Inc., New York, 1931.

BLAINE, JAMES G.: *Twenty Years of Congress,* The Henry Bill Publishing Co., Norwich, Conn., 1884–1886.

BOUTWELL, GEORGE SEWALL: *Reminiscences of Sixty Years in Public Affairs,* McClure, Phillips & Co., New York, 1902.

BURTON, THEODORE E.: *John Sherman,* Houghton Mifflin Company, Boston, 1906.

CAPERS, HENRY D.: *The Life and Times of C. G. Memminger,* Everett Waddey Co., Richmond, 1893.

COREY, LEWIS: *The House of Morgan; A Social Biography of the Masters of Money,* G. H. Watt, New York, 1930.

FESSENDEN, FRANCIS: *Life and Public Services of William Pitt Fessenden,* Houghton Mifflin Company, Boston, 1907.

FERLEGER, HERBERT R.: *David A. Wells and the American Revenue System, 1865–1870,* reproduced from typewritten copy, New York, 1942.

*HART, ALBERT B.: *Salmon Portland Chase,* Houghton Mifflin Company, Boston, 1899.

HIBBEN, PAXTON: *The Peerless Leader, William Jennings Bryan,* Rinehart & Company, Inc., New York, 1929.

JAYNER, FRED B.: *David Ames Welles: Champion of Free Trade,* The Torch Press, Cedar Rapids, Iowa, 1939.

KERR, WINFIELD S.: *John Sherman, His Life and Public Services,* Sherman, French & Co., Boston, 1908.

*LARSON, HENRIETTA M.: *Jay Cooke, Private Banker,* Harvard University Press, Cambridge, Mass., 1936.

LONG, JOHN C.: *Bryan, The Great Commoner,* Appleton-Century-Crofts, Inc., New York, 1928.

*McCulloch, Hugh: *Men and Measures of Half a Century; Sketches and Comments*, Charles Scribner's Sons, New York, 1889.

*Nevins, Allan: *Grover Cleveland; A Study in Courage*, Dodd, Mead & Company, Inc., New York, 1932.

*Oberholtzer, Ellis P.: *Jay Cooke, Financier of the Civil War*, G. W. Jacobs & Co., Philadelphia, 1907.

Olcott, Charles S.: *The Life of William McKinley*, Houghton Mifflin Company, Boston, 1916.

*Schuckers, Jacob W.: *The Life and Public Services of Salmon Portland Chase*, D. Appleton & Company, Inc., New York, 1874.

*Sherman, John T.: *John Sherman's Recollections of Forty Years*, The Werner Company, Chicago, 1895.

Warden, Robert B.: *An Account of the Private Life and Public Services of Salmon Portland Chase*, Wilstach, Baldwin & Co., Cincinnati, 1874.

Werner, Morris R.: *Bryan*, Harcourt, Brace and Company, Inc., New York, 1929.

*Williams, Wayne C.: *William Jennings Bryan*, G. P. Putnam's Sons, New York, 1936.

1900–1950

Baker, Ray S.: *Woodrow Wilson; Life and Letters*, 8 vols., Doubleday & Company, Inc., New York, 1927–1939.

Eccles, Marriner S.: *Beckoning Frontiers*, Alfred A. Knopf, Inc., New York, 1951.

Hinshaw, David: *Herbert Hoover—American Quaker*, Farrar, Straus & Young, New York, 1950.

Hoover, Herbert: *The Memoirs of Herbert Hoover*, The Macmillan Company, New York, 1951.

Johnson, Gerald W.: *Roosevelt: Dictator or Democrat*, Harper & Brothers, New York, 1941.

Jones, Jesse H.: *Fifty Billion Dollars: My Thirteen Years with R.F.C.*, The Macmillan Company, New York, 1951.

*Love, Phillip H.: *Andrew W. Mellon, The Man and His Work*, F. H. Coggins & Co., Baltimore, Md., 1929.

Lyons, Eugene: *Our Unknown Ex-President, A Portrait of Herbert Hoover*, Doubleday & Company, Inc., New York, 1948.

*McAdoo, William G.: *Crowded Years, The Reminiscences of William G. McAdoo*, Houghton Mifflin Company, Boston, 1931.

Morgenthau, Henry, Jr.: "The Morgenthau Diaries," *Collier's*, September–November, 1947.

O'Connor, Harvey: *Mellon's Millions, The Biography of a Fortune; The Life and Times of Andrew W. Mellon*, The John Day Company, New York, 1933.

Pringle, Henry F.: *Theodore Roosevelt, A Biography*, Harcourt, Brace and Company, Inc., New York, 1931.

———: *The Life and Times of William Howard Taft*, Rinehart Company, Inc., New York, 1939.

Sherwood, Robert E., *Roosevelt and Hopkins*, Harper & Brothers, New York, 1948.

Stephenson, Nathaniel W.: *Nelson W. Aldrich, A Leader in American Politics*, Charles Scribner's Sons, New York, 1930.

Tumulty, Joseph P.: *Woodrow Wilson as I Knew Him*, Doubleday & Company, Inc., New York, 1921.

White, William Allen: *A Puritan in Babylon*, The Macmillan Company, New York, 1938.

ARTICLES

The following list includes only those articles which the authors have found most helpful.

BACON, NATHANIEL T.: "American International Indebtedness," *The Yale Review*, Vol. IX, November, 1900.

BLAKEY, ROY G., and GLADYS C. BLAKEY: "Revenue Acts 1932–1941," *American Economic Review*, December, 1932, and 1935, September, 1936; December, 1937; September, 1938; December, 1939, 1940, and 1941.

BLOOMFIELD, ARTHUR I.: "Operations of the American Exchange Stabilization Fund," *The Review of Economic Statistics*, Vol. XXVI, No. 2, May, 1944.

BULLOCK, CHARLES J., JOHN H. WILLIAMS, and RUFUS S. TUCKER: "The Balance of Trade of the United States," *The Review of Economic Statistics*, Vol. VI, July, 1919.

EBERSOLE, J. FRANKLIN: "One Year of the Reconstruction Finance Corporation," *The Quarterly Journal of Economics*, Vol. XLVII, May, 1933.

FEIS, HERBERT: "The Export of American Capital," *Foreign Affairs*, Vol. III, No. 4, July, 1925.

FOSTER, WILLIAM F., and W. J. CATCHINGS: "Is the Reserve Board Keeping Faith?" *The Atlantic Monthly*, July, 1929.

HAMMOND, BRAY: "The Age of Jackson," a review, *The Journal of Economic History*, Vol. VI, No. 1, May, 1946.

————: "Jackson, Biddle, and the Bank of the U.S.," *The Journal of Economic History*, Vol. VII, No. 1, May, 1947.

HERSEY, ARTHUR: "Historical Review of Objectives of Federal Reserve Policy," *Federal Reserve Bulletin*, April, 1940.

LAKE, WILFRED S.: "The End of the Suffolk System," *The Journal of Economic History*, Vol. VII, No. 2, November, 1947.

PRESTON, HOWARD H.: "The Banking Act of 1933," *The American Economic Review*, Vol. XXIII, No. 4, December, 1933.

SELLERS, JAMES L.: "An Interpretation of Civil War Finance," *American Historical Review*, Vol. 30, January, 1925.

SLICHTER, SUMNER H.: "The Period 1919–1936 in the United States: Its Significance for Business-cycle Theory," *Review of Economic Statistics*, Vol. XIX, No. 1, February, 1937.

STUDENSKI, PAUL: "The Limits to Possible Debt Burdens," *American Economic Review*, Supplement, March, 1937.

————: "Federal Grants-in-Aid," *National Tax Journal*, September, 1949.

TAUSSIG, F. W.: "The Tariff Act of 1930," *The Quarterly Journal of Economics*, Vol. XLV, No. 1, November, 1930.

WHITE, GERALD T.: "Financing Industrial Expansion for War: The Origin of the Defense Plant Corporation Leases," *The Journal of Economic History*, Vol. IX, No. 2, November, 1949.

WILLIAMS, JOHN H.: "Deficit Spending," *The American Economic Review*, Vol. XXX, No. 5, February, 1941.

————: "The Implications of Fiscal Policy for Monetary Policy and the Banking System," *The American Economic Review*, Vol. XXXII, No. 1, Supplement Part 2, March, 1942.

YAPLE, MAXINE: "The Burden of Direct Taxes as Paid by Income Classes," *The American Economic Review*, Vol. XXVI, No. 4, December, 1936.

APPENDIX 1

Historical Series of Federal Receipts, Expenditures, Surplus or Deficit, and Debt, Fiscal Years 1789–1950*

(In millions of dollars)

Year	Net receipts	Expenditures	Surplus, or deficit (−)	Gross debt	Year	Net receipts	Expenditures	Surplus or deficit (−)	Gross debt through 1852; interest-bearing debt thereafter
1789–1791	$ 4.4	$ 4.3	$ 0.1	$ 77.2	1830	$ 24.8	$ 15.1	$ 9.7	$ 39.1
1792	3.7	5.1	− 1.4	80.4	1831	28.5	15.2	13.3	24.3
1793	4.7	4.5	0.2	78.4	1832	31.9	17.3	14.6	7.0
1794	5.4	7.0	− 1.6	80.7	1833	33.9	23.0	10.9	4.8
1795	6.1	7.5	− 1.4	83.8	1834	21.8	18.6	3.2	—
1796	8.4	5.7	2.7	82.1	1835	35.4	17.6	17.9	—
1797	8.7	6.1	2.6	79.2	1836	50.8	30.9	20.0	0.3
1798	7.9	7.7	0.2	78.4	1837	25.0	37.2	− 12.3	3.3
1799	7.5	9.7	− 2.1	83.0	1838	26.3	33.9	− 7.6	10.4
					1839	31.5	26.9	4.6	3.6
1800	10.8	10.8	0.1	83.0	1840	19.5	24.3	− 4.8	5.3
1801	12.9	9.4	3.5	80.7	1841	16.9	26.6	− 9.7	13.6
1802	15.0	7.9	7.1	77.1	1842	20.0	25.2	− 5.2	20.2
1803	11.1	7.9	3.2	86.4	1843	8.3	11.9	3.6	32.7
1804	11.8	8.7	3.1	82.3	1844	29.3	22.3	7.0	23.5
1805	13.6	10.5	3.1	75.7	1845	30.0	22.9	7.0	15.9
1806	15.6	9.8	5.8	69.2	1846	29.7	27.8	1.9	15.6
1807	16.4	8.4	8.0	65.2	1847	26.5	57.3	− 30.8	38.8
1808	17.1	9.9	7.2	57.0	1848	35.7	45.4	9.6	47.0
1809	7.8	10.3	− 2.5	53.2	1849	31.2	45.1	− 13.8	63.1

Year				
1810	9.4	8.2	1.2	48.0
1811	14.4	8.1	6.3	45.2
1812	9.8	20.3	−10.5	56.0
1813	14.3	31.7	−17.3	81.5
1814	11.2	34.7	−23.5	99.8
1815	15.7	32.7	−17.0	127.3
1816	47.7	30.6	17.1	123.5
1817	33.1	21.8	11.3	103.5
1818	21.6	19.8	1.8	95.5
1819	24.6	21.5	3.1	91.0
1820	17.9	18.3	—	90.0
1821	14.6	15.8	—	93.5
1822	20.2	15.0	5.2	90.9
1823	20.5	14.7	5.8	90.3
1824	19.4	20.3	—	83.8
1825	21.8	15.9	6.0	81.1
1826	25.3	17.0	8.2	74.0
1827	23.0	16.1	6.8	67.5
1828	24.8	16.4	8.4	58.4
1829	24.8	15.2	9.6	48.6

Year				
1850	43.6	39.5	4.1	63.4
1851	52.6	47.7	4.9	68.3
1852	49.8	44.2	5.7	66.2
1853	61.6	48.2	13.4	59.6
1854	73.8	58.0	15.8	42.0
1855	65.3	59.7	5.6	35.4
1856	74.1	69.6	4.5	31.8
1857	69.0	67.8	1.2	28.5
1858	46.7	74.2	− 27.5	44.7
1859	53.5	69.1	− 15.6	58.3
1860	56.1	63.1	− 7.1	64.7
1861	41.5	66.5	− 25.0	90.4
1862	52.0	474.8	−422.8	365.4
1863	112.7	714.7	−602.0	707.8
1864	264.6	865.3	−600.7	1,360.0
1865	333.7	1,297.6	−963.8	2,217.7
1866	558.0	520.8	37.2	2,322.1
1867	490.6	357.5	133.1	2,239.0
1868	405.6	377.3	28.3	2,191.3
1869	370.9	322.9	48.1	2,151.5

Historical Series of Federal Receipts, Expenditures, Surplus or Deficit, and Debt, Fiscal Years 1789–1950* (Continued)

Year	Net receipts	Expenditures	Surplus or deficit (−)	Interest-bearing debt	Year	Net receipts	Expenditures	Surplus or deficit (−)	Interest-bearing debt
1870	$411.3	$309.7	$ 101.6	$2,035.9	1910	$ 675.5	$ 693.6	$ − 18.1	$ 913.3
1871	383.3	292.2	91.1	1,920.7	1911	701.8	691.2	10.6	915.4
1872	371.1	277.5	96.6	1,800.8	1912	692.6	689.9	2.7	963.8
1873	333.7	290.3	43.4	1,696.5	1913	724.1	724.5	− 0.4	965.7
1874	305.0	302.6	2.3	1,724.9	1914	734.7	735.1	− 0.4	968.0
1875	288.0	274.6	13.4	1,708.7	1915	697.9	760.6	− 62.7	969.8
1876	294.1	265.1	29.0	1,696.7	1916	782.5	734.1	48.5	971.6
1877	281.4	241.3	40.1	1,697.9	1917	1,124.3	1,977.7	− 853.4	2,712.6
1878	257.8	237.0	20.8	1,780.7	1918	3,664.6	12,696.7	−9,032.1	11,985.9
1879	273.8	266.9	6.9	1,887.7	1919	5,152.3	18,514.9	−13,362.6	25,234.5
1880	333.5	267.6	65.9	1,710.0	1920	6,694.6	6,403.3	291.2	24,062.5
1881	360.8	260.7	100.1	1,625.6	1921	5,624.9	5,115.9	509.0	23,738.9
1882	403.5	258.0	145.5	1,449.8	1922	4,109.1	3,372.6	736.5	22,710.3
1883	398.3	265.4	132.9	1,324.2	1923	4,007.1	3,294.6	712.5	22,007.0
1884	348.5	244.1	104.4	1,212.6	1924	4,012.0	3,048.7	963.4	20,981.2
1885	323.7	260.2	63.5	1,182.2	1925	3,780.1	3,063.1	717.0	20,210.9
1886	336.4	242.5	94.0	1,132.0	1926	3,962.8	3,097.6	865.1	19,383.8
1887	371.4	267.9	103.5	1,007.7	1927	4,129.4	2,974.0	1,155.4	18,252.7
1888	379.3	267.9	111.3	936.5	1928	4,042.3	3,103.3	939.1	17,317.7
1889	387.1	299.3	87.8	815.9	1929	4,033.2	3,298.9	734.4	16,638.9

Year				
1890	403.1	318.0	85.0	711.3
1891	392.6	365.8	26.8	610.5
1892	354.9	345.0	9.9	585.0
1893	385.8	383.5	2.3	585.0
1894	306.4	367.5	−61.2	635.0
1895	324.7	356.2	−31.5	716.2
1896	338.1	352.2	−14.0	847.4
1897	347.7	365.8	−18.1	847.4
1898	405.3	443.4	−38.0	847.4
1899	516.0	605.1	−89.1	1,046.0
1900	567.2	520.9	46.4	1,023.5
1901	587.7	524.6	63.1	987.1
1902	562.5	485.2	77.2	931.1
1903	561.9	517.0	44.8	914.5
1904	541.1	583.7	−42.6	895.2
1905	544.3	567.3	−23.0	895.2
1906	595.0	570.2	24.8	895.2
1907	665.9	579.1	86.7	894.8
1908	601.9	659.2	−57.3	897.5
1909	604.3	693.7	−89.4	913.3

Year				
1930	4,177.9	3,440.3	737.7	15,921.9
1931	3,115.6	3,577.4	461.9	16,519.6
1932	1,923.9	4,659.2	−2,735.3	19,161.3
1933	2,021.2	4,622.9	−2,601.7	22,157.6
1934	3,064.3	6,693.9	−3,629.6	26,480.5
1935	3,729.9	6,521.0	−2,791.1	27,645.2
1936	4,068.9	8,493.5	−4,424.5	32,988.8
1937	4,978.6	7,756.0	−2,777.4	35,800.1
1938	5,761.6	6,938.2	−1,176.6	36,575.9
1939	5,103.4	8,965.6	−3862.2	39,886.0
1940	5,264.7	9,182.7	−3,918.0	42,376.5
1941	7,227.3	13,386.6	−6,159.3	48,387.4
1942	12,696.3	34,186.5	−21,490.2	71,968.4
1943	22,201.5	79,621.9	−57,420.4	135,380.3
1944	43,891.7	95,315.1	−51,423.4	199,543.4
1945	44,761.6	98,702.5	−53,940.9	256,356.6
1946	40,026.9	60,703.1	−20,676.2	268,110.9
1947	40,042.6	39,288.8	753.8	255,113.4
1948	42,210.8	33,791.3	8,419.5	250,063.3
1949	38,245.7	40,057.1	−1,811.4	250,761.6
1950	37,044.7	40,166.8	−3,122.1	255,209.4

SOURCE: *Annual Report of the Secretary of the Treasury*, 1950. * Fiscal years 1789–1842 ended on December 31; 1843–1950 on June 30. Receipts and expenditures on basis of warrants issued from 1789 through 1915 and of daily Treasury statements beginning 1916. General, special emergency, and trust accounts combined from 1789 through 1930. Trust accounts excluded beginning 1931. For Post Office only surpluses and deficits are included. The expenditures reported on basis of warrants issued constitute expenditures so far as appropriations against which they are charged are concerned. But they necessarily include unexpended balances in the hands of disbursing officers under these warrants, while not including the expenditures made by such officers during the year from unexpended balances under warrants issued in the previous years. For further explanation of differences between these figures and those given in the text see p. 3 above.

APPENDIX 2

Name	Whence appointed	Date of appointment	Expiration of service
Secretaries of the Treasury, 1789–1951:			
Alexander Hamilton	New York	Sept. 11, 1789	Jan. 31, 1795
Oliver Wolcott, Jr.	Connecticut	Feb. 2, 1795	Dec. 31, 1800
Samuel Dexter	Massachusetts	Jan. 1, 1801	May 6, 1801
Albert Gallatin	Pennsylvania	May 14, 1801	Apr. 20, 1813
George W. Campbell	Tennessee	Feb. 9, 1814	Sept. 26, 1814
Alexander J. Dallas	Pennsylvania	Oct. 6, 1814	Oct. 21, 1816
William H. Crawford	Georgia	Oct. 22, 1816	Mar. 3, 1825
Richard Rush	Pennsylvania	Mar. 7, 1825	Mar. 3, 1829
Samuel D. Ingham	Pennsylvania	Mar. 6, 1829	June 20, 1831
Louis McLane	Delaware	Aug. 8, 1831	May 29, 1833
William J. Duane	Pennsylvania	May 29, 1833	Sept. 23, 1833
Roger B. Taney	Maryland	Sept. 23, 1833	June 24, 1834
Levi Woodbury	New Hampshire	June 27, 1834	Mar. 4, 1841
Thomas Ewing	Ohio	Mar. 5, 1841	Sept. 11, 1841
Walter Forward	Pennsylvania	Sept. 13, 1841	Feb. 28, 1843
John C. Spencer	New York	Mar. 3, 1843	May 2, 1844
George M. Bibb	Kentucky	June 15, 1844	Mar. 7, 1845
Robert Walker	Mississippi	Mar. 6, 1845	Mar. 5, 1849
William M. Meredith	Pennsylvania	Mar. 8, 1849	July 22, 1850
Thomas Corwin	Ohio	July 23, 1850	Mar. 7, 1853
James Guthrie	Kentucky	Mar. 7, 1853	Mar. 6, 1857
Howell Cobb	Georgia	Mar. 6, 1857	Dec. 8, 1860
Philip F. Thomas	Maryland	Dec. 12, 1860	Jan. 14, 1861
John A. Dix	New York	Jan. 11, 1861	Mar. 6, 1861
Salmon P. Chase	Ohio	Mar. 7, 1861	June 30, 1864
Wm. P. Fessenden	Maine	July 1, 1864	Mar. 3, 1865
Hugh McCulloch	Indiana	Mar. 7, 1865	Mar. 4, 1869
George S. Boutwell	Massachusetts	Mar. 11, 1869	Mar. 16, 1873
Wm. A. Richardson	Massachusetts	Mar. 17, 1873	June 2, 1874
Benj. H. Bristow	Kentucky	June 2, 1874	June 20, 1876
Lot M. Morrill	Maine	June 21, 1876	Mar. 9, 1877
John Sherman	Ohio	Mar. 9, 1877	Mar. 3, 1881
William Windom	Minnesota	Mar. 5, 1881	Nov. 13, 1881
Charles J. Folger	New York	Nov. 14, 1881	Sept. 4, 1884
Walter Q. Gresham	Indiana	Sept. 24, 1884	Oct. 19, 1884
Hugh McCulloch	Indiana	Oct. 31, 1884	Mar. 6, 1885
Daniel Manning	New York	Mar. 7, 1885	Mar. 31, 1887
Charles S. Fairchild	New York	Apr. 1, 1887	Mar. 4, 1889
William Windom	Minnesota	Mar. 6, 1889	Jan. 29, 1891
Charles Foster	Ohio	Feb. 25, 1891	Mar. 6, 1893
John G. Carlisle	Kentucky	Mar. 7, 1893	Mar. 5, 1897
Lyman J. Gage	Illinois	Mar. 6, 1897	Jan. 31. 1902
Leslie M. Shaw	Iowa	Feb. 1, 1902	Mar. 4, 1907
George B. Cortelyou	New York	Mar. 4, 1907	Mar. 4, 1909

HISTORICAL LIST OF HEADS OF THE UNITED STATES TREASURY, THE FEDERAL RESERVE BOARD, AND THE GENERAL ACCOUNTING OFFICE   (*Continued*)

Name	Whence appointed	Date of appointment	Expiration of service
Secretaries of the Treasury, 1789–1951:			
Franklin MacVeagh	Illinois	Mar. 4, 1909	Mar. 4, 1913
William G. McAdoo	New York	Mar. 6, 1913	Dec. 15, 1918
Carter Glass	Virginia	Dec. 16, 1918	Feb. 1, 1920
David F. Houston	Missouri	Feb. 2, 1920	Mar. 3, 1921
Andrew W. Mellon	Pennsylvania	Mar. 4, 1921	Feb. 12, 1932
Ogden L. Mills	New York	Feb. 13, 1932	Mar. 3, 1933
William M. Woodin	New York	Mar. 4, 1933	Dec. 31, 1933
Henry Morgenthau, Jr.	New York	Jan. 1, 1934	July 23, 1943
Fred I. Vinson	Kentucky	July 23, 1945	Jan. 23, 1946
John W. Snyder	Missouri	June 24, 1946	
Governors and Chairmen of the Federal Reserve Board, 1914–1951:			
Charles S. Hamlin	Massachusetts	Aug. 10, 1914	Aug. 9, 1916
W. P. G. Harding	Georgia	Aug. 10, 1916	Aug. 9, 1922
D. R. Crissinger	Ohio	May 1, 1923	Sept. 15, 1927
Roy A. Young	Minnesota	Oct. 4, 1927	Aug. 31, 1930
Eugene Meyer	New York	Sept. 16, 1930	May 10, 1933
Eugene R. Black	Georgia	May 19, 1933	Aug. 15, 1934
Marriner S. Eccles	Missouri	Nov. 15, 1934	Jan. 31, 1948
Thomas B. McCabe	Pennsylvania	Apr. 15, 1948	Mar. 31, 1951
William McChesney Martin, Jr.	New York	Mar. 15, 1951	
Comptrollers-General of the United States, 1921–1951:			
J. R. McCarl	Nebraska	June 29, 1921	June 29, 1936
R. N. Elliott (acting)	Indiana	June 29, 1936	Apr. 3, 1939
Fred Herbert Brown	New Hampshire	Apr. 3, 1939	June 19, 1940
R. N. Elliott (acting)	Indiana	June 19, 1940	Aug. 1, 1940
Lindsay C. Warren	North Carolina	Aug. 1, 1940	

INDEX

Page references to basic tables on receipts and expenditures, debt operations, debt structure, and banking operations are given in **boldface** type.